Charles Howard

The Roads of England and Wales

An Itinerary for Cyclists, Tourists, and Travellers. Fifth Edition

Charles Howard

The Roads of England and Wales
An Itinerary for Cyclists, Tourists, and Travellers. Fifth Edition

ISBN/EAN: 9783337190613

Printed in Europe, USA, Canada, Australia, Japan

Cover: Foto ©Andreas Hilbeck / pixelio.de

More available books at **www.hansebooks.com**

REDUCED ORDNANCE MAP OF
ENGLAND AND WALES

Engraved on Sixty Five sheets and

PLANNED UPON A SCALE OF TWO MILES TO AN INCH

1/6 coloured 2/6 coloured & mounted

INDEX MAP

THE ROADS

OF

ENGLAND AND WALES;

AN ITINERARY FOR CYCLISTS, TOURISTS, & TRAVELLERS

CONTAINING

An Original Description of the Contour and Surface with Mileage of the Main (Direct and Principal Cross) Roads in England and Wales, and part of Scotland;

PARTICULARLY ADAPTED TO THE USE OF

BICYCLISTS AND TRICYCLISTS

TOGETHER WITH

TOPOGRAPHICAL NOTES OF THE CHIEF CITIES AND TOWNS, AND REFERENCES TO THE ANTIQUITIES, NATURAL CURIOSITIES, AND PLACES OF INTEREST ALONG THE VARIOUS ROUTES;

ALSO

A LIST OF HOTELS AND INNS IN EACH TOWN,

SUITABLE FOR CYCLISTS.

By CHARLES HOWARD.

(*Wanderers' B.C. and C.T.C.*)

FIFTH EDITION.

London:
MASON & PAYNE, 7, Gracechurch Street, E.C.
HUTCHINSON & CO., 25, Paternoster Square, E.C.
1889.
(*Copyright; entered at Stationers' Hall.*)

WILKINS & CO.,
CYCLE FITTINGS
AND
ACCESSORIES OF ALL KINDS.

SPRING BACK SAFETY LAMPS FROM 2/6.
LARGEST STOCK OF SUNDRIES IN THE TRADE.
Orders over 5s. Free by Parcels Post.

ILLUSTRATED CATALOGUE FREE.

66, HOLBORN VIADUCT, LONDON.

BOOKS FOR TOURISTS.

BICYCLES AND TRICYCLES OF THE YEAR. Descriptions of the New Inventions and Improvements for the present season. Designed to assist intending purchasers in the choice of a machine. Illustrated. By HARRY HEWITT GRIFFIN. Price 1s.
"It is as comprehensive as could be desired. . . . We can readily testify to the strict impartiality of the author."—*The Field.*

SEASIDE WATERING PLACES. A Description of nearly 200 Holiday Resorts on the Coasts of England and Wales, the Channel Islands, and the Isle of Man. Sixth Edition, with Illustrations. In cloth, price 2s. 6d.
"The information it gives is of a decidedly practical and reliable nature."—*The Spectator.*

TOUR IN THE STATES AND CANADA. Out and Home in Six Weeks. By THOMAS GREENWOOD. Illustrated. In cloth gilt, price 2s. 6d.
"We can confidently recommend this book."—*The Literary World.*

TOURIST'S ROUTE MAP of England and Wales, The. Third Edition, thoroughly Revised. Shows clearly all the Main, and most of the Cross Roads, and the Distances between the Chief Towns, as well as the Mileage from London. In addition to this, Routes of *Thirty of the most Interesting Tours* are printed in red. The Map is mounted on linen, so as not to tear, and is enclosed in a strong cloth case. In cloth, price 1s.
"Reliable and accurate; . . . an admirable companion to tourists and cyclists."—*The Tourist and Traveller.*

WATERING PLACES OF FRANCE, NORTHERN. A Guide for English people to the Holiday Resorts on the Coasts of the French Netherlands, Picardy, Normandy, and Brittany. By ROSA BAUGHAN. Price 2s.
"We have pleasure in recommending this work."—*Cook's Excursionist.*

LONDON: L. UPCOTT GILL, 170, STRAND, W.C.

PREFACE.

IT cannot be denied that Cycling, ever since its introduction into this country as a means of locomotion, has been in want of a reliable Road Book specially adapted for its requirements—in short, one that will afford full information as to mileage, hills, and surface of, at least, the great trunk roads. A strong proof of this, if any be needed, can be readily found by reference to the columns of the papers devoted to the pastime, where enquiries about roads, &c., may be seen almost every week.

Road Books are by no means a new invention, but without beginning so far back as the "Itinerarium" of Antoninus—the earliest specimen extant of a Road Book—it will suffice to mention *Cary's* and *Paterson's Roads*, both of which ran through many editions between 1780 and 1830, an interval that embraces the heyday of the coaching period. With the introduction of railways, travelling by road was gradually discontinued, and coaching almost died out. When, however, the bicycle was invented, the "Queen's highway" once more became extensively used, and wheelmen traversed the length and breadth of the island. Road information was eagerly sought for, and the bicycling press did its best to meet the requirements of the day, while the earlier Annuals contained a small collection of road routes described for bicycling. But the first public suggestion I can find of a Road Book specially adapted *ad usum bicyclicorum* was in a letter that appeared three or four years ago in *Bicycling News* over the then familiar *nom de plume* of "Essedarius." Since then several attempts have been made towards filling up the gap, but in my opinion none of them have yet produced anything of a sufficiently practical nature to commend itself to cyclists generally. The absence, therefore, of a Cyclist's Road Book has prompted me to make this compilation in the hope that it will supply what may well be called an acknowledged want.

As regards the work itself the chief aim has been to shape its contents in the most concise and intelligible form possible for the purpose of ready reference, by adhering to simplicity in matters of detail, but without degenerating into generalities in vagueness of description.

While professedly written in the special interest of cyclists it has been endeavoured, as far as the limits of such a class-work would allow, to embody in it also some general information suited to the wants of other travellers than wheelmen. "Where to go and what to see" has been construed in the barest and most literal meaning of the phrase, and long descriptions and minute particulars of the sights of our land have been invariably omitted. In this respect the tourist is referred for further information to county histories and local guide-books.

The roads are divided into *direct* and *cross*. All the former start from London, arranged in sections according to their several starting points (beginning with London Bridge), following the course of the sun from east to west, and continued round the compass. The cross roads are those which simply connect the large towns that are not on the same direct routes; they begin in the county of Kent and go round the map. The mileage is based upon that given in *Paterson's Roads* (18th ed., 1826), with some few corrections from the Ordnance Survey and milestones. As for the road descriptions, a fair proportion is the result of personal observation; a few routes have been gleaned from the "Bicycle" Annuals for 1877 and 1878; for information as to many others I am largely indebted to personal friends and bicyclical acquaintances; and I have obtained many miscellaneous details from some of the interesting accounts of tours contained in the pages of *Bicycling News*. To all I owe an acknowledgment. Yet even now I find that there are some roads about which I can obtain no reliable information; of these I can of course state the mileage only.

It will be observed that the road description is given from town to town, and this is followed at each stage first by the names (alphabetically arranged) of hotels; and then by a list of places of interest and notes of towns. It is not intended to recommend hotels, but to those that have adopted the Cyclists' Touring Club tariff are added the initials " B.T.C." or " C.T.C."

A copious Index will, it is hoped, complete the efficiency of the Volume.

It is hardly to be expected that a work of this kind in its first edition can be perfect; hence any additions and corrections will be thankfully accepted. All communications on this head should be addressed to me, care of the publishers.

In conclusion, while conscious that I may not have attained the standard of perfection in the eyes of all, yet I feel assured this volume containing, as it does, an amount of information at once unique and never before collected, will be acceptable to the great majority of my readers as a handbook of really practical utility, and I shall be satisfied if my efforts are a means of furthering the interests of the glorious pastime.

My task is now at an end. *Res ipsa loquatur.*

LONDON: *May* 1882.   C. H.

PREFACE TO THE FIFTH EDITION.

IN response to the general and generous appreciation of this work, and with the idea that the last should always be the best, I again gladly seize the opportunity of making some improvements in the road description and mileage, etc. These corrections are chiefly the result of my own close and personal observation, but, at the same time, for many of them I have to thank several gentlemen in various parts of the country.

We attain perfection gradually, and, therefore, I endeavour to correct all errors where possible, so that with the latest information we shall be at least nearest to perfection.

While thanking those who have been kind enough to point out errors, I hope their example will be followed by others wherever necessary.

March, 1889.   C. H.

FOR COMFORT,
When riding COOLNESS,
wear
CLEANLINESS,

CELLULAR

Without fear of Chill,

CYCLING SHIRTS,

AND

UNDERCLOTHING,

IN

COTTON, MERINO, WOOL, OR SILK.

Ecru Cotton, 6/-	Striped Cotton, 6/6	Ecru Silk and Cotton, 9/-
White Wool, 10/-	White Merino, 11/-	Striped Silk and Cotton, 17/-
	Striped Silk, 28/-	

C.T.C. Gazette—"Light, porous, and cool, and its use a pleasant relief."
Cyclist—"Cellular clothing a boon and a blessing."
Wheeling—"Much pleased with our experience."
Bicycling News—"Most comfortable and healthy garments for cycling."

Note the Label CELLULAR CLOTHING, PATENT, on all Garments.

A full selection of all garments made in Cellular Fabrics on view at OLIVER BROS., 417, Oxford Street, W.

OLIVER BROS. will cut any length of cloth or send a Sample Garment, post free to any address (on receipt of remittance), which will be exchanged or money returned if not approved of.

THE CELLULAR CLOTHING COMPANY, LD.,
75, ALDERMANBURY, LONDON, E.C.

INTRODUCTION.

THERE are two or three matters that appear to me to be of special interest to cycling tourists, as bearing more or less upon the subject of the following pages, and as to which I trust that the few observations I am tempted to make will not be thought out of place or superfluous in introducing this compilation to the cycling world.

ROADS: THEIR CHARACTERISTICS & COMPOSITION.

IN one respect our roads are in a state of transition. After a life of nearly 200 years the turnpike trust system is doomed; for many years past it has been in process of gradual abolition, the care of the roads being now transferred to the newly constituted County Councils.

Thanks, however, to the recently formed Roads Improvement Association, much useful information as to the proper system for the maintenance of roads is being disseminated, and will no doubt in time bear good fruit. Let us hope that the change will not be for the worse.

Since the decay of coaching some of the main roads have to a great extent become disused for travelling, but very few have seriously deteriorated. On the whole our roads will bear comparison with the continental roads. If Normandy, Central France, and Germany have good roads, so have we; but we have scarcely any of that horrid *pavé* that the French and Belgians seem to delight in.

Generally speaking, the roads in the South of England are better than those in the North; those again in agricultural districts, as a rule, are better than the roads in the manufacturing districts, chiefly, no doubt, owing to the heavy traffic the latter have to endure. Like most things also, roads differ in their composition as well as in their condition, the latter chiefly depending on the former; thus the phrase "state of the roads" is one of special significance to bicyclists.

The materials used in the composition of roads naturally vary to some extent according to the geological nature of the district. Taking that basis, roads may be classed as flint, gravel, limestone, macadam, oolite, sandstone, sandy, &c.

Undoubtedly the smoothest road-surface is that made of gravel, or, perhaps, gravel and flint combined, as gravel often contains a lot of flint. Gravel, geologically speaking, is a stratum of stones, large and small, deposited by the action of water after being broken and rounded by constant attrition or rubbing against each other; sometimes the term is used to mean all stones broken small, whether by nature or art, but the former is the more natural and the correct description. Gravel is very widely and indiscriminately distributed, but the chief gravel roads are in the counties of Kent, Surrey, Sussex, Hampshire, Middlesex, Berkshire, Buckingham, Hertford, Bedford, and Essex. As far as an imperfect and limited knowledge will enable me to judge, if not the majority, at least a large proportion of our roads are made of gravel or gravel and flint combined. Gravel roads, however, have a tendency to become sandy, and in wet weather very heavy.

Flint belongs to the chalk strata, and is the best material for roads, as it will stand rain much better than gravel alone. Purely chalk-flint roads chiefly occur in Hampshire, Wilts, Dorset, and Berkshire, and are to be found amongst the gravel in the south-eastern counties. Flint roads are the best for wet weather.

Limestone, or, more correctly speaking, mountain limestone, is principally confined to the hilly counties of Derby, York, Lancashire, Westmoreland, Cumberland, and Durham: but patches of it are also irregularly scattered about in all parts of the country. Limestone gives a good hard surface, but somewhat uneven, and, in wet weather, is liable rather to be greasy than merely soft or heavy, but is never dangerously so, like oolite; limestone roads when dry are generally white and dusty, the dust being very fine and powdery.

The term macadam was originally applied to a system of road-making invented by John Loudon Macadam. It was more especially intended for roads with heavy traffic, and the peculiarity of its construction was a surface covering of eight or ten inches of hard stone, preferably granite, broken small (not exceeding 6 oz. in weight), and well rolled or beaten in so as to present a fairly smooth and hard appearance. Though such, no doubt, is the correct meaning attached to the word, yet it is often applied to roads that have no granite at all in them, and it is entirely a popular error or misconception to imagine that all macadam roads are always made with granite. Thus the macadam roads in the environs of London are, I believe, made with a variety of grit-stone from North Wales. The roads in most of the large towns (where not paved) and in some few isolated districts are macadamised, but the proportion is small. Some 60 years ago the public mind was exercised by the question of the superiority of the rival road-making methods of Macadam and Telford (the great road engineer who effected many improvements in the Holyhead road). Telford's plan was to lay a foundation of large stones, with binding of gravel, or else a bed of rough concrete, and this is generally preferred.

Oolite, frequently, but wrongly, I think, called a variety of mountain limestone, is the worst kind of material for roads from a bicyclist's point of view. Happily the oolite district is not a large one, being almost entirely limited to the high grounds formed by the Cotswold Hills in West Oxfordshire, North Wilts, and Gloucestershire, and by the Mendip Hills in North Somersetshire. Here the roads will present anything but an inviting surface to the bicyclist, should he happen to traverse them in wet weather. The stone in appearance is something like granite, and in dry weather makes a hard and tolerably good surface, but when wet it is almost impossible to ride upon it with safety; the rain softens the material, and the traffic helps to convert it into a kind of greasy clay, very rutty and dangerously slippery. As many of these roads consist of one beaten track for vehicular traffic, the bicyclist has to choose between riding in the wheel-ruts or on the horse-hoof track, which, of course, on any kind of ground would require careful steering; when, however, he has to pass some vehicle in front or avoid another meeting him the danger of a fall is at once highly intensified; and it is only by the greatest dexterity that the wheel can be safely turned out of the rut. Portland stone and Purbeck stone are varieties of oolite.

Sandstone as a rule makes a good hard road, fairly smooth, and somewhat resembling gravel, to which it is in some respects superior, especially as rain has less effect on it. It is met with in various districts, such as West Sussex, East Hampshire, parts of Yorkshire, &c.

Sandy roads are usually met with in a flat country where stone is scarce; but very often gravel roads have a tendency to be sandy, instances of which are the Epsom road after Derby-day and parts of the Bath road.

In addition to the main roads, there are cross roads, bye-roads, and lanes, covering the country like a net-work, and at least five or six times as numerous as the main roads; to follow them one should have the 1-inch Ordnance Survey map, but it must not be taken for granted that all the bye-roads thereon displayed are really rideable, although many of them are as good as the main roads; on the other hand the greater portion are impracticable for bicycling, being merely used for agricultural purposes, and many are rough cart and horse tracks, or green lanes.

Of course it cannot be expected that roads always keep good and smooth, and it is not intended that the description of the surface of the roads should be taken as being the same all the year round. The state and condition of roads depend upon the time of the year, the weather, and the amount of traffic, not to mention the care bestowed in repairs. We have no really distinct and fixed rainy season; rain, snow, and frost, &c., are uncertain in their coming, and temporary in their effects; it would, therefore, be a work of supererogation to take note of them. Doubtless there are some roads that will stand almost any amount of rain, and are always hard and firm, or at least dry up hard and firm in a very short time after rain; but only a long experience of such roads, and that under rather trying circumstances, could enable anyone to speak of them with certainty. What is attempted to be described in the following pages is the ordinary state of the surface of the roads in fine weather, except only, that with regard to extremes of weather, in some instances the roads are described under both aspects.

MAPS.

This is an important subject for cyclists, as few start on a tour without a map of some kind, to give an idea of the country one is travelling through. From time to time queries appear in the bicycling papers asking which is the best map for bicycling.

For this purpose maps may be divided into two classes, sectional maps or county maps. Of the two it is generally admitted by those who have had experience that sectional maps are preferable. The chief objections to county maps are:—(1) the great number required for any ordinary tour (46 maps for England and Wales); (2) the difference of scale, scarcely two together being alike; (3) irregularity of their relative positions; (4) the awkwardness, if not difficulty, in tracing lines of road from one county to another, owing to inexactness of finish, and want of proper coincidence in the boundaries, which ought to fit into each other accurately. Then again, county maps seldom show the hills well, some indeed not at all.

The best sectional map, of course, is the Government Ordnance Survey of the British Isles, of which there are several scales; of these the smallest, 1m. to the inch, is the only one that I need refer to as being at all likely to be useful to bicyclists. The survey was commenced early in the present century, and though some parts of it are rather old—50 years or more—it is the basis of every other map published. For England and Wales the 1-in. scale map contains 110 sheets, each about 24in. by 35in. at 2s. 6d. per sheet; but for nearly all the country north of the Thames valley the map is also divided into quarter size sections at 1s. and 1s. 6d. each.

Doubtless many of my readers are familiar with its main features, but there are also many who are not. First of all the hills and elevations are shown by shaded lines, varying according to the height and steepness of the declivity; where the shading is engraved lightly and faintly, the undulations are only of a moderate character, and have nothing very high or steep; but where the shaded lines are dark and sharply defined they indicate that the slope is very high and steep —in fact, more or less precipitous—and consequently the roads on that gradient are proportionately dangerous. This, however, though on the whole giving one a good idea of the contour of the country, is not absolutely to be depended upon, as there are many dangerous hills as to which the shading affords no sufficient warning.

Next, every main road, bye-road, and lane is distinctly given, the main roads of course being the widest, and a very short study of them will enable anyone to distinguish them; further, a different kind of engraving is employed for all roads where they cross commons and heaths, the lines then being dotted and not continuous; there is, however, no distinction between ordinary carriage roads and merely occupation roads or green lanes.

In most instances the distances are marked on the main roads mile by mile, and in many places also the elevations are given in feet, both affording information most useful to bicyclists.

Then again, every town, village, hamlet, park, wood, and most residences and farms are noted, and numerous other objects are detailed, so that altogether the Ordnance Survey is quite an interesting study.

For practical use, bicyclists will find this map too cumbersome and costly for long distances; what is wanted is a map of small bulk, so as to be handy for the pocket, and of which several sections can be carried about one without the feeling that their room would be better than their company. For this reason, therefore, the 1-in. Ordnance is more suited for reference at home, or for the district in one's immediate neighbourhood, and for bye-roads.

Within the last few years a re-survey has been commenced, with the result of a great improvement on the original one, but it is not yet completed. It is divided into smaller sections (13¼in. by 11½in.) and will contain 360 sheets at 1s. each. The only drawback from a bicyclist's point of view in this new Ordnance Map is that the hill shading is entirely left out, lines of contour elevation being given instead; but the result is a poor exchange. I should not omit to mention that a small facsimile edition of above, reproduced by photography (on the suggestion of Mr. E. S. Gaisford, of the Temple B. C.), has been published on a ¼-in. scale at 6d. a sheet; but I hardly think the small printing will find favour with bicyclists.

The above prices do not include mounting or folding.

Besides the Ordnance Survey there are several smaller sectional maps. The first series is on a scale of 2m. to the inch, commonly, but not correctly, called the Reduced Ordnance; it is really older than the Ordnance, but has been corrected from it; there are 65 (or 60) sheets for England, Wales, and South Scotland, 20in. by 24in. each at 1s. 6d. Another series is on the scale of 4m. to the inch, being reduced from the 1m. Ordnance Survey; it consists of 14 sheets for England and Wales, about 25in. by 19in. (i.e. 100m. by 80m.) at 2s. 6d. This scale I would recommend as the most suitable map for tourists, showing not only main roads but bye-roads.

CYCLISTS' TOURING CLUB.

The history of this Association, originally called the "Bicycle Touring Club," has been one of remarkable progress; and, being formed solely for the benefit of Cycling Tourists, it is one worthy of continued support of all cyclists. Its object, or at least its main object, is to form a medium of mutual assistance for tourists, by giving each other information as to roads, hotels, sights, and other matters of common interest in the pastime. To carry out this, a system of local officers, called consuls, has been established in all the chief towns, and from them the desired information can always be obtained by the members.

Thus, to the combined energy of a corporate body is added an inherent vitality, essentially the outcome of the individual efforts of an army of enthusiasts. Under skilful guidance such an association ought never to look back; properly directed, its organization and influence are capable of becoming a power in the land, and an ever extending, never ceasing sphere of usefulness lies before it. Already it has done good work in assimilating hotel tariffs, and bringing them down to a figure suited to the pockets of cyclists, while we also owe to them a reduction in, and an almost uniform scale of the charges for carriage of bicycles by railway.

CORRIGENDA TO FIFTH EDITION.

The mileage of the English Southern and Midland Roads has been thoroughly revised in the Author's "Handy Route Book of England and Wales," Parts I. and II.; but with a few exceptions it has been impossible to incorporate such revision — in minute detail—in this work, on account of the cost it would involve. The following notes will, however, enable the reader to easily apply the chief alterations in the revised mileage of the Southern part of the "Handy Route Book" to the figures in this Road Book; in Middle England the alterations are too numerous to specify. The italics show actual alterations.

Page 5, line 20, to be read " *Whitstable, 55½.*"
,, 6, ,, 12, ,, " *Littlebourne to Deal (12½—71¼).*"
,, 6, ,, 14, ,, " *Upper Deal, 70¼.*"
,, 6, ,, 16, ,, " *Upper Deal, 72, to Deal, 73.*]"
,, 13, line 18, to be read " *Pembury Green to Goudhurst (7¼—42¼).*" After Goudhurst mileage to be decreased by ½m., and also in next route.
,, 14, lines 1 to 8, Decrease mileage by ½m.
,, 15, ,, 1 to 15, see Route Book, pp. 21 and 149.
,, 16, ,, 1 to 13, see Route Book, p. 24. Route to Rye, see p. 22.
,, 17, Routes to Rye and Hastings, see pp. 22-3.
,, 17, 18, Route to Eastbourne and Pevensey, see pp. 25-6.
,, 19, see p. 27.
,, 20, line 28, to be read " *Croydon to Caterham Junction (2¾—12¼).*"
,, 20, ,, 31, ,, " *Purley House 11⅝.*"
,, 20-23, above alteration necessitates increase of mileage by ½m. in this and the Seaford and the first Brighton routes.
,, 21, line 23, to be read " *Wych Cross to Maresfield (6—40½).*"
,, 21, ,, 32-3, ,, " *Duddleswell Gate, 37¼.*"
,, 21, ,, 34, ,, " *Maresfield, 41¼.*"
,, 21, ,, 37, ,, " *Maresfield to Eastbourne (21½—62).*"
,, 22, ,, 1 to 10, see p. 31.
,, 24, ,, 5, to be read " *London to Caterham Junction (12¼).*"
,, 24, ,, 8, ,, " *Red Lion, 13¼.*"
,, 24, ,, 6, ,, " *Merstham (5¾—18).*"
,, 24, ,, 14, ,, " *Merstham to Redhill, or Warwick Town (2¼—20¼).*"
,, 24, ,, 21, ,, " *Redhill to Horley Row, (4—24¼).*" In rest of page mileage to be increased by ½m.
,, 26 is revised.
,, 29, 30, Between West Grinstead and Worthing the mileage is revised, see p. 39.
,, 31, Mileage to Five Oaks Green on previous page being increased by ½m., requires rest of route to Littlehampton to be also increased.

Page 33-4, Mileage altered between Guildford and Milford, and rest of route requires to be increased by *1m.*; also other alterations, see pp. 44-5.
" 34-7, Next four routes, mileage to be increased by *1m.*
" 39, 42-5, Between Alton and Alresford mileage to be increased by *½m.*, which requires rest of route to be increased as well as mileage of the routes from Christchurch to Cadnam.
" 42, For Gosport, Botley, and Bishop's Waltham routes, see pp. 52-5.
" 53, line 9, to be read "Brockenhurst, *87¼*."
" 58, "Lobcombe," alter to "Lobscombe." Mileage slightly varied.
" 63, Route re-arranged after Torquay, see pp. 88-9.
" 73, Langport to Taunton revised, see p. 105.
" 75, Redlinch to Castle Cary revised, see pp. 108-9.
" 87-9, Bath road revised, see vol. ii.
" 94, Both Reading routes revised, see pp. 133-5.
" 95, Radstock and Bath roads revised, see pp. 136-8.
" 111, line 6, Abergavenny to Crickhowell, "*very good* road."
" 111, " 13, to be read "Llanham*lach*," also in line 18.
" 111, " 14, Crickhowell to Brecon, "*splendid* road."
" 162, " 1, to be read "Lindale."
" 175, " 12, " "Lindale," and in lines 13 and 18.

ERRATA.

Page 11, line 3: "(9—55)" *should be* "($7\frac{3}{4}$—55)."
" 11, " 4: "Goford Green *Tg.*" *should be* "Golford *Tg.*"
" 11, " 8: "($14\frac{1}{4}$—69)" *should be* "(14—69)."
" 14, " 1: "($2\frac{1}{2}$—$54\frac{3}{4}$)" *should be* "(3—$54\frac{3}{4}$)."
" 14, " 5: "Goford Green *Tg.*" *should be* "Golford *Tg.*"
" 14 " 9: "($13\frac{1}{2}$—$68\frac{1}{4}$)" *should be* "(14—$68\frac{3}{4}$)."
" 14 " 38: "(6—$56\frac{3}{4}$)" *should be* "(6—$56\frac{1}{4}$)."
" 25 " 25: "($3\frac{5}{8}$—$22\frac{1}{2}$)" *should be* "($3\frac{5}{8}$—$29\frac{1}{2}$)."
" 25, " 29: "($4\frac{3}{8}$—$23\frac{7}{8}$)" *should be* "($4\frac{3}{8}$—$33\frac{1}{8}$)."

THE Coventry Machinists' Co
LIMITED.
ESTABLISHED 1859.

By Special Appointment to H.R.H. the Prince of Wales.

SOLE MAKERS OF THE

"CLUB" BICYCLES & TRICYCLES.

The "SWIFT SAFETY."   The "MARLBORO' CLUB" TRICYCLE.

Head Office and Works: COVENTRY.
LONDON: 15 & 16, Holborn Viaduct.
MANCHESTER: 9, Victoria Buildings.
BIRMINGHAM, NEWCASTLE, etc.

Illustrated Catalogue, etc., etc., Post Free.

Coventry to Woodstock & to Kenilworth = perfect roads

DIRECT ROADS.

ABBREVIATIONS.

m.—Miles.	*Tg.*—Tollgate.	*M.P.*—Market Place.
l.—Left.	*ch.*—Church.	*P.O.*—Post Office.
r.—Right.	*M.H.*—Market House.	*Ms.*—Milestone.
Tp.—Turnpike.	*Ho.*—House.	*R.*—River.

THE FOLLOWING RELATE TO HOTELS ONLY:—

Hqrs.—Headquarters of a local Bicycle Club.
C.T.C. or *B.T.C.*—Hotel has adopted "Cyclists' Touring Club" Tariff.

NOTE.—The first of the two numbers within brackets denotes the mileage between the two places; the second number, gives the full distance from the starting point of the route to the place last named. A single number after the name of a place denotes its distance from the starting point.

SECTION I.

From London Bridge*; South Eastern Roads (Kent and East Sussex).

LONDON TO MARGATE AND BROADSTAIRS.

London Bridge (Surrey Side) to New Cross (3¾); beginning with a short descent from the bridge, after which it is level, the road is roughly paved along Borough High street, turning to the *l.* at St. George's *ch.*, ¼ *m.*, where tramway begins and continues the whole distance along Great Dover street to Old Kent road (Bricklayers' Arms, 1), and thence along Old Kent road, with a canal bridge to go over at 2 *m.*, and beyond New Cross Gate, 3¼, a railway bridge; all paved heavy traffic, and road generally bad and unfit for bicycling.

New Cross to Blackheath (1¼—5); the tramway with macadam continues through New Cross and Deptford, 4¼, which is a busy paved thoroughfare, to the bottom of Blackheath Hill, a very steep ascent for the last 250 yards, again macadam, and dangerous to ride down the reverse direction without a good brake, there being a bend towards the bottom.

Blackheath to Shooters Hill (3—8); having mounted the hill, it is a gentle undulating macadam road across Blackheath for about a mile,

---

* The roads on this Section are accessible from the other bridges, via the "Bricklayers' Arms," which is distant from them as follows:—From Southwark bridge, 1¼ *m.* nearly; from Blackfriars bridge, 1¼ *m.* nearly; from Waterloo bridge, 1¼ *m.* nearly; from Westminster bridge, 1¼ *m.* nearly; all meeting at the "Elephant and Castle," whence along the New Kent road to the "Bricklayers' Arms" is ¾ *m.* Also, from Vauxhall bridge by Kennington Oval, past Kennington *ch.*, along Camberwell New road, through Camberwell Green, and along Church street, Peckham High street, and Queen's road, to New Cross Gate, 4 *m.*; this is the best route from the West End, and has not so much traffic. Tramways are laid on all these roads, otherwise they are macadam, except Blackfriars road which is all paved.

and then soon improves to a more gravelly surface, generally good going, and is either level or slightly on the rise to the foot of Shooters Hill.
At Shooters Hill, on *r.*, Severndroog Castle.

Shooters Hill to Crayford (5—13); the steep and generally heavy ascent of Shooters Hill is followed by a corresponding fall down the opposite side, and it is not safe to ride *down either* descent without a reliable brake, the surface being often loose and stony; from the bottom, the road is very good and pretty level through Welling, 10¼, and Bexley New Town, 11½, with easy descent into Crayford, through which is macadam.
(*Welling :* Nag's Head.—*Crayford :* Bear Inn.)
At Welling, on *r.*, Danson Park.

Crayford to Dartford (2—15); long rise out of Crayford, and a steep descent into Dartford: good hard limestone road.
(*Dartford :* Bull; Odd Fellows' Arms; Railway; Royal Bull, *C.T.C.*)
At Dartford are remains of a magnificent nunnery, erected by Edward III.

Dartford to Gravesend (7—22); out of Dartford is an ascent, steep at first, but not long, followed by a level run across the Common, then two sharp falls into St. John's Hole, 16¼, and Horn's Cross, 17, with corresponding rises after; a little beyond the latter place occurs a long run down, but not steep (at the bottom of which, ½*m.* on *l.*, is *Greenhithe*, 18¼), then follow a rather stiff ascent and another long run down—Galley Hill—and shortly after the steep and lumpy macadam ascent of Northfleet Hill has to be climbed to Northfleet, 20½, and the rest is nearly level into Gravesend: good hard limestone road, tolerably smooth, to the bottom of Northfleet Hill, then rough macadam. At Gravesend, bells are compulsory.
[If not calling at Gravesend, the bicyclist will find a better road by turning to *r.* at the end of Northfleet (past Leather Bottle), avoiding nearly all the macadam and rejoining the main road ¾*m.* beyond Gravesend: there is one hill to go up and down, but good and smooth surface.]
(*Greenhithe:* Pier; Railway, *C.T.C.*; White Hart.—*Gravesend:* New Falcon; Old Falcon.—*Rosherville:* Terrace, *B.T.C.*)
At the top of the hill past Greenhithe, on *l.*, Ingress Park. Gravesend is the limit of the Port of London; opposite, across the River Thames, is Tilbury Fort.

Gravesend to Rochester *ch.* (7—29); rather lumpy macadam for a mile or so till clear of Gravesend, then very undulating through Chalk, 23¼, and past Halfway House, 25½, to the Falstaff Inn, at Gad's Hill, 26½, up to which there is a long stiff pull; then a steep fall, moderate rise, and the long steep descent of Coach and Horses Hill, 27½, should be carefully ridden down, there being a turn in it, to Strood, 28½, whence cross *R.* Medway bridge to Rochester: good hard road. Bells compulsory in Rochester.
(*Gad's Hill :* Falstaff Inn.—*Strood :* Bull; Crown; Victoria Tavern.—*Rochester :* Bull; Crown; King's Head, *B.T.C.*; Red Lion; Royal Crown; Victoria.)
At Gad's Hill was the residence of the late Charles Dickens, the celebrated novelist; 2*m.* or *r.*, on the line of the Roman Road, Watling Street, is Cobham Hall, the seat of Earl Darnley. At Rochester, the Cathedral and remains of the Castle; beyond Rochester, on *r.*, Fort Pitt and Fort Clarence.

Rochester to Key Street (9—38); rough macadam through the narrow main streets of Rochester and Chatham, 30, which form almost one continuous town; [instead of going through the main street of Chatham, there is a better route, of about the same distance, by turning to the *r.* up the hill by the theatre in Rochester (½*m.* beyond the *ch.*), leaving Chatham on the *l.*, and rejoining the main road near the railway, on the outskirts of that town at 30¼]; then there is the very steep ascent of Chatham Hill, which most riders will walk, and from the top of which the road is good and undulating past Star Inn, 32, and through Rainham, 34, Moor Street, 34¾, and Newington Street, 36¾, three of the hills being very stiff.

(*Chatham* : Globe, *Hqrs.*; Mitre and Clarence, *C.T.C.*; White Horse.—*Key Street* : Key.)

At Chatham are the extensive Government dockyards, naval arsenal, victualling office, hospitals, &c.; beyond, on *l.*, Brompton and Gillingham Forts, and across River Medway, Upnor Castle, which is best reached from Strood.

Key Street to Ospringe (8—46), is a good smooth road, undulating through Chalkwell, 39, to Sittingbourne, 40, where there is a very steep ascent, and then hilly through Bapchild, 41¼, and Green Street, 43, after which is a hill nearly 2*m.* long, and down again into Ospringe.

At Ospringe, on *l.* to *Faversham* (1—47).

(*Sittingbourne:* Bull, *Hqrs.*; Commercial; Lion; Shakespeare.—*Faversham*. Dolphin; Railway, *rec. C.T.C.*; Ship, *Hqrs.*)

At Sittingbourne, on *r.*, Gore Court; beyond Green Street, on *r.*, Norton Court. At Ospringe, on *r.*, Jud's Hill, Belmont, and Syndale Ho. At Sittingbourne, on *l.*, the village of Milton, famous for its oysters. At Faversham, remains of the Abbey.

Ospringe to Canterbury, King's Bridge (9¼—55¼); good, but hilly road through Preston, 46½, to Boughton Street, 49¼, beyond which there is the rather long and very steep ascent of Boughton Hill, 50¼, barely rideable; then a good undulating road with a stiff pull up to Harbledown Tp., 52½, whence there is a splendid run, mostly down hill, to beyond Harbledown, 54¼, with a level finish into Canterbury.

(*Canterbury:* Crampton's; Falstaff, *B.T.C.*; Fleur de Lis; Fountain; George and Dragon; Rose; Royal Fountain; Saracen's Head, *Hqrs.*; Station.)

Before Boughton, on *l.*, Nash Court. Canterbury has many interesting objects of antiquity; the magnificent Cathedral was begun in 1174, but not finished till the reign of Henry V.; St. Martin's *ch.*, the oldest Christian edifice in England, built with Roman bricks, and supposed to have been first erected in the second century; ruins of St. Augustine's monastery, remains of the Castle and city walls, Dane John Mound, &c.

Canterbury to Sturry (2½—57¾); in Canterbury, shortly after crossing the second bridge over *R.* Stour, turn sharp to *l.* up Guildhall St. nearly opposite the *P.O.*, and after getting clear of the streets it is a good hard road, fairly level, to Sturry, where is a level railway crossing.

Beyond Canterbury, on *l.*, Hales Place, the Jesuit College.

Sturry to Sarre (6—63¾); keeping to the *r.* after the railway, just out of Sturry is the stiff ascent of Staines Hill, then it is a good hard road, fairly level, through Upstreet, 61¼.

Sarre to Margate, High Street (7¾—71½); at Sarre take the left hand branch at the fork; through Birchington, 67¼, and Street, 69¼, the road is level except a few gentle undulations, and at first good, but gradually degenerates and becomes bad and loose approaching Margate. The country is very open and the road much exposed to the winds and sea breezes.

(*Margate:* Cliftonville; Elephant; Fountain; Hoy; King's Head, *C.T.C.*; Royal Assembly Rooms; Severn House; White Hart; York.)

At Birchington, on *r.*, Quex Park; 1½*m.* further on, on *l.*, Westgate-by-Sea. Margate is a favourite seaside resort, particularly noted for its excellent bathing.

Margate to Broadstairs (3½—75; turn to the *r.* in Margate, and by Draper's Hospital, 72¼, and through St. Peter's, 73¾, is a good undulating road.

(*Broadstairs:* Albion; Balmoral, *C.T.C.*; Victoria.)

Broadstairs is a small, quiet watering place; 1½*m.* N. is the promontory of North Foreland, with its lighthouse; it can be reached from Margate through North Down, 1½, and Kingsgate, 2¾, to North Foreland, 3½. From Kingsgate to Broadstairs, 2*m.*

LONDON TO RAMSGATE.

London to Sarre (63¾)—p. 3.

Sarre to Ramsgate (7¾—71½); at Sarre keep to the *r.*, and it is a capital undulating road through Monkton, 64¾, by Mount Pleasant, 66¾, Minster Mills, 67¾, and Nether Court, 70¼, and through St. Lawrence, 70¾: Ramsgate is mostly macadam.

(*Ramsgate:* Castle; Crampton; George and Dragon; Granville; Oak; Royal; Royal Albion; Spread Eagle, *Hqrs.*; Temperance; Wellington.)

At Mount Pleasant are some splendid views; 1*m.* on *r.* is the old picturesque village of Minster, with abbey and *ch.*, and in the neighbourhood are several ancient ruins. Ramsgate is a large watering place and seaport, its sands excelling those of Margate in extent.

Ramsgate to Broadstairs (2—73½).

LONDON TO ERITH.

London to New Cross (3¾)—p. 1.

New Cross to Greenwich (1½—5¼); the tramway and macadam continue all the way; at Deptford, 4¼, take the left hand road.

(*Greenwich:* Gloucester.)

At Greenwich, on *l.*, the Royal Seamen's Hospital; on *r.* the Park and Observatory.

Greenwich to Woolwich (3¼—8½) is all macadam.

[There is another road to Woolwich through *Blackheath*, 5—p. 1; on the top of the hill take the left hand road by Myrtle Place, 6, through Charlton, 7¼, and past the Artillery Barracks and over Woolwich Common to *Woolwich*, 9¼: pretty good road but partly macadam.

Or to *Shooters Hill*, 8—p. 1; then turn to *l.*, and it is a good road mostly on the fall to *Woolwich*, 9¾.]

At Woolwich is a Government dockyard and the Royal Arsenal. At Charlton, on *r.*, Charlton *Ho.*

(*Woolwich:* King's Arms, *C.T.C.*)

Woolwich to Erith (5½—14); through Plumstead, 9½, and over Bostal Heath, 10½.

Beyond Bostal Heath, a little on *l.*, Lesnes Abbey; 1*m.* before Erith, on *l.*, Belvedere *Ho.*

LONDON TO SHEERNESS.

London to Key Street (38)—p. 2.

Key Street to Sheerness ($10\frac{1}{2}$—$48\frac{1}{2}$); turn to the *l.* and through Bobbing, $38\frac{1}{2}$, Bobbing Street, $39\frac{3}{4}$, and Iwade, 41, a mile beyond which cross West Swale to Isle of Sheppey, and through King's Ferry, $42\frac{3}{4}$, Neatscourt, $44\frac{3}{4}$, (further on keep to *r.*) and by Halfway House, 46, (keep to *l.*) and Mile House, $47\frac{1}{2}$.

Beyond Neatscourt on *l.* to Queenborough (1—$45\frac{3}{4}$).

(*Queenborough:* Ship.—*Sheerness:* Fountain; Royal.)

At Sheerness are a royal dockyard, arsenal, and fortress, &c.

LONDON TO HERNE BAY.

London to Sturry ($57\frac{3}{4}$)—p. 3.

Sturry to Herne Bay (6—$63\frac{3}{4}$); after the railway crossing keep straight on (left hand road) and there is a long steep hill to climb (must be carefully ridden *down* the other way), shortly followed by a good run down and another stiffer but shorter rise up to Halfway House, $59\frac{1}{2}$, and the rest undulating with a long run down from Herne Common, $60\frac{3}{4}$, to Herne, $61\frac{3}{4}$: capital surface.

[Or to *Faversham*, 47—p. 3, then through Goodnestone, $49\frac{1}{4}$, and Graveney, $50\frac{1}{4}$, to Whitstable, 55, but not much more than a cart and horse track, and thence through Church Street, $56\frac{3}{4}$, and Swalecliffe to *Herne Bay*, $61\frac{3}{4}$, is nearly level and generally fairly good gravel road, a little loose in parts.

Or to St. Dunstan's *ch.* ($\frac{1}{4}$*m.* before Canterbury) 55—p. 3, and then turn to *l.*; steep loose ascent of Hackington Hill to walk up (unrideable *down* except with reliable brake), then two or three sharp ups and downs by Blean, 57, Honey Hill, $57\frac{3}{4}$, and Preen Hill, $58\frac{1}{2}$, shortly followed by Clapham Hill to walk up, steep, loose, and stony, and a very steep but short pitch to walk down Bostal Hill to Whitstable, 61.]

(*Whitstable:* Bear and Key; Duke of Cumberland, *B.T.C.*—*Herne Bay:* Brunswick; New Dolphin, *B.T.C.*; Victoria; Station.)

Whitstable is noted for its oyster fisheries; near it is Tankerton Castle. Herne Bay is much resorted to in summer for sea bathing. Nearly 5*m.* E. are the Reculvers towers, the site of the Roman Regulbium, and afterwards a royal residence of the Saxons; part of the *ch.* has been swept away by encroachments of the sea.

LONDON TO SANDWICH.

London to Canterbury, King's Bridge ($55\frac{1}{4}$)—p. 3.

Canterbury to Littlebourne ($3\frac{1}{2}$—$58\frac{3}{4}$) is a good road; follow the Dover road till nearly out of Canterbury, then turn to the *l.* up Lower Bridge Street; St. Martin's Hill to ride up out of the city, then nearly a mile run down, followed, after a rise, by level road to near Littlebourne, into which is a good descent.

Littlebourne to Ash ($5\frac{1}{2}$—$64\frac{1}{4}$); undulating road through Bramling, 60, to Wingham, $61\frac{3}{4}$, (turn to *l.*) out of which (keeping to *r.*) is a steep short hill to climb, generally rough, then a stiff descent, followed by a long incline, and a long gradual fall into Ash.

Past Littlebourne, on *r.*, Lee Priory. Past Bramling, a little on *r.*, Dane Court.

Ash to Sandwich (3¼—67¾) is an easy road, short descent at 1m. out of Ash, then level across the marshes; through Sandwich is paved and bad riding.

(*Sandwich:* Bell, *C.T.C.*; Fleur de Lis.)

About 1m. on *l.*, before Sandwich, the remains of Richborough Castle, the ancient Rutupiæ, one of the earliest Roman works in England; near it are remains of a Roman amphitheatre. Nearly 1m. N. of Sandwich, on Ramsgate road, is Great Stonar, now a farm-house, the site of a considerable town in Norman times. Sandwich is nearly enclosed by the old walls; it has two ancient churches.

LONDON TO DEAL.

London to Littlebourne (58¾)—p. 5.

Littlebourne to Deal (13¾—72½); undulating to Bramling, 60, where keep to *r.*, and through Knowlton, 64¼, over How Bridge, 68½, through Cottington, 69, Sholden, 70, and Upper Deal, 71.

[Or to *Sandwich*, 67¾—p. 5, then through Worth, 68¾, Hacklinge, 69¾, Cottington, 70¾, Sholden, 71¾, and Upper Deal, 72¾, to *Deal*, 74¼.]

(*Deal:* Black Horse, *C.T.C.*; Crown Inn, *Hqrs.*; Royal; Royal Exchange.)

Past Bramling, on *r.*, Dane Court and Goodnestone Park. At Knowlton, on *r.*, Knowlton Park. Deal Castle; 1m. on N. Sandown Castle, built by Henry VIII.; 1m. on S. is Walmer Castle.

LONDON TO DOVER.

London to Canterbury, King's Bridge (55¼)—p. 3.

Canterbury to Bridge (3¼—58½); continuing straight through Canterbury, there is a long rise out of the city, and then undulating with a short steep fall into Bridge.

Before Bridge, on *r.*, Renwell and Bridge Hill Ho.; on *l.* Bifrons.

Bridge to Lydden (7¾—66¼); out of Bridge there is a stiff hill to mount, then over Barham Downs the road consists of a series of little hills up and down to Halfway House, 63½, after which it is level for more than 2m., with the long but not steep descent of Lydden Hill into Lydden: splendid smooth and hard road, except on Lydden Hill.

Past Bridge, on *r.*, Bourne Ho.; on *l.*, Higham; about 3m. farther, on *r.*, Barham Court and Barham Place; on *l.*, Den Hill. Near Halfway House, on *r.*, Broom Park. About 3m. on *l.* is Barfreston *ch.*, an ancient and interesting structure.

Lydden to Dover (4¼—71); good road, undulating to Ewell, 68, and thence gently downhill through Buckland, 69½, and Charlton, 70¼; good road, but last 1½m. macadam streets.

(*Dover:* Dover Castle; Esplanade, *Hqrs.*; Harp; Shakespeare; Temperance; Victoria; Royal Oak, *C.T.C.*)

Dover lies in a valley, and eastward of it on a hill is the castle, an extensive fortification, part of it supposed to have been built by the Romans. St. Mary's *ch.* and St. James's *ch.*; Maison Dieu; Dover Priory. About ½m. S.W. is Shakespeare's Cliff, which of late years has been much undermined by the waves; 2½m. W. the ruins of St. Radigund's monastery (or Branside Abbey), founded at the end of the twelfth century.

LONDON TO CRAYFORD (by Eltham).

London to New Cross (3¾)—p. 1.

New Cross to Lewisham, Bridge (1¼—5); take the right hand fork by the "Marquis of Granby;" rough macadam road, with two sharp dips to cross.

Lewisham to Eltham (3—8); a short distance after crossing the R. Ravensbourne keep to the *l.*, and through Lee, 5¾, and past the "Tiger's Head," 6¼, the road is macadam all the way, and very bad and shaky; there is a long and stiff ascent to Eltham.

At Eltham, on *r.*, Eltham Place; near it the remains of the old royal palace erected in the thirteenth century, and now used as a barn.

Eltham to Bexley (5—13) is undulating, but inclined to be loose and sandy to Blendon, 11½, whence it is hilly with good surface to Bexley.

(*Bexley* : Bexley Arms.)

Past Eltham, on *l.*, Eltham Park. At Blendon, on *r.*, Blendon Hall.

Bexley to Crayford (1½—14½) is a good road, almost level.

LONDON TO FOLKESTONE.

London to Eltham (8)—above.

Eltham to Foots Cray (4¼—12¼); by the right hand road at the end of Eltham, then through Southend, 9, and Sidcup, 11½, is rather hilly, and there is a good downhill from Sidcup; pretty good surface.

(*Sidcup* : Black Horse.)

Before Sidcup, a little on *l.*, Lambabbey; further on, Foot's Cray Place.

Foots Cray to Farningham (5½—17½); there is a stiff ascent a short distance beyond Foots Cray, then undulating past Birchwood Corner, 14, to Pedham Place, 16½, whence there is a long descent into Farningham, the first part of which is safely rideable, but towards the bottom it becomes steeper and ends in the narrow winding street of the village, that must be ridden down very carefully if without a brake; very often, and especially in dry weather, the greater part of this stage is loose or sandy.

(*Farningham* : Ball; Lion. *rec. C.T.C.*)

Farningham to Wrotham (6½—24); stiff ascent out of the Darent valley, followed after a short interval by two still more difficult rises, the surface of which is often loose and stony; the top of the hill is reached some 2½m. out of Farningham, whence it is a good and gently undulating road past "The Cock," 20¾, Portobello, 21, and the "Horse and Groom." 22½; shortly beyond here commences a long and very steep fall of over a mile into Wrotham, which having several turns in it, and being often loose and stony, requires careful riding, and should not be descended without a reliable break.

(*Wrotham Hill* : Horse and Groom.—*Wrotham* : Bull, *rec. C.T.C.*)

Wrotham to Wrotham Heath (Royal Oak, 2¼—26¼) is a good undulating road, chiefly downhill.

Wrotham Heath to Maidstone (Rain's Cross, 8¼—34½); past the "Wheatsheaf," 28½, and through Larkfield, 30, and Ditton, 30¾, is up and down hill, but nothing difficult; after the first mile or so the surface becomes rough and lumpy, being made of a kind of limestone, which is greasy when wet, and is rather bad travelling; long run down into Maidstone, ending with a steep and rough descent to the bridge over the R.

Medway at the entrance of the town; thence a rise up High Street to Rain's Cross.

(*Maidstone:* Bell, *C.T.C.*; Mitre; Haunch of Venison; Queen's Head; Railway; Rose and Crown; Royal Star, *Hqrs.*; Ye Ancient Bell, *Hqrs.*)

At "Wheatsheaf," on *l.*, Leybourne Place; further on, ¼m. on *r.*, at West Malling, the abbey and ruins of Benedictine convent; West Malling *ch.* At Larkfield, on *r.*, Bradbourne *Ho.*; 1m. past Ditton, on *l.*, Preston Hall, and Aylesford Place, which is built from the remains of a Carmelite Friary. Near Aylesford was fought the battle where Vortimer defeated the Saxons in 455. About 1½m. N.E. is the cromlech known as Kit's Coty House; 2m. before Maidstone, 1m. on *l.*, ruins of Allington Castle, and 1m. further, of Boxley Abbey. Maidstone is the county town.

Maidstone to Lenham (9¼—43¾); keep straight on through Maidstone, and there are two or three sharp ascents in the first mile or so out of the town, then the road continues rather hilly, but nothing difficult through Bearsted, 36¾, Chrishmell *Tp.*, 37¾, past Park Gate Inn, 39½, and through West Harrietsham, 41½, beyond which is a long rise with a descent into Lenham; very good road and pretty country.

(*Lenham:* Dog and Bear, *B.T.C.*)

Beyond Maidstone, on *l.*, Vinters; further on, on *r.*, the Mote. At Park Gate Inn, on *r.*, the road skirts, for 1½m., the demesne of Leeds Park, with its castle, a fine old mansion; behind it the remains of the abbey. From Harrietsham the road runs at the foot of a range of hills, that bound it on the east, most of the way to Ashford; Lenham *ch.*

Lenham to Charing (3¼—47½); the road continues very good, and is easily undulating; pretty country.

(*Charing:* Swan, *rec. C.T.C.*)

Charing to Ashford (5¾—53¼); in Charing, first to *r.* and then to *l.*; there is a short ascent at Westwell Common, 49, and then the road continues undulating through Wooden Street, 50, over Hothfield Heath, 50½, and past Potters Corner, 51½, just beyond which is a sharp run down; very fair surface.

(*Ashford:* George, *B.T.C.*; Royal Oak; Saracen's Head; Wellesley Arms.)

At Hothfield Heath, a little on *r.*, Hothfield Park and Godington Park. At Ashford is an ancient *ch.* containing some interesting monuments.

Ashford to Hythe (12—65¼); steepish descent out of Ashford, which should be taken carefully, then an undulating road through Willesborough, 54½, Mersham Hatch, 56, Smeeth, 58, and Sellinge, 60, to New Inn Green, 62¾, whence there is a run down of 2m. through Pedlinge, 63¾, to Hythe *Tp.*, 64¾, and the road twisting somewhat, the slope should be ridden down carefully if without a brake; good road.

(*Hythe:* Swan, *B.T.C.*; White Hart.)

At Sellinge, on *l.*, Horton Priory. At Pedlinge, a little on *l.*, Westonhanger, an old manorial residence of the time of Richard I., and near it Fair Rosamond's Tower. At New Inn Green, 1½m. on *r.*, Lympne, the Portus Lemanus of the Romans, with remains of the castrum, &c., and also an old castle and *ch.*, and near it the magnificent ruins of Stutfall Castle. 1m. on *l.* of Hythe, the ruins of Saltwood Castle. On the coast are several forts or martello towers.

Hythe to Folkestone (4½—69¾); the road runs near the sea, through Shorncliff, 67, to Sandgate, 68, and is macadam and shaky most of the way. From Sandgate there are two roads to Folkestone, the lower road (to the right) is the better one, with slight undulations running at the base of the cliffs into Folkestone Old Town and the Harbour, but there is 1s. toll to pay on this road; by the upper road there is a long stiff hill out of the village, then level for a mile or so, and a sharp descent into Folkestone, entering by the Lees in the upper part of the town.

[There is another road to Folkestone by following the Dover road to *Bridge*, 58½—p. 6, and to within ½*m.* of Halfway House, then turn to the *r.*, skirting Broom Park to Denton, 64½, and through Maypole, 66¼, across Swingfield Minnis or Common, by Densell, 68½, Hawkinge Mill, 69½, Uphill, 69¾, Walton *Tp.*, 70¾, and Walton, 71¼, to *Folkestone*, 72½, into which is a descent of about 3*m.* long, very steep in parts, and not safe to ride down without a reliable brake.

Or 1*m.* beyond Bridge turn to *r.*, and through Bishopsbourne, 60, Kingston, 61, Barham, 62, Dorringstone, 62¼, Elham, 66½, Elham Mill, 67¼, and Acorise or Acryse, 68¾, to Hawkinge Mill, 70¾, and *Folkestone*, 73¾.]

(*Sandgate:* Royal Kent; Royal Norfolk.—*Folkestone:* Albion; Bates's; Clarendon; King's Arms; Pavilion; Rose; Shakespeare; West Cliff.)

On the top of the cliffs at Shorncliff is a large military camp. At Sandgate is a castle built by Henry VIII. At Folkestone are remains of a Norman Benedictine priory, founded 1095. The parish *ch.* contains some old monuments. N.W. of the town, on the Downs, is an ancient entrenchment called "Cæsar's Camp." Beyond Maypole, on Swingfield Minnis, 1*m.* on *l.*, ruins of St. John's Preceptory. At Elham, 2*m.* S.W. is Lyminge, the *ch.* of which was rebuilt *circ.* 1080, replacing an early Saxon *ch.*, and on the site of a Roman basilica, of which the foundations have been lately opened.

LONDON TO MAIDSTONE (by Rochester).

London to Rochester, Church (29)—p. 2.

Rochester to Maidstone (8½—37½); ¼*m.* past the *ch.* in Rochester turn sharp to the *r.*, and it is a steep ascent out of the town, by Upper Delce, 30¼, and through Bridge Woods and Boxley Wood to the Upper Bell, 33½ on Boxley Hill, and then all downhill, the first mile or two very steep, through Sandlin, 36, to Maidstone; very good road.

About 1*m.* past Upper Bell, on *r.*, close to road, is the cromlech of Kit's Coty House. Before Sandlin, on *l.*, ruins of Boxley Abbey; past Sandlin, on *r.*, across River Medway, ruins of Allington Castle.

LONDON TO NEW ROMNEY.

London to Maidstone (Rain's Cross, 34½)—p. 7.

Maidstone to Headcorn (9¼—43¾); at Maidstone turn to *r.* at the cross streets (or if coming from Rochester keep straight on), and after a short descent there is a rough ascent out of the town to the *Tg.* at the fork roads, where keep to *l.*, and it is undulating through Broadway, 37, Rumwood Green, 38, Langley, 38½, and Five Wents, 39, to Sutton Valence, 40¼, through and out of which is a steep, dangerous descent, 1*m.* long, with sharp turn in it, and again undulating to Headcorn.

(*Headcorn:* Railway, *B.T.C.*)

Headcorn to Biddenden (4¼—48); a short but stiff hill to mount about 1½m. beyond Headcorn, otherwise almost level.

1m. beyond Headcorn on *l.* to *Smarden* (2½—46½).

Biddenden to Tenterden (5—53); almost level to Castleton's Oak Inn, 49¾, where turn to the *l.*, and the road is undulating to Tenterden, which is situate on a hill. [Or take the left hand road, ¾m. out of Biddenden, and going by "Man of Kent," 50¾, London Beach, 51, Bird's Isle or Boar's Isle, 51¾, and Gallows Green, 52½, to Tenterden, 53¼, gently undulating all the way; but if not calling at Tenterden, keep to *l.* at Gallows Green straight to Lye Green (or Leigh Green), 53½, on the next stage, thus saving ¾m.]

(*Tenterden:* Eight Bells; Lion; Woolpack, *C.T.C.*)

Tenterden *ch.* steeple is a prominent object on the country side for miles round, and is a well-known land-mark to sailors coming up the channel. The country, south of Maidstone, is one of the chief hop growing districts in England.

Tenterden to Reading Street (3½—56½); through Tenterden keep to the *r.* [if coming by the alternative, or second of above roads to Tenterden, turn to *l.* entering the town,] and the road is all but level; through Lye Green (or Leigh Green), 54¼, beyond which begins a long and very stiff descent into Reading Street, which should be ridden down carefully.

Reading Street to Appledore (2½—59) is level, except a small hill to go over about half way.

Appledore to New Romney (8—67); after Appledore, cross the Royal Military Canal, and the road then traverses Romney Marsh, through Snargate, 61½, Brenzett Corner, 62¾, and Old Romney, 65; it is level, but a bad road, loose and stony.

(*New Romney:* New Inn, *rec. C.T.C.*; Ship.)

The Royal Military Canal extends from Sandgate to near Rye, 23*m.*; it was cut early in the present century. Old Romney was formerly a flourishing seaport; 4*m.* S. of New Romney is Dungeness Point.

LONDON TO NEW ROMNEY (by Staplehurst).

London to Maidstone (Rain's Cross, 34½)—p. 7.

Maidstone to Stile Bridge (5½—40); in Maidstone turn to *r.* at the cross streets (or if coming from Rochester keep straight on through the town), and after a short descent there is a rough and almost unrideable ascent out of the town, then at the fork roads turn to the *r.*, and shortly after is a steep descent into Loose, 37, whence there is a stiff climb with rather loose surface up to Cox Heath, then pretty level through Linton, 38¼, and Loddington Street, 38¾, with a steep downhill to Stile Bridge; good road, but loose in places.

At Linton, on *l.*, Linton Place.

Stile Bridge to Sissinghurst (7¼—47¼); past Stile Bridge, take the left-hand road, and by Cross in Hand, 41½, Swithland's Corner, 42, is a pretty level road, to Staplehurst, 43½, and by Iden Green, 44, Nock's Bridge, 44¾, and Camden Hill, 46½, is rather hilly, chiefly on the rise, otherwise good; beyond Camden Hill take the left hand-road (on *r.* by Willesly Green, 46¾, to *Cranbrook*, 48½).

(*Staplehurst:* Railway; South Eastern.—*Cranbrook:* George, *rec. C.T.C.*)

1 m. E. of Sissinghurst is Roundshill Park, and behind it the ruins of Sissinghurst Castle.

Sissinghurst to Tenterden (8—55); at Sissinghurst turn to the r. just before the *ch.*, and through Goford Green *Tg.*, 48 (where turn sharp to *l.*), and Forston Green, 5!, is nearly all up and downhill, but nothing difficult to Castleton's Oak Inn, 51¾, where join the road from Biddenden, and the rest is undulating with a rise up into Tenterden.

Tenterden to New Romney (14½—69)—p. 10.

LONDON TO ST. MARY'S CRAY.

London to Eltham (8)—p. 7.

Eltham to St. Mary's Cray (5½—13½); at the end of Eltham take the right hand road with a descent to Southend, 9, out of which, again to the *r.*, and through Chislehurst, 11¼, is a good road to St. Mary's Cray.

[There is another route by turning to the *r.* at the bottom of the hill 1m. before Eltham and through Mottingham, 8, Cold Harbour, 9, and Chislehurst, 10¾, to St. Mary's Cray, 13.]

Before Chislehurst, on *r.*, Camden Place.

LONDON TO RYE.

London to Lewisham (Bridge, 5)—p. 6.

Lewisham to Bromley (5—10); taking the right hand road, the macadam continues through Rushey Green, 6, and with some improvement, to Southend 7½, after which it is a good road, though sometimes sandy in dry weather; about 1m. beyond Southend there is a very stiff hill to mount, which is generally rather loose and rough, then level but indifferent road into Bromley, through which is macadam.

(*Rushey Green*: Black Horse, *Hqrs.*—*Southend*: Green Man.—*Bromley*: Bell, C.T.C.; Five Bells: White Hart; Prince of Wales.)

At Bromley Hill, on *r.*, Bromley Hill *Ho.*; on *l.*, Plaistow Lodge. Entering Bromley, on *l.*, the College; at the end of the town is the palace of the Bishop of Rochester.

Bromley to Green Street Green (5½—15½); short but stiff descent and ascent at Mason's Hill, 10½, and then slightly rising ground and undulatory over Bromley Common, 12 (where keep to the *l.*) to Lock's Bottom, 13, thence up and down hill to Farnborough, 14, just beyond which is a considerable descent, sometimes rather rough, otherwise good smooth road.

(*Mason's Hill*: Tiger's Head.—*Bromley Common*: Crown Inn.—*Farnborough*: New Inn.—*Green Street Green*: Rose and Crown.)

At Bromley Common, on *r.*, Oakley *Ho.* At Lock's Bottom, on *r.*, Keston Lodge, and further, Holwood *Ho.*

Green Street Green to Sevenoaks (*P. O.*, 8¼—23½); there is a continuous easy ascent for nearly the first 4 m. past Pratt's Bottom *Tg.*, 16½, to the "Polhill Arms," 19½, then a much steeper fall about 1m. long, down Madamscot or Sepham Hill, quite rideable, and forward the road is pretty level through Dunton Green, 21, and River Head, 22, with a very steep hill to climb entering Sevenoaks; capital smooth surface throughout.

[Or from Pratt's Bottom *Tg.* turn to *r.* up through Pratt's Bottom, 16¾, and Richmore Hill, 17½, to Knockholt Pound, 19, then a steep winding descent down Morant's Court Hill, 20, rejoining the other road at Dunton Green, 21.]

(Polhill Arms.—*River Head:* Amhurst Arms.—*Sevenoaks:* Bligh's; Bricklayers' Arms; Commercial; Crown; Railway; Rose and Crown; Royal Oak; Sennoaks Arms; Sargent's Railway and Bicycle; Sennocke.)

At Richmore Hill, on *l.*, Halstead Place. Splendid view from Morant's Court Hill; below, on *r.*, Chevening Park. At River Head, on *l.*, Bradbourn *Ho.*; on *r.*, Chipstead Place and Montreal Place.

Sevenoaks to Tunbridge (6½—30); long ascent a little beyond Sevenoaks by the side of Knole Park and past Sevenoaks Common, 24½, to the top of River Hill, 25, then there is River Hill to descend, ¾ of a mile long; and being very steep and winding it is not safe to ride down without a reliable brake (many accidents to bicyclists have happened on it); from the bottom it is easy riding by Watts Cross, 27¼, and Hildenboro', 27¾, over a good road, chiefly downhill to within a mile of Tunbridge, where is a sharp rise; fairly good and smooth road.

(*Tunbridge:* Rose and Crown; Bull, *B.T.C.*)

Just beyond Sevenoaks, on *l.*, Knole Park, with its fine old manorial mansion, chiefly built in the Tudor style of the fifteenth century, but some parts older. At Tunbridge (called also Tonbridge) are ruins of a castle and priory.

Tunbridge to Pembury Green (5—35); after crossing the River Medway and over the railway bridge at the other end of the town, turn to the *l.* up a stiffish hill; then, after a short fall, there is a long stiff pull up to Burgess Hill, 32¼, and the rest is rather hilly by Wood's Gate, 34¼; good hard road.

(*Pembury Green:* Camden Arms.)

Before Burgess Hill, on *l.*, Somerhill, once the residence of Lambert, the celebrated Puritan general.

Pembury Green to Lamberhurst (5—40); through Keys Green, 37, and Lindridge, 38, is not so hilly and more down than up, following the Goudhurst Road for nearly 4½m., and then turning to the *r.* for Lamberhurst, into which there is a steep descent, which requires careful riding; fair surface, but sometimes rough in places.

About 2m. on *r.* of Lindridge, and same W. of Lamberhurst, are the ruins of Bayham Abbey, which was founded about 1200. 1m. S.E. of Lamberhurst is Scotney Castle, an ancient mansion.

(*Lamberhurst:* Chequers.)

Lamberhurst to Flimwell (4¾—44¾); in the middle of Lamberhurst the road to the *l.* must be taken, up a stiff hill to Lamberhurst Down, then it is hilly but tolerably good road by Beals Bridge, 41½, and Stone Crouch, 43

Flimwell to Highgate (2¾—47½); turn to *l.* and it is almost level, running along the ridge of a hill through Seacock's Heath, 45¼, and High Street, 46½, with a fall and rise to Highgate.

(*Highgate:* Royal Oak.)

Highgate to Newenden (5¼—52¾); by Four Throws 48¾, Field Green, 49¼, Meagrim's Hill, 49¾, Sandhurst Green, 50¼, Cowbeach Green, 51, and Arnden, 51¾, is downhill nearly all the way, sharp descents to Field Green and into Newenden.

Newenden to Rye (8¾—61½); after crossing Newenden Bridge there is a short ascent, on the top of which keep to the *l.* and along White Bread Lane to Four Oaks, 55¾, and then through Peasmarsh, 57½, and Playden, 60½, is a very undulating road. [There is another road turning to the *r.* ½*m.* past Newenden Bridge and through Northiam, 54¾, and Beckley, 55¾, to Four Oaks, 57¼; more hilly and very bad road.] Rye is situate on a hill, and has roughly paved streets.

(*Rye:* Cinque Ports Arms, *C.T.C.*; Crown Inn; George.)

Rye is an old-fashioned town, with narrow streets; part of the walls and gates, erected by Edward I., still exist; the Ypres Tower, built in the reign of Stephen, and now a prison; Chapel of St. Clare, and Queen Elizabeth's Spring. A fine view is obtained from the *ch.* tower. 2*m.* S. is Winchelsea, formerly a large town, 2*m.* in circuit; fine old *ch.*, remains of gates and walls. Between Rye and Winchelsea are the ruins of Winchelsea or Camber Castle, built by Henry VIII. See Cross Roads, route I.

LONDON TO NEW ROMNEY (by Goudhurst).

London to Pembury Green (35)—p. 12.

Pembury Green to Goudhurst (7¾—42¾): through Keys Green, 37, and Lindridge, 38, is not so hilly, and for 4*m.* chiefly down hill to the bridge over the *R.* Teise, within a mile of Goudhurst, into which is the long ascent of Clay Hill, the top part very steep, and requiring care in descending; fairly good surface.

Before Goudhurst 1¼*m.* on *l.*, on an islet surrounded by the River Teise, is an ancient moated farmhouse.

(*Goudhurst:* Star and Crown.)

Goudhurst to Sissinghurst (4¾—47½); a very fair road, almost level by Iden Green, 44¼, and Barrack Farm, 46¾, the only hills worth mentioning, are a short descent and ascent beyond Iden Green; the road runs for the first 3*m.* along a high ridge of ground.

At **Iden Green** on *r.*, and 1¾*m.* farther to *l.*, mostly level, to *Cranbrook* (3—47¼); or at Barrack Farm, on *r.* to *Cranbrook* (1—47¾).

(*Cranbrook:* George, *rec. C.T.C.*)

At Iden Green, on *r.*, is Glassenbury, an ancient moated house, dating from the fifteenth century. Before Willesly Green, on *r.*, Angley Park. Cranbrook is an old-fashioned town, formerly a centre of the clothing trade.

Sissinghurst to New Romney (21¾—69¼)—p. 11.

LONDON TO NEW ROMNEY (by Rolvenden).

London to Goudhurst (42¾)—above.

Goudhurst to Hartley (3½—46¼); a very fair road, almost level by Iden Green, 44¼, where turn to the right.

At Iden Green, on *r.*, Glassenbury, an ancient moated house, dating from the fifteenth century.

Hartley to Rolvendon (6—52¼); at Hartley turn sharp to *l.* and then to *r.*, and it is rather uphill to Bennenden, 50, then nearly all down hill, but nothing difficult either way.

Before Bennenden, on *l.*, Hempstead Park.

Rolvenden to Tenterden ($2\frac{1}{2}$—$54\frac{3}{4}$); turning to *l.* and bearing slightly N.E., the road is on the fall for half the distance through Strood or Stroud Quarter, $52\frac{3}{4}$, and from Ashbourne Mill, $53\frac{1}{2}$, there is a good pull up, rather steep at first, then easier into Tenterden; bad road.

[There is another road by turning to the *l.* at *Hartley* to *Cranbrook*, $47\frac{1}{4}$, into which is a hill to mount, and thence up and downhill to Goford Green *Tg.*, 49, and thence to *Tenterden*, 56—as at p. 11.]

(*Tenterden:* Eight Bells; Lion; Woolpack, *C.T.C.*)

Tenterden to New Romney ($13\frac{1}{2}$—$68\frac{3}{4}$)—p. 10.

LONDON TO RYE (by Maidstone).

London to Reading Street ($56\frac{1}{2}$)—p. 10.

Reading Street to Rye (7—$63\frac{1}{2}$); take the right-hand road, and through some fields and three gates; then a short but rough stony hill to walk up, and (keeping to *l.* at first fork and to *r.* at next) the road, though nearly level, is rather rough to Wittersham Stocks, $58\frac{1}{2}$, whence is a very rough, steep, and *dangerous* descent to walk, with a similar hill to rise nearing Iden, 61; then down and up again to Playden, $62\frac{1}{2}$, beyond which is a long descent towards Rye.

LONDON TO RYE (by Goudhurst).

London to Hartley ($46\frac{1}{4}$)—p. 13.

Hartley to Highgate ($2\frac{1}{2}$—$48\frac{3}{4}$); fall out of Hartley, and downhill by Tubslake, 47 (keep to *r.*), and through Gills Green, $47\frac{1}{2}$, to within $\frac{1}{2}$*m.* of Highgate, to which is a stiff ascent.

Highgate to Rye (14—$62\frac{3}{4}$)—pp. 12-13.

[There is a little shorter route by turning to the *l.* at Tubslake, and by Furnace Mill, whence is a long rise to Four Throws, $1\frac{1}{4}$*m.* past Highgate.]

LONDON TO HASTINGS.

London to Flimwell ($44\frac{3}{4}$)—p. 12.

Flimwell to Hurst Green (3—$47\frac{3}{4}$) is hilly, but all rideable.

(*Hurst Green:* George, *C.T.C.*; White Horse.)

Hurst Green to Robertsbridge ($2\frac{1}{2}$—$50\frac{1}{4}$); about a mile beyond Hurst Green, at the right hand of the fork roads, is Silver Hill to descend, a long, steep fall with one or two nasty sharp turns, and not safe to ride down if without a reliable brake; at the top a B. U. "Dangerboard" has been set up.

(*Robertsbridge:* George.)

At Robertsbridge, on *l.*, are remains of the abbey.

Robertsbridge to Battle (6—$56\frac{1}{4}$); by John's Cross, $51\frac{3}{4}$ (keep to the *l.*), Vine Hall, $52\frac{3}{4}$ (a little further keep to *r.* twice), and Whatlington, $54\frac{1}{4}$, the road is rather loose and has some long and difficult hills, particularly the ascent up to Battle, through which there is a steep hill, narrow and rough. [From John's Cross a shorter road runs by the right hand fork direct to Battle, 55; the guide post says this is the "nearest road to Battle and Hastings," but it is not so good as that to the *l.*, second turning after Vine Hall, which avoids Battle Hill.—See Battle to Hastings.]

(*Battle:* George, *rec. C.T.C.*; Star, family and commercial).

Battle, till then called Epiton, was the scene of the victory of William the Conqueror; here are the ruins of Battle Abbey, founded by him, open to the public on Fridays; fine old Norman *ch.*, also Ashburnham *ch.* 2*m*. W.

Battle to Hastings (7¾—63¾); by Starr's Green, 57½, to Beauport Park, 59, is mostly uphill, and by Ore, 61½, is downhill to Fairlight Down, 62½, with a long steep descent, which requires careful riding, into Hastings; the road is rather lumpy in places. Or at Beauport Park turn to *r*. down a long hill through Hollington, 60¼, to Silver Hill, 61 (keep to *l*.), through Bohemia, 61½, with a sharp fall at Cuckoo Hill into *Hastings*, 62¾.—At Silver Hill on *r*. to *St Leonards*, 62.

[There is a shorter and better road from Vine Hall instead of the above, which is the old coach road, by taking the second turning to the *l*. and down to Kent Street, 56, whence it is chiefly uphill for about 2*m*. to where it crosses the old road beyond Beauport, and down the hill direct to Silver Hill, 60, whence to St. Leonards, 61, and *Hastings*, 61¾, as above.]

(*Hastings:* Castle; Havelock, *C.T.C.*; Marine; Pier, *Hqrs.*; Provincial; Queen; Royal Albion; Royal Swan; Swan, *Hqrs.*—*St. Leonards:* Albion; Denmark; Railway.—*Ore:* Kite's Nest.)

At Beauport, on *r.*, Crowhurst Park; on *l.*, Beauport Park. Beautiful view from the top of Fairlight Down. Hastings Castle was erected by the Normans, but is now in ruins; the town, with the handsome suburb of St. Leonards, is next after Brighton, the most fashionable watering place on the south coast, and a great resort for invalids; splendid pier and esplanade, baths, libraries, theatre, &c. There are many pretty walks and rides in the vicinity.

LONDON TO HASTINGS (by Tunbridge Wells).

London to Tunbridge (30)—p. 12.

Tunbridge to Tunbridge Wells (5¾—35¾); after crossing the *R*. Medway, and over the railway bridge, there is an easy rise out of the town, keeping straight on, followed shortly after by Quarry Hill, to climb, a steep ascent of nearly a mile; then a short descent to Southborough, 33, from which it is chiefly uphill, but an easy road, through Nonsuch Green, 34, with a run down into Tunbridge Wells; good surface. On entering the town keep straight on along Mount Ephraim, till you reach the common, where take the middle road, called the London road (the right one continuing along Mount Ephraim), and thence is a nice descent to the Parade, where the Frant and Eridge roads diverge, the latter to the *r. along Back Parade.*

(*Southborough:* Hand and Sceptre.—*Tunbridge Wells:* Calverly; Tu..lc, *C.T.C.*; Grosvenor; Royal Kentish; Royal Mount Ephraim; Royal Sussex..;

At Quarry Hill, on *r.*, Mabledon. At Southborough, on *r.*, Bounds. Tunbridge Wells is one of the chief inland watering places, and has long been celebrated for its chalybeate springs. The country around is very hilly and pretty.

Tunbridge Wells to Frant (2¼—38); keeping to left hand road from the Parade there is a stiffish rise all the way to the top of Rumbers Hill, 36½, then two short descents to the bottom of Frant Hill, which is a steep and difficult ascent (it is nearly straight, and may be ridden *down* in the reverse direction with a reliable brake).

(*Frant:* George Inn; Abergavenny, *recom.*, *C.T.C.*)
At Frant, on *r.*, Eridge Old Park.

Frant to Wadhurst (4¼—42¼); after passsing Frant Green (Sleech's Cross *Tg.*. 38½,) the left hand road must be taken, and a fall soon begins, which should be taken carefully, as though gradual at first it becomes steep

towards the bottom, to Riverhall Bridge, 40; about a mile beyond is a stiff pull up from Wadhurst Station to Sparrows Green, at the entrance of the village.
(*Wadhurst:* Greyhound.)

Wadhurst to Ticehurst (3—45½); the road continues uphill to Shover Green, 43½, when the top of the range is reached, and with a gradual, but not continuous fall runs to Ticehurst.
(*Ticehurst:* Duke of York.)

Ticehurst to Hurst Green (3¼—48¾); a little past Ticehurst keep to the *r.*, and the road is undulating but chiefly on the fall, joining the road from Flimwell on *l.*, ½*m.* before Hurst Green.

[There is another road to the *l.* just out of Ticehurst, and go through *Flimwell*, 47½, and then to Hurst Green, 50¼.]

Hurst Green to Hastings (16—64¾)—pp. 14-15.

LONDON TO TUNBRIDGE by (Ightham).

London to Farningham (17½)—p. 7.

Farningham to Ightham (7¾—25¼); follow the Wrotham road as at p. 7 to Portobello, 21, and 1¼*m.* further on take the right hand road, which is uphill for nearly ¾*m.* more, when the edge of the downs is reached; then bearing to the *l.* there is a very steep and winding descent which should be walked down for about a mile, and the rest is nearly all an easy down-hill into Ightham.
(*Ightham:* George and Dragon, *B.T.C.*)

About 1m. W. of Ightham, on Ightham Common, are the remains of a Roman camp.

Ightham to Tunbridge (7—32¼); leaving Ightham keep to the *l.*, and it is a very hilly road; for 1½*m.* chiefly uphill, then there is the long and very steep descent of Fair Lawn Hill to near Shipborn, 28½, and after that up and down hill—including the steep descent of Starve Crow Hill, 29¾—through Cage Green, 31¼, to Tunbridge; rather heavy to Shipborn, then sometimes bad and stony.

LONDON TO RYE (by Staple Cross).

London to Highgate (47½)—p. 12.

Highgate to Junction Inn (3—50½); turn to *r.* and down a steep descent to Hawkhurst, 48¼, then chiefly uphill, but good road.

[There is another road by *Hurst Green*, 47¾—p. 14; thence 1m. further turn to *l.*, and by Silver Hill, 49, and Springate's Hill *Tp.*, 49½, to *Junction Inn*, 50½; steep descent from Silver Hill.]
(*Hawkhurst:* Queen's.)

Junction Inn to Staple Cross (3¼—53¾); turn to the *l.* and down hill through Knowl Hill *Tp.*, 51½, to Bodyham Bridge, 52, followed by a long ascent.

Before Bodyham Bridge, on *l.*, the ruins of Bodyham Castle, erected 1386.

Staple Cross to Beckley (4—57¾); turn to the *l.*, and through Horns Cross *Tp.*, 56¼, is pretty level.

Beckley to Rye (7¼—65)—p. 13.

LONDON TO TUNBRIDGE WELLS (by Penshurst).

London to Sevenoaks—*P.O.* (23½)—p. 11.

Sevenoaks to Penshurst (8¼—31¾); follows the Tunbridge road as at p. 12, to Watts Cross, 27¼, then turn to *r.* and over a very undulating road through Stock's Green, 28½, and Leigh, 29¼, after which along the west side of Penshurst Park.

At Leigh, on *r*, Hall Place; Penshurst Place is a fine old castellated mansion; about 2*m.* on *r.* Chiddingstone Park.

Penshurst to Tunbridge Wells (4¾—36½); cross the *R.* Medway, and it is a very hilly road by Pounds Bridge, 33½, and Speldhurst, 34½.

LONDON TO RYE (by Udymer).

London to Junction Inn (50½)—p. 16.

Junction Inn to Cripp's Corner (3¼—53¾); at Junction Inn keep straight on down long descent; good but hilly road.

[Or to *Staple Cross*, 53¾, p. 16, and straight on to *Cripp's Corner*, 51½, slightly uphill.

Or to *Robertsbridge*, 50¼, p. 14, and then to Vine Hall, 52¾, p. 14, after which take first turn to *l.* to *Cripp's Corner*, 54¾; fairly level.]

Cripp's Corner to Rye—Strand Gate (10¼—64); turn to the *l.*, and through Goatham Green, 56¼, Broad Oak Cross *Tp.*, 57, and Udymer or Udimore, 59½, is an undulating road, with steep descent through Udymer, and sharp descent just before Rye, and rise into the town.

LONDON TO HASTINGS (by Sedlescombe).

London to Cripp's Corner (53¾)—above.

Cripp's Corner to Kent Street (3½—57¼); level for a mile, then short but sharp descent, on which turn to *l.*, into Sedlescombe, 55¼, and again downhill through Sedlescombe Street, 55¾, and uphill to Kent Street.

Kent Street to Hastings (5¾—63)—p. 15.

LONDON TO EASTBOURNE AND PEVENSEY.

London to Frant (38)—p. 15.

Frant to Mayfield (6½—44½); is a good but hilly road through Frant Green (Sleech's Cross *Tg.*, 38½), Mark Cross *Tp.*, 41½ (½*m.* beyond, turn to *l.*), and Lake Street, 42½.

Mayfield to Cross-in-Hand Tp. (6—50½); turn to *r.*, and the road continues hilly, by Wellbrook, 45½, Butcher's Cross *Tg.*, 47½, Croust Corner, 48¾, and Gate House, 49¾, where turn to the left.

[Or beyond Mark Cross *Tp.* there is a direct road on *r.* through Salter's Green to Butcher's Cross *Tg.*, 45½.]

Cross-in-Hand Tp. to Horsebridge (7—57½); ½*m.* past Cross-in-Hand turn to *r.*, through Little London, 52¼, Horeham *Tp.*, 53½, and Coggers Cross, 54½; it is rather hilly, but chiefly downhill; awkward twisting descent about 1*m.* before Horsebridge. (Returning, turn to *r.* out of Horsebridge).

At Little London, 1*m.* on *l.*, Heathfield Park.

Horsebridge to Hailsham (1½—59) is a splendid road, slightly uphill; out of Horsebridge keep to the r. (On return journey take the road to the l. out of Hailsham, and entering Horsebridge to l. again).

About 4m. E. of Hailsham the ruins of Hurstmonceux Castle, erected in the reign of Henry VI. At Mitchelham, 2m. W., the ruins of an Augustinian Priory, erected *temp.* Henry III.

Hailsham to Polegate Green (3½—62½); out of Hailsham keep to the r., and it is a very good undulating road, mostly downhill.

Near Wilmington, about 3m. W. of Polegate Green, is the figure of the "Long Man," 230 ft. high, cut in the turf on the side of the hill, and visible nearly 30m.; it is supposed to be of British origin.

Polegate Green to Eastbourne, Station (3½—66); past the railway crossing keep to l.; chiefly on the rise to Willingdon, 64, beyond which is a short descent, followed by a long stiff hill to mount, and some downhill into Eastbourne; good surface, gravel, and flint. The Seaside and Parade are 1½m. beyond the Station.

[There is another road by turning to the l. just beyond *Hailsham*, 2½m. further to the r., and by Stone Cross, 63, Langley *Tg.*, 65, Crumble Bridge, 65½, Sea Houses, 67, and South Bourn, 67¾, to *Eastbourne*, 68½,; hilly to Langley *Tg.*, then level: bad road, frequently loose and heavy.

About 1¼m. before Stone Cross on l., through Hankham Street, 62¼, to *Pevensey* (3¼—64¼); or 1m. before Langley *Tg.* on l. through Westham, 65½, to *Pevensey* (1¾—65¾).

Eastbourne: Albion; Anchor; Burlington; Cavendish; Devonshire; Diplock's; Lamb; Railway and Commercial; Railway; Wadey's.)

At Willingdon, on l., Ratton Park. At Eastbourne, Compton Place. Eastbourne is a thriving watering place and seaside resort; the old village is 1½m. distant from the sea and the parade, and pier, &c., which are at Sea Houses; it is greatly resorted to by invalids, the air being considered beneficial in pulmonary complaints. Fine old Norman ch. Several Roman remains have been found here. 3 or 4m. S.W. is Beachy Head, 575 ft. high, and containing several caverns; here are several barrows or British tumuli. At Pevensey, ruins of the castle, partly supposed to be Roman work. Pevensey is supposed to have been the Roman Anderida, and here landed William the Conqueror. Along the coast are many martello towers, and a battery at Langley Point.

LONDON TO EASTBOURNE (by Westerham).

London to Bromley (10)—p. 11.

Bromley to Keston (4½—14¾); short but stiff descent and ascent at Mason's Hill, 10¾, and then slightly rising ground and undulatory to Bromley Common, 12, where take the right-hand road, and through Keston Mark, 13, it is nearly all against the collar, ending with a sharp descent to Keston; good smooth road, but occasionally loose in the latter half.

S.E. of Keston is the pretty village of Down (1¼—15¾).
(*Keston*: Fox.—*Down*: Queen's Head.)

At Bromley Common, on r., Oakley *Ho.* At Keston Mark, on l., Keston Lodge, and further, Holwood *Ho.*; in the park are extensive remains of an encampment called Cæsar's Camp; opposite, on r., 1m. before Keston, is a pool called Cæsar's Well.

Keston to Westerham (7—21½); beyond Keston there are two or three sharp undulations, and then a stiff descent and similar ascent to

Leaves Green, 15½, after which it is an easy undulating road, with a gradual rising tendency, for 4*m*., through South Street, 18¾, when the top of a range of hills is reached, and immediately a very steep descent begins, dangerous to ride down, as the road makes a sudden turn to the *r*. a short way down, and the surface is very loose, rough, and stony for some distance; after that it is almost level and rather loose road to Westerham, with a short but very stiff rise just into the village.

At Westerham, on *r*., Squeries; on *l*., Hill Park.

Westerham to Eden Bridge (5¼—23¾); in the main street of Westerham, which runs E. and W., turn to the *l*., and, leaving the town, keep to the *r*., and there is a long stiff ascent of a mile to the top of Horns Hill, then pretty level for a mile over Westerham Common, followed by a long winding fall down Crockham Hill, 23¾, which must be taken carefully; then an undulating road through Linhurst, 25¼.

(*Eden Bridge:* Albion.)

Eden Bridge to Hartfield (7¼—34); at the *Tg*., ¾*m*. beyond Eden Bridge keep to the *l*., and through Stamford End, 27¾, Brook Street, 28¼, by Cowden Pound, 29½, Kent Water, 31, and Colestock Gate, 32, is an undulating road, but with two or three stiff hills.

At Stamford End, 2*m*. on *l*., ruins of Hever Castle, formerly the seat of the Boleyns.

Hartfield to Maresfield (7½—41½); at the fork roads just out of Hartfield keep to the *l*., and about 1*m*. further begins the long and in the latter part very steep ascent through Ashdown Forest to 37th *ms*., whence the road is pretty level to Duddleswell Gate, 38¾, from which there is a very steep descent, and the last 2*m*. are on a gradual fall; the surface is sometimes very loose and rough in places.

At Maresfield, on *r*., Maresfield Park.

Maresfield to Uckfield (1¾—43¼); in Maresfield keep to the *l*., and then to *r*., and it is almost level to Uckfield, through which is a long descent; good surface, but sometimes loose and rough in dry weather, and heavy when wet. (Returning, a little out of Uckfield keep to *l*.)

Uckfield: King's Head; Maiden's Head, *B.T.C.*)

Before Uckfield, on *l*., Buxted Place; on *r*., the Rocks; 1*m*. beyond, on *l*., Framfield Park.

Uckfield to East Hoathley (5—48¼); through Uckfield is a steep downhill to the railway crossing, beyond which is a stiff ascent, and at the top turn to the *l*., whence undulating over Crockstead Green, 46¼, to East Hoathley; splendid smooth gravel surface.

East Hoathley to Horsebridge (6—54¼); through Whitesmith Green, 50¼, and Dicker, 53½, the road is of an undulating character, but mostly on the fall: capital smooth gravel surface. (On the return journey keep to *r*. at the 51st *ms*.)

Horsebridge Tg. to Eastbourne Station (8½—62¾)—p. 18.

SECTION II.

From Westminster Bridge*; Southern Roads (East Surrey and Mid Sussex).

LONDON TO EASTBOURNE (by Godstone).

London, Westminster Bridge (Surrey side), **to Streatham** (5¼); level road along Kennington Road, by Kennington Gate, 1½ (keep to *l.* and a little further to *r.*), and along Brixton Road to Brixton (*ch.* 3), then a slight rise for nearly ½*m.* to foot of Brixton Hill, which is a stiff pull but not long, and from the top it is almost level: rough macadam road all the way, in wet weather heavy and greasy; tramway for first 3¼*m.*

Streatham to Croydon—George street, middle of the town (4¼—9¾); short stiff descent from Streatham, then gently undulating along Streatham Common, through Thornton Heath, 8, and Broad Green, 8¾; surface still macadam, generally very rough and in wet weather heavy and greasy; single line tramway, paved with asphalt, from Thornton Heath through and for a mile beyond Croydon. [In order to avoid the narrow main street of Croydon, which has its market day on a Saturday, take the right hand road at Broad Green, about ½*m.* further on go over the railway bridge, then along Church street (take second turning on *r.*) and along the right hand side of the *ch.*, and again to the *r.* of the second *ch.* at the next fork, which leads into the main road by a small turning—Southbridge Row—to the *l.* at the other end of Croydon: on coming the reverse direction this turning is the first on the *l.* (some 100 yards) after passing the "Swan and Sugar Loaf;" it is good and smooth nearly all the way.]

(*Croydon*: Bedford, *Hqrs*; Bridge; Green Dragon; Greyhound; Swan and Sugar Loaf.)

Beyond Streatham, on *l.*, see Crystal Palace.

Croydon to Caterham Junction (2½—12); the macadam ends a short distance out of Croydon, the tramway extending half-a-mile further (11th *ms.*); the rest is generally in good order, but sometimes loose and sandy, and heavy in wet weather; past Purley House 11½; all but level.

Outside Croydon, on *r.*, Hayling House; ½*m.* before Caterham Junction, on *l.*, Purley House, past which runs the old road over Riddlesdown, up a steep hill for ¾*m.*, and now very little used; rough unrideable *descent* either way.

Caterham Junction to Godstone Green (7¼—19¼); taking the left hand fork, the road is mostly on the rise, but easy going, past Kenley,

---

* These roads can be reached at Kennington Gate from the other bridges, as follows:—From London Bridge, 2*m.*; from Southwark Bridge, 2*m.* nearly; from Blackfriars Bridge, 2*m.*; from Waterloo Bridge, 1½*m.*; all meeting at the "Elephant and Castle," nearly 1*m.* before Kennington Gate; paved from London and Blackfriars Bridges to "Elephant and Castle" and lot of paving beyond it, otherwise macadam; heavy traffic. It is better to go by St. George's Circus and Lambeth Road to Kennington Road, ¼*m.* beyond Westminster Bridge.

The milestones on these roads are also reckoned both from Whitehall and Cornhill, the distance from the former being the longer by ½*m.*, and from Cornhill by 1*m.* than from Westminster Bridge.

13, "Rose and Crown Inn," 14¼, Warlingham Station, 15¼, to Caterham Station, 16¾, then two short rises followed by a longer and stiff ascent through a cutting, from which there is a long descent, rather steep at first, to Godstone Green; usually splendid smooth road, but in very dry weather occasionally loose in places as far as Caterham Station.

(Rose and Crown Inn.—*Caterham Station:* Clifton; Railway.—*Godstone Green:* Clayton Arms, *B.T.C.*)

Past Caterham Station, 1*m.* on *l.*, Marden House and Park.

Godstone Green to New Chapel (6—25¼); past Godstone Green keep to the *l.* (avoiding the long steep ascent by the old road over Tilburstow or Tilbuster Hill), and the road is up and down hill, but nothing to dismount for, through Stanstead Borough, 20¾, to Blindley Heath, 23¼; good gravel road for first 3*m.*, then rather rough and shaky.

New Chapel to East Grinstead (3½—28¾); keep to the *l.*, and the road is almost level to Felbridge, 27¼, out of which is a long rise to near East Grinstead; tolerably good going, but inclined to be shaky.

(*East Grinstead:* Dorset Arms; Railway; Swan.)

East Grinstead to Wych Cross (5½—34¼); about 1*m.* out of East Grinstead, after a short rise, there is a good long descent to Forest Row, 31¾; here take the middle road by *l.* of *ch.*, and it is all uphill, more or less steep, with rather uneven surface, and very trying traversing Ashdown Forest.

At Forest Row, on *r.*, Kidbrook Park. Wych Cross or Wytch Cross.

Wych Cross to Maresfield (5¾—40); take the *l.* fork at Wych Cross, and after a mile of pretty level but very indifferent road alongside Peppingford or Ashdown Park, a mile-long descent has to be carefully negotiated, the latter part being steep, and is followed by a stiff hill to mount (here leaving Ashdown Forest) to Nutley, 37¼; through and out of this is more or less downhill for nearly 2*m.*, again a sharp rise and rest level: tolerable surface in the latter part. (Returning, out of Maresfield keep to *r.*)

[There is another road from Forest Row, that to the *l.* through Ashdown Forest, chiefly uphill, and last mile or so rather steep to junction with Westerham road nearly 4*m.* further, then pretty level to Duddleswell Gate, 37¼, from which there is a very steep descent, and the last 2*m.* are on a gradual fall to Maresfield, 40; the surface is sometimes very loose and rough in places.]

At Maresfield, on *r.*, Maresfield Park.

Maresfield to Eastbourne (21¼—61¼)—p. 19.

This is the shortest and best route to Eastbourne.

LONDON TO SEAFORD.

London to Wych Cross Tg. (34¼)—above.

Wych Cross Tg. to Chailey (8½—42¾); at Wych Cross take the right hand road, and the ascent continues for a short distance, then level but indifferent road and rough in places to Charlwood Gate, 35½, afterwards all down hill to Dane Hill, 37, a stiff and rough ascent, followed by bad loose descent, and then very good and undulating with easy hills through Sheffield Green, 38½, and over Sheffield Bridge, 39¾, and Chailey Common.

Past Sheffield Green, on *l.*, Sheffield Park.

Chailey to Lewes—T.H. (6½—49¼), over South Common, 43½, Beverns Bridge, 44½, Cooks Bridge, 46½, and Offham Street, 47½, is a continuation of good road with easy hills, entering Lewes by the west end of the town, ¾m. on the road to Brighton, where turn to the *l.*

[There is another road from *Wych Cross* through *Maresfield*, 40, and *Uckfield*, 41¾, as at p. 21, and p. 19; then through Uckfield is a stiff downhill to the railway crossing, beyond which is a long stiff ascent and a downhill to Little Horsted, 43¾, whence it is tolerably level to within ½m. of Cliff, 49¾; downhill here to *R.* Ouse, at the entrance of *Lewes*, 50¼, and after crossing the river a very steep hill to climb through the town; good road, though sometimes rough and loose in dry weather.]

(*Lewes:* Bear, *C.T.C.*; Crown; Elephant and Castle; Star; White Hart.)

At Little Horsted, on *r.*, Horsted Place; 3*m.* before Lewes, on *l.*, Plashet Park; on *r.*, Malling *Ho.* and Malling Deanery. At Lewes the castle, built soon after the Conquest, is worth seeing, a fine view being obtained from the battlements; also ruins of St. Pancras Priory, the first of the Cluniac order in England, founded 1076. There are several old churches, one of which occupies the site of a Roman camp, St. John's. Near Lewes, in 1264, Simon de Montfort and the barons defeated Henry II. Town hall, theatre, library, archæological museum, &c.

Lewes to Newhaven—Bridge (7—56¼); in Lewes turn to the *r.* just before the railway, and through Iford, 51¼, Rodmill, 52¼, Southsease, 53, Deans, 54¼, and Piddinghoe, 55¼, is a good undulating road.

(*Newhaven:* Prince of Wales.)

At Southsease and Piddinghoe are Norman churches. Newhaven is a small, but rising seaport town, whence steamers ply to Dieppe, the shortest route to Paris; small Norman *ch.*, forts, &c. Above the town is a castle, and overlooking it is an ancient British earthwork.

Newhaven to Seaford—New Inn (3¼—59½); turn to *r.* and cross *R.* Ouse, and shortly after keep to *r.* twice; good road, but loose in places, level to near the Coastguard station, where there is a short, sharp descent to the beach, across which is unrideable, then a rise and fall, and up again to Seaford. [There is another but more hilly road by the left hand road at the second fork, through Bishopstone, 58½, and Blatchington, 59¼, to Seaford, 60.]

(*Seaford:* Boy; New Inn; Old Tree.)

Seaford *ch.* is Norman and early English; on Seaford heights are remains of a large Roman camp, and in the vicinity are remains of several deep entrenchments; Bishopstone *ch.* is a singular building with Saxon porch. Beyond the town, Corslea Hall.

LONDON TO LIMPSFIELD.

London to Croydon—George Street (9½)—p. 20.

Croydon to Warlingham (4¾—14¼); the macadam ends a short distance out of Croydon, the tramway extending half a mile further (to 11th *ms.*); here at the signpost take the road to the *l.*, and after passing under the railway bridge a long and severe uphill begins to Sanderstead, 12¼, divided by two short intervening falls into three stages, which require care in descending, especially the highest one, there being a sharp curve in it; after Sanderstead the road is level; fairly good surface after leaving the Brighton road. [The old road over Riddlesdown leaves the Brighton road ½m. further on at Purley House, with a stiff rough hill to climb in the first mile, and 1¼m. disused grassy lane to Hamsey Green, 14; ½m. longer.]

Outside Croydon, on r., Hayling *Ho*. On *l.*, Sanderstead Court.

Warlingham to Limpsfield (5½—19¾); slight gradual rise along Warlingham Common and Worms Heath, 15½, where is a very stiff hill to climb, rough, loose and stony, but not long, the top being reached at the 6th *ms.* from Croydon (from which they are measured); after this the road is fairly level and good for a couple of miles, running along the top of the hills to a cross road for Tatsfield; then the dangerous descent of Titsey Hill begins, 17½, and though it is gradual for the first ½m. bicyclists should not ride further than 100 yards beyond the 8th *ms.* from Croydon, as the fall soon becomes steeper and, curving to the *r.*, is too steep to be ridden down, besides being rough, for several hundred yards to Titsey *ch.*, 18¼; from here it is an easy and good ride, mostly on the fall, to Limpsfield.

LONDON TO BRIGHTON (by Lindfield).

London to New Chapel (25¼)—p. 21.

New Chapel to Turner Hill (5¼—30¾); turn to the *r.* and it is slightly undulating, but chiefly with an upward tendency, passing over Frogwood Heath, Copthorn Common, 27¼, and Crawleys Downs, 29¼, with a long stiff crooked ascent to Turner Hill, almost too steep and dangerous to be ridden *down* on the return journey except with a good brake; rather rough road.

About 1¼m. S.W. of Turner Hill is a curious rock, called Big upon Little.

Turner Hill to Hapstead Green (4¼—34¾); short descent out of Turner Hill, followed by a stiff pull up to Selsfield Common, then mostly on a gentle fall to Hapstead Green; good smooth road.

Before Hapstead Green, on *r.*, Wakehurst Place.

Hapstead Green to Lindfield (3—37¾), is rather hilly, with a short stiff ascent into Lindfield; good surface. Toll to pay at Lindfield gate.

Lindfield to Hayward's Heath (1½—39¼) is easy travelling and a good road, though sometimes loose and sandy.

[Or from *Hapstead Green* keep to *r.*, and stiff descent to *R.* Ouse bridge, 36¼, then sharp rise, long fall, and again an ascent to *Hayward's Heath*, 38½.]

Hayward's Heath to Ditchling (5½—44¾); rather hilly but nothing very difficult to Wivelsfield, 41, and then pretty level, passing over Ditchling Common; the road is generally loose and heavy. Toll to pay at Wivelsfield and Ditchling gates.

Ditchling to Brighton—Aquarium (8—52¾); a short distance out of Ditchling begins a very steep and winding ascent, with rough and stony surface, and too steep to be ridden either up or down, leading to the top of the South Downs; on the top the road becomes a mere cart and hoof track for about 3m. over the Downs, which must be walked, then it improves and is rideable, all up and down hill, but still rough and very stony for 2m. more till clear of the Downs, and the last 1½m. are all down hill into Brighton. [Or beyond *Ditchling* turn to *r.* to *Clayton*, 47, whence to *Brighton*, 7—54, as by next route.]

(Brighton hotels, &c., see *post*, p. 25.)

At the top of the Downs, on r., the road passes close to Ditchling Beacon; about 3m. before Brighton, on l., is Hollingsbury Castle, a Roman encampment on a high hill.

LONDON TO BRIGHTON (by Cuckfield).

London to Caterham Junction (12)—p. 20.

Caterham Junction to Merstham (5¾—17¾); following the right hand road up the valley of Smitham Bottom, it is a gradual but barely noticeable rise to the "Red Lion," 13½, just beyond which a moderate ascent begins, and is continued more or less for nearly 3½m., but no part of the gradient is difficult, and the last ¾m. is a stiff downhill into Merstham; the surface is smooth and generally in good order, but sometimes sandy, and in wet weather heavy.

(*Merstham:* Feathers.)

Merstham to Red Hill (2¾—20¼) is nearly all up and down hill but easy riding; pretty fair surface, but inclined to be uneven, and through Red Hill is macadam; take the left hand road at the bifurcation about 1¼m. beyond Merstham.

(*Red Hill:* Warwick, rec., C.T.C.)

Beyond Merstham, on r., Gatton Ho. and Park; here also formerly stood the village of Gatton, long famous as a rotten borough.

Red Hill to Horley (3½—24); out of Red Hill there is the very stiff ascent of that name to mount, but which a good rider need not dismount for, then across Earlswood Common it is undulating, though more down than up, over a rough and shaky macadam road; leaving the Common there is a good rise and fall, then the road is almost level to Horley, with better surface. [An easier road up Red Hill is to take the first turn on r. past the railway, then keeping to l. up a gradual rise, and joining the main road again nearly at the top; good surface.]

(*Horley:* Chequers.)

Horley to Balcombe (8¾—32¾); at the entrance of Horley where the road forks keep straight on by the left hand branch over the railway bridge, after which the road continues fairly level for about 4m., rough for half that distance over Horley Common, and good and smooth for the other half past Black Corner, 27 (where enter Sussex); then it becomes hilly, beginning with the short but stiff ascent of Pound Hill (top of) 28¾, and past Worth Bridge, 29½, while the long rise of Whitely Hill, 2m. before Balcombe, particularly requires some collar work, but fairly good surface.

(*Pound Hill:* King's Head).

At Worth Bridge, on l., Worth Park. Worth has an ancient Saxon *ch.* After Pound Hill the road runs through part of Tilgate Forest. At Balcombe, on l., Balcombe Ho.

Balcombe to Cuckfield (4¼—37); a little beyond the *ch.* keep to r., and through Brook Street, 35¼, is undulating but good road; a stiff ascent to mount to Whiteman's Green, 36½, and down to and through Cuckfield.

(*Cuckfield:* King's Head; Talbot; *B.T.C.*)

Beyond Balcombe, 1m. on l., Ouse Viaduct. At Cuckfield, on r., Cuckfield Place, the original of Ainsworth's "Rookwood Hall."

Cuckfield to Clayton (7½—44½); by Anstey Cross, 38 (first l., then r.), Bridge Farm, 40¼, St. John's Common, 40¾, Friar's Oak Inn, 42¼, and

Stonepound, 43¾, the road is undulating, some of the hills being of rather stiff gradient in either direction. [Or in Cuckfield turn to *l.* to Butler's Green, 38¼, whence on *r.* to Bridge Farm, same distance.]

Clayton to Piecombe, opp. *ch.* (⅞—45⅝); out of Clayton there is a very steep ascent which it is impossible to ride up (and bicyclists should not attempt to ride *down* it); then easy descent to Piecombe.

Piecombe to Brighton—Aquarium (6⅛—51¾), through Pangdean, 46⅜, Patcham, 48¼, Withdean, 49⅜, and Preston, 49⅞, is all down hill or level; very good and smooth surface to Old Patcham Gate, 3*m.* from Brighton, after which the road gets rather bumpy and is often wet and greasy into Brighton.

(*Brighton:* Albermarle; Albion; Albion Temperance; Egremont; Emery's Temp.; Gloucester, *C.T.C.*; Golden Fleece; Marine; New Steine; New Ship; Old Ship; Pump House; Royal Marine; St. James's; Victoria; Ward's; White Horse; Woodman's Cot; Olive Branch; Castle, Middle Street, *C.T.C.*)

Brighton is a large and well-built town, being the principal seaside watering place on the south coast; there are some fine buildings, notably the Royal Pavilion, erected by George IV., town hall, the old church, etc.; splendid promenade nearly 3*m.* long, from suburb of Kemptown on the east to Hove and Cliftonville on the West. The Aquarium is one of the best in England. Bells are compulsory in Brighton.

LONDON TO BRIGHTON (by Handcross).

London to Horley (24¼)—p. 24.

Horley to Povey Cross (1⅝—25⅞); at the entrance of Horley take the right-hand fork, and it is a capital nearly level road.

Povey Cross to Crawley (3⅜—22½); over Kimberham Bridge, 26¼, and Lowfield Heath, 27¼, is a capital road, nearly level.

(*Crawley:* George; George and Dragon; Railway, *C.T.C.*; Station.)

In the middle of Lowfield Heath, at the County Oak, enter Sussex.

Crawley to Handcross (4⅜—23⅞); a short distance out of Crawley a long but not difficult hill begins, which continues with one intermission to within about ½*m.* of Pease Cottage Gate, 31¼, and the rest is a level and capital road of 2½*m.* to Handcross.

(*Handcross:* Red Lion, *rec. B.T.C.*)

Handcross to Hickstead (6⅜—40¼); going out of Handcross turn first to the *l.*, then to the *r.*, and past Slaugham Park is the long descent of Handcross Hill, at first rather steep, then towards the bottom the fall becomes more gradual, and sometimes being rough and loose, it requires care in descending; out of the valley there is a long but not steep hill to mount, and then several more by Bolney Common, 37⅞, and Rice Bridge, 39¾; generally good road but sometimes rather loose in places.

Hickstead to Piecombe—Plough (5¾—46); rather hilly road but nothing difficult through Sayer's Common, 41⅓, and Albourne Green, 42½, to the bottom of Dale Hill, 45⅛, which is a long stiff hill right up through Piecombe Street, 45½, and the rest down hill. (Dale Hill should be *descended* carefully when returning, as many accidents have occurred there.)

The height on the *l.* of Dale Hill is Wolsonbury Beacon.

Piecombe to Brighton—Aquarium ($5\frac{7}{8}$—$51\frac{7}{8}$); just beyond the "Plough" join the Clayton road, and by Pagdean, $46\frac{1}{2}$—as at p. 25.

The above route and the Reigate route are the best roads to Brighton.

LONDON TO BRIGHTON (by Crawley and Cuckfield).

London to Hand Cross ($33\frac{1}{2}$)—p. 25.

Hand Cross to Cuckfield ($4\frac{1}{2}$—38); going out of Hand Cross the main road to the *l.* must be taken, and there is a long downhill past Staplefield Common, $34\frac{3}{4}$ (where again keep to the *l.*), then two stiff ascents to Slough Green, $36\frac{1}{4}$, and level to Whiteman's Green, $37\frac{1}{2}$, and down into Cuckfield; shaky macadam surface.

Cuckfield to Brighton—Aquarium ($14\frac{1}{2}$—$52\frac{1}{2}$)—pp. 24-25.

[Or a little past Slough Green turn to *r.*, and go straight to Anstey Cross, $38\frac{1}{2}$, and on to *Brighton*, 52.]

LONDON TO BRIGHTON (by Reigate).

London, Westminster Bridge (Surrey side), **to Clapham**—The "Plough" ($3\frac{1}{2}$); level road along Kennington road, by Kennington Gate, $1\frac{1}{2}$ (keep to the *r.*), along Clapham road and through Stockwell ("Swan," $2\frac{1}{4}$), whence it is slightly undulating; macadam surface, rough and greasy, except past Stockwell and for the last 300 yards or so, where patches of wood paving are laid; tramway the whole distance.

Clapham to Tooting Cross or Lower Tooting ($2\frac{2}{3}$—6); keeping along the left-hand side of Clapham common, the road is fairly level except a slight descent just beyond the Common at Balham, $4\frac{1}{4}$, and another, steeper, at Upper Tooting, $5\frac{1}{2}$; bad surface, being macadam, very shaky, and generally wet and greasy.

Tooting Cross to Sutton, "Cock" Inn ($5\frac{1}{4}$—$11\frac{1}{4}$); taking the left-hand fork, the road continues macadam across Fig's Marsh to Upper Mitcham (Green) $7\frac{1}{2}$, and is all level through Lower Mitcham, $8\frac{1}{4}$, to past the *R.* Wandle, $8\frac{3}{4}$, then rather hilly—two ups and downs—to Sutton, with a very stiff pull in the town up to and past the "Cock" Inn at the cross roads: the last $3\frac{1}{2}$m. are good going, though sometimes sandy in dry weather.

(*Lower Mitcham:* White Hart, *B.T.C.*—*Sutton:* Cock, *B.T.C.*; Grapes; Greyhound; Station.)

Sutton to Burgh Heath (4—$15\frac{1}{4}$); the hill past the "Cock" Inn ends at the railway bridge a little further on, but is followed by two easy rises to California, $12\frac{1}{2}$, and again by another uphill of $1\frac{1}{2}$m., the first part rather stiff, over Banstead Downs, across which the surface is generally loose, and in dry weather very sandy; after leaving the Downs, $13\frac{3}{4}$, the road continues uphill for about $\frac{1}{4}$m., and then is gently undulating to Burgh Heath, with good surface.

At the end of the Downs, 1m. on *l.*, is the pretty village of Banstead, and $1\frac{1}{4}$m. further on, Woodmanstone, near which is the Oaks Park; good and easy road. Before Burgh Heath, a little on *r.* Nork Park.

Burgh Heath to Reigate—*M.H.* ($5\frac{3}{4}$—21); across Burgh Heath and Walton Heath (keeping to *l.* at 16th *ms.*), the road is undulating for a couple of miles, with a steepish descent beyond Kingswood *ch.*, then it is more or less on the rise past the "Fox" Inn, 18, to the top of Reigate Hill, $19\frac{1}{4}$, all with a capital smooth hard surface; here the bicyclist should dismount (B. U. "danger board" is erected on *l.*) for the long winding descent of Reigate Hill, running right down into the town: the first part, $\frac{1}{3}$*m.* long, is very steep, with its surface for half the width on the left formed of loose stony gravel, and extremely rough, while on the other half a double row of flagstones is laid for upward vehicular traffic; this descent is unrideable except with a very powerful brake, though it has been ridden down and can be just ridden up by a good rider keeping to the flagstones, but in any case it is dangerous, as one is not able to see to the bottom: the rest of the descent is comparatively easy, passing over a level railway crossing, and finally debouching through a short tunnel under the Castle grounds into the market-place. The total fall is 420ft., and the average gradient on the flagstones is 10ft. in 100ft.

At Tadworth Court, 16, on *r.* to *Walton-on-the-Hill* ($1\frac{1}{4}$—$17\frac{1}{4}$); and to *Box Hill* ($4\frac{3}{4}$—$20\frac{3}{4}$).

(*Reigate:* Grapes, *B.T.C.*; Swan; White Hart.)

Beyond Burgh Heath, on *r.*, Tadworth Court, and further on, Dundrum Castle. Before Reigate Hill, 1*m.* on *r.*, Upper Gatton *Ho.*, and on the Hill, a little on *l.*, Gatton Park and Gatton village, now consisting of two or three houses, famous as a rotten borough. The view from the top of Reigate Hill is very fine. At Reigate are remains of the old castle, now a well-laid-out public garden, with a large cavern underneath. The Priory.

Reigate to Povey Cross ($5\frac{1}{2}$—$26\frac{1}{2}$); long moderate ascent out of Reigate ending in a cutting, and followed by a good descent to Woodhatch, $22\frac{1}{4}$, then undulating over Kennersley Bridge, $23\frac{1}{4}$ (*R.* Mole), and Hookwood Common, $25\frac{3}{4}$; capital smooth road.

Povey Cross to Brighton—Aquarium (26—$52\frac{1}{2}$) by Hand Cross, $34\frac{1}{4}$, and Hicksted, $40\frac{3}{4}$—pp. 25-26.

LONDON TO REIGATE (by Croydon.)

London to Merstham ($17\frac{3}{4}$)—p. 24.

Merstham to Reigate ($3\frac{1}{2}$—$21\frac{1}{4}$); follow the Red Hill road to the bifurcation at the top of a short rise by the 19th *ms.*, and then take the right-hand branch; for about a mile there are three very stiff uphills, but with good smooth surface, to Wray Common, and thence is a long gradual run down into Reigate over a macadam road.

LONDON TO SHOREHAM.

London to Hand Cross ($33\frac{1}{2}$)—p. 25.

Hand Cross to Cowfold (6—$39\frac{1}{2}$); take the right hand road, and it is undulating by Ashfold Crossways, 35, and Lower Beeding, $36\frac{1}{2}$ (keep to *l.*), with a steep descent at Crabtree, $37\frac{3}{4}$. (Returning, keep to *r.* on top of Crabtree Hill.)

Cowfold to Partridge Green ($3\frac{1}{4}$—$42\frac{3}{4}$); very undulating road by Corner House *Tg.*, $41\frac{1}{2}$ (where turn to *r.*)

Partridge Green to Steyning (5¼—48); hilly road over Bines Bridge, 43¾, through Ashurst, 45, and Horse Bridge Common, 45¾, and over Broadbourn Bridge, 47¼.
(*Steyning:* White Horse.)
Steyning *ch.* is in part early Norman and supposed to have been portion of a Benedictine monastery, and to contain the remains of Ethelwulf, father of Alfred the Great.

Steyning to New Shoreham (5½—53½); through Bramber, 49½, over Bramber Bridge (*R.* Adur), 49½, (just beyond keep to *r.*) along the valley of the *R.* Adur to Old Shoreham, 52¾, where turn to the *l.* at the *ch.*, and shortly after to the *r.*; good road, undulating for first 1½*m.*, then level.
At Bramber, on *l.*, remains of a castle erected by the Saxons, probably on a Roman foundation. At Old Shoreham the *ch.* is a fine old Norman building.

LONDON TO WORTHING.

London to Tooting Cross (6)—p. 26.

Tooting Cross to Merton—Double Gates (1½—7½); the macadam soon ends, then there is a short descent and a railway bridge to go over, the slopes of which are generally very loose and sandy; after this the road is level and tolerably good going, though sometimes sandy.

[In order to avoid the bad road through Balham, &c., most riders leave Clapham Common by Nightingale lane, a little to the right of the main road, where there is a stiff descent and ascent, then over Wandsworth Common, along Burntwood Lane with another descent, turn to *l.* at Garratt Green, again sharp to the *l.* and immediately after to the *r.*, and through Somerstown; at the next cross roads keep to the *l.* over the railway bridge, and along Haydon's Lane to Merton, joining the main road just before the Double Gates; the surface is good as a rule, but occasionally a little loose and heavy in places; distance from "Plough," 4¾—8.]

(*Merton:* Bay Tree, temp.; Duke of Edinburgh.)

Merton to Ewell (5½—13); taking the left hand fork there are two railway bridges to go over, then from the next bifurcation (where keep to *r.*) there is a long gradual rise of over a mile to Morden, 9½; out of here is a short steep fall, followed by a long moderate rise and another steep descent to Pylford Bridge, 10½, and after a short pull-up the road is gently undulating for ¾*m.* past the "Victoria Inn" at North Cheam, 11¼, when an easy run-down occurs, then level, with again a short drop into Ewell; it is much easier going to Ewell than the reverse journey, but there is nothing an ordinary rider need dismount for; good gravel road on the whole, but in dry weather the greater part is often loose and sandy.

(*Ewell:* Glyn Arms; King's Head; King William IV.; Spring.)

At Morden, on *r.*, Morden Park; before Ewell, on *l.*, Nonesuch Park, where formerly stood a palace of Henry VIII. and Queen Elizabeth. The *ch.* is modern, but the ivy-clad tower of the old one is preserved just behind it.

Ewell to Epsom—King's Head (1½—14½); short stiff rise out of Ewell, then almost level to Epsom; capital smooth road.

(*Epsom:* King's Head; Spread Eagle.)

Epsom was formerly celebrated for its mineral springs, whence Epsom salts derived their name. About 1*m.* S.W. of Epsom, on the Downs, is the racecourse, where the Derby and Oaks races are held.

Epsom to Leatherhead—*ch.* (4—18½); at the end of the *M.P.* in Epsom keep to the *l.*, then keeping to the *r.* the road rises gradually for about a mile terminating with a rather stiff pull on to Ashtead Common, directly followed by a steepish fall generally very loose and heavy; after that the road is very undulating through Ashtead, 16¾, to Leatherhead, into which is a good run down.

(*Leatherhead:* Bull, *Hqrs.*; Duke's Head; Swan.)

Beyond Epsom, on *l.*, Woodcote Park and Ashtead Park. Leatherhead *ch.* was built about the middle of the fourteenth century.

Leatherhead to Dorking—M.H. (5—23½); turn sharp to the *l.* in Leatherhead opposite the "Swan;" just out of the town is a steep rough fall, then the road is undulating to Mickleham, 20½, through and out of which is a long steady rise, followed by a stiff descent, then another short very stiff ascent through a cutting and a long fall to Burford Bridge, 21¾ (*R.* Mole); the rest is almost level with an easy rise into Dorking; good smooth road, but in dry weather apt to be sandy for the first mile or so; macadam through Dorking.

(*Burford Bridge:* Burford Bridge; a little further, Beehive.—*Dorking:* Red Lion; Swan; Three Tuns; Wheatsheaf; White Horse.)

This stage of the road runs up the valley of the *R.* Mole, the scenery being very pretty. Before Mickleham, on *r.*, Norbury Park. At Burford Bridge, on *l.*, the North Downs break off in the precipitous height of Box Hill, whence a splendid view of the Dorking valley can be gained; it is easily accessible to cyclists from 16th *ms.* on the Reigate road. On the S.E. side of Dorking is the beautiful seat of Deepdene, and about 1 m. further E. are the ruins of Betchworth Castle.

Dorking to Bear Green (4—27½); in Dorking take the left hand road and again *l.*, just leaving the town, then beginning with a moderate ascent through a cutting the road continues rather hilly over Holmwood Common and past Holmwood Station, 26¾; pretty good road, though sometimes rather lumpy.

At Holmwood Station, 1½m. on *r.*, Anstiebury Hill, a Danish encampment.

Bear Green to Horsham (9—36½); through Capel, 29, Clark's Green, 30, by Shiremark Mill, 31½, Kingsfold *Tp.*, 32, and Slaughter Bridge, 33½, (where keep to *l.*) is a hilly road, but nothing difficult; good smooth surface; at the fork roads just before entering Horsham keep to the *r.* for the direct Worthing road, if not wishing to call in the town.

(*Horsham:* Anchor; Bedford; Crown; King's Head; Queen's Head.)

Beyond Bear Green, on *r.*, see Leith Hill and tower 2½m. off. Entering Horsham on *l.*, Horsham Park, and on *r.*, Springfield. Horsham *ch.* is Early English restored, and contains many old monuments.

Horsham to West Grinstead—Burrel Arms (6¼—42¾); through Southwater, 38½, is a splendid undulating road.

1m. S. of Horsham, on *l.*, Den Park, and beyond it, Chesworth. At West Grinstead, on *l.*, West Grinstead Park; a little further on *r.*, Knep Castle, an old castellated mansion. The chief part of the village of West Grinstead lies a little *l.* of the main road.

West Grinstead to Washington Common (5¼—48½) is undulating, with a splendid surface, through Dial Post *Tp.*, 44, and Ashington, 47, nearing which keep to the *l.*, and at the bottom of the descent out of the village is a *Tg.*, where take the right hand road.

Washington Common to Worthing (7½—56); from the common there is a steep hill to ascend over part of the South Downs, which is followed by a good undulating road through North End, 50¾, and Finden, 51½; 2m. beyond this it is joined by the Arundel to Brighton road, where turn to the *l.*, and at the next fork roads (54¼) keep to the *r.*, and it is then a splendid level road through Broadwater, 54¾, into Worthing.

(*Worthing:* Albion, *C.T.C.*; Brunswick; Gibbs's Private; Marine; Sea House.)

1½m. S.E. of Washington Common, on the Downs, is an old entrenchment, called Chanctonbury Ring; 1m. E. of Finden is Ciscbury Hill, a large entrenchment surmounted by remains of a fort said to have been erected by the early Saxons. Worthing is a rising watering-place with excellent bathing and a very mild climate.

LONDON TO SHOREHAM (by Horsham).

London to West Grinstead—Burrel Arms (42¾)—p. 29.

West Grinstead to Partridge Green (2½—45¼); at the Corner House turn to the *l.*, and it is a good undulating road skirting West Grinstead Park and across Joulsfield Common.

Partridge Green to New Shoreham (10¾—56)—p. 28.

LONDON TO LITTLEHAMPTON.

London to Bear Green (27½)—p. 29.

Bear Green to Stone Street or Ockley Green (2¾—30¼); turning to the *r.* at the sign-post the road is level for a mile, then turning to the *l.* undulating for another mile, when it joins the line of the ancient Roman Road, now known as Stone Street Causeway, and the rest consists of a couple of sharp descents to Stone Street; pretty good road.

(*Stone Street:* Red Lion; King's Arms.)

Before joining Stone Street Causeway, nearly 2m. on *r.*, Leith Hill, 967 ft. high, the highest ground in Surrey, and from which the sea is visible in clear weather.

Stone Street to Roman Tp. (5½—35¾); the old Causeway continues in a straight line for almost 2m., very undulating, and with a capital hard surface, then it breaks off and the road bears a little to the *r.* down a short decline, which is followed by the ascent of Oakwood Hill to climb, not long but much too steep to ride up or down, the surface being rather rough; from the top the road is undulating but with indifferent stony surface, keeping to the *l.* at the first two forks, and afterwards passing two sign-posts on the *r.*, and by Rowhook, 35¼. [There is another road turning to the *l.* just before the end of the Causeway and by Denne Bridge, 33, to Roman Turnpike, 36; it is very hilly, but pretty good hard road.]

Roman Tp. to Five Oaks Green (3¼—39); here the old Roman Causeway recommences, and is a fairly good undulating road through Park Street, 37, and by Buckman's Corner, 38¾. [There is another road by turning to the *r.* at Slaughter Bridge, 33½, on the Horsham road, p. 29, and through Warnham, 33¾, and over Broadbridge Heath, 35¼, to Five Oaks Green, 39¼; a good undulating road.]

Five Oaks Green to Billinghurst—*ch.* (1¾—40¼); splendid road, chiefly down hill, with a pull up into Billinghurst.

Billinghurst to Pulborough—*ch.* (5—45¼); through Adversane, 42¼, and Codmore Hill, 44¼, is a splendid road, rather hilly, but with some fine stretches of level ground; steep hill to descend into and through Pulborough.

(*Pulborough:* Railway; Swan, *rec. C.T.C.*)

Pulborough to Arundel—*ch.* (9¼—54½); at the bottom of the hill in Pulborough turn to *r.* and directly after to *l.* across *R.* Arun; after a short level, there is a stiff hill to mount to Hardham, 46¼, followed by a longer descent to Coldwaltham, 47½, and then the road is undulating over Watersfield Common, through Watersfield, 48¼, Bury *Tp.*, 48¾ (where leave Stone Street Causeway), and Bury Common to Bury, 50¼; from here a long steep ascent leads to the summit of Houghton hill, 51¾ (the descent of which in the reverse direction is dangerous, owing to a sharp turn to the *l.* near the bottom), and then there is a capital run, mostly down hill, alongside Arundel park, with a steep fall into the town.

(*Arundel:* Castle; Norfolk Arms, *C.T.C.*; Railway.)

At Bignor, 2 or 3*m.* W. of Bury, are remains of Roman pavement and villa; about 1*m.* S.W., on the top of the Downs the line of the Stone Street Causeway reappears, and runs direct to Chichester. On top of Houghton Hill, 52¼*m.*, are some ancient earthworks. At Bury, on *l.*, across *R.* Arun, is Amberley Castle. In Arundel Park, N. of the town, is Arundel Castle, founded in the ninth century; it was partly ruined by the Parliamentarians, and was magnificently restored by the late Duke of Norfolk; it is open to the public on Mondays and Fridays. Ancient Gothic *ch.*, containing many old monuments.

Arundel to Littlehampton (3¾—58¼); after crossing the River Arun, short rise out of Arundel, followed by another soon after, at the top of which turn to the *r.* and go down a long hill, then level through Leominster, 56½, and Wick Street, 57½, the road taking several turns.

(*Littlehampton:* Dolphin; Norfolk; Terminus, *rec. C.T.C.*)

LONDON TO TWICKENHAM.

London, Westminster Bridge (Surrey side) to Wandsworth (5); turn to *r.* along Albert Embankment to Vauxhall, 1, paved, then rough macadam with tramway along Wandsworth Road, all level to Lavender Hill, 3½, which is a short descent, followed by a longer rise (on *r.* Clapham Junction Station), and presently a stiff fall into Wandsworth; the tramway ends at the top of the hill.

[Or to *Clapham*, (3½)—p. 26; then keep to *r.* along the north side of Clapham Common, whence short sharp descent at Battersea Rise, with corresponding ascent after, and join the above road on *r.* on the top of the hill before *Wandsworth*, 5½; all macadam.

Wandsworth to Richmond (5—10); stiff ascent out of Wandsworth, then (keeping to *r.*) almost level and rough macadam through Putney, 6, along Barnes Common, 7¼, and through East Sheen, 8¼.

Richmond to Twickenham (1½—11½): in Richmond turn first to *r.*, then *l.*, and to *l.* again over Richmond Bridge (*R.* Thames), and fairly level, but still macadam to Twickenham.

SECTION III.

From Hyde Park Corner*; South Western Roads (West Surrey, West Sussex, Hampshire, Dorset, Devon, Cornwall, Somerset, South Berkshire, South Wilts).

LONDON TO CHICHESTER AND BOGNOR.

London, Hyde Park Corner, to Putney Heath (5½); macadam road, very rough all the way, and generally wet and greasy, through Knightsbridge, ½ (turn to *l.*), along Brompton road (at 1*m.* turn again to *l.*), Fulham road through Brompton, West Brompton, 2, Walham Green, 2¾, to Fulham, 3¾, whence cross River Thames to Putney, 4, out of which is a stiff rough hill to mount.

Putney Heath to Kingston—*M.P.* (4½—10); across the Heath the road is pretty good, and undulating with a long run down to the "Halfway House," 7, then beyond the "Robin Hood" and *Tp.*, at Kingston Bottom, 8, there is a steep and bad ascent followed by a long rough descent down Kingston hill to Norbiton, 9, whence it is all level, and macadam very rough and shaky into Kingston, where turn to *l.* before the *ch.* for *M.P.*

[From *Westminster Bridge* there is another road *viâ Merton*, 7½, p. 28; at the Double Gates keep straight on to the *r.*, the road is level, but macadam for ½*m.* through Merton till past the level railway crossing; then along Combe Lane past Raynes Park, 9½, the surface improves, being gravel and flint, generally in good order, and still level to the bottom of Combe Hill, 10½, which is a long and stiff ascent, shortly followed by a shorter but steeper fall down the other side (care should be exercised in taking either of these descents, as they are often loose and rough, with turns in them); the rest is all but level, with good surface as far as Norbiton, 11¾, where it joins the other road.]

[Or from *Richmond*, (10)—p. 31, turning first to *l.* and then to *r.*, and a little farther is a sharp fall on *r.* to Petersham, 11, and thence level but bumpy through Ham, 11⅛, and across Ham Common, the last 1½*m.* tolerable going, to *Kingston*, 13].

(*Kingston:* Bell; Griffin; The Sailors; White Hart.)

Before Kingston Hill, on *r.*, Richmond Park. On N. side of Kingston *ch.* is the coronation stone of the Saxon kings.

Kingston to Esher (4—14) is level except a gradual rise for the last ½*m.*; the macadam continues through and out of Kingston to Ditton Marsh for about 3*m.*, but for the latter half there is good riding at the

---

* These roads can also be reached from the previous routes, as follows :—From Westminster Bridge to Clapham, 3¼, p. 26, thence along the north side of Clapham Common with a sharp descent at Battersea, then an ascent and fall again to Wandsworth, 5¼, all macadam, very rough and bumpy; thence another stiff climb followed by long gradual rise with better surface to Putney Heath, 7¼. Or from Westminster Bridge turn to *r.*, and as on p. 31 to Wandsworth, 5, thence to Putney Heath as above, 6¾. From London Bridge these routes can be joined—either No. 1 at Kennington Gate, 2*m.*, p. 20; or No. 2, turning to *r.*, ½*m.*, past "Elephant and Castle," along Kennington Lane to Vauxhall, 2½*m*.

sides, and the rest is fairly good and smooth, though sometimes heavy up the rise.

At 12m. on r. to Thames Ditton (½—12½).
(*Thames Ditton:* Angel; Swan.—*Esher:* Bear; Marquis of Granby.)
Before Esher, on r., Sandown racecourse.

Esher to Ripley (7¾—21¾); the rise into Esher is continued through the village and is followed by a very stiff descent, then there is up and down hill twice—the last fall called Horseshoe-clump Hill—past Claremont Park and across Esher Common, with another stiff pull up to Fair Mile Common, exactly a mile across, as the name implies, and level running; from the Fair Mile is a sharp but short drop, then a little level ground through Cobham Street, 17½ (where turn to r.), and after crossing the *R.* Mole, Pain's Hill has to be climbed, the steepest rise from Kingston to Guildford; at the top take the left hand road and, except the rather steep fall of Red Hill entering Wisley Common about a mile further on, the remainder is an easy undulating road over Wisley Common ("The Hut" 20) with a sharp drop entering Ripley. The surface is good and smooth all the way, except the rise to Fair Mile, and Red Hill descent, and across Wisley Common, which are often loose and heavy. Pretty scenery.

Just before "The Hut" a good road branches off on *l.* to *Ockham* (1¼—21¼); greatly frequented by cyclists.
(*Cobham Street:* White Lion, *rec. C.T.C.—Ockham:* Hautboy and Fiddle, *rec. C.T.C.—Ripley:* Anchor, *rec. C.T.C.*; Talbot.)

Beyond Esher, on *l.*, Claremont Park. On *l.*, Pain's Hill Park; 1m. on *r.*, on St. George's Hill, a large ancient entrenchment; before Ripley, en *l.*, Ockham Park. 1m. N.W. of Ripley, on banks of *R.* Wey, are the ruins of Newark Abbey.

Ripley to Guildford—"White Hart" Inn (5¾—27½) is a capital smooth and undulating road; Guildford is paved, and there is a very steep descent down the High street, which should not be ridden without a powerful brake, though it can just be mounted by a good rider.

(*Guildford:* Angel; Central Dining Rooms; Cannon; Ram; Stoke, *C.T.C.*; White Hart; White Horse; White Lion.)

The road from Esher to Guildford is one of the finest near London, not only for the pretty and varied views of scenery it is bordered with, but also on account of the uniform goodness of its surface. Before Guildford, on *r.*, Stoke Place. Guildford is the county town of Surrey. There are ruins of a Norman castle. St. Mary's is the oldest *ch.*; also Grammar School, Abbot's Hospital, Guildhall, &c.

Guildford to Godalming (4—31½); after crossing the bridge (*R.* Wey) turn to *l.* and there is an ascent out of Guildford up to St. Catherine's Hill, 28½, then nearly level across Pease Marsh, 29¾, but not at all a smooth or good road; Godalming is paved with round cobbles, and very jolty.

(*Godalming:* Angel; King's Arms; Railway; West Surrey, *rec. C.T.C.*)

On St. Catherine's Hill are remains of a decorated chapel, dating from Edward I.'s reign.

Godalming to Haslemere (8½—40) is a very hilly road; beginning with a stiff rise out of Godalming it is up and down hill, chiefly the former, but nothing difficult through Milford, 33 (where keep to *l.* and ½m. after to *r.*) to Brook Green or Street, 36½, then undulating and more downhill through Gray's Wood, 38½, and Gray's Wood Common; pretty good surface.

(*Haslemere:* White Horse, *C.T.C.*)

D

Haslemere to Midhurst (7¼—47¾); steep hill to climb out of Haslemere (dangerous to ride down the other way on account of a sharp turn to the r. and another at the bottom to the l.) then fairly good and undulating road past Sussex Bells, 41, and over Friday Hill to Fernhurst, 43, beyond which is a long rise for nearly 2m. past Henly Green, 44½, to top of Henly Hill, followed by a long run down over North Heath and through Easebourn, 47, where turn sharp to r.

(*Midhurst:* Angel; Eagle.)

At Midhurst, on l., Cowdry Park, in which are the ruins of Cowdry House, destroyed by fire 1793.

Midhurst to Singleton (5½—53½): out of Midhurst is a stiff ascent up to Lavington Common, followed by a run down, then level to Cocking, 50¼, out of which (keeping to l.) there is a steep, long hill to climb and the road continues more or less on the rise to Singleton.

Singleton to Chichester—Market Cross (7—60½); taking the right hand fork in Singleton and again just outside the village, it is a good undulating road through West Dean, 54, to Binderton, 56, and thence downhill or level through Mid Lavant, 58. [There is a more direct road by keeping to the l. at the fork outside Singleton and going over Rook's Hill and through East Lavant, 57, joining the other road ½m. further on; it is half uphill and half down over Rook's Hill, the ascent of which on either side is very severe. It passes close by an ancient Beacon and earthworks, beyond which is Goodwood race-course and the Park.]

(*Chichester:* Anchor, *B.T.C.*; Dolphin; White Horse.)

At West Dean, on l., Cannon *Ho.*; on r. Binderton *Ho.*; at Mid Lavant, on r., West Lavant *Ho.*; 2m. on l. is Goodwood Park. Chichester was an important city in Roman times, and the walls, 1½m. in extent, are supposed to be chiefly Roman work. The town was besieged by the Parliamentarians in 1642. The cathedral was erected in the twelfth century, but has undergone frequent repairs, including a new tower, the old one having fallen in 1861. St. Mary's Hospital, Market Cross, Town Hall (part of a Grey Friars Monastery *ch.*), Bell Tower, St. Olave's *ch.*, &c., &c.

Chichester to Bognor (7¾—68); in Chichester turn to l., and outside the city walls take middle of three roads, and then first on r.; it is a level and very fair road by Merston Stream, 62¾, Elbridge, 64¼, and South Berstead, 66⅜.

[Or to *Arundel*, 54½, p. 31, then to r. up a good ascent out of the town on the Chichester road, which follow for more than 2m., then turn to l., and through Walberton (end of), 57¾, Yapton, 59½, Felpham, 63½, to *Bognor*, 65.]

(*Bognor:* Bedford, *C.T.C.*; Claremont; Norfolk.)

LONDON TO CHICHESTER (by Petworth).

London to Godalming (31½)—p. 33.

Godalming to Chiddingfold (6½—38); stiff rise out of Godalming, and undulating through Milford (where keep to l. twice) with a steep uphill to mount to Witley, 35; from it is more or less downhill, in some parts rather steep, over Hambledon Heath and Hurst to North Bridge *Tg.*, 37½.

Chiddingfold to Petworth (9—47); very hilly road over Cripple

Crouch Hill, 40¾ (at the top keep to the *l.*), through Fisher's Street, 41, North Chapel, 42, and over Hoad's Common, 41½.

[There is another road to Petworth by *Billinghurst*, 40¼, p. 31; then turn to the *r.* over New Bridge, 41½ (just beyond keep to *l.*), through Wisborough Green, 42¾, Idehurst, 44¼, Strood Green, 44¾, and over Brinkshole Heath, 47¼, to *Petworth*, 49¼, very hilly.]

(*Petworth:* Half Moon; Swan.)

At Fisher's Street, a little on *l.*, Shillinglee Park. Before Petworth, for 1¼*m.* on *r.*, the road skirts Petworth Park, with its splendid mansion containing some fine paintings that can be seen on certain days.

Petworth to Duncton—*ch.* (4¼—51¼); descent out of Petworth, then almost level, by Coultershaw Mill *Tp.*, 49, cross *R.* Rother, and over Duncton Common.

Before Duncton, on *l.*, Burton Park.

Duncton to Chichester—Cross (10½—61¾); steep winding ascent out of Duncton on to the South Downs (dangerous to ride *down*), followed by another hill beyond Upper Waltham, 53¾, to Benge's Wood, 54; then long downhill past North Wood to Halnaker, 58, and level through Maudlin, 59¾, and West Hampnet, 60¼, and entering Chichester by the East gate.

[For Bognor turn to *l.* at entering Chichester, which will make it ½*m* shorter to *Bognor*, 69. There is also another road to Bognor by turning to *l.* beyond Benge's Wood and through Eartham, 56¾, Eastergate, 59½, Woodgate, 60½, Shripney, 62, and South Berstead, 63¼, to *Bognor*, 65.]

At Halnaker join the old Roman Stone or Stane Street Causeway.

LONDON TO LITTLEHAMPTON (by Petworth).

London to Petworth (47)—p. 34.

Petworth to Fittleworth—*ch.* (3—50); in Petworth turn to *l.*, and down a steep hill, followed by a long and very steep ascent with two or three sharp turns in it (dangerous to ride *down*) to climb, through Byworth Street, 48 (where keep to *l.*), and over Low Heath, Egdean Common, and Codmoor Hill, the road continues up and down hill, and requires careful riding.

Fittleworth to Arundel—*ch.* (8¼—58¼); the descent from Codmoor Hill continues through Fittleworth and Lower Fittleworth, 50½, to Fittleworth Bridge, 50¾ (*R.* Rother) whence almost level over Horncroft Common to Bury *Tp.*, 52¼, where join the road from Pulborough, for remainder of which see p. 31.

Arundel to Littlehampton (3¾—62)—p. 31.

LONDON TO PORTSMOUTH.

London to Godalming (31½)—p. 33.

Godalming to Liphook (12½—44); beginning with a stiff rise out of Godalming, it is up and downhill to Milford, 33 (where turn to *r.*), then there are a couple of stiff pulls over Mouse Hill, 33¾, and Witley Common, with a good run down of about ½*m.* to the "Anglers' Rest," at the Hammer Ponds, 35¾; from here begins the long and severe ascent of over 2*m.* up Hind Head Hill, 39, the latter part of which is very steep, followed by a long run down for about 3m., over the Common and Cold Ash Down, passing by the "Royal Huts," and "Seven Thorns Inn," 41¾, after which there are one or two sharp pulls before Liphook is reached; good hard road.

(*Liphook*: Anchor; Royal Anchor, *C.T.C.*)

From the top of Hind Head Hill the prospect is extensive and beautiful; on r. is the deep dell of Hackham Bottom, commonly called Devil's Punch Bowl.

Liphook to Petersfield—"Red Lion" (8¼—52¼); there are two or three stiff ascents, the last—Gravel Hill—being rather severe, over Milland Common to and out of Rake, 47½, then over Rake Down it is all downhill to Sheet Bridge, 51: uneven surface to Rake, over the Common, and often very loose for first 5m., then good.

[There is another way by going to *Haslemere*, 40, p. 33, and to the Sussex Bells, 41, just before which turn to r., and over Lynchmere Common, to the "Jolly Sailor" on Milland Common, 1¾m. before Rake, 48¼.]

(*Petersfield*: Dolphin, *B.T.C.*; Red Lion.)

Petersfield to Horndean (7½—59¾); soon after leaving Petersfield the ascent of Butser Hill has to be climbed, about 2m. long, and the last ½m. rather steep but very smooth; from the top, 55, the road descends for a mile, and with one or two short rises is chiefly on the fall to Horndean; good road.

(*Horndean*: Ship and Bell.)

Magnificent view from Butser Hill, 917 ft. high; on a clear day Salisbury Cathedral is visible 40m. distant.

Horndean to Cosham (6—65¾); at Horndean turn sharp to the r. up the hill, the road straight on going to Havant; the road is undulating, and traverses the Forest of Bere to Purbrook, 63¾, after which there is Portsdown Hill, 65, to mount, rather long and steep, the descent of which on the other side is rather steep and rough to Cosham.

From Portsdown Hill capital views of Portsmouth, Southampton, and Isle of Wight are obtained; eastward the spire of Chichester Cathedral is visible. On r. are three forts, and in front ruins of Porchester Castle in which is an ancient Saxon ch.

Cosham to Portsmouth (4¾—70½) is level, but, being mostly macadam, is bad and shaky, especially after crossing Portsea Bridge, 66¼; tramway for last 2m.

(*Portsmouth*: George, *C.T.C.*; York and Pier.—*Portsea*: Kepple's Head; Royal Oak; Totterdell's.—*Landport*: Smith's Commercial; Sussex.—*Southsea*: Bush, *C.T.C.*; Marine Mansion; Pier; Portland; Queen's; Sussex.)

Portsmouth, with its suburbs of Portsea, Landport, and Southsea, is the chief naval station of Britain, containing a large dockyard and naval arsenal. There is a splendid land-locked harbour, the whole being strongly fortified. The suburb of Southsea is greatly resorted to as a watering-place.

LONDON TO HAYLING.

London to Horndean (59¾)—above.

Horndean to Havant (4¾—64½), through the Forest of Bere is a good road, slightly downhill; keep to r. at St. John's, 62¼.

(*Havant*: Bear; Dolphin, *C.T.C.*; Star.)

Havant to Hayling (5—69½); the road soon crosses from the mainland to Hayling Island, and is very sandy and heavy all the way.
(*Hayling:* Royal, B.T.C.)

LONDON TO GUILDFORD (by Leatherhead).

London to Leatherhead (18½)—p. 29.

Leatherhead to East Horsley (5½—24); keep straight on down the hill through Leatherhead, passing the Dorking road on *l.*, and over the bridge (*R.* Mole); ¼m. farther on a long steep hill has to be climbed, generally covered with loose stones (and on the reverse journey should be descended with great care, but is best walked down); from the top the road is undulating to Great Bookham, 20¾, then up and down continually, but nothing difficult, through Great Effingham, 22¼; the surface is hard and smooth. [There is an easier road by turning to the *r.* at the foot of Leatherhead hill and through the pretty village of Fetcham, 19¾, out of which is a short but stiff pull, then over a good undulating road through the lower end of Great Bookham, 20¾, Little Bookham, 21½, to the lower end of Effingham, 22¼, where turn to the *l.* and join the other road at the top of the village; ¼m. longer.]
(*East Horsley:* Duke of Wellington.)

Before East Horsley, on *r.*, Horsley Towers, the residence of the Earl of Lovelace.

East Horsley to Guildford—"White Hart" Inn (6½—30½); through West Horsley, 24½, East Clandon, 26½, and Merrow, 28½, the road is nearly all up and down hill, with good smooth surface.

On *r.*, Horsley Place, Hatchland Park, and Clandon Park.

LONDON TO CHERTSEY.

London to Kingston—M.P. (10)—p. 32.

Kingston to Hampton Court (1¾—11¾); in Kingston keep straight on past the *ch.* and cross bridge over *R.* Thames, after which the macadam ends, and (bearing to the *l.*) the road is level, but still rather rough and bumpy riding in the middle, passing the Lion Gates, 11½.
(*Hampton Court:* Greyhound; King's Arms; Mitre.)

Hampton Court Palace, built by Cardinal Wolsey, can be seen on certain days. On *r.* is Bushey Park, famous for its avenue of chesnut trees. Hampton Court Green and Bushey Park are the scene of the great annual "Hampton Court Meet" of metropolitan bicyclists.

Hampton Court to Walton-on-Thames (4¼—16) is level all the way; at the Green keep to *l.* and cross *R.* Thames by Hampton Court Bridge, over a pretty fair road through East Moulsey, 12½ (where turn sharp to *r.*) and West Moulsey, 13¼, to Apps Court gates, 14, just beyond which turn to the *r.*, and the surface is very good and smooth past Apps Court Tavern, 15, at which, on coming the reverse direction the right hand road must be taken. [There is also another road by turning to the *r.* after crossing the river, and by the lanes and across Moulsey Hurst or Common to Apps Court Tavern, being the left hand road there on the reverse journey; level and good but sometimes sandy. Or follow the Esher road as on p. 32

for 2m. beyond Kingston, then take first turn on r. through Thames Ditton, 12¼ (where keep to r. and then to l.), and it is a level and good road except a level railway crossing and a ford across R. Mole, which is rideable on right-hand side, then turn to r. to East Moulsey, 13½.]

(*East Moulsey:* Bell, *rec. C.T.C.*; Carnarvon Castle; Duke's Head.—*Thames Ditton:* Angel; Swan.—*Walton-on-Thames:* Crown; Duke's Head; Swan, *C.T.C.*; White Hart.)

Walton-on-Thames to Chertsey (5—21); in Walton turn to r., then to l., and again to l. just before the bridge, and a good undulating road runs through Oatlands Park, at the end of which keep to r., and then —instead of straight down the hill which only leads to the riverside—to the l. into Weybridge, 18; through Weybridge, at the guide-post, keep to the r., and having crossed two bridges the remainder is level, except a stiff hill, up and down, about halfway. On the whole very good road, but in places near the river, where liable to be flooded, it is sometimes rather sandy.

(*Weybridge:* Hand and Spear; Lincoln Arms; Queen's Head; Ship, *C.T.C.*—*Chertsey:* Chertsey Bridge; Railway; Swan, *R.T.C.*)

Just below Walton Bridge are Cowey Stakes, where Cæsar is supposed to have crossed the R. Thames. At Chertsey are some traces of a Benedictine monastery, founded 666; here is Cowley Ho., an Elizabethan mansion, in which the poet Cowley died, 1667. From St. Ann's Hill, 1m. beyond Chertsey, St. Paul's Cathedral and Westminster Abbey are visible.

LONDON TO CHERTSEY (by Shepperton).

London to Hampton Court (11¾)—p. 37.

Hampton Court to Sunbury—*ch.* (3¼—15); keeping to the r. along the Green the road is level all the way, generally sandy and heavy to Hampton, 12¾, just beyond which turn to l. by the waterworks, and for nearly a mile the road is narrow and rather rutty and rough, and then pretty good to Sunbury, but apt to get loose in dry weather and very heavy in wet weather.

(*Sunbury:* Flowerpot; Magpie; Weir.)

Sunbury to Chertsey.—(4¼—19½) through Lower Halliford, 16¾, (just beyond keep to l.) and Shepperton, 17¼, is a good level road, though in dry weather apt to be rather loose in places, especially beyond Shepperton where it is frequently loose and shingly. About a mile beyond Sunbury a brook crosses the road, but is fordable in dry weather. Cross over Chertsey Bridge.

Or to Walton-on-Thames, 16, p. 37, whence cross over R. Thames by Walton Bridge to Lower Halliford, 17½; good road.]

(*Halliford:* Ship.—*Shepperton:* Anchor.)

This is a very pretty ride in summer.

LONDON TO LYMINGTON.

London to Guildford—"White Hart" Inn (27½)—p. 33.

Guildford to Farnham (10¼—37¾); just after crossing the bridge (R. Wey), at the bottom of the hill in Guildford, turn off sharp to the r. in a narrow street, which directly after bears to the l. again, and then there is an ascent for over 2m. leading up to the Hog's Back, the first part too steep to ride *down* except with great care, but the rest is rideable either way; on reaching the top there is a splendid level road for about 5m. along the crest of the Hog's Back, which is a narrow straight ridge running nearly due west, and the last 3m. are more or less downhill into Farnham.

The usual main route from London is by Brentford, Staines, and Bagshot, to Farnham, 38½, p. 52; the Guildford route is shorter and better.

(*Farnham:* Bush; Lion; Lion and Lamb.)

About 2m. S.E. of Farnham, on the banks of the River Wey, is Waverley Abbey. At Farnham the castle, now the residence of the Bishop of Winchester.

Farnham to Alton (9¼—47); a little out of Farnham keep to the *r*., and there is a gentle rise to Bentley Green, 41¾, then slightly undulating through Froyle, 44, and Holybourne, 45¾; very good smooth road.

(*Alton:* Butcher's Arms; Crown; Duke's Head; Matchwick's; Railway; Royal Oak; Swan.)

Alton to Alresford (9¼—56¼); level to Chawton, 48¼, where take the right hand road, and there is a long stiffish climb of 2½ to 3m., but nowhere at all steep, to the White Horse Inn at Medstead Station; then a short run down and a similar up are followed by a rather steep fall, which should be taken carefully as the road has two or three sharp turns in the middle, nearly to Ropley Stoke, 52½, past which there is a gradual run down through Ropley Dean, 54¼, to Bishop's Sutton, 55½, and the rest is level to Alresford; good surface.

(*Alresford:* Swan.)

Alresford is a pretty old-fashioned town; the streams in the neighbourhood abound in trout. About 2m. S.W. are Tichborne village and Ho.

Alresford to Winchester (7¾—64½); over Seward's Bridge, 57¼, is a first-rate hard and smooth road, but very hilly; there is very little level ground, but the hills are not long or difficult either way, except the dangerously steep and crooked descent of Morn Hill into Winchester, which should be walked down; on the top of the hill on *l*. is a B.U. "Danger" board; at first the fall is moderate, then suddenly becoming steep the road turns sharp to *l*., shooting for 300 or 400 yards down the side of the hill, which rises in an almost precipitous cliff above the R. Itchen, and commands a splendid view of the town, the descent ending with another sharp turn to *r*. into the town; the surface is not very smooth: through Winchester is macadam and rough, and there is a sharp rise through the town. In Winchester bells are compulsory. [In order to avoid the hilly road from Alresford to Winchester, at the bottom of the descent about ½m. out of Alresford, take the road to *r*. by the railway, running along the Itchen valley and through the villages of Itchen Abbots, Martyr Worthy, and Abbots Worthy and falling into the Basingstoke road 2m. north of Winchester; this is about 1½m. farther round but not hilly, though inclined to be rough in places; pretty country.]

(*Winchester:* Black Swan; Eagle; George; Royal.)

At Winchester two of the Roman gates are said to be still remaining. It was besieged and dismantled by Cromwell, and the castle (founded by William the Conqueror) blown up, only the foundations of it being visible; in the cathedral, part of which was erected 980, are the bones of Alfred the Great, Canute, William Rufus, and many Saxon kings, besides various ancient monuments, &c. Other buildings are St. Mary's College (built by William of Wykeham), Hospital of St. Cross, Museum, &c. On St. Catherine's Hill, 1m. S.E., are remains of fortifications and entrenchments, and vestiges of the great Roman road to Porchester.

Winchester to Southampton (12—76½); in Winchester turn to *l.*, and for a short distance past the abbey or Hospital of St. Cross, 65½, the road is level, then begins a long gradual rise followed after a little level by a long descent to Compton, 67, thence undulating to Otterbourn, 69, out of which is a severe hill to mount; after that it is almost level past Half-way House to Chandler's Ford Bridge, 71, beyond which is a short stiff rise; the next 2½*m.* are rather hilly but nothing difficult, and the last 3*m.* are down hill; tolerably good going all the way, in many parts very good; tramway in Southampton and macadam streets. On the milestones about here Winchester is called "Winton," and Southampton "Southon."

(*Southampton:* Alexandra, *Hqrs.;* Bedford ; Canute ; Cliff ; Crown, *B.T.C.;* Dolphin : Dock ; Flowers, temp. ; Fountain ; Imperial ; Railway ; South Western · Star ; Sun.—*West End:* Swan.)

At Otterbourn, on *r.*, Cranbury *Ho.;* 2*m.* past Chandler's Ford Bridge, on *l.*, Stoneham Park. Southampton is an important seaport and steam packet station. There are remains of the old walls still left, and one of the old gates--Bargate. About 3*m.* S.E. are the ruins of Netley Abbey.

Southampton to Totton (3¼—80¼); instead of going into the town, turn off to *r.* and through suburb of West End (just beyond keep to *l.*) for the Lyndhurst road, which is a dead level through Milbrook, 78½, and Redbridge, 79¾, and after getting clear of the town of Southampton is a pretty good road ; part of the way it skirts the top of Southampton Water. [There is a short cut from the Winchester road to Milbrook, striking off to *r.* 2 or 3*m.* before Southampton and going across country through Shirley, situate in a valley, into and out of which are rather stiff and loose descent and ascent, otherwise nearly level and a good road: distance about 3*m.*]

In Totton is a level railway crossing.

Totton to Lyndhurst (5½—85¾); turning to *l.* in Totton it is a very fair level road to bottom of Houndsdown Hill, 82¼, which is a good stiff ascent, then after a gradual slope to past the level railway crossing at Lyndhurst Road Station, 82¾, where it enters the New Forest, the remainder is a capital undulating road to Lyndhurst, at the entrance of which instead of going through the village turn to *l.* for the Brockenhurst road.

(*Lyndhurst:* Crown; Railway ; Stag's Head.)

Pretty scenery through the New Forest. At Lyndhurst *ch.* there is a beautiful altar fresco by Sir F. Leighton, R.A. King's *Ho.* and King's stables.

Lyndhurst to Brockenhurst (3½—89¼); a capital easy road through the New Forest, on the rise for some distance, then presently a little downhill, and the latter half level : railway crossing in Brockenhurst.

Brockenhurst *ch.* is partly Saxon; near to is Watcombe *Ho.*

Brockenhurst to Lymington (5—94¼); through Batramsley, 91¾, is rather hilly, but nothing difficult either way ; not quite so good surface as the last stage : pretty scenery.

(*Lymington:* Angel ; Nag's Head ; Londesborough, *B.T.C.*)

Past Lyndhurst, on *r.*, Cuffnels; at Brockenhurst, on *l.*, Brockenhurst Park. At Lymington is good bathing. About 3*m.* S. is Hurst Castle, built by Henry VIII.; Charles I. was confined here.

LONDON TO LYMINGTON (by Beaulieu).

London to Southampton (76½)—above; in Southampton, keep straight through the town.

Southampton to Hythe (2—78½); cross Southampton Water by ferry.
(*Hythe :* Drummond Arms.)

Hythe to Beaulieu (4½—83); long rise over Beaulieu Heath to Hill Top, 82: splendid road.

At Beaulieu are remains of a Cistercian abbey, founded 1204; also of a Hospital of Knights Templars. About 5m. E., or 4m. S. of Hythe, is Calshot Castle.

Beaulieu to Lymington (6½—89½); through Hatchet Gate, 84⅓, across Beaulieu Heath, and by Newtown Park, 87¾, is a splendid road, with no difficult hills.

LONDON TO PORTSMOUTH (by Farnham).

London to Farnham (37¾)—p. 38.

Farnham to Petersfield (17—54½); turn to *l.* just out of Farnham, and through Alice Holt or Alder Holt Wood, Woolmer Forest, Greatham, 48¼, and Lyss, 50, is a good road with no difficult hills.

Petersfield to Portsmouth (18¼—73)—p. 36.

LONDON TO GOSPORT.

London to Alton (47)—p. 39.

Alton to Filmer Hill (9—56): level and very good through Chawton, 48¼ (keep on to *l.*), Farrington, 50, and East Tisted, 51¾, then a gradual ascent for about 2m. past Basing Park and the Devil's Jump, with a steep fall at Filmer Hill, quite safe to ride down.

Beyond Chawton, on *l.*, Chawton *Ho*. At East Tisted, on *r.*, Rotherfield *Ho* and Park. Near Filmer Hill, on *l.*, Basing Park.

Filmer Hill to Corhampton (6—62); a long rise past the Hut, 57¼ (where the Winchester and Petersfield road crosses) nearly to West Meon, 58½, into and through which there is a stiff long hill down that requires to be ridden carefully, as the road turns sharp to the *r.* and then to the *l.* about halfway down; after that the road is all that can be desired, through Warnford, 60, and Exton, 61½, mostly on a slight decline.

At Warnford, on *l.*, Belmont, in the grounds of which are ruins of an old mansion called King John's House. At Exton, 2m. on *l.*, a Roman camp. At Corhampton, 1 or 2m. on *l*, is Old Winchester Hill, 900 ft. high, from which the Isle of Wight is visible; many tumuli on the top.

Corhampton to Cold Harbour Tg. (6½—68½); an easy uphill out of Corhampton, then a steep rough descent into Droxford, 63½, and a corresponding hill to mount out of it; after that is a long run down, in parts rather steep, till about 2m. past Hill Pound Inn, 65¼, followed by a long rise and a gradual but rough descent to the junction of the road from Bishop's Waltham, ½m. beyond Cold Harbour *Tg.*; for the last 3m. the road traverses Waltham Chase; capital surface.

Cold Harbour Tg. to Fareham (4—72½); good easy road, except a bad hill to mount out of Wickham, 69.

(*Fareham :* Bugle; Golden Lion; King's Arms; Railway; Red Lion; Royal Oak, *B.T.C.*; White Hart.)

Wickham *ch.* contains several ancient monuments. On *r.* Park Place, 1*m.* before Fareham, on *l.*, is Roche Court, a mansion nearly 700 years old. Beyond Fareham, on *l.*, Cams Hall. Before Fareham, on *l.*, on Portsdown Hill, is Nelson's monument.

Fareham to Gosport (5½—78): in Fareham turn to *r.*, and a little after to *l.*, and it is a good road through Brockhurst *Tp.*, 75¾, and Forton, 77.

From Gosport cross by ferry to Portsmouth. Through Gosport to Stokes Bay is 2*m.* farther. Beyond Gosport, Haslar Hospital and Fort Monkton.

LONDON TO SOUTHAMPTON (by Botley).

London to Cold Harbour Tg. (68½)—p. 41.

Cold Harbour Tg. to Botley (3¼—71¾): follow the Fareham road for ¼*m.*, then turn to *r.*, and it is a good but rather hilly road over Curbridge Common to Botley.

(*Botley:* Railway.)

Botley to Southampton (6½—78¼); long rise out of Botley, then (keeping to *l.*) pretty level through Bittern, 76, and over Northam Bridge, 77¼; capital road. If intending to get to the New Forest road through Totton, this road from Northam Bridge runs straight into it, through the upper part of Southampton. Returning, just before Bittern keep to *l.*

This is a better road to Southampton than that through Bishop's Waltham.

Bittern was the Roman Clausentum, and Roman remains have been found here.

LONDON TO SOUTHAMPTON (by Bishop's Waltham).

London to Filmer Hill (56)—p. 41.

Filmer Hill to Bishop's Waltham (8¾—64¾); at Filmer Hill turn to *r.*, and follow the old coach road. [There is also another road, through Corhampton, 62, p. 41; then turn to *r.* for Bishop's Waltham, 65½.]

(*Bishop's Waltham:* Crown.)

At Bishop's Waltham are remains of a castle or palace, built by the brother of King Stephen, Bishop Henry de Blois, but demolished in the Civil War.

Bishop's Waltham to Botley (3½—68¼); out of Bishop's Waltham take the right hand road, joining the Droxford road on Curbridge Common.

Botley to Southampton (6½—74¾)—above.

LONDON TO CHRISTCHURCH.

London to Lyndhurst (85¾)—p 40.

Lyndhurst to Holmesley Station (6½—92¼); entering Lyndhurst keep to *r.* up the village, and a little past the *ch.* turn to the *l.*, it is rather hilly through the middle of the New Forest by Allum Green, 87½, and Blackwater Bridge, 89½; the road is good for a mile, then it becomes bad for the rest of the stage, being chiefly covered with loose sand and gravel, which makes riding heavy work, especially up the hills. [The old road used to pass a little to the *l.* by New Forest Gate and Rhinefield Lodge, 89¼, to Wilverley Bridge just past Holmesley Station.]

The country is wild and bleak, but it is only at intervals that the timber comes close up to the road; very often the ground on either side is open, or covered with furze or bush.

Holmesley Station to Christchurch (7—99¼); the surface now improves again, and after ascending a hill beyond the bridge the road is level and tolerable going to Hinton, 96¼ (before which the Forest ends), from here is an easy run down, and the last 2*m.* are level and very good into Christchurch; heavy going in wet weather.

(*Christchurch :* Antelope; King's Arms; Newlyn's; Ship, *B.T.C.*)

At Christchurch are remains of an Augustine priory, founded in early Saxon times. The *ch.* contains some curious monuments. Near the town are Heron Court and Landhills; also remains of a camp and entrenchments, and several tumuli.

LONDON TO POOLE AND BOURNEMOUTH.

London to Totton (80¾)—p. 40.

Totton to Cadnam (4½—84¾); in Totton keep straight on, and it is an undulating road with very gentle gradients.

(*Cadnam :* Sir John Barleycorn; White Hart.)

Cadnam to Ringwood (11½—96¼); the road now enters the New Forest, taking the left hand fork just out of Cadnam; ascent for ½*m.*, rather steep at the top but smooth surface, and shortly after is another rise, then a long fall, the latter part of which is very stony and steep to Stoney Cross, 87; this is followed by another long ascent, smooth and not so steep, on the top of which are long stretches of nearly level ground with good surface for about 4*m.*, then another descent and a long rise again to the toll-bar at Picked Post, 93¼, whence it is slightly downhill into Ringwood; some parts of the road are generally rather loose in dry weather.

(*Ringwood :* Crown; White Hart, *B.T.C.*)

At Stoney Cross, on *r.*, is Rufus Stone, commemorating the death of William Rufus.

Ringwood to New Bridge (4¼—100¼); cross River Avon, and keeping first to *r.*, then to *l.* at Ashley Cross, 96¾, just past the railway, the surface continues good for a mile, then rough and rutty over St. Leonard's Bridge, 99¾, to New Bridge; there is only one hill to speak of, which is short but rough.

New Bridge to Poole (8½—108¾); keep to the *l.* and it is an undulating very good road, but a little loose in places over Parley Common, through Long Ham, 103½ (cross River Stour), thence over Canford Heath and through Parkstone Green, 107.

Past Long Ham there is branch road to *Bournemouth*, turning to *l.* through Kinson or Kingston, 104½, then capital road to Winton, and rather rough to top of Richmond hill, which is a stiff descent into Bournemouth, about 6*m.* in all.

(*Poole :* Antelope; Crown; Furmage's; London, *B.T.C.—Bournemouth :* Bath; Bellevue; Grand; Hickson's; Newlyn's; Pembroke, *B.T.C.*; Stewart, Family.)

At Long Ham, on *l.*, an ancient entrenchment called Dudsbury Camp. In Poole Harbour, on Brownsea Island, Brownsea Castle. Bournemouth has sprung up as a watering-place during the last twenty years; it has a very mild climate, and is a winter resort for invalids.

LONDON TO WEYMOUTH.

London to New Bridge (100½)—p. 43.

New Bridge to Wimborne Minster (5¼—105¾); keep to r. beyond New Bridge, and it is an easy road as to hills, but the surface is rather rough and sandy to within 3m. of Wimborne.

(*Wimborne Minster:* Crown; Griffin; King's Arms, *B.T.C.*; King's Head; Laing's, *B.T.C.*; Railway.)

At Wimborne Minster the *ch.* is mainly Saxon, and here Ethelred, brother of King Alfred, was buried. About 3m. N.W. of Wimborne, on the Blandford road, is Badbury Rings, an ancient British hill fortress of great extent.

Wimborne Minster to Lytchett Minster (7½—113); in Wimborne Minster turn sharp to *l.* and follow the Poole road for ¼m beyond Bushels Mill, 110, to which it is rather hilly but easy riding, then turn to *r.* through the toll-gate and over the railway bridge (bicyclists coming the contrary direction should beware of this gate), then undulating for 1¼m. to a second toll-gate and the rest level; first rate smooth road.

[There is another route by following the Poole road through *New Bridge* to 3m. beyond Long Ham, 103½, p. 43, then turn to *r.* and strike across to the Poole and Wareham road, 107½, and follow it to the toll-gate near Bushels Mill, 108½ (where turn to *l.*), shortening the distance to *Lytchett Minster* to 111¼.

Or just before entering Poole turn to the *r.* and follow the Wareham road to the toll-gate, then to Lytchett Minster, 113, as above.]

Lytchett Minster to Wareham (4¾—117¾); just beyond Lytchett Minster keep to *l.* and it is almost level and a pretty good road over King's Bridge, 113¾, and Gore Heath.

(*Wareham:* Black Bear; Red Lion, *B.T.C.*)

Wareham is supposed to have been the site of a British town, and afterwards of a Roman station; it is surrounded on three sides by a high rampart of earth of Saxon origin. In St. Mary's *ch.* is a Saxon chapel, supposed to have been the burial-place of the early Saxon kings.

Wareham to Wool Bridge (6—123¾); in Wareham turn to *r.*, and through Stoke Green or Stokeford, 121¼, is a good road but rather uphill.

At Wool Bridge, on *l.*, are the remains of Bindon Abbey, founded 1172. 3m. S. is Lulworth Castle, a splendid residence.

Wool Bridge to Warmwell Cross (6½—130¼); the road continues chiefly level till past Portway, 126¾, then gradually becoming more undulating toward Warmwell Cross.

Warmwell Cross to Weymouth (5¼—135¾); take the left hand road for Poxwell, 131¼, through which is a long run down with one short break to Osmington, 132¾; out of this is a very stiff pull, the road crossing a big hill (from the top of which Weymouth and Portland Isle are visible). with a long rather winding descent down the other side, the last bit rather steep, into Preston, 133¼, and the rest is almost level into Melcombe Regis, 135¼, skirting the shore of Weymouth Bay; good road.

(*Weymouth:* Burdon; Crown, *B.T.C.*; Golden Lion; London; Marine; Queen's.)

On the hill, N.W. of Preston, is an old circular earthwork called Charlebury. Weymouth, with its twin town of Melcombe Regis, is a fashionable watering-place, pleasantly situated, and with some fine buildings and esplanade. There is the modern fort, Sandsfoot Castle (built by Henry VIII., but now in ruins), Portland Isle, with convict prison, the Verne Citadel, ruins of Rufus Castle, Bow-and-Arrow Castle, Pennsylvania, Quarries, &c. About 9m. W., near the end of the Chesil Bank, is Abbotsbury, where are ruins of the old abbey, of St. Catherine's Chapel, and Abbotsbury Castle; here is also the Swannery. A little more N., near Portisham, is a Druidical cromlech, and on Blagdon Hill the Hardy monument,

LONDON TO SWANAGE.

London to Wareham (117¾)—p. 44.

Wareham to Corfe Castle (4—121¾); through Stowborough, 118¼, is a tolerably good road, with one or two moderate hills; Corfe is entered by a very steep ascent, on which are several deep cross-ruts, and it is hardly safe to ride down as the road twists about.

Corfe, or Corfe Castle, is a very ancient town. The castle, now in ruins, from which it derives its name, was founded by King Edgar, and was a residence of the Saxon kings; it was of great strength, and was dismantled by the Parliamentarians.

Corfe Castle to Swanage (6—127¾); there are two roads, the upper and the lower; from the little square in Corfe take the left hand road, and at the bifurcation just outside the town keep to r. for the upper road which is nearly all uphill to Kingston, 123½, then (turning to l.) downhill through Langton Matravers, 125¾, a very bad road, and in wet weather slippery and dangerous riding: for the lower road, which is nearly a mile shorter, keep to l. just outside the town, and after mounting a short but very steep rise (some 60 or 70 yards) it rapidly deteriorates, being but a narrow, rough, and rutty lane; soon after there are several nasty ascents and descents, the surface being very bad and with the least wet slippery and greasy, till the upper road is joined ½m. before Swanage; into and through the town is a narrow winding descent, too steep to be ridden down.

[Instead of either of the above routes, a better one will be found by turning to l. in front of the castle and not going through the town; the roads run along the north side of Nine Barrow Down, passing Rempston House, and is rather hilly for 3 or 4m., then leaving Studland Bay on the l. turn to r. over the hill, and there are two short but steep pitches to walk down, gates being at the bottom, and the rest is more or less downhill through Ulwell to Swanage, but should be ridden very carefully; capital smooth gravel surface; distance about 6m.]

(*Swanage:* Anchor; Purbeck.)

This district is called the Isle of Purbeck, and is noted for the Purbeck stone which is largely quarried.

LONDON TO CADNAM (by Romsey).

London to Winchester (64½)—p. 39.

Winchester to Hursley—*ch.* (4½—69); leaving Winchester by Westgate there is a steep unrideable hill a mile long to climb out of the town, and afterwards it is a hilly but good hard road by Pitt Pond, 66½, and Standen, 68.

On r. Hursley Park, once the property of Richard Cromwell.

Hursley to Romsey—*P.O.* (6—75); ½m. out of Hursley keep to r. and through Amfield, 71½, the road continues hilly, the hills being short but steep, and there is a long descent into Romsey; good gravel road, but after rain heavy.

(*Romsey:* Market Inn; White Horse, *B.T.C.*)

Romsey *ch.* was formerly part of a Benedictine monastery, founded by King Edgar, and contains some fine monuments, &c. On S. Broadlands.

Romsey to Ower or Oux Bridge (2¼—77¾); after crossing *R.* Test keep to *l.*, and ½ *m.* out of Romsey there is a steep hill to walk up, then a good undulating road by Ranvild's Gate, 76¼.

Ower Bridge to Cadnam (3—80¼); at the bifurcation a little beyond Ower Bridge keep to *r.*, over Shorne Hill Common; undulating at first, then it becomes fairly level; good surface.

LONDON TO LAND'S END.

London (Hyde Park Corner) to Hounslow (9¾); through Knightsbridge, ½, Kensington, 1½, Hammersmith, 4, Turnham Green, 5, Brentford, 7, and Smallbury Green, 9, is level but a macadamised road, lumpy and greasy most of the way, with heavy traffic; at the beginning of Knightsbridge, and in Kensington and Hammersmith are sections of wood pavement.

(*Hounslow:* Palmerston).

Past Brentford, a little on *l.*, Sion Ho.; across River Thames, Kew Gardens.

Hounslow to Staines 6¼—16¼); in Hounslow at the two bifurcations keep first to *r.* and after to *l.*; past the Powder Mills, 11¾, and through Bedfont, 13¼, is a good and almost level road, but sometimes sandy.

(*Staines:* Angel; Angel and Crown; Jolly Farmer; Crooked Billet; Packhorse; Railway; Swan).

Staines to Virginia Water (4½—21) after crossing *R.* Thames there is a very sandy bit of road, quite level, into Egham, 18, out of which is the long and stiff ascent of Egham Hill to mount, then it is fairly level for a mile, followed by a long run down to Virginia Water; good smooth road, but apt to be loose and sandy at times.

(*Egham:* Packhorse.—*Sunningdale:* Sunningdale.)

At Egham, 1*m.* N., are Magna Charta Island and Runnymead. At Virginia Water, on *r.*, Windsor Great Park.

Virginia Water to Bagshot (5½—26¼); long rise from Virginia Water, then an undulating road by Shrub's Hill, 22, and Broomhill Hut, 23, where is a level railway crossing; tolerably good road but sometimes loose and sandy.

[There is another road to Bagshot by *Weybridge*, 18, p. 38; about 1*m.* further turn to *l.*, and crossing the railway at a level go through Addlestone, 19½, to Ottershaw, 21, here take the third road from the *r.*, past Ottershaw Park, keeping twice to *r.* and twice to *l.* through Chobham, 24½, (turn to *r.*) Burrow Green, 25, where turn to *l.*, then next to *r.*, and to *l.* at Westley Green, 26¼, and through Windlesham, 27½, (where keep first to *r.* and then to *l.* twice) to *Bagshot*, 29; sharp descent before Ottershaw, loose and stoney ascent and descent past Ottershaw Park and sharp stony descent into Windlesham, otherwise fairly level and good road.]

Bagshot: Cricketers' Arms; Fighting Cocks; King's Arms, *B.T.C.*)

At Broomhill Hut, a little on *l.*, is a large ancient entrenchment. 1*m.* before Bagshot, on *l.*, Hall Grove; further on, on *r.*, Bagshot Park.

Bagshot to Blackwater (4¼—30½): out of Bagshot a couple of ascents, the latter rather steep and rough towards the top, lead up to the "Jolly Farmer," 27½, (formerly the "Golden Farmer") on Chobham Ridges; here take the right hand fork, and after a mile or so of undulating road it is downhill into York Town, 29¼, and rest level; capital smooth road; level railway crossing in Blackwater.

(*York Town:* Duke of York.—*Blackwater:* Red Lion; Swan; White Hart, B.T.C.)

The curious obelisk or tower on the *l.* is said to be visible from Hampstead Heath. At York Town, on *r.*, Royal Military College.

Blackwater to Hartley Row (5¾—36¼); there is a long stiff ascent on leaving Blackwater, then the road is level or slightly undulating for about 4*m.* over Yateley Heath and Hartford Bridge Flats, from which there is a rather steep descent to Hartford Bridge, 35½, and then level; splendid smooth road.

(*Hartley Row:* White Lion.)

Hartley Row to Basingstoke (9—45¼); a mile past Hartley Row keep to *r.*; through Murrell Green, 38¼, Hook, 39¼, Hook Common and Mapledurwell Hatch, 42¾, is an undulating road, but no difficult hills; good smooth surface.

(*Basingstoke:* Angel; Blackboy; Feather; Red Lion; Wheatsheaf, B.T.C.)

2*m.* before Basingstoke, on *r.*, the ruins of Basing *Ho.*, celebrated for its brave defence for two years against the Parliamentarians. N. of Basingstoke, just outside the town, are the ruins of the Holy Ghost Chapel.

Basingstoke to Popham Lane (5¾—51); leaving Basingstoke keep to *l.*; good road but some long hills over Basingstoke Down.

About 3*m.* beyond Basingstoke, on *l.*, Kempshot *Ho.*

Popham Lane to Sutton Scotney (8—59); take the right hand road, it is hilly but good going.

Sutton Scotney to Stockbridge (7½—66½); across Barton Down, by Leckford Hutt, 63, and Worlby Hill, 65; long descent into Stockbridge.

(*Stockbridge:* Grosvenor Arms, B.T.C.; Vine.)

Stockbridge to Lobcombe Corner (6¼—73¼); in Stockbridge turn to *r.*, steep hill out of the town, and then rather hilly and not a good road, rather rough and heavy in wet weather, very open and exposed road.

Lobcombe Corner to Salisbury (7¾—81); past The Pheasant Inn or Winterslow Hut, 74½, the road continues very hilly, some of the ascents being rather steep, and the surface is very rough and stony for 5*m.*, then mostly downhill and fair going over St. Thomas's Bridge (River Bourne), 79.

(*Salisbury:* Angel; Crown; Four Swans; Plume of Feathers; Red Lion, B.T.C.; Shoulder of Mutton; Three Swans; White Hart.)

3*m.* past Winterslow Hut, on *r.*, a large entrenchment called Clorus' Camp. Salisbury was founded in the early part of the thirteenth century, consequent upon the removal of the cathedral from Old Sarum, of which the remains, now uninhabited, are still to be seen on the hill 2*m.* N. of Salisbury. The present cathedral, founded 1220, and recently restored, is one of the most elegant in England, and is rich in sepulchral monuments. About 4*m.* W. of Salisbury, the ruins of Clarendon Castle, where were framed the famous "Constitutions of Clarendon" in the reign of Henry II. 2 or 3*m.* more S. is Longford Castle, containing a splendid collection of pictures. About 8*m.* N. of Salisbury, on the Plain, is the celebrated Druidical temple of Stonehenge.

Salisbury to Barford St. Martin (6—87); in Salisbury ask for the Wilton road, keeping to *l.* opposite the gaol in the suburb of Fisherton, 81½, it is a nearly level and good road through Fugglestone or Foulstone, 83¾ (where turn to *l.* and cross River Avon), Wilton, 84½, Ugford, 85¼, and Burcombe, 85¾.

(*Wilton:* Pembroke Arms.)

On *l.* Wilton *Ho.*, where Sir Philip Sydney wrote his "Arcadia." At Barford, on *r.*, Hurdcott *Ho.*

Barford St. Martin to Shaftesbury (14—101); in Barford turn to *l.*, and the road is hilly through Compton Chamberlain, 89¼, Fovant ("Pembroke Arms"), 90¾, Swallowcliff, 92¾, Ansty, 93½, White Sheet *Tp.*, 95¾, Brook Hill, 97, and Ludwell, 98, to Shaftesbury, which stands on the top of a steep hill; the surface is not so good as the previous stage.

[There is another road from Salisbury by taking the Dorchester road, through Harnham and up Harnham Hill, at the top of which, 82½, turn to *r.*, then over Combe Down past the racecourse, 85, and along the ridge of the hills by Compton Hill, 87½, Fovant Hut, 90¾, and White Sheet Hill, 94¼, where there is a steep descent to White Sheet *Tp.*, 95¾; not a good road.

Or at Wilton take the left hand road, and there is an ascent of 1¾*m.* on to the ridge of the hill, 2*m.*, before Compton Hill, 88, whence to White Sheet *Tp.*, 95¾; as above.]

(*Shaftesbury:* Grosvenor Arms; Crown, *B.T.C.*; Railway.)

Before Fovant, on *l.*, close to the upper road, is an ancient entrenchment, called Chiselbury. At Compton Chamberlain, on *r.*, Compton *Ho.* At Swallowcliff, on *r.*, Castle Ditches, an ancient entrenched hill fort; also another called Castle Rings, 2*m.* N.E. of Shaftesbury. Beyond Ansty, on *r.*, Wardour Park, in which are the ruins of the old castle, twice besieged in the Civil War; the modern mansion is very beautiful. Shaftesbury was formerly a considerable town, with a splendid nunnery and twelve churches, only three of which remain. Fine view from the castle hill.

Shaftesbury to Henstridge Ash (9½—110½); very steep unrideable hill to walk down out of Shaftesbury, then the road is pretty fair to East Stour, 105¼, after which it gets rough and lumpy again, and is rather hilly through West Stour, 106¾. (The roads about here are often spoiled by sheep in wet weather.)

At West Stour, on *l.*, Fifehead *Ho.* At Henstridge Ash, is the Old Virginia Inn, where Raleigh first smoked tobacco in England.

Henstridge Ash to Sherborne (6½—117); long hill to descend from Henstridge Ash, then hilly but with splendid surface through Milborne Port, 114½, and Oborne, 116. The principal part of Sherborne lies on the *l.* of the main road.

(*Sherborne:* Antelope; Half Moon, *B.T.C.*)

At Sherborne, on *l.*, the castle. Fine old *ch.*

Sherborne to Yeovil (5¼—122¼); the road is neatly level past Nether Compton (Halfway *Ho.*), 119¼, to Babylon Hill, 120¼, whence is a long descent to Penn Mill, 121¼, on River Yeo, and then pretty level into Yeovil; very good surface. Entering Yeovil keep straight on, without going through the chief part of the town, which lies on the *l.*

(*Yeovil:* Three Choughs, *B.T.C.*)

Yeovil to Crewkerne (9¾—132); through Preston Plucknett, 123¼ (a mile beyond keep to *l.*), Brimpton, 125¼, East Chinnock, 127¼, and

Haselbury, 129½, is a good road with some stiff hills. [Or turn to *l.* into Yeovil, and when through the town keep to *r.* and through West Coker, 125¾, to East Chinnock, 127¼.]
(*Crewkerne*: George, *B.T.C.*)
Crewkerne *ch.* is a fine Gothic structure.

Crewkerne to Chard (8—140); out of Crewkerne an ascent for about 3*m.* has to be climbed to the top of White Down Hill, 135 (½*m.* before keep to *l.*), which can all be ridden, except perhaps the first part, with a fair wind; from the top it is nearly level to Windwhistle, 136 (a little beyond keep to *r.*), after which comes a gradual downhill of 2*m.* and the rest level; capital road, generally in good order.
(*Chard*: Crown, *Hqrs.*; George, *B.T.C.*; Railway).
From top of White Down Hill the English and Bristol Channels are visible. Chard *ch.*, an ancient Gothic building, is worth seeing. About 3*m.* S.E. is Ford Abbey.

Chard to Honiton (12—152); hilly for the first 3*m.* to the top of Balay Down (808ft. high), then a sharp descent down the other side, and easy riding over Long Bridge, 145, and for a mile beyond Stockland, 146, when there is a steep ascent up Stockland Hill with a crooked descent on the other side; after 2*m.* of nearly level there is a long hill down into Honiton, which is a long straggling town situate on an incline. (Returning, take the right hand road ¾*m.* out of Honiton.) [London to Honiton, through Amesbury and Ilchester, is 2½*m.* shorter—see p. 71.]
(*Honiton*: Angel; Dolphin, *B.T.C.*; Star).
On Stockland Hill, on *l.*, an ancient circular entrenchment. Honiton is celebrated for its lace manufacture. The old parish *ch.* contains an elaborate rood screen, &c. 2*m.* N. an old entrenchment called Dumpdon Hill or Castle; 3*m.* S. Farway Castle; also near it Blackberry Castle.

Honiton to Rockbere (10¼—162¼); another descent from Honiton, then a less hilly and much easier road through Weston, 153½, Fenny Bridges, 155¼, and Tallford, 157¼, then a long stiff hill to mount to Straightway Head, 159, followed by a sharp descent to "Fair Mile Inn," 160, and pretty level to Rockbere; the road is fairly good except for about 2*m.* beyond Fenny Bridges, where it is little used and very rough.

Rockbere to Exeter (6¼—168½); through Honiton-Clyst, 164¼, East Wonford, 166¾, and Heavitree, 167¼, is rather hilly, and there is a steep hill to descend through Exeter; pretty good road.
(*Exeter*: Black Horse; Bude; City Temperance; Clarence; Elmfield; Gidley's Refreshment Rooms; Globe; Half Moon; Museum; New London; Plymouth Arms; Royal Clarence; Rougemont, *B.T.C.*)
Exeter, the capital of Devonshire, was the Roman Isca Damnonii. There are the ruins of Rougemont Castle, said to have been founded by the Romans, and afterwards the residence of the West Saxon kings. Magnificent cathedral, Guildhall, &c.

Exeter to Cheriton Cross (9½—178); in Exeter, after passing through High street, go down Fore street hill to the *R.* Exe, and when over the bridge turn to *r.*; a mile out of the town is a very steep hill, quite impossible to ride up (and dangerous to ride *down*), with a descent on the other side; after this the road continues hilly through Adderwater, 170¼, Heath Cross, 173¼, Lilly Bridge, 174¾, and Tap House, 175½; the road is occasionally bad going, being loose and flinty in many places.
Beyond Tap *Ho.*, on *l.*, Fulford *Ho.*, an old mansion.

Cheriton Cross to Okehampton (12¾—190¾); rough descent and ascent to Crockernwell, 179½, then almost level through Merrymeet, 183½, and across Whiddon Down to near South Zeal, 186½, into which is a winding descent, then up and down into Low Sticklepath, 187¼ (where cross *R.* Taw); out of this is another rise, then level with a rather steep descent into Okehampton; the surface continues loose and stony in places.

(*Okehampton:* Fountain; London; Plume of Feathers; White Hart, *B.T.C.*)

2*m.* S. of Crockernwell, on banks of River Teign, are three ancient camps—Preston Berry Castle, Wooston Castle, and Cranbrook Castle; beautiful scenery: also a cromlech. For last 6 or 7*m.* the road runs close to Dartmoor, on *l.* Okehampton (or Oakhampton) is a small picturesque town. The castle is in ruins, having been dismantled by Henry VIII.

Okehampton to Launceston (18½—209¼); after crossing *R.* Okement keep to *l.* in Okehampton, and long hill to ascend out of the town, then a good run down and again a long uphill on to Sourton Down, at the top of which, 3½*m.* from Okehampton, keep to *r.* (on *l.* to Tavistock); next is a long hill to descend to Bridestow, 196¾, beyond which is an easy rise followed by a steep descent to Kimbo or Point Bridge, 198¾, then after a gradual ascent of a mile it is undulating through Lew Cross, 200¾, past New Inn, 201¼, and over Old Street Down, with a sharp fall to Tinhay Bridge, 205; out of Lifton 205¾, there is a steep uphill to Lifton Down and down again through Cadron, 207, to Poulston, 207¼, (where cross *R.* Tamar) whence there is a long hill to mount to Launceston; good road, the surface being firm and fairly smooth; it passes through a wild and open country.

(*Launceston:* King's Arms; London; Templar; White Hart, *B.T.C.*)

At Launceston are ruins of a castle supposed to have been erected by the Britons, and known as Castle Terrible. About 1*m.* N. is Werrington *Ho.*

Launceston to Bodmin (21—230¼); keeping straight through the town, it is a continuation of hills through Trebursey, 211¼, (a mile further take the middle road) by Hick's Mill, 214¼,—to which there is a descent of nearly 2*m.*—Trerethick or Trevithick Bridge, 215½, Five Lanes Inn, 217, Trewint, 217½, long downhill again to Palmer's Bridge, 220, (cross R. Fowey) with ascent to Jamaica Inn, 220½, on Temple Moors, passing over the moors by Four Holes Cross, 221½, Temple, 224¼, and Colvanick, (London Inn) 226¼, where the moors end, and finally descending a very steep hill near Bodmin. The road goes through a very wild country, not a house or tree to be seen for miles; the surface is hard, and in wet weather tolerable but never very good; through Bodmin is paved for about 1*m.*

(*Bodmin:* Queen's Head; Royal, *B.T.C*).

Bodmin had formerly a cathedral, with priory and thirteen churches. On a hill near the town are some large stones called The Hurlers, supposed to have been a Druidical temple. In the churchyard remains of a chapel.

Bodmin to Fradden (9—239¼)); a succession of sharp ups and downs by Lanivet Ford, 232¼, Grigland, 234¾, and East Lane End, 237.

At Lanivet, on *l.*, remains of an ancient monastery.

Fradden to St. Michael (4½—243¾); through Summer Court, 242¼; the road continues hilly, but the surface improves.

St. Michael, usually pronounced Mitchell, was formerly a large town.

St. Michael to Truro (7—250¾); ¾*m.* beyond St. Michael turn to *l.*, and soon after there is a steep descent shortly followed by a stiff hill to mount, then the road becomes easier through Trespen, 247, and Buckshead, 249¾; the surface continues excellent; Truro is paved.

[From *Fradden* there is another and better road on *l.* through Ladock, 244¼, to Tresilian, 247¾, on the Plymouth road, (where on returning keep to *l.*); the road is very good and nearly all downhill to Kiggon Mill, 249, then comes a hill to mount about a mile long, and a mile downhill into *Truro*, 251.]

(*Truro:* Red Lion; Royal; Star, *B.T.C.*; Temperance).

Truro is now an episcopal see. Formerly there was a castle here, of which only a mound is left. Within a short distance are the seats or residences of Polwhele, Trowarthenick, Trelissick, Tregolls, and Killiganoon.

Truro to Perranwell (5—255¾); in Truro keep to *l.*; a very steep hill leads out of the town, and after a slight descent to Calenick, 252, another long ascent follows, then downhill through a wood (keeping to *r.*) to Carnan, 254¾, and level to Perranwell.

(At Perranwell, on *l.*, Carclew).

Perranwell to Helstone (12—267¾); keep to the right hand road, and through Tregolls, 259¾, Bultris, 262¼, Polgrean, 263¼, Menchy, 264¾, Trevennen, 265¼, and Trewenick, 266¼, is a very good road but hilly to within a mile of Helstone, when there is a descent into the town.

[Or from Perranwell keep to *l.*, and 1½*m.* beyond is a long hill to mount, and after crossing the railway turn to *l.* at the cross roads and there is a descent into *Penryn*, 259½, where turn to *r.* and for 3*m.* it is rather uphill, with good surface, to the junction with the direct road, ¼*m.* before Bultris, 263½, and thence on to *Helstone*, 269, as above.]

From *Penryn*, on *l.*, to *Falmouth* (3¼—262¾).

(*Penryn:* Elephant and Castle; King's Arms.—*Falmouth:* Green Bank; Commercial; Royal, *B.T.C.*—*Helstone:* Angel; Star.—*Lizard:* Lugg's. *B.T.C.*)

Falmouth is the most westerly seaport in England. About 1½*m.* further, at the mouth of the bay, is Pendennis Castle, which stood a six-months' siege against the Parliamentarians; opposite it is St. Mawes Castle. About 4*m.* further is the beautiful seat of Penrose; also near it the huge Tolman, or Cornish Pebble, a granite block of 800 tons weight: Arwenack Manor House. Helstone is the centre of a mining district, and is remarkable for its May games or festival, held on May 8th, a relic of the Roman Floralia. From Helstone is a splendid run of about 11*m.* to Lizard Town, with a descent at 4*m.* and another at 5*m.*; from Lizard Town is a short walk to the Point and to Kinance Cove, &c.

Helstone to Marazion (9—276¾); rather hilly for half the distance through St. Breage, 270¾, followed by a long down hill through Chywoon, 273¾, and Roost, 275, into Marazion.

(*Marazion:* Thomas's).

At St. Breage the celebrated tin and copper mine of Huel Vor; also remains of Pengerswick Tower. At Roost, 1*m.* on *l.*, Acton Castle. Marazion, or Market Jew, is supposed to be the oldest town in the county, and derived its importance as a resort of pilgrims to the well-known St. Michael's Mount, a remarkable rock in the bay, 1*m.* from the town, and on which is an ancient castle.

Marazion to Penzance (4—280¾); along the margin of Mount's Bay is level, but a very rough bit of macadam road; Penzance is paved.

(*Penzance:* Mount's Bay House; Queen; Railway; Star; Union; Western, *B.T.C.*)

Penzance is the most westerly town in England; the climate is very mild and salubrious.

Penzance to Land's End (11—291¾); the first 2*m.* are rather hilly through Newlyn, 282¼, then rough and hilly through Trevelloe, 28¼, St. Buryan or St. Burien, 286¾, Trebear, 288¼, and Trevescan, 291; bad but mostly rideable road. [There is another road from Penzance by keeping to r. and through Trembeth, 282¼, and Sennen, 289½, to Land's End, 291.]

From St. Buryan on l. to Logan Rock or Stone 2m., at first pretty good and level, till a steep hill is reached leading down to the rock, which must be walked. From the Logan Rock to the Land's End is a good and level road.

From Penzance to Gunard's Head, 7m.; leaving the east end of the town turn to the r. twice, uphill road except a sharp descent halfway, which should be walked; grand scenery.

From Trembeth on r. to *St. Just*, (6—288¼); near it Cape Cornwall.

(*St. Just*: Commercial; Wellington).

At Newlyn, on r., Castle Hornick. There are numerous natural curiosities and cromlechs in the vicinity of Penzance; also at St. Buryan very old *ch.* and singular cross. 1m. W. is a Druidical circle—Boscawen Urn; on l., near the coast, is another—The Merry Maidens and the Pipers; near Boskenna, a cromlech; further on coast, Treroen Castle. Near St. Just is Carniajack Castle, Clum Castle.

LONDON TO FARNHAM (by Bagshot).

London to Bagshot (26¼)—p. 46.

Bagshot to Farnborough (5¾—32); out of Bagshot a couple of ascents, the second rather steep and rough towards the top, lead up to the "Jolly Farmer," 27½ (formerly the "Golden Farmer"), on Chobham Ridges; here take the left hand road which continues rather hilly, though mostly downhill, to Frimley, 30¼, and thence pretty level; very good road.

Farnborough to Farnham (6½—38½) is an easy undulating road, passing Basingstoke Canal, 34, and through Aldershot Camp; very good road.

LONDON TO ALTON (by Odiham).

London to Hartley Row (36¼)—p. 47.

Hartley Row to Odiham (4—40¼); a mile out of Hartley Row keep to l. and a beautiful road runs near Winchfield Station, 38½, on Shapley Heath and through Odiham Wood, with a steep canal bridge to mount just before the town. [At Odiham on r. through North Warnborough, 41¼, and Mapledurwell Hatch, 45¾, to *Basingstoke*, 48; fairly level and good.]

(*Odiham*: George).

There are ruins of a castle at Odiham.

Odiham to Alton (9—49¼); keeping to l. out of Odiham, the road rises pretty sharply for some distance to the cross road on the l. for Farnham, a little before South Warnborough, 42¾; thence keep straight on up a very steep hill, but with very good surface, to a turnpike gate, after which the road falls gently until the Golden Pot, 46½, is reached, when turning to l. it is slightly downhill, with a capital surface, to Alton.

LONDON TO LYMINGTON, CHRISTCHURCH, POOLE, WEYMOUTH, & SWANAGE (by Basingstoke).

London to Popham Lane (51)—p. 47.

Popham Lane to Winchester (11½—62½); keep to *l.* and through Popham, 52¼, East Stratton, 53½, by Lunway's Inn, 57½, and through Worthy, 60¼, is a capital road but hilly.

Before East Stratton, on *l.*, Stratton Park.

Winchester to Lymington (29¾—92¼); through Southampton, 74½, Lyndhurst, 83¾, and Brockenhurst, 78¾—p. 40. [Or Southampton through Beaulieu, 81, to *Lymington*, 87½—p. 41.]

Winchester to Christchurch (34¾—97¼); by Lyndhurst, 83¾—p. 40; thence to Christchurch—pp. 42-43.

Winchester to Poole (40¼—102¾); by Hursley, 67, Romsey, 73, Cadnam, 78¾—p. 46; thence by Ringwood, 90¼, and New Bridge, 94½—p. 43.

Winchester to Weymouth (67¼—129¾); by New Bridge, 94½, above, thence by *Wimborne Minster*, 99¾, Lytchett Minster, 107, Wareham, 111¾, and Warmwell Cross, 124¼—p. 44.

Winchester to Swanage (59¼—121¾); through Wareham, 111¾, above, and Corfe Castle, 115¾—p. 45.

LONDON TO POOLE (by Cranbourn).

London to Salisbury (81)—p. 47.

Salisbury to Cranbourn (11¼—92¼); on south side of Salisbury after crossing *R.* Avon, take the Blandford road (to the *r.*) up Harnham Hill (on the top of which, nearly 1*m.* further, keep to *l.*), then down a sharp fall to Combe Bissett, 83¾, out of which is a stiff hill up to Combe Common, where keep to *l.* for Cranbourn; rough and hilly road over Comber and Tile Downs to Tidpit (or Tipput), 88¾, and then over Damerham Down and through Bowridge, 91, to Cranbourn.

(*Cranbourn :* Cross Keys; Fleur de Lis.)

On Comber Down cross an ancient entrenchment, called Grims Dyke, 5 or 6*m.* long, running in a U-shaped form to Castle Ditches, a circular camp near Whichbury, 3*m.* W. of Tidpit. Cranbourn *ch.* was formerly part of a Benedictine Priory. On Castle Hill, outside the town, are remains of a circular encampment.

Cranbourn to Wimborne Minster (9¼—101½); a rough and hilly road past Horton Inn, 96¼, and Stanbridge Chapel (or Ashton), 99.

Beyond Cranbourn, on *r.*, is St. Giles's Park.

Wimborne Minster to Poole (6½—108); first rate road, rather hilly, but easy riding past Bushels Mill, 106.

LONDON TO LAND'S END (by Dorchester and Plymouth).

London to Salisbury (81)—p. 47.

Salisbury to Blandford (22—103); on south side of Salisbury after crossing River Avon keep to *r.* up Harnham hill, on the top of which, nearly 1*m.*, further keep to *l.* and down a sharp fall to Combe Bissett, 83¾, out of which is a stiff hill up to Combe Common (where keep to *r.*), then across Crowdon Down past Drove End, 89, to Woodyates Inn, 90¾, thence past Achling Ditch end, 92¼, and over Pentridge and Workly Downs to Thorny Down Inn, 94¾, over Thorny Down past Cashmoor (or Caishmore) Inn, 95¾, across Thick Thorn and Launceston Down, through Tarrant Hinton, 98, and Pimperne, 100¼, the road is hilly and rough in places, not good for travelling, it goes over a loose sandy common for many miles. Returning, a little out of Blandford keep to r.

(*Blandford*: Crown; King's Arms, *B.T.C.*; Railway.)

Beyond Woodyates Inn, on r., is Cranbourn Chase. Achling Ditch is the line of a Roman road which is supposed to have led to Wareham. At Tarrant Hinton on r., East Bury Park. At Blandford, on r., Bryanstone Park. Blandford is also called Blandford Forum.

Blandford to Piddletown (11—114); after crossing the River Stour keep to r., and the road is up and down hill over Charlton Down and through Whitechurch, 108¼, and Milborne St. Andrews, 110¾, but the surface is good and smooth.

At Milborne, on r., 2m., is Milton Abbey Park, with the pretty village of Milton Abbas; good easy road: the Abbey was founded by King Athelstan. On l. 1m. is an old entrenched hill called Weatherbury Castle. At Whitechurch on r., Whatcomb Park.

Piddletown to Dorchester (5—119); long stiff ascent to climb out of the former through Troy Town, 115½, and a mile beyond a capital run down Yellowham hill, the surface being simply perfect, and after mounting a slight incline there is a nice run into Dorchester, the approach to which is very pretty, the road running through an avenue of fine trees; there is a short but stiff rise through the town, the surface being macadam.

[There is another road to Dorchester by *Wareham*, 111¾ to *Warmwell Cross*, 124¼—p. 53; then keep to r., through Broad Moigne (or Maine), 125¾, and Whitecomb, 127, to *Dorchester*, 4¾—129.]

(*Dorchester*: King's Arms, *B.T.C.*; Royal Oak.)

About 1m. before Dorchester, on l., Stinsford. Dorchester was a military station of the Romans; N.W. of the town is a hill called Poundbury, supposed to have been a Roman entrenched camp, also on the S. near the L. & S. W. Railway Station is the Maumbury, a Roman amphitheatre; the foundations of the old walls are still to be seen, now utilised as a pretty walk lined with trees. About 2m. S.W. is Maiden Castle, an ancient British hill fortress on a large scale.

Dorchester to Bridport (15¼—134¼) is more hilly than the last stage, as the road passes over some high ground; it is very undulating to beyond Winterborne Abbas, 124, and at Longbredy *Tp*., 127¼, after a short fall there is a high hill to climb, from the top of which the sea is seen, then the road runs along a ridge for several miles past Askerwell, and there is a steep descent to the "Travellers' Rest," 131, with a further run down into Bridport. Bridport Harbour is 1½m. S. of the town.

(*Bridport*: Bull, *B.T.C.*; Greyhound; Star.)

At Winterborne Abbas; 2m. on l., Blagdon Hill, Hardy's Monument; at Portisham, further south, a cromlech; and 2m. W. at Abbotsbury, ruins of the old abbey, St. Catherine's chapel, and Abbotsbury Castle; here also is a royal swannery. On the coast, 3m. S.E. of Bridport, is Burton Castle.

Bridport to Charmouth (6¾—141); a mile out of Bridport is a very steep but not long hill to mount, followed by another steep and difficult ascent, then a rather stiff descent to Chidiock, 137; after which is another hill to climb worse than the two last, being 1½m. long and very steep, and then a run down of 2*m.* into Charmouth, not steep and quite safe; very good surface, pretty views.

(*Charmouth:* Coach and Horses; George; New Inn; Royal Oak.)

Charmouth to Axminster (5¼—146¼); out of Charmouth keep to *r.*, and past Penn Inn, 143, and Hunter's Lodge, 144½, is hilly, but the hills are not so severe as the last stage,; 2*m.* downhill into Axminster, which must be taken carefully. Returning, keep to *r.* at the fork roads just out of Axminster, and to *l.* at Hunter's Lodge.

(*Axminster:* Bell; Commercial; George, *B.T.C.*; Grey's; Old Bell.)

Axminster is noted for its manufacture of carpets; 1*m.* S. are the ruins of Newhenham Abbey; 5*m.* S. are ruins of Colcombe Castle, destroyed in the civil war; near it Musbury Castle, a British hill fort.

Axminster to Honiton (9¾—156); a mile out of Axminster and through Kilmington, 147¾, is a long hill to climb, rather stiff, to the top of Shute Hill, 148¾, directly followed by a descent, with continuation of more or less downhill to Wilmington, 152¼, then a 2*m.* ascent to walk up to Mount Pleasant, 154½, and a steep winding decline into Honiton; not a very good road, in some places rough and stony. Returning, take first turn to *r.* at the end of Honiton.

S. of Wilmington, near Widworthy *ch.*, are two ancient entrenchments.

Honiton to Exeter (16½—172½)—p. 49.

Exeter to Chudleigh (9½—182); in Exeter after passing through High street, go down Fore street hill to the *R.* Exe, and when over the bridge turn to *l.*; the road is good through Alphington, 174½, out of which at the fork roads, ¼*m.* past the *ch.*, keep to *r.* up the hill (the road to *l.* by the telegraph wires is the old coach road, and is not so good), and it continues nearly all up hill to Shillingford, 176, then downhill to Clopton Bridge, 177; from here is a a 2*m.* hill to ascend, some of it rather severe, till the top of Haldon Hill is reached, whence a splendid view is obtained, and the rest is a long descent into Chudleigh.

(*Chudleigh:* Clifford Arms, *B.T.C.*; Ship, *B.T.C.*)

Past Clopton Bridge on *r.*, Haldon *Ho.* The district round Chudleigh is very pretty, and is noted for its orchards and cider; ½*m.* W. of town, Chudleigh Rock and cavern are worth seeing. A little E. is Ugbrook Park, and the splendid mansion; in the park is a Danish encampment.

Chudleigh to Ashburton (9½—191½); a fair road, but hilly over Chudleigh Bridge, 183 (River Teign), through Knighton, 184, over Jews Bridge, 185 (West Teign River), and through Bickington, 188, and Lemonford, 188½.

(*Ashburton:* Globe; Golden Lion, *B.T.C.*; London.)

On *r.* extends Dartmoor Forest. Ashburton *ch.* was formerly a collegiate one. About 3*m.* on *r.* are Brook Abbey, Holne Chase, and Henbury Fort (a Danish encampment) near the *R.* Dart; pretty scenery.

Ashburton to South Brent (7½—199); through Ashburton take second turn to *r.*, and by Dart Bridge, 193½, through Buckfastleigh, 194, Dean Prior, 195½, and Brent Harberton Ford, 197, is a good undulating road.

At Buckfastleigh, on *r.*, Buckfast Abbey. The road skirts Dartmoor Forest on *r.*

South Brent to Ivy Bridge (5¼—204¼); sharp descent to Brent Bridge, 199½ (cross *R.* Avon), then hilly but nothing difficult by Kingsbridge

Road Station, 201, and Bittaford (or Bideford) Bridge, 202¼, with a long downhill to Ivy Bridge; good road.

Before Cherston, on *l.*, is a circular camp. Beyond Cherston, on *r.*, are Ugborough Beacon and Western Beacon, the two most southerly spurs of Dartmoor. About Ivy Bridge (*R.* Erme) the scenery is very pretty.

Ivy Bridge to Plymouth (11¼—215½); easy undulating road through Woodland, 205, Cadleigh, 205½, and Lee Mill, 206¾ (cross *R.* Yealm), to Ridgeway, 210¾, through which is a very steep descent, dangerous to ride down without brake, and the rest is almost level over New Bridge, 212 (cross *R.* Plym), and through Crab Tree, 212¾; very good road except the last 2*m.*, which are very bad and rough.

[Or to *Exeter*, 168½—p. 49, thence by *Chudleigh*, 178, *Ashburton*, 187½, *South Brent*, 195, and *Ivy Bridge*, 200¼, to *Plymouth*, 211½.]

(*Plymouth:* Albion; Chubb's; Cousins; Duke of Cornwall; Farley, *B.T.C.*; Globe; Harvey's; Imperial; Royal; Temperance; Victoria.—*Plympton:* George.)

At Ridgeway, on *l.*, at Plympton Earl, are ruins of a once magnificent castle, erected in the reign of Henry I.; also remains of Priory. Plymouth, at the mouths of Plym and Tamar, is one of the chief naval stations of the kingdom, with the neighbouring town of Devonport, and there are extensive dockyards at both. Plymouth Sound or harbour is protected by the well-known breakwater, and will hold the largest ships afloat. The town is defended by a citadel and several strong fortifications. On the opposite side of the harbour is the splendid mansion, Mount Edgecumbe. Beyond Ridgeway, on *l.*, Saltram *Ho.*

Plymouth to Torpoint (2½—218); continue through Plymouth, then past the Royal Hospital and through Stonehouse, 216¾, to Devonport, 217½, whence cross *R.* Tamar, here called the Hamoaze, by ferry to Torpoint. Plymouth, Stonehouse, and Devonport form almost one town, houses extending the whole distance.

(*Devonport:* Royal, *B.T.C.*)

Devonport has a large Dockyard; it is surrounded by a wall on the land side, and is protected by the fortress of Mount Wise, besides other forts.

Torpoint to Polscove (5¾—223¾); rather hilly, but splendid road through St. Anthony, 221¼, (keep to *r.*) and Sheviock, 223¼.

[There is another route from *Plymouth*, by crossing the Sound to Cremill Passsage, 217½, on the north point under Mount Edgcumbe; here is a steep hill to climb, after which it is a rather hilly road through Millbrook, 220, and *Crafthole*, 223¾, to Polscove, 224½.]

Beyond Torpoint, on *r.*, Thanks, and further on, East Anthony Park. At Crafthole, on *r.*, Sheviock *ch.*

Polscove to Liskeard (9½—233¼); keep to *r.* at 2*m.* farther, it is a good but hilly road, by Trerule Foot, 227 (keep to middle road), Catchfrench, 228½, and Buckapit Bridge, 229½ (cross *R.* Seaton). On the reverse journey, just before Trerule Foot, keep to the *r.* of two main roads, and again to *r.* at Trerule Foot.

About 1¼*m.* beyond Polscove on *r.* to *St. German's* (1—226¼).

[There is another route from *Plymouth*, by turning sharp to *r.* when nearly through the town, a little further keeping to *l.*, and past Mile House 216¾, Weston Mill, 218¼, to Passage on *R.* Tamar, opposite *Saltash*, 220, to which cross by Ferry; 1*m* beyond Saltash keep to *l.* and over Nottar Bridge, 223¼, through Landrake, 224, and Tidiford, 225½, and over Heskin Bridge,

226, to the junction of the road on the previous route just beyond Trerule Foot, 227; hilly road].

At Heskin Bridge on *l.* to *St. German's* (1½—227½)

(*Saltash :* Commercial; Green Dragon; Railway.—*Liskeard :* Bell; Venning's London, *B.T.C.*; Webb's.)

St. German's was anciently the seat of a bishopric; there was also a priory, to which the present parish *ch.* belonged. Close adjoining is Earl St. German's seat, Port Eliot, on the site of the old Priory. 1*m.* beyond Saltash, 1*m.* on *l.*, Trematon Castle. Before Buckapit Bridge, on *l.*, Blackaton, and 1*m.* on *r.*, Padderbury Top, both hills with circular entrenchments; a little further on *r.*, Coldrenick *Ho.*; 2*m.* N. of Liskeard is St. Cleer, the *ch.* of which is partly Saxon; also St. Cleer's Well and stone Cross, and a cromlech called Trevethy Stone; 2*m.* further N. are the Hurlers and the Cheesewring, the latter a curious pile of rocks.

Liskeard to Tap House (6¾—240); beyond Liskeard is a winding descent to Looe Mills, 235¼, then hilly through Dobwalls, 235¾, and Eastern Tap House, 237¾; a good road with beautiful scenery.

Tap House to Lostwithiel (4—244); ½*m.* beyond Tap House keep to *l.* (the right-hand road goes to *Bodmin*, (6¼—246¼); good road with a long run downhill to Lostwithiel.

[Or to *Bodmin*, 230¼—p. 50; thence, on *l.*, to *Lostwithiel*, 6—236¼.]

(*Lostwithiel :* King's Arms; Talbot, *B.T.C.*)

2½*m.* beyond Tap House, on *r.*, Boconnoc. At Lostwithiel, the old palace, formerly a residence of the Dukes of Cornwall, now a prison; fine early English *ch.*; 1*m.* N. of the town, the ruins of Restormel Castle.

Lostwithiel to St. Austell (8½—252½); very steep hill to walk up out of the former, followed by a long run down, and then undulating through St. Blazey, 248½, and Tregrehan *Tp.*, 249½.

(*St. Austell :* Globe; Queen's Head; White Hart, *B.T.C.*)

St. Austell is the centre of the chief tin mining district, and there are also copper and china clay mines; handsome *ch.* Just beyond, on *r.*, St. Mewan *ch.* and Mewan Beacon.

St. Austell to Truro (13¼—265¾); hilly through Higher Sticker, 255, and Hewes Water, 255½, to Teags *Tpg.*, 256 (keep to *r.*), then good undulating road through Grampound, 258, and Probus, 260¼, whence it is downhill through Tresilian, 262½, to Kiggon Mill, 263¾: then there is a hill to mount about a mile long, and a mile downhill into Truro, through which is paved. [There is another road by keeping to *l.* at Teags *Tpg.*, and through Tregony, 260¼, where keep to *r.*, joining the other road ½*m.* before Tresilian, 264; see p. 51.]

At Higher Sticker, 1*m.* on *r.*, Trethullan Castle, a circular entrenchment. Near Grampound are 6 ancient camps or entrenchments, within 2*m.* of the town.

Truro to Land's End (41—306¾)—p. 51.

LONDON TO DORCHESTER (by Bere Regis).

London to Wimborne Minster (99¾)—p. 53.

Wimborne Minster to Bere Regis (11½—111¼); through Wimborne keep to *l.*; for 3*m.* splendid road, very smooth and almost level, through Corfe Mullen, 102, then rough in odd places, and more undulating to Alner, 105½, and after that (keeping to *r.*,) rather hilly but capital going through Winterborne Zelstone, 107¾, and Winterborne Thompson, 108¾, with a nice run down just before Bere; all the hills are easy both ways.

[Or to *Lytchett Minster*, 107, p. 53; turn to *r.* at the sign post beyond it, then a long but slight incline is encountered, and the road continues to rise, except for two short dips, for 6*m.*, past Morden Park on *l.*, ending with a straight sharp descent, quite safe, into *Bere Regis*, 7¾—114¾.]

Bere Regis to Piddletown (6¾—117½); after passing through the toll bar at the end of Bere, the steep ascent of Rogers Hill has to be climbed, too steep to ride up, from the top of which a good road runs through Tolpiddle, 115, and Burleston, 116.

Piddletown to Dorchester (5—122½)—p. 54.

LONDON TO LAND'S END (by Andover).

London to Basingstoke (45¾)—p. 47.

Basingstoke to Whitchurch (11¼—56½); leaving Basingstoke keep to *r.*; good road though hilly through the pretty villages of Worting, 47½, Clerken Green, 50, Dean, 51, Ash, 52, Overton, 53, and Freefolk, 55; pretty country.

(*Whitchurch:* White Hart, *B.T.C.*)

At Overton, in middle of August, is held one of the largest sheep fairs in England, the traffic of which cuts up the roads. A little further on *r.*, at Laverstock, the Bank of England paper mills. On *r.*, Worting *Ho.*, Ash *Ho.*, Laverstock Hall; on *l.*, Ash Park.

Whitchurch to Andover (7—63½); is the same kind of road, through Hurstbourne Priors, 58½, skirting Harewood Forest on *l.*, and by Down House, 61½; there is one steep hill to walk up.

(*Andover:* George; Globe; Goodden's; Railway; Star; Star and Garter; Station; Temperance Rooms; White Hart, *B.T.C.*)

Beyond Whitchurch, on *r.*, Hurstbourne Park and *Ho.* About 1½*m.* before Andover cross the old Roman road from Winchester to Cirencester. Andover *ch.* dates from the Saxon times.

Andover to Lobcombe Corner (10¼—73¾); just out of Andover at the railway station keep to *l.*; long ascent through Little Ann, 65½, then fair road crossing the Downs past Down Farm, 68¼, and Kent Barrow, 69, to the village of Middle Wallop, 71, after which it is very hilly and begins to be rough.

At Little Ann, on *l.*, is Bury Hill, a large circular entrenchment. At Kent Barrow, 2*m.* on *l.*, Danebury Hill, a circular entrenched camp.

Lobcombe Corner to Land's End (218½—292¼)—pp. 47-51.

LONDON TO EXETER (by Colyford).

London to Charmouth (141)—p. 54.

Charmouth to Lyme Regis (1¾—142¾); a mile long hill to walk up out of Charmouth, followed by a very steep unrideable descent, keeping to *l.* at the cross roads, into Lyme Regis.

(*Lyme Regis:* The Cups.)

At Lyme Regis the Duke of Monmouth landed, 1685.

Lyme Regis to Colyford (5¾—148½); by the left hand road out of the town there is a steep winding hill to climb (not safe to ride *down*) to Ware Cliff House, 149½, then a pretty level ride of nearly 3*m*. along the top of the hills, ending with a walk down to Axe Bridge, ½*m*. before Colyford: good surface.

At *Colyford* on *r*. to *Colyton*, (1—149½).

On the top of the hill before descending to Colyford, 1*m*. on *r*., Musbury Castle, an ancient hill fortress, from which 12 others can be seen; also another at Hawksdown Hill, 1*m*. on *l*.

Colyford to Sidford (8¼—156¾); after walking up the mile hill out of Colyford on to Seaton Down, it is undulating for about 6*m*., over Starford Common, 151, and past Hangman Stone, 152, (about 1*m*. further keep to *l*.), and then a descent to Sidford, not steep at first, but towards the bottom dangerously so even with a brake; good surface.

[There is another route to Sidford by *Axminster*, 146¼—p. 55; then to Kilmington, 147¾, where turn to *l*. and it is chiefly downhill through Whitford, 149¾, to *Colyton*, 150¾, then long severe uphill and across Colyton Hill to Starford Common, 153½, where join the above road ½*m*. before Hangman Stone, and to *Sidford*, 158¾.]

About half-way on *r*. Blackberry Castle, an old British hill fortress. On the hill 1*m*. N. of Sidford is an ancient entrenchment, called Sidbury Castle; 1*m*. further is an earthwork, supposed to be of Roman origin.

Sidford to Bishop's Clyst (10¼—167); long uphill out of Sidford, with longer descent to walk down into Newton Poppleford, 159½, then another 2*m*. hill to walk up to the 8th *Ms*. from Exeter, and the rest is all downhill; good surface on the whole.

About 2*m*. on *l*. at the top of the hill beyond Newton, is Woodbury Castle, an old British entrenchment.

Bishop's Clyst to Exeter (3¼—170¼); short rise out of Bishop's Clyst and downhill to East Wonford, 168¼, out of which is the steep ascent of Heavitree Hill, through Heavitree, 169, and similar down again into Exeter. On the reverse journey keep to *r*. just beyond East Wonford.

LONDON TO EXETER (by Sidmouth).

London to Sidford (156¾)—above.

Sidford to Sidmouth (1½—158¼); at the end of Sidford turn to *l*., and it is nearly all downhill into Sidmouth, the frightfully steep descent into which must be walked.

(*Sidmouth:* Bedford; London, *B.T.C.*; Royal York.)

Sidmouth is a small sea-bathing resort, with a very mild climate.

Sidmouth to St. George's Clyst (10—168¼); out of Sidmouth the road ascends the cliffs by a steep winding hill, and then there is a long descent into Otterton, 161½, beyond which it is almost all uphill through Yattington, 163¼, on to Woodbury Common, 164¾, and the rest is downhill, except a short hill beyond Woodbury, 166¼.

Beyond Otterton, on *r*., Bicton Lodge. On Woodbury Common, ¾*m*. on *r*., Woodbury Castle, an old British entrenchment. 2*m*. S.W. of Woodbury, on banks of *R*. Exe, Nutwell Court.

St. George's Clyst to Exeter (5—173¼); turn sharp to *l*. at St. George's Clyst and over Topsham Bridge to Topsham, 169½, and thence through Northbrook, 171½, and St. Leonards, 172½, up and downhill all the way. [Or at St. George's Clyst keep straight on and through *Bishop's Clyst*, 170, to Exeter, 173¼—p. 59.]

Beyond Topsham, on *r.*, Wear and Higher Newcourt. Before Bishop's Clyst on *l.*, Winslate *Ho*. Beyond Topsham, on *l.*, Retreat, Low Wear, High Wear, and Northbrook.

LONDON TO EXMOUTH.

London to Sidmouth (158¼)—p. 59.

Sidmouth to Exmouth (9½—167½); out of Sidmouth the road ascends the cliffs by a steep, winding hill, and then there is a long descent into Otterton, 161½; after crossing *R*. Otter turn to *l.* and the road is nearly all uphill through East Budleigh, 162½, and Knoll, 164, to Knoll Hill, 164⅞, some parts of it very steep, and the rest is downhill more or less, ending with a steep and crooked descent into Exmouth; bad road, many parts being merely cart and horse track.

(*Exmouth :* Imperial ; London, *B.T.C.* ; Royal Beacon ; South Western.)

From Exmouth by ferry across *R.* Exe to Starcross.

LONDON TO EXETER (by Ottery St. Mary).

London to Colyford (148½)—p. 59.

Colyford to Ottery St. Mary (12—160½); after walking up a mile long hill out of Colyford on to Seaton Down, it is undulating over Starford Common, 151, and past Hangman Stone, 152 (about 1*m.* further keep to *r.*), then it is uphill for a couple of miles across Broad Down, and again almost level past Rondcomb Gate, 155½, and across Farway Hill (keep to *l.*) to Gittisham Hill, 157¼, whence a couple of steep descents, 1*m.* and 2*m.* long, lead down into Ottery.

Ottery St. Mary to Rockbere (5—165½); from Ottery St. Mary it is nearly all uphill to "Fair Mile" Inn, 163¼ (where join the main London road), and then pretty level to Rockbere.

Rockbere to Exeter (6¼—171¾)—p. 49.

LONDON TO EXETER (by Beaminster).

London to Dorchester (119)—p. 54.

Dorchester to Maiden Newton (8—127) : in Dorchester turn to *r.* and sharp hill to descend out of the town, after which it is level (at 1½*m.* keeping to *l.*) crossing some marshes to Charminster, 121 (keep to *l.* again), and then gently undulating through Stratton, 122¼, and Frampton, 125.

(*Maiden Newton :* White Horse, *B.T.C.*)

Maiden Newton to Beaminster (9½—136½); following the Crewkerne road, after having mounted a steep ascent out of Maiden Newton, a beautiful undulating road runs along a ridge of hills to Catsley Down Gate, 133, then turn to *l.* and go down a steep descent, followed by an equally sharp ascent, after which is a capital run down of 2*m.* into Beaminster. [There is another road through Hook, 132½, a little more south.]

(*Beaminster :* White Hart.)

S. of Beaminster is Parnham House.

Beaminster to Broadwindsor (4½—141); a short distance out of Beaminster there is a stiff uphill, and then a nasty downhill which should be ridden carefully, and easy road to Broadwindsor. [There is another road straight from Catsley Down Gate to Broadwindsor, 5—138.]

Broadwindsor to Axminster (10½—151½); out of Broadwindsor there is another steep hill to walk up, from the top of which it is rather collar work through Marshalsea, 144¾, to Lambert's Castle Hill, 146½, whence it is an easy ride over Hawchurch Common, 148 (where keep to *r.*), with a 2*m.* descent into Axminster.

S. of Broadwindsor is Lewesdon (or Lewston) Hill; 2*m.* beyond Broadwindsor on *r.* Pillesden Pen, a large entrenched hill. On Lambert's Castle Hill is also a great triple entrenchment.

Axminster to Exeter (26½—177½)—p. 55.

LONDON TO PLYMOUTH (by Totnes).

London to Exeter (168½)—p. 49.

Exeter to Newton Abbot (15—183½); in Exeter, after passing through High street, go down Fore street hill to the *R.* Exe, and when over the bridge turn to *l.*; the road is good through Alphington, 170½, out of which at the division in the road ¼*m.* past the *ch.* keep to *l.* by the telegraph wires, and there is a rather steep ascent, presently followed by a winding descent to Kenford, 172½, then a walk of about 2*m.* to the top of Haldon Hill (800ft. high); for 2 or 3*m.* the road runs along the ridge of the hill, and is pretty level, keeping to *r.* at the bifurcation 2*m.* on, then it is more or less on the fall past Ugbrook Park, 179½, and Sandy Gate, 181, to Teign Bridge, 182¼, and the rest nearly level; not so good surface as the Chudleigh road, and from Haldon Hill much of it is loose and stony, requiring careful riding. On the reverse journey keep to *r.* leaving Newton.

(*Newton Abbot :* Commercial; Globe, *B.T.C.*; Magor's, *B.T.C.*; Queen.)

Magnificent view from Haldon Hill; on *l.* Castle Lawrence. Newton Abbot, formerly called Newton Bushel.

Newton Abbot to Totnes (8—191½); in Newton turn to *r.*, and by Two Mile Oak, 185½, Bow Bridge, 188, and Netherton, 190, it is mostly uphill for the first half, then up and down hill, one or two of the inclines too steep for riding, and the last mile is all downhill to the *R.* Dart, after crossing which there is a steep hill up through the town.

[There is another route by *Ashburton*, 187½, p. 56; at the end of the town keep to *l.* up a long hill, presently followed by a long downhill to Staverton Bridge, 192¼; after a stiff ascent the rest is pretty level to Totnes, 195¼.]

(*Totnes :* Castle; Commercial; Royal Seven Stars; Seymour, *B.T.C.*)

At Netherton, 1*m.* on *l.*, ruins of Berry Pomeroy Castle. Totnes is surrounded by very pretty scenery; there are remains of a castle erected in the time of William I.

Totnes to Venn Cross (8—199½); a very steep hill to climb out of Totnes, then hilly road through Wonton, 197, with a long descent to New Bridge, 198, and a long hill to rise beyond it; the road for the first 3 or 4*m.* is macadam and rather loose, then very good.

Venn Cross to Ivy Bridge (4½—204); take the right hand road, rather undulating to Bittaford or Bideford Bridge, 202 (where join the direct Exeter and Plymouth road through Ashburton), then a short rise and long downhill to Ivy Bridge; easy and very good road.

Ivy Bridge to Plymouth (11¼—215¼)—p. 56.

LONDON TO DARTMOUTH.

London to Exeter (168½)—p. 49.

Exeter to Star Cross (9¼—177¾); in Exeter after passing through High street, go down Fore street hill to the R. Exe, and when over the bridge turn to l.; the road is good and undulating through Alphington, 170¼ (in the middle of which turn sharp to l.), to Exminster, 173, then it becomes very hilly through Kenton, 176; keep close to the estuary of the R. Exe all the way.

At Kenton, on l., on banks of R. Exe, is the splendid mansion of Powderham Castle.

Star Cross to Dawlish—(3¾—181½); very hilly but good road through Cockwood, 178½, and over Shutton Bridge, 180¼.

(*Dawlish*: Southwood's London, B.T.C.; Queen's.)

Dawlish is a fashionable watering-place; on r. Luscombe Castle.

Dawlish to Teignmouth (3¼—184¾) is nothing but hills; there are three to walk up with intervening descents, which at least require very careful riding, and finally a descent to walk down into Teignmouth ¾m. long, very steep, with two sharp turns at the bottom, "Danger Board" on top; good surface, except on the hill.

[Or from *Exeter* follow the Newton Abbot road to the top of Haldon Hill, as at p. 61, then, at the bifurcation 2m. on, keep to l.; a mile further on is a steepish descent, then after some level is a gradual rise on to Little Haldon Hill, whence it is downhill for nearly 3m. into *Teignmouth*, 182½.]

(*Teignmouth*: London; Queen's, B.T.C.)

Teignmouth is a noted seaside resort; here are ruins of a fort.

Teignmouth to Torquay—Strand (8—192¾); cross the bridge over R. Teign to Shaldon, 186¼, whence is a very steep ascent, 1m. long, with rather good surface, to Stoke Common (dangerous to *descend* from sharp turn at bottom), then the road is level for about 3m., except a short descent and ascent, followed by a mile descent to St. Mary's Church, 190¼; here keep to r., and it is chiefly uphill through West Hill, 190¾, and Upham, 191¼, to Tor Mohun, 191¾ (keep to l. at Brunswick square), and slight fall into Torquay; this is much the worse road. [There is another road from St. Mary's Church by keeping to l. by the seaside; it is a capital road through Babbacombe or Babbicombe, 191¼, and close by Hope's or Bob's Nose, with a moderate descent into Torquay, 193½, at the eastern end.]

[Or through *Newton Abbot*, 183½, p. 61; from here keep straight on through Ford, 184¼, whence there is a steep ascent on to Milber Down, 185¼, then it is fairly level by Barton Cross, 187¼, to Barton, 187½, where either keep to l. down through the village into St. Mary's Church, 188, or to r. and ½m. further on is sharp descent, with similar ascent nearly to Tor Mohun, 189½, and thence to *Torquay*, 190½.]

(*Torquay:* Queen's; Imperial; Jordan's; Pavilion Refreshment Rooms; Queen's; Royal, *B.T.C.*; Union; Victoria and Albert.)

Torquay is the chief watering-place in the South of Devon; its mild and salubrious climate is peculiarly adapted for invalids; it is surrounded by picturesque scenery. At Tor Mohun on *r.*, in the mansion of Tor Abbey, some few remains of the ancient monastery are visible. E. of the town is Kent's Hole, a cavern interesting to geologists on account of its ossiferous remains. Hope's or Bob's Nose is the headland E. of Torquay. On Milber Down the road passes through an old triple entrenched camp.

Torquay to Paignton ($2\frac{3}{4}$—$193\frac{1}{2}$); turn to *r.* along the bay, with one short rise on the cliffs, and through Preston, 195; at Paignton, if not calling, keep straight on to left.

(*Paignton:* Crown and Anchor; Esplanade, *C.T.C.*; Gerston; Parkfield.)

Paignton is greatly resorted to as a watering place and for sea bathing, having very fine sands.

Paignton to Brixham ($5\frac{1}{2}$—201); by the Naval Hospital and Goodrington Sands is pretty level to Goodrington, $196\frac{3}{4}$; then gradual rise to Galmpton Warborough *Tp.*, 198, and level (keep to *l.* past Churston station, $198\frac{3}{4}$) to Churston Ferrers, $199\frac{1}{2}$, and mostly downhill to Brixham. [Or at Paignton, and again at Paignton Cross keep to *r.* to Langstone, $196\frac{1}{4}$, on the Newton Abbot road, where turn to *l.* to Galmpton Warborough *Tp.*, $198\frac{3}{4}$; very hilly road.]

(*Brixham:* Bolton, *C.T.C.*; Globe.)

Beyond Churston Ferrers, on *r.* Lupton *Ho.* Brixham is a small fishing port; a bone cave similar to Kent's Hole has been found near it. The quay is $\frac{3}{4}$m. further north of the town.

Brixham to Dartmouth (5—206); long rise out of Brixham to the junction with the Newton Abbot road at Raddicombe *Tp.* or Brixham Cross, $203\frac{1}{4}$, and $\frac{1}{4}$m. farther on begins a long, steep, and winding descent to Kingswear, $205\frac{1}{2}$, whence cross by ferry to Dartmouth. Or past Raddicombe *Tp.* keep to *r.* down a very steep and winding descent to Old Rock Inn, whence cross by floating bridge to *Dartmouth,* $205\frac{1}{2}$. [Or keep to *r.* past Churston Station, $198\frac{3}{4}$, and it is all uphill to Brixham Cross, $200\frac{3}{4}$, and to *Dartmouth,* $203\frac{1}{2}$, or 206 as before.]

(*Dartmouth:* Royal Castle, *B.T.C.*)

Dartmouth is a small seaport, built on a succession of terraces; fine old parish *ch.* Beautiful scenery up the *R.* Dart. Remains of castles at Dartmouth and Kingswear.

LONDON TO DARTMOUTH (by Newton Abbot).

London to Newton Abbot ($183\frac{1}{2}$)—p. 61.

Newton Abbot to Dartmouth (16—$199\frac{1}{2}$); in the former turn to *r.* and follow the Totnes road for $1\frac{1}{2}$m., then turn to *l.* to Abbots Kerswell, $185\frac{1}{2}$, the road being on the rise mostly, then up a winding ascent and over an undulating road through Compton, $188\frac{1}{2}$, to Marldon, $189\frac{1}{2}$, after which it becomes more hilly by Five Lanes, 190, Langstone, 192, and Galmpton *Tp.*, 194, whence by Brixham Cross, $196\frac{3}{4}$, to Kingswear, 199, and by ferry or floating bridge to Dartmouth as above. [Or in Newton Abbot keep straight on to Ford, $184\frac{1}{4}$, here turn to *r.* for King's Kerswell, 186, all an undulating road; out of this is a long, stiff ascent, and after a couple of miles of level riding, join the above road at Five Lanes, 190.]

At Five Lanes on *l.* to *Paignton* (1½—191½); nearly all downhill.
At Galmpton *Tp.* on *l.* to *Brixham* (2¼—196¼).

LONDON TO DARTMOUTH (by Totnes).

London to Totnes (191½)—p. 61.

Totnes to Dartmouth (10—201½) is a very hilly and very bad road; through Totnes turn sharp to *l.*; an ascent (keeping to *l.* again at ¾*m.*), and a mile of level and downhill lead to Bow Bridge, 194½; about ½*m.* farther, beyond Tuckenhay, 195, is a steep and winding ascent, and then all up and downhill by Tidaford, 196½, and Ditsham Cross, 197¾, to Norton House, 199½, soon after which begins a long and, in places, steep descent into Dartmouth.

Before Norton House, on *l.*, Woodbury Camp.

LONDON TO KINGSBRIDGE.

London to Totnes (191½)—p. 61.

Totnes to Kingsbridge (12—203½); through Totnes turn sharp to *l.*, and beginning with an ascent the road is all up and down hill through Harbertonford, 194½, to Halwell, 196½, then (keeping to *l.* and shortly after to *r.*) there is a long, but comparatively easy pull up by Stanborough House to Mounts, 200½, then level, with a short but steep descent into Kingsbridge.

(*Kingsbridge:* King's Arms, *B.T.C.*)

LONDON TO PLYMOUTH (by Modbury).

London to Venn Cross (199½)—p. 61.

Venn Cross to Modbury (4—203½); keep to *l.*; undulating road by Dunwell Cross, 201¼, Ball Cross, 201¾, and Mary Cross, 202½. On the reverse journey keep to *l.* at Mary Cross.

[There is another route by *Totnes*, 191½, p. 61, thence to Halwell, 196½, above; here turn to *r.*, and level by Morleigh, 197¼, except steep winding descent at Storridge Mill, 199¼, to Gerah Bridge, 199¾, followed by long ascent and descent to Brownstone, 201½; from here is a long rise most of the way to Mary Cross, 203½.

Or from *Totnes* through Inglebourn and Luckbridge to Brownstone, 200½; very hilly.]

(*Modbury:* Davis's, *B.T.C.*)

At Modbury are to be seen remains of a Benedictine priory, also ruins of Modbury *Ho.*

Modbury to Brixton (7—210½); in Modbury turn to *r.*, and the road continues rather hilly over Sequer's Bridge, 205½, Yealm Bridge, 208¼, and through Yealmpton, 209.

Before Brixton, on *l.*, Kitley Park.

Brixton to Plymouth (5½—216); to Elburton, 212½, is very undulating, and then on the fall to the Laira Bridge, a mile before Plymouth, where cross the Catwater or *R.* Plym, and directly after join the road from Ridgeway on *r.* [Or in Brixton turn to *r.*, undulating for a mile, then a stiff hill to climb, with steep descent to walk down into Plympton Earle, 212½, whence to Ridgeway, 213, and to Plymouth, 217¾, p. 56.]

At Plympton Earle, remains of Castle.

LONDON TO LAND'S END (by Tavistock).

London to Exeter (168½)—p. 49.

Exeter to Moreton Hampstead (12—180½); in Exeter, after passing through High street, go down Fore street hill to *R.* Exe, and when over the bridge, keep straight on by the middle road through the suburb of St. Thomas, over the hill and down to Pocomb Bridge, 171; from here is an ascent to Longdown, and after Longdown End, 172½, it is down hill by Culverhouse, 174½, to Great Oak, 175½, and a rise and fall to Dunsford, 176½; shortly after cross *R.* Tamar, and there is a long rise through Bridford Wood and again by Doccombe, 179, followed by stiff descent to King's Bridge, 180, and rise into the town.

(*Moreton Hampstead:* White Hart, *B.T.C.*)

Moreton Hampstead is on the verge of Dartmoor, has a handsome *ch.*, and remains of two castles. In the neighbourhood are several Druidical remains, and 2 or 3*m.* N. are three ancient hill fortresses, Cranbrook Castle, Preston Berry Castle, and Wooston Castle.

Moreton Hampstead to Two Bridges (13¾—194¼); by Bughead Cross, 182, the road is undulating to Worm Hill Bridge, 183, then it begins to ascend over Worm Hill, 183½, and by Beetor Cross, 183¾, a little beyond which enter Dartmoor Forest, and the ascent continues more or less past New House, 187½, to Merripit Hill, 188½, followed by a mile run down to Post Bridge (*R.* Dart); the rest is nearly half uphill and half down.

Beyond Two Bridges, on *l.*, is the large convict prison.

Two Bridges to Tavistock (8—202¼); take the right hand road, and after a stiff ascent the road falls rapidly to Merivale Bridge, 197¼, then another short ascent and again downhill (leaving Dartmoor Forest 2*m.* further) through Tavy Town, 201½, to Tavistock, crossing *R.* Tavy at the entrance of the town.

(*Tavistock:* Bedford, *B.T.C.*; Queen's Head.)

At Tavistock there are remains of the splendid abbey founded in the 10th century; ancient parish *ch.*

Tavistock to Callington (9—211¼): in Tavistock turn to *l.*, and and from Lumber Bridge, 203¾, is a stiff hill up to Gulworthy, 204¾, followed by a similar descent to New Bridge, 205¾ (*R.* Tamar), then (keeping to *l.*) a long steep hill to walk up on to Hingston Down, after crossing which a 3*m.* descent, in some parts very steep, leads down into Callington.

(*Callington:* Golding's, *B.T.C.*)

Callington to Liskeard (8—219¼); downhill to New Bridge, 212¼, then a short steep ascent, and after a little level past Appledore Down the road is nearly all downhill through St. Ive, 215¼, to Cornbrow, 216½, uphill to Pengover, 217½, and another down and up to Liskeard.

Liskeard to Land's End (73½—292¾); through *Lostwithiel*, 230, and *St. Austell*, 238½—p. 57.

¼*m.* before Lumber Bridge on *l.* to Beer Alston (6—209¾), thence to *Beer Ferris* (2—211¾); hilly road by Roman's Lee and over Morwell Down and Alston Down.

LONDON TO TAVISTOCK (by Okehampton).

London to Okehampton (190¾)—p. 50.

Okehampton to Downton (8—198¾); follow the Launceston road to Sourton Down, as at p. 50, and $3\frac{1}{2}$*m.* out of Okehampton take left hand road, all up and down hill through Sourton, $195\frac{1}{4}$, and Southerleigh, $196\frac{3}{4}$.

Downton to Tavistock ($8\frac{1}{2}$—$207\frac{1}{4}$); taking the right hand road, after a short pull up there is a sharp fall into and through Lidford, $199\frac{3}{4}$, out of which a short but very awkward drop should be walked down to the bridge over the *R.* Lid; from here it is nearly all uphill to Brent Tor *Tg.*, $203\frac{1}{4}$, on Heath Field, and thence downhill to Tavistock. [Or from Downton by the left hand road, crossing over Black Down a part of Dartmoor, half chiefly uphill and half down; about same distance.]

At Lidford are the ruins of a castle; pretty scenery. On Brent Tor is a *ch.*, which forms a prominent landmark at sea.

LONDON TO FOWEY.

London to Plymouth ($211\frac{1}{2}$)—p. 56.

Plymouth to Crafthole ($8\frac{1}{4}$—$219\frac{3}{4}$)—p. 56.

Crafthole to East Looe ($9\frac{1}{2}$—$229\frac{1}{4}$); keep to *l.* and up a gradual ascent along the top of the cliffs to St. German's Beacon, $221\frac{3}{4}$, followed —turning inland—by a downhill more or less past Minerd Cross, $223\frac{3}{4}$, to the pretty village of Hessenford, $224\frac{3}{4}$; out of this, after crossing *R.* Seaton there is another long hill to mount past Short Cross, $226\frac{1}{4}$ (where keep to *l.*), on to Bin Down, then mostly on the fall to St. Martin's, $228\frac{1}{4}$, from which is a winding descent through a wood into East Looe.

At St. Martin's, 1*m.* on *r.* across *R.* Looe, is Trenant Park.

East Looe to Fowey (*ch.*, $9\frac{3}{4}$—239); cross the narrow bridge over the *R.* Looe to West Looe, $229\frac{1}{2}$, out of which is a hill to ride up with a short fall into Talland, 231, and then a fairly level road runs through Polperro, $232\frac{1}{2}$, and Carneggan, 236, to Treduduell, $236\frac{1}{2}$, descent to Gregon, $237\frac{1}{2}$, another rise out of it, and a sharp downhill leads into Bodinnock, $238\frac{3}{4}$, whence cross the harbour to Fowey; splendid road, except from West Looe to Polperro which is said to be impracticable even for carriages. The better way is to keep to *r.* $\frac{1}{2}$*m.* beyond West Looe and by South Wayland Pulpit, $230\frac{1}{2}$, (keep to *r.*) Wayland, $231\frac{1}{2}$, (keep to *l.* and again 2nd on *l.*) to Polperro, 234.

[Or to *Lostwithiel*, 230, p. 65, thence *l.* to *Fowey*, $5\frac{1}{2}$—$235\frac{1}{2}$.]

(*Fowey:* Commercial; Ship, *B.T.C.*)

Fowey is an old-fashioned seaport; close to, amidst pretty scenery, are the old Castle and the ruins of St. Saviour's Chapel; handsome *ch.* Near the town, Menabilly *Ho.*

LONDON TO MEVAGISSEY.

London to St. Austell ($238\frac{1}{2}$)—p. 65.

St. Austell to Mevagissey (7—$245\frac{1}{2}$); in St. Austell turn to *l.* by the *ch.*, and for a considerable distance a tramway is laid along the road, which follows the valley of a small stream down to Pentewan, $243\frac{1}{2}$, on the coast, then a hill has to be mounted, and after 1*m.* of level is a short but sharp descent into Mevagissey.

LONDON TO FALMOUTH (by Tregony).

London to St. Austell ($238\frac{1}{2}$)—p. 65.

St. Austell to Tregony ($7\frac{3}{4}$—$246\frac{1}{4}$); hilly through Higher Sticker

241, and Hewes Water, 241½, to Teags *Tpk.*, 242, where turn to *l.*, and it is an undulating road with a descent into and through the town.

About 2*m.* before Tregony, 1*m.* on *l.*, is a large ancient circular camp or entrenchment.

Tregony to St. Mawes (9½—255¾); undulating road by Little Trengrowse, 248 (keep to *r.*), Three Gates 250, Trewarlas, 251, Cargurrel, 252, and Trewithian, 252½ (keep to *r.*), to Tregear, 253 (a little after keep to *r*), then short fall and rise to St. Just, 254¼, and after a mile of level a descent into St. Mawes.

At St. Mawes is an old castle.

St. Mawes to Falmouth (2½—258¼); cross Falmouth Harbour by steamer.

LONDON TO LAND'S END (by Redruth).

London to St. Michael (243¾)—p. 50.

St. Michael to Redruth (13—256¾); a short distance beyond St. Michael keep to *r.*, and through Zealla, 247¼, past Perran's Alms Houses, 249¼, and through Black Water, 253¾.

1*m.* before Black Water on *r.* to *St. Agnes*, (3¼—256.)

[Or to *Truro*, 250¾, p. 50, thence on *r.* to *Redruth*, 8½—259¼; or to junction of the road 1*m.* before Black Water, 258½, and forward to *Redruth*, 261½.]

(*Redruth :* Tapp's.)

About 1*m.* S.W. of Redruth is Carn Brea Hill, on which are several Druidical remains, and near to is Carn Brea Castle. Redruth is the centre of a tin and copper mining district.

Redruth to Camborne (3½—260¼); through Pool, 258¾.

(*Camborne :* Commercial; Tyack's.)

2*m.* *l.* of Camborne is Pendarves. On the coast, 2*m.* on *r.*, Tehidy Park. Between the two towns are the Dolcoath and Cook's Kitchen mines, the former the deepest in the county.

Camborne to Guildford (5¼—265½); through Treswithian, 261, Conner, 262½, and Angarrack, 264¾.

From Guildford on *r.* to *St. Ives*, (5¼—270¾).

(*St. Ives :* Queen's; Trewren's; Western.)

At Conner, on *r.*, Clowance Park. St. Ives is chiefly devoted to the pilchard fishery. 2*m.* *r.* of Conner on the shore of St. Ives' Bay, remains of the *ch.* of St Gwythian, which was buried in the sands for centuries.

Guildford to Penzance (9¼—274¾); through St. Erth, 268, Treloweth, 269, Ludgwan, 271¼, and Gulvall, 273¼.

At Ludgwan on *l.* to *Marazion* (2—273¼)

At Treloweth on *r.* to *St. Ives* (4¼—273¼), through Lelant, 270½.

Penzance to Land's End (11—285¾)—p. 51.

LONDON TO TRURO (by Camelford).

London to Launceston (209¼)—p. 50.

Launceston to Hallworthy (9—218¼); in Launceston turn to *r.*, and from the suburb of Newport, 209¾, there is a long gradual ascent through St. Stephen's, 210¼, on to St. Stephen's Down, 210¾, (at the beginning of which turn to *l.*), and then an undulating road through Egloskerry, 212, over Tremeer Down, 214½, and by Trenegloss (near on *l.*) 215¼, with a long rise to Hallworthy; limestone road, rather rough. [Or keep straight through Launceston, long hill out of the town, through Trebursey, 211¼, then ¼m. beyond take right hand road and it is pretty level by Piper's Pool, 214, and over Lancast Down.]

At Hallworthy on *r.* to *Bossiney* (7½—225¾).
(*Bossiney :* Warncliffe Arms, *B.T.C.* ; Fry's Boarding House.)
Near Bossiney are the ruins of Tintagel Castle, or King Arthur's Castle. Grand scenery. 4m. N. is Boscastle, over moderate but hilly road.

Hallworthy to Camelford (5½—223¾); pretty level to Davidstow, 219¾, out of which is a long descent and then long hill to mount.

[Or ¾m. beyond Hick's Mill, 214½—p. 50, by right hand road through Lower Tregunnan, 216¼, to *Camelford*, 224½.]

At Davidstow on *r.* to *Bossiney* (6—225¾), bad road for bicycling. Or from *Camelford* to *Bossiney* (5—226¾), but it is a rather difficult road to find.
(*Camelford :* Darlington ; King's Arms, *B.T.C.*)
Near Camelford was fought the battle that proved fatal to King Arthur.

Camelford to Wadebridge (10¾—234½); beyond Camelford ascent for 3m., through Tremagennow, 224¾, (keep to *r.*), and Helson or Helstone, 225¾, to St. Teath, 227¼, then undulating through Treelill, 229½, Highway, 231, and Three Holes Cross, 233, with a stiff descent to Wadebridge.

At St. Teath on *r.* through St. Endellion to *Padstow* (11½—238¾). Or from Wadebridge by Halsar's Grave, 236¾, on *r.* to St. Issey, 238½, and Little Petherick, 239¼, to *Padstow*, 242.
(*Wadebridge :* Commercial, *B.T.C.* ; Molesworth Arms).
2 or 3m. W. of Wadebridge, Trevose Head, Pentire Point, St. Enodock *ch.*, De la Bole slate quarries ; good undulating roads.

Wadebridge to St. Columb (9—243½); very good and fairly level road by Halsar's Grave, 236¾, and No Man's Land, 237¾, to within 3m. of St. Columb, when it becomes bad and hilly.
(*St. Columb :* Barley Sheaf ; King's Arms ; Red Lion, *B.T.C.*)
At St. Columb is a fine gothic *ch.*

St. Columb to Fradden (3½—247); bad and hilly road for 3¼m., when it joins the main Bodmin and Truro road.

Fradden to Truro (11½—258½)—p. 50.

LONDON TO STRATTON.

London to Exeter (168½)—p. 49.

Exeter to Crediton (7½—176); keep straight through Exeter and then up a gradual ascent through St. David's, 169, and most of the way to Cowley Bridge, 170¼ (cross *R.* Exe), whence the road is rather hilly, following the edge of the valley through Newton St. Cyres, 173, to Crediton.
(*Crediton :* Angel ; Railway ; Ship.)
At Crediton, elegant *ch.* with fine altar-piece. N. of the town Creedy *Ho.*

Crediton to Bow *alias* **Nymet Tracey** (7½—183½); in Crediton turn to *l.*, and out of the town is an ascent of 2m. but not difficult, then level past Barnstaple Cross, 178½, with a short descent into and ascent out of Colford, 180, and except another fall and rise at Gay's Lake, 181¾, the rest is level with a downhill through Bow. [Or at Barnstaple Cross by the right fork, and, except a descent into and ascent out of Copplestone, 180¼, where keep to *l.*, it is fairly level, joining the above road entering Bow.]

Bow to Hatherleigh (13—196½); up and down hill all the way through Stone Cross, 186 (keep to *r.*), North Tawton, 187½, Sampford Courtney, 189¾, Exbourne, 191¾, across *R.* Okement, through Jacobstow, 193, over Beckamoor and through Bassels Gate, 195¼.

[Or to Okehampton, 190¾—p. 50; thence, after crossing *R.* Okement, keep to *r.* and by Five Oaks, 192½, to *Hatherleigh*, 197½; rather hilly.]

Hatherleigh to Holsworthy (13½—210); in Hatherleigh keep to *l.*, and it is a very hilly road over Rundon Moor (at 2½m. from Hatherleigh keeping to *r.*, on *l.* to Launceston, 17½m.) and Pulworthy Moor to Golden Inn, 200½, then taking second turn to *r.* 1¼m. further, over Hill, King's, and Gadand's Moors, past Brandis Corner, 205, over Beacon Field, Eastcombe Moor and Simpson Moor.

At "Golden Inn," on *r.* to *Sheepwash* (1½—202).

(*Holsworthy:* Brendon's Stanhope, *B.T.C.*)

Holsworthy to Stratton (8—218); in Holsworthy turn to *r.* and through Ridon, 211, over Killatree Moor, Weekstone Bridge, 213½, and Tamerstone Bridge, 214½ (where cross *R.* Tamar); hilly road, and long descent into Stratton.

(*Stratton:* Tree.)

Nearly 2m. beyond Stratton is Bude Haven.

LONDON TO EXETER (by Amesbury).

London to Andover (63½)—p. 58.

Andover to Amesbury (14—77½); just out of Andover at the railway station keep to *r.*, and through Weyhill, 66¾ (keep to *l.*), by Mollen's Pond, 68¼, near Thruxton and Quarley, past Park House, 72½, and Haradon Hill, 74, is a difficult bicycling road; there are two high hills to cross, and the surface is rough in many places; a lot of walking is necessary in either direction, and the last descent into Andover on the reverse journey should be taken cautiously.

(*Amesbury:* George.)

At Weyhill a large sheep fair is held for the week after 28th Sept. Near Quarley, 2m. S. on Quarley Hill, is an old British entrenchment. At Amesbury, on *r.*, Amesbury H?., where the poet Gay lived with his patron, the Duke of Queensbury. Beyond Park House, 1m. on *l.*, Wilbury Park.

Amesbury to Long Barrow Cross (3½—81); leaving Amesbury, after crossing *R.* Avon, the road bears to *r.* up a short rise and down again; after this a long and very stiff ascent has to be mounted leading on to Salisbury Plain, and after a little level ground Stonehenge comes in sight on an opposite hill, before which two short but sharp falls with an intervening rise have to be negotiated; at the bottom of the second descent keep to *l.*, at 79½m., just before crossing to Stonehenge (which is close to the road side at the top of a very stiff ascent on the right hand fork), and having mounted a rather steep hill the rest is pretty level to Long Barrow

Cross, where the Salisbury and Devizes road crosses; except for a few stones sometimes on the hills the surface (flint) is capital and smooth to the fork roads, but thence deteriorates to the Devizes road, being rough and stony.

Nearly 1m. out of Amesbury on r., an old British earthwork, called Vespasian's Camp. The interesting and wonderful remains of Stonehenge, generally supposed to have been a Druidical Temple, consists of two circles of stones, the outer of 24 and the inner of 19, more than half still standing; it is surrounded by numerous barrows on the Downs; on the N. is a wide avenue leading to the Cursus, which is 2m. in length, the whole being enclosed between 2 ditches. On the southern horizon the spire of Salisbury Cathedral is visible 7m. distant.

Long Barrow Cross to Deptford Inn ($5\frac{1}{4}$—$86\frac{3}{4}$); after $\frac{1}{2}$m. there is a steep descent to Winterbourne Stoke, $82\frac{1}{2}$, then a good rise out of it, and a pretty level run across Salisbury Plain for $2\frac{1}{2}$m., with a long downhill to Deptford Inn; not a very good road.

2 or 3m. past Winterbourn, on r., Yarnbury Castle, a British entrenchment and Roman camp.

Deptford Inn to Willoughby Hedge ($9\frac{1}{4}$—$96\frac{1}{4}$); keeping to l., cross the valley to Wiley, $87\frac{1}{2}$, out of which is a steep ascent, then a hilly road past Stockham Wood, by New Inn, $92\frac{1}{4}$, up Chicklade Bottom, and through Chicklade, $93\frac{3}{4}$; this road is almost unrideable. [Or at New Inn turn to l. and go through Hindon, $94\frac{1}{4}$, to Willoughby Hedge, 97.]

At Hindon, 1m. on l., ruins of Fonthill Abbey. At Willoughby Hedge, on l., Knoyle Court.

Willoughby Hedge to Mere (4—$100\frac{3}{4}$); a mile beyond Willoughby Hedge keep to l.; a long descent into Mere.

(*Mere*: Talbot, *B.T.C.*)

At Mere, on Castle Hill, slight remains of a castle.

Mere to Wincanton ($7\frac{1}{4}$—$107\frac{1}{2}$); a mile out of Mere keep to l., and it is very undulating through Long Cross, $101\frac{3}{4}$, Zeal's Green, $102\frac{1}{4}$, Bourton, $103\frac{3}{4}$, Leigh Common and Bayford, $106\frac{1}{2}$; a rough macadam road made of a soft greasy looking stone.

(*Wincanton*: Greyhound, *B.T.C.*)

At Zeal's Green, on r., 1m. Stowhead Park and *Ho.*, also, near the village of Penselwood, or Penzlewood, are the Pen Pits, of great extent, and supposed to be the site of a prehistoric British town: Castle Orchard.

Wincanton to Sparkford ($7\frac{1}{2}$—115); in Wincanton turn to l., and keeping to r. 1m. beyond, it is an up and down hill road, through Holton, $109\frac{1}{2}$, Blackford, $111\frac{1}{4}$, and Cadbury, 113; bad macadam surface, of a soft and greasy looking stone.

Near Cadbury, on l., Cadbury Castle or Camalet, an ancient British hill fortress, said to have formerly been a mile in circuit, guarded by 4 trenches and ramparts, and in the centre is a mound, called King Arthur's Palace; numerous antiquities have been found here.

Sparkford to Ilchester ($5\frac{1}{2}$—$120\frac{1}{2}$); out of Sparkford is a steep ascent over Camel Hill (near to the top keep to the r.) and after a little level ground there is a long descent, and then (at the next bifurcation taking left hand road) nearly level through Northover *Tp.*, $120\frac{1}{4}$.

Ilchester was the Roman Ischalis, and an important town in Saxon times, but it is now in a declining state; the old fosse way from Lincoln and Bath passes through it; very old *ch.* Roger Bacon was born here.

Ilchester to Petherton Bridge (6—126½) is a straight undulating road, following the old Roman Fosse Way.
½m. before Petherton Bridge on *l.* to *Crewkerne* (6—132).

Petherton Bridge to Ilminster (6—132½); rather hilly road by Watergure, 127¾, and White Cross, 128½, to Seavington, 129½, then a long ascent to White Lackington, 131, followed by a hill to ride down into Ilminster; rather bumpy road to White Cross, then capital surface to Ilminster. [Or just beyond Petherton Bridge on r. through South Petherton, 127½, and by Lopen Head to Seavington, distance about the same; road very bumpy to Lopen Head, and then good.] On the reverse journey just out of Ilminster keep to *l.*

(*Ilminster :* Dolphin; George, *B.T.C.*)
Near Seavington, 2m. on *l.*, Hinton *Ho.* and Park; on *r.*, Dillington *Ho.* At Ilminster, fine old Gothic *ch.*

Ilminster to Honiton (17—149½); through Horton, 134, and by Broadway, 135½, after which the road goes throug.. a wild mountainous tract of country, passing Buckland St. Mary, 138½, Heathfield Arms, 141, Knightshayne, 142, and Devonshire Arms, 143¾, whence it is mostly downhill through Monkton, 147¼. [Or in Ilminster turn to *l.*, and a little downhill to Sea, 134½, then chiefly uphill over Chard Down to *Chard*, 5—137½, thence to *Honiton*, 12—149½—p. 49.]

At Buckland St. Mary, 2m. on *r.*, Castle Nereche, an immense entrenched hill.

Honiton to Exeter (16½—166)—p. 49.

LONDON TO EXETER (by Hindon).

London to Barford St. Martin (87)—p. 48.

Barford St. Martin to Hindon (9½—96½); through Dinton, 89½, Teffont Magna, 91½, Chilmark, 92¾, Bishops Fonthill, 95, and Berwick St. Leonards 95¾, an up and down road, two or three stillish hills, and gentle descent into and through Hindon; chalk flint, fairly good road; scenery dreary.

At Fonthill, on *l.*, Fonthill Abbey *Ho.*, in beautiful grounds.

Hindon to Willoughby Hedge (2¼—99¼) is a similar kind of road.

Willoughby Hedge to Exeter (69¾—169)—p. 70 and above.

LONDON TO AXMINSTER (by Crewkerne.)

London to Crewkerne (132)—p. 48.

Crewkerne to Marshalsea (5½—137½); through Crewkerne keep to *l.*, and almost level through Hewish, 133, to Seaborough, 134¼, then hilly.

Marshalsea to Axminster (6¾—144¼)—p. 61.

[Or through Crewkerne to Windwhistle, 136—p. 49, then a little further keep to *l.*, and through White Gate, 138½, Titherleigh 141½, and over Weycroft Bridge, 143, to *Axminster*, 145½]

LONDON TO WINCANTON (by Shaftesbury.)

London to Shaftesbury (101)—p. 48.

Shaftesbury to Gillingham ($4\frac{1}{2}$—$105\frac{1}{2}$); long and steep zigzag descent to walk down from Shaftesbury, then the road is undulating over Ledden Bridge, 105, and the railway bridge.
(*Gillingham* : Phœnix, *B.T.C.*; South Western.)

Gillingham to Wincanton ($6\frac{1}{2}$—112); rather rough and narrow road through Cucklington. 109, out of which is a steep descent, then undulating through Stoke Trister, 110, and Bayford, 111, where join the main London road through Mere. [Or instead of turning to *l.* for Cucklington keep straight on and join the London road 2*m.* before Bayford.]

LONDON TO SHERBORNE (by Wincanton.)

London to Wincanton ($107\frac{1}{2}$)—p. 70.

Wincanton to Sherborne ($9\frac{1}{2}$—117); a mile out of Wincanton, on the Sparkford road, turn to *l.*, and shortly after take the road to *r.*, which is uphill for nearly 2*m.*; then comes a steep winding descent to Charleton Horethorne, $112\frac{1}{4}$, which the bicyclist must beware against riding down, and after that the road is more or less downhill to Sherborne.

LONDON TO YEOVIL (by Sparkford.)

London to Sparkford (115)—p. 70.

Sparkford to Yeovil ($7\frac{3}{4}$—$122\frac{3}{4}$); out of Sparkford is a steep ascent over Camel Hill (near the top of which keep to *l.*), followed by a steep crooked descent into Queen Camel, $116\frac{1}{4}$, then undulating through Marston Magna, $118\frac{1}{2}$, and Mudford, $120\frac{1}{2}$.

LONDON TO ILMINSTER (by Yeovil.)

London to Yeovil ($122\frac{3}{4}$)—p. 48.

Yeovil to Petherton Bridge ($7\frac{1}{2}$—$129\frac{3}{4}$); rough and very bumpy road through Preston Plucknett, $123\frac{1}{2}$ (a mile beyond keep to *r.*), Odcomb, $125\frac{1}{4}$, Montacute, $126\frac{1}{2}$, Stoke-under-Handon, $127\frac{1}{4}$, and West Stoke, $128\frac{1}{4}$, joining the road from Ilchester $\frac{1}{4}m.$ before Petherton Bridge.

Petherton Bridge to Ilminster (6—$135\frac{3}{4}$)—p. 71.

LONDON TO HARTLAND.

London to Sparkford (115)—p. 70.

Sparkford to Langport ($12\frac{1}{2}$—$127\frac{1}{2}$); out of Sparkford is a steep ascent over Camel Hill (near the top keep to *r.*), and after a little level ground there is a long descent, and then at the next bifurcation 3*m.* from Sparkford keep to *r.*; it is a good road and nearly level through Pudimore Milton, 119, a mile beyond which cross the old Fosse Way from Bath to Ilchester, and then through Long Sutton, $124\frac{1}{4}$, Pisbury, $126\frac{1}{4}$, and Huish Episcopi, 127.

(*Langport* : Langport Arms, *B.T.C.*)

Langport to Taunton (13½—141); ascent out of Langport, then pretty level through Curry Rivell, 129¾, to Swell Hill, 131½, where there is a long descent, which is continued more or less past Rock House Inn, 133¾, (keep to r.) to Wrantage, 134½, and then undulating by Mattock Tree, 137, to Taunton; excellent road. At Mattock Tree on the reverse journey keep to l. at the top of the hill.

(*Taunton:* Blue Anchor; Castle; Clarke's, *B.T.C.*; George; London; Railway.)

At Taunton, remains of the castle, founded by Ina, 700, and rebuilt after the conquest, but the west wing is supposed to be part of the original building; St James' *ch.* is supposed to have been erected in the 13th century; St. Mary's *ch.* is a handsome building, with curious roof, &c.

Taunton to Wellington (7—148); long but easy rise out of Taunton, and the rest through Bishop's Hull, 142¾, Rumwell, 144, and Chilson, 147, is an undulating and splendid road.

(*Wellington:* Half Moon; Squirrel, *B.T.C.*; Temperance Refreshment Rooms.)

About 1m. before Chilson, on r., Heatherton Park. Wellington *ch.* has a magnificent tomb of Sir John Popham, and the altar-piece is considered one of the finest in England.

Wellington to South Appledore (6½—154½); after passing Rockwell Green, 149, good and fairly level road to Beambridge, then long and rather steep ascent to White Ball Inn, 151, situate on a part of the Black Down Hills, which cross to Maiden Down, 152½, and the rest is chiefly down hill, the last part being a very dangerous descent into South Appledore, steep and covered with loose stones.

At Maiden Down, on *l.*, the Wellington Monument, in commemoration of Waterloo, from which is a fine view, including the Welsh Coast and the Mendip Hills. About 4m. S.E., on Black Down Hills, Hemyock Castle, a large entrenched hill.

South Appledore to Tiverton (7¾—162¼); long and easy descent from South Appledore (a mile beyond keep to r.), then uphill over Ashford Moor and through Sampford Peverel, 157¼, followed 1m. further by easy descent into Halberton, 159½, and the last 2m. down hill; good road. On the reverse journey, just out of Tiverton keep to *l.*

(*Tiverton:* Angel; Palmerston, *B.T.C.*)

At Tiverton, remains of castle, built in 1106; fine modern *ch.*, with beautiful altar-piece, &c.; free grammar school, town hall, &c. The chief manufactory is lace. S. of town is Collipriest *Ho.*

Tiverton to South Molton (18½—180¾); after a stiff ascent out of Tiverton, the road continues more or less on the rise through Calverleigh, 164¼, and North Sidborough, ending with a rather long and stiff ascent on to Gibbet Moor, 167¾, then a descent of 2m., followed by a steep hill to climb through Rackenford, 170¼, (where turn to r.); after that the road is very hilly, crossing over Ash Moor, 172½—174½, and by Ash Mill, 176, and Bush Bridge, 178½, where the Dulverton Road joins in on r.; for the most part the road is very rough and rutty.

(*South Molton:* George, *B.T.C.*; White Hart.)

South Molton *ch.*, erected in the 15th century, has a fine carved stone pulpit and altar-piece, &c. In the parish is the Flitton Oak, of great age and size. N. of the town extends Exmoor, the haunt of the red deer.

South Molton to Barnstaple ($11\frac{1}{2}$—$192\frac{1}{4}$); 1*m*. beyond the former keep to *r*., and the road affords capital running through North Hill, $182\frac{1}{4}$, Filleigh, $183\frac{3}{4}$, Kerscot, 186 (keep to *l*.), Hanaford, $187\frac{1}{2}$, Landkey, 190, and Newport, $191\frac{1}{2}$; rather hilly, but there are no hills of any difficulty.

(*Barnstaple:* Gaydon's Restaurant; Golden Lion; King's Arms; Royal and Fortescue, *B.T.C.*; Trevelyan Temperance.)

At Filleigh, on *r*., Castle Hill, the splendid mansion of Earl Fortescue. At Barnstaple was formerly a castle built by King Athelstan, but only a mound now marks its site. SS. Peter and Paul *ch.* was built about 1318; the bridge over the *R.* Taw is older still. Beyond the town, Pilton *ch.*, formerly part of a priory founded by King Athelstan, and containing a curious pulpit. There are many pretty rides and drives in the neighbourhood; 3*m*. S.W., Tawstock *ch.*

Barnstaple to Bideford ($8\frac{1}{2}$—$200\frac{3}{4}$); in Barnstaple turn to *l.* and cross *R.* Taw, $\frac{3}{4}$*m*. further keep to *r*., and the road is undulating but chiefly uphill for 2 or 3*m*., then is on the fall through Holmacot, $196\frac{3}{4}$, and East Leigh, $198\frac{1}{4}$; fair road.

At *Bideford* on *r.* through Northam to *Appledore* (3—$203\frac{3}{4}$), near which is Westward Ho! both at the mouth of the Taw.

(*Bideford:* Commercial; New Inn, *B.T.C.*; Newfoundland.)

Bideford to Hartland ($13\frac{1}{2}$—$214\frac{1}{4}$); rather hilly road by Knotty Corner, $203\frac{1}{2}$, Fairy Cross, $204\frac{1}{4}$, Horn's Cross, $205\frac{3}{4}$, Holwell, $206\frac{3}{4}$, West Buckish, $208\frac{3}{4}$, and Ditchen Hills, $210\frac{3}{4}$.

At Ditchen Hills on *r.* to Clovelly ($1\frac{1}{4}$—212); a small village romantically situated on the coast.

(*Clovelly:* King's Arms.)

At Clovelly is Clovelly Court. At Hartland remains of the abbey.

LONDON TO TAUNTON (by Ilminster).

London to Ilminster ($132\frac{1}{4}$)—p. 71.

Ilminster to Taunton ($12\frac{1}{2}$—145); keep straight through Ilminster and descent from the town, then very hilly road through Horton, $134\frac{1}{4}$ (turn to *r*.), Ashill, $136\frac{1}{4}$, over Ashill Forest, through Hatch Beauchamp, $139\frac{1}{4}$ (keep to *l*.), to Mattock Tree, $141\frac{1}{2}$, where join the main London road.

Beyond Horton, on *r*., Jordans. At Hatch Beauchamp, on *r*., Hatch Court.

LONDON TO TIVERTON (by Honiton).

London to Honiton ($149\frac{1}{2}$)—p. 71.

Honiton to Cullompton ($10\frac{1}{2}$—160); in Honiton turn to *r*., and through Awliscombe, $151\frac{1}{2}$, the road is a succession of small hills for the first 3*m*., then a steep ascent over a spur of the Black Down Hills to Hembury Fort House, $153\frac{1}{4}$, and descent to be walked down the other side to Colleton, 155, the rest being a good but rather hilly road through Dilford, $156\frac{3}{4}$, and over Kentisbeare Moor.

$\frac{1}{4}$*m*. before Colleton on *r.* to Broadhembury (1—$156\frac{3}{4}$).

On *r.* pass Hembury Fort, a Roman encampment. At Cullompton, fine old *ch.*

Cullompton to Tiverton ($5\frac{1}{2}$—$165\frac{1}{2}$); in Cullompton turn first to *l.* and then to *r.*; the road is chiefly uphill to White Down, 163, whence there is a steep winding descent into Tiverton. On the reverse journey keep to

r. just out of Tiverton. [Or a better road, though rather hilly, is to take the Taunton road from Cullompton to Willand, 2¼, and at Willand Moor ½m. further turn to l. to Halberton, 5¼, on Taunton and Tiverton road, whence to Tiverton, 3—8¼—as at p. 73.]

LONDON TO HARTLAND (by Somerton.)

London to Willoughby Hedge (96¼)—p. 70.

Willoughby Hedge to Redlinch (11—107¼); a mile beyond Willoughby Hedge keep to r., and over Mere Down for 2 or 3m., then, after a steep crooked descent, an undulating road by Red Lion, 101¼, Long Lane End (Kilmington) 101¾, past Stourhead Park for 2m., when there is King's Settle Hill to descend, and the rest pretty level through Hardway, 105¾.

On the edge of Mere Down, on l., White Sheet Castle, an ancient encampment. At Kilmington, on l., Stourhead *Ho.* In the Park at the top of King's Settle Hill, on l., Alfred Tower, from which is a splendid view; 1m. beyond it, Jack's Castle, an ancient encampment.

Redlinch to Castle Cary (Almsford Inn, 4¼—111½); past Redlinch Park, through Shepton Montague, 108¾, Higher Shepton, 109¼, and then take 4th turning on r. for Castle Cary. [Or at Redlinch turn to r. through *Bruton*, 108¾, and Pitcombe, 110¼, joining the other road 1m. beyond to Castle Cary, 113. Or beyond railway, out of Bruton, keep to r. and through Honeywick, 110¾, to Castle Cary, 111¼.]

(*Bruton:* Blue Ball, *B.T.C.*—*Castle Cary:* George, *B.T.C.*)

At Bruton, fine *ch.* Castle Cary is a small old-fashioned town, lying chiefly on l. of the road; the Castle, from which the name was derived, was destroyed in the reign of Stephen, and only a mound marks the site; in the old manor house, now in ruins, Charles II. took refuge after the battle of Worcester. Beautiful *ch.* of the time of Henry VI.

Castle Cary to Somerton (10½—122); through Clanville, 112¼, Alford, 113½, Lydford, 116½ (where cross the Fosse Way), Keinton Mandeville, 117½, and King Weston, 118½, is a hilly road, with a long downhill to Somerton.

(*Somerton:* Red Lion, *B.T.C.*)

Somerton is supposed to have been a Roman fortress, it was afterwards a residence of the Saxon Kings; there are some slight remains of the castle; ancient *ch.*

Somerton to Langport (4—126); on the reverse journey keep to l. in Langport.

Langport to Hartland (86¾—212¾) through Taunton, 139½, Wellington 146½, South Appledore, 153, Tiverton, 160¾, South Molton, 179¼, Barnstaple, 190¾, and Bideford, 199¼—pp. 73-74.

LONDON TO EXETER (by Redlinch.)

London to Castle Cary (111½)—above.

Castle Cary to Sparkford (4½—116); keep to l. and through Galhampton, 113; hilly road.

Sparkford to Exeter (51—167); through Ilchester, 121½, Petherton Bridge, 127½, Ilminster, 133½, and Honiton, 150½—pp. 70-71.

LONDON TO EXETER (by Taunton.)

London to South Appledore (153)—p. 75.

South Appledore to Cullompton ($5\frac{3}{4}$—$158\frac{3}{4}$); descent out of the former, a mile beyond it keeping to the *l.*, and then the road is mostly up and down hill over Leonard Moor, Willand Moor, from which is a winding descent into Willand, $156\frac{1}{2}$, and then over Five Bridges, $157\frac{1}{2}$.

(*Cullompton:* Railway; White Hart, *B.T.C.*)

Cullompton to Exeter (12—$170\frac{3}{4}$); through Bradninch, $161\frac{1}{4}$, by Atherleigh Mill, $163\frac{3}{4}$ (cross *R.* Culm, and $\frac{1}{2}$*m.* beyond keep to *l.*), and through Broad Clyst, $166\frac{1}{4}$, Brock Hill, Langaton, $168\frac{1}{2}$, and Whipton, $169\frac{1}{2}$, is an indifferent and undulating road. [Or $\frac{1}{2}$*m.* beyond Atherleigh Mill turn to *r.* and through Hatchleigh, $166\frac{1}{4}$, whence it is a steep ascent up to Stop Gate, $167\frac{3}{4}$, and after two steep descents join the other road just before Exeter, $170\frac{1}{2}$.]

(*Bradninch:* Castle.)

At Atherleigh Mill, on *r.*, Killerton Park. At Bradninch, on *l.*, Hele *ch.*, where is a beautifully painted screen, quite unique.

LONDON TO OKEHAMPTON (by Tiverton).

London to Tiverton ($160\frac{3}{4}$)—p. 75.

Tiverton to Crediton (12—$172\frac{3}{4}$); after crossing *R.* Exe at Tiverton turn to *l.*, and the road is level for $3\frac{1}{4}$*m.*, following the valley of the Exe, to the bridge near Bickleigh (on *l.* $164\frac{1}{4}$), where keep straight on and there is a long ascent followed by an equally long descent to Stokeleigh Pomeroy, $169\frac{1}{4}$, and the rest undulating through Little Gutton, $170\frac{1}{2}$, and over Creedy Bridge, $171\frac{3}{4}$; not very good surface, greasy in wet weather.

At Bickleigh Bridge, on *l.*, Bickleigh Court. About 2 *m.* further, on the top of the hill, on *l.*, Cadbury Castle, an ancient hill fort. Beyond Little Gutton, on *l.*, Fulford Park. Beyond Creedy Bridge, on *r.*, Creedy *Ho.*

Crediton to Bow ($7\frac{1}{2}$—$180\frac{1}{4}$)—p. 68.

Bow to Okehampton (11—$191\frac{1}{4}$); rather hilly road by Stone Cross, $182\frac{3}{4}$ (keep to *l.*), Newland Bridge, $184\frac{1}{4}$, over Greenslade Moor and by Belstone Corner, $186\frac{1}{4}$, with a descent into the town.

LONDON TO STRATTON (by Tiverton).

London to Bow ($180\frac{1}{4}$)—above.

Bow to Stratton ($34\frac{1}{2}$—$214\frac{3}{4}$); through Hatherleigh, $193\frac{1}{4}$, and Holsworthy, $206\frac{3}{4}$—p. 69.

LONDON TO TORRINGTON.

London to South Molton ($179\frac{1}{4}$)—p. 75.

South Molton to Atherington ($8\frac{1}{2}$—$187\frac{3}{4}$); 1*m.* beyond South Molton keep to the *l.* and over Bray Bridge, $181\frac{3}{4}$, by Chittlehampton, $184\frac{3}{4}$, and over Umberleigh Bridge, $186\frac{1}{2}$, is a hilly road, and generally rather rough.

Before Chittlehampton, on *l.*, Hudscot *Ho.*

Atherington to Torrington (7—194¾); by Langridge, 188¾, Cranford Moor, 190¼, and High Bullen, 191¾, there are several short but stiff ascents and descents; generally rather rough road.
(*Torrington* : Globe, *B.T.C.*)

LONDON TO ILFRACOMBE.

London to Barnstaple (190¾)—p. 75.

Barnstaple to Ilfracombe (10—200¾); go straight through the High street of Barnstaple, or through Boutport street, over the causeway bridge, from which a hill leads up through the suburb of Pilton, 191¾, at the end of which keep to *l.*, and the road is undulating for a mile beyond Prexford, 193¾; then comes a steep ascent for more than a mile over Swinham Down, and the rest is mostly down hill by Hore-down gate, 198¼, with a steep descent into Ilfracombe. The road is very picturesque, winding over deep valleys, through a richly wooded country and with splendid views.
At Pilton on *r.* through Muddiford, 3*m.* and over Hewish and Berry Downs to *Combe Martin*, (9¼—201).
(*Ilfracombe* : Bailey's Private; Britannia; Clarence; Gardiner's Private; Ilfracombe; Lewis' Private; London; Pier; Queen's; Royal Clarence, *B.T.C.*; Royal Britannia; Star; Victoria.)

LONDON TO TORRINGTON, HARTLAND, AND ILFRACOMBE (by Dulverton).

London to Taunton (139½)—p. 75.

Taunton to Milverton (8¼—147¾); in Taunton turn to *r.* by the *ch.*, and cross *R.* Tone, then the road is on the rise through North Town to Staplegrove, 141¼, and after that is undulating over Langford Bridge, 141¾, (just beyond keep to *l.*) and through Norton Fitzwarren, 142¼, Heathfield, 144¾, Hale Common, 145¾, and Preston Bower, 146½; very good road. On the reverse journey keep to *r.*, just out of Milverton.
Near Norton Fitzwarren is a British Camp; the *ch.* dates from Saxon times, and has some antique carvings.

Milverton to Wiveliscombe (4—151¾); over Slade's Moor Bridge, 150, is rather more hilly, and fairly good road.
(*Wiveliscombe* : Lion, *B.T.C.*)
On Castle Hill, on *r.*, 1*m.* before Wiveliscombe is the site of a Roman camp. Wiveliscombe is situate in a deep valley, nearly surrounded by wooded hills; there are ruins of a palace of the Bishop of Wells, which existed here prior to 1256.

Wiveliscombe to Dulverton (12—163¾); in the former turn to *l.*, and a little further to the *r.*; there is a long steep ascent out of the town, then an undulating fairly good road through Chipstable, 154¼, Skilgate, 158¾, and Bury, 161¼, (turn to *l.*) and over *R.* Exe at Hele Bridge, 162½. On the reverse journey, after crossing Hele Bridge, take the middle road.
[There is another route from *Wiveliscombe*, by going on *l.* through Shillingford over a hilly road to *Bampton*, 8—159¾, out of which is a sharp ascent, presently followed by a steep winding and rough descent of a mile to Exe Bridge at Ripway Corner, 162¾, and the rest almost level alongside the *R.* Barle to *Dulverton*, 5¾—165½.]

(*Dulverton:* Carnarvon Arms, *B.T.C.*; Lamb; Lion; Red Lion, *B.T.C.*—*Bampton:* White Horse, *B.T.C.*)

On *r.* are Heydon Down and Haddon Down Hills, the southern flanks of Exmoor, whence some splendid views are to be had. Just before Dulverton, on *l.*, Pixton Park. Dulverton is surrounded by romantic scenery, and the Exe and Barle are noted trout streams; ancient *ch.* recently restored. Up the Exe Valley, 1½*m.* N.E., are the ruins of Barlinch Abbey. At Bampton is a fine Norman keep.

Dulverton to South Molton (13—176¾); cross *R.* Barle, and the road continues very wild and hilly through Durleyford, 169¾, and over Bush Bridge, 174¾, just beyond which join the Tiverton road on the *l.*

South Molton to Torrington (15½—192¼), through *Atherington* 185¼—pp. 76-77.

South Molton to Hartland (33½—210¼), through *Barnstaple*, 188¼, and *Bideford*, 196¾—p. 74.

South Molton to Ilfracombe (21½—198¼), through *Barnstaple*, 188¼—p. 74, and to *Ilfracombe*—p. 77.

LONDON TO ILFRACOMBE (by Lynmouth.)

London to Taunton (139¼)—p. 75.

Taunton to Gore Inn (5¼—144¾); in Taunton turn to *r.* by the *ch.*, and cross *R.* Tone, then the road is on a very gentle rise through North Town to Staplegrove, 141¼, followed after by a short easy decline to Langford Bridge, 141¾ (just beyond keep to *r.*), and the rest undulating good road.

Gore Inn to Washford (11¾—156½); uphill nearly to Handy Cross, 147¾, and again a long climb nearly all the way to Hartrowgate, 150¾, on a spur of Brendon Hill; after a mile or so of pretty level, the road falls sharply, with two or three rectangular dangerous turns to Monksilver, 153¾, then slightly downhill with ½*m.* ascent to Fair Cross, 155¼, and descent into Washford.

Beyond Hartrowgate on *r.* to Stogumber (1¼—152). At Washford on *r.* to Watchet (2¼—158¾); or at Fair Cross on *r.* (2½—157¾).

[There is another and better route by turning to *r.* at Gore Inn and through Bishop's Lydeard, 145¼, Seven Ash, 148¼, Crowcombe, 150½, Halfway 152¼, Bicknoller, 153¾ (½*m.* further turn to *l.*) over Woolston Moor, through Woolston, 155¼, and Sampford Brett, 155¾, to Williton, 156¾, to Washford, 158¾; undulating for first 2 or 3*m.*, then hilly, all up and down and running close under the Quantock Hills on *r.* to Bicknoller, whence downhill into Sampford Brett, after which it is undulating, and the going improves.

Or after crossing the *R.* Tone out of Taunton turn to *r.*, and it is chiefly uphill through Mill Cross, 142¾, Kingston, 143¼, Coombe and Yawford to the cross-roads ½*m.* beyond Bishop's Lydeard, whence as above to Washford, 159¾.]

(*Williton:* Egremont, *B.T.C.*; Railway.—*Watchet:* West Somerset, *B.T.C.*)

Beyond Gore Inn, on *l.*, Lynchfield and Sandhill Park. Before Hartrowgate, on *r.*, Willet Hill Tower. N. of the small old town of Williton is a field called Battlegore, the scene of a battle with the Danes. Watchet is situate at the mouth of a romantic valley. St. Decuman's *ch.* contains some old monuments. A little W. on the coast, an ancient entrenched camp, called Dart's Castle. On *r.*, just before Washford, the ruins of Cleeve Abbey, founded by the Cistercians, 1188.

Washford to Dunster (4—160½); in Washford turn to *l.*, and the road is fairly good and undulating through Bilbrook, 157½, and Carhampton, 159; at the bifurcation, ¾*m.* before Dunster, turn to *l.*

(*Dunster:* Luttrell Arms, *B.T.C.*)

Dunster, a quaint and pretty little town, was once on the sea shore, which has receded 1*m.* from it. S. is Dunster Park and Castle, of which the tower is Norman. Just beyond it, Conegar Tower and a Roman camp. There are remains of a Benedictine Priory, founded soon after the conquest. Large gothic *ch.*, dating from Henry VI.'s reign.

Dunster to Porlock (7½—168); in Dunster turn to *r.* by the *ch.*, and the road is undulating to Alcombe, 162, [or instead of turning to *l.* just before Dunster, the road straight on runs direct to Alcombe, 161½]; out of Alcombe keep to the *l.* and the road is mostly uphill through Perryton, 163½, on to Heyden Down, then downhill again through Holnicote, 166, to Brandy Street, 166½; beyond is another stiff ascent, and entering Porlock is a steep descent with a sharp turn in it. [Or beyond Alcombe take the right hand road to *Minehead*, 162¾—if not going through Dunster, the distance to Minehead is 162¼—and out of the town by the present coach-road is a steep ascent, after which it is mostly up and down hill, some of the gradients severe, by Bratton Court, Hinon, and through the pretty village of Selworthy, joining the other route at Holnicote, into which is a steep descent; distance about ¾*m.* longer; the surface is inclined to be rough.] Pretty scenery. 1½*m.* N. of Porlock is Porlock Weir in the bay.

(*Minehead:* Beach; Feathers, *B.T.C.*; Wellington.—*Porlock:* Rose and Crown; Ship.—*Porlock Weir:* Anchor Inn.)

Minehead is a small seaport; handsome *ch.* with curious monuments, &c.; good bathing. The railway only extends to Minehead. Above the town is an ancient camp, Bury Castle. In Porlock *ch.* are some beautiful alabaster effigies, &c.; large yew tree in the churchyard 4*m.* S. is Dunkerry Beacon, the highest point of Exmoor, from which 15 counties can be seen.

Porlock to Lynmouth (11½—179½); just beyond the "Ship" hotel take the left hand road; long steep and zigzag ascent leads out of Porlock, exceedingly rough and quite unrideable either up or *down*, followed by a more gradual ascent, in all 1½*m.* before the top of Porlock Hill is reached, whence there is a splendid view, then the road is up and down with moderate gradients along the ridges of Porlock and Oare Hills, part of Exmoor, and by Cosgate, 174½, and Wingate, 175½, to Countisbury, 177¾, where a long downhill begins, quite safe till about ½*m.* from Lynmouth, when it approaches the sea coast, and is very steep, being cut out of the face of the cliffs, with loose and rough surface, and should be walked down; some of the road is not at all good for bicycling, and it is frequently sandy and loose; beautiful scenery.

(*Lynmouth:* Bath; Lyndale.—*Lynton:* Crown, *B.T.C.*; Queen; Royal Castle; Valley of Rocks.)

Beyond Porlock, on the coast, Ashley Combe, the charming residence of Earl Lovelace; a little further, the romantic hamlet of Culbone with its small *ch.*; these can be reached on foot by a private road through Porlock Weir. About 3*m.* W. is Glenthorne *Ho.*, with its pleasure grounds. Beyond Cosgate, on *r.*, is an ancient British camp on old Barrow Hill; also a Roman camp near Countisbury. From Oare Hill, on *l.*, the pretty valley of the East Lyn *R.* runs parallel to the road; a turning before Cosgate leads down into it, and it is traversed by a good road down to Lynmouth, except one or two unrideable ascents and descents.

There are numerous walks and rides about Lynmouth; the chief objects of interest are Mount Sinai, Valley of Rocks, Watersmeet, The Torrs, Glen Lyn, West Lyn R., Guildhall, Ley Abbey, &c.

Lynmouth to Combe Martin (10¾—190); beyond Lynmouth turn sharp to r. to Lynton, 180, which lies on the slope of the opposite hill, and is approached by an exceedingly steep and zigzag ascent; then keeping to r. another steep hill rises out of Lynton, and an undulating road traverses the Valley of Rocks, and past Ley Abbey, 181¼, and through Slattenslade, 182½, to Martinhoe, 183¼, from which is a steep winding descent into the valley of Heddon's Mouth, followed by a steep hill winding up through a wood to Trentishoe, 184¾, thence the road becomes very hilly, stretching across the moorland for several miles, keeping to r. at the first fork, and ends with a long winding descent into Combe Martin, which should be ridden down carefully if without a good brake.

[There is another more inland road keeping to the l. out of Lynmouth, up a stiff ascent along the pretty valley of the West Lyn to Barbrook Mill, 180¾, where keep to r. and the road continues hilly, with a dangerous descent into Paracombe, 184, and a steep ascent out of it (keeping to r.), presently followed by a couple more descents and ascents alternated and joining the other road near the top of the second rise, 2 or 3m. further on; pretty good surface on the whole, but it should be ridden with caution; distance nearly the same.] On these roads much walking will be necessary.

(*Combe Martin :* King's Arms; Valley.)
Beautiful scenery. At Slattenslade, on r., Wooda Bay and Heddon's Mouth. Combe Martin is a long, straggling place, extending for 1½m. down a narrow valley to the sea shore. In the vicinity were formerly lead and silver mines, now worked out. Overlooking the little bay or cove is the Castle.

Combe Martin to Ilfracombe (5¾—195¾); beginning with a sharp steep ascent from Combe Martin Cove the road is all up and down through Berry Narbor, 192, and Hele, 194, with a long descent into Ilfracombe; pretty good surface.

[There is another route, but more devious, by going through Paracombe, 184, as above; then keeping to l. there is a steep hill to climb out of the village, very loose and stony (not safe to be ridden down), from the top of which it is a nice undulating road (turning to r. at Blackmoor *Tpg.*, 186½) to within 3m. of Ilfracombe, where join the Barnstaple road at Horedown Gate, and the remainder is downhill into the town; distance 2 or 3m. longer.]

(*Ilfracombe*, hotels—p. 77.)
At Berry Narbor, ancient *ch.*; at Hele, on r., on the coast, Helesborough, an ancient hill fort. Ilfracombe is the chief watering place on the North Devon coast, with a good harbour; fine old *ch.*; the chief objects of interest are Capstone Hill, Lantern Hill, Rapparee Cove, Watermouth Castle and Caves, Smallmouth Caves, Sampson's Caves at Rillage Point, Torrs Walks, Runnacleaves, Crewkhorn, &c.

LONDON TO ILFRACOMBE (by Bridgewater).

London to Castle Cary (111½)—p. 75.
Castle Cary to Piper's Inn (13¼—125); follow the Somerton road

to King Weston, as at p. 75; then turn to r., and up very stiff ascent on to Polden Hill, along the top of which the road runs past Marshes Elm, 121¾.

Piper's Inn to Bridgewater (10½—135½); taking the right hand road, from Piper's Inn there is a downhill to Ashcot, 126, whence ascend again on to Polden Hill, along which the road runs for several miles, then descends through Bawdrip, 132, to Crandon Bridge, 132½, where turn sharp to l. and cross Sedgemoor Cut, and the rest is level to Bridgewater; all a good road.

(*Bridgewater*: Reed's Arms: Royal Clarence, B.T.C.)

At Weston, 3 or 4m. E. of Bridgewater, was fought the battle of Sedgemoor.

At Bridgewater; the Castle, built by King John; the *ch.* has a fine altar-piece by Guido.

Bridgewater to Rydon (15½—151); nearly through the town turn to the r., and the road is chiefly uphill for 3m., when turn to r. with a descent to Cannington, 140; here turn to l. and it is more or less uphill through Ashford, 141, to Kinthorn, 142½, then descent with two or three turns in it to Nether Stowey, 144, and again a long uphill through Doddington, 145, on to the lower slopes of the Quantock Hills followed by a steep fall to Holford, 146½, which is continued in a more gradual decline to Putsham, 148, whence it is up and down hill to Rydon.

At Holford, on l., Alfoxton *Ho.* Beyond Cannington, on r., Brymore *Ho.*

At Doddington, 1m. on l., an old encampment, called Danesborough. Before Rydon, on l., St. Audries.

Rydon to Dunster (7¾—158¾); keep to r., up a short hill and longer steep descent to Donniford, 151¾, whence level to Watchet, 153; from here is a long stiff uphill along the coast with run down to Blue Anchor, 155½, and another short up and down just before Carhampton, 157¼, where join the Taunton road. [Or from Watchet take the valley road to Washford, 155, whence to *Dunster*, 159, as at p. 79. Or at Rydon take left hand road down to High Bridge, 152, thence undulating through Williton, 153, to *Washford*, 155.]

Dunster to Ilfracombe (35¼—194); through Alcombe, 159¾, Minehead, 161, *Porlock*, 166¼, *Lynmouth*, 177¾, Lynton, 178¼, Martinhoe, 181½, Trentishoe, 183, *Combe Martin*, 188¼, Berry Narbor, 190¼: or by Paracombe, 182¼; pp. 79-80.

LONDON TO TAUNTON (by Piper's Inn).

London to Piper's Inn (125)—p. 80.

Piper's Inn to Taunton (17½—142½); take the left hand road which crosses Sedgemoor; descent through Pedwell, 126, to Greinton, 127½, then level through King's Sedgemoor *Tp.*, 128, Blindman's Gate, 129¼, Othery, 130¾, Burrowbridge, 132 (cross *R.* Parrett), by King Alfred's Pillar, 133, East Lyng, 134, West Lyng, 135½, Durston, 137, Walford Bridge, 138½, and Bath Pool End, 140¾. On the reverse journey turn to l. 1¼m. out of Taunton, and to r. ¼m. beyond Walford Bridge; bad road for bicycling, first 10m. being little more than a grass grown cart track, and frequently very stony.

At Burrowbridge, on l., a large burrow or mound, on which are ruins of a chapel. At East Lyng, on r., the Isle of Athelney, the refuge of King Alfred, where he founded a Benedictine Abbey, not a vestige of which is left.

LONDON TO DULVERTON (by Bridgewater).

London to Bridgewater (135½)—p. 81.

Bridgewater to Willet (12½—148); long rise out of the town, turning to *l.* down a short pitch just before Durleigh, 137 (where turn to *r.*), and then it is nearly all uphill for 6*m.*, through Enmore, 139½, Water Pitts, 141½, and over Buncombe Hill and the Quantock Hills, followed by steep descent into West Bagborough, 144½, whence it is hilly to Willet.

At Enmore, on *r.*, Enmore Castle; 1*m.* on *l.*, Halswell *Ho.*

Willet to Dulverton (14½—162½); there are two or three long and steep ascents to encounter, mounting the slopes of the Brendon Hills to Raleigh's Cross, 152, whence it continues very hilly, but mostly downhill, through Holwelslade, 153½, and Woolcot, 156¾, to Hele Bridge, 160¾, where join the Wiveliscombe road. The whole of this road from Bridgewater is extremely hilly and rough, and a great deal of walking will be necessary.

LONDON TO ILFRACOMBE (by Glastonbury).

London to Amesbury (77½)—p. 69.

Amesbury to Maddington (5¾—83¼); follow the Long Barrow Cross road as at p. 69, to 79½*m.*, just before Stonehenge, where take the right hand road up a very stiff ascent, after which it is up and down hill.

Before Maddington, on *r.* are some ancient earthworks.

Maddington to Heytesbury (9—92¼); a little out of Maddington is a long uphill, followed by 2 or 3*m.* of fairly level, then there is a very steep hill to descend, with vile surface, to Chiltern, 88½, with a hill to mount out of it, and the rest hilly. On the reverse journey keep to *l.* just out of Heytesbury.

[There is another route by *Deptford Inn*, 86¾, whence, keeping to *r.*, through Fisherton-de-la-Mere, 87½, Codford St. Mary, 89¾, Upton Lovel, 91½, and Knook, 92½, to *Heytesbury*, 93, is a good road with easy hills in both directions.]

(*Heytesbury*: Angel; Red Lion.)

2*m.* beyond Chiltern, on *r.*, Knook Castle, an ancient encampment. At Codford, on *r.*, is an old entrenchment. Heytesbury *ch.*, ancient cruciform building. On *r.*, Heytesbury Park.

Heytesbury to Warminster (4—96¼); just beyond Heytesbury keep to *r.* and through Boreham, 94¾, is a capital undulating road

(*Warminster*: Anchor, *B.T.C.*; Bath Arms, *B.T.C.*; Bell and Railway; Pack Horse Inn.)

On *r.* pass 3 ancient camps, or hill forts, Battlesbury, Middlebury, and Scratchbury. Warminster is an ancient town, and the neighbourhood abounds in antiquities.

Warminster to Frome (7—103¼); level to Bugley, 97¼, from which is a good hill to mount over Cley Hill, then mostly downhill through Whitbourn, 99¼, and Corsley Heath, 100¼, and past the station. On the reverse journey keep to *r.* after passing the station.

(*Frome:* George, *B.T.C.*)

At Whitbourn, 1*m.* on *l.*, Longleat Park, the magnificent seat of the Marquis of Bath; near it, Boddenbury, an old entrenchment. Beautiful rocky scenery.

Frome to Shepton Mallet (12—115¼); in Frome beyond the *ch.*

turn to *l.*, and short steep ascent out of the town, then rather hilly, but nothing difficult, through Nunney, 106¾, Holwell, 107, Leighton, 109 (keep to *r.*), East Cranmore, 110¼, Dean, 111, and Doulting, 112¾; very steep descent, but with good surface, and safe with a good brake, into Shepton; good surface, and on the whole a capital run; beautiful scenery. [Or in Frome turn to *l.* before the *ch.*, and through Marston Bigot and Nunney Catch, joining the other road 1*m.* beyond Nunney.] In Shepton Mallet turn first to *l.* then to *r.*

(*Shepton Mallet:* Commercial; George; Hare and Hounds, *B.T.C.*)

At Nunney, the ruins of the castle. Shepton Mallet, on the line of the old Fosse Way, is very irregularly built, consisting of three parallel streets running N. and S., ⅓*m.* apart; it contains some fine buildings, and there is a curious old market cross, erected 1500. Before Marston Bigot, on *l.*, Marston *Ho.* At Doulting are large freestone quarries.

Shepton Mallet to Glastonbury (8½—123¾); leaving the former, keep to *l.*, and over Lambert's Hill, 116¼, descents into and out of Pilton, 117¾, and through West Pennard, 120¾, and Edgarley, 122¼.

(*Glastonbury:* Crown; George, *B.T.C.*; Red Lion.)

At Edgarly, on *r.*, St. Michael's tor or hill, on which are a tower and St. Michael's *ch.*, built circ. 1280. Beyond it are some British earthworks, and Ponter's Wall crosses the road. Glastonbury was long famous for its magnificent Abbey, now in ruins, stated by the old monkish chroniclers to have been founded by St. Patrick, circ. 440, on the site of the first Christian *ch.* in Britain; here are said to have been buried St. Patrick, Arthur and his Queen, Bede, and several Saxon kings. The district was called by the Romans the Island of Avalon. The earliest part of the Abbey now existing dates from 1186; the *ch.* of St. Peter and St. Paul was erected 1189—1303, now also in ruins. Other buildings are Abbot's Kitchen, Abbot's Barn, Pilgrim's Inn, The Tribunal, St. John the Baptist *ch.*, St. Benedict's *ch.*, Market Cross, &c.

Glastonbury to Piper's Inn (4¾—128½); downhill through Glastonbury, then rough and often heavy through Street, 125¾, (just before it keep to *r.*) and Walton, 127¼, to Piper's Inn at the cross roads, on the Polden Hills, up to which is a stiff ascent.

At Walton, on *r.*, Sharpham Park. S. of the Polden Hills is Sedgemoor.

Piper's Inn to Ilfracombe (69—197½)—p. 81.

LONDON TO BRUTON (by Heytesbury).

London to Heytesbury (92¼)—p. 82.

Heytesbury to Longbridge Deverill (3¾—96); ½*m.* out of Heytesbury keep to *l.*, and through Newham, 94.

Longbridge Deverill to Maiden Bradley (4—100).

At Maiden Bradley, on *l*, Bradley Park.

Maiden Bradley to Bruton (8—108); through Yarnfield *Tp.*, 102½ (keep to *r.*), and North Brewham, 105; rather hilly. On the reverse journey keep to *r.* ½*m.* beyond Yarnfield *Tp.*

LONDON TO WESTON-SUPER-MARE.

London to Frome (103¼)—p. 82.

Frome to Wells (17—120¼); past the *ch.* in Frome take the middle road, and 1¼m. further keep to l.; it is undulating through Whateley, 105¾, and Little Elm, 107½, (1m. beyond which keep to l.), then 2 or 3m. further it ascends the Mendip Hills, and after traversing the top of the ridge for 3 or 4m., it descends through East Horrington, 118½, to Wells.

[Or from Frome go to *Shepton Mallett*, 115¼, p. 82; out of which is a long descent, and then go along the valley through Dinder, 118½, and Dulcot, 119½, to *Wells*, 120¼; good road and pretty scenery.]

(*Wells:* Mitre; Star, B.T.C.; Swan.)

At Whateley, on r., Tedbury, an ancient entrenchment. At Little Elm, on r., Mells Park. On the Mendip Hills, on r., Maesbury Castle, or Masbury Ring, an ancient entrenchment. Wells is noted for its splendid cathedral, begun in Henry III.'s reign, containing many old monuments, and recently restored. Also Bishop's Palace, St. Cuthbert's ch. The environs are very picturesque.

Wells to Cheddar (7¾—128); through Wokey, 121¾, Easton, 123, Westbury, 124, Stoke Rodney, 125¼, and Draycott, 126¼; is a hilly road with rutty oolite surface.

(*Cheddar:* Cliff, B.T.C.; Lion Rock House.)

At Wokey, on r., Wokey Hole. At Cheddar, on r., the cliffs and stalactite caverns; pretty scenery. The ch. was built in the 15th century. The well-known Cheddar cheese derives its name from here.

Cheddar to Axbridge (2¼—130¼); oolite road.

(*Axbridge:* Lamb, B.T.C.)

Axbridge ch. contains some ancient monuments.

Axbridge to Banwell (5—135¼); beyond Axbridge turn to r., and there is an ascent to mount, the road crossing a spur of the Mendip Hills, on the other side of which is a downhill through Winscombe, 132¼, followed by a dangerous descent, best walked down into Banwell.

(*Banwell:* Bell, B.T.C.; Ship.)

At Winscombe, interesting old ch., built 1329. At Banwell, the castle; on r., an ancient camp; and 3m. E., another, Dolebury Camp. Banwell Cave.

Banwell to Weston-super-Mare (6—141¼); through Locking, 137¾, is an extremely bad road, rough and dangerous riding; no hills. Pretty scenery.

[There is another road by keeping to l. ¼m. before Locking, and instead of going through that village go through Hutton, 138, Oldmixton, 138¾, and Uphill, 139¼, to Weston-super-Mare, 141¾; rather undulating.

Or from *Axbridge* keep to l. and through Bleadon, 137½, where keep to r., and Uphill, 139¼, to *Weston-super-Mare*, 141¼; not so hilly, the only ones of any consequence being rise out of Bleadon, and short but sharp fall into Uphill.]

(*Weston-super-Mare:* Plough; Pier; Railway, B.T.C.; Royal; York, B.T.C.)

Weston is a fashionable watering-place, and a great resort for invalids, possessing a very bracing air, with fine sandy beach. Fine old ch. N. of town, on Worle Hill, is Worlebury, an ancient entrenchment; further on to r., Pass of St. Kew, ruins of Woodspringe Priory, Worle Castle, &c. At Uphill, on l., on Brean Down, is a powerful battery.

LONDON TO FROME (by Westbury).

London to Andover (63½)—p. 58.

Andover to Ludgershall (7¼—70¾); just out of Andover, at the railway station, keep to r. and through Weyhill, 66¼ (keep to r.), is a fair road, chiefly on the rise. On the reverse journey the last descent into Andover must be taken carefully.

At Ludgershall, ruins of the castle, erected soon after the Conquest; ancient market cross.

Ludgershall to Up Avon (9¼—80½); through East Everley, 75½, and West Everley, 76¾, the road is very hilly all the way, crossing over the Downs, with long steep fall into the Avon valley, at the bottom of which turn to *r.* ¾*m.* before Up Avon.

At East Everley, on *r.*, Everley *Ho.* Before Up Avon, 1*m.* on *l.*, Chisenbury Priory.

Up Avon to Connock or Coule (5¼—85¾); through Rushall, 81½, and Charlton is undulating and a pretty good road.

2*m.* W. of Up Avon, on Salisbury Plain, Casterly Camp, a large entrenchment; 2*m.* past Charlton, on *l.*, Broadbury Camp.

Connock to Market Lavington (4—89¾); keep to left and through Urchfont, 87¾, and Easterton, 88¾, is a similar kind of road.

At Rushall, on *r.*, Rushall Park. Market Lavington *ch.*, erected in the reign of Richard III, contains many curious monuments, &c.

Market Lavington to Tinhead (5—94¾); after Littleton Pannel, 90¾, long descent through Little Cheverel, 91¼, then rather hilly through Earl Stoke, 93½.

Beyond Market Lavington, on *l.*, Cleeve Hall. Before Earl Stoke, on *r.*, West Coulston *Ho.* and Earl Stoke Park.

Tinhead to Westbury (4—98¾); through Edington, 95½, and Bratton, 96¾, is rather hilly.

Beyond Bratton, on Bratton Down, on *l.*, a large entrenchment, called Bratton Castle. Near Westbury is a gigantic figure of a white horse, cut in the chalk on the side of a hill, and visible 20*m.* Westbury *ch.* was built in the 13th century.

Westbury to Frome (6¾—105½); at Westbury Leigh, 99¼, turn to *r.* and by Broomfield *Tp.*, 101¾, and Chapman's Lade, 102½. [At Broomfield *Tp.* on *r.* to *Beckington*, 3—104¾, or at the end of Westbury Leigh on *r.* to *Beckington*, 4—103½.)

Beyond Westbury Leigh, on *r.*, Chalcott *Ho.* 2*m.* before Frome, on *r.*, Berkeley *Ho.*

LONDON TO RADSTOCK.

London to Market Lavington (89¾)—above.

Market Lavington to Bulkington (6—95¾); in the former turn to *r.* and presently descend a long hill, then undulating through Cuckold's Green, 92¾ (turn to *l.*), and Worton, 93½, keeping to *l.* again about 2*m.* further. [Or through Littleton Pannel, 90¾, as at above, then turn to *r.* to *Bulkington*, 96½.]

Bulkington to Trowbridge (6—101¾); through Keevil, 97¾, beyond which is a stiff descent to Ashton Common, 99¾ (where turn to *r.*), and undulating through Hilperton, 100¾, with a long steepish hill through Trowbridge. On reverse journey at Hilperton turn to *r.*

[Or to *Tinhead*, 94¾, above; then turn to *r.* and stiff hill to mount to Steeple Ashton, 96, and downhill to Ashton Common, 99¾.]

(*Trowbridge:* George, *B.T.C.*; Woolpack.)

Trowbridge and Bradford are the chief broadcloth and kerseymere manufacturing towns in Wilts.

Trowbridge to Farleigh Hungerford (4—105¾); through Trowbridge, cross canal and railway to Studley, 102, then straight on, crossing R. Frome just before Farleigh, into which there is a short but very steep hill to climb (dangerous to ride down on account of a sharp turn at right angles.)

After crossing the railway beyond Trowbridge on r. to *Bradford-on-Avon*, (2—103¾), an undulating road. Or at Hilperton turn to r., cross Hilperton Marsh, Kennet and Avon Canal, railway and R. Avon, just beyond which keep to l. to *Bradford* (3½—104¼.)

At Farleigh, the ruins of Farleigh or Farley Castle. At Bradford the *ch.* is said to be Saxon.

Farleigh Hungerford to Radstock (6½—112¼); take the left hand road through Norton St. Philip, 107¼, Faulkland, 109¼ (1½m. further keep to l.), and Writhlington, 111½. [Or by the right hand road through Charterhouse Hinton, 107¾, and Wellow, 109¾, about 2½m. further turning to l. along the road from Bath to *Radstock*, 113½.]

(*Radstock:* Waldegrave, *B.T.C.*)

LONDON TO RADSTOCK (by Devizes).

London to Connock (85¾)—p. 85.

Connock to Devizes (5—90¾); take the right hand road ½m beyond Connock, and it is pretty good but rather hilly, chiefly downhill through Lide, 87¾, and Nursteed, 89¾; entering Devizes turn to l. Returning keep to l. ¼m. past Lide.

(*Devizes:* Bear; Castle, *B.T.C.*)

At Devizes there are slight remains of a castle erected in the reign of Henry I, and besieged and demolished by Cromwell. St. Mary's *ch.*, the chancel of which is Saxon; 1m. N. is New Park; on S., South Broom *Ho.* and Old Park *Ho.* 3m. N. is Roundaway Down, the scene of a Parliamentarian defeat. Oliver's castle, or camp.

Devizes to Trowbridge (9¾—100½); in Devizes turn to r. just before the railway, and when through the town cross the canal, then keeping to l. there is a long descent with another to Summerham or Seend Bridge, 93¼, whence by the left hand road is a hill to rise into Seend, 94¾, followed by another downhill out of it; the rest is an easy undulating road through Hilperton, 99½, with a long steepish hill through Trowbridge.

Trowbridge to Radstock (10½—111); through Farleigh Hungerford, 104½, Norton St. Philip, 106, Faulkland, 108, Charterhouse Hinton, 106½, and Wellow, 108½—above.

LONDON TO KINGSCLERE.

London to Basingstoke (45¼)—p. 47.

Basingstoke to Kingsclere (9¾—55); in Basingstoke turn to r., passing by the ruins of the Holy Ghost Chapel, and a little further, when clear of the town, keep to l. and up a long ascent on to Rooks Down, having crossed which, there is a long descent from Shothanger, 48¼, into Ramsdell, 49½, whence over West Heath to Stoning Heath or Baughurst Street, 52, then turn to l. and through Woolverton, 52½.

On r., Woolverton Park. Kingsclere was formerly a residence of the Saxon kings. 1m. beyond Ramsdell, on l., Ewhurst Park.

SECTION IV.

From Hyde Park Corner and Marble Arch;* Western Roads, (West Middlesex, Berkshire, North Wiltshire, North Somerset, South Buckingham, South Oxford, South Gloucester, Monmouth and South Wales).

LONDON TO ST. DAVID'S.

London (Hyde Park Corner) to Hounslow (9¾)—p. 46.

Hounslow to Colnbrook (7½—17¼); in Hounslow, keep to *r.* twice and the road is fairly level all the way; the macadam continues, but with very tolerable riding at the sides, over Cranford Bridge, 12¼, to Harlington Corner, 13, then it gradually gives way to gravel, and after Longford, 15¼, the surface becomes fairly good and smooth, but inclined to be dusty; the narrow street of Colnbrook is half paved with cobbles.

(*Colnbrook:* George; King's Head.)

Colnbrook to Slough (3¼—20½) is a good and almost level road, but in dry weather very loose and heavy.

At 18¾ m. on *l.*, through Datchet, 20½, where turn to *r.* cross R. Thames and through the Little Park to *Windsor*, (3¼—22); or from turn to *l*, cross R. Thames by Albert Bridge and turn to *r.* to *Windsor* (3¾—22¼); Windsor is paved.

At Slough on *l.* through Eton, 22, and across R. Thames to *Windsor*, (2¼—22¾).

(*Datchet:* Manor House; Royal Stag's Head.—*Windsor:* Castle; Datchet; Royal Adelaide; Royal Oak; Star and Garter; Three Tuns, *Hqrs.*; White Hart.—*Eton:* Bridge House; Christopher.—*Slough:* Dolphin; Eagle; Swan, *B.T.C.*; White Hart.)

At Eton, on *l.*, the celebrated college, founded by Henry VI. Before Datchet, on *r.* pass Ditton Park. At Windsor, the magnificent castle, founded by William the Conqueror; the state apartments are superbly fitted up, and there are many celebrated paintings, &c.; it is situate on a hill overlooking the Thames, and commands a view over a charming landscape. S. extends Windsor Great Park. 2 m. N. of Slough is Stoke Pogis, where the poet Gray is buried; also Stoke Place and Stoke Park.

Slough to Maidenhead (5½—26) is a gently undulating road, chiefly downhill, through Salt Hill, 21¼; good smooth surface, but inclined to be loose and sandy occasionally, with a bad and heavy bit just before Maidenhead Bridge, 25¼, where cross R. Thames; macadam through the town.

(*Maidenhead:* Bear; Bell; Cleare's; Cliveden, Queen St., *Hqrs.*; Lewis's; Queen's Arms; Ragmead; Railway; Saracen's Head; Thames; White Hart.)

2 or 3 m. on *r.*, Burnham Beeches, lately purchased for public recreation by

---

* From Hyde Park Corner to Marble Arch is a little over ¾ mile N., along Park Lane, a wood pavement.

the Corporation of London. At Maidenhead Bridge, on *r.*, Taplow *Ho.*, and 3*m.* N., Cliefden and Dropmore Lodge. 1m. S. of Maidenhead, the village of Bray, of "The Vicar of Bray" fame.

Maidenhead to Twyford (8—34); hill to mount out of the town, then first rate level road to Stubbings Heath or Maidenhead Thicket, 28 (where keep to *l.*), and the rest is rather hilly by Littlewick Green, 29½, Knowl Hill, 30½, Kiln Green, 31½, and Hare Hatch, 32; capital smooth and hard road. Pretty scenery.

Twyford to Reading (5—39) is undulating, chiefly on the rise for two-thirds of the distance, ending with a long gradual fall just before Reading; capital smooth road, but not quite so firm a surface as the preceding stage; macadam through the town, in which turn to *l.* into Minster street for the Bath road.

(*Reading*: Black Horse; George, *B.T.C.*; Great Western; New Albion; Queen's; Upper Ship; Wheatsheaf.)

2*m.* past Twyford, on *r.*, Holme Park. At Reading are remains of a Benedictine Abbey, built 1121. St. Mary's, St. Lawrence, and the old Greyfriars are the most interesting churches. Here is the large biscuit manufactory of Huntley and Palmer. On *r.*, across R. Thames, Caversham Park.

Reading to Jack's Booth (6½—45½); level, but not so smooth for a mile or two out of Reading, then at Calcot Green, 41½, a sharp descent occurs, after which it is a dead level road through Theale, 43½, with capital smooth surface, but inclined to be sandy in very dry weather and heavy when wet.

On *r.* pass Prospect Hill and Calcot Park. Past Theale, on *r.*, Englefield *Ho.* and Beenham *Ho.* 1½m. on *l.*, Sulhampstead *Ho.*

Jack's Booth to Newbury or Speenhamland (10¾—56); the road continues level through Woolhampton, 49¼, to Thatcham, 53, whence it is somewhat undulating to near Newbury; inclined to be sandy for the first few miles, but the greater part is a capital smooth road on which a good pace can be kept up. Newbury proper lies just on the south of the road, the town here being called Speenhamland.

(*Newbury*: Chequers; Jack; Queen's, *B.T.C.*; Sun; White Hart.)

The scenery on this road from Reading is very monotonous; the road runs along the Kennet Valley the whole distance, and the prospect is confined by a range of hills on each side. Past Woolhampton, on *r.*, Midgham *Ho.* Entering Speenhamland on *r.*, Shaw *Ho.*, the headquarters of Charles I. before the last battle of Newbury. Through the town, on *r.*, the ruins of Donnington Castle, the residence of Chaucer.

Newbury to Hungerford (8½—64½); short ascent up Speen Hill to Speen, 57, followed by another and much stiffer pull, then level for some distance, and a steep but not long fall occurs near Halfway House, 60, after which is some more hilly riding, but nothing difficult, for 2 or 3*m.*; tolerably good road but rather loose in places.

(*Hungerford*: Black Bear; Red Lion; Three Swans, *B.T.C.*)

Speen occupies the site of the Roman Station, Spinæ; 1m. past, on *l.*, Benham Place. Beyond Halfway *Ho.*, on *r.*, Elcot Park, and further, on *l.*, Barton Court. Hungerford town lies on the *l.* of the main road; here are the headquarters of the Craven Hunt; ancient *ch.*

Hungerford to Marlborough (10—74½); very stiff ascent out of Hungerford, and up and down hill work to Froxfield, 67½, whence begins the long but easy ascent past and through the remnant of Savernake Forest; passing Cross Ford, 69, the road very gradually winds up a narrow valley for nearly 4m.—part of the way under a fine avenue of trees—when the Forest proper is reached, 71¾; in the next 1½m. there are three rather stiff pulls to the top of the range of hills, then begins a long steep descent, generally rather rough, and a little twisting at first, which should be ridden carefully if without a strong brake; then after a level run to Marlborough, another sharp pitch has to be mounted into the main street; good smooth surface. [Or an easier road is to turn to r. in Hungerford and follow the left (N) bank of the *R.* Kennet, through the villages of Chilton Foliat, 66, Ramsbury, 69, Axford, and Mildenhall, about 2m. longer.]

At Cross Ford on *l.* to *Great Bedwin* (3—72).

(*Marlborough*: Ailesbury Arms, *B.T.C.*; Castle and Ball; Savernake Forest.)

At Savernake Forest, on *l.*, Savernake Lodge. Past Ramsbury, on *l.*, Ramsbury Manor *Ho.* At Chilton on *l.*, Littlecot Park. Marlborough contains some old-fashioned houses, and in the main thoroughfare is a unique piazza, or colonnade, forming a pleasant promenade. The College, formerly the Castle Inn, occupies the site of the old castle. St. Mary's *ch.* has a Norman doorway. At Great Bedwin is an ancient *ch.*

Marlborough to Beckhampton Inn (6¾—81¼); at the end of the main street of the town turn to *r.* up a short rise, and it is a capital but rather hilly road through Fyfield, 77, Overton, 78½, West Kennet, 79¼, and past Silbury Hill, 80½; there are a couple of stiff pulls after Fyfield, and past Silbury Hill is a good descent which should be ridden with care, as a turn in it prevents seeing to the bottom.

Beyond Marlborough, on *l.*, the figure of a white horse is seen on the hill side. At Fyfield, on *r.*, a cromlech, called the Devil's Den; the remarkable tumulus of Silbury Hill is supposed to be a British barrow. From West Kennet, and also from Beckhampton Inn, 1¼m. on *r.*, (over a rather hilly road) at the village of Avebury, are the remains of a large Druidical temple, surrounded by a high rampart; also 1m. N., a large cromlech. Past Silbury Hill leave the line of the old Roman road which runs in a direct line to Bath on *l.*

Beckhampton Inn to Calne (5¾—87); keeping to the *r.* it is a good undulating road across the Downs and through Cherhill, 84½, into which there is a long descent.

(*Calne*: Lansdowne Arms, *B.T.C.*; White Hart.)

Just before Cherhill, on *l.*, an ancient hill fort, called Oldbury Camp, or Oldborough Castle, on the slope of which is cut the figure of a white horse. Calne was a residence of the Saxon Kings; ancient *ch.* with fine carved roof. 2m. S. of the town, on the old Roman road to Bath, is the supposed site of the Roman station, Verlucio. Before Calne, on *l.*, Blackland *Ho.*

Calne to Chippenham (6½—93½); through Calne turn to *l.*, and after crossing the Wilts and Berks canal 2m. out, there is a short but stiff hill (Burk Hill) to mount, and shortly after one to descend at Derry Hill, 91, otherwise pretty level; macadam and rather shaky. On the reverse journey keep to *l.* at Derry Hill.

(*Chippenham*: Angel, *B.T.C.*; Commercial; Great Western; Lansdowne Arms.)

Past Calne, on *l.*, Bowood Park (Marquis of Lansdowne); on *r.*, Stanley Abbey. Chippenham was a seat of the Wessex Kings; ancient Gothic parish *ch.*; the town mainly consists of a street nearly a mile in length.

Chippenham to Bath (12½—106); at the end of Chippenham, after crossing *R.* Avon, keep to *l.*, and the road is rather uphill through Pickwick, 97½ (at 96¾m. keep to middle road and to r. ½m. beyond Pickwick), and after a slight rise descend Box Hill, 98¾, which is not steep, to Box, 100¼, and the rest is almost level through Bathford Tg., 103, and Batheaston, 104, with an ascent into Bath; the macadam continues most of the way, and for the last 2 or 3m. the road is made of oolite, very greasy in wet weather. On the reverse journey keep to r. outside Bath, again at and beyond Batheaston, and ½m. before the railway at Bathford Tg., take the left hand road; 1½m. E. of Box keep to r. and entering Pickwick to l. [Or ½m. before Pickwick take right hand fork, rejoining the other road 1¼m. beyond it and going through Hills Green, 98.]

At 96¾m. on l. to Corsham (¾—97½).

(*Bath :* Angel; Christopher; Castle; Fisher's Restaurant; Full Moon; Grand Pump Room; London Dining Rooms; Railway, Charles street; Railway, Railway place; Royal; Saracen's Head; Stead's; White Lion, *Hqrs.*, *B.T.C.*; York *Ho.*)

Magnificent view from Box Hill. Bath, the most elegant city in England, is noted for the beauty of its buildings. The Romans had a station and baths here. The chief buildings are, the Abbey ch., founded 1495, King's Baths, Pump Room, Assembly Rooms, Guildhall, Circus, &c. Bath is still regarded as the chief of our inland watering-places. At Corsham. on l., Corsham *Ho.* At Pickwick, ½m. on r., Hartham *Ho.*

Bath to Keynsham (8½—114½); leaving Bath by the lower Bristol road, down Southgate street, cross R. Avon and turn to r.; good but hilly road through Twerton, 108¾, and Newton St. Loe, 110, for 5 or 6m., when there is a rather steep and very rutty hill to mount (rather dangerous to descend on the reverse way), after which the road becomes rough. On the reverse journey 1m. past Newton St. Loe turn to l.

(*Keynsham :* Lamb and Lark, *B.T.C.*)

At Twerton, on l., Englishcombe Barrow and Camp. At Newton St. Loe, on l., Newton Park, and beyond it, Stantonbury Hill Camp, an ancient entrenchment.

Keynsham to Bristol (5¼—119¾); a rather rough but fairly level road through Brislington, 117¼, entering Bristol by Redcliff Bridge: Bristol is hilly and roughly paved, with tramway through the city.

[There is another route from *Bath* by keeping to the right bank of the R. Avon, through Kelston, 109½, Bitton, 111¾, over Wills Bridge, 113½, and through Henton, 114¼, West Hanham, 115¼, and St. George, 116½, to *Bristol*, 118½. On the reverse journey keep to r. at St. George.]

(*Bristol :* Bank; Cathedral; Clifton Down; Draw Bridge; Guildhall; Hope and Anchor; Nicholas Temperance, *Hqrs.*; Royal; Royal Talbot, *B.T.C.*; Three Lamps; Victoria.)

At Kelston, on l., Kelston *Ho.* Bristol is the chief seaport and capital of the West; the streets are often narrow and ill constructed, but there are numerous imposing buildings; the chief objects of interest are the Cathedral, Mayor's Chapel, Abbey Gateway and Civic Cross, St. Mary ch. (Redcliffe), Colston Hall, Academy, and St. James' ch., founded 1130. From Brandon Hill a fine view of the city is to be had. At Clifton, the western suburb of Bristol, are St. Vincent's Rocks, Suspension Bridge, Observatory, Zoological Gardens; and on Clifton Downs, Cook's Folly Tower. The scenery about here is very fine; in the vicinity are Ashton Court, Leigh Court, Leigh Woods, and Nightingale Valley, with the old Camps of Abbot's Leigh and Borough, or Bower Walls. 2m. N. is Stoke Park.

Bristol to New Passage (10½—130¼); leave Bristol by Queen's Road and White Ladies' Road, then (keeping to r.) across Clifton Downs and there is a long hill to walk down into Westbury-on-Trym, 123½, after which it is level through Compton Greenfield, 126¾ (2½m. further keeping to l.); very greasy and slippery as far as Westbury, where the road improves and is wide and smooth to New Passage.

(*Westbury :* White Lion.)

Beyond Bristol, on l., Stoke Giffard Park; further, on r., Henley *Ho.* Beyond Westbury, on l., Henbury Park and Blaize Castle, on r., Pen Park and Pen Park *Ho.* Before Compton, on l., Holly Hill. Pretty scenery.

New Passage to Black Rock Inn (3—133¼); cross *R.* Severn by ferry; about 15 minutes steaming. [Or take train to Portskewit by Severn tunnel; fare 4d., bicycle 6d.]

Black Rock Inn to Crick (2½—135¾); just beyond the railway keep to l. and at Portskewit, 134¼, to r.

Near Portskewit are the remains of a Roman camp, and a little beyond, the ruins of Caldecot Castle.

Crick to Newport (12—147¾); turn to l., and except a steep ascent beyond Caerwent, 137¼ (keep to l.), the road is undulating by Five Lanes, 138¼, Rock and Fountain, 139¼, Penhow, 140¾, Unicorn, 141¼, Hendrew, 142, (¾m. further keep to l.) and Christchurch, 145¼, crossing *R.* Usk just before Newport.

Beyond Hendrew ¾m., on r. to *Caerleon* (1½—144¼); or at Christchurch on r. (1½—146¾).

(*Newport :* King's Head; Westgate.)

At Penhow, on l., the ruins of the castle; 2m. S., Pencoed Castle; beyond Hendrew, 1m. on l., Llanwern *Ho.* At Caerwent are some Roman remains. Caerleon was an important town in the Roman period, and even now has some considerable remains. In the neighbourhood are many Roman encampments. 2m. N.W., in Llantarnam Park, the remains of the Abbey. On the Newport road are remains of St. Julian's Abbey. At Newport, the Castle and Malpas *ch.*

Newport to Cardiff (12½—160¼); in Newport keep first to l. and then to r., and by Tredegar House, 150½, Halfway House, 153½, through St. Mellons, 155½, over Rumney Bridge, 157, and through Roath, 158¾, is not so hilly and is a good macadam road. [Or in Newport take first to r. after railway, then to l., and again to l. at Bassaleg, 150¾, joining the other road at St. Mellons, 155¼.]

(*Cardiff :* Cardiff Arms; Imperial; Queen's, *B.T.C.*; Royal.)

At St. Mellons is a small encampment. At Bassaleg, on r., Rogerston Castle. At Cardiff, remains of the Norman castle, in which Duke Robert was confined 26 years. Cardiff lies on l. of the road, it is chiefly the seaport of the Merthyr Tydvil coal and iron district. 2m. on r., at Landaff, the ruins of the Abbey or Cathedral and Palace.

Cardiff to Cowbridge (12½—172¾); soon after leaving Cardiff cross *R.* Taff, then a hill has to be climbed, more than a mile long and rather too steep to be ridden, and followed by a steep fall to Ely Bridge, 162¾; after that it is a good but hilly road through St. Nicholas, 166¼, Bonvilston or Tresimon, 168¼, and over Staton Down, 170¼; fine scenery.

At Cowbridge on l. through St. Athan's, 176¾, to *Gileston*, 177¼.

(*Cowbridge :* Bear, *B.T.C.*; Duke of Wellington.)

At St. Nicholas, on l., Duffryn *Ho.*, near which are several large cromlechs; 1m. further S., Wenvoe Castle. At Bonvilston, on r., Cottrell, on l., Llantrithyd Park. At Cowbridge, a Gothic built gate, part of the old wall still remains

Singular embattled *ch.*, near which are remains of a Druidical temple. Llanbethian Castle and Penlline Castle. South Glamorganshire abounds in old castles and castellated mansions, &c.

Cowbridge to Ewenny Bridge (6½—179), is a fair undulating road through Corntown, 178. Past Ewenny on the reverse journey keep to *l.*

At Ewenny Bridge, on *r.*, the Priory; 4m. on *l.*, on the coast, Dunraven Castle.

Ewenny Bridge to Aberavon (13—192); by the left hand road over Newbridge, 181, by Pyle Inn, 185½, Margam Park, 187¼, and through Taibach, 191, is a good road for Wales. On the reverse journey keep to *r.* ¾m. before Newbridge. [Or keep to *r.* from Ewenny Bridge, and through Bridgend, 181, and Lalestone, joining the other road ¼m. past Newbridge; 1¼m. longer.]

At Newbridge, on *l.*, ruins of Ogmore Castle. At Bridgend, the ruins of Coity Castle. At Margam, old Saxon *ch.*, Abbey ruins, Margam Park, Roman camp, &c. At Aberavon, large copper works.

Aberavon to Neath (6—198); through Briton Ferry, 195, is a similar kind of road.

(*Neath :* Castle.)

Near Briton Ferry, on *r.*, Baglan Hall. Neath is a small seaport with iron and copper works; here are ruins of castle and Cistercian monastery; Gno'l Castle.

Neath to Swansea (8½—206½); after crossing R. Neath, turn to *l.*, and over Morriston Bridge, 203½, (turn to *l.*) is not quite so good and more hilly, but nothing a bicyclist need fear; it is rather bumpy owing to so much local traffic.

(*Swansea:* Bush; Cameron Arms; Castle; George; Mackworth Arms; Royal, B.T.C.; Temperance.)

Past Morriston Bridge, on *r.*, Morris Castle. Swansea is one of the chief seaports in South Wales, and has extensive docks; north is a large coal and iron, &c. district. St. Mary's *ch.*, and St. John's *ch.* Swansea Castle, erected 1099. Beyond are Woodland Castle, Oystermouth Castle ruins, King Arthur's Stone, &c.

Swansea to Llanelly (10½—217); at the entrance of Swansea turn to *r.*, and about 2½m. out to *l.*; it is nearly all up and down as far as Loughor or Llwchyr Ferry, 212½, with hills averaging ¾m. long, but a good rider can mount them; the remainder is easier: the surface is something between macadam and paved, and does not suit a light machine. Returning 2m. out of Llanelly, keep to *r.*

At Loughor, ruins of the castle; near it is an immense cromlech, Arthur's Stone.

Llanelly to Kidwelly (9—226); in Llanelly turn to *l.*; good macadam road, running close by the coast, with a few ups and downs to Pembrey, 222, entering which village is a short steep fall, where the rider should be careful; the other 4m. are quite level, except a short rise followed by a descent into the old town at Kidwelly; rather heavy going. [Or by the main road is 1m. shorter; keep through Llanelly bearing to the *r.*, then turn to *l.* at the railway; it is half up hill and half down, passing over Mynydd Pembrey.]

At Kidwelly, the remains of the castle, founded 1094.

Kidwelly to Carmarthen (Ivy Bush, 9—235); through Llandefeilog, 229½; there are some rather steep ups and downs, including one stiff hill a mile long, the first half of which can be ridden by a good rider; good surface all the way.

[There is a shorter route from *Neath* over Morriston Bridge, 203½ (keep straight on), through Llangervelach, 205½, Cross Inon, 207½, Pontardulais, 211 (turn to *r.* and 1½*m.* further keep to *l.*), Gibranlwy, 212¾, Brymind, 213½, *Llannon*, 216 (shortly after keep to *l.*), Pont-y-berem, 219½, and Llangendrian or Llangyndeyrn, 223½, to *Carmarthen*, 228¾; this is the old mail-coach road, but there are two or three long hills to walk up and down.

Or from *Llanelly* by Morning Star, 221, Pont Yates, 223½, Maingeeu, 225, and Pont Anton, 227, joining the last road nearly 3*m.* further, to *Carmarthen*, 232.

Or from *Swansea*, 2½*m.* beyond keeping to *r.*, through Cadley, 210, to Cross Inon, 211½, whence to *Carmarthen*, 21¼—232¾, as above.]

(*Carmarthen :* Boar's Head, *B.T.C.*)

From Kidwelly, 4*m.* before Carmarthen, on *l.*, Towy Castle, on *r.*, Parr's Castle. At Carmarthen was born the bard Merlin. 2*m.* off are Merlin's Hill and chair. The remains of the castle are now used as a gaol.

Carmarthen to St. Clears or St. Clare's Bridge (Blue Boar, 9½—241½); in Carmarthen keep to *l.*, and by Stony Bridge, 236½, and Banc-y-fetin, 241, is an undulating road, all rideable.

At St. Clears on *l.* to *Laugharne* (3—247½.)

Past Stony Bridge, on *r.*, Castle-y-Gaer, an old entrenchment. Laugharne, at the mouth of the *R.* Taff, the ruins of the castle. 1*m.* distant, Roche Castle and Llanstephan Castle.

St. Clears to Canaston Bridge (13½—258); take the right hand road through Bethlem, 245½, Pont-y-Fenny, 247½, Whitland, 249½, and Robeston Wathen, 257; it is a continuation of long ups and downs, some of them almost too steep to be ridden up, but can be descended with safety by a careful rider; steep descent for ½*m.* to Canaston Bridge, hardly rideable the reverse way; good surface. On returning, keep to *l.* from Canaston Bridge and also at Robeston Wathen. [Or at St. Clears take the left hand road through *Llandowror*, 246½, where keep to *r.*, over Brandy Hill, 249, by Tavernspite, 251½, Princes Gate, 254½, whence either by *r.* straight to Narberth, or by *l.* through *Cold Blow*, 255½, and Narberth, 257¼, to *Robeston Wathen*, 259.]

(*Narberth :* Angel; Court House; De Rutzen.)

At Whitland, on *r.*, ruins of the Abbey. At Canaston Bridge, on *r.*, Ridgway *Ho.*, and beyond it, ruins of Llawhadden Castle. At Narberth are the remains of a castle.

Canaston Bridge to Haverfordwest (8—266); just beyond Canaston Bridge is a steep, rough climb of about a mile, which requires care in descending; from the top a good level road extends past Mid-County House, 260¾, with another stiff descent of nearly ½*m.* to Deeplake Bridge, 263, and the rest is good easy running to within ½*m.* of Haverfordwest, where a steep descent, Scurry Hill, has to be negotiated.

(*Haverfordwest :* Castle; Marine; Salutation.)

At Midcounty *Ho.*, 1*m.* on *l.*, Picton Castle and Rose Castle; on *r.* ruins of Wiston Castle. Haverfordwest is a small seaport town; there are remains of an ancient castle, now the gaol.

Haverfordwest to St. David's (15¾—281¾); through the town keep to *r.*, and by Pelcomb Bridge, 267½, Keeston Bridge, 269¼, over Keeston

Hill, through Roche, 272½, by Newgate Sands, 274, and Solva, 279; it consists throughout of steep unrideable ascents and descents, the surface being loose and dangerous.

(*St. David's* : Georgo; Prospect.)

At Roche are the ruins of an old castle. St. David's was formerly for 600 years a Metropolitan see, having been founded, it is said, by King Arthur. The cathedral is a venerable Gothic built structure; there are ruins of the Bishop's Palace, also of St. Stephen's Chapel and the Nuns' Chapel, and remains of a camp.

LONDON TO READING (by Wokingham).

London to Virginia Water (21)—p. 46.

Virginia Water to Wokingham or Oakingham (10¾—31¾); turning to the *r.* it is a pretty undulating road for about 3*m.*, skirting the south side of Windsor Park, with a stiff hill to mount at Sunninghill, 24, then a mile level past Ascot race ground, followed by a long downhill, and the road continues hilly for a mile beyond Bracknell, 28, after which it is pretty level into Wokingham: good gravel road but sometimes loose and sandy in dry weather, especially alongside the park.

At Sunninghill, on *r.*, Sillwood Park: 2*m.* S. of Bracknell is Easthampstead Park.

Wokingham to Reading (7—38¼); very good easy road through King Street, 33¾, and over Loddon Bridge, 35½, except a long hill to mount just before Reading, followed by a good downhill into the town.

At Loddon Bridge, on *l.*, Maiden Early; a little further, White Knights.

LONDON TO READING (by Winkfield).

London to Egham (18)—p. 46.

Egham to Winkfield (7½—25½); at the foot of Egham Hill turn to *r.*, and through Englefield Green, 19½; it is chiefly on the rise to Bishop's Gate, 20¼, where enter Windsor Great Park; then taking the right hand fork, across the park (2*m.*) by the end of the Long Walk, 21, through Cranbourn Wood, 22¼, just beyond which at 23½*m.* turn to *r.* at the forks, (the road straight on to *l.* is to *Wokingham*, 32½), and over Lovell Hill, 24½, is up and down hill; through the park the road is sometimes heavy, otherwise good. 1*m.* before Winkfield on *r.* to Windsor 5*m.* On the reverse journey, just inside the park, keep to *r.*; on *l.* to Windsor, 3*m.*

Within Windsor Park, on *l.*, Cumberland Lodge and the cottage. Out of Egham, on *r.*, Egham Park, Kingswood Lodge, &c. At the end of the park, on *r.* Cranbourn Lodge; 1½*m.* beyond it, near the Windsor road, St. Leonards Hill *Ho.*, on the site of a Roman Camp. Before Winkfield, on *l.*, Ascot Place.

Winkfield to Binfield Bridge (3½—29); stiff rise to Maiden Green, 26, (turn to *l.*) then short fall and another rise to Haley or Holly Green, 27, and undulating by Newell Green, 27¾, Bol Bridge, 28, and Cabbage Hill: very good road. [Or at Lovell Hill on *l.*, along Hatchet Lane and Winkfield Row to Newell Green; not quite so hilly; ½*m.* shorter.]

Binfield Bridge to Reading (9½—38½); long stiff hill to mount beyond Binfield Bridge, then undulating by Tippen's Hill, 30½, and Bill Hill, 31¾, joining the Wokingham road, 1¼*m.* further on: very good surface. Returning, take second left hand turn past "Pheasant" public-house.

LONDON TO KINGSCLERE (by Reading).

London to Jack's Booth (45¼)—p. 88.

Jack's Booth to Kingsclere (10¼—55½); follow the Bath road for 2½m. further, then keep to *l*. and through Aldermaston, 49½, a little further turn to *r*., through Wasing, 51½, over Ashford common, and by Fair Oak, 53½.

At Aldermaston, on *l*., Aldermaston Park: at Wasing, on *l*., Wasing Ho. About 4m. E. of Aldermaston, at Silchester, the remains of the Romano-British city of Calleva, destroyed in the 6th century; the wall is still standing, 12 to 30 ft. high; also the amphitheatre.

LONDON TO RADSTOCK (by Marlborough).

London to Beckhampton Inn (81¼)—p. 89.

Beckhampton Inn to Devizes (7½—88¾) by the left hand fork is a capital road and level for most of the way.

On *r*. pass close by Roundaway Down, where the Parliamentarians were defeated in the civil war; Oliver's Camp and Beacon Down. Before, at 84¼m., cross Wans Dyke, an ancient entrenchment running across the Downs for 7 or 8m.

Devizes to Radstock (20¼—109); through *Trowbridge*, 98½—p. 86.

LONDON TO BATH (by Devizes).

London to Trowbridge (98½)—above.

Trowbridge to Bradford-on-Avon (2—100½)—p. 86.

Bradford-on-Avon to Stoke Viaduct (4—104½); keep along the edge of the Avon valley through Winsley, 101½, and going down a long hill, cross *R*. Avon by Stoke Bridge to Limpley Stoke, 104, where turn to *r*. to Stoke Viaduct at the junction of the new road from Beckington. [Or through Trowbridge cross railway, turn to *r*., and ½m. further to *l*., and through Westwood-with-Ilford and Freshford, to Limpley Stoke.]

At Freshford, on *l*., Hinton Abbey.

Stoke Viaduct to Bath (4¼—108¾); at the sign-post at the foot of Stoke Hill the road to the *r*. should be taken through Claverton, 105¾, and Bathampton, following the left bank of *R*. Avon; it is undulating, with a descent into Bath that requires care; this is much the easier road. [The other road on *l*. through Widcombe, 106½, is 1½m. shorter, but a steep ascent has to be negotiated, and a long, very steep descent to be walked down into Bath, 107¾. Coming from Bath bear to *l*. after crossing *R*. Avon and railway.] Oolite surface.

[Or in Bradford turn to *r*., and shortly after keep to *l*., and by Farleywick, 103½, and through Bathford, 105¾, and Bathford *Tg*., 106, where join the Chippenham road, and to *Bath*, 109—p. 90. It is not so pretty as the other road. From Farleywick the road runs close to *R*. Avon on *l*. Returning keep always to *r*.]

Pretty scenery. In the Avon valley the road, canal, railway, and river run parallel all the way to Bath. Before Widcombe, on *l*., Prior Park. Bath, p. 90.

LONDON TO BATH (by Melksham).

London to Devizes ($88\frac{3}{4}$)—p. 95.

Devizes to Melksham ($7\frac{1}{4}$—96); follow the Trowbridge road as at p. 86, to Summerham or Seend Bridge, $91\frac{3}{4}$, where keep to *r.*, and the road is nearly level, and very good to Melksham, through which is a descent. [Or beyond Devizes keep to *r.* and through Rowde and Selves Green, joining the other road further on.]

(Melksham : King's Arms, *B.T.C.)*

Melksham to Bathford (8—104); good road, past the railway station, through Shaw, $97\frac{3}{4}$, over Shaw Hill, 98, through Atford, $99\frac{1}{2}$, by Horse and Jockey, 101, and Kingsdown Hill, 103. [Or in Melksham, after crossing *R.* Avon, turn to *l.*, shortly after to *r.*, and through Wroxall to Kingsdown Hill.]

Bathford to Bath ($3\frac{1}{4}$—$107\frac{1}{4}$)—p. 90.

LONDON TO WESTON-SUPER-MARE (by Bath).

London to Bath (106)—p. 89.

Bath to Marksbury ($6\frac{3}{4}$—$112\frac{3}{4}$); follow the Keynsham road, as at p. 90, to Newton St. Loe, 110, just beyond which turn to *l.* and through Corston, $110\frac{3}{4}$, keeping to *l.* 1m. before Marksbury.

Before Marksbury, on *l.*, Stantonbury Hill Camp.

Marksbury to West Harptree ($9\frac{1}{2}$—$122\frac{1}{4}$); keep to *r.* through Chelwood, $116\frac{1}{4}$, Stanton Wick, $117\frac{3}{4}$, Knighton Sutton, $118\frac{3}{4}$, and Stowey, $119\frac{1}{4}$.

At Chelwood, on *r.*, Houndstreet Park : at Stowey, on *r.*, Sutton Court, on *l.*, Stoway *Ho.* At Stanton Drew, 1m. on *r.* of Stanton Wick is a large Druidical temple.

West Harptree to Churchill (8—$130\frac{1}{4}$) ; take the right hand road, running under the north side of the Mendip Hills, through Compton Martin, $123\frac{1}{4}$, Ubley, $124\frac{1}{4}$, Blagdon, 126, and Burrington, $127\frac{1}{2}$.

At Churchill, on Mendip Hills, Dolebury Camp.

Churchill to Banwell (3—$133\frac{1}{4}$) ; at the entrance of the former take the middle road through Sandford, $131\frac{3}{4}$; or keep through Churchill, then to *l.* and through Sandford Hill, 132.

Banwell to Weston-super-Mare (6—$139\frac{1}{4}$)—p. 84.

LONDON TO WESTON-SUPER-MARE
(by Marshfield and Bristol).

London to Chippenham ($93\frac{1}{2}$)—p. 89.

Chippenham to Marshfield ($9\frac{1}{2}$—103); keep straight on through Chippenham to the railway station, then to *l.* under the railway; $2\frac{1}{2}$m. further keep to *l.*, and at Ford Mill, 99, to the *r.* and through Wraxall, $100\frac{1}{2}$; it is a macadam road, but on the whole tolerable.

At Ford Mill, 2m. on *r.*, Castle Combe *Ho.* ; $\frac{1}{2}$m. beyond Wraxall cross the Fosse Way. S. of Marshfield are some Druidical stones.

Marshfield to Bristol (11—114); by Tog Hill, 106, Wick, 107¼, Warmley, 109¼, Kingswood Hill, 110¼, and St. George, 112, is a poor macadam road, inclined to be rutty in places. Returning, at St. George keep to *l*.

Wick is situate on a small stream that runs down the Golden Valley to the R. Avon; S. are some Druidical stones, and near the R. Avon is a Roman camp.

Bristol to Brockley (9½—123½); in Bristol turn to *l.* along Victoria street to the Keynsham road, crossing the R. Avon, by Redcliff Bridge, then turn to *r.* along Redcliff Crescent, and to *l.* through Bedminster, 115 (where keep to *r.*), Long Ashton, 117, Flax Bourton, 120, and Backwell West Town, 122. [Or from Redcliff Crescent continue along the riverside through Coronation road to beyond the railway, when turn to *l.* for Long Ashton.]

Before Long Ashton, on *r.*, Ashton Court. At Bourton, on *r.*, Bourton *Ho.*, on *l.*, Barrow Court. At Brockley, 5m. on *r.*, on Severn Channel, Clevedon Court, Walton Castle, and Cadbury Camp.

Brockley to Weston-super-Mare (10—133½); very rough road through Congresbury, 126 (turn to *r.*), Puxton, 128, Banwell Station, 130½, and Worle, 131½; after Congresbury it is but a lane.

LONDON TO ST. DAVID'S (by Marshfield).

London to Bristol (114)—above.

Bristol to St. David's (162—276)—pp. 90-94; the distance to Bristol by this route is 5¼m. shorter than through Bath.

LONDON TO ST. DAVID'S (by Aust).

London to Chippenham (93½)—p. 89.

Chippenham to Nettleton (8½—102); keep straight on through Chippenham to the railway station, then to *l.* under the railway; 2½m. further on turn to *r.*, and gentle rise to Yatton Keynell, 97½, and then hilly with sharp ups and downs through Upper Castlecombe, 99; surface inclined to be rough and rutty.

On *l.*, Castle Combe *Ho.* Beyond Chippenham, on *r.*, Hardenhuish *Ho.* Beyond Upper Castle Combe cross Fosse Way.

Nettleton to Chipping Sodbury (6—108); by the right hand road through Acton Turville, 102¼, by Cross Hands Inn, 105½, whence (keeping to *r.* a little further) is downhill, the first bit rather steep, through Old Sodbury, 106¾.

(*Chipping Sodbury:* Portcullis, B.T.C.; Cross Hands Inn.)

At Acton Turville, 2m. on *r.*, Badminton Park. At Cross Hands Inn, on *l.*, Doddington Park.

Chipping Sodbury to Iron Acton (3½—111¼); through Yate, 109, and over Westerleigh Common, 110 (keep to *r.*).

Iron Acton to Alveston (4—115½); through Iron Acton turn to *r.* and through Lotteridge, 112½, and over Earthcote Common, 113¾.

Alveston to Olveston (2¼—117½); out of Alveston turn to *l.*, and at the Royal Oak, 116, turn to *r.*, and through Tockington, 116¾. Returning, from Olveston take right hand road.

Olveston to Aust Passage (2½—120).

Aust Passage to New Passage (2½—122½); turn to *l.* and through Northwich, 121½.

New Passage to St. David's (151½—274); by *Black Rock Inn*, 125½, *Crick*, 128, *Caerleon*, 136½, *Newport*, 140, *Cardiff*, 152½, *Cowbridge*, 165, *Ewenny Bridge*, 171¼, *Aberavon*, 184¼, *Bridgend*, 173¾, *Neath*, 190¼, *Swansea*, 198¾, *Llanelly*, 209½, *Kidwelly*, 218¼, *Llannon*, 208¼, *Carmarthen*, 227¼ or 221, *St. Clears*, 236¾, *Canaston Bridge*, 250¼, and *Haverfordwest*, 258¼.—pp. 91-94. The old passage was by Chepstow.

LONDON TO PENRICE AND RHOSSILI.

London to Swansea (198¾)—above.

Swansea to Penrice (14—212¾); keep straight through Swansea, then bear to *r.* and through Olchfa, 201¾, and Penmaen, 209¾.

2*m.* beyond Olchfa on *r.* to *Rhossili* (8—209¾).

Penrice Castle, Oxwich Castle, Weobley Castle, &c.

LONDON TO PEMBROKE.

London to St. Clears (236¾)—above.

St. Clears to Llandowror (2—238¾)—p. 93.

Llandowror to Begelly (10—248¾); take the left hand road and through Cronware, 243¾. [Or to *Cold Blow*, 9—247¾—p. 93; here turn to *l.* and again to *l.*, through Templeton, 248¾, to *Begelly*, 251¼.]

Begelly to Tenby (4—252¾); turn to *l.* and through Wooden, 250½, and Tenby Gate, 252½. [If from Cold Blow keep straight through Begelly].

(*Tenby*: Coburg; Gordon's; Lion; Royal Gate House; Royal White Lion; Vine.)

At Begelly, on *l.*, Hean or Hên Castle; before Begelly, on *l.*, Amroth Castle, and, on *r.*, Kilgatty or Celgetty Park. Tenby is a great resort for invalids, and for sea bathing; here are St. Catherine's Rock and Fort, Castle Hill, Merlin's Cave, &c.; St. Mary's *ch.* has many ancient monuments.

Tenby to Pembroke (10—262¾); about 1*m.* out of Tenby is a long steep hill to climb on the Ridge Way, on the top of which the road runs for several miles almost level, then there is a steep descent to Lamphey, 260¾, and the rest level or slightly downhill.

[Or from *Begelly* through Redberth, 251¾, Sageston, 253¾, *Carew*, 254¾ and Stupelake, 256½, to *Pembroke*, 258.

Or from Templeton on *r.*, through Yerbeston Gate, 251½, Cressilly, 253¼, and over Carew Bridge, 255, to *Carew*, 255¾, and *Pembroke*, 259.

Or from *Canaston Bridge* on *l.*, to Yerbeston Gate, 254¾.

Or from *Tenby* a good undulating road to Ivy Tower, 256¼, with a very steep rough ascent into Gumfreston, 254¼, and the rest rather hilly but splendid hard road to *Carew*, 259¾.]

(*Pembroke*: Lion.)

Splendid view from the Ridge Way; on *l.*, on the coast, Lydstep Caverns, Manorbier Castle ruins and *ch.* At Lamphey, ruins of the palace. At Carew, on *r.*, castle ruins, and 2*m.* beyond it, Upton Castle. Pembroke was formerly surrounded by a wall, part of which still exists; ruins of Castle, and Monkton Priory *ch.*, Wogan Cavern, &c., Orielton *Ho.*, Stackpole Court, St. Govan's chapel.

LONDON TO MILFORD.

London to Haverfordwest (258¼)—p. 98.

Haverfordwest to Johnston (4—262¼); through the former keep to *l.*, and just out of the town is Merlin's Hill, a very sharp descent to Merlin's (or Mawdlen's) Bridge, 259¼, over which take the middle road, and after a short stiff climb the long severe ascent of Dredgman Hill has to be negotiated, the rest being likewise hilly; good surface all the way.

At Merlin's Bridge on *r.* by Tears or Tier's Cross, 263¼, and Hubberstone, 266½, to Hakin, 267½.

On *l.* across Milford Haven by the ferry to Pembroke (12—271¼)—see cross roads—p. 331.

At Merlin's Bridge, on *l.*, Fern Hill, and Boulston *Ho.*

Johnston to Milford (3½—265¾) is capital going over a good undulating road, with one difficult hill to mount at Stainton, 263¾.

(*Milford*: Lord Nelson.)

Milford, commonly called Milford Haven, has large docks and quay; the harbour is one of the finest in the kingdom; here is an observatory. Beyond Johnston, on *l.*, Harmestou *Ho.* At Stainton, on *r.*, Thornton, Robeston Hall, &c. At Milford, on *l.*, Castle Hall, on *r.*, Nieston *Ho.*, St. Botolph's, Sandy Haven *Ho.*, Butter Hill, and Dale Castle, &c.

LONDON TO MERTHYR TYDVIL.

London to Newport (147¾)—p. 91.

Newport to Caerphilly (12¼—160); in Newport keep first to *r.* after the railway, then to *l.* for Bassaleg, 150¾, where keep to *r.* through Machen (keep to *l.*) and Rudry.

At Caerphilly, remains of castle.

Caerphilly to Merthyr Tydvil (16—176); by Bridgewater's Arms, 163, whence follow the valley of the *R.* Taff, by Pontypridd or Newbridge, 164, Traveller's Rest, 167, and Quaker's Yard, 168, alongside river, railway, and canal. [Or to *Cardiff*, 160¼, p. 91, then turn to *r.* before crossing *R.* Taff, which follow up the valley through Whitchurch, 163½, and joining the other road at Bridgewater's Arms, 171¼; the roads are good, and there are several hills which can be easily mounted. Picturesque scenery.]

At Traveller's Rest on *l.*, along canal and railway up a branch valley by Mountain Ash to *Aberdare*, 184¼.

(*Aberdare*: Black Lion, B.T.C.; Boot.)

Merthyr Tydvil is the largest town in Wales, and the chief ironworks centre. Dowlais *Ho.*, Cyfarthfa Castle, &c.

LONDON TO ALDBOURN.

London to Reading (39)—p. 88.

Reading to Pangbourne (6—45) is level or slightly rising ground along the *R.* Thames and through Purley, 44; flint road with good and smooth hard surface. Pretty ride.

(*Pangbourne*: Swan.)

Near Pangbourne, on *l.*, Purley Hall and Bere Court.

Pangbourne to Streatley (4—49), is a good but rather hilly road through Basildon, 47½, running close by R. Thames; flint road.
On *l.*, Basildon Park. Pretty scenery.

Streatley to East Ilsley (5—54); in Streatley turn to *l.* and through Compton, 52, crossing the Downs.

East Ilsley to Fawley (5¼—59¼); through West Ilsley, 55, and Farnborough, 58.
Before Fawley, on *l.*, Woolley Park.

Fawley to Lambourne (5—64¾); across Eastbury Down; steep descent into Lambourne.
[Or to Speenhamland, 56, p. 83; thence on *r.* through Welford, 61½, Little or East Shefford, 63¼, Great or West Shefford, 64, East Garston, 65¼, and Eastbury, 66½, to *Lambourne*, 68; pretty level.]
On *l.*, Welford Park.

Lambourne to Aldbourn (6—70¾); through Baydon, 68¼.
[Or to Ramsbury, 69—p. 89; then on *r.* to *Aldbourn*, 73.]

LONDON TO WICKWAR.

London to Maidenhead (26)—p. 87.

Maidenhead to Henley-on-Thames (9—35); follow the Reading road to Stubbings Heath or Maidenhead Thicket, 28, where keep to *r.* across Stubbings Heath; then come two or three short stiff ascents and descents followed by a gentle rise for 2m., and descent again to Hurley Bottom, 32; hence the steep ascent of Rose Hill has to be mounted, followed by the long and very steep descent of White Hill leading down to the bridge over R. Thames, riding down which is dangerous, if not impossible, on account of the steepness and generally loose stony state of the surface: otherwise good road.

[Or another road, not near so hilly, is to follow the Reading road to Hare Hatch, 32—p. 83; and shortly beyond turn off to *r.* for Wargrave, 34, thence on to Henley is a good, smooth, gravel road, with one or two short but very steep ups and downs: very pretty scenery.]
(*Henley*: Red Lion; Royal; White Hart.)

2m. before Hurley Bottom, on *r.*, remains of Augustine Priory at Bisham; across R. Thames, Medmenham Abbey. Henley is famous for its annual regatta in July. On *l.*, Henley Park, and on *r.*, Fawley Court, both elegant mansions in beautiful grounds; the neighbourhood abounds in residences of the gentry, interspersed with beautiful scenery.

Henley-on-Thames to Nettlebed (5—40); for the first mile it is level, then there are about 3m. of continuous uphill, but not steep, through Assington Cross, 37, and Bix *Tp.*, 37¾; the surface is generally very smooth, so all the 5m. can be ridden up.
(*Nettlebed*: Red Lion.)

At Bix *Tp.*, on *r.*, Henley Park; 3m. beyond it, Stonor Park, in which deer are kept.

Nettlebed to Wallingford (6—46); rather steep descent out of Nettlebed, then undulating for nearly 2m. through Nuffield Heath, 41½ (where keep to *l.*), and long descent to Crowmarsh Gifford, 45¼, whence cross R. Thames to Wallingford, over bridge of 19 arches, gravel road.

(*Wallingford:* George; Lamb; Nuffield Heath; Crown.)
On *l.*, Ipsden *Ho.* and Woodcot *Ho.* On Crowmarsh, on *l.*, Mongewell *Ho.* At Wallingford, remains of castle, St. Peter's *ch.*, Castle Priory.

Wallingford to Harwell (8—54); through Brightwell, 48 (turn to *l.*), and Didcot, 52¾; good chalk road.

[Or to *Streatley,* 49—p. 100; at the fork roads beyond keep to *l.*, and it is very hilly and rough as far as Blewberry, 54½, and then it improves through Upton, 56, to *Harwell,* 58.]

Harwell to Wantage 6—60) is a good chalk road through East Hendred, 56, and Ardington, 57¾. This road is called the Port Way.

(*Wantage:* Bear, *B.T.C.*)

Wantage was the birthplace of Alfred the Great, and was a royal town of the Saxons. On the range of hills on *l.* runs an old British road, called the Ridgeway or Ickleton street; many barrows are scattered about.

Wantage to Swindon (17—77); beyond Wantage turn to *l.*, and through Childrey, 62¼, Woolston, 66½, Ashbury, 69½, Bishopstone, 71½, and Wanborough, 73, is a very loose and rough road, with many steep little hills, which require careful riding.

(*Swindon:* Bell; Goddard Arms, *B.T.C.*; King's Arms.)

About 3m. beyond Wantage, the road goes through the Vale of White Horse, the figure of which is seen on the hill side, on *l.* For several m. the road runs close under the north side of the hills, being the old Port Way. There are several objects of antiquity, &c., as the Punch Bowl, Letcombe Castle, Blowing Stone, White Horse, Dragon Hill, Offington Castle, Wayland Smith's Cave or Forge, Alfred's Castle, and Hardwell Camp.

Swindon to Malmesbury (15—92); rough descent out of Swindon, then a good gravel and flint road through Brinkworth, 86½, with no difficult hills till just before Malmesbury, when there are two which require careful riding. Returning, when nearly through Malmesbury, turn to *l.*

4m. further, ½m. on *l.*, Wootton Bassett, a small old-fashioned town, 83½.

(*Malmesbury:* King's Arms, *B.T.C.*; King's Head.—*Wootton Bassett:* Angel; Royal Oak.)

2m. beyond Swindon, on *r.*, Lydiard Park. Malmesbury was formerly an important town, and parts of the walls are left, but the castle has disappeared; there are ruins of the splendid Abbey, built in the 9th century, and containing King Athelstane's tomb; fine market cross.

Malmesbury to Great Sherston (5½—97½); through Westport, 92¼, and Easton Grey, 95½, undulating and fair road.

About half-way cross the old Fosse Way, or Akeman Street, and 1m. on *l.* at Whitewalls, is the site of the Roman station of Matuardonis.

Great Sherston to Dunkirk (4½—102), through Sopworth, 99½. Returning, just out of Dunkirk keep to *r.*

1m. before Dunkirk, on *l.*, Badminton Park (Duke of Beaufort).

Dunkirk to Wickwar (5—107); through Hawkesbury Upton, 103 (½m. beyond which keep to *l.*).

LONDON TO CHIPPENHAM (by Swindon).

London to Wootton Bassett (83½)—above.
Wootton Bassett to Lyneham (4¼—87¾).

Lyneham to Chippenham (9¼—99); at Lyneham keep to *r*. and through Christian Malford, 91¾, Sutton Benger, 93, and Langley Burrell, 95½.

At Sutton Benger, on *r*., Draycot *Ho*.

LONDON TO THORNBURY.

London to Wantage (60)—p. 101.

Wantage to Faringdon (8—68) is a splendid flint road through East Charlow, 61, Stanford, 64¾, and Stanford Plain, 65¾; after East Charlow the road bears away to N.W., and there is a long descent into Faringdon. Returning, keep to *r*. out of Faringdon.

Before Faringdon, on *l*., Shillingford Castle; on *r*., Wadley *Ho*. Interesting old *ch*. at Faringdon, with many old monuments. N. of town, Faringdon *Ho*.; near to it is a circular camp.

Faringdon to Highworth (6½—74½); beyond Faringdon is a long uphill to mount, then descent and ascent to Coleshill, 71¾, out of which is a steep fall and long pull up to Highworth.

(*Highworth*: King and Queen; Saracen's Head.)

On *l*., Coleshill *Ho*.; at Highworth, on *l*., at Sevenhampton, Warneford Place.

Highworth to Cricklade (7½—81¾); after some undulating road a long rise to "Cold Harbour" Inn, 78, where turn to *r*. down a long, steep hill, and through Water Eaton, 80¼, and over Colcut Bridge; good flint road.

[Or to *Swindon*, 77—p. 101; thence to *Cricklade*, 8—85, by "Cold Harbour" Inn, 81¼.]

(*Cricklade*: White Hart; White Horse.)

About 3m. past Highworth, on *r*., Castle Hill. At "Cold Harbour" Inn join the Roman Ermine Way. At Cricklade, St. Sampson's *ch*. and St. Mary's *ch*.

Cricklade to Charlton (9¾—91½); rather up and down hill, but nothing difficult, through Leigh Common, 84¾, by Cove House, 85¾, Minety station, 86¾, and over Broadwater Bridge, 91; gravel road, very good going. Pretty scenery.

Charlton to Tetbury (5½—97); turn to *r*. and skirt north side of Charlton Park, and through Five Lanes *Tp*., 93, and Long Newton, 95¼; rather hilly, and steep ascent into Tetbury.

[Or forward to *Malmesbury*, 93¾; then turn to *r*. and through Long Newton, 96¾, to *Tetbury*, 98½; very shaky road, with some sharp little hills to ascend.

Or to *Malmesbury*, 92—p. 101, thence to *Tetbury*, 4¾—96¾—above.]

(*Tetbury*: White Hart, *B.T.C*.)

Before Tetbury, on *l*., Eastcourt *Ho*. At Tetbury, fine *ch*.

Tetbury to Kingscote, Hunter's Hall (5¼—102¼); through Tetbury turn to *l*. and through Beverstone, 99, and past Calcott Farm, 100½.

At Beverstone, on *r*., Chevenage *Ho*. On *r*., Kingscote Park; on *l*. 1m., Lasborough Park.

Kingscote to Wotton-under-Edge (4¼—106½); beyond Kingscote keep to *l*. twice.

(*Wotton*: Royal Oak, *B.T.C*.; Swan, *B.T.C*.)

At Wotton, 1m. on *l*., Newark Park.

Wotton-under-Edge to Thornbury (8½—115).

LONDON TO BRISTOL (by Malmesbury).

London to Malmesbury (92)—p. 101.

Malmesbury to Acton Turville (8¾—100¾); beyond Malmesbury turn to *l.* and through Foxley, 94½, and Lackington, 99.

[Or to *Great Sherston*, 97½, p. 101; there turning to *l.* is a sharp awkward fall, which requires caution in descending, and almost level through Lackington, 101¼, to *Acton Turville*, 103; surface inclined to be stony.]

At Lackington, on *r.*, Badminton Park.

Acton Turville to Bristol (15½—116¼); through Tormarton, 103½, Codrington, Whimsey, and Ridgway.

[Or at Acton Turville turn on *l.* to *Nettleton*, 101½, whence by Toll Down Inn, 105½, Hinton, 107, through Pucklechurch, 109, Mangotsfield, 110¼, and Ridgway, where join the other road to *Bristol*, 117.]

At Tormarton, on *r.*, Dodington Park; before Ridgway, on *r.*, Cleeve Lodge and Cleeve Hill. Beyond Toll Down Inn, on *l.*, Dirham Park; beyond Pucklechurch, on *l.*, Siston Court; at Mangotsfield, on *r.*, Hill *Ho.*

LONDON TO WICKWAR (by Tetbury).

London to Tetbury (97)—p. 102.

Tetbury to Dunkirk (7½—104½); in Tetbury turn to *l.* and through Doughton, 98, by Hare and Hounds, 99, and through Didmarton, 102½, is an easy road as to hills; oolite surface, slippery and rutty in wet weather.

Dunkirk to Wickwar (5—109½)—p. 101.

[Or to *Wotton-under-Edge*, 106½, p. 102, then follow the Thornbury road for 3*m.*, and turn to *l.* to *Wickwar*, 111½.]

LONDON TO ST. DAVID'S (by Malmesbury).

London to Acton Turville (100¾)—above.

Acton Turville to St. David's (171¼—272)—pp. 97-98.

LONDON TO BERKELEY.

London to Faringdon (68)—p. 102.

Faringdon to Lechlade (5¾—73¾); in Faringdon turn to *r.* and through Buscot, 72, and over St. John's Bridge, 73, is perfectly level and first rate gravel road.

(*Lechlade:* New Inn; Swan.)

Lechlade is the highest point to which the *R.* Thames is navigable; the *ch.* was erected in the 15th century; on *r.*, Buscot Park.

Lechlade to Fairford (4¼—78) is a fairly good road, and quite level.

(*Fairford:* Bull, *B.T.C.*)

At Fairford, very fine *ch.* with beautiful windows; on *r.*, Fairford Park.

Fairford to Cirencester (8¾—86¾); through Poulton, 81½, Easington, 82¾, and Ampney Crucis, 83¾, fairly level road, with one or two slight undulations; fairly good surface, but being composed of oolite stone is dangerously rutty and greasy when wet. Returning, turn to *r.* outside Cirencester.

(*Cirencester*: Fleece, *B.T.C.*; King's Head.)

On *r*. pass Ampney Park and *Ho*. Cirencester was an important station of the Romans, situate at the junction of Ermine Way, Fosse Way, Ikenild street, and Akeman street; many antiquities have been found in the vicinity. Gothic ch. of the 14th century, recently restored, one of the finest in England. Near the town is the Agricultural College. Old Roman Museum.

Cirencester to Frampton Tp. (6¼—93¼); ¾m. out of Cirencester keep to *r*.; very undulating road, skirting south side of Oakley Park for 4m., then over Sapperton Tunnel.

On *l*., the village of Cotes, which gives its name to the Cotswold Hills; beyond is the source of R. Thames; also an old entrenchment called Trewsbury Castle.

Frampton Tp. to Minchin Hampton (3¼—96½); ¼m. beyond, turn to *l*., and again to *l*. before Minchin Hampton.

(*Minchin Hampton*: Crown, *B.T.C.*)

Before Minchin Hampton, on *r*., Hyde Court, and Minchin Hampton Park; on *l*., Gatcombe Park. Fine *ch*. at Minchin Hampton, founded in the reign of Henry III.

Minchin Hampton to Nailsworth (2—98½); entering Nailsworth turn to *l*.

(*Nailsworth*: George, *B.T.C.*; Railway.)

Nailsworth to Dursley (7—105½); through Horsley, 99¾, and 2m. further turn to *l*., then ½m. further to *r*., and again to *r*. shortly after, and through Uley, 103¾.

[Or to *Kingscote*, 102¼,—p. 102; beyond which take second turn on *r*. to *Dursley*, 106¾.]

(*Dursley*: Old Bell, *B.T.C.*)

At Dursley, on *l*., Stancombe Park; on *r*. Ferney Hill and Kingshill *Ho*.

Dursley to Berkeley (5¾—111¼); a mile beyond Dursley keep to *l*., and ½m. further to *r*., and 2m. again join the Gloucester and Bristol road; at "Old Bell," 109¾, turn to *r*.

(*Berkeley*: Berkeley Arms; White Hart.)

At Berkeley, on *l*., Berkeley Castle, built soon after the Conquest. Fine old *ch*., containing some ancient monuments, and with a separate tower.

LONDON TO STONEHOUSE.

London to Frampton Tp. (93¼)—above.

Frampton Tp. to Stroud (5¾—99); take right hand road ¼m. further on, then there is a long hill to mount, followed by 1½m. descent, in some parts steep, through Chalford, 95¼, to near Brimscombe, 97, whence it is a level run into Stroud, running alongside railway and canal. Pretty scenery.

[Or to *Minchin Hampton*, 96½, above; then on *r*. through Rodborough, 99¾, to *Stroud*, 100¼.]

(*Stroud*: Albany; George; Imperial; Royal George, *B.T.C.*; Swan.)

At Chalford 2m. on *r*. Lypial Park. Beyond Minchin Hampton, on *r*., Road *Ho*., and on *l*. Hill *Ho*. At Rodborough Hill, the Fort; on *l*., Stanley Park. Stroud is the chief seat of the West of England woollen trade; on every side but W. it is surrounded by steep hills.

Stroud to Stonehouse (2¼—101¾); through Cain's Cross, 100, and Ebley, 100½, is a good level road.

(*Stonehouse :* Crown and Anchor.)

2*m.* S. of Stonehouse is Woodchester Park, where remains of a large Roman villa have been found.

LONDON TO GLOUCESTER.

London to Cirencester (86¾)—p. 103.

Cirencester to Birdlip (10¾—97½), along the old Roman Ermine Way, and crossing the Cotswold Hills; through Stratton, 89¼, is an undulating road, quite straight for 8*m.*, with no heavy hills, but descent into Birdlip; oolite road, good in dry weather, bad and slippery when wet.

About 3*m.* before Birdlip, on *l.*, Miserden Park. 2*m.* N. of Birdlip, the *R.* Churn rises, one of the highest affluents of the *R.* Thames. Fine views.

Birdlip to Gloucester (7¼—104¾); leaving the Cotswolds the long and very steep descent of Birdlip Hill continues through Birdlip to Whitcomb, 99, dangerous to ride down and should be walked; then it is a level and very good road through Cross Hands, 100, Brockworth, 100½, Hucclecote, 101¾, and Barnwood, 102¾, with an ascent into Gloucester: Bristol stone.

(*Gloucester :* Albion; Greyhound; Lower George; New Inn; Ram; Spread Eagle, *B.T.C.*)

At Whitcomb, on *l.*, remains of a Roman villa; beyond, Prinknash Park. At Gloucester, the cathedral, a fine Gothic building, commenced in 1407.

LONDON TO GLOUCESTER (by Abingdon).

London to Nettlebed (40)—p. 100.

Nettlebed to Bensington or Benson (6—46); rather steep descent out of Nettlebed, then uphill for nearly 2*m.* through Nuffield Heath, 41½ (keep to *r.*); after that is the long and rather stiff descent of Gangsdown Hill, followed by another descent just after the 43rd *ms.*, then undulating through Beggar's Bush, 44, and the last mile level into Bensington; good surface, but sometimes dusty.

Bensington to Dorchester (3¼—49¼); capital level road through Shillingford, 47½, running close by *R.* Thames all the way.

(*Shillingford :* Swan.)

In Saxon times Dorchester was a bishop's see; interesting old *ch.*; remains of priory of Black Monks. At the junction of Thames and Isis is an ancient camp.

Dorchester to Abingdon (6½—55¾); by left hand road, is almost level through Burcot, 50¾, and Clifton, 52, and over Culham Bridge, 54¾ (*R.* Thames); capital going, pretty scenery.

(*Abingdon :* Lion, *B.T.C.*; Nag's Head; Queen.)

At Abingdon, St. Nicholas *ch.*, erected in the latter part of the 13th century. Slight remains of a Benedictine Abbey, founded by the Saxons.

Abingdon to Fyfield (5½—61¼); through Shippon, 56¾, and Tubney, 60½, fairly level and good road, but mostly oolite.

On *r.*, Oakley *Ho* and Tubney *Ho.*

Fyfield to Faringdon (9¼—70½); by Kingston Inn, 62½, and Pusey Furze, 65¾, is a perfectly level road ; oolite surface, but fairly good going.

At Pusey Furze, on *r.*, Buckland *Ho.*; on *l.*, Pusey *Ho.*; and beyond Cherbury camp, an old entrenchment. Near Faringdon, on *r.*, Wadley *Ho.*

Faringdon to Cirencester (18¾—89½)—p. 103.

Cirencester to Gloucester (18—107¼)—p. 105.

LONDON TO ST. DAVID'S (by Oxford and Gloucester).

London (Marble Arch) to Acton (5); level road through Bayswater, ¾, to Notting Hill, 2, whence there is a good longish descent nearly to Shepherd's Bush, 2½ ; here take right hand road at the Common, and the rest is level except a hill to rise into Acton; except a few 100 yards of wood paving through Notting Hill, the surface is macadam all the way, consequently rough and bumpy, and often wet and greasy; tramway from Shepherd's Bush to near Acton.

Close to Marble Arch formerly stood Tyburn Turnpike; here also for many years was the execution place of London. For the first 1½ m. the road skirts the north side of Hyde Park and Kensington Gardens; at Notting Hill, on *l.*, Holland *Ho.*

Acton to Southall (4½—9½); sharp descent out of Acton and similar rise after, then past Ealing Common, 6, it is level for a mile or so, followed by a long gentle descent past Ealing Dean to Hanwell, 8; from here the road descends sharply down Hanwell Hill to R. Brent, followed by a rise past the Asylum and a gradual slope up to Southall: still macadam and rough, but after Ealing Common it improves slightly.

(*Ealing*, on *l.* : Bell.)

On *r.*, Hanger Hill, Castle Bear Lodge and Hanwell Park. Near Hanwell, on *l.*, Osterly Park.

Southall to Uxbridge (5½—15); on the rise nearly all the way through Hayes End, 12½, to Hillingdon, 13½, out of which is a sharp descent, then nearly level to Uxbridge; macadam road, with pretty fair riding at the sides.

(*Hayes* : Adam and Eve ; Angel.—*Uxbridge* : Chequers ; Eight Bells ; King's Arms.)

The main street of Uxbridge is almost a mile long. Before Uxbridge, on *r.* Hillingdon *Ho.*

Uxbridge to Beaconsfield (8½—23½); the macadam ends with Uxbridge, out of which is a short dip, and then two bridges to go over (R. Coln and Grand Junction Canal); after that the road is level, but not very smooth, to the foot of Red Hill, 17¼, which, though rather rough and generally loose and heavy, can be mounted by an ordinary rider, as it is not steep; thence undulating past Tatling End, 18, to Gerard's Cross, 20, beyond which are two or three sharp descents and ascents skirting Bulstrode Park (Duke of Somerset), and then it runs up a narrow well-wooded valley by a gradual rise with a few undulations to Beaconsfield ; gravel surface, in dry weather sandy and heavy for the first 3m., then good except sometimes rather loose and heavy in places on the long slope past Bulstrode Park.

(*Beaconsfield* : Old Swan, B.T.C.; Saracen's Head ; White Hart.—*Gerard's Cross* : Bull.)

In Beaconsfield *ch.* Edmund Burke is buried, and in the churchyard, the

Poet Waller. On r., before Beaconsfield, is Wilton Park. In Bulstrode Park is an ancient entrenchment. S. of Beaconsfield is Hall Barn Park.

Beaconsfield to High Wycombe (5¼—29); sharp descent from Beaconsfield, which is rather stony, followed by a gradual rise to Hotspur Heath, 24¾, then a long hill down into Loudwater, 26½, whence an all but level road runs up the valley past Wycombe Marsh, 27¼, to High Wycombe; capital smooth surface.

(*High Wycombe*: Coach and Horses; Falcon; Red Lion, B.T.C.; Swan Inn.)

High Wycombe possesses a handsome town hall; the *ch.*, All Saints', was built in the 13th century and has fine altar-piece and monuments. On *l.* is Wycombe Abbey. High Wycombe is noted for the manufacture of chairs.

High Wycombe to Stokenchurch (7½—36½); out of High Wycombe there is nearly a mile of easy uphill, then nearly all down to West Wycombe, 31¾; from here a gently rising road runs for ¾m. to the foot of Dashwood Hill, which leads on to the Chiltern Hills, and is a very steep but straight ascent of some 400 yards in length; riding up is almost impossible and bicyclists coming the contrary direction should beware against riding *down*, as it is often very loose, besides being dangerous on account of its steepness; once on the top it is an easy undulating road across the Chilterns to Stokenchurch: good surface on the whole.

(*West Wycombe*: White Horse.—*Stokenchurch*: Barley Mow; Red Lion.)

N. of High Wycombe is Hughenden Lodge. At West Wycombe, on *l.*, Wycombe Park; on *r.*, overlooking the road, is an elegant mausoleum.

Stokenchurch to Tetsworth (6—42½) is a capital going road; after a gradual ascent to the *Tg.* about a mile beyond Stokenchurch, the descent from the Chilterns begins, the road gradually winding down the hillside through a wood for nearly 2m., rideable either down (with caution) or up; after this comes a splendid stretch of smooth and nearly level road, on which almost any pace can be maintained, till a mile beyond Postcombe, 40½, when there is a long stiff hill to run down, followed by a short up and down into Tetsworth.

(*Tetsworth*: Red Lion; Swan.)

At the foot of the Chilterns, 3m. on *l.*, is the splendid mansion of Shirburne Castle (Earl of Macclesfield) containing large armoury and many celebrated paintings; on *r.*, Aston Rowant; on *l.*, Nethercote Park. 3m. N. of Postcombe is Thame Park, the house of which is built on the site of an ancient abbey.

Tetsworth to Wheatley, entrance of (6½—48½); past the "Three Pigeons," 44¾, is a good undulating road, with a long descent to Wheatley Bridge, 47½, on the *R.* Thame, and an easy rise to the entrance of Wheatley, which the main road does not go through, but passes to the right of.

(*Wheatley*: Crown; King's Arms; Railway.)

At Wheatley Bridge, 1m. on *l.*, Cuddesden Palace, residence of the Bishop of Oxford; on *r.*, Holton Park.

Wheatley to Oxford (5½—54); turning to *r.* entering Wheatley, and ½m. beyond to *l.*; the road continues good and undulating to Headington *Tg.*, 52½, whence it is all downhill, the surface being macadam and very bumpy, ending with a sharp descent at St. Clement's, 53¾, and after some rough paving, cross the Magdalen Bridge (*R.* Cherwell) into Oxford; through the town is partly cobble paved and bad for bicycling.

[From Wheatley Bridge by the Old Road through Wheatley and over Shotover Hill to Oxford, 7m.]

(*Oxford:* Black Horse; Clarendon; Jones' Railway, B.T.C.; Mitre; Randolph; Roebuck; Three Cups; Ship.)

Oxford is one of the most beautiful and elegant cities of England, both on account of the picturesqueness of its situation and the number and architectural richness of its public edifices; its University, England's chief seat of learning, has a world-wide reputation. There are 25 colleges and halls, the oldest, University College, said to have been founded in 872. The cathedral and churches are very handsome; also library, museums, observatory, &c. Some remains still exist of the old castle and walls. Splendid view of the town from Headington Hill.

Oxford to Witney ($11\frac{1}{4}$—$65\frac{1}{4}$); keeping straight on through Oxford, pass under the G. W. Ry., close to the station and over several bridges (*R.* Isis), then very good and smooth road, quite level, by Botley Hill, $55\frac{1}{4}$, to Ensham or Eynsham Bridge, called also Swinford Bridge, 59 (over *R.* Isis), which is a private bridge, and there is toll, $2d.$, to be paid; from Ensham, $59\frac{3}{4}$ (turn to *r.*), there is an ascent followed by a long descent, but the road becomes level approaching Witney.

(*Witney:* Marlborough.—*Ensham:* Swan.)

$3m.$ N. of Oxford, near the Isis, are the ruins of Godstow Nunnery. Witney is celebrated for its blankets; it has a large and handsome cruciform *ch.* $2m.$ S. of Ensham, at Stanton Harcourt, a fine old *ch.*; the manor house is an interesting building. On the *r.*, $3m.$ before Witney, is Ensham Hall; near it are two ancient camps. $2m.$ before Burford, the old Roman Akeman street crosses the road.

Witney to Burford (7—$72\frac{1}{4}$); after crossing the *R.* Windrush, instead of following the main road right through Witney, turn sharp to *r.*, by which some distance is saved; then keeping straight on there are two or three hills, otherwise a good easy road; at the bifurcation just before Burford if not wishing to go into the town take the left hand and more direct branch, following the telegraph wires and skirting the town on the south side; by the other road it is downhill to Burford, turning to *l.* into the main street, which is on a slope, then turn again to N. and up a long hill, at the top of which join the former road.

(*Burford:* Bull; Lamb.)

Burford is an old-fashioned town; large *ch.*, chiefly Norman; fine old manor house; also that at Asthall, on *r.*, $3m.$ before Burford.

Burford to Northleach (9—$81\frac{1}{4}$), through Little Barrington, $75\frac{1}{2}$, is fairly good and level most of the way, except two hills to descend into the town.

(*Northleach:* Union; Wheatsheaf; New Inn, nearly $2m.$ beyond Burford.)

On *r.*, at a little distance, Barrington Park and Sherborne Park; on *l.*, about halfway, is an old camp.

Northleach to Andoverford ($7\frac{3}{4}$—89); the road now crosses the Cotswold Hills, from which there are some fine views; the first $2m.$ are slightly downhill, then there is a long stiff ascent, followed by downhill for about the same length, by Frog Mill Inn, 88, into Andoverford: the surface is of oolite stone, and, although good in dry weather, it is rutty and dangerously greasy when wet.

Just out of Northleach the old Roman Fosse Way is crossed; $2m.$ on *l.* is Stowell Park.

Andoverford to Cheltenham ($5\frac{1}{4}$—$94\frac{1}{4}$); after a little level, there is a long hill to descend from Andoverford to Dowdeswell, 90, then a splendid run of 2*m.*, and another long descent to Charlton Kings, 93, and the rest level; good road at first, but afterwards it gets loose and rough, and the last 2*m.* are very bad, and through the town it is very rough and lumpy; chiefly mountain limestone.

(*Cheltenham:* Belle Vue; Fleece, *B.T.C.*; Lamb, *B.T.C.*; Plough.

Cheltenham is one of the most fashionable and elegant of our inland watering places: it has 14 springs, all saline; its climate is very salubrious. The chief parts are the High street, Promenade or Well Walk, Lansdowne, Pitville Spa, and Christchurch.

Cheltenham to Gloucester (9—103½); turning to *r.* from Lansdowne, take the left of the next two main roads; when out of the town the road is smooth at first, but soon becomes rough again; it is level till nearing Gloucester, when there is a short uphill, after which turn to *r.* and entering the town is a slight incline.

[This is the best road to Gloucester, as every hill between Oxford and Gloucester can be ridden up.]

Gloucester to Newnham (12¼—115½); turn to *r.* at the Post Office down a slight descent, then cross canal and *R.* Severn, and through Over, 104¾, Highnam Court, 105¼ (turn to *l.* and again ½*m.* further on), Minsterworth, 107¾, and Westbury, 112¼, is a rather narrow but good road, with a few easy hills; steep ascent through Newnham; though macadam, there is nothing a bicyclist need complain of.

At Westbury, 1*m.* on *r.*, is Flaxley Abbey.

Newnham to Lydney (7—122½); through Blakeney, 119, is much the same quality of road, but it has very long ups and downs, some of which are too steep to ride up and must be descended carefully.

On *r.* lies the Forest of Dean.

Lydney to Chepstow (9¼—131¾); through Ailberton (or Aylburton) 124, Alvington, 125½, Woolaston, 127, Stroute, 128¼, and Tiddenham, 129¾, is rather better going but hilly; into Chepstow there is a steep hill to descend.

(*Chepstow:* Beaufort Arms; White Hart.)

At Ailberton, 3*m.* on *r.*, remains of St. Briavel's Castle. Chepstow, on the *R.* Wye, is surrounded by grand and beautiful scenery. The ruins of the castle, built in the 11th century, are very extensive; the *ch.* originally formed part of the chapel of a Benedictine priory, erected shortly after the Conquest. The tide in the *R.* Wye here sometimes rises 50 and even 70 feet. Near Chepstow, the fine mansion and park of Piercefield.

Chepstow to Crick (4—135¾); long steep hill to walk up out of Chepstow followed by a steep descent to Poolmeyrick, 133¼, then undulating by St. Pierre's Park Gate, 134½: good wide road with a sound surface.

Near Crick, on *l.*, ruins of Caldecot Castle.

Crick to St. David's (146—281¾)—pp. 91-94.

LONDON TO OXFORD (by Maidenhead).

London to Dorchester (49¼)—p. 105.

Dorchester to Oxford (8¾—58); keep to *r.* out of Dorchester, and through Nuneham Courtney (or Courtenay), 52¾, Sandford, 54¾, and Cowley, 55½, is an undulating road, but the hills are not difficult: good surface to Cowley, and then it is macadam, very rough and shaky, for the last 2*m.*, joining the Wycombe Road just before St. Magdalen's Bridge.

On *l.*, at Nuneham Courtney, is Nuneham Park, the magnificent seat of the Vernon Harcourts: the road after that runs near the *R.* Thames.

LONDON TO GLOUCESTER (By Oxford and Birdlip).

London to Frog Mill Inn (88)—p. 108.

Frog Mill Inn to Birdlip (8¼—96¼); turn sharp to *l.* and the road goes downhill to Kilkenny, 89½, and should be ridden carefully as the last part is rather steep; then hilly and rough road by Seven Wells, 92¾ (keep to *r.*), and Balloon Inn, 95 (keep to *l.*)

Beyond Seven Wells the *R.* Churn takes its rise, said by some to be the highest source of the Thames. Very fine views.

Birdlip to Gloucester (7¼—103½)—p. 105.

LONDON TO ST. DAVID'S (by Brecon).

London to Gloucester (103¼)—p. 109.

Gloucester to Huntley (7¾—111); turn to *r.* at the *P.O.* down a slight descent, then cross canal and *R.* Severn, and keep straight on through Over, 104¾, Highnam Court, 105¼, Churcham, 107¼, over Birdwood Common, and through Birdwood, 109¾; good flat road.

Huntley to Ross (9¼—120¼); good road through Mayhill, 112, Dorsley Cross, 112¾, Longhope, 114¼, Lea, 115¾, Ryford, 117¼, and Weston, 118¼; good scenery. [Better road than through Newent.]

(*Ross:* Lamb Inn)

Ross is surrounded by picturesque scenery, especially down the Wye Valley. Here lived John Kyrle, celebrated as the "Man of Ross." On the S. are the ruins of Wilton Castle; handsome *ch.*

Ross to Monmouth (10½—130¾); keep straight through Ross, cross *R.* Wye, and at Wilton *Tq.*, 121, take left hand road; rough and rather hilly road through Pencraig, 123¼, Goodrich, 125, Whitchurch, 126½, and Ganarew, 127¾; last 2*m.* downhill: Monmouth is paved.

(*Monmouth:* Angel; Beaufort Arms; King's Head; White Swan.)

Beautiful scenery. Near Goodrich, the ruins of Goodrich Castle, besieged and dismantled by the Parliamentarians. Near Whitchurch, on Symond's Yate Hill, is an ancient encampment, whence a fine view is obtained. At Monmouth are remains of the Norman castle in which Henry V. was born; of a priory house; and the old town walls near Welshgate, on Monnow Bridge. St. Mary's *ch.* once the priory *ch.*, is of early English style, with a spire 200 feet high. On Kymin Hill is Nelson's Pavilion. At Troy *Ho.* (Duke of Beaufort) are preserved the cradle of Henry V., and the armour he wore at Agincourt.

Monmouth to Abergavenny (16½—147¼); through Monmouth turn to *r.*, and shortly after to *l.*; through Wonastow, 133½ (a little further keep to *r.*), Dingestow, 134½ (2*m.* beyond keep to *r.*), Tregare (or Tregaer), 137¼, Bringwyn, 138½, Croes-bychan, 139 (turn to *r.*), Llanvihangel, 142¼, and Llangattock, 143¼. Returning, 1*m.* out of Abergavenny, keep to *l.* under the railway. [Or a little out of Monmouth keep to *r.* to Rockfield, 133, where keep to *l.*, and through Llanvapley to Abergavenny, 145¾.]

(*Abergavenny:* Angel; Great Western; Greyhound; Swan.)

Beyond Monmouth, on *l.*, Troy *Ho.*, Dingestow *Ho.*, and Bringwyn *Ho.*, and on *r.*, Llanarth Court. 2*m.* past Bringwyn, on *r.*, Clytha Castle. At Abergavenny, ruins of the castle. St. Mary's *ch.* was originally the chapel of the ancient priory, 2 or 3 *m.* N.W., Sugar Loaf and Holy Mountains. At Langwn *ch.* is a fine screen.

Abergavenny to Crickhowell ($6\frac{1}{4}$—$153\frac{1}{2}$); through Pentre, $148\frac{3}{4}$, Llanwenarth, $149\frac{1}{2}$, and Llangranach, $151\frac{1}{2}$, up the Usk valley; bad road. [Or in Abergavenny turn to *l.*, and, crossing *R.* Usk, through Llanfoist and Govilon, about 1*m.* longer.]

Before Crickhowell, on *r.*, Col-y-Gollen and Greenhill Cottage; beyond, Gwernvale, and $1\frac{1}{2}m.$ on *r.*, More Park. At Crickhowell are slight remains of castle.

Crickhowell to Brecon or Brecknock ($13\frac{3}{4}$—$167\frac{1}{4}$); through Llanvair, $154\frac{1}{4}$, Tretower, $155\frac{3}{4}$, Bwlch, 159 (keep to *l.*), Llansaintffraid, $161\frac{1}{4}$, Skythrog, $162\frac{3}{4}$, and Llanhamlog, 164; still up the Usk valley, with one very steep hill up to and down from Bwlch; bad road.

(*Brecon:* Castle; George; Wellington.)

Beyond Crickhowell, on *l.*, Glan Usk Park. At Tretower, ruins of the castle. At Bwlch, on *l.*, Buckland *Ho.* At Brecon, ruins of the castle and priory; St. John's and St. Mary's Churches. At Llanhamlog, on *r.*, Peterstone Court.

Brecon to Trecastle ($9\frac{3}{4}$—178); in Brecon turn to *l.* and up the Usk Valley, through Llanvaes, 168, (keep to *r.*) Llanspyddyd, $169\frac{1}{2}$, Penpont, $172\frac{1}{2}$, and Rhyd-y-Brew, $175\frac{3}{4}$.

On *r.*, Penpont *Ho.*

Trecastle to Llandovery ($9\frac{1}{4}$—$187\frac{1}{4}$); now leave *R.* Usk and up a small branch valley, through Llywel, 179, by Halfway *Ho.*, $182\frac{3}{4}$, and downhill through Velindre, $186\frac{1}{4}$.

(*Llandovery:* King's Head; North Western.)

Llandovery to Llandilo (12—$199\frac{1}{4}$); at Llandovery cross *R.* Brane and *R.* Towy, then turn to *l.* and through Llwynjack, $188\frac{1}{2}$, Croes-ceilog, $191\frac{1}{4}$, and Rhoesmaen, $198\frac{1}{4}$, down the Towy valley. [Or at Llwynjack turn to *l.* and through Dol-y-carreg, $190\frac{1}{2}$, Llangadock, $193\frac{1}{2}$, and 1*m.* further rejoining the other road, a little longer.]

[Or from *Trecastle* on *l.* up the Usk Valley for 2 or 3*m.* and then across the hills, through Talsarn, $185\frac{3}{4}$, Pontarlleche, $189\frac{1}{4}$, 1*m.* further keeping to *l.* and by Penachamawr, $193\frac{1}{4}$, and Maneravon, $195\frac{1}{2}$, to *Llandilo*, $198\frac{1}{2}$.]

(*Llandilo:* Castle; Cawdor Arms; Half Moon; King's Head; Salutation.)

2*m.* beyond Croesceilog, on *r.*, Abermarlais. $1\frac{1}{2}m.$ before Rhoesmaen, 1*m.* on *r.*, Taliaris. At Landilo (called also Llandilo-Vaur), Dynevor Park and Castle ruins. 1*m.* beyond Penachamawr., on *l.*, Carreg Cennin, Castle ruins.

Llandilo to Carmarthen ($14\frac{3}{4}$—214); turn to *r.* and past Dynevor Park, by Rhuradar, $201\frac{3}{4}$, Cross Inn, $204\frac{1}{4}$, Cothy Bridge, $207\frac{1}{4}$, White Mill, $210\frac{1}{2}$, and Abergwylly, 212.

Beyond Rhuradar, on *l.*, Aberglasney, and beyond it, Golden Grove. Beyond Cross Inn, on *l.*, Dryslwyn Castle ruins. At Abergwylly, Bishop of St. David's Palace, and Merlin's Cave and Grave.

Carmarthen to St. David's ($46\frac{3}{4}$—$260\frac{3}{4}$)—pp. 93-94.

LONDON TO ST. DAVID'S (by Cardigan).

London to Llandovery ($187\frac{1}{4}$)—above.

Llandovery to Lampeter (18—$205\frac{1}{4}$); through Llandovery turn to r., and by Pumsant, 197¼, and Lampeter Mountain, 201¼; two big hills to cross.

(*Lampeter:* Black Lion.)

2*m*. beyond Llandovery, on *l*., Henllys. At Pumsant, on *r*., Dolancothi and Brunant. At Lampeter, the *R*. Teifi is noted for its salmon. Ancient *ch*. and College.

Lampeter to Newcastle-in-Emlyn (20—225¼); entering Lampeter turn to *l*. and through Llanwinnen, Llanwenog, by Allt Yr Odyn Arms, 213¾, Rhydowen, 215¼, and through Llandyfriog, 223½; hilly road.

At Lampeter on *r*. to *Tregarron* (11—216¼).

(*Newcastle-in-Emlyn:* Emlyn Arms.)

Newcastle is situate amid beautiful scenery on *R*. Teifi. There are ruins of a castle.

Newcastle-in-Emlyn to Cardigan (10—235¼); at Newcastle turn to *l*. and cross *R*. Teifi and then turn to *r*.; through Kenarth, 228¼ (where recross *R*. Teifi), by Stradmore *Ho*., 229¾, Llechrhyd, 232¼, and Llangoedmore, 234; the road keeps close to the river as far as Llechrhyd, and is almost level; delightful ride through fine scenery. [Or at Newcastle keep straight on instead of crossing the river, and long ascent and descent to Pont Hirwen, 229¼, again ascent out of it and more or less down to Llangoedmore.]

(*Cardigan:* Black Lion.)

At Llechrhyd, on *l*., across *R*. Teifi, Castle Mal-gwyn; 2*m*. farther (8*m*. from Newcastle-in-Emlyn) is the pretty village of Kilgerran, with the ruins of its castle. Cardigan is a small seaport near the mouth of *R*. Teifi. Ancient *ch*. and ruins of castle dismantled by the Parliamentarians.

Cardigan to Newport (10½—245¾); in Cardigan turn to *l*., cross *R*. Teifi and turn to *r*., through St. Dogmael's, 236½, and Velindre or College, 242¾.

(*Newport:* Queen's, *B.T.C.*)

At St. Dogmael's, remains of abbey.

Newport to Fishguard (7—252¾).

(*Fishguard:* Commercial; Great Western.)

Fishguard to St. David's (14¾—267½); about 2*m*. out of Fishguard keep to *r*. and through Mathry, 258¾, Penlan, 260½, and Hendre, 265¼.

LONDON TO CARDIGAN (by Carmarthen).

London to Carmarthen (214)—p. 111.

Carmarthen to Conwyl-Elfed (7—221); in Carmarthen turn to *r*. (if coming from Llanelly way it is the 2nd turn after crossing *R*. Towy), and it is a good macadam road by Llan-newydd or Newchurch, 217½; there is a slight but barely perceptible rise all the way to Conwyl-Elfed, otherwise Conwil-in-Elvet.

Conwyl-Elfed to Llangeler (7¾—228¾); keeping to *r*. at the bifurcation, the road now runs up the valley and is good and nearly level to Cwmdeant or Dolau-Saison, 223¾, then uphill, rather too steep to be ridden, to Blaen-Bargoed, 225¼, on the top of a bleak mountain; the descent of the other side begins immediately after, and continues more or less gradual by Bwlch-clawdd, 226½, and Croes-ffordd, 227½ (keep to *l*.), ending with a steep pitch of 100 yards, where the road is cut through the solid rock.

Llangeler to Newcastle-in-Emlyn (5½—234¼); by Henllan, 230½, Pentre-cagyl, 232, and Aber-arad, 233¾, the road follows the left bank of the *R.* Teifi, and is slightly on the fall all the way, with one steeper hill about ½*m.* long, though it can be ridden down with safety.

[Or from Conwyl-Elfed by the left hand road, and keeping to *r.* about 3½*m.* farther on, to Pentre-cagyl, a little shorter.

Or keep to *l.* at Conwyl, and again to *l.* 3½*m.* further, by Pont-y-bwlch (keep to *r.*) to Aber-arad.]

Newcastle-in-Emlyn to Cardigan (10—244¼)—p. 112; join the Cardigan road just before Newcastle, and keep straight on instead of going through the town. [Or at Pont-y-bwlch keep to *l.* straight to Kenarth, 235½, and Cardigan, 242½. Or from *Carmarthen* by Llanelnwth *ch.*, 217½, The County Stone, 226¾, Kilrah Kilrhedyn, 228, Velindre Mill, 230½, and Bridell, 237, to *Cardigan*, 240.]

LONDON TO NEWPORT (by Monmouth.)

London to Monmouth (130¾)—p. 110.

Monmouth to Raglan (8—138¾); through Monmouth turn to *r.* and shortly after to *l.*; through Wonastow, 133½ (a little further keep to *l.*) is a good macadam road, rather hilly. [Or out of Monmouth turn to *l.* and shortly after to *r.* and through Mitcheltroy, joining the other road a little further, past Wonastow.]

At Raglan, ruins of the once magnificent castle, dismantled in the Civil War

Raglan to Usk (5¼—144); take second turn to *l.* ¼*m.* past the Beaufort Arms; there is the long ascent of Lancayo Hill to mount, followed by a run down for the last 2*m.*; not so good road as the preceding.

(*Usk:* Three Salmons.)

Usk was the birthplace of Richard III. and Edward IV.; ruins of ancient castle. *R.* Usk is famous for its salmon.

Usk to Caerleon (7—151); after crossing the *R.* Usk, turn to *l.*, and it is a capital undulating road, but more down than up, through Llanbadock, 144½, Llangibby, 146½, and Llanhennock, 149¾.

Near Llangibby are the ruins of Llangibby Castle. Caerleon was a Roman city, and there are many remains of it still to be seen. In the vicinity are large tin mines and works.

Caerleon to Newport (4—155); cross *R.* Usk and it is a hilly but good road through Christchurch, 152½, when you join the New Passage and Chepstow road.

LONDON TO MONMOUTH (by Coleford).

London to Newnham (115½)—p. 109.

Newnham to Littledean (2—117½); turn sharp to *r.* in Newnham; it is a fair but uphill road. [A shorter way is by turning off to *r.* 1*m.* beyond Westbury, 112¼—p. 109, saving nearly 2*m.*]

Just before Littledean is an ancient camp.

Littledean to Coleford (6¾—124¼) through the Forest of Dean, by

Cinderford, 119, Speech House, 120¼, and Winnett's Hill, 122¾, is not a very good road, and rather hilly.
(*Coleford:* Angel.)

Coleford to Monmouth (5—129¼); a considerable rise out of Coleford, and another before Stanton, 126¼, then a very steep and dangerous descent through splendid scenery. [There is another road, turning to l. ½m. out of Coleford and through High Meadow, 125¼, to Upper Redbrook, 127, on the *R.* Wye, thence up the river side; same distance.]

LONDON TO MONMOUTH (by Mitcheldean.)

London to Huntley (111)—p. 110.

Huntley to Mitcheldean (4¾—115¾) by the left hand road and past Longhope station, 113½; hilly, but good road. Good scenery.

Mitcheldean to Coleford (8—123¾); turn sharp to l. in Mitcheldean, and up a steep hill; the road goes through the Forest of Dean by Drybrook, 117 (keep to l. and shortly after to r.), Camomile Green, 120, and Mile End, 122¾; very hilly road.

Coleford to Monmouth (5—128¾)—above.

LONDON TO ABERYSTWITH.

London to Ross (120¼)—p. 110.

Ross to Hereford (15—135¼); keep straight through Ross, cross *R.* Wye, and at Wilton *Tg.*, 121, take the middle road; through Peterstow, 123¼, by Harewood End Inn, 126¼, Llandinabo, 127¼, and Much Birch, 128¾, to Cross-in-Hand *Tg.*, 130½, is a good road, with some rather long hills, but none which cannot be ridden up; then a long and heavy hill to descend down Callow Pitch, and rough road through Callow, 131¼; the streets of Hereford are macadamised. Returning, keep to l. near top of Callow Pitch. [Or ½m. past Wilton *Tg.*, on *r.*, through Pig's Cross, 123¾, Hoarwithy, 125½, Little Dewchurch, 127½, and Aconbury, 129, it is not near so hilly, joining the other road just before *Hereford*, 133½.] Fine scenery.

(*Hereford:* Green Dragon; Mitre, *Hqrs.*; Nelson Inn.)

At Hereford there are slight remains of the old walls and the castle; it was a diocese in British-Roman times. The cathedral was erected in the 11th century; it has been recently restored, and contains many old monuments. A triennial musical festival is held here in conjunction with the choirs of Gloucester and Worcester. The town was besieged twice in the Parliamentary War. David Garrick was born here. Beyond Peterstow, on *r.*, Pengethly; on *r.*, Harewood Park. On Aconbury Hill, top of Callow Pitch, on *r.*, an ancient camp; also Dindor or Dynedor Hill, on which are remains of an ancient camp, 2m. on *r.* before Hereford.

Hereford to Norton Canon (9½—144¾); in Hereford turn to *l.*, and by White Cross, 136¼, King's Acre, 137¾ (keep to *r.*), Stretton, 138½, Creden Hill, 140, Mansell Lacy, 142, and Yazor, 143½; good road.

Note the elegant White Cross. At Stretton, cross line of Roman way. At Creden Hill, 2m. on *l.*, the site of Roman station, Kenchester, where many remains are to be seen. On *r.*, an entrenched camp on Creden Hill.

Norton Canon to Kington (10—154¾); by left hand road through Eccles Green, 146, Sarnesfield, 147½, Woonton, 149, Holmes Marsh, 151, Lyonshall, 152¼, and Penrhôs, 153¼; good road.

[Or at White Cross, on *r.* through Cross Elms, 137½, keep to *l.*, Tillington, 140¼, Burghill, 139¼, Brinsop Court, 141½, Wormesley, 143½, over Wormesley Hill, through *Weobley*, 146¾, to Sarnesfield, 148¾.

Or at Norton, on *r.* to *Weobley*, 147¼, and thence direct to Lyonshall, 153¼.]

(*Kington*: Oxford Arms.)

1*m.* before Weobley, between the two roads, Garnstone Castle. Past Lyonshall, on *r.*, Castle Woore or Weir; on *l.*, Moor Court.

Kington to New Radnor (7¼—162) is a splendid road, rather undulating, passing close to Old Radnor on *l.* about halfway.

(*New Radnor*: Eagle.)

2*m.* before New Radnor, on *l.*, Harpton Court; 1*m.* further, on *r.*, Downton Hall.

New Radnor to Rhayader (19—181); turn to *l.* and there is a long pull uphill through and for 3*m.* beyond Llanfihangel-Nant-Melan, 165 (just beyond keep to *r.*), then a similar run down through Llandegley, 169, to Pen-y-bont, 171, and undulating but chiefly on the rise to Nantmel, 175, and then downhill. Returning, keep to *r.* at Pen-y-bont; very good road.

(*Rhayader*: Lion; Lion and Castle.)

Pretty scenery. Before Llanfihangel, 1*m.* on *r.*, the cascade of Water-break-its-neck. On *r.*, Pen-y-bont Court; on *l.*, Pen-y-bont Hall.

Rhayader to Devil's Bridge (18¼—199¼); leaving Rhayader cross *R.* Wye, and the road then goes over the mountains: chiefly uphill for about 4*m.*, with descent into the Afon Elan valley, which follow up for 4 or 5*m.* farther, then down the Ystwith valley by Cwm Ystwith, 192¼, to Pentrebrunant ("Fountain" Inn), 195¼; here bear to *r.* out of the Ystwith valley, a stiff ascent followed by long downhill to Devil's Bridge in the Rheidol valley; the surface is very rough and scarcely rideable, and much walking will be necessary; very wild and rugged scenery. [Or in Rhayader turn to *r.* and run up the valley of the *R.* Wye, by Severn Arms and Llangurig for about 17*m.* to Steddfor-gurig Inn, at the foot of Mount Plynlimmon, and downhill, more or less, for 7 or 8*m.*, by Yspytty Cynfyn to Devil's Bridge, in some parts too steep to ride.]

At Devil's Bridge, the Falls of Mynach and Devil's Punchbowl; 2*m.* up the Rheidol Valley, Parson's Bridge. 8*m.* S. are the ruins of Strata Florida Abbey, past Hafod mansion and park.

Devil's Bridge to Aberystwith (11½—210¾); the road is rather on the rise for 2½*m.*, then commencing at the 9th *ms.* from Aberystwith (971ft. high) it is a gradual downhill with scarcely a break, winding along the hill sides on the left bank of the Rheidol valley, by Eskynald, 202¼, and through Piccadilly, 208¾ (where on return journey keep to *l.*); good road.

(*Aberystwith*: Bellevue; Queen.)

2*m.* before Piccadilly, on *l.*, Nanteos Park. At Aberystwith, ruins of the castle, founded 1277, and dismantled by Cromwell; there are library, theatre, assembly rooms, baths, &c. Many pretty walks in the neighbourhood: Plas-crug, Pen-dinas, Pen-glais, Vale of Clarach, Gogerddan Park, Tan-y-castell, Crosswood Park or Trawscoed, &c. Excellent sea-bathing. There are many lead mines in the neighbourhood.

LONDON TO HEREFORD (by Ledbury).

London to Gloucester (103¼)—p. 109.

Gloucester to Newent (8½—111¾); turn to *r.* at the *P.O.* down a slight descent, then cross canal and *R.* Severn, and along an avenue of trees, through Over, 104¾, to Highnam Court, 105¾ (where turn to *r.*), and through Highnam, 107, and Highleadon Green, 109¼, the road is rather hilly and very dusty and rutty on account of coach traffic; oolite surface, slippery in wet weather and requiring careful riding.

At Newent are remains of an ancient priory.

Newent to Ledbury (8—119¾); long hill to mount out of Newent to Hill End, 113¾, followed by a corresponding descent to Dymock, 115¾, and then nearly level to Ledbury, the streets of which are paved. Returning, a mile out of Ledbury keep to *l.*

(*Ledbury:* Feathers; New Commercial; Royal Oak.)

Ledbury is a small old-fashioned town; the *ch.* was originally Saxon, but from numerous alterations is now mostly Norman, with detached tower and fine altar-piece. On *r.*, near Ledbury, is Eastnor Castle, the elegant residence of Earl Somers.

Ledbury to Hereford (15¾—135½); ½*m.* out of Ledbury turn to *l.*, and through Ledbury Mills, 120¾, Trumpet, 123¾, Pool End, 124¾, Tarrington, 127, Stoke Edith, 128, Dormington, 129½ (keep to *r.*), Bartestree, 131, Lugwardine, 132½, and Tupsley, 134; undulating all the way, nowhere dangerous or difficult, except a ½*m.* hill to walk down at Lugwardine; generally a bad road.

Beyond Ledbury, on *l.*, Wall Hill Camp. At Trumpet, on *r.*, Mainstone Court. On *l.*, pass Stoke Edith Park, Sufton Court and Hom-Lacey, where Pope wrote his "Man of Ross." At Lugwardine, on *r.*, New Court. At Bartestree, on *l.*, Hagley Park and Longworth Court.

LONDON TO BRECON (by Hereford).

London to Hereford (135¼)—p. 114.

Hereford to Hanmer's Cross (10½—145¾); in Hereford turn to *l.*, and by White Cross, 136¼ (keep to *l.*), King's Acre (Green Man), 137¾ (keep to *l.*), Sugwas Pool, 139¼, New Ware, 140¼, Bridge Sollers, 141½, and Portway, 144.

At Sugwas Pool, on *r.*, the site of the Roman Station of Kenchester, where many remains are to be seen. At Sugwas Pool, on *l.*, Sugwas Court. At Hanmer's Cross, on *l.*, Moccas Park.

Hanmer's Cross to Hay (9—154¾); keep to *l.* over Tin Hill and cross *R.* Wye to Bredwardine, 147¾, and through Clockmill, 150¾, and Hardwick Green, 152¾. [Or by the right hand road through Letton, 147, Willersley, 149 (keep to *l.*), Winforton, 150, Whitney, 152 (just beyond cross *R.* Wye), and Clifford, 154¼, to Hay, 156½.]

(*Hay:* Blue Boar.)

On *l.*, Letton Court. Beyond Clockmill, on *r.*, ruins of Clifford Castle. On *l.*, Hardwick Court and The Moor; on *r.*, Whitney Court. At Hay, the castle.

Hay to Brecon (15¼—170); just out of Hay keep to *r.* and through Glasbury ("Cock" Inn), 158¼, Bronllys, 162¾, and Vellinvach, 165¾. [Or beyond Hay keep to *l.* and through Talgarth, 162¼, where turn to *r.*, to Bronllys, 163¾.]

At Glasbury, on *r.*, across R. Wye, Maeslough and Tregoyd. At Bronllys, on *r.*, Pontywall; on *l.*, Tregunter *Ho.*

LONDON TO KNIGHTON.

London to Hereford (135¼)—p. 114.

Hereford to Stretford Bridge (11—146¼); in Hereford turn to *l.*, and by White Cross, 136⅜ (keep to *r.*), Cross Elms, 137½ (keep to *r.*), Portway, 139¾, and Bush Bank, 143¼.

Note the elegant White Cross. 1½m. past Portway, on *l.*, Burghill Lodge.

Stretford Bridge to Presteign (12—158¼); by left hand road, through Ridge Cross, 148¾, Pembridge, 150½ (turn to *r.*), Byton Lane, 154, and Cwm or Combe, 156.

(*Presteign:* Castle.)

At Cwm, on *l.*, an ancient camp.

Presteign to Knighton (7—165¼); out of Presteign keep to *r.*, and through Norton, 161¾, and over Llanwen Hill. Returning, out of Knighton keep to *r.*, and 1m. further to *l.*, before crossing Llanwen Hill.

Beyond Presteign, on *r.*, Boultibrook. About 3m. N. of Knighton, on Stow Hill, is an ancient entrenchment, called Caer Caradoc, by some supposed to be the scene of the last battle fought by Caractacus against the Romans.

LONDON TO LEDBURY (by Stanton).

London to Gloucester (103¼)—p. 109.

Gloucester to Stanton (9—112¼); a mile out of Gloucester, after the railway and before crossing the *R.* Severn, turn to *r.* from the Highnam Court road, then cross the *R.* Severn 1m. further on, and through Maisemore, 105¼ (4m. further keep to *l.*), is a rather hilly but good road; Bristol stone.

Stanton to Ledbury (7¾—120) is more hilly; steep ascent into Redmarley, 115¼, and then hilly through Little London, 117; Malvern stone; good scenery.

LONDON TO TEWKESBURY.

London to Cheltenham (94¼)—p. 108.

Cheltenham to Tewkesbury (9—103¼); keep straight on through Cheltenham, and then level by Bedlam, 96, and Uckington, 97, to Piff's Elm, 98½, when there is a short ascent to mount at Comb Hill to Swan Inn, 99¼, where join the Gloucester road and keep to *r.*, and after this it is undulating, but no steep hills; good road all the way; Bristol stone.

(*Tewkesbury:* Anchor; Hop Pole; Swan.)

Tewkesbury, at the junction of the Severn and Avon, is pleasantly situated; the parish *ch.* was formerly part of an abbey founded by the Saxons, and contains many fine monuments. In the neighbourhood was fought a bloody battle in 1461, when Edward IV. totally defeated the Lancastrians.

SECTION V.

From Marble Arch and General Post Office; North Western Roads (North West Middlesex, West Herts, Buckinghamshire, Oxfordshire, Worcestershire, Shropshire, South Northamptonshire, Warwickshire, Staffordshire, South Cheshire, and North Wales).

LONDON TO BARMOUTH.

London to Oxford (54)—p. 107.

Oxford to Woodstock (8—62); at the further end of Oxford, instead of crossing the *R.* Isis turn to *r.*, and the road is level past the Observatory, through Summerstown, 55½, and by Wolvercot, 56½, and Yarnton *Tp.*, 58, to Begbrook, 59½, from which there is a long rise and gentle fall into Woodstock; bad macadam road, rough and bumpy all the way, and in wet weather greasy.

(*Woodstock*: Bear; King's Arms, *B.T.C.*)

On *l.*, near Wolvercot, the ruins of Godstow Nunnery. On *l.* at Begbrook, on Worton Heath Hill, an old camp called Round Castle. Woodstock was a residence of several English sovereigns, from Alfred downwards: here Henry II. wooed the fair Rosamond. The palace stood in Blenheim Park, which was presented by the nation to the Duke of Marlborough, and the modern stately pile since erected was designed by Sir John Vanbrugh.

Woodstock to Enstone (7—69); the road continues bad past Slape Bridge, 64¼, to Over Kiddington, 66¼, after which it is slightly better, but becomes greasy and heavy with the least wet; stiff pull out of Woodstock, the rest undulating with rough and stony descent into Enstone.

1½m. beyond Woodstock, the line of the old Roman road, Akeman Street, crosses the road. A little further, on *l.*, are extensive remains of ancient earthworks, under the name of Grime's Dyke, and Callow Hill. Close to, is Ditchley Park, Earl of Normanton. On *r.*, Glympton Park and Kiddington House; in the grounds of the latter is a baptismal font, said to be that in which Edward the Confessor was baptized.

Enstone to Chipping Norton (4½—73½); first a short stiff rise, followed by a gentle incline for nearly a mile up Broadstone Hill, and then level; rough road to the toll-bar, 72¼, where turn to *l.*, and the rest is good smooth road to Chipping Norton.

On *r.*, Heythrop Park, the elegant mansion of the Duke of Beaufort. At Chipping Norton, fine ancient *ch.*, with many old monuments; slight remains of a castle erected in the reign of Stephen.

Chipping Norton to Moreton-in-the-Marsh (8¼—81¾); the road gradually improves through Salford, 75½, Salford Hill (or Cross Hands), 76½, and over Chastleton Heath to Four Shire Stone, 80, where take left hand road.

At Salford, on the hill on *l.*, is Cornwell *Ho.* On Chastleton Heath is an ancient camp. At Four Shire Stone the counties of Oxford, Gloucester, Warwick, and Worcester meet. Here Edmund Ironside defeated the Danes in a severe battle.

Moreton-in-the-Marsh to Broadway (8¼—90); good road to Bourton-on-the-Hill, 83½, but again becomes worse and is all rather hilly to Broadway Quarry on the top of Broadway Hill, which is a very long and winding descent, and should not be ridden down except with a good brake, into Broadway.

(*Broadway*: Lygon Arms.)

At Bourton, on *l.*, Seizincote Park; on *r.*, Batsford (Lord Redesdale). Fine views of the Avon and Severn Valleys are obtained from Broadway Hill. Before Broadway is Northwick Park. On *r.*, at Broadway Hill, Farncombe Abbey; on *l.*, Spring Hill.

Broadway to Bengeworth (5¼—95¼) by Wickhamford Bridge, 93¼, is a fairly level and good road.

At Bengeworth, ¼m. on *r.*, across *R.* Avon, is *Evesham*, 95½, into which is a stiff descent.

(*Evesham*: Cross Keys; Crown; Northwick Arms; Rose and Crown; Star; Railway.)

Evesham is pleasantly situated on the *R.* Avon, in the midst of a beautiful and fertile tract of country, called the Vale of Evesham; a magnificent abbey formerly existed here, but only a few remains are now to be seen, the fine bell tower of St. Laurence's *ch.*, erected 1533, having belonged to it, but was spared at the dissolution. Near the town Prince Edward in 1265 defeated Simon Montfort, who was slain with his son.

Bengeworth to Pershore (6¾—102); turn to *l.* in Bengeworth; the road follows down the valley of the Avon through Great Hampton, 96¼, and is chiefly on the fall to the Avon Bridge at Wick, 101, where turn to *r.*; good surface. Pershore is paved.

(*Pershore*: Angel; Three Tuns.)

At Pershore, fine old abbey *ch.* There are ruins of a large Benedictine Abbey. Pretty scenery. Good bathing to be had in the *R.* Avon.

Pershore to Worcester (9—111); long steep hill out of Pershore, and three more steep hills to climb at short intervals to Stoulton, 106¼, and the rest undulating and pretty good road through Whittington, 108¾: descent at Redhill.

[From *Bengeworth* there is another road through Evesham, down the right bank of the *R.* Avon, turning to *l.* at Red House, 96½, and by Chedbury Farm, Fladbury Station, and Moore to Wyre Piddle, 102, a mile beyond which on *l.* to *Pershore*, 103½, or straight on by Stonebow Bridge, 104¾, Egdon Hall, Spetchley Station, 107¼, and Swineshead, 109½, to *Worcester*, 111½.]

(*Worcester*: Bell, *Hqrs.*; Crown; Hop Market; Pinkett's; Punchbowl; Railway, *R.T.C.*; Star; Talbot Commercial; Unicorn; Watton.)

At Worcester are remains of the castle and walls, erected by the Normans; fine early English cathedral (1218-1386) originally a priory *ch.*, containing many monuments, and recently restored. There are numerous public buildings. The chief manufactures are porcelain and stone-china and leather gloves. Here Charles II. was defeated by Cromwell in 1651.

Worcester to Hundred House Inn (11—122); in Worcester turn to *l.*, cross *R.* Severn and turn to *r.*, then running near *R.* Severn and through Hallow, 113¾, to Holt Heath, 117½ (where turn to *l.*), and through Witley, 119½, and past Witley Park.

2*m.* out of Worcester, on *l.*, Henwick *Ho.* At Hallow, on *r.*, Hallow Park; a little farther on *l.*, Thorngrove Lodge. On *r.*, Holt Castle; on *l.*, Witley Court.

Hundred House Inn to Tenbury (10¾—132¾); keep to *r.* and 1*m.* farther to *l.*, and through Stockton, 124½, Eardistone, 126, Lindridge, 127¼, and Newnham, 129¾; for last 6 or 7*m.* the road runs near to *R.* Teme.

[Or from *Worcester* turn to *l.* about 1½*m.* after crossing *R.* Severn, and through Peachley, 114½, Martley, 118¼, over Ham Bridge, 119½ (*R.* Teme), through Clifton-upon-Teme, 121¾, by High House, 123¼, Broad Heath, 125¾, Round Oak, 126½, and Wood Park, 128½, to *Tenbury*, 130½.]

(*Tenbury:* Swan.)

At Hundred House Inn, on *l.*, Woodbury Hill, an ancient encampment; on *r.*, Abberley Lodge. At Stockton, on *l.*, across *R.* Teme, and at High *Ho.*, on *r.*, Stanford Court. At Ham Bridge, on *r.*, Ham Castle. At Broad Heath, on *r.*, Hanley Court. On *r.*, Eardistone *Ho.* Tenbury lies on S. side of *R.* Teme.

Tenbury to Brimfield Cross (4—136¾); through Burford, 133¾, and Little Hereford, 135½ (just beyond cross *R.* Teme.)

At Little Hereford, on *r.*, Easton Court. On *l.*, Brimfield Court. On *l.*, Burford House.

Brimfield Cross to Ludlow (5—141¾); turn to *r.* and it is pretty level and fair going, except a steep ascent into Ludlow from *R.* Teme, through a narrow archway, dangerous to ride down. [Or at Little Hereford turn to *r.* to Ludlow, 140¾.] Returning, out of Ludlow, after crossing *R.* Teme, keep to *l.* at the *Tg.*

(*Ludlow:* Angel; Feathers.)

About half-way, on *l.*, Ashford Hall and Moor Park. Before Ludlow, on *l.*, Ludford *Ho.* and Ludford Park. At Ludlow, ruins of castle; fine *ch.*, containing many ancient monuments.

Ludlow to Newton Green. Guide Post (8—149¾); about 1¼*m.* from Ludlow keep to *l.* and through Bromfield, 144¼ (keep to *r.*), and Onibury, 146¾, and Stoke Say, 149, on the rise most of the way, being up the Teme valley; rather rough road.

At Bromfield, on *l.*, Oakley Park; and 4*m.* beyond it, Downton Castle. On *l.*, Stoke Castle; on *r.*, Norton Camp. The Guide Post enumerates the distances of 48 cities and towns.

Newton Green to Bishop's Castle, *M.H.* (9—158¾); keep straight on to New Inn, 150¼, where turn to *l.*, and by Basford *Tg.*, 153¼, Edgeton Farms, 153¾, and Red House Farm, 155¼ (keep to *r.*); very hilly road, especially a very steep hill to go over between Red House Farm and Bishop's Castle. [Or at Red House Farm keep to *l.*, and through Lydbury and Brocton, avoiding the hill, 1*m.* longer. Or at Newton Green turn to *l.*, and by the new road through Aston, 152¾, Brampton, 153¾, keep to *r.* for Kempton, 154¾, Lydbury or Walcot Park, 155¾, Brocktor, 157¼, and Bishop's Castle, 159¾.]

(*Bishop's Castle:* Castle.)

About 1½m. past Newton Green, between the two roads, Sibdon Castle. At Red House, on *r.*, Plowden Hall; on *l.*, 1*m.*, Walcot Park, W. of which, on Tongley Hill, are some remains of extensive British earthworks, called Bury Ditches.

Bishop's Castle to Montgomery (9—167¾); by Bishop's Moat, 160¾, and Red Court House, 163½. [Or beyond Bishop's Castle keep to *r.*, and through Snead and Church Stoke to Red Court House, 164½.]

(*Montgomery:* Dragon.)

Beyond Bishop's Castle, on *r.*, Oakley *Ho.* At Snead, on *r.*, Boveries *Ho.*, and beyond it, Castle Ring, an ancient entrenched hill. At Red Court *Ho.*, on *l.*, Millington Hall; 1*m.* farther, on *r.*, Brompton Hall. Before Montgomery, on *r.*, Lymore Lodge and Park. At Montgomery, ruins of the castle, and near to it, on a hill, a large fortified camp.

Montgomery to Welshpool (8½—176); through Forden, 171½, and (keeping to *l.*) cross *R.* Severn 2*m.* further. [Or at Church Stoke turn to *r.*, and through Cherbury, joining the other road a little beyond Forden; about 1½*m.* shorter.]

(*Welshpool:* Mitre; Royal Oak; Star.)

At Forden, on *r.*, Nantfribba Hall; 1*m.* farther, on *l.*, Edderton Hall. At Severn Bridge, on *r.*, Leighton Hall. Before Welshpool, on *l.*, Powis Castle and Park.

Welshpool to Llanfair (7½—183½); in Welshpool turn to *l.*; 4¼*m.* farther, at the bifurcation, keep to *l*, the road on *r.* being 2¼*m.* longer.

[Or from *Montgomery*, leaving by the Old Castle, turn to *r.* 2*m.* beyond the town, and through Garthmyl, 169¾, to Effelfach ½*m.* farther, turn to *l.* to Berriew; leaving this by the *l.* to Castle Caereinion, 175½, and 1*m.* farther join the other road to *Llanfair*, 179¼.]

(*Llanfair:* Fox's.)

Beyond Welshpool, on *r.*, Llanerchydol. At the fork roads. 1*m.* on *r.*, Gyfronydd; on *l.*, Dolerddyn Hall. At Llanfair, interesting old *ch.* Before Berriew, on *r.*, Glan Severn.

Llanfair to Cann Office Inn (7—190½); through Llanerfyl, 188½. At Llanerfyl, on *r.*, Llyssin. Near Cann Office Inn, on *l.*, a large tumulus.

Cann Office Inn to Dinas Mawddwy (13—203½); a little farther than the Inn keep to *l.*, and for about 6*m.* the road gradually rises up a valley, followed by similar downhill to Mallwyd, 202½, where turn to *r.*

(*Mallwyd:* Pencarth Arms.)

Dinas Mawddwy to Dolgelly (9—212½); turn to *l.* and it is nearly half uphill and half down, passing through a wild and mountain district.

(*Dolgelly:* Golden Lion; Royal Ship; Ship.)

S. of Dolgelly is Cader Idris Mountain.

Dolgelly to Barmouth (9½—222); in Dolgelly turn to *r.*, cross river, and then to *l.*, and again to *l.* at Llanelltid, 214, whence the road runs close to *R.* Mawddach, through Glandwr, 220; pretty fair road.

(*Barmouth:* Arthog Hall; Barmouth, *B. T. C.*; Cousygedol Arms; Kynoch's; Lion.)

Beyond Dolgelly, on *r.*, Hengwrt Hall, Cymmer Abbey and Nannau Hall. Barmouth is a small town and watering place at the mouth of the *R.* Mawddach. There is a castle built by Edward I.

LONDON TO KNIGHTON (by Worcester).

London to Worcester (111)—p. 119.

Worcester to Bromyard (14—125); in Worcester turn to *l.*, cross *R.* Severn, and through Cotheridge, 115, Broadwas, 117, Dodenham Lane, 118, and over Knightsford Bridge, 119¼.

(*Bromyard:* Falcon; Hop Pole.)

2*m.* out of Worcester, on *l.*, Crownest; on *l.*, Cotheridge Court. At Knightsford Bridge, on *r.*, Whitbourne Court; on *l.*, Gaines. 2*m.* farther, on *r.*, Brockhampton Park; on *l.*, Clater Park.

Bromyard to Leominster (12—137); steep ascent to Bredenbury, 128¼, and by New Inn, 129¼, Blatchley Green, 130, Docklow, 131¾, Steen's Bridge, 133, Trumpet, 134, and Eaton Bridge, 136.
On r., Bredenbury Ho. At Docklow, on l., Buckland.

Leominster to Mortimer's Cross (6½—143¾); 1m. out of Leominster keep to r., and again at Cholstry, 139½, and by Cobden's Ash, 140½, and through Kingsland, 141¼.
At Leominster, on l., Ryelands. At Mortimer's Cross was fought the last battle in which Edward IV. defeated the Lancastrians. 1m. N., Yatton Court. On E., in Croft Park, remains of Croft Castle and a British entrenchment. 4m. N., are Wigmore Hall, and ruins of the castle, a very ancient building. 2m. beyond it, Aldferton Abbey ruins and Brandon Camp.

Mortimer's Cross to Presteign (8—151¾); turn to l., and through Shobden, 145, Byton Lane or Cross, 147, and Cwm or Combe, 149.
On r., Shobden Court.

Presteign to Knighton (7—158¾)—p. 117.
[Or at *Mortimer's Cross* keep straight on through Aymestrey, 144½, Wigmore, 147¼, Aldferton, 149, *Walford*, 150, turn to l. and then to r. and through Brampton Bryan, 151½, to *Knighton*, 157¼.]
On l., Brampton Bryan Park; on r., Brampton Hall; on r., at Coxwall Knoll, an old British hill fortress. 2½m. before Knighton, on l., Stanage Park.

LONDON TO TOWYN.

London to Bishop's Castle (158¾)—p. 120.

Bishop's Castle to Newtown (16—174¾); by Bishop's Moat, 160¼, and Red Court House, 163½, and 1¼m. farther turn to l. and through Kerry, 171¾.
[Or from *Montgomery*, 167¾—p. 120; here turn to l., and there is a steep unrideable hill to mount and walk down into Llandyssil, 169¾, whence it runs close by the R. Severn, and is almost level and fairly good to *Newtown*, 176½.]
(*Newtown*: Bear's Head, B.T.C.; Bear; Elephant; Unicorn.)
At Kerry, on r., Dolforgan Hall.

Newtown to Talerthig (14—188¾); through Newtown cross R. Severn, then turn to l. and the road is more or less on the rise through Aberhavesp, 177¾, Llanwnnog, 181¾, and Carno, 185¾.
On r., Aberhavesp Hall.

Talerthig to Machynlleth (14—202¾); keep to r., and downhill through Capel, 190¾, to "Wynnstay Arms," 191¾, then 3 or 4m. uphill and down through Pen-y-goes, 200¾.
[Or from *Mallwyd*, 202½—p. 121; then turn to l. down Dovey Valley and through Cemmes, 206½, joining the above road 1½m. farther, and to *Machynlleth*, 213.]
2m. before Pen-y-goes, on r., Aber-gwidol; farther on, on r., Dolguog.

Machynlleth to Towyn (12—214¾); in the former turn to r., cross R. Dovey or Dyfi, and turn to l. through Pennal, 206½.
(*Towyn*: Browyu; Cambrian; Corbet; Temperance.)
At Pennal, on l., Telgarth. 1m. before Towyn, on r., Bodtalog. 1m. N., Ynysymaengwyn.

LONDON TO CARNARVON.

London to Dolgelly (242½)—p. 121.

Dolgelly to Maentwrog (18—230½); in Dolgelly turn to *r.*, cross river, and then turn to *l.*, and at Llanelltid, 214, keep to *r.* up the Mawddach valley, by Pont-ar-garfa, 218, and Pontdelgofylia, 220½, and through Trawsfynayd, 225½.

Maentwrog to Beddgelert (9—239½); cross the river, and at Tan-y-Bwlch Inn, 231½, keep to *r.*, and by the old *Tp.* road and up the Pass of Aberglassllyn and over Pont-Aberglassllyn, 238, is a wretched road, very rough and stony; this road cannot be recommended for bicycling, in some parts quite unrideable. [A better road is to go round by *Tremadoc*, 240, to Beddgelert, 246.]

(*Tremadoc*: Maddock Arms.—*Beddgelert*: Goat; Prince Llewellyn; Saracen's Head.)

On *r.*, Tan-y-Bwlch Hall. Fine scenery.

Beddgelert to Carnarvon (12—251½); keep to *l.* and it is uphill for 3m., then downhill through Bettws Garmon, 246½. [Or from *Tremadoc* through Penmorfa, 240½, Dolbenmaen, 244½, Llanllyfni, 250½, Llanwnda, 255½, to *Carnarvon*, 258½.]

LONDON TO TEWKESBURY (by Stow-on-the-Wold).

London to Burford (72¼)—p. 108.

Burford to Stow-on-the-Wold (10—82¼); in the middle of Burford turn to *r.* past the *ch.*, and a short distance farther out of the town keep to *l.*; beginning with a ¼m. mile walk out of the town, it is an almost continual ascent for 7m., then the surface improves, and there is a mile run down to the railway, followed by a mile walk up into Stow.

(*Stow*: Talbot, *B.T.C.*; Unicorn.)

Stow is built on the top of a hill, and in a bleak and exposed situation; the *ch.* was erected at different periods of the 14th and 15th centuries.

Stow-on-the-Wold to Stanway (9¾—92); steep descent from Stow to Upper Swell, 83¼, and thence through Ford, 89, and Coscomb Cross, 90.

Stanway to Tewkesbury (10½—102½); level road by Toddington, 93½, Alderton, 95¾, Little Washburn, 96½, to Isabel's Elm, 99½, after which is a long and gradual decline through Ashchurch, 100½, down to Tewkesbury; rutty road, very rough and bumpy.

On *r.*, Toddington *Ho.*, and on *l.*, Toddington Park.

LONDON TO ENSTONE (by Islip).

London to Wheatley (48½)—p. 107.

Wheatley to Islip (7½—56); turning to *r.* at the entrance of Wheatley, and ½m. beyond keep again to *r.*, leaving the Oxford road; after a little uphill, presently there is a sharp descent to Forest Hill, 50, then the road is level by Stanton, 51¼, and for some distance past New Inn, 52, when a stiff and stony descent occurs, followed after another mile by a tolerable rise with a sharp drop into Islip; the road gradually deteriorates, and after New Inn is rather rough and rutty, and inclined to be greasy when wet.

At Forest Hill is a pretty old *ch.*, surrounded by fine yew trees. Islip is a village on the *R.* Ray.

Islip to Enslow Bridge ($4\frac{1}{2}$—$60\frac{1}{2}$); straight through Islip is but a narrow lane, so very steep and rough as to be utterly unrideable; to avoid this, after crossing the bridge turn to *l.* through the lower part of the village, then to *r.*, when the ascent is much easier; from the top the road is slightly undulating and tolerably good, crossing the Oxford and Bicester road at 57, and through Bletchingdon, $58\frac{3}{4}$, to Enslow Wharf, 60, where there is a short but sharp and loose descent into Cherwell valley, across which, over canal and *R.* Cherwell, it is rough, and, when wet, greasy.

On *r.*, Bletchingdon Park, and beyond it, Kirtlington Park.

Enslow Bridge to Enstone (8—$68\frac{1}{2}$); a stiff rise, rather rough and bumpy, leads out of the valley (care should be taken in descending it, as there is a *Tg.* at the bottom and also a sharp turn to the *r.*); from the top it is undulating for about 2m., crossing the Oxford and Banbury road at 61m. and the Woodstock and Banbury road at the *Tg.*, $61\frac{1}{2}$m., then there is a steep crooked descent, best walked down, to Dornford Cottage, $62\frac{3}{4}$, followed by a long and rather stiff hill to grind up, and again a little level past the Killingworth Castle, $63\frac{1}{2}$, with another steep winding descent, very awkward to ride down, to Glympton, $64\frac{1}{2}$; here turn sharp to *l.*, and directly after the road curves sharp round again to *r.* up a steep ascent (dangerous to ride down) which gradually becomes easier and soon turns to level, joining the main Oxford road just before Over Kiddington, $65\frac{3}{4}$, and the rest undulating, with a rough and stony descent into Enstone; surface inclined to be rough and greasy when wet.

Dornford, on the Dorne Brook, and Glympton, on the *R.* Glyme, are two pretty hamlets. At Glympton is Glympton Park, and further on, Kiddington Park, where is preserved a font in which Edward the Confessor is said to have been baptized.

LONDON TO HOLYHEAD.

London to Enstone (69)—p. 118.

Enstone to Chapel House ($3\frac{1}{4}$—$72\frac{3}{4}$); a short stiff rise is followed by a gentle incline for nearly a mile up Broadstone Hill, and then level: rough road to the toll-bar, $72\frac{1}{2}$, where keep to *r.* (the Chipping Norton road to *l.*) and the rest is good and smooth.

On *r.*, pass Heythrop Park, the elegant mansion of the Duke of Beaufort.

Chapel House to Long Compton ($4\frac{1}{4}$—77) is a hilly ride; keeping to *r.* at the bifurcation $\frac{1}{4}$m. past Chapel House Inn, there are three moderate ascents in the first mile, then a considerable descent, with two turns in it and rather loose and stony, but not very steep, into a narrow valley, up the opposite side of which is a stiff pull of nearly a mile through a deep cutting to the top of Bright Hill, followed by a long run down into Long Compton; pretty good surface on the whole.

On Bright Hill, a short distance on *l.*, are the Rollerich Stones, locally known as the King, King's Men, and Five Knights; they are supposed to be remains of a Druidical Temple.

Long Compton to Shipston-on-Stour ($5\frac{1}{4}$—$82\frac{1}{4}$); at the toll-bar at the end of Long Compton keep to *l.* and through Burmington, $80\frac{3}{4}$, and Tidmington, $81\frac{1}{2}$, is a capital undulating road, with several sharp rises, but nothing difficult either way; easier going than returning. Pretty country.

(*Shipston*: Bell; George; White Horse.)

On *r.*, Weston *Ho.*; on *l.*, Tidmington Hall.

Shipston-on-Stour to Stratford-upon-Avon (10½—93¼); rough and lumpy with several small hills through Tredington, 84¾, to Newbold, 86¼, and thence nearly all downhill or level; the surface improves gradually to Alderminster, 88¾, and the rest is fairly good going. Cross R. Avon just before entering Stratford. (This road has been very much cut up by a traction engine, but it is improving again.)

(*Stratford*: Falcon, *Hqrs.*; Golden Lion; Red Horse; Red Lion; Shakespere, *Hqrs.*, *B.T.C.*; Washington Irving's.)

Beyond Tredington, cross the old Roman Fosse Way. On *r.*, Honington Hall, and Lower Eatington Park at Newbold. Beyond Alderminster, on *l.*, Alscot park. Stratford-upon-Avon is chiefly famous as being the birth-place of Shakespeare; the house in which he was born is dedicated to the nation; he was buried in the parish *ch.*, which also contains many fine monuments. The scenery of the Avon valley is very beautiful.

Stratford-upon-Avon to Alcester (8—101¼); for the first 4m. it is a little lumpy, and there are three long slopes to pull up, to top of Red Hill, 97¼, which is a steep hill to go down, smooth surface and safe with a good brake, after which it is a capital road, mostly level or gentle downhill into Alcester.

(*Alcester*: Swan, *B.T.C.*)

Alcester contains many old houses, and has a fine old *ch.*

Alcester to Headless Cross (6¼—107¾); capital smooth road and level, except a short hill at Coughton, 103¾, through Spernall Ash, 104½ (keep to *l.*; the right hand road leads to Birmingham), to Littlewood Green, 105, after which are two long hills, the second one roughish and barely rideable, at the top of which is Crab's Cross, 106¾, and the rest not very good.

[There is another route to Crab's Cross, taking the left hand fork just outside Alcester, and by the Droitwich road to New Inn, which is hilly and roughish, then to *r.* along the Ridge Way, very good; longer and not so good as the other route.]

At *Headless Cross* on *r.* to *Redditch* (1—108¾), all downhill, and sharp descent into the town.

(*Redditch*: Crown; Unicorn; Warwick Arms, *B.T.C.*—*Headless Cross*: White Hart, *B.T.C.*)

On *l.*, Coughton Park; on *r.*, Coughton Court; on *r.*, Studley Castle and Priory. Redditch is the chief seat of the needle and pin manufacture.

Headless Cross to Bromsgrove (6¾—114½); good road, with two stiff hills to pull up, through Webb Heath, to Tardebigge, 111¼, then not so good, being rather rough and hilly, two of the descents also being generally very loose; long stiff downhill, loose and rough, approaching Bromsgrove, and a narrow street leads into the town; turn to *l.* in the main street.

(*Bromsgrove*: Crab Mill Inn.)

At Tardebigge, on *r.*, Hewell Grange. Bromsgrove is the centre of the nail and button trades, which are also carried on in the surrounding villages; the parish *ch.* is situated on an eminence, and is approached by 50 steps; it has a fine tower.

Bromsgrove to Kidderminster (9½—124); turn to *r.* up a narrow turning out of the main street of Bromsgrove, and then through Chaddesley Corbett, 119½, Winterfold, 120¾, and Stone, 122, is a very undulating road, with scarcely any level stretches in the whole distance; all the hills, however, are rideable, though one or two are stiffish; entering the town is a very bumpy, but not very steep descent over the railway bridge.

Kidderminster is noted for its carpets.

Kidderminster to Bridgenorth (13¼—137¾); the first half is hilly, with two very stiff and long ascents to walk, but a moderate surface through Frainch, 124¾, and Shatterford, 128, to Allum (or Alam) Bridge, 131¼, then it is easier riding through Quatt, 133¼, over a good smooth road with a gradual fall towards Quatford, 135¼; thence take the left hand road by the side of the *R.* Severn, which is fairly level into Bridgenorth though somewhat shaky; the other road to the right is hilly.

(*Bridgenorth:* Crown and Royal.)

At Frainch, on *r.*, Sion Hill; on *l.*, an ancient earthwork, Warshill Camp. Across the *R.* Severn is the Forest of Wyre. Past Quatt, on *l.*, Dudmaston *Ho.* Bridgenorth is said to resemble ancient Jerusalem; many of the houses are built on the rock. The Saxons erected a fortress here, and there are still remains of a castle.

Bridgenorth to Much Wenlock (8¼—146); cross *R.* Severn: before a mile is traversed a stiff hill has to be mounted, and the road continues hilly and on the rise most of the way through Morville, 140¾, and by Muckley Cross, 142¾.

Past Morville, on *r.*, Aldenham Hall. At Much Wenlock are remains of an abbey, founded in 680, including the chief part of the *ch.*, a fine Gothic building of the 13th century.

Much Wenlock to Shrewsbury (12—158); a mile out of Wenlock a stiff hill begins, which ends on the top of Wenlock Edge; having crossed the summit there is a steep descent through a deep cutting, down which it is not safe to ride, as it is long, very rough, and stony, into Harley, 148; from here (keeping to *r.*) the remainder, through Cressage, 150, Cound, 152, Brompton, 154, Weeping Cross, 154¼, St. Giles, 156¾, and Abbey Foregate, 157½, except a short hill into Cressage, is good riding through an undulating and pretty country; enter the town over English Bridge, from the suburb of Abbey Foregate.

[At Shrewsbury we join the Holyhead Road proper—the old coach road—the first part of which is described *infra*, pp. 137-140. The above route to Shrewsbury is better travelling.]

(*Shrewsbury:* Eagle; Raven.)

At Cressage, on *r.*, across *R.* Severn, is the Wrekin Mountain. At Cound, across the Severn, are the remains of the Roman city of Uriconium, now Wroxeter. It was on the decay of this that Shrewsbury was founded in the 5th century by the British Princes of Powysland. There are remains of Shrewsbury town walls built in Henry III's reign, also of the old castle; the Benedictine Abbey, founded in 1083, and part of which is incorporated in the *ch.* of Holy Cross, noted for its handsome window. There are several old churches and many fine public buildings. N. of the town, at Battlefield, is the scene of the great battle between Henry IV. and Hotspur, in 1403.

Shrewsbury to Nesscliff (8½—166½); leave the town by Welsh Bridge, over *R.* Severn, and through the suburb of Frankwell, then through Shelton, 160 (keep to *r.*), over Montford Bridge, 162½ (recross *R.* Severn), and by Ensdon House, 164, is good riding, though rather hilly, and chiefly on the rise.

At Shelton, Berwick *Ho.*, Great Berwick and Down Rossall. At Nesscliff, **Great Ness.**

Nesscliff to Oswestry (9½—176); through West Felton, 171¼, and Queen's Head *Tg.*, 172 (keep to *l.*), is not quite so hilly as the last stage; surface still keeps smooth and good.

(*Oswestry:* Bell; Boar's Head; Cross Keys; George; Osburne; Queen's; Wynnstay Arms.)

On *l.*, on the Breiddin Hills, see Lord Rodney's Pillar. At Aston, pass Aston Hall. Oswestry had formerly a castle and walls, a mound marks the site of the former, and the latter have disappeared. About 3*m.* E. are the ruins of Whittington Castle.

Oswestry to Chirk (5¼—181¼); through Gobowen, 178½ (keep to *l.*), is a good road, nearly level; railway crossing at Gobowen.

[From Queen's Head *Tg.* on *r.*, a shorter and better road goes direct through Whittington to Gobowen, instead of through Oswestry; it passes through a lower country, and is more level; 1*m.* shorter.]

(*Chirk:* Hand.)

On *l.*, pass old Oswestry, Mount Sion, and l'entre-pont. 2*m.* before Chirk, on *r.*, Belmont. At Chirk, on *l.*, Chirk Castle, and on *r.*, Brynkinalt. Pretty country.

Chirk to Llangollen (6¾—188); at Whitehurst *Tg.*, 183, the road turns to *l.* and enters the valley of the *R.* Dee, called also the Vale of Llangollen; it is undulating with one or two stiff hills in the first half, then mostly downhill: good smooth road.

There is not a hill between Shrewsbury and Llangollen that cannot be ridden.

(*Llangollen:* Bridge End; Hand; Royal.)

Beautiful scenery. On *r.*, at Llangollen the ruins of Caer Dinas Bran, or Crow Castle, formerly a place of great strength. At the entrance of the Dee Valley, on *r.*, Wynnstay Park, and farther on, Trevor Hall. On *l.* of Llangollen is Plas Newydd.

Llangollen to Corwen (10¼—198¼); continuing up the valley of the Dee past Carrog Station and Llansaintffraid *Tg.*, 195¾, through Glyn Dyfrdwy, the road consists of a series of very long but gradual slopes up and down, mostly the former, especially in the first half, but the surface is very good. Splendid scenery.

(*Corwen:* Owen Glyndwr; Queen.)

Beyond Llangollen, on *r.*, Dinbryn Hall. 1*m.* farther on the road to Ruthin is the picturesque ruin of Valle Crucis Abbey, founded 1200; beyond it, Eliseg's Pillar, and the remains of Owen Glendwr's Palace. 1*m.* farther, on the banks of the Dee, is Llandysilio Hall. Before Corwen, on *r.*, Caer Drewyn, an ancient fortification. Beyond Llangollen, on *l.*, Craig-y-Gadd, an old encampment.

Corwen to Cerrig-y-Druidion (10—208¼); out of Corwen take right hand road, and cross *R.* Dee; the road now leaves the valley of the Dee and goes up the Alwen valley; it is good past Druid Inn, 201¼ (keep to *r.*), with a moderate rise to the Goat Inn at Maes Mawr, 203¼, then leaving the Alwen valley on *r.* is a long and trying ascent up the pass of Aber Geirw, and except in dry weather an indifferent road. [There is another and better way by going up the Alwen valley, 1½*m.* out of Corwen, and joining the road from Ruthin.]

(*Cerrig-y-Druidion:* Lion, B.T.C.)

Pretty scenery. 1½*m.* past Maes Mawr, on *l.*, on the top of a hill, see Glyn Diffwys bridge and pretty waterfall. ½*m.* before Cerrig, on *r.*, is Pen-y-Gaer, an ancient entrenchment.

Cerrig-y-Druidion to Pentre Voelas (5¼—213½); long drag uphill for about 3*m.* till the summit of the pass is reached at Cernioge Mawr, 211¾, and then it is level or slightly downhill, with capital surface.

Pentre Voelas to Bettws-y-Coed (7¼—220¾) is a splendid smooth road all level or downhill, following the valley of the *R.* Conway, but nearing Bettws it requires careful riding, as the road has very sudden turns and corners. Just before Bettws turn to *l.* and cross *R.* Conway.

(*Bettws:* Glan Ober; Gwyder; Royal Oak; Waterloo.)

Beyond Pentre Voelas, on *r.*, Voelas Hall and Lima Hall. 1*m.* before Bettws, on *l.*, the Conway Falls, and Bridge over *R.* Conway. Pretty scenery: also Fairy Glen before Bettws.

Bettws-y-Coed to Capel-Curig (5—225¾); turn to left out of Bettws and it is a good road, but slightly on the rise all the way, running up the valley of the Llugwy, a tributory of the *R.* Conway: keep to the *r.* at Capel-Curig.

(*Capel-Curig:* Royal; Tan-y-Bwlch.)

About 2*m.* beyond Bettws, on *r.*, the Waterfall of Rhaiadr-Wennol, or Swallow Falls, and just beyond the road crosses to the *l.* bank of the river at Miner's Bridge.

Capel-Curig to Bangor (15—240¾); keeping to *r.* at the *Tp.*, the road ascends a fairly easy incline for nearly 4*m.* up the Llugwy valley, then it is downhill past Ogwen Lake (Llyn Ogwen), 230, from the bottom end of which a long and rather steep descent runs down the Ogwen valley, here called the pass of Nant Francon, partly winding through woods, with 2 or 3 ups and downs past Ogwen Bank, 235¼, to Bethesda, 236; thence the road falls to Llandegai, 239, with good surface: long narrow street through Bangor.

(*Bethesda:* Douglas Arms, *B.T.C.*—*Bangor:* British; Castle; George; Penrhyn Arms; Railway.)

On *l.*, about 2*m.* before Bethesda, the celebrated Penrhyn Slate Quarries, of tremendous extent, and employing some 7000 men. At Llandegai, on *r.*, Penrhyn Castle, built in the reign of Henry VI.; also Lime Grove. At Bangor, the cathedral.

Bangor to Menai Bridge (2½—243¼); turn to *r.* before the station up a hill, and then a gentle descent to the bridge, which can be ridden over; 1*d.* toll to pay. On *r.* to Beaumaris, 4*m.*

Menai Bridge is 560 feet between the points of suspension, and 100 feet high, it was built by Telford, 1819—1826. 1*m.* on *l.* is the remarkable Britannia Tubular Bridge, 1513 feet long; it was erected by Robert Stephenson, and opened in 1860.

Menai Bridge to Holyhead (21½—264¾); through Llanfair, 245¼, Gaerwen, 248¼, Pentre Berw, 249¾, across Malldreath Marsh to Llangristiolus, 251, Cefn Cumyd, 251¾, Caea Mona Inn, 252¾, Gwalchmai, 254¾, Ceirchiog, 256¼, Bryn, 257, Caer-Caeliog (ceiliog?), 260, and across Stanley Sands, 262, is a good straight road right across Anglesea Island; rather hilly, but nothing difficult, the chief inclines being ½*m.* and 7*m.* from Menai Bridge.

(*Holyhead:* Marine; Royal.—*Beaumaris:* Liverpool Arms, *B.T.C.*)

LONDON TO SHREWSBURY (by Ironbridge.)

London to Bridgenorth (137¾)—p. 126.

Bridgenorth to Broseley (6½—144¼); turn to *r.* in Bridgenorth, then a fair undulating road through Norley, 140, over Norley Common, and through Linley, 141¾ (just beyond which keep to *r.*), and a long ascent to Broseley.

1m. before Norley, on *r.*, Stanley Hall. On *l.*, Linley Hall, and beyond it, Willey Hall.

Broseley to Buildwas (3¼—147½); in Broseley keep to *r.* and there is a long rough descent to Iron Bridge, 145¼, which must be carefully ridden as the road is also crossed at intervals by tram lines belonging to brick and tile works; ½d. toll across Ironbridge (R. Severn), then turn sharp to *l.* and a moderately good but somewhat hilly road leads to Buildwas alongside the river.

At Buildwas, on *l.*, the abbey.

Buildwas to Shrewsbury (12½—160); moderately good but somewhat hilly road, running near R. Severn, through Leighton, 150¼, and over Tern Bridge, 155¼, where join the Watling Street road from Wolverhampton, to Atcham, 156 (cross R. Severn), and keeping to *r.* the rest is an excellent road into Shrewsbury, through St. Giles, 158½.

At Iron Bridge, on *r.*, near Coalbrookdale, are large ironworks. On *l.*, Leighton Hall, and 2m. on *r.*, the Wrekin mountain, on which is an ancient camp; splendid view. Below it, Neves Castle. Before Tern Bridge, on *l.*, at Wroxeter, are the remains of the Roman town of Uriconium. At Atcham, on *r.*, Allingham Hall and Longnor Castle and Hall.

LONDON TO HOLYHEAD (by Banbury).

Marble Arch (Oxford street) **to Edgware** (8); wood pavement for nearly a mile along Edgware road, through Paddington, ¾, then a bad macadam road, rough and shaky all the way; level as far as Kilburn, 2¾, whence there is a stiff rise up Shoot-up Hill, 3, and it continues hilly, and chiefly on the rise, by Cricklewood, 4, past the "Welsh Harp" at Hendon, 5¼ (Brent Bridge), and The Hyde, 6¼; very heavy traffic for first 3m., and the surface generally heavy and greasy, but after Hendon it improves somewhat, with tolerable riding at the sides.

(*Hendon :* Welsh Harp.—*Edgware :* Bald Faced Stag, *rec. C.T.C.*)

Edgware to Watford (6¾—14¾); the road continues lumpy and uphill through Little Stanmore for a mile beyond Edgware, then turn to *l.* at the fork, and it is level but loose and not very smooth going to Great Stanmore, 10¼, through and out of which (keeping to *r.*) is a hill, a mile long to mount, rather stiff at first, but rideable (it should be ridden *down* with care); then good almost level run for a couple of miles, over Bushey Heath, followed by the steep descent of Clay Hill, generally very loose, stony and rough, and requiring great care in riding down, to Bushey, 13¼, and beyond that is another long but moderate downhill, and the last mile level; except Clay Hill, it is a good gravel and flint road from Stanmore. Watford is a long (1m.) straggling town, nearly all on a gentle rise.

(*Stanmore :* (half way up the hill), Abercorn Arms; Crown, *rec. C.T.C.*—*Watford :* Clarendon; Essex Arms, *C.T.C.*; George; Green Man; Rose and Crown.)

Beyond Edgware, on *l.*, Canons Park; beyond Stanmore, on *l.*, Bentley Priory; 1m. distant is a line of ancient earthworks. At Bushey, Hartsbourne Manor Ho., Bushey Manor Ho. and Aldenham Abbey.

Watford to Two Waters (7¼—22); after leaving Watford it is a splendid level road, partly skirting Cashiobury Park, to Upper Highway, 18, then it crosses the valley by Hunton Bridge, 18¼, to the left, and is on a

K

gradual rise through King's Langley, 19¾, to within a mile of Two Waters, then undulating; good smooth surface on the whole, but sometimes sandy between Upper Highway and King's Langley.

On *l.*, Cashiobury Park, Grove Park and Langley Bury.

Two Waters to Berkhampstead (4¼—26½); through Box Moor, 23¼, and Bourn End, 24½, is gently undulating; capital smooth going.

(*Berkhampstead:* Goat Inn; King's Arms.)

On *r.*, Berkhampstead Castle (remains of), Monte Cavallo, and Berkhampstead Place; on *l.*, Ashlyns Hall and Haresfoot. At Berkhampstead the poet Cowper was born. The *ch.* is Gothic and contains many ancient monuments.

Berkhampstead to Tring (5—31¼); level to Northchurch, 27½, whence it is all uphill for nearly 3*m.*, ending with a rather stiff pull opposite Tring Park, and the rest is a gentle fall into Tring; splendid smooth road.

(*Tring:* Rose and Crown, B.T.C.; Royal.)

Past Berkhampstead, on the hill, on *l.*, are the remains of an ancient earthwork, called Græme's Dyke. At Tring, ancient *ch.*, with some old monuments.

Tring to Aylesbury (7—38¼); three short rises in the first mile or so out of Tring, followed by a long descent, rather steep but perfectly safe and good, to near Aston Clinton, 34½; the rest is level to Aylesbury, with a short pull up just in the town; splendid smooth surface all the way: the middle of Aylesbury is paved.

(*Aylesbury:* Crown, *B.T.C.*; George; Greyhound; Red Lion; Star.)

From near Watford the road follows a low valley right through the Chiltern Hills, which are crossed between Berkhampstead and Aston Clinton. Aylesbury is situate in a fertile tract of country, called the Vale of Aylesbury, and regarded as the dairy of England; the town is irregularly built, but has some fine public buildings, county hall, corn exchange, infirmary, St. Mary's *ch.*, &c. Chief manufactures are lace and straw plait, and the vicinity produces large numbers of ducks and geese for the London market.

Aylesbury to Winslow (10½—48¾); turn to *r.* in Aylesbury opposite the George Hotel, and when beyond the paving (keeping to *r.* again) there is a sharp hill to go down out of the town, then fair and almost level road to Hardwick, 41¾, shortly after which is the long rise of Holborn Hill, rather stiff towards the top, and generally very rough, being loose and stony, up to Whitchurch, 43; ½*m.* beyond this village is a rather steep but not long descent, with a turn in the middle and loose and stony at the bottom, and the rest is an easy undulating ride, with a stiffish hill to mount just before reaching Winslow, through which is rough and bumpy; capital road on the whole.

(*Winslow:* Bell Inn.)

At Whitchurch, on *l.*, is the site of an old castle.

Winslow to Buckingham (6¾—55½); a fair level road to within ½ a mile of Padbury, 52¾, into which is a gradual rise and a sharp descent out of it, then nearly 1*m.* level and 1½*m.* chiefly of a moderate uphill, followed by a short but steepish fall to the bridge over the *R.* Ouse entering Buckingham, whence keep to *r.* into the square; fairly good surface on the whole: macadam through Buckingham.

(*Buckingham:* Swan and Castle; Whale; White Hart, *Hyrs.*, B.T.C.)

At Buckingham was formerly a castle, but its site, an artificial mound, is now occupied by the *ch.*, a large and handsome structure. About 3*m.* N. is Stowe, the beautiful seat of the Duke of Buckingham, the road to it being along an avenue of lofty trees.

Buckingham to Aynho-on-the-Hill (11¼—66¾); leave the Square by Castle street on *l.*, down a short hill, and turning to *r.* at the bottom over the bridge (*R.* Ouse), it is up and down hill, but good and easy riding till having mounted the hill beyond Tingewick, 58, then almost level, with capital gravel surface past Finmere, 59¼, to Monk's House, 61¾, after that the road begins to be undulating again and changes to limestone, hard but rather shaky, past Barley Mow, 63, to Croughton, 64¼, out of which is a sharp fall followed by a similar rise, both very rough, and thence good and undulating to Aynho.

At Finmere, the old Roman way through Bicester crosses; 2*m.* further, on *r.*, near Mixbury, is Beaumont, supposed to be a Roman remain; 1*m.* N. of Barley Mow, is an ancient entrenched camp, also another a mile N.E. of Aynho, called Rainsborough Camp. At Aynho, on *l.*, Aynho Park.

Aynho to Banbury (6¼—73); keeping to *r.* there is a long descent winding through and out of Aynho into Cherwell valley, then except a short rise beyond Nett Bridge, 68¼ (over *R.* Cherwell and canal), it is a nearly level and good road by Adderbury, 69¼, and Weeping Cross, 71¼, to Banbury, entering the town by a rather steep descent, which should be ridden down carefully.

[There is another road from Buckingham through Brackley to Banbury, 1¾*m.* shorter, but not so good and more hilly—*vide infra*, p. 136.]

(*Banbury:* Crown; George and Dragon Inn; Red Lion; Crown Inn; White Horse, *B.T.C.*; White Lion, *Hqrs., B.T.C.*)

Banbury *ch.* was rebuilt in 1790. At the bottom of the hill is the famous cross. A castle of great strength formerly existed, but after sustaining two sieges in the Civil War, it was demolished, and only very slight remains of it are left. At Banbury are some good baths.

Banbury to Upton (7¼—80¼); keep straight on through Banbury, then turn to *l.*, and after Neithrop, 73½, the road rises gently to Drayton, 75, out of which is a sharp descent and ascent to Wroxton, 76, and then there is a long but gradual hill to mount past New Inn, 78¼, to the verge of Edge Hill at Upton; good surface. On Edge Hill is a B.U. "Danger" board.

On *l.*, Wroxton Abbey: beyond it, on the hill, is an old entrenchment. On *l.*, Upton *Ho.*

Upton to Upper Eatington (7¼—87½); take the left hand road at the sign post, and from the "Rising Sun," on the top of Edge Hill, 81, there is a tremendously steep hill to descend, about a mile long, and very loose and rough, down which it is impossible to ride; from the bottom the road is level, but with a wretched surface the whole distance, through Pillerton Lazer, 84, and Pillerton Priors, 85½; the road is made with ironstone, and when wet, forms into ruts, and prevents quick riding.

From the top of Edge Hill a fine view can be obtained. On the *r.*, in the plain below, 2 or 3*m.* distant, is the scene of the battle of Edge Hill, on 23rd October, 1642, the first in the Civil War.

Upper Eatington to Stratford-upon-Avon (5—92½); long gradual downhill through Goldicote, 89, to the *Tg.* 2*m.* before Stratford, and then undulating to Bridge Town, 92, where the Oxford road is joined; poor surface.

Stratford-upon-Avon to Holyhead (171½—264)—pp. 125-8.

[On the whole the above route to Stratford-upon-Avon is better and easier than that through Oxford; it can be shortened 1¾m. by going from Buckingham through Brackley to Banbury.]

LONDON TO BANBURY (by Bicester).

London to Aylesbury (38¼)—p. 130.

Aylesbury to Waddesdon (5—43¼); turn to *r.* in Aylesbury, opposite the George Hotel, and when clear of the paving, keep to *l.* at the bifurcation, and there is a moderate downhill out of the town; then it is a fair road, pretty level to Fleet Marston, 41, and thence rather hilly to Waddesdon.

Waddesdon to Bicester (10¾—54); the road continues fair through Ham Green, 46, to Sharp's Hill, 47, which is a long rise, followed by a descent on the other side; after this it gets rapidly worse, and then is very bad, being nothing more than a cart track, and traverses a very wild and desolate tract of country for about 6m., over Blackthorn Heath, 51¼, whence there is a stiff ascent up Blackthorn Hill, and on through Wretchwick, 52½, to Bicester.

(*Bicester:* Crown, B.T.C.; King's Arms; King's Head; White Lion.)

This road partly follows the line of the Roman Akeman Street. At Ham Green, 1m. on *l.*, Wotton Ho.; at Blackthorn Hill on *l.*, Ambrosden Park. Bicester was a Roman station and is situate near the junction of several Roman roads; about 1½m. S.W., are the traces of the ancient city of Alchester. The *ch.* was erected about 1200, and contains many old monuments.

Bicester to Aynho-on-the-Hill (8¼—62¾); keep to *r.* in Bicester, and at the *Tg.* outside the town to *l.*; the road is very hilly, through Caversfield, 55¾, Baynard's Green, 58¾, past Souldern, 60¾, and joining the Buckingham road ½m. before Aynho; very steep descent and ascent just before Baynard's Green; bad road, rough and bumpy, very little better than the last stage.

On *r.* Caversfield Ho.; farther on *l.*, Bucknell Ho., and Swift's Ho. At Souldern on *l.* is an ancient entrenchment called Ploughley Hill; from here, stretching in S. and S.W. direction, is a line of entrenchment 7 or 8 miles long, extending to the old Akeman Street, near Kirtlington; it is known variously as Ashbank, Wattlebank, or Avesditch, and overlooks the valley of the Cherwell.

Aynho-on-the-Hill to Banbury (6¼—69)—p. 131.

LONDON TO AYLESBURY (by Uxbridge).

London to Uxbridge (15)—p. 106.

Uxbridge to Chalfont St. Peters (5½—20½); the macadam ends with Uxbridge, out of which is a short dip, and then two bridges to go over (R. Coln and Grand Junction Canal); after that the road is level, but not very smooth, to the foot of Red Hill, 17¼, which though rather rough and generally loose and heavy, can be mounted by an ordinary rider, as it is not steep; thence it is undulating to Tatling End, 18, where leave the Oxford road and turn to *r.*, and directly after there is a rather steep fall with loose surface and a turn at the bottom; then the road is shaky and stony for a mile, owing chiefly to the traffic of some brick and tile works at Oak End, 19, and after passing them it gets better, and is undulating all the way, but no other difficult hill; in dry weather very loose and sandy for first 3m.; ford to cross in Chalfont.

At Red Hill on *l.*, Denham Mount; 1m. before Chalfont on *r.*, Chalfont Ho. From Tatling End the road runs up a narrow valley nearly all the way to Wendover, through the Chiltern Hills.

Chalfont St. Peters to Amersham (5½—26); hill out the former, then the road is a series of short stiff rises and falls, running along the right hand hill-side of the valley, with a gentle descent into Amersham; good road to Chalfont St. Giles, 22½, then rather sandy.

(*Amersham:* Crown Inn; Griffin.)

At Chalfont St. Giles, (which lies a little to the left of the road) Milton resided during the great plague, and here he finished "Paradise Lost." Amersham *ch.*, in the middle of the town, contains some old monuments: the town hall was built in 1612.

Amersham to Wendover (9½—35½); first-rate smooth gravel road through Little Missenden, 28½, and Great Missenden, 31; for about 8m. level and gently rising ground alternate, with a few moderate undulations, the only one of any consequence being a sharp descent out of Great Missenden; the last 1½m. into Wendover are downhill.

Beyond Amersham on *l.* Shardeloes; a mile past Little Missenden on *l.*, Little Missenden Abbey. On *r.* Great Missenden Abbey, of which part of the old cloisters still remains; 3m. W., up a side valley, is Hampden Ho., where John Hampden was born, and near which he is buried. Wendover is a small old fashioned town.

Wendover to Aylesbury (5—40½); is almost level and a good road but in dry weather rather sandy; from Walton Tg., (entrance of Aylesbury 40, it is paved into and through Aylesbury, which is entered from the south, and crossed through the market place.

LONDON TO AMERSHAM (by Harrow).

Marble Arch to Harlesden (or Holsden) Green (4½); wood pavement along the Edgware Road for ½m., then turn to *l.* along the Harrow Road, and the rest is macadam: level through Paddington Green, ⅜m., and Westbourne Green, 1½, to Kensal New Town, 2½, whence it is on a gradual rise past Kensal Green, 3, over Honeypot Hill and past Willesden Station, 4.

(*Harlesden Green:* Royal Oak.—*Willesden:* Junction Arms.)

Harlesden Green to Harrow-on-the-Hill (5½—10); pretty good road over Stone Bridge, 5½, to the top of the hill by Oakington Farm, 6½, and then both rough and hilly to the "Swan" at Sudbury Green, 8½, where keep to *l.*, and there is a steep winding hill up into Harrow. [There is another road avoiding the steep hill into and out of Harrow, by taking the right hand road at Sudbury Green, and passing by Harrow on *l.*, turn to the *l.* again beyond it into the road for Pinner.]

(*Harrow:* King's Head.—*Roxeth:* 1m. on *l.*, Three Horse Shoes.)

At Stone Bridge on *l.*, Twyford Abbey; 2m. farther, 1m. on *r.*, Wembley Park; before Harrow on *r.*, Sudbury Grove, and on the Hill, The Hermitage. At Harrow is the celebrated school.

Harrow-on-the-Hill to Pinner (3—13); dangerous winding descent out of Harrow, then level over Hooking Green, 12, and a steep but not long ascent into Pinner.

Pinner to Rickmansworth (5—18); [instead of going through Pinner, there is an easier route by taking the left hand road just before the village, going by Pinner Marsh, and joining the main road at the bottom of the hill through Pinner;] an awkward rough descent in Pinner by the church; then undulating road through Pinner Green, $13\frac{1}{2}$, and over Ruislip Common, with a rather steep hill, loose and stony, to descend at North Wood, $15\frac{3}{4}$, after which the road is pretty level and good through Batchworth Heath, $16\frac{1}{2}$, and skirting the west side of Moor Park, and a very bad hill leading down into Rickmansworth, which is best walked. [At Batchworth Heath, permission may be obtained at the lodge, to pass through Moor Park, but beyond the mansion there is a loose and steep hill to go down, with a gate at the bottom.]

(*Rickmansworth:* Swan.)

Beyond Pinner, 1m. on *l.*, Ruislip Park. Moor Park was formerly the residence of Cardinal Wolsey, and also of the Duke of Monmouth; it now belongs to Lord Ebury.

Rickmansworth to Green Street, before Cheneys ($3\frac{1}{4}$—$21\frac{1}{4}$); passing the *ch.* on *l.* take the new road for Chesham, as the hill leading to the old one is unrideable; there is a stiff hill to mount, and at the top is a very good and fairly level road over Chorleywood Common, 20, to Green Street. At Green Street, $\frac{1}{4}$m. on *r.*, is Cheneys, $21\frac{1}{2}$, whence is a steep descent into the valley of *R.* Chess, up which a fairly level road leads to *Chesham*, $26\frac{1}{4}$.

(*Chesham:* Crown, B.T.C.)

Green Street to Amersham ($4\frac{1}{2}$—$25\frac{3}{4}$); take the left hand road, which is undulating for nearly 2m., when there is a steep and very rough hill, which requires careful riding down, to Loudhams, $23\frac{1}{4}$; then very good and level over Amersham Common for $1\frac{3}{4}$m., where turn to *l.* by a small inn, and there is a capital run down to Amersham. Returning, $\frac{3}{4}$m. out of Amersham, turn to *l.*

LONDON TO ENSTONE (by Bicester).

London to Bicester (54)—p. 132.

Bicester to Middleton Stoney ($3\frac{1}{2}$—$57\frac{1}{2}$); keep to *l.* in the middle of Bicester, and nearly $\frac{1}{2}$m. further on to *l.* again, and shortly after that to *r.*; it is a fair road, slightly uphill.

Just beyond Middleton Stoney is Middleton Park.

Middleton Stoney to Hopcroft's Holt ($4\frac{3}{4}$—$62\frac{1}{4}$); skirting the north side of Middleton Park the road continues level to Lower Heyford, $60\frac{1}{2}$, into and through which is a long decline to the *R.* Cherwell, followed by a rise again to Hopcroft's Holt, on the Oxford and Banbury road; bad surface.

Just past Middleton Park, cross the Avesditch, and $\frac{1}{2}$m. farther on the Port Way. Beyond Lower Heyford on *l.*, Rousham Park.

Hopcroft's Holt to Church Enstone ($5\frac{3}{4}$—68); rather hilly road till clear of Westcot Barton, $64\frac{3}{4}$, then fair and almost level through Gagingwell, $66\frac{1}{4}$: $\frac{1}{4}$m. beyond Church Enstone, after a short descent and like ascent, join the road from Oxford on *l.* just outside Enstone. This road should be ridden only in dry weather, as in wet weather and winter time it is mostly covered with mud and water, and is inclined to be rutty and greasy.

LONDON TO WORCESTER (by Alcester).

London to Stratford-upon-Avon (92½)—p. 131.

Stratford-upon-Avon to Alcester (8—100½)—p. 125.

Alcester to Flyford Flavel (8½—109); mostly on the rise for the first mile through Arrow, 101¼, to Ragley Park, at the end of which turn sharp to *r.* uphill, and it continues hilly to Dunnington, 103½ (where turn to *r.* at the sign post and take left hand road nearly a mile farther on), and then good with a few small hills through Abbots Moreton, 106, and Radford, 107¼; gravel surface.

Flyford Flavel to Worcester (9—118); over Grafton Bridge, 110, and through Upton Snodsbury, 111½, and Spetchley, 114½, is a good undulating road with a long run down, followed by a steep descent into the town, rideable with a good brake.

LONDON TO CARNARVON (by Llanberis).

London to Stratford-upon-Avon (92½)—p. 131.

Stratford-upon-Avon to Capel Curig (132½—225)—pp. 125-8.

Capel Curig to Pen-y-gwryd (4¼—229¼); taking the left hand road at the turnpike and past Royal Hotel, it is an almost continuous ascent with several steep and rough pitches up the narrow valley of Nant-y-gwryd; the surface is rough and abounds in loose stones. The country is very wild and open. From near Pen-y-gwryd the ascent of Mount Snowdon can be made.

(Pen-y-gwryd Hotel.)

Pen-y-gwryd to Llanberis (6¾—236); keeping to *r.* there is a stiff ascent of ¾m. to the summit of the pass of Llanberis at Gorphwysfa (the Resting Place), 231, then the descent of the pass begins and is steep, rough, and stony for about ½m., when it improves, and though still downhill it is not so steep, and can be ridden with safety. For the last 2m. it skirts the shores of Llyn or Lake Peris.

(*Llanberis*: Castle; Dolbadarn, *B.T.C.*; Padarn Villa; Pen-y-pass; Royal Victoria; Snowden Valley.)

The road skirts the foot of Mount Snowdon all the way, the summit being 3 or 4m. from Gorphwysfa: there is another road from Llanberis by Ceunant Maur, where is a fine waterfall. Before Llanberis on *r.* below Llyn Peris is Dolbadaru Castle.

Llanberis to Carnarvon (8—244); one steep hill up past Glyn Peris Hotel, 237, otherwise easy road, but rough and bumpy, and after heavy rain very loose, as Lake Padarn, which it skirts for 3m., overflows: from Cwm-y-Glo, 240, the country becomes more open and the road is rather better, though much up and down through Llanrug.

(*Carnarvon:* Arvonia, *Hqrs.*; Castle; Prince of Wales; Queen's; Royal; Royal Sportsman, *B.T.C.*)

Just beyond Llanberis on *l.*, is a large slate quarry, employing 3,000 men. Carnarvon is an ancient town and is surrounded by a wall with round towers, the streets are narrow: the chief building is the castle erected by Edward I., and is that in which Edward II. was born; it was 12 years in building. About a mile from the town are remains of the Roman town of Segontium.

LONDON TO BANBURY (by Brackley).

London to Buckingham (55½)—p. 130.

Buckingham to Brackley (7¼—62¾); through Westbury, 60¼, is a hilly road, but all the hills are rideable; a mile before Brackley is a stiff descent, followed by a long and very stiff pull up into the town. The greater part of the road is generally rough.

(*Brackley*: Cross Keys; Crown; Wheatsheaf.)

On *r.* 2m. N. is Stowe, the magnificent seat of the Duke of Buckingham.

Brackley to Banbury, Cross (9¾—72½); through Farthingho, 66¼, and Middleton Cheney, 69¼, is a rather undulating road, but not so hilly as the last stage, though nearing Banbury there are one or two stiffish hills to mount, followed by a run down for nearly 1½m. Indifferent surface for first few miles, then very good.

[This road is not used so much as that by Aynho.]

LONDON TO STRATFORD-UPON-AVON (by Kineton).

London to Upton (80¼)—p. 131.

Upton to Kineton (5—85¼) keep to *r.* at the guide post, and at Edge Hill, 81, there is a long and very steep descent, which is loose and unrideable; after that it is a rather rough road, slightly down hill at first, then level.

(*Kineton*: Oxford Arms.)

On *l.*, just under Edge Hill, the beautiful residence of Radway. On *r.* on the top of the hill, is an old entrenchment called Nadbury Camp. Beyond Edge Hill the road skirts the field of the Battle of Edge Hill, which on the 23rd October, 1642, began the Civil War. Kineton or Kington, was once a royal residence, and there was a castle said to have been built by King John.

Kineton to Wellesbourne Hastings (4¼—89½); leaving Kineton, there are two rather stiff hills to mount and then an extremely pretty road through Compton Verney Park and Compton Verney, 87¼, a mile beyond which is a very steep and rather rough hill (Friz Hill) to ride down, and nearing Wellesbourne Hastings the road becomes very good.

Wellesbourne Hastings to Stratford-upon-Avon (5—94½); by Alveston, 92½, and through Tiddington, 93, and Bridge Town, 94, is a good, fairly level road, with gravel surface, but in wet weather becomes soft and heavy: for the last 3m, it runs close to *R.* Avon.

On *r.* pass Charlecote Park.

LONDON TO BRIDGENORTH (by Stourbridge).

London to Alcester (100½)—p. 135.

Alcester to Bromsgrove (13¼—113¾)—p. 125.

Bromsgrove to Stourbridge ($9\frac{1}{2}$—$123\frac{1}{4}$); crossing the main street, a little to the *r.*, keep straight on through Bromsgrove, and then through Barnsley, $115\frac{3}{4}$, Forfield, $116\frac{3}{4}$, Gost, $117\frac{1}{4}$, Hollow Cross, $118\frac{3}{4}$, Clent, $119\frac{1}{2}$, Hagley, 121, Pedmore, $121\frac{3}{4}$, and Old Swinford, $122\frac{1}{2}$; there are several stiff and loose hills to mount in the first half, in the rest nothing difficult; otherwise good road. Through Stourbridge is macadam.

(*Stourbridge:* Bell; Talbot, *C.T.C.*; Vine.)

On *r.* is the range of the Lickey Hills; on *r.* Hagley Park, and Hollow or Holy Cross.

Stourbridge to Bridgenorth (14—$137\frac{1}{4}$); through Stewponey, $125\frac{3}{4}$, Stourton, $126\frac{1}{4}$ (cross Canal and *R.* Stour), Enville, $128\frac{3}{4}$, Broad Oak, $131\frac{1}{2}$, and St. James's, $136\frac{1}{4}$, where cross *R.* Severn; hilly road. Returning, at St. James's turn first to *r*, then to *l.*

At Stewponey, 1*m.* on *r.*, Prestwood *Ho.*; on *r.* remains of Stourton Castle; on *l.* Enville Hall; at Broad Oak on *r.* Gatacre Park.

LONDON TO HOLYHEAD (by Coventry).

(The old Parliamentary and mail coach road. This road after Dunstable to Daventry is not a favourable one for quick travelling, especially with a light machine.)

London (General Post Office) **to Highgate Archway** ($4\frac{1}{4}$); wood pavement for $\frac{1}{2}$*m.* along Aldersgate Street, then granite paving with tramway along Goswell road, past the "Angel" Islington, $1\frac{1}{4}$, along High street and Upper street, a short distance down which the paving gives way to ordinary macadam, and along Holloway road; the tramway extends to the Archway. There is a moderate rise up to the "Angel," otherwise level: heavy traffic for first $1\frac{1}{2}$*m.*, and road generally bad for bicycling. At the "Archway" Tavern, $\frac{1}{4}$*m.* before the Archway, keep to *r.*, that to *l.* over the hill being the old road through Highgate town.

Highgate Archway to Barnet (7—$11\frac{1}{4}$); undulating road, with two rather stiff descents at East End Station, $5\frac{3}{4}$, and past the St. Pancras Cemetery, to the "Green Man," Brown's Wells, 7, then undulating over Finchley Common and through Whetstone, $9\frac{1}{4}$, and Greenhill Cross, $10\frac{1}{4}$, and a long stiff and rough ascent to Barnet; the macadam continues, bad and shaky, to Finchley Common, then the road gradually improves, and is generally fair riding.

(*Whetstone:* Bull and Butcher, *C.T.C.*—*Barnet:* King of Prussia; Old Salisbury; Red Lion; Salisbury Arms, *C.T.C.*—*Chipping Barnet:* Lion.)

A short distance beyond the Archway, on Muswell Hill, 1*m.* on *r.* Alexandra Palace. Just N. of Barnet on *r.* an obelisk marks the site of the last battle of the Wars of the Roses in 1471, when the Earl of Warwick was defeated and slain. Barnet *ch.* was erected in 1400, and contains many old monuments.

Barnet to St. Albans ($9\frac{1}{2}$—$20\frac{3}{4}$); instead of taking the old road from Monken Hadley, and turning off at the Obelisk (which is not now much used and in bad condition) turn to left (second turning) in the middle of Barnet, $\frac{1}{2}$*m.* *before* reaching the Obelisk, and a good road runs direct to South Mims, $14\frac{1}{2}$, thus saving $\frac{1}{2}$*m.*; then the road continues good, with a long gradual rise to the top of Ridge Hill, $15\frac{3}{4}$, the northern slope of which is a steep descent, generally somewhat rough and loose, and thence it is fairly good and nearly level through London Colney, $17\frac{1}{2}$, to St. Albans, with a long hill up into the middle of the town.

(*South Mims:* Green Man Inn; Wheatsheaf.—*St. Albans:* Bell Inn; Cock; Cross Keys; Crystal Palace, *Hqrs., rec. C.T.C.*; George; Peahen.)

2m. beyond Barnet on *l.* Derham Park; at London Colney on *l.*, Colney Ho., on *r.* Tittenhanger Park. St. Albans is noted for its abbey ch., lately restored after being long in ruins. A short distance west of the town is the site, with some slight vestiges of the old Roman town of Verulamium.

St. Albans to Dunstable (12½—33¼); turn to *r.* a short distance beyond the cross streets in St. Albans, and out of the town there is a hill to descend, after which it is a capital smooth and gently undulating road, with two long gradual ascents through the villages of Redbourn, 25, and Markyate Street, 29, followed by a long and steeper one—Spittol Hill—just before Dunstable, and a long gradual fall entering the town: red sandstone road.

(*Dunstable:* Red Lion; Saracen's Head, *B.T.C.*; Sugar Loaf.)

2m. out of St. Albans on *l.*, Gorham Bury Park. At Dunstable, the Priory ch. is worth a visit; 2m. distant on *l.*, Totternhoe Castle, an extensive ancient British earthwork; also near it Maiden or Madning Bower, a Roman camp. The chief manufacture of Dunstable is straw hats.

Dunstable to Hockliffe (3¾—37); for 2m. the road continues good and chiefly on a slight fall to the other side of the chalk cutting, when the surface begins to be uneven and rough, and there is a stiff descent over a high embankment; the rest level into Hockliffe.

Hockliffe to Fenny Stratford (7¾—44¾); long steep hill to mount out of Hockliffe, and the road continues rather hilly, but none of the gradients are steep, though there is a long and rough descent at Brickhill, 43, hill up through Fenny Stratford: the surface is rather shaky for quick riding, and in places is very rough and lumpy, with many loose stones.

Beyond Hockliffe, 1m. on *r.*, Battlesden Park.—(*Fenny Stratford:* Swan.)

Fenny Stratford to Stoney Stratford (7¼—52) through Shenley, 48¼; hilly road, but none of the gradients are steep, though some of them are long; rough and shaky, and in places very rough and lumpy; near Stoney Stratford is a sudden dip in the road which has a double row of flagstones on the left hand side of each ascent, like Reigate Hill.

(*Stoney Stratford:* Bull; Cock Inn, *C.T.C.*; George Inn; Plough.)

2½m. W. of Shenley is Whaddon Hall: a little farther, on *r.* Bradwell Abbey.

Stoney Stratford to Towcester (7¾—59¾); hill out of Stratford, to Old Stratford, 52¾, and then there are two stiff and rough hills to Potterspury, 54¾, and in the rest through Heathencote, 58¾, there is nothing difficult, but the road continues rough and bad the whole distance.

(*Towcester:* Pomfret Arms, *rec. C.T.C.*; Talbot.)

At Potterspury on *l.*, Whittlewood Forest and Wakefield Lodge; on *r.* Grafton Park. At Heathencote 2m. on *r.* Stoke Park. At Towcester on *r.*, Easton Park and *Ho.*

Towcester to Weedon (8—67¾); undulating and easy going to Foster's Booth, 62½, after which there are some long hills up and down, but nothing steep, to the top of the hill above Weedon tunnel, whence there is a capital long run down into Weedon: the surface is much better, but still inclined to be shaky and loose.

(*Weedon:* Globe, *C.T.C.*; Horse Shoe Inn; New.)

At Weedon, called also Weedon-on-the-Street, leave the old Roman Watling Street which keeps straight on, on *r.* to Atherstone, &c., but it is not rideable for a bicycle for about 10m.

Weedon to Daventry (4½—72); leaving the former there is a long stiff ascent to climb past the railway and barracks, which most tourists will walk up; then it is a good up and down hill ride, with a stiff pull up into Daventry, which is situate on the top of a hill.

(*Daventry:* Wheatsheaf, *B.T.C.*)

On *l.* 3*m.* distant, Fawsley Park, an old mansion. At Daventry, remains of a Cluniac Priory: near Daventry on *r.*, Danes or Borough Hill, one of the largest encampments in England.

Daventry to Dunchurch (7¾—79¾); short but rather steep descent going through and out of Daventry, followed by another hill to mount, then undulating but easy going to Braunston, 74¾, into which there is a long stiff descent; thence through Willoughby, 76½, is nearly level, with a stiff ascent into Dunchurch: capital surface: the last 2*m.* under a fine avenue of trees.

(*Dunchurch:* Crown; Dun Cow, *C.T.C.*)

At Braunston, handsome *ch.* and a curious stone cross.

Dunchurch to Ryton (6¾—86¼); the road leaves the former village on a slight descent beneath a long avenue of fir trees, and then it traverses Dunsmore Heath to Frog Hall, 84¾, and on by Knightlow Cross or Hill, 85, to Ryton, where there is a hill to descend, the first part steep and usually rough; otherwise excellent road.

(*Ryton:* Bull and Butcher.)

At Frog Hall the road crosses the old Roman Fosse Way, and a short distance on *l.* is Stretton-on-Dunsmore. At Ryton, or Ryton-on-Dunsmore, 2*m.* on *r.* Brandon Castle.

Ryton to Coventry (4½—91); about a mile beyond Ryton, at the bridge over *R.* Avon, the Southam road joins in, and it is gently undulating through Willenhall, 88¼, and over Whitley Bridge, 88¾: excellent going at first for 1 or 2*m.*, but the latter part is macadam, rough and bumpy, which continues through Coventry: here the street is rather narrow as far as the cross roads, then there is a longish but gradual fall down Smithford street, at the bottom of which the traveller will see the words "Holyhead Road," directing him up a short rise out of the town.

(*Coventry:* Craven Arms; George, *Hqrs.*; Kenilworth Castle; King's Head; Knight's; Lord Nelson; Pitt's Head; Queen's, *C.T.C.*)

Coventry may be called the headquarters of bicycle manufacturing, and a visit to some of the great bicycle works will prove of interest to the tourist. The chief buildings are St. Michael's *ch.*, Trinity *ch.*, St. John's *ch.*, St. Mary's Hall, &c.; the town was once surrounded by a wall 3*m.* in circuit, which was pulled down by Charles II. At Whitley Bridge on *l.*, Whitley Abbey.

Coventry to Stone Bridge (8½—99½); after mounting the rise out of Coventry, it is a level road to Allesley, 93¾, over rather shaky macadam, but good riding can generally be had at the sides; thence it is a capital smooth road, chiefly on a gentle rise for the next 3*m.*, with a good stiff descent into Meriden, 97¼, and the rest undulating.

On *l.*, Allesley Park and Meriden Park; just before Stone Bridge on *r*, Packington Hall, (Earl of Aylesford). Near Meriden is an obelisk said to be in the exact centre of England.

Stone Bridge to Birmingham (9¾—109¼); good undulating road, but not quite so smooth as the last stage, through Wells Green, 103¾, to Yardley, 106½, then rough and shaky macadam into and through the town:

short stiff descent at Bordesley, 107¾, a suburb of Birmingham, and a steep hill to mount at the Bull Ring, in the town: New street, running nearly east and west, is the central thoroughfare of Birmingham.

(*Birmingham:* Grand, *C.T.C.*; King's Head; Midland; Queen's; Swan.)

Before Wells Green on *l.*, Elmdon Hall. Birmingham, the metropolis of the Midlands, is celebrated for its manufactures of hardware, guns, plated metals, and other kindred objects. The appearance of the town in general is mean, though it has of late years been much improved, and has some fine buildings; it is very smoky and dirty. For a town it is very hilly and bicyclists had best give it a wide berth.

Birmingham to Wolverhampton (13¼—122½); leave the former by the suburb of Soho, 110¾, and then through Soho street, 111¾, and Sandwell Green, 112¾, to West Bromwich, 114¼; a mile beyond this keep to *r.*, and by Wednesbury, 117¼, Moxley, 118½, and Bilston, 119¾; it is a macadam road, and very bad for bicycling, being extremely rough and full of holes; tramway laid, and heavy traffic. [From West Bromwich there is another road to Bilston, keeping to *l.* a mile beyond the former, and through Great Bridge and Horsley Heath, ½*m.* longer.]

(*Wednesbury:* Dartmouth.—*Bilston:* Lion; Pipe Hall, *C.T.C.*; Queen's Arms.—*Wolverhampton:* Commercial Exchange; Corn Exchange; Coach and Horses, *C.T.C.*; Peacock; Star and Garter; Swan.)

This is a most undesirable road to travel, being through the middle of the "Black Country;" the better way is to go by railway which runs parallel to the road all the way. The country is more or less a desert of blasted fields and furnace heaps, varied by a succession of dirty and dingy towns and villages, intermixed with furnaces and manufactories of all kinds. Just before West Bromwich on *r.*, Sandwell Hall. At Soho is Messrs. Boulton & Watts' extensive manufactory of engines, plated goods, &c., one of the largest in the world. Wednesbury is of great antiquity, and its *ch.* is supposed to have been built in the 8th century; here also are traces of a Saxon fort.

Wolverhampton to Shifnal (12½—135); after leaving Wolverhampton keep to *r.*, and it is a good road, being level or downhill for about 1¾*m.* through Tettenhall, 124½, then Tettenhall Rocks to climb, a stiff ascent of ½*m.*,—16 ft. in the 100—(best walked *down* on the reverse journey); from the top is a fairly level and good road by the Wergs, 125¾ (1½*m.* beyond keep to *l.*), and through Boninghall (or Boningale), 129½, and Upton 134¼.

(*Shiffnall:* Jerningham Arms, *B.T.C.*; Star.)

At the Wergs on *l.*, Wrottesley Park, and farther on Patshill Park; on *r.* 2*m* off, Chillington Park. In Shiffnall *ch.* is a monument to one Wm. Wakely who is said to have lived to 124 years of age.

Shifnal to Watling Street (6½—141½); through Priors Lee, 138, and past Ketley Iron Works, 140¾, is a bad road. [At Watling Street the town of *Wellington* lies a short distance off on right; ¾—142¼.]

(*Wellington:* Charlton Arms, *B.T.C.*; Wrekin.)

Beyond Shifnal on *r.*, Haughton Hall and Priorslee Hall; nearly 2*m.* beyond the Watling street again joins the road. 2*m.* S. of Wellington is the Wrekin hill, on which is an ancient fortification, and embracing an extensive view.

Watling Street to Shrewsbury, Town Hall (11½—153); over Tern Bridge, 148¼, and Atcham Bridge, 149, where cross the *R.* Severn, then turn to *r.* and past Lord Hill's column, 151¾; the road gradually declines most of the way to Atcham Bridge, and being made with Mount Sorrel stone has a splendid smooth surface and is always dry: enter Shrewsbury through the suburb of Abbey Foregate and over the R. Severn by English Bridge.

Shrewsbury to Holyhead (106¼—259¾)—pp. 126-8.

LONDON TO ST. ALBANS (by Edgware).

London to Edgware (8)—p. 129.

Edgware to Elstree (3—11); the road continues lumpy and uphill through Little Stanmore (keeping to r. at the sign-post 1m. beyond Edgware) for 1½m., then up Brockley Hill, 10, and another hill going up into Elstree, both stiff ascents, the crown of each being almost unrideable: tolerably good road.

(*Elstree :* Plough; Red Lion.)

Beyond Edgware on l., Canon's Park. At Brockley Hill on r., have been discovered Roman remains.

Elstree to St. Albans (8¼—19¼); downhill leading out of Elstree, then hilly, but good give-and-take road through Cobden Hill, Radlet, 14, Colney Street, 16¼, Park Street, 17¼, and St. Stephen's; there is a loose rough hill at Park Street, and a very steep hill—Holywell Hill—to mount into St. Albans, otherwise capital surface.

On r. Kendall Hall, Old Organ Hall, and Old Park Bury.

LONDON TO TOWCESTER (by Buckingham).

London to Buckingham (55½)—p. 130.

Buckingham to Towcester (10½—66); through Maid's Moreton, 56½, Akeley, 58, Lillingston Dayrell, 59½, across Whittlewood Forest and through Whittlebury, 62½, is hilly but an indifferent road; in dry weather it is lumpy, and the least rain makes it very soft and heavy.

LONDON TO STONE BRIDGE (by Banbury).

London to Banbury (73)—p. 131.

Banbury to Gaydon—or Gaydon Inn, (10—83); keep straight on through Banbury, then first turn to l., and through Neithrop, 73½, after which is a gentle rise for about a mile, the road being very smooth, then it is level and a fairly good road, running along the ridge of a hill to Warmington, 78, where is a long and very steep hill to descend, which requires great caution, the first part being crooked; from the bottom it is almost level, one or two short but sharp falls excepted, but most of it rough and rutty to Gaydon.

Gaydon to Warwick (9—92); the road is undulating and rather rough for nearly 2m., when there is a short winding descent, after which it is almost level for 3m., passing Harwood House, 86¼, and the surface having changed to gravel, is very good and smooth all the way to Warwick; the last 4m. are hilly but nothing difficult, there being 4 descents and 2 ascents, with another stiff pull entering Warwick.

[Or to *Wellesbourne Hastings*, 89½—p. 136; thence through Barford,

93¾, where cross R. Avon, and Longbridge, 94½, to *Warwick*, 96¼; level road except sharp ascent to Warwick; gravel surface and splendid going.]

At Warwick, on r. to *Leamington*, (2¼—94¼); a first rate broad and level road, smooth as asphalt. For Leamington, see p. 144. Bells are compulsory in Leamington.

(*Warwick:* Crown; Globe; Warwick Arms; Woolpack, *C.T.C.*)

At Harwood's *Ho.* the old Roman Fosse Way crosses the road. Pretty country. Before Warwick, on *l.*, Warwick Park. Warwick, on the *R.* Avon, is supposed to be of Saxon origin, and was formerly a walled town. St. Mary's *ch.* is erected over the site of one of the old gates, with the carriage way passing beneath it; contains many interesting monuments and a beautiful lady chapel, dating from 1443. Leicester's hospital is a fine specimen of old half-timbered house. The castle is on *l.* entering the town; the interior is splendidly adorned, and there is a valuable collection of paintings, ancient armour, and the Warwick vase, &c.

Warwick to Kenilworth (5¼—97¼); at the top of the hill in Warwick, turn to *r.*, through the gateway under the *ch.*, when there is a short descent, and at the end of the street keep to *l.* past the station; the road is a little hilly, chiefly on the rise through Guy's Cliff, 93, and Leek Wotton, 95, and is only indifferent going; loose and dusty in dry weather.

(*Kenilworth:* Globe, *Hqrs.*; King's Arms, *C.T.C.*)

On *l.*, nearly half-way, on Blacklow Hill, is Gaveston's Cross, where Piers Gaveston was beheaded in 1312: on *r.* romantic seat of Guy's Cliff. Kenilworth is noted for the remains of its magnificent castle, built in the reign of Henry I., and chiefly remarkable as belonging to the favourite of Elizabeth, the Earl of Leicester. It now belongs to the Earl of Clarendon, and is open to visitors at a small fee. There are also remains of an abbey.

Kenilworth to Stone Bridge (8¾—106); keep to *l.* out of Kenilworth, and in the next 2 or 3*m.* there are several stiff rises, rather loose and stony, then a long gradual ascent and the remainder is level past George-in-the-Tree (or Wootton Green), 101¾, and Moulding Bridge, 105: on the whole it is a good and easy road, but loose and stony in places.

On *r.*, beyond George-in-the-Tree, are Berkswell *Ho.* and Meercot Hall.

LONDON TO COVENTRY (by Banbury).

London to Banbury (73)—p. 131.

Banbury to Southam (13¾—86¾); keep straight on through Banbury, and at the fork just outside the town; nearly a mile beyond is a stiff hill to mount, then almost level for 2 or 3*m.* through Little Bourton, 75, after which it is hilly through Mollington, 77½, and for about 4*m.* beyond but more down than up; several of the falls are steep but nothing dangerous, the last of any moment being over the canal bridge at 81½*m.*, near Fenny Compton; then it is level for some distance, and after a little more uphill, the last 2½*m.* are on a gradual slope through Ladbroke, 84¾, to Southam: easier going to Southam than coming the contrary direction: good surface throughout.

(*Southam:* Bull, *C.T.C.*)

Southam to Princethorpe (6½—93); stiff hill to mount going out of Southam, followed by a descent, then nearly level (except sharp fall over a canal bridge at Long Itchington, 88¾), through Marton, 91¼.

(*Princethorpe:* Three Horse Shoes.)

At Princethorpe cross the old Roman Fosse Way.

Princethorpe to Coventry (6¼—99¼); mostly uphill for first 2*m.*, then a succession of descents to the junction with the Holyhead road at the Avon Bridge, 96¼, from which it is gently undulating through Willenhall, 97½, and over Whitley Bridge, 98: good road for half the distance, and the latter part macadam, rough and bumpy into Coventry.

At the Avon Bridge, 1*m.* on *l.*, Baginton Hall; and beyond, Stoneleigh Park and Abbey.

LONDON TO BIRMINGHAM (by Warwick).

London to Warwick (92)—p. 141.

Warwick to Solihull (13¾—105¾); keep straight on in Warwick, and then through Hatton, 95, Wroxall, 98, Bedlams End 99½, Chadwick End, 100, Henfield, 101¼, Rotten Row, 102, and Knowle, 102¾, is a moderate not over good road, being loose and rough in places.

(*Solihull:* George; Saddler's Arms.—*Knowle:* Greswolde Arms, *B.T.C.*)

On *l.* Wroxall Abbey; 1*m.* on *r.* Camp *Ho.*; before Solihull, on *l.*, Malvern Hall and Langdon Hall.

Solihull to Birmingham (7½—112¾); through Ulverley, 107¼, Acock's Green, 108¼, Greet or Greet Bridge, 110¼, and Spark Brook, 111¼, is a fair road to the latter place, then macadam, and shortly after join the Coventry road.

LONDON TO BIRMINGHAM (by Henley-in-Arden).

London to Stratford-upon-Avon (92½)—p. 131.

Stratford-upon-Avon to Henley-in-Arden (8—100½), through Hardwick, 95½, past Bearley Cross, 96¼, and through Wootten Wawen, 98½, where turn to *r.*, and also ½*m.* farther on; good undulating road.

(*Henley-in-Arden:* Bear, *rec. C.T.C.*; Hen and Chickens.)

Beyond Stratford, on *r.*, Clopton *Ho.*; at Bearley Cross, on *r.*, Edstone Hall: on *r.* Wootton Hall. At Henley is an ancient market cross. "Arden" was the name of the forest that formerly overspread the district.

Henley-in-Arden to Birmingham (15¼—115¾); about 2*m.* out of Henley is the steep ascent of Liveridge Hill, with good surface, thence undulating by "Hockley House" Inn, 105½, Box Trees, 106½, Monksford (or Monkspath) Street, 107¼, Shirley Street, 110¼, Six Way, 111, and Hall Green, 112, to Spark Brook, 114¼, where the macadam begins. [From Wootton Wawen there is another road, keeping to *l.* about ¼*m.* beyond it, and through Ullenhall Street, Ullenhall Cross, Bramstone Cross, by Forshaw Park, over Trumans Heath, Kings Norton Heath, by Holly Wood, Lane End, and Moseley: distance nearly the same.]

Beyond Henley, on *l.*, Beaudesert Park: before Hockley *Ho.*, 1*m.* on *l.*, Umbersdale Park.

LONDON TO WOLVERHAMPTON (by Alcester).

London to Stourbridge (123¼)—p. 137.

Stourbridge to Wolverhampton (9¾—133); in the middle of Stourbridge is a moderate fall, near the bottom of which an open line of rails crosses the road; long stiff rise out of the town over macadam, which

continues through Wordesley, 125; then it gives way to ordinary flint road but not very good, and it is pretty level through Himley, 127¾, and Wombourn, 129, to Upper Penn, 130½, where there is a steep stony descent, and after a short rise the rest is level and macadam into Wolverhampton.
On r. Himley Park, and about a mile farther Wood Ho. and Lloyd Ho.

LONDON TO WARWICK (by Southam).

London to Daventry (72)—p. 139.

Daventry to Southam (10—82); in Daventry take second turn to l., and it is a good hard road; Staverton, 73¾, is reached up a long winding hill, with a descent on the other side; the rest is undulating through Lower Shuckburgh, 77¼, but nothing difficult for an ordinary rider.
On Staverton, 1m. on l., Catesby Park; farther, Newbold Grounds and Shuckburgh Park.

Southam to Leamington (7—89); ½m. out of Southam is a steepish fall, then nearly all uphill to Ufton, 84½, from which there is a long descent, sharp at first with a curve; thence two more stiff pulls alternate with easy riding through Radford Semele, 87¼, and Leamington Priors, 88¼.
(*Leamington*: Angel, B.T.C., Hqrs.; Avenue; Bath; Clarendon; Manor House; Regent; Warwick Arms.)
At Radford, on r., Offchurch Bury, a fine old mansion. Leamington, or more correctly called, Leamington Priors, fifty or sixty years ago was a village; it is one of the most important inland spas or watering places of England. The springs are chiefly saline. Bells are compulsory at Leamington.

Leamington to Warwick (2¼—91¼) is a first rate broad and level road, smooth as asphalte.

LONDON TO KENILWORTH (by Daventry).

London to Leamington (89)—above.

Leamington to Kenilworth (4—93) is a good but very undulating road by Blakedon Hill and over Chesford Bridge, 91¼ (R. Avon). Pretty country.
On r., at Chesford Bridge, 2m. distant, is Stoneleigh Abbey, and beyond, Stoneleigh Park.

LONDON TO STOURBRIDGE (by Birmingham).

London to Birmingham (109½)—p. 139.

Birmingham to Halesowen (7¾—117) by the Black Boy Inn, 114½, is a good road after first 3m.
Before Halesowen, on l., Leascowes; beyond, Halesowen Abbey. Pretty country. On r. Warley Abbey.

Halesowen to Stourbridge (4½—121½); through Cradley, 119, and The Lye, 120½, is a pretty good road.

LONDON TO HOLYHEAD (by Chester).

London to Stonebridge (99½)—p. 139.

Stonebridge to Coleshill (4—103½); turning to r. there are three short but very loose and stony rises in the first mile, and on the last the road forks, here keep to *r.* and it is level and good to Coleshill ; steep and stony descent in the main street of Coleshill.

(*Coleshill :* Swan.)

At Coleshill, 1*m.* on *r.,* Maxstoke Castle and Park and ruins of Maxstoke Priory ; on *l.* Coleshill Park.

Coleshill to Bassets Pole (8—111½) ; about ½*m.* out of Coleshill the right hand road must be taken, up a steep, rugged and stony hill, impossible to ride up and dangerous to ride down ; this is shortly followed by a moderate and smoother fall, then the road is almost level, but bad in places on account of the coal traffic, over Curdworth Bridge, 105½, (*R.* Tame) and a mile beyond, over the Birmingham Canal to Wishaw, 107½, from here (leaving the Fazeley road on *r.* at the guide post, and afterwards bearing first to *r.* and then to *l.* twice) it is chiefly a succession of long gradual inclines for about 2*m.*, the last part rather stiff, then after a little level, a good run down, again a rise and level to the cross roads at Bassets Pole ; from Wishaw the surface is not so good, there are many loose and stony patches, and the country is cheerless, lonely and moorlike.

At Curdworth Bridge, 1*m.* on *r.,* Hams Hall ; at Wishaw, on *r.,* Moxhull Hall. At Bassets Pole cross the Birmingham to Tamworth road.

Bassets Pole to Lichfield (7—118½) ; the road soon improves and from Canwell, 112, there is a grand run down, nearly continuous all the way to Weeford, 114½, with capital smooth surface, and the rest, except a short pull up, is fairly level with good smooth surface, through Swinfen, 116¼ where turn to *r.* and afterwards to *l.*; macadam through Lichfield.

(*Lichfield :* George ; Swan.)

On *r.* Canwell Hall and Swinfen Hall. At Weeford, on *l.,* Thickbroom Manor. Lichfield is of great antiquity, and close to is the supposed site of the Roman station of Etocetum at Wall on the Watling Street. The cathedral is a fine early English building, and is worth an inspection. Dr. Johnson was a native of the town, also Addison and Garrick.

Lichfield to Rugeley (7½—126) ; shortly after leaving Lichfield, there is a sharp descent, upon which the road divides and the left hand fork must be taken ; the road is good through Longdon Green, 121¾, and Longdon, 122½, then a stiff ascent over Brereton Hill and a good run down through Brereton, 124½, to Rugeley. [There is another road by keeping sharp to *r.* at the above-mentioned divide, and up a slight hill ; then the road winds round to *l.* again with an easy gradient, and at the next fork the left hand road must be taken, and at Handsacre, 124, again keep to *l.* through Armitage, 124½, and after a descent join the other road just before Rugeley ; it is a mile longer, but better and not so hilly.]

(*Rugeley :* Shrewsbury Arms.)

On *r.* pass Elmhurst Hall, Lissways Hall, and Armitage Park. At Longdon, 1*m.* on *l.,* Beaudesert Park, in which is Castle Hill, an ancient encampment ; at Rugeley, on *l.,* Hagley Park. On the *l.* Cannock Chase stretches the whole way, formerly covered with oaks.

Rugeley to Stafford (9¾—135¾) is a fair undulating road by Wolseley Bridge, 128¼ (where keep to *l.*), Milford, 132, and Weeping Cross, 133¾ ; the road runs alongside the *R.* Trent, and afterwards the *R.* Sow.

(*Stafford :* North Western ; Pine, *Hqrs.*; Railway Junction ; Swan ; Vine.)

On *r.* Wolseley Hall ; further on Shugborough, on *l.* Brockton Hall. Stafford was formerly walled, but the walls were demolished by Cromwell. It has two

L

ancient churches. S. of the town are the remains of the Castle, and beyond it, Bury Ring, an old fortified hill.

Stafford to Eccleshall (7—142¾) through Great Bridgeford, 139, and Walton, 140¾.

(*Eccleshall* : Crown ; King's Arms ; Royal Oak.)

At Eccleshall the Castle, erected in 1310, and now the Episcopal residence.

Eccleshall to Woore (12½—155¼), through Pershall, 144½, Croxton, 146, Broughton, 148, Muckleston (or Muxton), 151¾, Knighton, 153¾, and Dorrington, 154½.

On *r.* Broughton Hall.

Woore to Nantwich (9—164¼) through Bridgemore, 157¼, Walgherton, 160¼, and Stapeley, 162.

(*Nantwich* : Crown, *Hqrs.* ; Lamb ; Swan Inn, *Hqrs.*)

At Bridgemore, on *l.*, Doddington Park. Nantwich is in the centre of the Cheshire salt district.

Nantwich to Tarporley (9—173¼) through Acton, 165¼, Hurleston, 166¾, Wardle (or Barbridge), 167¾, and Highway Side (or Albraham), 170¼, Tilston Fernall, 171¼, and Tiresford, 172¼.

(*Tarporley* : Swan ; 2*m.* off, Tollemache Arms.)

At Tilston, 2*m.* on *l.*, the ruins of Beeston Castle, (erected 1220) ; past Barbridge on *r.* Calveley Hall ; further, Tilston Lodge ; at Tarporley, Eaton Banks.

Tarporley to Tarvin (4¼—177½) through Clotton, 175, and Duddon, 176.

Tarvin to Chester (6—183½); turn to *l.* in Tarvin, and up a slight ascent, over bad ground; on the other side of the hill the road improves, and is good over Stamford Bridge, 179, and by Vicar's Cross, 180¾, to within 2*m.* of Chester, and the rest is rough through Boughton, 182¼ ; entering the town, cross a bridge and turn to *r.* for High street, which is roughly paved with cobble stones.

(*Chester* : Grosvenor ; Liverpool Arms ; Queen.)

Chester is an old-fashioned place, surrounded by walls, which, with the Rows, are most striking to a stranger. Some of the houses are built on excavations in the rock. The castle is said to have been erected by William I. ; St. Werburgh's Abbey and St. John's *ch.*, are supposed to have been founded in the 7th century. The cathedral was built in the 15th century.

Chester to Broughton (5—188½); turn to *l.* in the middle of Chester and cross the *R.* Dee, then through Handbridge, 184¼, and Bretton, 188, the road is very hilly but very good, though heavy after rain.

At Handbridge, 3*m.* on *l.*, Eaton Hall, the magnificent seat of the Duke of Westminster.

Broughton to Hawarden (2—190½); keep to *r.* past the railway, and the road continues good.

On *l.* pass Broughton Hall and Hawarden Castle, the latter the residence of Mr. W. E. Gladstone. On the other side of the town are the ruins of the old castle.

Hawarden to Northop (5—195½) through Ewloe, 193.

On *r.* pass the ruins of Ewloe Castle.

Northop to Holywell (6½—202) through Halkin, 198¼, and Pentre Halkin, 199.

(*Holywell* : Red Lion.)

At Holywell, 1*m.* on *r.*, Basingwerk Abbey ; there is a line of ancient fortification running N.E. from the town and known as Watts Dyke. The town derives its name from St. Winifred's Wells, formerly of repute in the cure of diseases.

Holywell to St. Asaph (10—212); about 2½m. out of Holywell, at the fork at the bottom of a descent, keep to *l.*, and at Travellers' Inn, 207¾, to *r.*; a moderate road with one fearful hill to cross.

(*St. Asaph*: Kinnel Arms; Mostyn Arms, *B.T.C.*; Plough.)

Beyond Travellers' Inn (or Brick Kiln) 2*m.* on *l.*, Brynbella. St. Asaph is an ancient but small town; a see was founded here about 540, and the present cathedral is one of the smallest in England or Wales. Pretty scenery. 3*m.* S. Llannerch Park, Wigfair, Ffynnon-y-Capel, and Cefn, where there are some caves.

St. Asaph to Abergele (7—219); after crossing the *R.* Elwy, there is a long rise to mount over Rose Hill, then it is a good road, downhill nearly all the way but nothing difficult, by Cross Foxes, 215, and through St. George or Llan-St. Sior, 216¾.

(*Abergele*: Bee; Cambrian.)

On *r.* pass Bodlewyddan Castle and Kinmel Hall. At St. George, on *l.*, Parc-y-Meirch, an old hill fort, and another called Castle Cann, *l.* of Abergele, near which at Cefn-yr-Oge are some stalactite caverns. Abergele is much frequented for its bathing in summer.

Abergele to Conway (11½—230½); rather hilly road through Llandulas, 221¾, Colwyn, 224¼, and Mochtre, 228½; on the whole not a good road, at Colwyn it is simply execrable for about a mile, and beyond that is very rough and dusty; cross *R.* Conway before entering the town, the railway also crossing alongside by a tubular bridge.

Before crossing to Conway, on *r.* to Llandudno, 3*m.*, not a good road and a nasty little hill to cross

(*Colwyn*: Baukes; Colwyn Bay; Station, *B.T.C.*; Pwllycrochan.—*Llandudno*: Adelphi; Imperial; Prince of Wales; Queen; Royal.—*Conway*: Castle; Castle View; Erskine; George.)

Beyond Abergele on *l.* Gwrych Castle. The road runs by the sea nearly the whole distance. Conway, or Aber-Conway, was formerly surrounded by walls, of which most of the towers and four gateways remain. There are remains of a magnificent castle erected by Edward I.

Conway to Aber (9¼—239¾); following the coast it is an excellent road by Pont Lychnant (or Pendyffryn), 233, to beyond Penmaenmawr, 235½, when a long, rough and very stiff ascent has to be climbed over the headland of that name, followed by a long steep hill to descend on the other side and through Llanfairfechan, 237¾, the road becomes very indifferent, but is fairly level.

(*Aber*: Bulkley Arms, *B.T.C.*)

At Aber on *r.*, across the bay, is Beaumaris.

Aber to Bangor (5¼—245); through Talybont, 242¾, and Llandegai, 243¼, is an indifferent road, very hard, but no hills; long narrow street through Bangor.

Bangor to Holyhead (24—269)—p. 128.

LONDON TO CHESTER (by Malpas).

London to Wolverhampton (122½)—p. 140.

Wolverhampton to Newport (17¾—140¼); after leaving Wolverhampton keep to *r.*, and it is a good road, level or downhill, for about 1¼m.

through Tettenhall, 124½, then Tettenhall Rocks to climb, a stiff ascent of ½ a mile—16 ft. in the 100—(best walked down on the reverse journey); from the top is a fairly level and good road for 1½m., past The Wergs, 125¾, where take the right hand fork, and it is a good road, with one or two hills, through Albrighton, 130¼, Tong, 132, King Street, 136, Bloomsbury, 136¾, and Woodcote, 137¼.

(*Newport:* King's Arms; Victoria.)

Beyond Tettenhall on *l.*, Wrottesley Hall. At Albrighton, 2m. on *r.*, Chillington Park. At Tong, Tong Castle; on *r.* 2m., Boscobel House, with the Royal Oak where Charles II. took refuge after his defeat at Worcester. 2½m. beyond Tong, cross the old Roman Watling Street (Holyhead road), which runs in a straight line E. and W. for many miles; on *r.* Weston Park. At Woodcote, 2m. on *l.*, ruins of Lilleshall Abbey, and near it Lilleshall Hall.

Newport to Tern Hill (12—152¼); excellent road through Chetwynd, 141¾, Stanford Bridge, 144½, Hinstock, 146 (where keep to *l.*), Shakeford, 148¼, and Sutton Heath, 150¼.

On *l.* Chetwynd Park and Stanford Hall. At Newport on *r.* Aqualate Hall.

Tern Hill to Whitchurch (9—161¼); through Bletchley, 153½, Sandford, 156¼, and Great Ash, 159¾, is not so good as the last stage.

(*Whitchurch:* Fox and Goose; Victoria.)

At Sandford 2m. on *l.*, Hawkstone, a beautifully situated mansion, with ruins of Red Castle. Whitchurch has a handsome *ch.*, in which are several effigies of the Talbots. 3m. on *r.*, Combermere Abbey.

Whitchurch to Malpas (5—166¼); good road over Grindley Bridge, 163¼ (keep to *l.*), and through Bradley, 165.

Malpas to Handley (7½—173½); first-rate road through Hampton, 169¾, Broxton, 170¼, and Barnhill, 171¼.

[From Grindley Bridge there is another road, on *r.*, by Bell-on-the-Hill, 164¼, and No Man's Heath, 166¼, to Hampton; same distance.]

At Hampton, 3m. on *r.*, Cholmondeley Castle. At Barnhill, 1m. on *r.*, Bolesworth Castle. At Broxton, on *l.*, Carden Hall.

Handley to Chester (7¾—181¼); first-rate road through Milton Green, 174¼, over Golbourn Bridge, 174½, and through Higher Hatton, 176¼, to Boughton, 180, then rough; entering Chester cross a bridge and turn to *r.* for High street, which is roughly paved with cobble stones.

Beyond Handley, 3m. on *l.*, Eaton Hall, the magnificent seat of the Duke of Westminster.

LONDON TO DENBIGH.

London to Chester (181¼)—above.

Chester to Broughton (5—186¼)—p. 146.

Broughton to Mold (7½—193¾); keep to *l.* when past the railway, and it is a very hilly but good road.

(*Mold:* Black Lion; Boar's Head; Royal Oak; Star, *B.T.C.*)

Mold is a small neat town; the *ch.* contains some fine monuments. On the hill, Moel Fammau, 4m. W. is the tower erected on the jubilee of George III.

Mold to Nannerch (6—199¾) is a good road, following up the course of the *R.* Alyn and Afon Wheeler, but not very hilly.

The railway runs alongside the road all the way from Mold to Denbigh. Beyond Mold on *l.* Rhual, and on *r.*, Gwysaney Hall. Before Nannerch on *l.*, Penbedw; on *r.*, Plas Cilcen.

Nannerch to Bodfary ($5\frac{1}{4}$—205) is a similar kind of road through Ysceifiog, $201\frac{1}{2}$.

2*m*. N. of Bodfary is Bryn Bella.

Bodfary to Denbigh ($4\frac{1}{4}$—$209\frac{1}{4}$); over Pont Ryffydd, 206 (*R*. Clwyd), shortly after which take the left hand road.

(*Denbigh:* Bull, *B.T.C.*; Crown.)

Denbigh is pleasantly situated on an eminence in the vale of Clwyd, and overlooked by the ruins of the castle, founded in the reign of Edward I., and formerly of immense strength. The old town walls are still standing. Beyond Denbigh is Gwaenynog, the seat of the Middletons, one of whom was the Sir Hugh Myddleton who brought the New River into London.

LONDON TO ST. ASAPH (by Mold).

London to Bodfary (205)—above.

Bodfary to St. Asaph ($5\frac{1}{2}$—$210\frac{1}{2}$); over Pont Ryffydd, 206 (*R*. Clwyd), shortly after which keep to *r*. and by Trefnant Station and over the *R*. Elwy; it is a good road.

Beyond Trefnant, on *r*., Llannerch; on *l*., Ffynnon-y-Capel, Wigfair, and Cefn, near which are some caves on the banks of *R*. Elwy.

LONDON TO ST. ASAPH (by Ruthin).

London to Stratford-upon-Avon ($92\frac{1}{2}$)—p. 131.

Stratford-upon-Avon to Llangollen ($94\frac{3}{4}$—$187\frac{1}{4}$)—pp. 125-7.

[The shortest way is by Coventry to Shrewsbury (153*m*.)—p. 140; thence to Llangollen (30—183)—pp. 126-7]

Llangollen to Ruthin ($13\frac{1}{2}$—$200\frac{3}{4}$); cross *R*. Dee, and at Pentrefelin, $188\frac{3}{4}$, leave the main valley and proceed up the Valle Crucis and past the ruins of the Abbey and Eliseg's Pillar, shortly after which the road ascends the long hill of Bwlch, and after going down the farther side there is some more hill work, and then enter the vale of Clwyd, and the last 5 or 6*m*. are more or less downhill through Llanfair-Dyffryn-Clwyd, $198\frac{1}{2}$; the road crosses the mountains and is dreadfully bad, being nothing more than a bridle-path, up and down hill, and necessitates a deal of walking. Beautiful scenery.

(*Ruthin:* Castle, *B.T.C.*; Cross Keys; George House; Wynnstay Arms.)

Ruthin stands on a hill, and took its rise and name from the old castle (the Red Castle), built in the reign of Edward I., but which no longer exists, the site being occupied by a modern building. There was formerly a convent here, the choir of which is now represented by the parish *ch*.

Ruthin to Denbigh (8—$208\frac{3}{4}$) through Llanrhaiadr, $205\frac{1}{4}$.

Denbigh to St. Asaph ($5\frac{1}{4}$—214) is a very good bit of road. 2*m*. before St. Asaph, cross *R*. Elwy.

Beyond Denbigh on *l*., Plas Heaton; further on Ffynnon-y-Capel, Wigfair, and Cefn, near which are some caves on banks of *R*. Elwy. On *r*. Llannerch Park.

LONDON to CONWAY (by Llangollen).

London to Llangollen [$187\frac{1}{4}$)—above.

Llangollen to Bettws-y-Coed ($32\frac{3}{4}$—220)—pp. 127-8.

[The shortest way is by Coventry to Llangollen (183)—p. 149; thence to Bettws-y-Coed (32¼—215¾).]

Bettws-y-Coed to Llanrwst (3½—223½); cross the R. Llugwy over Pont-y-Pair, and follow down the Conway Valley, by the left bank of the river; for 3m. the road runs through a wood, twists a good deal and has several sharp ups and downs, with a rutty surface, to Gwydir, 223, where turn to r. and cross R. Conway to Llanrwst.

[Another road is, to keep to the r. ¾m. before Bettws-y-Coed and follow down the r. bank of the R. Conway. There is also a shorter way by taking the right hand road at Pentre Voelas, 212¼, and going direct to Llanrwst, 217¼, but the road is more hilly].

(*Llanrwst :* Eagles and Cwyder Arms ; Victoria.)

Llanrwst is situate in the midst of charming scenery, and is a favorite resort of tourists, artists, and anglers.

Llanrwst to Conway (13—236½); keep to the road on the right side of the river which is much the better one, and with but one hill; it goes by Tal-y-Cafn, 230¼ and through Llansantffraid-glan-Conway, 233¼, joining the Chester road a mile further on. [For the other road down the left hand or Conway side of the river, instead of turning to r. for Llanrwst, keep straight on at Gwydir, 223 ; the road now improves, being through a little more open country, to Trefriw, 224½, * when it becomes good and firm, though occasionally stony, and is fairly level to Caer Hûn Hall, 229½, when the hills become numerous and formidable, through Arianos, 231½, and there is a steep hill, twisting two or three times and dangerous to ride down, into Conway, 234½.]

3m. beyond Llanrwst on r. bank, the Abbey ; on l. bank Gwydir and Caer Hûn Hall.

LONDON TO HOLYWELL (by Flint).

London to Chester (181¼); through Malpas—p. 148.

[The route through Lichfield and Stafford to Chester is 2¼m. longer (183½) p. 146.]

Chester to Queensferry, R. Dee, (6—187¼); keep straight on through Chester, and turning to r. at the archway, a capital going level road thence runs through Waterloo, 185, to Queensferry, except the last mile.

Queensferry to Flint (6—193¼); turn to r. a short distance past Queensferry Station, and then through Weypre, 189¼, and St. Marks, 190¼; it is a shocking bad road on account of the coal traffic, but no hills.

[The best road is through *Northop* to *Flint* (3m.—196¼).]

(*Flint :* Cross; George and Dragon ; Royal Oak, *B.T.C.*)

Flint is supposed to have been a Roman station from its formation and the numerous antiquities that have been found here. There are ruins of the old castle.

Flint to Holywell (5½—198¾); through St. Mary's, 194¾, and Bagillt, 195½, is a rough macadam road ; no hills.

---

* Through Llanrwst these distances will be 1m. longer than here reckoned through Gwydir alone.

SECTION VI.

From General Post Office; Midland Roads, (Mid Herts, West Bedfordshire, North Buckinghamshire, Northamptonshire, North Warwickshire, Leicestershire, North Staffordshire, Derbyshire, West Notts, East Cheshire, Lancashire, West Yorks, Westmoreland, and Cumberland.)

LONDON to LIVERPOOL.

London to Chester (181¼) through Malpas—p. 148.

Chester to Birkenhead (16½—197¾); splendid road through Upton, 183, Backford, 184½, Great Sutton, 188, Eastham, 190¾, Bromborough, 192, and Great Bebbington, 194½, to Tranmere, 196¾.

(*Birkenhead:* Queen's, *B.T.C.*; Woodside.)

Beyond Great Sutton on *r.*, Hooton Hall. Birkenhead has risen into existence as a seaport town, within the last 50 years. Beyond, at the mouth of the Mersey, is the fort at New Brighton and Leasowes Castle.

Birkenhead to Liverpool (¾—198¼); by the steamboat ferry across the R. Mersey.

(*Liverpool:* Angel, *Hqrs.*; Compton; Havana; Railway; Neptune, *B.T.C.*; Washington.)

Liverpool, the second city in England, is the great seaport for America; there are immense docks; many fine public buildings.

LONDON to LIVERPOOL (by Knutsford).

London to Rugeley (126)—p. 145.

Rugeley to Sandon (10¼—136¼); is a fair undulating road by Wolseley Bridge, 128¼, (where turn to the *r.* and cross the R. Trent and Grand Trunk Canal) to Colwich, 129, whence is a steep ascent and good long descent to Great Haywood, 130½, and at the bottom turn to *r.* through a *Tg.*, then fine road through Shirleywich, 133, and Weston, 133¼, running almost level with and alongside the canal.

On *l.* pass Wolseley Park, Shugborough Park, Tixall Hall, and Ingestre Hall. Before Sandon on *r.*, Sandon Hall.

Sandon to Stone (4¼—140½); through Stoke, 139½, is continuation of the same kind of road; Stone is cobble paved.

(*Stone:* Bell and Bear; Crown; Talbot; Unicorn.)

At Stone are remains of an Augustinian monastery founded in Saxon times.

Stone to Trentham (5¼—145¾); out of Stone keep to *l.* and cross the canal, and after crossing R. Trent keep to *r.*; the road is good but rather hilly through Darlaston, 142, and by Titensor Mill, 144.

On *l.* Trentham Park, the magnificent seat of the Duke of Sutherland. **Pretty country.**

Trentham to Newcastle-under-Lyme (3¾—149½); from Trentham the road begins to ascend and rapidly deteriorates to Handford, 146½, after which it is bad and hilly through Flask, 147¼, in some places very bad, being made with loose cinders and sand; at Flask, after crossing R. Trent and the canal, keep to *l*.

(*Newcastle*: Borough Arms; Castle.—*Stoke-upon-Trent*: West End, *Hqrs.*; North Staffordshire.)

The road now passes through the "Potteries" district, a dirty and smoky neighbourhood. Stoke-upon-Trent and Hanley are distant on *r*. 1½*m*. and 2½*m*.

Newcastle-under-Lyme to Church Lawton (6¼—155¾); ascent through the town, then a little level, and another long rise followed by a descent and ascent passing through Chesterton, 151¼; after this it is level past some collieries and Talk-on-the-Hill, 154¼, and keeping to *r*. further on a very rough and bad descent occurs, then it is level again, and the surface improves nearing Church Lawton; this is an extremely rough and very bad road, besides being loose and heavy; in some parts it is scarcely rideable.

(*Talk-on-the-Hill*: Swan.)

This is a colliery district, and is full of shafts and furnaces. The village of Talk-on-the-Hill lies a little *l*. of the main road, and there is a steep hill to descend out of it.

Church Lawton to Holmes Chapel, or Chapel Hulme (9—164¾); about a mile beyond Church Lawton keep to *r*.; in the first half there are 3 or 4 short undulations, the surface being like good macadam, a little stony but never greasy; after that it is fairly level and smooth through Brereton Green, 162¾; Holmes Chapel is paved.

Beyond Church Lawton, on *r*., Rode Hall, and at Brereton Green, Brereton Hall.

Holmes Chapel to Knutsford (7¼—172); sharp stony descent and ascent just out of Holmes Chapel, and the road continues rough to the toll-gate a mile further on; at the fork beyond keep to *r*., and it is level for about 2*m*., then a long gradual rise, shortly followed by a stiff ascent before Toft, 170, and a mile beyond that a sharp descent and stiff ascent: on the whole a tolerable though not very smooth road, being made of material like macadam, but without being greasy or so bumpy as that kind of road near London; through Knutsford is cobble paved.

(*Knutsford*: Angel; Royal George.)

About half-way on *r*. Over Peover Hall; on *l*. Toft Hall.

Knutsford to Warrington (11¾—183¾); the road is almost level, with fairly good macadam-like surface (out of Knutsford keep to *l*., a little further to *r*., and at the *Tg*. 1*m*. beyond to *l*.), through Mere, 174¾, and Hoo Green, 175¾, to High Leigh, 177; then through Kirkman's Green, 178, it falls gradually for about 3*m*., ending with a steep and rather rough descent, after which it is nearly level to Warrington; at Grappenhall, 180¾, the road passes under the Bridgewater canal, and is very bad and rough; shortly after there is a level crossing, and the last 2*m*. through Latchford, 182⅝, are rough and shaky: cross R. Mersey into Warrington, the main street of which is narrow and paved.

(*Warrington*: Patten Arms; Red Lion; Ring of Bells.)

Beyond Knutsford, on *r*., Tatton Park; on *r*. Mere Hall. Warrington is an ancient town, and its bridge was for many ages the chief communication across the Mersey. The first stage-coach from Lancashire to London ran from here in

1757, the time of the journey being three days and nights. It carries on cotton, iron, glass, and heavy leather manufactures. The parish *ch.* is of Saxon origin and has many old monuments.

Warrington to Prescot (9¼—193½); by turning to *l.* when across the bridge, and bearing to the *r.* by the railway station over a fair macadam road the main paved street is avoided, and the Prescot road is joined in the outskirts of the town: otherwise, turning to *l.* in the middle of the town, it is level but all paved with large square setts to Sankey Bridge, 185, where is a patch of cobble paving, then gently undulating and tolerable macadam road through Great Sankey, 186, and Rainhill, 190½, with a stiff descent into Prescot: this town is paved with square setts.

(*Prescot:* King's Arms.)

Prescot is noted for the manufacture of watch movements and files, &c. N. of the town is Knowsley Park and Hall, the residence of the Earl of Derby.

Prescot to Liverpool (8—201½); rather steep descent out of the former, then fairly level and good macadam road to Knotty Ash, 197½, after which it is rather uneven and rough into Liverpool.

LONDON to WARRINGTON (by Northwich).

London to Church Lawton (155¾)—p. 152.

Church Lawton to Sandbach (6¼—162); follow the Knutsford road for a mile, then turn to *l.*, and it is fairly good through Oddrode, 158, and Dean Hill, 160.

(*Sandbach:* George; Swan and Chequer; Wheatsheaf.)

Sandbach to Middlewich (5—167); take the middle road, which runs by the side of a canal and affords good and level running, through Boothville or Booth Lane Head, 163¼.

(*Middlewich:* Wagings.)

Middlewich to Northwich (7—174); take the right hand road, (the left going to Nantwich); the surface of the road continues fairly good, but there are several hills, at the top of the first of which one must again keep to the *r.*, and through High Bostock Green, 170, and Davenham, 171¾: Northwich is paved.

(*Northwich:* Angel; Crown and Anchor, *B.T.C.*; Lion.)

On *r.* Bostock Hall and Davenham Hall. Northwich is the centre of the Cheshire salt works. 2m. W. of Davenham is Vale Royal Abbey, the residence of Lord Delamere.

Northwich to Warrington (11½—185½); through Great Budworth, 177, Higher Whitley, 180, Stretton, 182, and Wilderspool, 184½.

LONDON to WARRINGTON (by Congleton).

London to Church Lawton (155¾)—p. 152.

Church Lawton to Congleton (6—161¾); keep to *r.* and it is an excellent undulating road by Moreton Hall, 158¾, and through Astbury, 160¼, with one or two sharp hills; long descent into Congleton, rather steep.

(*Congleton:* Bull's Head; Lion and Swan.)

Congleton to Siddington, *Tp.* (4¾—166½); after crossing the *R.* Dane outside Congleton, there is a long and severe ascent to be climbed, from the top of which a good macadamised and undulating road runs through Marton, 165½.

Beyond Congleton, on *r.*, Eaton Hall.

Siddington to Knutsford (9¾—176¼); keep to *l.* at Siddington *Tp.*, and it is an undulating road through Chelford, 171, and by Ollerton or Ollerton Gates, 174, to Knutsford: macadam-like surface, but pretty good going. Pretty scenery.

(*Chelford:* Dixon Arms.)

At Chelford, on *l.*, Astle Hall. Before Knutsford, on *r.*, Booth Hall.

Knutsford to Warrington (11¾—188)—p. 152.

LONDON TO LICHFIELD (by Hinckley).

London to Hockliffe (37)—p. 138.

Hockliffe to Woburn (4¼—41¼) is a good but rather hilly road; turn to *r.* in Hockliffe.

At Woburn is a handsome modern *ch.*, the windows all of painted glass, and the great bell weighs three tons; it was erected by the Duke of Bedford, whose magnificent mansion (formerly Woburn Abbey) and park are east of the town.

Woburn to Newport Pagnell (8½—49¾); a somewhat hilly road over Wavendon Heath, through Wavendon, 44¾, Broughton, 47¼, and Tickford End, 49¼; rather rough, but good travelling on the whole; the road only goes through the eastern end of Newport Pagnell, which lies to *l.*, on the cross road to Stoney Stratford.

Newport Pagnell to Northampton (16—65¾); after crossing *R.* Ouse, keep to *l.* out of the town, and through Lathbury, 50¾, Gayhurst, 52¾ (again to *l.*), Stoke Goldington, 54¼, near Horton (on *r.*), 58¼, through Hackleton, 59¾, and Queen's Cross, 63¾; after the first 2*m.* the road is generally loose and rather rough; no hills of any consequence, but steep and rough ascent in the middle of Northampton up to the *M.P.*

(*Northampton:* Angel; Cross Keys, *Hqrs.*, *B.T.C.*; Franklin, *B.T.C.*; George, *Hqrs.*; Peacock; Royal.)

At Gayhurst, on *r.*, across the *R.* Ouse, Tyringham; on *l.* Gayhurst; on *r.* Horton House. At Stoke Goldington, 2*m.* on *l.*, Hanslope Castle, built in the 12th century. Before Northampton, on *r.*, Delapre Abbey, a fine mansion. At Northampton St. Sepulchre's *ch.*, built early in the 12th century by the Knights Templars, is one of the few round churches in the kingdom. All Saints' *ch.* and St. Peter's *ch.* are also fine structures, and St. Giles' *ch.* contains some curious monuments. The hospitals of St. Thomas and St. John were formerly religious houses. Of the old castle only some earthworks now remain. Northampton is celebrated for its horse fairs. The chief manufactory is boots and shoes, &c.

Northampton to Welford (14½—80¼); through Kingsthorpe, 67¼ (keep to *l.*), Chapel Brampton, 70, Spratton, 72¼, Creaton, 73½, and Thornby, 77, is not a very good road; the only hill of any consequence is a stiff ascent before Spratton.

Beyond Creaton, 1*m.* on *r.*, Cottesbrook *Ho.* At Thornby, 2*m.* on *r.*, Naseby Field, the scene of the defeat of Charles I. by Cromwell. At Welford, 1*m.* on *r.*, Sulby Abbey. Naseby village is regarded by some as the centre of England;

near it rise the three rivers, Welland, Nene, and Avon. To the *l.* of Creaton is Holmby *Ho.*, where Charles I. was imprisoned.

Welford to Lutterworth ($8\frac{1}{2}$—$88\frac{3}{4}$); keep to *l.* and through North Kilworth, $83\frac{1}{2}$, and Walcote, $86\frac{1}{4}$, the road improves considerably.

(*Lutterworth:* Denbigh Arms; Hind; Stag.)

At Lutterworth is preserved part of the pulpit from which the celebrated reformer, Wycliffe, is said to have preached; also the chair in which he died.

Lutterworth to High Cross (6—$94\frac{3}{4}$); through Bitteswell, $89\frac{3}{4}$, and Claybrook, $92\frac{3}{4}$, is a good road.

At High Cross is the junction of the two Roman roads, Watling Street and the Fosse Way.

High Cross to Hinckley ($4\frac{1}{2}$—$99\frac{1}{4}$); follow Watling Street for $\frac{1}{2}$ a mile beyond Smockington, $95\frac{3}{4}$, when turn off it to *r.* and go through Burbage, $98\frac{1}{4}$; fairly good road.

(*Hinckley:* George; Greyhound.)

About 4*m.* N. of Hinckley was fought the battle of Bosworth Field, in 1485, when Richard III. was defeated and slain. There are some slight remains of a castle at Hinckley, and also of a bath supposed to be Roman.

Hinckley to Atherstone (8—$107\frac{1}{4}$); 2*m.* beyond Hinckley, rejoin Watling Street, which runs in almost a straight line through Witherley, $106\frac{1}{4}$, to Atherstone; good road. [If not calling at Hinckley, keep straight on along Watling Street, just beyond Smockington, joining the Atherstone road as above.]

At Watling Street, 3*m.* on *l.*, Nuneaton, beyond which are ruins of the abbey. Before Witherley the road crosses the site of the Roman station, Manduessedum. 2*m.* on *l.* Oldbury Hall, occupying the site of a Roman camp, and near it Hay's Castle. At Atherstone, on *l.*, Bentley Park.

Atherstone to Tamworth (8—$115\frac{1}{4}$); through Hall End, $111\frac{1}{4}$, and Wilnecote, $112\frac{3}{4}$, just beyond which turn to *r.* from the Watling Street for Tamworth: or cross the *R.* Tame to Fazeley, $114\frac{1}{4}$, and then on *r.* to Tamworth, $115\frac{1}{2}$; it is somewhat rough, but a comparatively good road. [Or turn to *r.* in Atherstone, $1\frac{1}{2}$*m.* further to *l.*, and through Grendon, Polesworth, Glascote and Bolehall, to Tamworth, 9*m.*] Enter Tamworth by a narrow awkward old bridge over the *R.* Anker.

(*Tamworth:* Castle.)

At Tamworth is a fine old castle erected by the Normans. On *l.*, at Fazeley, is Drayton Manor, the residence of Sir R. Peel.

Tamworth to Lichfield (8—$123\frac{1}{4}$) through Hopwas, $117\frac{1}{2}$.

LONDON TO TAMWORTH (by Coventry).

London to Coventry (91)—p. 139.

Coventry to Over Whitacre (9—100); in Coventry turn to *r.* at the cross streets, and straight on with a steep descent through the town; then hilly through Radford, 92, Kersley (or Carsley) Green, $93\frac{1}{4}$, Corley, $95\frac{1}{4}$, out of which is a stiff hill to mount and another to descend through Corley Ash, $96\frac{1}{4}$, and then through Fillongley, 97; it is not a very good road, heavy and muddy when wet.

At Corley, on *l.*, 2*m.* off, Titbury Castle. At Fillongley, on *l.*, Castle Yard; 2*m.* on *r.* Astley Castle.

Over Whitacre to Tamworth ($9\frac{3}{4}$—$109\frac{3}{4}$); very hilly road through Nether Whitacre, $102\frac{1}{2}$, and Kingsbury, $104\frac{3}{4}$; some of the ascents steep; $3\frac{1}{4}m.$ beyond Kingsbury cross Watling Street and join the Atherstone road. [It is a better road from Coventry to go by Nuneaton, Atherstone, and the old Roman Watling Street, and not so hilly—*vide infra.*]

LONDON TO NORTHAMPTON (by Stoney Stratford).

London to Stoney Stratford (52)—p. 138.

Stoney Stratford to Northampton ($13\frac{3}{4}$—$65\frac{3}{4}$); after crossing the *R.* Ouse turn to *r.* at Old Stratford, $52\frac{1}{2}$, and through Cosgrove, $53\frac{1}{2}$, Yardley Gobion, $54\frac{3}{4}$, Grafton Regis, $56\frac{1}{4}$, Stoke Bruern, $57\frac{3}{4}$, Roade Lane, $58\frac{3}{4}$, Wootton Bridge, $62\frac{1}{4}$, and by Queen's Cross, $63\frac{3}{4}$; this is rather unfavourable for bicycling, there are some long hills, and the road is made of soft stone and has a very uneven surface; in wet weather it is very bad.

Queen's Cross is one of the crosses erected in memory of Queen Eleanor by Edward I.

LONDON TO BURTON-UPON-TRENT.

London to Coventry (91)—p. 139.

Coventry to Nuneaton ($8\frac{1}{2}$—$99\frac{1}{2}$); turn to *r.* at the cross streets in Coventry, through the market place, from which is a sharp descent partly paved; then take the second turn on *r.*, and through Longford, $93\frac{3}{4}$, Bedworth, $95\frac{3}{4}$, Griff, $97\frac{1}{4}$, and Chilvers Coton, 99, is a bad road, loose and shaky, on account of the coal traffic; one or two short hills.

(*Nuneaton:* Newdegate Arms.)

At Griff, 1*m.* on *l.*, Arbury Hall, and beyond it Astley Castle. Near Nuneaton are remains of the abbey and also of the castle.

Nuneaton to Atherstone ($5\frac{1}{2}$—105); keep to *l.* through Nuneaton, and a mile beyond to *r.*; it is a good road, though somewhat rough in parts.

(*Atherstone:* Angel; New Swan; Red Lion; White Hart.)

Atherstone to Burton-upon-Trent ($18\frac{1}{2}$—$123\frac{1}{2}$); turn to *r.* in Atherstone and again $1\frac{1}{2}m.$ further on, and it is a nice road, but hilly through Sheepy, 108, Twycross, $110\frac{1}{4}$ (just beyond take the left hand road), Norton, $111\frac{3}{4}$, Appleby, $113\frac{1}{4}$ (beyond which again to *l.*), Stretton-en-le-Field, $115\frac{1}{4}$, Crickett's Inn, $116\frac{1}{4}$, Over Seal, $117\frac{3}{4}$, Castle Gresley, $119\frac{3}{4}$, Stanton, $121\frac{3}{4}$, and Stapenhill, $122\frac{3}{4}$. [There is another road from Twycross on *r.* through Snareston, $113\frac{3}{4}$, and Measham (Union Inn), $115\frac{1}{4}$, to Crickett's Inn, $117\frac{1}{4}$.]

(*Burton-on-Trent:* Queen.)

At Twycross, on *r.*, Gopsal Hall. Burton is chiefly known for its breweries: there are remains of a large abbey founded in 1002: the *R.* Trent is crossed by a remarkable old bridge.

LONDON TO BURTON-UPON-TRENT (by Hinckley).

London to Hinckley ($99\frac{1}{4}$)—p. 155.

Hinckley to Ashby-de-la-Zouch ($16\frac{1}{4}$—$115\frac{1}{2}$); good but hilly road through Stapleton, $102\frac{1}{4}$, Cadeby, $104\frac{3}{4}$, Osbaston, $106\frac{1}{2}$, Nailstone, $107\frac{3}{4}$, Ibstock, $110\frac{1}{4}$, and Ravenstone, $112\frac{1}{2}$ (just before that turn to *l*); it is a cross country road, and difficult to follow on account of the turnings.

(*Ashby:* Queen's Head ; Royal.)

Before Cadeby, on *l.*, Bosworth Field, where Richard III. was defeated and slain in 1485. At Ravenstone, 3*m.* N.E , Whitwick Castle on the borders of Charnwood Forest ; 2*m.* further N. are the ruins of Grace Dieu Abbey. Ashby is celebrated for its castle (now in ruins), where Mary, Queen of Scots, was imprisoned. Handsome ancient *ch.*

Ashby-de-la-Zouch to Burton-upon-Trent (9—124½) ; very hilly road by Butt House, 119, Midway Houses, 120½, and Bretby Park, 121¾ ; macadam all the way.

[Or from Cadeby through Market Bosworth, 106½, Carlton, 107½, Barton-in-the-Beans, 108½, Oldby, 109½, Newton Burgoland, 112½, Nethercote, 113, Cross Lane, 114, Measham, 116½, and through the Wolds to Butt House, 121½.]

North of Ashby, 4*m.* off, is Calke Abbey.

LONDON to GLASGOW.

London to Warrington (183¾)—p. 152.

Warrington to Newton (5—188¾); after leaving the former it is an indifferent road by Langford Bridge, 184¼, to Holme (or Hulme) 186¼, then it is paved most of the way and almost unrideable except with a stout machine, through Winwick, 186¾.

(*Newton:* Legh ; Pied Bull.)

On *l.*, Winwick Hall. According to tradition, Winwick was the residence of Oswald, King of Northumbria, and near the *ch.* an ancient building with many monuments, is pointed out as the spot where he fell, fighting against the pagans of Mercia, in 642 ; near to is St. Oswald's Well. At Newton (called Newton-in-Makerfield, and Newton-le-Willows), is an old hall, said to have been a royal residence.

Newton to Wigan (7¼—196); the paving continues almost without intermission through Ashton-in-Makerfield, 191¼, and Goose Green, 193¾, and for the last mile into Wigan is a line of tramway, at the end of which, in the centre of the town, is a short ascent followed by a very steep descent, all paved; the main street is 1¼*m.* long.

(*Ashton:* King's Head.—*Wigan:* Eagle and Child ; Railway ; Victoria.)

Wigan is an ancient town ; there is a tradition that the Saxons were defeated here by the Britons, while numerous remains have been found in the vicinity. It is in the centre of the Lancashire coalfield, and here is the deepest mine in England, if not in the world, Rose Bridge Main, 808yds ; at the bottom the temperature is 93½ degs. At Ashton, on *l.*, New Hall ; on *r.*, Haydock Lodge.

Wigan to Chorley (8—204); long steep hill to ascend out of Wigan, the lower part of which is paved, and the remainder is a good hard and fairly smooth road ; at 198*m.* keep to *r.* at the bifurcation, and the road continues good, but there are one or two steep and crooked hills, until ½*m.* before Yarrow Bridge, 202¼, where, join the old coach road from London through Manchester ; this is paved for half the width but the other half affords pretty fair riding.

(*Chorley:* Royal Oak.)

About half way on *r.*, Adlington Hall, and before Yarrow Bridge, on *r.*, Duxbury Hall. Beyond Wigan, on *r.*, Haigh Hall.

Chorley to Preston (9¼—213¼); through Whittle-in-the-Woods, 206¼, Clayton, 208, Bamber Bridge, 209½, and Walton-le-Dale, 211½, is fair riding over a good hard road: cross *R.* Ribble, ¾*m.* beyond Walton-le-Dale, and then steep ascent entering Preston: pretty scenery.

[There is another road from Wigan, keeping to *l.* 2*m.* beyond and through Standish, 199, Welch Whittle, 202, Bolton Green, 204, and Euxton, 205½, to Bamber Bridge, 209; it is a good hard road, tolerably smooth with no very difficult hills.]

(*Preston:* Bull; Castle; Victoria.)

At Whittle-le-Woods, on *l.*, Shaw Hall; at Bamber Bridge, on *l.*, Cuerden Hall. Preston is a very ancient town, a seaport, and a large portion of its population is engaged in the cotton trade; there are remains of a monastery of Greyfriars.

Preston to Garstang (11¼—224½) is a fairly level road, with good surface, by Cadley Moor, 215½, Broughton Bridge, 217, Four Lane Ends, 217¾, Barton, 219¼, Bilsborough, 220¾, Brocks Bridge, 221½, and Claughton *Tp.*, 222½.

(*Garstang:* Eagle and Child; King's Arms; Royal Oak.)

On *r.*, Broughton Hall and Tower, and Claughton Hall. At Garstang are the remains of Greenhalgh Castle.

Garstang to Lancaster (11¼—235¾); the road is fairly level through Cabus, 226½, Hole of Ellel, 229¾, over Galgate Bridge, 231¼, and by Borough, 233¼, to Scotforth, 234¼, whence there is a long descent to Lancaster; rather rough and shaky, very bad in wet weather. Pretty scenery.

(*Lancaster:* County; Feathers, *B.T.C.*; Queen's; Royal County.)

Beyond Garstang, a few miles on *r.*, are Bleasdale Moors; on *l.*, Lancaster Bay. At Lancaster, the principal object is the castle, founded before the Conquest, and enlarged by Edward III.; it is now the county gaol: the principal *ch.*, St. Mary's, is an ancient edifice with carved stalls, screens and monuments. At Borough, on *l.*, Ashton Hall (Duke of Hamilton).

Lancaster to Carnforth (6—241¾); after crossing the *R.* Lune the road presently skirts the shores of Morecambe Bay, the estuary of the *R.* Kent, and becomes rather hilly through Slyne, 238¼, and Bolton-le-Sands, 239¾, the ascents being rather sharp, and the surface is not very good.

(*Carnforth:* Grange.)

Near Bolton-le-Sands is a large cavern, called Dunal Mill Hole.

Carnforth to Burton-in-Kendal (5—246¾); over Keer Bridge, 243¾, is a pretty good road and not so hilly; at Carnforth keep to *r.*

Burton to Kendal (10¾—257½); good road with some stiff hills, through Farlton Lane, 248¾, End Moor, 252, Barrow Green, 254½, and Mill Beck, 256¼. [Or keep to *l.* beyond *Burton* and go through Holme, 248¼, Milnthorpe, 251¼, Heversham, 252¼, Levens Hall, 253½, and Syzergh, 255½, to *Kendal*, 259½; a very pleasant road, but with one or two severe ascents; from Heversham it follows the valley of the *R.* Kent, and after the least rain the road becomes sticky and heavy.]

(*Kendal:* Commercial; Railway; Railway and Commercial.)

On *l.*, near Heversham, is Levens Hall, which contains some rich carvings; Syzergh Hall, the ancient seat of the Stricklands. At Kendal, on *r.*, Abbot Hall. Kendal, otherwise Kirkby-in-Kendal, is situate in a valley. There are remains of the castle, and on the opposite side of the town is Castlelow Hill. 1*m.* S., are traces of the Roman station Concangium.

Kendal to Shap (15¾—273¼); for the first mile or so the road is bad, and soon after leaving Kendal the ascent up to Shap Fells begins, and continues for some 10m.; it is not difficult to Otter Bank, 260¾ (whence a capital view can be obtained of Kendal), and then it becomes more or less steep—many parts too steep to be ridden up, and too dangerous to be ridden down in the reverse direction—passing Gate Side post office. 262½, Banisdale Bridge, 263¾, then down a dangerous hill to High Barrow Bridge, 265½, and again up a very steep ascent under Bretherdale Bank to Demmings, 267½, and for a mile or so on to and over the top of Shap Fells, the highest point of which is 1,304 feet above sea level; then the descent begins, part of it very steep, and with one break in it of about ½m., where there is a slight ascent; in descending either side great care should be taken. The greater part of this stage is very bad, some of it being overgrown with grass and covered with loose stones, so that it is no better than a mere mountain track for miles, especially so after High Barrow Bridge to within 2m. of Shap, when it is much better, though still rather rough, and the descent is easy.

(*Shap:* Greyhound; King's Arms.)

The scenery on the road is very fine. About 4m. before Shap, on r., is Shap Wells Hotel, possessing a medicinal spring similar to that of Leamington, and much resorted to. About 2m. farther on, by the roadside, on r., are two rows of huge unhewn granite blocks, called Karl Lofts; 1m. N.E. of Shap, at Gunnerskeld Bottom is a circle of large stones; both are supposed to be Druidical remains. 1m. E. of Shap, on the banks of the R. Lowther, are ruins of Shap Abbey; Hawes Water lies 6m. W.

Shap to Penrith (10¼—283½) is a tolerable road with some more hills, but nothing difficult through Thrimby, 276½, Hackthorpe, 279, and Clifton, 281, over Lowther Bridge, 282 (then turn to r.), and Eamont Bridge, 282½, whence there is a short but stiff hill to mount into Penrith.

(*Penrith:* Agricultural; Crown; Fish; George, *C.T.C.*; Gloucester Arms; New Crown; Old Crown; White Hart.)

There are some splendid views on this road; Helvellyn and Saddleback are visible. At Clifton, on l., Lowther Park and Castle, the magnificent seat of Earl Lonsdale; also Clifton Hall, an old turreted mansion. At Lowther Bridge, 1m. on r., Brougham Castle, a fine ruin, is supposed to occupy the site of a Roman station; before Eamont Bridge, down a lane on l., King Arthur's Round Table, and Mayborough. At Penrith are the ruins of the castle, dismantled by the Parliamentarians; also the Beacon, Giant's Grave, Giant's Caves, etc. Ulleswater is 5m. S.W.

Penrith to High Hesket (9¼—292¾); the first mile or so is uphill, then the road is undulating to Salkeld Gate, 288, and thence rather hilly (one or two of the gradients each way being very sharp), with a long ascent to High Hesket; capital hard and smooth surface, not much affected by rain.

6m. N.E. of Penrith, near Little Salkeld, and passing Eden Hall, is a Druidical remain, a large circle of 67 stones, bearing the name of Long Meg and her Daughters. At Old Penrith, 5m. N.W., are the remains of a Roman station, Voreda. Near High Hesket is Armathwaite Hall; also ruins of Castle Hewin.

High Hesket to Carlisle (8¾—301½); beyond High Hesket is a long steep hill to go down, which is generally rather rough, to Low Hesket, 294¼, followed by a hill to climb out of the village, and then it is easy riding over an undulating road, through Carleton, 299, and Harraby, 300, whence it is more or less downhill to Carlisle; after leaving Low Hesket,

It is a capital, smooth, hard road; the streets of Carlisle are paved with square setts, but rideable.

(*Carlisle*: Bush; County; Great Central; Crescent, *Temp.*; Jenk's; Red Lion, *C.T.C.*; Turf.)

Carlisle was early fortified by the Romans; a small portion of the old Norman wall remains, but the most striking feature of the town is the castle, founded by William Rufus. The cathedral, restored in 1856, is a venerable building of red freestone, some parts dating from Norman times.

Carlisle to Gretna Green (9¼—310¾); after crossing the bridge over the *R.* Eden there is a stiff hill to mount going through Stanwix, 302½, a suburb of Carlisle; here the road to Newcastle must be passed on the right and a mile farther on keep again to the *l.*, and through Todhills, 305½, Floriston, 306¾, over the Metal Bridge, 307¾, through Lennoxtown, 309½, and across *R.* Sark into Scotland, 310, is a fair road almost level.

Gretna Green to Ecclefechan (9¾—320¼); fair road, but rather hilly by Newtown Inn, or Kirkpatrick, 314¾, Woodhouse Inn, 315¾, and Kirtle Bridge, 317¾; rough for about a mile on either side of Kirtle Bridge.

About ⅞m. before Gretna Green cross the small *R.* Sark and enter Scotland. On *l.*, Solway Firth. Gretna Green was famous many years ago as the scene of runaway marriages, now illegal. At Ecclefechan are shown the birthplace and tomb of Thomas Carlyle; 1m. on *l.*, Hoddam Castle and the Tower of Repentance, or Tower of Trailtrone.

Ecclefechan to Dinwoodie Green (11—331¼); long ascent out of Ecclefechan, and fall into Lockerbie, 326¾, whence undulating through Nethercleugh, 330; easy going and good road.

At Lockerbie, on *r.*, Lockerbie *Ho.*: at Dinwoodie Green, on *l.*, Jardine Hall. 1¾m. beyond Ecclefechan, on *l.*, Castlemilk *Ho.*

(*Ecclefechan*: Bush, *C.T.C.*—*Lockerbie*: Blue Bell, rec. *C.T.C.*)

Dinwoodie Green to Beattock, Bridge Inn (9½—341); is a good undulating road, chiefly on the rise up the valley of the *R.* Annan; at Dinwoodie, 333, keep to *l.*, and a mile beyond cross to the right bank of the *R.* Annan.

At Beattock, 1m. on *r.*, Moffat town, and near it Marsdale Park; on *l.*, Cragielands. Beyond Dinwoodie, on *r.*, ruins of Lethan Hall.

Beattock to Crawford (16—357); leaving the main Annan valley on *r.*, the road follows up that of its tributary, Evan Water, past Longbeddom, 343½, Greenhill, Raecleugh, 347, Howcleugh and Bedhouse, for about 10 miles to Little Clyde, where the top of the hill is reached, and there is a long descent down the valley of the *R.* Clyde, past Newton and Elvanfoot Inn, 354½, to Crawford; generally speaking it is a good undulating road, but rough in places.

Before Newton, on *r.*, Bodsbury Camp; a Roman road runs on the *r.* here for several miles. At Crawford, on *r.*, ruins of castle. At Raecleugh, 2m. on *r.*, source of *R.* Tweed and Deil's Beef Tub. Beyond Beattock, on *l.*, Auchen Castle. At Little Clyde, on *r.*, source of *R.* Clyde.

Crawford to Douglas Mill, Inn (12—369); through Abington, 360, hilly road, leaving the Clyde valley on *r.* and going over some very high moorlands, with long and severe gradients, rough in places; long descent to Douglas Mill.

1m. beyond Crawford, on *r.*, Roman camp, and further on a Roman road. Abington *Ho.* 1m. on *l.*, Douglas Castle and the old castle ruins beyond.

Douglas Mill to Hamilton (17½—386¼); cross the moors from Fauld House to Lesmahagow, 375¼, and again to Larkhall, 382¼; hilly but not so difficult as the last stage; fair road.

At Lesmahagow, about 3m. on r., are the falls of the R. Clyde, Corra Linn, etc. 3m. further, on r. 2m., Craignethan Castle. Before Hamilton, on l., Chatelherault with its deer park; ruins of Cadzow Castle; ruins of Woodhouse with park of old British cattle. At Hamilton, on r., the Palace (Duke of Hamilton).

(*Hamilton:* Commercial, *C.T.C.*)

Hamilton to Glasgow (11—397¼); cross the R. Clyde at Bothwell Bridge, 388, and then through Bothwell, 288½, Uddingston, 390, and Broomhouse, 391¾, is rather rough and hillier than the last stage.

(*Glasgow:* Grand, *C.T.C.*; McLean's; Victoria.—*Uddingston:* Royal.)

Bothwell Bridge is the site of the battle in 1679, between the Covenanters and the Duke of Monmouth. At Bothwell, on l., Bothwell Castle.

LONDON TO BLACKPOOL.

London to Preston (213¼)—p. 157.

Preston to Freckleton (7½—220¾); through Ashton, 216½, and across the marshes is quite level, and in fair weather a good hard road.

Freckleton to Lytham 4½—225¼); through Warton, 222½, is a first rate road.

(*Lytham:* Clifton Arms, *C.T.C.*; Market and Commercial; Ship and Royal.)

Lytham is a small watering-place, pleasantly situated on the north side of the Ribble; beyond is Lytham Hall.

Lytham to Blackpool (8—233¼); through Hey Houses, The Folds, and Blown Sands is a very fair road on the whole, but varies with the time of the year.

(*Blackpool:* Bailey; Beach; Imperial; Royal; Victoria, *C.T.C.*)

Blackpool, on the shore of the Irish Sea, is a large watering-place, and has greatly increased of late years; it may, indeed be called the Brighton of Lancashire and the North; fine pier and aquarium.

LONDON TO WIGTON (by Keswick and the Lakes).

London to Carnforth (241¾)—p. 158.

Carnforth to Milnthorpe (7¼—249); from Carnforth keep to l. and through Hale, 246¾, to Beetham, 247¾, is very level, but owing to its not being much used is very bad and loose, being nothing but cart ruts, after that it is better to Milnthorpe. [After crossing the R. Keer just beyond Carnforth there is another road on l. through Warton and Yealand to Milnthorpe, 250½.]

(*Milnthorpe:* Cross Keys.)

At Milnthorpe, 1m. on l. Dallam Tower.

Milnthorpe to Levens Hall (2¼—251¼); long rise to ascend from Milnthorpe, and good road through Heversham, 250.

On r., Levens Hall.

Levens Hall to Lindale (7—258¼); after crossing the R. Kent leave the Kendal road and turn sharp to l., and it is level but a very loose road through Underbarrow Beck Tp., 252¾, to Town End (Derby's Arms), 255½, after which it begins to be hilly but good across R. Winster, 257¼, to Lindale.

At Lindale, on l., Castle Head Ho.; 3¼m. l. of Lindale is Cartmel.

Linsdale to Staveley (5½—263¾); very long steep hill to climb to Upper Allithwaite and Newton, 260, (from the top of which is obtained a beautiful view of Morecambe Bay and the surrounding country,) and then a long gentle descent, over good roads, through Hayside to Staveley and Newby Bridge: grand scenery.

(*Newby Bridge:* Swan.)

Staveley and Newby Bridge are at the foot of lake Windermere, the largest and most beautiful of the English lakes.

Staveley to Bowness (8½—272¼); the road now follows the eastern shore of Lake Windermere; it undulates considerably, and there are several short sharp pitches; good going.

(*Bowness:* Crown; Lake; Royal.)

3*m.* before Bowness, on *l.*, Storr's Hall. Pretty scenery.

Bowness to Ambleside (5½—277¾); continuing along the shore of the lake, about ¾*m.* beyond Bowness the road ascends a steep hill, and then pursues a level course to Cook's House, 273½, where the Kendal road joins in; thence it is undulating over Troutbeck Bridge, 274¼, past Low Wood Inn, 275¾, and Waterhead, 277, to Ambleside; good road, but heavy in wet weather.

(*Low Wood Inn.—Ambleside:* Commercial; Queen; Salutation; Waterhead; White Lion.)

Beyond Bowness on *l.*, Rayrigg Ho., and at Troutbeck Bridge, Calgarth: before Waterhead, on *r.*, Dove's Nest. On *l.*, see Bowfell, Scawfell and Langdale Pikes, &c. Fine scenery. Ambleside is prettily situated 1*m.* above the head of the lake, surrounded by fine scenery of mountain, dale, lake, and stream. On *l.*, Loughrigg Fell, on *r.*, Wansfell Pike and Stockgill Force.

Ambleside to Grasmere, Town End (4¾—282¼); the road is good and undulating through Rydal, 279, and winding round the wooded shores of Rydal Water and Grasmere Lake. Grasmere village lies a short distance on *l.*

(*Grasmere:* Lake; Hollins and Lowther; Prince of Wales; Swan, *B.T.C.*)

On *r.*, Rydal Hall and Rydal Mount, the latter formerly the residence of the poet Wordsworth; he also lived at Allan Bank, Grasmere, and at Town End; and lies buried in Grasmere churchyard. In Rydal Park are the celebrated Falls. On *r.*, is Knab Scar.

Grasmere to Keswick (11¼—293¾); there is a long steep hill to climb from Grasmere, very steep for the first ½*m.*, ending in the pass of Dunmail Raise, 283½, which reaches an elevation of 720 feet, then a long run down through Wytheburn, 285, to the head of Thirlemere Lake, 286, which lies at the foot of Helvellyn, the scenery here being very wild; alongside the lake it is a good undulating road to Smalthwaite Bridge, 289, from which is steep hill to climb, then downhill to Causeway Foot, 291¾, where another stiff bit to walk up intervenes, and there is an exceedingly steep and unrideable descent leading into Keswick.

(*Keswick:* Borrowdale; Keswick; King's Arms; Lake; Queen's; Royal Oak, *B.T.C.*; Skiddaw, temp.)

This is a lovely ride, new views of scenery opening out at every mile. 2*m.* before Keswick, on *l.*, Castle Rigg Hill; also 1*m.* on *r.* of it, remains of a Druidical temple; near the town Castle Hill. 3*m.* N. is Skiddaw mountain; 1*m.* on Penrith road is Greta Hall. S. are the pretty lake of Derwent Water, Lodore Falls, Borrowdale, &c., &c.

Keswick to Uldale (10½—304): very poor and rather hilly road, scarcely fit for cycles, through Crossthwaite, 294½ (keep to *r.*), Little Crossthwaite, 297¾, and High Side, 299¾, to Castle Inn, 301½, and another hill up and down to Uldale. [Or to Pheasant Inn, 300¾, as at p. 176, a fairly good road with no difficult hills, and ¼*m.* beyond keep to *r.*, and a good road over Ouse Bridge (*R.* Derwent), 301¾, to Castle Inn, 303.]

For several miles the road skirts the shores of Bassenthwaite Water.

Uldale to Wigton (7—311); turn to *l.* and through Ireby, 305½.

Ireby: Black Lion.—*Wigton:* King's Arms, *C.T.C.*)

LONDON TO AMBLESIDE (by Kendal).

London to Kendal (257½)—p. 158.

Kendal to Cook's House (8¾—266¼); when clear of the houses keep to *l.*, and the very steep ascent of House of Correction Hill has to be climbed (should be *descended* carefully even with a brake), then capital road, rather undulating and with fair surface (keeping to *r.* at 259*m.*) through Staveley (Westmoreland), 261¾, and Ings, 263¼, nearly a mile beyond which is another steep hill to mount, followed by the very steep descent of Bannerigge Brow to walk down (unrideable both ways) to Windermere, 265¾, where bear to *r.*

(*Windermere:* Crown; Ferry; Lowwood; Old England; Queen's; Rigg's; Windermere.)

At Windermere is the railway terminus.

Cook's House to Ambleside (4¼—270½)—p. 162.

LONDON TO GLASGOW (by Dumfries).

London to Gretna Green (310¾)—p. 160.

Gretna Green to Annan (9—319¾); the road follows the north shore of Solway Firth through Dornock, 316¾.

1½*m.* from Annan on *l.* Newby Ruins.—(*Annan:* Queensberry Arms, *C.T.C.*)

Annan to Dumfries (17—336¾); by Cumbertrees, 323½, Ruthwell, 326¼, and Mousewald, 330¼, is rather hilly but not a bad road.

(*Dumfries:* Commercial, *B.T.C.*; King's Arms; Queensberry Arms.)

At Mousewald, Duke of Buccleugh; 3*m.* on *l.* Camlungan Castle. Dumfries is situate on the *R.* Nith; there is a fine monument here to Burns.

Dumfries to Thornhill (16—352¾); first rate road up the valley of the *R.* Nith, through Millhead, 340¾, Dalswinton, 343½, Forest, 345¼, by Algirth Bridge, 346 (cross to left bank of *R.* Nith), Steep Ends, 347½, and Gateside, 349¼. Fine scenery.

Beyond Dumfries on *r.*, the Old College of Linncluden ruins; on *l.*, Terregles *Ho.*; at Dalswinton on *r.*, is the site of the ancient castle of the Cummings; at Gateside on *r.*, the Academy of Closeburn and Closeburn Castle.

Thornhill to Sanquhar (12—364¾); excellent road, still up the valley of the *R.* Nith and by Carron Bridge, 354¾.

At Carron Bridge on *l.*, across the Nith, is Drumlanrig Castle. At Sanquhar on *l.*, are the castle ruins.—(*Sanquhar:* Queensberry Arms, *C.T.C.*

Sanquhar to Muirkirk (16—380¾); the road now leaves the valley of the Nith and crosses the hills through Fingland, 370½, and Tarkhill, 379.

Muirkirk to Strathaven (13¼—394) is a hilly road through picturesque scenery.

At Strathaven on *r.*, castle ruins and waterfall.

Strathaven to Kilbride (8—402); through Chapleton, 397, and Shawton, 399.

Kilbride to Glasgow (8¾—410¾); through Rutherglen, 408.

LONDON TO LEEK.

London to Lichfield (118½)—p. 145.

Lichfield to Abbots Bromley (10—128½); a mile out of Lichfield keep to *r.*, and 1¼*m.* further on to *l.*; very good road through Handsacre, 122½, Hill Ridware, 124, and Blithbury, 125½; there are a few hills but nothing difficult.

Abbots Bromley to Uttoxeter (6¾—135¼); through Bagots Bromley, 129½, and Blount's Green, 134¾, is a good road.

(*Uttoxeter:* Cross Keys; White Hart.)

Beyond Abbots Bromley, on *l.* Blithfield Park, and on *r.* Bagots Park.

Uttoxeter to Cheadle (10¼—145½); through Stramshall, 136¾, Beanshurst, 138½, Checkley, 140¾, Lower Tean, 141¾, and Upper Tean, 142½.

(*Cheadle:* Royal Oak; Wheatsheaf.)

About 4*m.* E. of Cheadle are Alton Park and Towers.

Cheadle to Leek (10¾—156¼); through Kingsley Lane, 147½ (a mile beyond to *r.*), Wetley or Wetley Rocks, 150¾, Cheddleton, 153¼, and Cornhill, 155½. [Or from Cheadle, through Holt, 147¼, Ipstones, 150¼, by Bottom House, 152¼ (keep to *l.*), and Ashtonsitch, 154, to Leek, 156½.]

(*Leek:* For hotels and notes see p. 169.)

LONDON TO BURSLEM.

London to Upper Tean (142½)—above.

Upper Tean to Stoke-upon-Trent (10—152½); through Draycott, 144¼, Blythe Marsh, 145¼, Meere (or Mear) *Tp.*, 147¼, Longton, 148½, Lane End, 149¼, and Lane Delph, 150¼.

(*Stoke:* North Staffordshire; West End, *Hqrs.*)

For the latter half of the stage, the road traverses the Potteries district.

Stoke-upon-Trent to Burslem (3¼—155¾); through Etruria, 153¾, (leaving Hanley ½*m.* on *r.*) and Cobridge *Tp.*, 154½.

[Or instead of going through Stoke, keep to *r.* at Lane Delph, and go through *Hanley*, 153, to Cobridge *Tp.*, 154.

Or to Flask, 147¼, p. 152, then on *r*, to *Stoke-upon-Trent*, 1½—148¾, and *Hanley*, 2½—149¾.]

(*Burslem:* Leopard; Marquis of Granby.)

LONDON TO UTTOXETER (by Nuneaton).

London to Burton-upon-Trent (123½)—p. 157.

Burton-upon-Trent to Sudbury (9½—133); through Horninglow, 125, Tutbury, 128, Foston, 131, and Aston, 132½.

Beyond Horninglow on *r.*, Rolleston Hall. At Tutbury, on the *R.* Dove, are ruins of a magnificent castle built by the Normans, besieged and dismantled by the Parliamentarians; there are also remains of a priory.

Sudbury to Uttoxeter (5½—138½); good undulating road through Doveridge, 136½.

[Or from *Burton-upon-Trent* by Henhurst, Anslow Leys, over Coulter Hills, and through Marchington; a little shorter.]

LONDON TO LEEK (by Sandon).

London to Sandon (136¼)—p. 156.

Sandon to Hilderstone (3—139¼).

Hilderstone to Meere Tp. (5—144¼); over Meere Heath (or Barlaston Common) 142¾, and Shooters Hill, 143¼.

Meere Tp. to Wetley Rocks (4½—148¾); through Weston Coyney 145¾ (keep to *r.*), and Cellar Head, 147¼.

At Cellar Head on *r.*, Wetley Abbey.

Wetley Rocks to Leek (5½—154¼)—p. 164.

LONDON TO MANCHESTER.

London to Siddington Tp. (166½)—p. 154.

Siddington to Wilmslow (8—174½); keep to *r.* and it is a good undulating road to Alderley Edge Hill where is a long and very steep descent to Alderley, 170¾, beyond which it is level but lumpy and rough through Chorley, 172½, to Wilmslow; in the middle of the latter is a short patch of cobble stone paving.

(*Wilmslow:* Swan.)

Beyond Siddington on *l.*, Capesthorn Hall; on *r.*, Alderley Park and Birtles Hall. The range of hills on the right here is Alderley Edge.

Wilmslow to Cheadle (4¾—179¼); descent out of Wilmslow, followed by a short ascent, then level for a mile through Finney Green, 175¼, and a descent and steep rise to Handforth, 176, whence it is level and fairly good through Hurlbote Green, 176½, to Cheadle, except a short fall ¾*m.* before the village.

(*Cheadle:* George and Dragon; White Hart).

Cheadle to Manchester, St. Ann's Square (7—186¼); ¾*m.* beyond Cheadle cross the *R.* Mersey; the road soon changes to macadam, very rough and bumpy through Didsbury, 181, Withington, 182¼, and Birch, 183¾, to Rusholme, 184½, which is now a part of Manchester, and whence it is paved and very rough into the town along Oxford road, Moseley street, and Market street; level all the way, tramway from Withington.

For hotels and notes on Manchester, see p. 168.

LONDON TO GLASGOW (by Derby and Manchester).

London to Northampton (65¾)—p. 154 or p. 156.

Northampton to Lamport (8½—74¼); long hill out of Northampton, and all up and down hill through Kingsthorpe, 67¼, Boughton, 69, Pitsford, 70, and Brixworth, 72; excellent hard road.

(*Lamport:* Lamports Inn.)

On r., Boughton Park; before Lamport on r., Lamport Hall.

Lamport to Market Harborough (9—83¼); descent out of Lamport, at the bottom of which there is a level railway crossing, and the hill should be descended carefully as the gate cannot be seen from the top; out of this valley is Hopping Hill to climb, not very long but part of it very steep, then excellent but rather hilly road through Maidwell, 76, Kelmarsh, 78, Great Oxendon, 80¾, and Little Bowden, 82½; through Market Harborough the sides of the street are paved.

(*Market Harborough:* Angel; George; Hind; Peacock, *C.T.C.*; Three Swans.)

3m. W. of Kelmarsh is Naseby Field, the scene of the defeat of Charles I. by Cromwell; Kelmarsh Hall. Market Harborough is a small old town; many Roman antiquities have been found here; fine ch.

Market Harborough to Leicester (14½—97¾); through Kibworth, 88¾, Great Glen, 91½, and Oadby, 94¼, is a first rate undulating road; hill to mount into Oadby, but nothing difficult, and from here is tramway into Leicester, and slightly downhill; most of Leicester is cobble-paved, with tramways through the town.

Leicester: Barley Mow; Bell, *C.T.C.*; Bull's Head; Carlton; Cook's, temp.; George; Stag and Pheasant; Wellington.)

At Kibworth, 2m. on r., Carlton Curlieu Hall, a fine old Elizabethan mansion. Leicester is supposed to have been the Roman station Ratæ or Ragæ, which survives in the name of Raw Dykes, a bank outside the town; there are also remains of the old wall; the castle was a most extensive building, and part of it is now the Assize Hall. There are ruins of the abbey, where Cardinal Wolsey died; there are some fine churches and public buildings. The town is celebrated for its hosiery.

Leicester to Loughborough (11—108¾); tramway through and out of Leicester to Belgrave, 99½ (just before which turn to r.), and then a very smooth and hard road, with no hills to speak of, through Birstal, 101, Mount Sorrel, 104¾, and Quorndon, 106¼.

(*Loughborough:* Bull's Head; Bull & Anchor; King's Head; Red Lion, *C.T.C.*)

On r., Birstal Hall, and 1½m. further, Wanlip Hall. Mount Sorrel was famous in the Plantagenet period for its fortress of great natural strength, situate on a steep hill overhanging the town, and demolished by Henry III. A few miles on l., lies Charnwood Forest. Quorndon gives the name to the celebrated Quorn Hunt. 2m. on l. is Beaumanor Hall.

Loughborough to Kegworth (6—114¾) is a capital level road through Dishley, 110½, and Hathern, 111½.

(*Kegworth:* Flying Childers.)

At Dishley, 1m. on l., Gavendon Park.

Kegworth to Derby (11—125¾); cross *R.* Trent at Cavendish Bridge, 118½, and then through Shardlow, 119¼, and Alvaston, 122¼, is nearly all on the level and capital road till close to Derby.

(*Derby:* Bell; Midland; Royal; St. James', *Hqrs.*, *B.T.C.*; Wheel.)

Before Cavendish Bridge, 2m. on l., Castle Donington. On r., Alvaston Castle. Derby is pleasantly situated, and of late years has greatly improved in its buildings. The chief manufacture is silk, and the first silk mill in England still exists here.

Derby to Belper (7¼—133½); rather up and down hill past Darley Chapel and through Allestree, 128½, Duffield, 130½, and Milford, 132 (where cross R. Derwent); first 2 or 3m. the road is good, then it deteriorates.

(*Belper:* George; Lion; Nag's Head; New Inn; Red Lion, *C.T.C.*; Rose and Crown; White Swan.)

Beyond Derby, 1m. on r., Darley Abbey. On l., Allestree Park. Belper owes its prosperity to the large cotton factories of the Messrs. Strutt, employing about 1200 persons.

Belper to Matlock (10¾—144¼); the road follows close by the R. Derwent all the way, through Ambergate, 136¾ (keep to l.), 2¼m. further cross the Derwent and keep to r. through Cromford, 142¼ (keep to r.), and Matlock Bath, 142¾; it is nearly level but a rough road; before Matlock cross the Derwent.

(*Matlock Bath:* Bath Terrace; Devonshire Arms; New Bath, *C.T.C.*; Temple; Walker's.—*Matlock:* Midland.)

Beautiful scenery all the way. Beyond Ambergate, on l., Alderwasley Hall. At Cromford is a cotton mill, erected by Sir Richard Arkwright, the inventor of the spinning frame, and now belonging to his descendants. On the r. is Willersley Castle, an elegant mansion belonging to the Arkwright's. Matlock is a favourite summer resort of invalids and tourists; the former for the sake of its mineral springs, the latter to visit the beautiful scenery: there are also several natural caverns, and numerous Druidical and other antiquities in the neighbourhood. All the roads round Matlock have a good surface, and afford capital riding, but being hilly a good brake is required. There are some pretty rides to be had; such as through Bonsal Hollow, the Via Gellia, up the hill, and then to the Black Rock and back, a very pretty ride.

Matlock to Rowsley (5¼—149¾); up the left bank of the Derwent valley, through Darley, 147½, is undulating, but the road still continues rough; just before Rowsley turn to l. and cross the Derwent.

3m. north of Rowsley, up the Derwent valley is Chatsworth Ho. (Duke of Devonshire), which can be viewed any day. 1½m. beyond Rowsley, on the Bakewell road, is Haddon Hall (Duke of Rutland). Pretty scenery. At Stanton, on the l., are rocking stones and a Druidical circle.

Rowsley to Bakewell (3¼—153); the road now leaves the Derwent valley and runs up that of the R. Wye, which it crosses to the right bank at Fillyford Bridge, 150¾; pretty level, but the road still continues rough.

(*Bakewell:* Castle and Commercial, *B.T.C.*; Rutland Arms.)

Beyond Fillyford Bridge on r., Haddon Hall. Bakewell is a great resort of tourists and anglers; there are also some warm baths of great repute: fine old ch., partly Saxon, with several curious monuments. Castle Hill.

Bakewell to Buxton (12—165); the road now improves, and for the first 2 or 3m. through Ashford, 154¾, is pretty level and affords good running, up Ashford Dale, crossing the R. Wye twice; at Lees Bottom, 156½, leave the Wye valley on r. (Monsal Dale and Miller's Dale) and there is a long, very steep hill to walk up to Taddington, 158¾ (this hill has a sharp turn, and bicyclists coming the contrary direction must be careful not to attempt riding down); from beyond Taddington is a long and steep descent with a sharp turn at the bottom, which should not be ridden down without a powerful brake, then following the right bank of the R. Wye the road is pretty level for last 3m., but bad again going into Buxton.

(*Buxton:* Burlington; Cheshire Cheese; Crescent; George; Grove Commercial; Lee Wood; Old Hall; Palace; St. Ann's; Station; Shakesperian Commercial; Swan.)

Buxton is surrounded by bleak hills and moors, amongst which is some pretty scenery. It was celebrated for its hot baths in the time of the Romans, and is now greatly frequented in the summer and autumn. In the market place is a curious old cross. The chief objects of interest are Poole's Hole, Diamond Hill and Tower, Chee Tor (4m. before Buxton on r.), Axe Edge, Marvel Stone, &c.

Buxton to Whaley Bridge ($6\frac{1}{2}$—$171\frac{1}{2}$); for 2m. out of Buxton there is a steep hill to walk up, then the road winds about amongst the hills, and is downhill for nearly all the remaining $4\frac{1}{2}$m. into Whaley Bridge: good hard road.

Whaley Bridge to Disley ($3\frac{1}{4}$—$174\frac{3}{4}$); after Whaley Bridge the road becomes rough, but is level.

At Disley, 1m. on l., Lyme Park and Hall.

Disley to Stockport ($6\frac{1}{4}$—181); short ascent out of Disley, then downhill over bad pavement and macadam through Hoo Lane, $176\frac{1}{2}$, and Norbury, $177\frac{1}{4}$, to Bullock Smithy, $178\frac{1}{2}$, whence it is level, but more or less paved through Hazelgrove, $178\frac{3}{4}$, to Stockport, into and through which is a long stiff descent.

(*Stockport*: George ; Vernon Arms.)

Stockport is a large town on the R. Mersey, chiefly engaged in the cotton business.

Stockport to Manchester, St. Ann's Square ($6\frac{3}{4}$—$187\frac{3}{4}$); paved through Stockport, and long gradual rise out of the town, then level but nearly all paved, through Heaton Norris, $182\frac{1}{2}$, Levenshulme, $183\frac{3}{4}$, Longsight, $184\frac{3}{4}$, and Ardwick Green, $185\frac{3}{4}$, a suburb of Manchester, and along the London road, with a short stiff ascent before Piccadilly, and through that and Market street : tram lines all the way.

(*Manchester*: White Bear, Piccadilly, Hqrs.)

Manchester is the great centre of the cotton manufacture, for which it contains mills and warehouses of leviathan proportions. The Cathedral, formerly a collegiate ch., was erected in 1422, and is a handsome edifice. The chief public buildings are the Town Hall, Exchange, Assize Courts, Infirmary, Cheetham's Hospital School, Grammar School, Owen's College, Free Library, &c.

Manchester to Bolton (11—$198\frac{3}{4}$); in Manchester, at the bottom of Market street, turn to l. and along Deansgate, Bridge street, over Albert Bridge (R. Irwell) into Salford, $188\frac{1}{2}$, then to l. along Chapel street, in continuation of which the road rises gradually for half the way to Pendleton, 190, and so far it is all paved ; thence it is undulating and nearly all roughly paved through Irlam-on-the-Height, $191\frac{1}{4}$ (keep to r.), Pendlebury, $192\frac{1}{4}$ (keep to r. and shortly after to l.), Clifton, $193\frac{1}{2}$, and Farnworth, $196\frac{1}{4}$: this road is not fit for bicycling.

(*Bolton*: Levar's Arms; Swan; Talbot's, temp.; Victoria.)

Bolton, or Bolton-le-Moors, is a large manufacturing town, chiefly engaged in the cotton trade, and is in the midst of a coal-mining district. At Farnworth, on r., Darley Hall.

Bolton to Chorley ($11\frac{1}{2}$—$210\frac{1}{4}$); loose undulating road through Horwich, $203\frac{3}{4}$, Smithy Bridge, $204\frac{3}{4}$, Duxbury, $207\frac{1}{4}$, and Yarrow Bridge, 209.

[There is another and shorter road from Irlam-on-the-Height by turning to l. and 1m. beyond to r., and then through Swinton, $192\frac{3}{4}$, Stanney street, Walkden Moor, $194\frac{3}{4}$, Little Hulton, Peel, $195\frac{3}{4}$, Middle Hulton, $198\frac{3}{4}$, Over Hulton, $199\frac{3}{4}$, Wingates (or Win Yate), $201\frac{3}{4}$, Blackrod, 205, and

Adlington, 206½, joining the above road at Duxbury, 207, thence through Yarrow Bridge, 208¾, to *Chorley*, 210.]

Beyond Horwich, on *r.*, Rivington Reservoir, which supplies Liverpool with water. On *l.*, pass Hulton Park, Adlington Hall, and Duxbury Hall.

Chorley to Glasgow (193¼—403¼); through Preston, 219½, Garstang, 230¾, Lancaster, 242, Carnforth, 248, Burton, 253, Kendal, 263¼, Shap, 279½, Penrith, 289¾, and Carlisle, 307¼—pp. 157-61.

LONDON TO MANCHESTER (by Macclesfield).

London to Derby (125¾)—p. 166.

Derby to Ashbourne (13¼—139); through Mackworth, 128½, Kirk Langley, 130¼, Brailsford, 132¾, Shirley Bridge, 135¼, and Penters Lane, 137, is a capital smooth road but hilly, some of the gradients being very steep; into Ashbourne is a considerable descent, generally loose and stony.

(*Ashbourne :* Green Man; Royal.)

Beyond Derby, on *r.*, Markeaton Hall. At Kirk Langley, 2*m.* on *r.*, Kedleston Hall. Ashbourne is beautifully situated in the valley of the *R.* Dove, which forms the well-known and pretty Dove Dale, 3*m.* north of the town: fine old church built in the 13th century.

Ashbourne to Leek (15—154); cross *R.* Dove at Hanging Bridge, 140¾, and past the Red Lion, 143¾, over Calton Moor, to Winkhill Bridge, 148, through New Street, 148½, Bottom House, 149½, and Ashtonsitch, 151; long hill to climb out of Ashbourne, and for the first 4 or 5*m.* the road passes through a wild, bleak and desolate country; after that it is very pretty, and is all up and down hill, nearly all of which can be ridden, but some of the ascents are very steep, and one or two rather dangerous to ride down in the reverse direction, the surface sometimes being rather stony.

(*Leek :* Buck; George; Swan.)

At Hanging Bridge, 3*m.* on *l.*, Colwich Abbey; 1*m.* on *r.*, is Okeover Hall. Further on is Blore Heath, the scene of one of the battles in the Parliamentary War. At Mayfield, on *l.* is the house where Moore wrote "Lalla Rookh." In Leek churchyard is a curious old cross. Here also are the remains of Dieu la Croix Abbey. In the neighbourhood is some romantic scenery.

Leek to Macclesfield (13—167); out of Leek is a steep hill to descend from the Market place (almost too steep to ride up), then the road ascends more or less all the way for 1½*m.* beyond Pool End, 155½, after which there is a long steady descent for about 3*m.* past Rudyard Lake or Reservoir and Rushton Marsh, 158¾, to Hog or Hug Bridge (*R.* Dane), 160, and the rest is easy riding through Bosley, 161½: good limestone road; through Macclesfield is paved.

(*Macclesfield :* Alcock's; Feathers; George; Macclesfield Arms; Queen's, *B.T.C.*)

Before Macclesfield, on *l.*, Park *Ho.* Macclesfield is one of the chief seats of the silk manufacture, and is a long straggling town. Beyond Macclesfield, on *r.*, Hurdsfield *Ho.*

Macclesfield to Stockport (12—179); very good undulating road through Flask, 169, Butley, 170½, Hope Green, 173¼, Poynton, 174¼, Norbury, 175¼ (¾*m.* beyond join the Buxton road), to Bullock Smithy, 176¼, whence it is level, but more or less paved through Hazelgrove, 176¾, to Stockport, into and through which is a long stiff descent.

Stockport to Manchester (6¾—185¾)—p. 168.

LONDON TO MANCHESTER (by Ashbourne and Buxton).

(This is the shortest route to Manchester).

London to Ashbourne (139)—p. 169.

Ashbourne to Buxton (20½—159½); through Sandy Brook, 140, Fenny Bentley, 141½, by New Inn, 144½ (near Alsop-in-le-Dale), Old Bear, Jug and Glass, Newhaven Inn, 148, Hen Moor, 152, Hurdlow House, 152¾, and Over Street, 153¾; it is continually up and down hill, but a very smooth road.

The road goes through some pretty scenery; for many miles it runs parallel with Dove Dale on *l.*; in the latter half of the stage it follows the line of the old Roman road, and close to it on *l.*, is the old High Peak Mineral Railway. Near Newhaven Inn, on *r.*, is a Druidical circle.

Buxton to Manchester (22¾—182¼)—p. 168: through Whaley Bridge, 166, Disley, 169¼, and Stockport, 175½.

LONDON TO BURTON-UPON-TRENT (by Leicester).

London to Leicester (97¾)—p. 166.

Leicester to Ravenstone (14—111¾) through Grooby, 101¾, Markfield, 104¾, and Hugglescote, 109¼.

On *r.* is Charnwood Forest.

Ravenstone to Burton-upon-Trent (12—123¾); by Ashby-de-la-Zouch, 114¾—pp. 156-7.

LONDON TO DERBY (by Ashby-de-la-Zouch).

London to Ashby-de-la-Zouch (114¾)—above.

Ashby-de-la-Zouch to Derby (14½—129¼); by Staunton Harrold, 119, Melbourne, 121¾, Swarkestone, 124½, and Osmaston, 127¾.

LONDON TO MANCHESTER (by Wirksworth).

London to Derby (125¾)—p. 166.

Derby to Cross Hands Inn (8¾—134½) by Kedleston Inn, 129, and Weston-under-Wood, 132; keep to *r.* ¼m. before Cross Hands Inn.

On *l.*, Kedleston Park, the magnificent seat of Lord Scarsdale.

Cross Hands Inn to Wirksworth (5¼—139¾); by the Black Swan at Idridgehay Green, 136½, Bateman Bridge, 138, and Wall Brook Bridge, 139½.

[From Derby there is another road through *Belper*, 133½ (p. 167), and thence by Belper Lane End, 135¼, and over Wirksworth Moor to *Wirksworth*, 140.]

(*Wirksworth*: Red Lion.)

Wirksworth is prettily situated in an amphitheatre of hills.

Wirksworth to Cromford (2—141¾); into the latter is a fearful hill to descend, quite impossible to ride down.

Cromford to Manchester (45½—187¼); through Matlock, 143¾, Rowsley, 149¼, Bakewell, 152½, Buxton, 164½, &c.—pp. 167-8.

LONDON TO MANCHESTER (by Chapel-en-le-Frith).

London to Bakewell (153)—p. 167.

Bakewell to Chapel-en-le-Frith ($14\tfrac{3}{4}$—$167\tfrac{3}{4}$); the road now improves and is pretty level, and affords good running to Ashford, $154\tfrac{3}{4}$, just before which cross R. Wye; then keep to r. and the road becomes very hilly through Little Longstone, $155\tfrac{3}{4}$, Wardlow, 158, Wardlow Tp., $158\tfrac{1}{2}$, Tideswell Lane End, $160\tfrac{1}{4}$, New Dam, $163\tfrac{3}{4}$, and Sparrow Pit, $165\tfrac{3}{4}$.

At Tideswell Lane End on *l.* to *Tideswell* ($\tfrac{1}{2}$—$160\tfrac{3}{4}$).

(*Chapel-en-le-Frith:* King's Arms; Royal Oak.)

A few miles north of Chapel-en-le-Frith is the Peak mountain with Mam Tor, Peak Cavern, Odin Mine, Peak Castle, &c., and more east Eldon Hole.

Chapel-en-le-Frith to Whaley Bridge ($3\tfrac{1}{2}$—$171\tfrac{1}{4}$).

Whaley Bridge to Manchester ($16\tfrac{1}{4}$—$187\tfrac{1}{2}$)—p. 168.

LONDON TO GLASGOW (by Ashbourne and Manchester).

London to Manchester ($182\tfrac{1}{4}$)—p. 170.

Manchester to Glasgow ($215\tfrac{3}{4}$—398); through Bolton, $193\tfrac{1}{4}$, Chorley, $204\tfrac{3}{4}$, Preston, 214, Garstang, $225\tfrac{1}{2}$, Lancaster, $236\tfrac{1}{2}$, Carnforth, $242\tfrac{1}{2}$, Burton, $247\tfrac{1}{2}$, Kendal, $258\tfrac{1}{4}$, Shap, 274, Penrith, $284\tfrac{1}{4}$, and Carlisle, $302\tfrac{1}{4}$—pp. 168-9.

LONDON TO KENDAL (by Clitheroe).

London to Manchester ($182\tfrac{1}{4}$)—p. 170.

Manchester to Bury (9—$191\tfrac{1}{4}$); from the Exchange in Manchester turn to *r.* along Corporation street, then up the long gradual ascent of Cheetham Hill, a suburb of Manchester; it is paved to Cheetham, 184, then (keeping to *l.* and shortly afterwards to *r.*) it is rough macadam through Great Heaton, $186\tfrac{1}{2}$, to Whitefield (or Stand), $188\tfrac{1}{2}$, whence, over Blackford Bridge, $189\tfrac{1}{2}$, it is paved with large square stones, and also through Bury. [From Manchester there is a little shorter road by going through Strangeways, up the gradual rise of Broughton Hill, and through Prestwich, 186, to Whitefield, 188; the pavement extends for about a mile, then macadam.]

At Cheetham, on *l.* (and at Broughton Hill, on *r.*) is Broughton Hall; further on, on *r.*, Heaton Hall.

Bury to Edenfield (6—$197\tfrac{1}{4}$); through Walmsley, $193\tfrac{1}{4}$, and Shuttleworth, $196\tfrac{1}{4}$, is an undulating road with good hard surface, except for the pavement through the villages.

At Shuttleworth, on a projecting spur of the hills, on *r.*, is the Grant Tower, erected by the brothers W. & C. Grant, the original of the Cheeryble Brothers of Charles Dickens. On Holcombe Hill, across the Irwell valley, is the Peel Monument.

Edenfield to Haslingden (3—$200\tfrac{3}{4}$); through Edenfield is half a mile of pavement, and leaving the village keep to *l.*, then it is downhill—the last bit rather stiff—to Ewood Bridge, $198\tfrac{3}{4}$, where cross the railway and R. Irwell; on the other side of the valley there is a gradual ascent of half a mile, and after another stretch of pavement, there is a long steady rise to Haslingden: good smooth and hard road;* Haslingden is paved.

Haslingden is the highest town in England.

(*Haslingden :* Bay Horse Inn; Roebuck.)

Haslingden to Accrington (4—204¾); through Baxenden, 202¾, is a good and gently undulating road, with scarcely any pavement between the two towns; Accrington is all paved.

(*Accrington :* Hargraves Inn, B.T.C.)

Accrington to Whalley (5½—210¼); stiff pull out of Accrington, then moderately good road, with considerable fall at Clayton-le-Moors, 206½, and another to Cock Bridge, 208½ (R. Calder), from which there is a steep ascent, all paved with large stones, which on the top of the hill continue for ½m., and then very steep, dangerous descent into Whalley, where it meets the street at right angles; short patch of cobble-stone paving through Whalley.

On r., Clayton Hall; at Cock Bridge, on l., Moreton Hall. At Whalley are remains of the Cistercian Abbey; the *ch.* dates from 1100, and contains some curious carved stalls and monuments. On l., by R. Ribble, is Mitton Hall, and beyond it Bashall and Whaddow Hall, all surrounded by charming scenery. Mitton Church is one of the smallest in the kingdom. About 4m. N.W. is Stonyhurst, the celebrated Jesuit College.

Whalley to Clitheroe (4—214¼); in Whalley turn to r. and it is a good undulating road, with a very sharp ascent just after entering Clitheroe, followed by a corresponding sharp descent at the other end of the town.

(*Clitheroe :* Brownlow Arms; Pendle; Starkie Arms; Swan.)

At Clitheroe are remains of the castle erected by the Lacys soon after the Conquest, and dismantled by the Parliamentarians. About 3m. E. is Pendle Hill, 1831 ft. high. 4m. N.W. is Browsholme Hall, erected in the 15th century, and containing the original seal of the Commonwealth.

Clitheroe to Gisburn (7—221¼); fairly good and undulating road up the valley of the R. Ribble, through Chatburn, 215¼, to Sawley, 217¼, where turn to r. by the " Sawley Arms," and then you have Sawley Brow to climb, which is very steep, loose, and stony (not safe to ride *down* the other way); this is followed by two or three shorter but stony ascents at intervals in the next 2m., and the rest is downhill, in one or two parts rather sharp, into Gisburn; after Sawley the surface for the most part is generally loose and stony.

At Sawley, are remains of the Abbey.

Gisburn to Long Preston (6½—227¾); through Newsholme, 222¾, and Nappa, 224¼, is rather hilly, but good travelling in fine weather.

Long Preston to Settle (4½—232¼) is a good limestone road, but sometimes rather rough; downhill out of Long Preston, then almost level, running up the valley of the R. Ribble.

(*Settle :* Commercial; Golden Lion.)

---

* The roads in N.E. Lancashire are nearly all made of the peculiar stone of the district, a kind of hard durable limestone, geologically known as "millstone grit," similar to the London flagstones, and here largely used in building; it is much superior to the granitic macadam, as it binds well, is not lumpy and uneven, and though slightly inclined to be greasy when wet, is never dangerously so, as the water runs well off; in dry weather the dust formed is very powdery.

Settle is remarkable for its situation at the foot of an overhanging limestone rock. A few miles E. are Malham Tarn and Malham Cove.

Settle to Clapham (6¾—239); cross *R.* Ribble to Giggleswick, 233, whence the road now ascends gradually for about 2*m.* over Giggleswick Scar or Craven Ridge, down the other side of which it falls away very sharply, and the last 3*m.* are level; good running.

(*Clapham:* New Inn.)

N. of Clapham are Ingleborough, Wharnside, and Penygant mountains, Thornton Force cascade, and two caves of Yordas and Weathercote.

Clapham to Ingleton (4—243); through Newby, 240¼, is a comparatively good hard road, but greasy when wet.

Ingleton to Kirkby Lonsdale (7—250); hilly and rough road through Thornton, 244, and over Cowan Bridge, 247¾.

Kirkby Lonsdale to Kendal (12—262); good road through Kearswick, 251, Old Town, 253, and Old Hutton, 257¼.

LONDON TO BLACKBURN.

London to Manchester (182¼); by Ashbourne and Buxton—p. 170.

Manchester to Bolton (11—193¼)—p. 168.

Bolton to Blackburn (13—206¼); through Sharples, 195, Walmsley, 196½, Egerton, 197, and Over Darwen, 202¼, is a hilly road. [There is an easier route, but longer round through Turton on *r.*]

(*Blackburn:* Old Bull.)

Near Turton is Turton Tower, and on Turton Heights is a Druidical circle.

LONDON TO SKIPTON.

London to Edenfield (197¼)—p. 171.

Edenfield to Rawtenstall (2¾—200); through Edenfield is ½*m.* of pavement, and leaving the village keep to *r.*, then it is a fairly good undulating road, with a long descent to Rawtenstall, entering which is a level crossing; ½*m.* of square sett pavement through the town.

Rawtenstall to Burnley (7¾—207¾); except for two or three patches of pavement it is a tolerable and fairly level road to Crawshaw Booth, 202¼, whence it is fairly good and hard, and gradually rises for about 2*m.* to the head of the valley, and there is a winding descent of about 2½*m.*, in some parts rather steep, into Burnley, and which should be ridden down with great care; Burnley is paved.

(*Burnley:* Bull; Commercial; Old Red Lion; Thorn.)

Burnley to Colne (6½—214¼); undulating road through Little Marsden, 210¾, Higher Bradley, 211¼, and Nelson, 212 (keep to *r.*).

Colne to Skipton (13—227¼); keep straight on through Colne, ½*m.* beyond to *r.*, and then it is hilly by Laneshaw Bridge, 216¾, and through Ickornshaw, 219, to Glusburn, 221¼, a mile beyond which join the Bradford road and turn to *l.* up the valley of the Aire; bad for the first half, then a fair road almost level. [Or turn to *l.* at Colne and through Foulridge,

215½, Kelbrook, 217, Thornton, 220, and Broughton, 223, to Skipton, 226; it is much easier, and after the first 2 or 3*m.* is level or gently downhill.]

(*Skipton:* see post p. 179.)

LONDON TO SKIPTON (by Bacup).

London to Manchester (182¼); by Ashbourne and Buxton—p. 170.

Manchester to Middleton (6½—188¾); by the old road along Corporation street and up the long gradual ascent of Cheetham Hill, a suburb of Manchester; it is paved to Cheetham, 184, then keep to *r.* and through Rhodes, 187¾, is a macadam road, but with patches of paving, and where not paved is generally loose and dusty. [The new road along Rochdale road and through Harpurhey, 185, and Blackley, 186, to Middleton, 188, is more hilly; partly paved and partly macadam, which is generally rough and loose.]

Just before Middleton, on *r.*, Alkington Hall,

Middleton to Rochdale (6—194¾); through Trub Smithy (or Blue Pits), 191¾, is a bad macadam road with a good deal of paving, and where not paved is generally loose and rough, and in dry weather dusty; long steep hill to descend into Rochdale, pavement through the town.

(*Rochdale:* Duke of Wellington, *Hqrs.*; Reed.)

Rochdale to Bacup (7—201¾); macadam road, alternating with pavement through Shawclough, 195½, Whitworth, 197¼, and Leavengreave, 198, to Shawforth, 198¾, to which it is more or less on a gradual rise; the rest is macadam and chiefly downhill to Bacup, with a steep paved descent into the town.

Bacup to Burnley (8—209¾); the road runs up the valley of the *R.* Irwell; for a mile or so the pavement continues till clear of the houses, then it gives way to very fair macadam, the road gradually rising for a couple of miles to the head of the valley and the last 3 or 4*m.* being downhill into Burnley, the gradient being nowhere very steep, but the hill should be ridden down carefully.

Before Burnley, on *r.*, Townley Hall.

Burnley to Skipton (19½—229¼)—p. 173.

LONDON TO BURNLEY (by Todmorden).

London to Rochdale (194¾)—above.

Rochdale to Todmorden (9—203¾); through Smallbridge, 196¼, Littleborough, 198¼, and Hundersfield, 199¼, is a good hard road, undulating with two or three stiff hills either way; Todmorden is not paved.

(*Todmorden:* Golden Lion; Queen's; Stansfield's Temp.; White Hart.)

Todmorden to Burnley (9½—213¼); good macadam road, slightly uphill, through Portsmouth, 206½, to Calder Head, 207½, then nearly all downhill through Cliviger (or Holme), 209, except a moderate ascent about 2*m.* before Burnley.

LONDON TO APPLEBY.

London to Kendal (257½)—p. 158.

Kendal to Orton (14—271½); when leaving Kendal turn to r. from the Shap road, and go through Lambrigg, 264, Grayrigg, 264½, over Low Borrow Bridge, 267½, and through Tebay, 269½ (keep to r.), and across Orton Common ; steep hill up into Orton.

The terminal "rigg," in the Lake District, means ridge or hill. All places with this ending are on a hill—usually a long or steep one.

Orton to Appleby (10—281½): keep to r., and over Orton Moor, and Ravensworth and Meaburn Moors, and through Hough, 279½, and Burwall, 280½.

(*Appleby:* King's Head ; Tufton Arms.)

Appleby Castle was rebuilt in 1686. It contains many curious portraits and relics.

LONDON TO WORKINGTON AND ALLONBY.

London to Lindale (258¼)—p. 161.
Lindale to Cartmel (3¼—261½).
(*Cartmel:* Cavendish Arms, *Hqrs.*)
At Cartmel is an ancient *ch.*, once a priory, founded 1138.

Cartmel to Ulverston (7—268½); through Holker, 263½, and then cross the Leven Sands to Ulverston.

[There is a better road from Lindale by going to Staveley, 263½, as at p. 162; then turn to l., cross over Newby Bridge, 264½, and again to l. through Haverthwaite, 266½, to *Ulverston*, 272½.]

(*Ulverston:* Railway ; Sun ; Queen's.)

On l., Holker Hall. At Ulverston, on l., Conishead Priory, a beautiful mansion, on the site of the ancient priory.

Ulverston to Dalton-in-Furness (4—272½) through Lindal, 271.
(*Dalton:* Furness Abbey.)
About 1½m. S. of Dalton are the ruins of Furness Abbey.

Dalton-in-Furness to Kirkby (6½—279) through Kirkby Ireleth, 275½.

[Or, go direct from Lindal to Kirkby Ireleth (3—274). There is also a shorter road from Ulverston to Kirkby, 274½, but it crosses over the mountains.]

Kirkby to Broughton-in-Furness (3½—282½).
(*Broughton-in-Furness:* King's Head.)

Broughton-in-Furness to Ravenglass (9—291½); cross Duddon Bridge, 283, and then over the moors at the back of Black Comb Mountain. [There is another road not so hilly by Whicham, 289½, Whitbeck, 290½, Bootle, 293½, Park Nook, 297, to Ravenglass, 301.]

At Ravenglass, 1m. on r., Muncaster Castle ; 1½m. further E. are remains called Barnscar, according to tradition a Danish city.

Ravenglass to Egremont (12½—304½); through Carleton, 294½, Gosforth, 297½, and Ponsonby, 299¾.

On l., Ponsonby Hall ; on r., Calder Abbey ruins, founded 1134. At Egremont are ruins of the castle. From Egremont, a good road runs up on r. to foot of Ennerdale lake, 7m.

Egremont to Whitehaven (5—309½).
(*Whitehaven:* Albion ; Black Lion ; Globe ; Golden Lion.)
On l., St. Bees Head and College. At Whitehaven the castle.

Whitehaven to Workington (8—317¼); through Moresby, 311¼, and Distington, 313¼, (a mile beyond keep to *l.*)

(*Workington:* Green Dragon; Station.)

At Distington, on *l.*, ruins of Hayes Castle. On *r.*, Workington Hall.

Workington to Maryport (5—322¼); through Flimby, 320¼.

(*Maryport:* Golden Lion; Senhouse Arms.)

Maryport to Allonby (5—327¼).

LONDON TO MARYPORT (by Keswick).

London to Ambleside (270½); by Kendal—p. 163.

Ambleside to Keswick (16—286½)—p. 162.

Keswick to Cockermouth (12—298½); through Portinscale, 288, (1*m.* beyond keep to *l.*) Braithwaite, 289½, and Lorton, 294½. [Or take the right hand fork 1*m.* beyond Portinscale, and through Thornthwaite, 290 by Swan Inn, 290¾, and along the west shore of Bassenthwaite Water, by Smithy Green, 292¾, Pheasant Inn, 293½, quarter of a mile beyond which, join the Carlisle road and turn to *l.* to Cockermouth, 299.] Pretty scenery.

(*Cockermouth:* Globe; Peelwyke; Sun.)

At Cockermouth, ruins of the castle. In the neighbourhood are tumulus of Toots Hill, remains of an entrenchment, &c., at Fitt's Wood, and at Pap Castle traces of a Roman camp. At Lorton, 4*m.* on *l.*, is Crummock Water.

Cockermouth to Maryport (7½—306); through Davenby, 301, and Ellenborough, 304½.

LONDON TO BROUGH.

London to Lancaster (235¾)—p. 158.

Lancaster to Hornby (9—244¾); the road runs up the valley of the *R.* Lune through Bulk, 236¾, Caton, 240¾, Claughton, 243¼, and Farlton, 244; it is loose in many places, and very rough.

Pretty scenery. Beyond Bulk, on *r.*, Quernmoor Park. At Hornby, the castle.

Hornby to Burrow (6—250¾); at Hornby keep to *l.* and the road follows the Lune Valley through Melling, 246¾, (1¼*m.* beyond, keep to *l.*), and Tunstall, 248¾.

[Or from *Lancaster* by Halton, 238¼, Red Well, 242¾, Arkholme, 245¼, Newton, 247¼, and Whittington, 248¼, to the junction of the roads 1*m.* beyond Burrow, and to Casterton, 251½.]

At Tunstall, on *r.*, Thurland Castle: 1¼*m.* beyond Burrow, on *l.*, ½m. to Kirkby Lonsdale.

Burrow to Sedbergh (11½—262¼); the road still follows the Lune valley; 1*m.* beyond Burrow join the Settle road, and ¼*m.* further keep to *r.*, and through Casterton, 253¼, and Middleton, 257¼, and over New Bridge, 259¾, beyond which keep to *r.* for Sedbergh.

(*Sedbergh:* Black Bull; Bull Inn; King's Arms.)

Sedbergh to Kirkby Stephen (13—275¼); from Sedbergh, keep to *l.* up the valley of the *R.* Rother to Rother Bridge, 267¼, then a steep hill to climb and over the moors to Ravenstonedale, 270¾, whence it is chiefly downhill to Kirkby Stephen.

(*Kirkby Stephen:* Fleece; King's Head; King's Arms, *B.T.C.*)

2m. before Kirkby Stephen, on *r.*, Wharton Hall. Near the town are the ruins of Hartley Castle.

Kirkby Stephen to Brough (4¾—280); through Brough Sowerby, 278¾.

(*Brough:* Ferry; Station.)

LONDON TO ROCHDALE (by Oldham).

London to Buxton (159½)—p. 170.

Buxton to Stockport (16—175½)—p. 168.

Stockport to Denton (4¼—179¾); in Stockport turn to *r.* and through Haughton, 178¾.

Denton to Ashton-under-Lyne (3—182¾); by Hooley Hill, 181, the road is paved all the way from Stockport, except a few occasional stretches of macadam at the sides.

(*Ashton-under-Lyne:* Commercial.)

Ashton-under-Lyne to Oldham (4¼—187); in Ashton turn sharp to the left, and it is a straight road to Oldham.

(*Oldham:* Angel.)

Oldham to Rochdale (6—193); through Royton, 189 (just before which keep to *l.*), and Bolderstone, 191½.

LONDON TO TODMORDEN (by Oldham).

London to Oldham (187)—above.

Oldham to Todmorden (13½—200½); 1¼m. beyond Oldham, turn to *r.* and through Shaw, 190, Littleborough, 195, and Hundersfield, 196.

LONDON TO HUDDERSFIELD.

London to Buxton (159½); by Ashbourne, p. 170.

Buxton to Chapel-en-le-Frith (5¼—164¾); turn to *r.* in the middle of Buxton, and down the hill to *R.* Wye, when turn to *l.*, up a steep hill to Fairfield, 160¼, and through Plumpton, 163¼, where turn to *l.*

[Or London to *Chapel-en-le-Frith*, 167¾—p. 171.]

Chapel-en-le-Frith to Tintwistle (12¼—177); turn sharp to *r.* in the former, and through Milton, 166, whence it is uphill through Chinley Head, 167½, nearly to Hayfield, 169¼; after that it is downhill or undulating by Abbots Chair, 171½, Chunal, 172½, Whitefield, 173¾, through Howardtown, 174, by Glossop Hall, 175¼, and through Hadfield, 176.

Beyond Hayfield, on *r.*, is the mountain of Kinderscout, 1981 ft. high, the loftiest summit of the Peak, whose huge mass lies behind it. At Howardtown, on *r.*, is Glossop, a cotton manufacturing town. On *l.*, 1m. distant, is Melandra Castle, the site of a Roman camp; a little further on *l.*, Mouslow Castle.

Tintwistle to Holmfirth (12—189); the road now runs up the valley of the *R.* Etherow (Longden Dale), past the Woodhead Reservoirs to Woodhead, 180¼, a little beyond which, take the left hand road up a side valley for a couple of miles; then cross Holme Moss Moor, and there is •

steep winding descent of a mile to Holme, 186, and thence downhill through Holmbridge, 187½.

Holmfirth to Huddersfield (6—195); take the left hand road which runs down the valley of and close to *R*. Holme all the way, over Thong Bridge, 190, and through Honley, 191½, and Lockwood, 193¼.

2*m.* S. of Huddersfield, on Castle Hill, are remains of the Roman city of Cambodunum.

LONDON TO KENDAL (by Wakefield).

London to Derby (125¾)—p. 166.

Derby to Ripley (9½—135¼); through Little Chester, 126¼ (keep to *l.*), Little Eaton, 128¾, Coxbench, 130¼, Kilburn *Tp.*, 132¼, and Smithy Houses, 133¼, is nearly level all the way; in dry weather it is a good road, but when wet is very heavy, on account of the coal traffic.

(*Ripley:* Cock; Red Lion; Temperance; Thorn Tree; White Lion.)

1*m.* beyond Derby, on *l.*, Darley Abbey; at Little Eaton, 1*m.* on *r.*, the Priory; at Coxbench, on *r.*, Horsley Castle.

Ripley to Alfreton (3½—138¾); through Swanwick, 137¼, is very hilly; long descent into Alfreton.

(*Alfreton:* Angel; Castle Inn; George.)

At Alfreton is a very old *ch*.

Alfreton to Chesterfield (11¼—150); long ascent out of Alfreton, then rather hilly through Shirland, 140¾, Higham, 141¾, Stretton, 143, Clay Cross *Tp.*, 144½, and Tupton, 145½: the surface is at times rather shaky for quick travelling.

(*Chesterfield:* Angel; Scarsdale; Star; Temperance.)

2*m.* before Chesterfield, on *l.*, Wingerworth Hall. Chesterfield *ch.* was erected in the 13th century, and possesses a curious crooked spire.

Chesterfield to Dronfield (5½—155½); over Whittington Common, 151½, and through Unston, 154¼, is very hilly, with long ascent through Dronfield: macadamised, rough and shaky, all the way, bad travelling in wet weather.

(*Dronfield:* Red Lion, *Hqrs.*)

On Whittington Moor, on the *r.*, was a public house called Revolution House, where the Revolution of 1688 was planned.

Dronfield to Sheffield (6½—162); through Little Norton, 157¼, and Heely *Tp.*, 160, is a similar kind of road, but much more up hill than down: through Sheffield is paved.

(*Sheffield:* Black Swan; Buncliffe Oaks; Clarence; King's Head, *B.T.C.*; Yellow Lion.)

At Little Norton, 1*m.* on *l.*, is Beauchief Abbey, founded in 1163 for White Canons, in expiation of the murder of Thomas à Becket. Sheffield is noted as the chief seat of the cutlery trade, with manufactories of plated goods and similar articles. It has some fine public buildings, as Cutlery Hall, Corn Exchange, Assembly Hall, Public Baths, Botanical Gardens, Theatre, Institutes, &c.

Sheffield to Barnsley (13½—175½); long ascent out of Sheffield to Pittsmoor, 163, then through Chapel Town, 168, to Wood Hill, 169½, is a very hilly road, some of the hills being dangerously steep, especially one or two near Chapel Town; from Wood Hill it is nearly all a gradual down hill into Worsborough, 173, then come a steep ascent and another run down of 2m. into Barnsley: first half a macadamised road, but after Wood Hill it is very good and smooth.

(*Barnsley:* King's Head; Royal, *B.T.C.*)

At Worsborough, 1m. on *l.*, is Wentworth Castle, a modern elegant mansion, occupying the site of an ancient fortress.

Barnsley to Wakefield (10½—186); long ascent out of Barnsley, and it is a good road all the way through Staincross, 179, by New Miller Dam, 182½, and through Milnthorpe, 183½, and Sandal Magna, 184: paved through Wakefield.

(*Wakefield:* Bull; Royal; Stratford Arms.)

Beyond Staincross, on *r.*, Notton Hall; further on, on *l.*, Wooley Hall; 1m. farther on *r.*, Chevet Hall. On *l.*, Sandal Castle. Wakefield is one of the chief markets of the corn trade; All Saints ch. has the loftiest spire in the county; there is also a beautiful Gothic chapel, erected by Edward IV.

Wakefield to Bruntcliff (7¼—193¾); through East Ardsley, 189½, and Tingley, 191, is a fair road.

Bruntcliff to Bradford (6¼—200); through Drighlington, 195, Wisket Hill, 196½, and Dudley Hill, 198; the road rapidly deteriorates and becomes very bad for the last few miles, being mostly made with slagg and dross from ironworks in the neighbourhood. The streets of Bradford are paved.

(*Bradford:* Belle Vue; Commercial; George Inn; New Imperial, *Hqrs.*; Spotted House; Talbot Inn; Victoria.)

About 5m. E. of Bradford and N. of Drighlington, is the Moravian colony or settlement of Fulueck. Bradford is a large well-built town, remarkable as being nearly all of stone.

Bradford to Keighley (10¼—210¼); the first 2m. are paved, then a good ironstone road without any hills all the way through Cottingley, 203¾, over Cottingley Bridge (*R.* Aire), 204¾, then up the valley of the Aire and through Bingley, 206, and traversing Nab Wood; 1m. before Keighley, re-cross *R.* Aire; entering Keighley is a level railway crossing, and through the town is paved and rather rough. [There is another road on *r.* through Manningham, where there are large silk mills employing 6,000 to 7,000 hands, and by the model town of Saltaire, both of which are worth seeing: nearly 1m. longer.]

(*Bingley:* Fleece.—*Keighley:* Devonshire.)

In Keighley churchyard is a gravestone bearing date 1023. At Bingley, on *l.*, Harden Grange.

Keighley to Kildwick (5¾—216); a good road and nearly level running up the valley of the *R.* Aire, through Steeton, 213¼, Eastburn, 214½, and Cross Hill, 215¼, where keep to *r.*

Kildwick to Skipton (4½—220½) is a fair road almost level, up the Aire valley. Pretty scenery.

(*Skipton:* Black Horse, *B.T.C.*; Craven; Devonshire; Ship.)

At Skipton is the old castle, erected soon after the Conquest; it was besieged for several months by Cromwell, in 1645. About 6m. E., are the ruins of Bolton Priory, in the romantic Wharfedale, a mile distant being the chasm of the Strid, and in the vicinity the ruined fortress of Barden Tower.

Skipton to Gargrave (4½—224¾); it is quite level through Sturton, 221¾, Thorlby, 222½, and Holme Bridge, 224, and a good limestone road.

At Gargrave are traces of a Roman encampment.

Gargrave to Long Preston (7—231¾); the road continues nearly level to Cold Coniston, 226¾, then it begins to rise over Coniston Moor and there is a long hill to climb; after traversing Coniston Moor it descends again at Hellifield, 229¾, and is pretty level to Long Preston; it is a good limestone road on the whole, but sometimes rather rough.

Long Preston to Kendal (34¼—266)—pp. 172-3.

LONDON TO KENDAL (by Halifax).

London to Barnsley (175½)—p. 178.

Barnsley to Hill Top (9¼—184¾); hill to climb out of Barnsley, then the road for the first 4m. is all downhill, but rather rough, through Darton, 178½, to Upper and Lower Swithen, 180, after which there are some very trying ascents and descents through Bretton, 182, Midgeley, 183¼, and Cold Henley, 184¼.

Before Bretton, on *l.*, Haigh Hall and Bretton Hall.

Hill Top to Huddersfield (7¾—192½); the road continues rather hilly through Flockton, 185½, to Lepton, 188, beyond which there is a very long and trying descent, the last mile of which is just too steep to ride down; from the bottom the road is very rough through Dalton Green, 191½, into Huddersfield, the streets of which are paved.

[There is another road keeping to *l.* 2m. out of Barnsley and going through Cawthorne, Sude Hill, Honley, and Lockwood, the distance being about the same.]

(*Huddersfield:* Cherry Tree.)

Huddersfield to Halifax (8—200½), by Fixby Hall, 194½, and through Elland, 197½, and over Salter Hebble Bridge, 198¾.

(*Halifax:* White Swan.)

Halifax to Denholme Gate (5½—206), through Wheatley, 201½, Ovenden, 202, Illingworth, 203, St. Johns, 204, and Swillhill End, 204¾.

[Or from Huddersfield through Brighouse, Ripperholme, and Queenshead; about the same distance; a very steep hill to walk up out of Huddersfield, then the road is fair for a few miles, then comes a very steep hill down into Brighouse, out of which is another hill to climb, and the rest pretty level but rather rough road.]

Denholme Gate to Keighley (6½—212½), through Denholme, 207, Denholme Park, and Cullingworth, 209.

Keighley to Kendal (55¾—268¼)—p. 179, and above.

LONDON TO CHESTERFIELD (by Heage).

London to Derby (125¾)—p. 166.

Derby to Duffield (4½—130¼); rather up and down hill past Darley Chapel and through Allestree, 128¼; the road is good for the first 2 or 3m., then it deteriorates.

Duffield to Heage (5¾—136); cross the R. Derwent, and through Bargate, 132¾.

Heage to Higham (5¾—141¾); by Peacock Inn, 139¾.

At Peacock Inn, on *l.*, Wingfield Manor Ho, in ruins.

Higham to Chesterfield (8¼—150)—p. 178.

[There is another road through Belper 133½, as at p. 167, and thence to Heage: about the same distance. Or to Ambergate, 136¾, as at p. 167, then keep to r. and join the above route about 1m. beyond Heage; nearly 1m. longer.]

LONDON TO SHEFFIELD (by Baslow).

London to Bakewell (153)—p. 167.

Bakewell to Baslow (3½—156½); ½m. out of Bakewell keep to r., and 1m. afterwards to l.

[There is another road from *Rowsley*, 149¾—p. 167, through Edensor, along the right bank of the R. Derwent: or along the left bank and by Chatsworth *Ho*.: by either route to *Baslow*, 4½—154¼.]

(*Baslow:* Devonshire Arms; Peacock; Wheatsheaf.)

Baslow to Sheffield (12¾—169¼); at the Wheatsheaf, ½m. out of Baslow keep to l., and also again a short distance further on; the road runs up a valley for 2 or 3m., then cross East Moor by Car Top, 160½, to Totley, 163, whence it is downhill or level into Sheffield.

2 or 3m. beyond Baslow, on a hill on the r., Nelson's Monument.

LONDON TO SHEFFIELD (by Hassop).

London to Bakewell (153)—p. 167.

Bakewell to Hassop (2¾—155¾); ½m. out of Bakewell take the left hand road.

Hassop to Grindleford Bridge (3¾—159½), through Calver, 157½, a little beyond which keep to l.

Grindleford Bridge to Sheffield (10—169½); cross R. Derwent and follow up a small valley for a mile or two, then, a very steep hill to climb on to High Moors, which cross to Ringinglow *Tp*., 164½, and then through Bent's Green, 166¼, and Little Sheffield, 168¼.

About 2m. beyond Grindleford Bridge, on the hill on l., is a remarkable rocking stone.

LONDON TO HATHERSAGE.

London to Grindleford Bridge (159½)—above.

Grindleford Bridge to Hathersage (3—162½); turn sharp to l. at Grindleford Bridge instead of crossing the R. Derwent, and follow up the Derwent valley.

(*Hathersage:* George.)

LONDON TO LEICESTER (by Welford).

London to Welford (80¼)—p. 154.

Welford to Husband's Bosworth (2½—82¾).

Husband's Bosworth to Leicester (13½—96¼); hill out of Husband's Bosworth, descent into Shearsby, 87½, then through Arnesby, 88½, Wigston, 92¾, and Knighton, 94¼.

LONDON TO HUDDERSFIELD (by Penistone).

London to Sheffield (162)—p. 178.

Sheffield to Penistone (12½—174½); through Owlerton, 163¾, where take the right hand road over Wadsley Bridge, 164½, then a long steep hill to mount to Greenoside, 166¾, and through Wortley, 170, and Thurgoland, 171½. [There is another road to Wortley by turning to *l.* at Chapel Town on the Barnsley road, p. 178: distance the same.]

Penistone is situate on the *R.* Don, a few miles from its source, and in a wild and dreary district, all westward being moorlands.

Penistone to Huddersfield (13¼—187¾); through Ing Birchworth, 176½, Over Shepley, 180, High Burton, 183, Fenay Bridge, 184¼, and Dalton Green, 186¼. [Or a mile before Over Shepley turn to *l.* down to Sude Hill, and through Honley and Lockwood. Or there is another road from *Sheffield*, by keeping to *l.* at Owlerton, whence the road runs up the valley of the *R.* Don, close by the side of the river, through Oughtibridge to Deep Car; here follow the valley of the Little Don through Middopstones, a couple of miles beyond which the road leaves the valley and crosses over the moors to Sude Hill: by this road 25*m.*]

LONDON TO HINCKLEY (by Rugby).

London to Dunchurch (79¾)—p. 139.

Dunchurch to Rugby (2½—82¼); turn to *r.* in Dunchurch, and ¾*m.* further on to *l.*: good road with a stiff hill to rise to Rugby.

(*Rugby*: George; Railway Inn; Royal George.)

At Rugby is the celebrated school: there are also remains of a castle. On *l.*, Bilton Hall.

Rugby to Wolvey (10½—92¾); cross the *R.* Avon 1*m.* out of Rugby and through Newbold-upon-Avon, 83¾, Harborough Magna, 85¼, Pailton, 87 (keep to *l.*), Stretaston, 88, and Withybrook, 90¼: very good going.

Wolvey to Hinckley (4¼—97); about half way, cross Watling Street: very good road.

LONDON TO RUGBY (by Northampton).

London to Northampton (65¾)—p. 154. or p. 156.

Northampton to West Haddon (11—76¾); in Northampton turn to *l.*, and 1*m.* further keep to *r.* and through Dallington, 67¼, Harlestone, 69¾, and East Haddon, 73¼.

Beyond Harlestone, on *l.*, Harlestone Hall and Althorp Park.

West Haddon to Rugby (8—84¾); through Crick, 79¼, a mile beyond cross Watling Street, and a steep hill up to Hill Morton, 82¼, a mile beyond keep to the *r.*, and then down into Rugby.

LONDON TO LUTTERWORTH (by Daventry).

London to Daventry (72)—p. 139.

Daventry to Kilsby (6—78); turn to *r.* when leaving Daventry, and through Ashby St. Ledgers, 76: hilly road, descent into Kilsby.

Kilsby to Lutterworth (10—88); 1½*m*, beyond Kilsby, join the Watling Street, and over Dove Bridge (*R.* Avon), 83, and through Shawell, 85.

LONDON TO NUNEATON (by Rugby).

London to Wolvey (92¾)—p. 182.

Wolvey to Nuneaton (5½—98¼); ½*m.* beyond Wolvey turn to *l.* and through Shelford, 99¾.

LONDON TO EDINBURGH.

London to Carlisle (301½)—p. 159.

Carlisle to Longtown (8¾—310¼); after crossing the bridge over the *R.* Eden there is a stiff hill to mount going through Stanwix, 302¼, a suburb of Carlisle; here the road to Newcastle must be passed on *r.*, then it is good and nearly level, a mile further on keeping to *r.* through Blackford, 305¼, and West Linton, 307¼.

(*Longtown:* Graham's Arms.)

Longtown to Langholm (11½—321¾); through Kirk Andrews, 313, Scots Dyke *Tg.*, 313¾ (here enter Scotland), Cannobie Kirk, 316, and Gilnockie Ruins, 317; the road runs up the valley of the *R.* Esk, and continues good, but is undulating and gradually gets more hilly: pretty scenery.

(*Langholm:* Crown, *B.T.C.*)

Gilnockie Hall and Hallows Tower were formerly the residence of the renowned Johnny Armstrong. On *l.*, Langholm Castle (Duke of Buccleugh).

Langholm to Mosspaul Inn (10—331¾); the road now leaves the valley of the *R.* Esk, and follows that of the Ewes Water, up amongst the Cheviot Hills, through Ewes Kirk, 326, Redpath, 326¼, and Fiddleton *Tg.*, 329½; it is mostly on the ascent, but nearly all of it can be ridden: very good road. At Mosspaul Inn the summit of the Cheviot Hills is reached.

2*m.* from Redpath, on *r.*, chapel ruins. Grand scenery.

Mosspaul Inn to Hawick (12¾—344½); the road runs for some distance through a mountain pass on the top of the Cheviots, then down the valley of a tributary stream of the *R.* Teviot, and, except a few short rises, is on the fall through Binks, 335¼, and Allanmouth, 340¼, to Hawick: very good surface.

(*Hawick:* Buccleugh Arms; Tower, *B.T.C.*)

At Binks are ruins of Carlowrie Chapel; at Allanmouth, on *r.*, are ruins of the castle; 2*m.* further Goldiland ruins. Fine scenery.

Hawick to Selkirk (11¼—355¾); cross the *R.* Teviot, and then there is a long steep hill out of Hawick to Wilton Kirk, 345, with some more hilly riding through Newtown, 346¾, and over the moors to Ashkirk, 350¾; out of here there is another long ascent, and the road continues hilly through Selkirk *Tg.*, 352¾, to Selkirk.

(*Selkirk:* County, *B.T.C.*; Cross Keys, *Hqrs.*)

On *l.* of Selkirk is Philiphaugh, were the Royalist army under Montrose wa. defeated by the Parliamentarians.

Selkirk to Crosslee Tg. (9—364¾); long descent out of Selkirk to the bridge over the *R.* Ettrick, and a corresponding ascent on the other side of the river, then another descent to Fernielie Bridge, 359¾, over the *R.* Tweed, and hilly and indifferent road to Crosslee. [There is another and easier road from Selkirk by following the *R.* Ettrick down to its junction with the Tweed, 359, then cross the river and it is hilly through Galashiels, 361¼, to Crosslee; about the same distance.]

(*Galashiels:* Maxwell's, *B.T.C.—Melrose:* Station.)

From Galashiels, on *r.*, to Melrose, 4½*m.*, very good but undulating road. Here are the ruins of the celebrated abbey, the finest specimen in Scotland of rich Gothic architecture.

Crosslee Tg. to Bankhouse Inn (6—370¾); rather hilly and indifferent road through Stagehall, 368.

About 1½*m.* beyond Crosslee, on *l.* 1½*m.*, upon Lugate Water the ruins of Lugate Castle.

Bankhouse Inn to Middleton (8¾—379½); a similar kind of road through Heriot House *Tg.*, 376, and Swirehouse, 377¾.

Before Heriot Tollgate, on *r.*, Kaythe Castle, and in the neighbourhood are the remains of several camps. Near Middleton, on *r.*, ruins of Borthwick Castle, and beyond ruins of Crichton Castle. ½*m.* before Middleton, about ¾*m.* on *r.*, Half Law Kiln, Roman camp in connection with that above Dalkeith.

Middleton to Laswade (6¾—386¼); rather hilly but good road through New Byers, 382½, Dalhousie, 384¾, and Hillhead, 385¾; pretty scenery.

At New Byers, ruins of the castle; beyond, Cockpen *Ho.* At Dalhousie, on *l.*, Dalhousie Castle. At Hillhead, on *r.*, Newbattle Abbey; near Laswade, Melville Castle, Roslin Castle, and Hawthornden *Ho.*

Laswade to Edinburgh (6¼—392½); through Nellifield, 388¾, Libberton Kirk, 389¼, and Powburn, 390¾; approaching Edinburgh the road becomes macadamised and is rather shaky.

(*Edinburgh:* Imperial; Princes; Rutland; Waverley Temp.; Windsor; Young's *B.T.C.*)

LONDON TO KENDAL (by Nottingham).

London to Barnet (11¼)—p. 137.

Barnet to Hatfield (8½—19¾); keep to *r.* past the obelisk at Monken Hadley, 12, and through Ganwick Corner, 13, Potters Bar, 14½ (beyond here take the left hand road), Little Heath Lane, 15¼, and Bell Bar, 17½ (keep to *l.*), is a splendid smooth road, for the most part gently undulating; past Potters Bar a long hill to run down followed by one or two hills to rise, and a long gradual decline approaching Hatfield.

(*Potters Bar:* Old Robin Hood, *B.T.C.—Hatfield:* One Bell; Red Lion, *B.T.C.*; Salisbury Arms; Swan.)

At Monken Hadley, on *l.*, Wrotham Park. At Potters Bar, on *r.*, Clock *Ho.*; 2*m.* further on *l.*, Gobions and Brookmans Park. Before Hatfied, on *r.*, Hatfield *Ho.* (Marquis of Salisbury).

Hatfield to Welwyn (5½—25¼); in Hatfield take the left hand road, and after crossing over the railway bridge it is pretty level for about a mile through Stanborough, 21½, then uphill for 1½*m.* near by Lemsford Mills, 22½, to Brickwall, 23½, and downhill from Digswell Hill, 23¾, into Welwyn, the last part of it being rather steep and winding, and should be ridden carefully; very good road.

(*Digswell Hill:* Red Lion.—*Welwyn:* Wellington Commercial; White Hart.)
At Lemsford Mills, on *l.*, Brocket Hall. At Welwyn, on *r.*, Danesbury.

Welwyn to Hitchin (9—34¼); rather uphill out of Welwyn through Codicote, 26¾, to Knebworth, 29¼, thence through Langley, 29¾; a mile of downhill aud uphill twice, alternate, then downhill to near Ippolits, 33, 1*m.* uphill, and a rather steep fall past Priory Park into Hitchin: splendid road.

(*Hitchin:* Sun; Swan.)

On *r.*, Knebworth Park, the residence of the late Lord Lytton, the celebrated novelist. Hitchin *ch.* dates from the time of Henry VI., and contains a fine altar-piece by Rubens.

Hitchin to Shefford (7—41¼); very fair road with no hills to speak of

About 2*m.* beyond Hitchin, cross Icknield way or road; about 2*m.* on *r.*, is an ancient entrenchment called Wilbury Hill.

Shefford to Bedford (9—50¼); long rise out of Shefford, then level by Deadman's Cross, 43¼, Herring Green, 46¼, Cotton End, 46½, and Harrowden, 47½, except descent to Herring Green and another to Harrowden: excellent gravel road.

(*Bedford:* Bear Inn; Bedford Arms; Clarence, *Hqrs.*, *B.T.C.*; George; Lion; Rose, *Hqrs.*, *B.T.C.*; Swan.)

1*m.* beyond Shefford, on *l.*, Chicksand Priory; beyond Deadman's Cross, on *r.*, Warden Abbey. In Bedford gaol, Bunyan wrote "Pilgrim's Progress;" he was born at Elstow, a village 1½*m.* S.W., where the cottage still stands.

Bedford to Bletsoe (6½—56¾); through Clapham, 52½, and Milton Ernest, 55¼, is a good undulating road with an excellent surface, but in wet weather heavy; part of the way it runs alongside the *R.* Ouse.

(*Clapham:* Swan.)

Bletsoe to Higham Ferrers (8¼—65); at Bletsoe keep to *l.*; good undulating road through Knotting, 60¼, Westwood *Tp.*, 60¾, and Rushden, 63¾; two very steep hills to walk up: excellent surface but in wet weather heavy.

(*Higham Ferrers:* Green Dragon.)

1*m.* beyond Bletsoe, on *r.*, Bletsoe Park; beyond Notting, on *r.*, Higham Park. At Higham Ferrers are traces of the castle. The *ch.* contains some fine monuments. A college was founded here by Archbishop Chichele, in 1422, and some remains of it still exist. Curious old market cross.

Higham Ferrers to Finedon (4—69); very rough macadam road, crossing the *R.* Nen a mile beyond Higham Ferrers, and then through Irthlingborough, 67, where keep to *r.* by the *ch.*

Irthlingborough is locally shortened to Artleboro'. At Finedon, on *l.*, Finedon Hall.

Finedon to Kettering (5¾—74¾); through Burton Latimer, 71¼, and Barton Seagrave, 73, is a hilly and very bad macadam road, frequently very rough and rutty.

(*Kettering:* George; Royal; Railway Commercial.)

At Warkton *ch.*, 2*m.* on *r.* of Kettering, are some old monuments of the Montagu family; beyond it Boughton *Ho.*

Kettering to Rockingham (8¾—83½); by Oakley Inn, 79½, is macadam all the way, and the first 6*m.* very bad; there is one steep ascent to climb, and a very steep hill with 3 or 4 sharp turns to walk down into Rockingham, not safe to ride down.

The road passes through part of the district known as Rockingham Forest, which formerly extended as far as Oundle. There are remains of a strong castle fortress, erected by William the Conqueror. The *ch.* was partially destroyed by Cromwell, but contains some fine monuments. At Oakley Inn, 1m. on *l.*, Ripwell Abbey.

Rockingham to Uppingham (5½—89); cross the *R.* Welland, and the road is very good and quite level to Caldecot, 85, then it is macadam, and undulating to Uppingham; the last 2m. are very bad, with two very steep hills—too steep to ride either up or down—going into Uppingham.

(*Uppingham:* Cross Keys; Falcon.)

Ancient Gothic *ch.* at Uppingham; also free school and hospital, founded in 1584. The town is in the form of a square.

Uppingham to Oakham (6—95); leave Uppingham by the N.E. corner, and it is a little better going through Preston, 90¾, and Manton, 92¼; very good undulating road for first few miles, terminating with a very steep descent, too steep to be ridden with safety, then a corresponding ascent, from the top of which the road is very good and nearly level into Oakham.

(*Oakham:* Crown.)

Oakham, the county town of Rutland, is situate in the Vale of Catmos. There are remains of a castle erected in the reign of Henry II., frequently in the occupation of the Plantagenet princes, part of it now used as the county hall. Oakham is remarkable for its ancient custom of claiming a horse shoe from a peer who passes through it for the first time. About 2m. on *r.*, is the magnificent seat of Burley-on-the-Hill.

Oakham to Melton Mowbray (10½—105½); keep to *l.* entering Oakham, and through Barleythorpe, 96½, Langham, 97½, Leesthorpe, 101, and Burton Lazars, 103¾, is a very good undulating road with no very steep hills. Melton Mowbray is paved with cobble stones.

(*Melton Mowbray:* Bell and Swan; Flying Childers; George, Harboro' Arms; White Lion.)

Melton Mowbray is the centre of a great hunting and sporting district, more particularly the Melton Hunt takes its name from here.

Melton Mowbray to Nottingham (18½—124); the first 2m. out of Melton are all uphill, but rideable, then pretty level for a short distance, after which it is very hilly, as the road begins to rise over the Wolds, and a lot of walking up and down has to be done; through Kettleby, 108½, and Nether Broughton, 111¼, to Upper Broughton, 112; from here, by Widmerpool Inn, 115, and through Plumptree, 118¼, it is nearly all down hill to Trent Bridge, 123, a splendid road for about 8m., but the last 4m. being rather bumpy; between Upper Broughton and Plumptree it crosses over the Wolds: through Nottingham is paved.

(*Nottingham:* Clarendon; Commercial; Flying Horse; George; Globe; Half Moon; Lion and Maypole; Ramsden's; Wellington.)

Nottingham is a large town, chiefly engaged in the silk, lace, and hosiery manufactures. The principal public buildings are Exchange, County and Town Halls, St. Mary's *ch.*, &c.; there is also a museum. The market place is the largest in England; it is celebrated for the annual goose fair. The castle was founded by William the Conqueror, and after being dismantled by the Parliamentarians, was rebuilt at the Restoration; it was sacked and burnt during the Reform Riots, and is now in ruins.

Nottingham to Mansfield (14—138); just out of Nottingham there are three very stiff hills to mount, the first two rideable and not very difficult, but the last one, Red Hill, 128¼, being much steeper, and almost too much to ride up; after this the road is nearly level, with a splendid surface, through the old Sherwood Forest, and past the Hutt Inn, 133¾; downhill into Mansfield.

(*Mansfield:* Swan; White Bear.)

3*m.* beyond Red Hill a little on *l.*, Papplewick Hall. At the Hutt Inn, on *l.*, Newstead Abbey, once the property of the Byron family. 2*m.* on *r.*, are some Druidical remains. At Red Hill, on *r.*, is the site of an ancient camp. About 1½*m.* N.W. of Mansfield are the remains of two Roman villas, discovered in 1786. N.E. of the town are Hallam's Grave; further on an ancient camp, and at Clipstone, a few miles off, the ruins of a palace of Henry II. and King John. Sherwood Forest abounds in reminiscences of Robin Hood.

Mansfield to Clown (10—148); keep to *l.* out of Mansfield and the road is very hilly to Pleasley, 141, where take the right hand fork, and it is tolerably level through Stone Houghton, 142, and Scarcliff, 144.

At Pleasley, a little on the *r.*, is the site of a Roman villa. Beyond Scarcliff, on *l.*, is Bolsover Castle (Duke of Portland).

Clown to Rotherham (12—160); through Knitacre, 149½ (½*m.* beyond turn to *l.*, and after crossing the Chesterfield canal, 153, keep to *r.* for) Aughton, 156, and Whiston, 158; the road gradually becomes more hilly, some of the hills too steep to be ridden either up or down; the streets of Rotherham are paved.

(*Rotherham:* Crown; Red Lion.)

At Knitacre, on *l.*, Barlborough Hall.

Rotherham to Wentworth (5¼—165¼); after crossing the *R.* Don, and keeping first to *r.* then to *l.*, there is a tremendously steep hill to climb out of Rotherham, then there is a very good road through Greasborough, 161¾, and Nether Hough, 162¾, to Wentworth.

Just before Wentworth, on *l.*, is Wentworth *Ho.*, the magnificent seat of Earl Fitzwilliam.

Wentworth to Barnsley (7¼—172½); 1¼*m.* beyond Wentworth join the Sheffield road; splendid road, with a surface like a billiard table, nearly all a gradual downhill into Worsborough, 170, then comes a steep ascent and another run down of 2*m.* into Barnsley.

[There is another road from Rotherham by turning to *l.* when across the *R.* Don, and through Kimberworth, 162½, to Chapel Town on the Sheffield road, thence to Barnsley as at p. 178; a mile longer.]

Barnsley to Kendal (90½—263); through Wakefield, 183, Bradford, 197, Keighley, 207¼, Skipton, 217¼, Settle, 233¼, Clapham, 240, Ingleton, 244, and Kirkby Lonsdale, 251, pp. 179-80.

LONDON TO HITCHIN (by St. Albans).

London to St. Albans (20¾)—p. 137.

St. Albans to Hitchin (16¾—37½); take the right hand road at the cross roads, and through Sandridge, 23, Wheathampstead, 25¼, Kimpton, 28¼, St. Paul's Walden, 31¼, and Shilley Green, 32, it is nothing but a series of hills to be encountered, some pretty stiff; surface of the road perfect; a mile beyond Shilley Green join the Hatfield road.

LONDON TO BEDFORD (by Luton).

London to St. Albans ($20\frac{3}{4}$)—p. 137.

St. Albans to Luton ($10—30\frac{3}{4}$); in St. Albans, turn to *r.* at the cross roads, and $\frac{1}{2}$*m.* further on keep to *l.*, and it is a rather hilly road, otherwise good, through Chilwick Green, 23, over Harpenden Common, through Harpenden, 25, and by Gibraltar Inn, $28\frac{1}{4}$.

(*Harpenden:* Railway.—*Luton:* Bell: George; Midland; Queen's.)

Luton *ch.* contains some ancient and curious monuments, font, and windows. On *l.*, Chilwick Bury; at Harpenden Common, on *l.*, Hothampstead; before Luton, on *r.*, Luton Hoo Park.

Luton to Clophill ($11\frac{1}{4}—42$); a capital road over Luton Downs, through Barton-in-the-Clay, $37\frac{1}{4}$, and Silsoe, $40\frac{1}{4}$; there are some long gradual hills, but nothing difficult to mount; a stiffish descent into Barton, and another into Clophill.

(*Silsoe:* George Inn.)

At Silsoe, on *r.*, Wrest Park.

Clophill to Bedford ($8\frac{3}{4}—50\frac{3}{4}$); gradual rise out of Clophill, then pretty level through West End, 44, with a long downhill to Willshampstead, $46\frac{3}{4}$, whence it is almost level through Elstow, 49, to Bedford. (Coming back from Bedford to Luton there is more collar work.)

At Elstow is the cottage where Bunyan was born.

LONDON TO BEDFORD (by Ampthill).

London to Dunstable ($33\frac{1}{4}$)—p. 138.

Dunstable to Ampthill ($11\frac{3}{4}—45$); turn to *r.* either in Dunstable or $\frac{1}{2}$*m.* beyond, and then through Houghton Regis, $34\frac{3}{4}$, Chalgrave, $37\frac{1}{4}$, Toddington, $38\frac{1}{4}$ (turn to *r.*), Westoning, $41\frac{1}{4}$, Flitwick, $42\frac{1}{2}$, Dennel End, $43\frac{1}{2}$, and How Green, 44; a rather hilly road but nothing difficult, except a stiff ascent into Ampthill.

[There is another road from *Woburn*, $41\frac{1}{4}$—p. 154, to *r.*, through Ridgemont, $43\frac{1}{2}$, Lidlington *Tp.*, $45\frac{3}{4}$, and Millbrook, $47\frac{1}{2}$, to *Ampthill*, $48\frac{3}{4}$.]

(*Ampthill:* White Hart.)

On *l.*, Toddington Park and Manor *Ho.* Beyond Ampthill, on *l.*, Ampthill Park, and on *r.*, Houghton Park.

Ampthill to Bedford ($8—53$); the road is almost level, passing between Ampthill and Houghton Parks to Houghton Conquest *Tp.*, $46\frac{1}{2}$, and then through Kempston Hardwick, 49, and Elstow, $51\frac{1}{4}$.

LONDON TO KETTERING (by Wellingborough).

London to Newport Pagnell ($49\frac{3}{4}$)—p. 154.

Newport Pagnell to Olney ($5—54\frac{3}{4}$); keep to *r.* after crossing the *R.* Ouse outside Newport, and again cross the Ouse at Sherrington Bridge, $50\frac{3}{4}$, shortly afterwards taking the left hand road, and through Sherrington, $51\frac{3}{4}$, out of which there is a long rise, presently followed by a steep descent into Emberton, otherwise fairly level, but very rough road; just before Olney cross *R.* Ouse again.

(*Olney:* Bull; Queen.)

At Olney, 1*m.* on *l.*, Weston Park; on *r.*, Clifton Hall. At Weston the poet Cowper resided for many years.

Olney to Wellingborough (12—66¾); very hilly and rough road through Warrington, 56¼, Bozeat, 59¾, and Wollaston, 62¾, and over the *R.* Nen at Long Bridge, 65¾.

(*Wellingborough :* Angel; Hind.)

At Bozeat, about 2*m.* on *l.*, is Castle Ashby (Marquis of Northampton). Wellingborough was formerly celebrated for its medicinal springs; Charles I. and his Queen lived here a whole season in tents to drink the waters.

Wellingborough to Kettering (7—73¾); a fine undulating road through Great Harrowden, 68¼, and Isham, 70¼.

LONDON TO NORTHAMPTON (by Bedford).

London to Bedford (50¼)—p. 185.

Bedford to Turvey (8—58¼); a little out of Bedford keep to *l.*, and the first 4*m.* are good to Bromham Bridge, 54¼, over *R.* Ouse, and after that the road is rather rough and bumpy; at the cross roads with a stone cross, beyond Bromham Bridge, keep to *r.*, and at Grange, 54¾, turn to *l.*, then there is a long hill to mount, with a run down into Turvey.

Turvey to Northampton (13¼—71½); cross *R.* Ouse, and 1*m.* further keep to *r.*, and up a steep ascent to Lavendon, 60¾, and then through Yardley Hastings, 64½, Denton, 66, Brayfield-on-the-Green, 67¼, Little Houghton, 68½, and over *R.* Nen, 1½*m.* before Northampton; very rough road.

[From Bedford to Northampton by Higham Ferrers and Wellingborough is a better road but much longer.]

On *r.*, the remains of Lavendon Castle. At Yardley Hastings, on *r.*, Castle Ashby.

LONDON TO LEICESTER (by Bedford).

London to Kettering (74¾)—p. 185.

Kettering to Market Harborough (11¼—86); turn to *l.* in Kettering and down a hill out of the town; the road is very rough and hilly; there is a very steep hill to mount into Rothwell, 78¾, whence there is a steep and rough descent, followed by another very steep hill to mount through Desborough, 80¼, after which there is a long gradual run down past the "Fox Inn," 82¼, the road being rather rough, and then a long steep descent into Market Harborough.

(*Desborough :* Angel.)

Market Harborough to Leicester (14½—100½)—p. 166.

LONDON TO NOTTINGHAM (by Leicester).

London to Loughborough (108¾)—p. 166.

Loughborough to Nottingham (15—123¾); turn to *r.* in Loughborough, and the road is fairly level and good through Cotes, 109¾, and Hoton, 111¾, to Rempstone, 113¼, to which there is a short descent, then a run down to Corlingstock (locally called Costock), 114½, out of which is another rise followed by the long steep descent of Bunny Hill, very loose, lumpy, and rutty, and dangerous to ride up or down on account of loose stones, to Bunny, 116¾; from here the road is undulating through Bradmore, 117¾, and Ruddington, 118¾, with a good long descent down into the Trent valley and over Trent Bridge, 122¾.

[There is another road turning to *l.* a little out of Loughborough, and through Stanford, East Leake, and Bunny, which avoids the worst hill, Bunny Hill.

Or from East Leake through Gotham, Clifton, and Wilford to Trent Bridge or Nottingham; but sometimes this road is cut up with the gypsum traffic about Gotham.

Another route is to follow the Derby road through Hathern and Kegworth to within ½ mile of Cavendish Bridge, then turn to *r.* and through Sawley, Long Eaton, Chilwell, and Beeston to Nottingham; many prefer this, though the longest.]

Near Clifton is an ancient entrenchment, and 1*m.* S. are remains of a tesselated pavement.

LONDON TO ALFRETON (by Nottingham).

London to Nottingham (124)—p. 186.

Nottingham to Moor Green (7½—131½); in Nottingham turn to *l.*, and at New Radford, 125, keep to *r.* by Bobbers Mill, 125½, and again to *r.* a mile further on, and the road is then on the rise through Cinder Hill, 127½, to Nuthall, 128¾, out of which (keeping to *r.*) is a steep ascent, followed by a fall at Watnall, 130, and a hill into Greasley, 131.

Moor Green to Alfreton (8½—140); beyond Moor Green there is a steep hill to climb, and the road continues hilly to Selston, 136½ (keeping to *l.* twice), after which it is downhill to Pye Bridge, 137¼, and through Somercotes, 138.

LONDON TO CHESTERFIELD (by Mansfield).

London to Mansfield (138)—p. 186.

Mansfield to Chesterfield (12¼—150¼); keep to *l.* out of Mansfield, and the road is very hilly to Pleasley, 141, where take the left hand road, which continues very hilly through Glapwell, 143 (out of which is a steep descent), Heath, 145, and Hasland, 149.

At Glapwell, on *l.*, Hardwick Hall, an interesting Elizabethan mansion, containing some rare portraits and tapestry, &c. At Heath, on *r.*, Sutton Hall.

LONDON TO ROTHERHAM (by Chesterfield).

London to Chesterfield (150)—p. 178.

Chesterfield to Staveley (4½—154½); in Chesterfield turn to *r.*, and through Birmington, 152¼.

Staveley to Rotherham (11½—166); at Staveley turn to *l.* and the road is very undulating past Renishaw Park to Eckington, 157½, but from here through Beighton, 160, and Aughton, 162, it is very hilly, the greater part being unrideable, as the hills are too steep to ride either up or down; the streets of Rotherham are paved.

LONDON TO SHEFFIELD (by Mansfield).

London to Clown (148)—p. 187.

Clown to Sheffield (13½—161½); a mile beyond Clown turn to *l.*, and through Barlborough, 150, Renishaw, 152, Eckington, 154½, Masborough, 155¾, and Birley Vale, 158½.

LONDON TO SKIPTON (by Leeds).

London to Wakefield (186)—p. 179.

Wakefield to Leeds (9—195); through Newton, 187, Lofthouse, 189¾, Thorpe-on-the-Hill, 190¾, Woodhouse, 192¾, and Hunslet, 193¼; the heavy traffic on this road makes it bad for bicycling; paving and tramways through Leeds.

(*Leeds*: Griffin, B.T.C.; Queen.)

Leeds, the largest town in Yorkshire, is the metropolis of the woollen manufacture. 3m. beyond Leeds, on N.W., are the ruins of Kirkstall Abbey, picturesquely situate on the banks of the R. Aire; it was founded in 1152 for the Cistercian monks. 3m. E. is Temple Newsome, the elegant residence of the Marquis of Hertford.

Leeds to Otley (10—205); a fair undulating road through Headingley, 197, and Cookridge, 200½, ending with a descent of 2½m. from Pool Bank into Otley.

(*Otley*: Black Horse; White Horse.)

Otley to Ilkley (6—211); the road goes up the R. Wharfe valley through Burley, 207, and is not so hilly, but is not very good.

(*Ilkley*: Crown; New Inn.)

Just before Ilkley, on l., Ben Rhydding, which has come into notice of late years as a watering-place.

Ilkley to Skipton (9—220); up the right bank of the R. Wharfe to Addingham, 214, beyond which keep to r., and the road leaves Wharfedale and goes through Draughton, 217. [There is another road from Addingham turning sharp to r. before the village, up Wharfedale to Bolton Bridge, 217; the road is hilly but good except in wet weather: from Bolton Bridge to Skipton, 5¼—222¼, turning to l., the road is good for 2m., for the next 2m. bad, and the remainder indifferent.]

(*Bolton Bridge*: Devonshire Arms.)

Fine scenery. N. of Bolton are the ruins of Bolton Abbey or Priory; 1m. further is the Strid, a narrow chasm where the R. Wharfe has worn a passage for its bed through the solid rock. In the vicinity are the ruins of Barden Tower.

LONDON TO RIPON.

London to Leeds (195)—above.

Leeds to Harewood (8½—203½); after leaving the town it is a rough road and rather hilly through Chapel Allerton, 197¼, Moor Town, 199, and by Alwoodley Gates, 200¼.

On l. Alwoodley old Hall. On l., Harewood Ho., and remains of Harewood Castle. The ch. is an ancient building, and contains some old monuments, amongst others the tomb of Judge Gascoigne.

Harewood to Harrogate (7½—210¾); through Dunkeswick, 205, and by Spacey House, 208, is very hilly, but pretty good surface; at the obelisk entering Harrowgate keep to left, and go through that part of the town called Low Harrowgate.

(*Harrogate*: Commercial, B.T.C.; Crown; George; Prospect.)

Harrogate is celebrated for its mineral springs, and is a great resort for invalids. About 3m. E. is Knaresborough, on the R. Nidd, surrounded by romantic scenery. About 9m. N.W. are Brimham Rocks, a singular natural curiosity, to which there is a fair road.

Harrogate to Ripley (4—214¾); very trying hill to climb out of Harrogate, followed by a long and steep run down, perfectly safe, through Killinghall, 213½; excellent smooth surface.

At Ripley, on *l*., the castle. Before Ripley cross the R. Nidd.

Ripley to Ripon (7¾—222½); leaving Ripley turn to right, and it is a splendid road and first rate travelling through South Stainley, 217¼; stiff climb into Ripon.

(*Ripon*: Black Bull; Crown and Anchor: Unicorn.)

Ripon, on the R. Ure, is an ancient town; the cathedral, founded in 1331, is said to be one of the best proportioned buildings in England. Near it is a tumulus or artificial mound, called Ellshaw or Ailcey Hill, supposed to be a memorial of a battle in which the Saxons were defeated by the Danes. About 3m. W. is Studley Royal, the seat of Earl Grey; in the park grounds are the ruins of Fountains Abbey, founded in 1132 by the Cistercian monks, and said to be the most perfect monastic building in England. Near it is the mansion of Fountains Hall. 4m. E. of Ripon is Newby Hall. 6m. distant is the romantic Hackfall, or Witches' Valley.

LONDON TO PATELEY BRIDGE AND LOFTHOUSE.

London to Ripley, Yorks (214¾)—above.

Ripley to Pateley Bridge (9¼—224); out of Ripley turn to *l*., and it is a fairly good undulating road, from Summer Bridge, 220, running near R. Nidd.

(*Pateley Bridge*: George.)

Pateley Bridge to Lofthouse (9—233); by Ramsgill, 230, and up the valley of the R. Nidd, the road is fairly good, and there are a few small hills.

LONDON TO BOROUGHBRIDGE.

London to Harrogate (210¾)—p. 191.

Harrogate to Knaresborough (3—213¾); at the Obelisk entering Harrogate keep to the right through High Harrogate, and it is a good road, all downhill.

(*Knaresborough*: Crown; Elephant and Castle.)

Knaresborough, on the R. Nidd, is surrounded by pretty scenery. There are remains of a castle erected soon after the Conquest. The chief objects of interest are the Petrifying or Dropping Well, St. Robert's Chapel, ruins of the priory, and St. Robert's Cave, remarkable for the murder for which Eugene Aram was convicted.

Knaresborough to Boroughbridge (7—220¾); through Ferensby, 216½, and Minskip, 219¼, the road is good on the whole, but loose in places, and there are no hills of any consequence.

LONDON TO WANSFORD.

London to Bedford (50¼)—p. 185.

Bedford to Kimbolton (14—64¼); when through Bedford turn to r., and through Ravensden, 54¼, Wildon, 55¼, Bolnhurst, 57½, Keysoe, 60, and Pertenhall, 61¾; undulating road, rather stiff hill down into Kimbolton.

(*Kimbolton*: George; White Lion.)
On *l.*, Kimbolton Castle (Duke of Manchester). At Bolnhurst, 2m. on *r.*, Bushmead Priory, and near it an old encampment.

Kimbolton to Brington (6—70¼); keep to *r.* out of Kimbolton, and through Catworth, 68¼.

Brington to Oundle (9—79¼); through Clapton, 74¾, and Barnwell St. Andrews, 77¼.
(*Oundle:* Talbot.)
Before Barnwell St. Andrews, on *l.*, Lilford Hall. At Barnwell, on *r.*, ruins of the castle, which was erected in 1132.

Oundle to Elton (5¼—84½); turn to *r.* in Oundle, cross R. Nen and through Warmington, 82¾, is almost level, following the valley of the *R.* Nen.
At Elton, 1½m. on *l.*, the ruins of Fotheringhay Castle, which was founded shortly after the Conquest. Richard III. was born here, and here Mary, Queen of Scots, was imprisoned, tried, and beheaded.

Elton to Wansford (3¾—88¼).

LONDON TO OUNDLE (by Thrapston).

London to Higham Ferrers (65)—p. 185.

Higham Ferrers to Thrapston (8½—73½); cross the *R.* Nen to Irthlingborough, 67, where turn sharp to *r.* and through Little Addington, 68½, Great Addington, 69¼, and Woodford, 71, recrossing the *R.* Nen just before Thrapston.
(*Thrapston:* White Hart.)
About 2m. W. of Thrapston is Drayton *Ho.*, erected about the middle of the 15th century. Irthlingborough is locally called Artleboro'.

Thrapston to Oundle (8—81½); in Thrapston take the left hand road and through Thorpe Waterville, 76, and Barnwell St. Andrews, 79½; the road follows the Nen valley all the way from Higham Ferrers.

LONDON TO DONCASTER.

London to Mansfield (138)—p. 186.

Mansfield to Worksop (12—150); keep to *r.* at the bifurcation in Mansfield, and it is very hilly work through Market Warsop, 142¾, Church Warsop, 143¼, Cuckney, 145, and Norton, 145½, with a stiff hill down into Worksop; an uneven and rutty road.
(*Worksop:* Red Lion.)
Beyond Norton, on *l.*, Welbeck, the magnificent mansion of the Duke of Portland; further on, Worksop Manor *Ho.*; about 2m. on *r.*, Clumber Park. At Worksop are remains of a priory, erected in the reign of Henry I.; part of it is now embodied in the *ch.* This district is generally called the Dukery, from there having been here at one time no less than four ducal seats.

Worksop to Tickhill (9—159); just out of Worksop keep to *r.*, and through Carlton, 153¼, and Goldthorpe, 156.
At Tickhill are remains of a castle.

Tickhill to Doncaster (7½—166½), through Wadworth, 162, Loversall, 163, and Balby, 165.

SECTION VII.

From General Post Office; Great Northern Roads (East Middlesex, East Herts, East Bedford, Huntingdonshire, West Cambridge, East Northamptonshire, Rutlandshire, East Nottinghamshire, Lincolnshire, East Yorkshire, Durham, and Northumberland.)

LONDON TO EDINBURGH (by Stamford, &c.).
(THE GREAT NORTH ROAD.)

London to Welwyn (25¼)—p. 184.

Welwyn to Stevenage (6½—31¾); at Welwyn, bear to r. at the bottom of the hill, then to l. at the church, and again to r. further on; very good road through Woolmer Green, 27¼, and Broadwater, 29½; there are some long ascents and descents, two of the former in particular.
(*Stevenage*: Old Castle; White Lion.)
Before Stevenage, on r., is a row of six large barrows, supposed to be of Danish origin.

Stevenage to Baldock (5¾—37½); taking the right hand fork at the end of Stevenage, it is a very good road through Graveley, 33½; long ascent out of Stevenage, one or two stiff hills to mount afterwards, and a long fall approaching Baldock.
(*Baldock*: Rose and Crown; White Horse Commercial.)
At Baldock, the *ch.* is a handsome building, and contains some ancient and curious monuments, &c.

Baldock to Biggleswade (7¾—45¼), is good going by New Inn *Tp.* 40½, and Bleak Hall, 42¼; undulating road, with two long and rather steep descents: just before Biggleswade keep to l.
(*Biggleswade*: Crown, *Hqrs.*; George; Rose; Royal Oak; Swan, *B.T.C.*; White Horse.)
A little beyond Baldock, on l., at Radwell, a Roman encampment called Cæsar's Camp, where many Roman antiquities have been found. A little further, 2 or 3m. on r., near Ashwell, is an ancient entrenchment called Harborough Banks.

Biggleswade to Tempsford (6—51¼); turn to l. out of the town and cross the bridge over *R.* Ivel; then an excellent road through Lower Caldecote, 46¾, Beeston Cross, 48¾, a little beyond which (keeping to r.) recross *R.* Ivel, and through Girtford, 49½.
At Tempsford, on r., Tempsford Hall.

Tempsford to Eaton Socon (4—55¼); ½m. beyond Tempsford keep to l., cross *R.* Ouse, and down the valley through Wiboston, 54; loose road.

Eaton Socon to Buckden (6—61¼); is a good level road, following the Ouse valley through Cross Hall, 56¾, Little Paxton, 58, and Diddington, 60

[Better to go through St. Neots, 56, keeping to right bank of *R.* Ouse which cross at St. Neots, and join the G. N. road at Cross Hall, 57¼.]

On *r.*, Paxton Place; on *r.*, Diddington *Ho.*; at Buckden, Bishop of Lincoln's Palace.

Buckden to Alconbury Hill (6¾—68); keeping to *l.* ½*m.* beyond Buckden, it is a fair easy road by Brampton Hut, 63¾, and through Alconbury, 66¼, to Alconbury Weston, 67, whence, bearing to *r.*, there is a long stiff hill to mount.

Beyond Buckden, a little on *r.*, Brampton Park, and farther on *r.* Hinchinbrook *Ho.* and Huntingdon town.

Alconbury Hill to Norman Cross (8—76); after ½*m.* is a considerable descent, then through Sawtry St. Andrews, 71½, and Stilton, 75¼, out of which is a short steep hill; otherwise a good easy road.

(*Stilton:* George and Dragon Inn.)

Norman Cross to Wansford (7¾—83¾); keep to *l.*, and by Kate's Cabin Inn, 79½, and through Water Newton, 81¼, and Sibson, 82, the road is pretty level, but rough and loose, though fair going at the sides.

(*Wansford:* The Haycock Inn.)

This road is part of the Roman Ermine Street, which ran through Huntingdon. 1*m.* beyond Sawtry St. Andrews, on *r.*, Conington Castle. At Stilton, the cheese which bears this name, was first sold, though made in Leicestershire. At Kate's Cabin Inn, on *r.*, Alwalton Castle. 1*m.* beyond Kate's Cabin Inn, on *r.*, an ancient entrenchment, supposed to be the site of the Roman station Durobrivæ; the old line of the Ermine Street ran through it.

Wansford to Stamford (5¾—89½); out of Wansford take the right hand road, and for the first 3*m.*, through White Water *Tp.*, 85½, it is rather hilly, then fairly level for next 2*m.*, after which there is a long gradual descent into Stamford; very rough road, rutty and greasy when wet.

(*Stamford:* Crown; George.)

Before Stamford, on *r.*, Burghley Park, the splendid mansion of the Marquis of Exeter, and on *l.*, ruins of Wothorpe Hall.

Stamford to South Witham (9¾—99¼); through Bridge Casterton, 91½, Horn Lane *Tp.*, 95½, and by Stretton, 96, and Ram Jam House, 97½, the road on the whole is very undulating, with some level bits here and there; soon after leaving Stamford the surface becomes bad and rough, and in wet weather is rutty and dangerous.

Bridge Casterton occupies the site of a Roman station on the ancient Ermine Street, and there are still the remains of a Roman encampment S.E. of the village. The *ch.* is an ancient Gothic structure. At Horn Lane *Tp.*, on *l.*, Exton Hall, a fine mansion partly of the 16th century. Exton *ch.* is a beautiful specimen of Gothic architecture.

South Witham to Grantham (11—110¼); the road continues bad through North Witham, 100½, to Coltersworth, 102¼, after which it becomes rather better through Stoke Rochford, 104½, Great Ponton, 106¾, Little Ponton, 108¾, and Spittlegate Hill *Tp.* 109¾; hilly road, with one or two steep but short pulls, and the last mile is downhill and rather rough; in wet weather it is rutty and dangerously greasy, and sometimes it is almost unrideable.

(*Coltersworth:* Blue Lion; Red Lion.—*Grantham:* Angel and Royal; Blue Lion: George; Red Lion.)

Near Coltersworth, Sir Isaac Newton was born. At Grantham, there were formerly several religious houses, remains of which still exist. St. Wulfstan's *ch.* contains a curious font and several monuments. On St. Peter's Hill is Queen Eleanor's Cross. 5m. W., in Belvoir Vale, is Belvoir Castle, the magnificent seat of the Duke of Rutland.

Grantham to Newark (14¼—124½); long uphill out of Grantham to Great Gonerby, 112, then there is a long gradual descent, after which the road is nearly level through Marston *Tp.*, 114¼, Foston, 116, Long Bennington, 118¼, over Shire Bridge, 120½, and through Balderton *Tp.*, 122¼; the surface continues lumpy and very rutty, in wet weather greasy and dangerous for the first 10m., then it is hard and good: the streets of Newark are paved.

(*Newark*: Clinton Arms; Gilstrap; Ram; Royal Oak.)

Beyond Grantham, 2m. on *r.*, Belton *Ho.* and Syston Park. Newark is a neat town; St. Mary Magdelene *ch.* is one of the largest and finest in the kingdom, partly rebuilt in the reign of Henry VI., and contains many old monuments, brasses, &c. There are ruins of a castle, and many Roman antiquities have been found in the neighbourhood.

Newark to Carlton-on-Trent (7—131½); after crossing *R.* Dean keep to *r.* just out of Newark, and then cross *R.* Trent, and it is a very good road, slightly undulating, following the Trent valley, and through South Muskham, 127, North Muskham, 128, and Cromwell, 130.

Carlton-on-Trent to Tuxford (6¼—137¾); very good road, almost level to Sutton-on-Trent, 133, then a moderate rise up Crown Hill, and a run down to Weston, 134¾, whence slightly undulating past Scarthing Moor Inn, 135½, and a rather steep hill down into Tuxford.

(*Tuxford*: Newcastle Arms.)

From the top of Crown Hill, the tower of Lincoln Cathedral is visible, 16m. distant on the *r.*

Tuxford to Retford (7¼—145); out of Tuxford is the steep ascent of Cleveland Hill to climb, then easy undulating road through West Markham, 139½, Markham Moor *Tg.*, 140¼, and Gamston, 141½; good road. Retford is paved.

(*Retford*: Crown; Queen's; Swan; White Hart.)

Retford is sometimes called East Retford; 2m. on *l.*, Babworth Hall.

Retford to Bawtry (8¼—153¼); take left hand road in Retford, and when just out of the town keep to *r.*; it is very bad for the first 3 or 4m., being rutty and very loose and stony, past Barnby Moor Inn, 148, where turn to *r.* up a stiff hill, and it is a good road through Torworth, 149½, Ranskill, 150¼, and Scrooby, 152, to which there is a long run down.

(*Bawtry*: Black Bull; Crown; Granby.)

Before Scrooby, on *l.*, Serlby Hall. At Scrooby formerly stood the palace of the Archbishop of York; part has been pulled down, and the rest is now a farm house.

Bawtry to Doncaster (9—162¼); splendid smooth undulating road over Rossington Bridge, 157¾, and through Tophall, 158¾, with a descent into Doncaster; the surface is of a sandy nature and sometimes is soft and heavy going: about the time of Doncaster races, in September, the last mile is generally very rough.

(*Doncaster*: Angel; Elephant, B.T.C.; Royal; Temperance.)

Doncaster is a fine town, occupying the site of a Roman station, many coins and other antiquities having been found here; it has one of the largest corn markets in the kingdom. There are some good swimming baths here. St. George's *ch.* is an elegant building, well worth seeing.

Doncaster to Red House (5—167¼): rather hilly and rough road through York Bar, 164, where keep to *r.*

Red House to Went Bridge (5¼—172¼); keeping to *r.*, steep hill to ascend from Red House, then rather hilly by Robin Hood's Well, 169¼, with a steep and winding descent into Went Bridge; rough road.

(*Went Bridge:* Coach Horse Inn.)

Went Bridge to Brotherton (5¾—178½), is a hilly and good road; very steep winding ascent (rather awkward to ride down on the reverse journey) out of Went Bridge, and at Darrington, 174½, are steep descent and ascent, and again hilly through Ferry Bridge, 177½ (cross *R.* Aire), to Brotherton, entering which turn to *l.*

2*m.* W. of Darrington is the town of Pontefract or Pomfret, with ruins of the castle, in which it is said that Richard II. was foully murdered. At Brotherton, on *l.*, Fryston Hall.

Brotherton to Aberford (8¼—186¾); through Fairburn, 180, Peckfield *Tp.*, 182½ (keep to *r.*), and Micklefield, 184, is a fairly good road, though, being made of limestone, it is inclined to be rough and heavy after rain; a few more hills.

At Micklefield, 1*m.* on *r.*, Huddleston Hall. At Aberford, ruins of the castle, which was built soon after the Conquest. At Peckfield *Tp.*, on *l.*, Ledstone Hall.

Aberford to Wetherby (7½—194¼); through Bramham, 190¼, a rough and hilly road, but none of the hills difficult; cross *R.* Wharfe entering Wetherby.

(*Wetherby:* Angel; Brunswick; White Hart.)

1*m.* beyond Aberford, on *r.*, Hazlewood Hall, which has remained in the Vavasour family since the Conquest. Before Bramham, on *l.*, Bramham Park. Wetherby, on the *R.* Wharfe, is situated amidst pleasant scenery. A little below the town is St. Helen's Ford, where the Roman military way crossed the river.

Wetherby to Boroughbridge (12—206¼); leaving Wetherby keep to *l.*, a mile after to *r.* and over Walshford Bridge, 197¼ (*R.* Nidd); on the whole a good undulating road, with easy hills; a few loose patches in dry weather, and in wet very heavy.

[From Boroughbridge, instead of keeping to the Great North Road proper, which goes through Northallerton and Darlington to Durham, the road through Leeming and along Leeming Lane is interposed here, as it is the route most generally followed, the distance being the same. The Northallerton route is given in the next route—pp. 201-2.

(*Boroughbridge:* Crown.)

Beyond Walshford Bridge, on *l.*, Ribstone Hall, where the "Ribstone Pippin" apples were first cultivated; in the chapel is a monument to the standard bearer of a Roman legion, discovered at York, in 1688. Before Boroughbridge, on *l.*, are 3, originally 4, huge pyramidal stones, called the Arrows. 2*m.* beyond Walshford Bridge, on *r.*, Allerton Park, where was formerly a Benedictine priory. 1*m.* E. of Boroughbridge is Aldborough, occupying the site of a Roman station; in the *ch.* and churchyard are some Roman and Saxon remains.

Boroughbridge to Leeming (15½—221¾); having crossed *R.* Ure outside Boroughbridge, keep to *l.*, and at Kirkby Hill, 207½, to *r.*, then past York Gate Inn, 213¼, and through Leeming Lane (New Inn), 218¼, and Londonderry, 220¼, being the well-known "Leeming Lane," a straight stretch of splendid undulating road, chiefly on the rise, with some long gradual slopes, none of which are in the least difficult; the surface is as smooth as a racing path, except for some loose patches which occur at intervals.

At Leeming on *l.* to *Bedale* (2—223¾), or ½*m.* beyond New Inn, Leeming Lane, turn to *l.* and through Burmeston and Exilby to *Bedale* (4½—223½).

(*Bedale:* Black Swan.)

At York Gate Inn, 2*m.* on *l.*, Norton Hall; on *r.*, Newby Park.

Leeming to Catterick Bridge (7½—229¼) is a continuation of the same kind of road, the last 2½*m.* being on an easy incline through Catterick, 228¼; at Catterick Bridge cross *R.* Swale; picturesque scenery.

(*Catterick:* Angel; George; Golden Lion.)

2*m.* before Catterick, a little on *l.*, Hornby Castle (Duke of Leeds); on *r.*, Kiplin Park.

Catterick Bridge to Scotch Corner (3½—232¾) is an easy undulating road, very good and smooth, but heavy in wet weather: pretty scenery.

Scotch Corner to Pierce Bridge (6½—239¼) is principally slightly downhill, with a very steep and abrupt descent at Hang Bank, about 1½*m.* beyond Scotch Corner.

About half way, a little on *l.*, Stanwick Hall. At Pierce Bridge is the site of a Roman station.

Pierce Bridge to Heighington (5¼—244½); turn to *r.* beyond Pierce Bridge, and it is a fair road, but rather hilly.

About half way on *r.*, Walworth Castle.

Heighington to Sunderland Bridge (10¾—255¼); hilly road through Eldon, 248¼, and Merrington, 251¼; at 253¾ join the road from Bishop Auckland on *l.*, and just before Sunderland Bridge rejoin the Great North road from Darlington on *r.*

[Or from *Pierce Bridge* keep straight on through West Auckland, 246¼, and St. Helens, 246¾, where there is a level railway crossing, to *Bishop Auckland*, 249¾, thence through Spennymoor, 253¾, to *Sunderland Bridge*, 256¼; very hilly road.

Or from Heighington turn to *r.* and it is nearly all downhill to Aycliffe, 247, on the Darlington road, whence to *Sunderland Bridge*, 256.]

Near West Auckland, on *r.*, Brusselton Tower; 2*m.* W., the ruins of Evenwood Castle. At Bishop Auckland, the castle, now the residence of the Bishop of Durham. From Merrington *ch.*, which is situated on a hill, there is a most extensive view, and it is said that York Minster can be seen with a glass. At Sunderland Bridge, on *r.*, Croxdale Hall; 2*m.* on W., Brancepath Castle.

Sunderland Bridge to Durham (4¼—259½); after crossing *R.* Wear there is a long steepish hill to mount, presently followed by a long very steep descent, which is partly paved, to walk down into Durham; in going through Durham cross *R.* Wear twice, and there another very steep paved descent just before crossing *R.* Wear for the second time.

(*Durham:* County; Rose and Crown.)

Durham is remarkable for the singularity of its position—on an eminence nearly surrounded by the *R.* Wear. The venerable and magnificent cathedral was founded in 1093; it contains the remains of St. Cuthbert, Bede, and others, and numerous interesting monuments, &c. There is also a castle, built soon after the Conquest, and the Guildhall, erected in 1555: the other objects of interest are the University; the remains of the city walls; Maiden Castle, an ancient fortification, ¾*m.* distant, ascribed to the Romans; Nevill's Cross, 1*m.* W.; and the ruins of Finchale Abbey, a few miles N.E., on the banks of the Wear.

Durham to Chester-le-Street (6—265½); after crossing R. Wear the second time keep to r. and there is a hill to walk up out of the town on to Durham Moor, 260½, then an excellent road, level nearly all the way, over Durham Moor and through Plausworth *Tp.*, 263 ; rather stiff but safe descent into Chester-le-Street.

(*Chester-le-Street :* Lambton Arms.)

At Plausworth *Tp.*, the ruins of Finchale Abbey are 2 *m.* on *r.* At Chester-le-Street, on *r.*, across *R.* Wear, is Lumley Castle, the seat of the Earl of Scarborough.

Chester-le-Street to Newcastle-upon-Tyne (8½—274); undulating road, but not with good surface through Pelaw, 266½, Birtley, 268½, and Ayton Bank, 270; in several places the colliery lines cross the road, and the rider must be on the look out for the wagons, then the surface deteriorates considerably about Low Fell, 271½, and is generally exceedingly bad to Gateshead, 273, where there is a very steep descent, with an awkward turn and crossing at the bottom of West street; High street is more gradual but for this turn to *r.* shortly after entering the town ; thence cross *R.* Tyne over the High Level Bridge, along which is wood pavement and good riding (½d. toll to pay), and entering Newcastle there is a descent down Moseley street and a rise up Grey street (turn to *r.*), Blackett street and then to *l.* up Northumberland street. Tram line in Gateshead.

(*Newcastle-upon-Tyne :* Alexandra ; Alliance ; Crown and Thistle ; Queen's Head, *Hqrs.* ; Royal Turf, *B.T.C.* ; Station.)

At Ayton Bank, 2 *m.* on *l.*, Ravensworth Castle. Newcastle is a large town, in the midst of the chief coal district of England ; it has also manufactories of glass, pottery, iron, steel, engines, &c. The castle, from which its name is derived, was erected by Robert, eldest son of the Conqueror. The chief public buildings are St. Nicholas' *ch.*, St. Andrew's *ch.*, St. John the Baptist *ch.*, Royal Arcade, Stephenson's Double Bridge, Museum, Library, &c.

Newcastle-upon-Tyne to Morpeth (14¾—288¾); over the Town Moor there are tram lines all the way to Gosforth, 277, and then a fair give and take road over Three Mile Bridge, 277½, by Six Mile House, 280, and Shotton Edge, 282, to Blagden Bank, whence there is a long run down to Stannington Bridge, 283½ (over *R.* Blyth), and through Stannington, 284, and Clifton, 286 ; generally very fair surface, and it is about the best road in the vicinity of Newcastle ; there is a rather steep descent into Morpeth past the Castle and the Jail, and then over the bridge (*R.* Wansbeck).

(*Morpeth :* Black Bull ; Newcastle Arms, *B.T.C.* ; Queen's Head ; Turk's Head.)

At Three Mile Bridge, on *r.*, Gosforth *Ho.* At Shotton Edge, on *l.*, Blagdon Park. At Morpeth, 2 *m.* on *l.*, ruins of Mitford Castle, and near it Mitford *Ho.*, on the banks of the *R.* Wansbeck, and surrounded by beautiful scenery. At Morpeth are remains of the old castle.

Morpeth to Alnwick (19¼—308); through Loaning *Tp.*, 291 (keep to *r.*), Shield Green, 293, West Moor, 297¾, West Thirston, 298¾, Felton, 299, by Nelson's Monument, 300¾, and through Newton, 302¼, is a fair going road, but loose in places, and with plenty of hills, the last 5 *m.* are a nice run nearly all downhill into Alnwick ; steep descent into Felton, with an awkward right-angle turn over the bridge.

(*Alnwick :* White Swan.)

At Shield Green, 4 *m.* on *r.*, Widdrington Castle near the coast. At West Thirston, 4 *m.* on *l.*, Brinkburn Priory. At Newton, 4 *m.* on *r.*, Warkworth Castle and Hermitage. At Alnwick the Castle and Hulne Abbey, both the seats of the

Duke of Northumberland. Part of the walls of Alnwick are still standing, and also of the Abbey. The castle can be seen on Thursdays.

Alnwick to Belford (14½—322½); steep descent going out of Alnwick (keeping to r. by the Castle), then cross the R. Aln, and it is uphill for 1½m. over Heffler Bank and hilly through North Charlton, 314¼, and Warrenford, 318¼, otherwise a good road.

(*Belford*: Blue Bell.)

Beyond Alnwick, 2m. on r., Howick, the handsome seat of Earl Grey. 2m. further N., the remains of Dunstanburgh Castle on the coast. At Warrenford, on l., Twizel Ho. At Belford, 4m. on r., Bamburgh Castle, said to have been founded by the Saxons in the 6th century.

Belford to Berwick-upon-Tweed (15—337½); stiff ascent of Belford Hill to be mounted out of the former, then through Detchent, 324¼, Fenwick, 327½, Haggerston, 330½, and Tweedmouth, 337, is a fair road, but the last part hilly, in wet weather it is rather rough and greasy; steep descent of 2m. through Tweedmouth, and then over Border Bridge into High street, Berwick.

(*Berwick-upon-Tweed*: King's Arms; Red Lion.)

Opposite Fenwick, on r., Holy Island or Lindisfarne, containing the ruins of an ancient monastery. At Berwick, the remains of the castle, a fortress of great strength and importance before the union of England and Scotland; near it is the Bell Tower.

Berwick-upon-Tweed to Ayton (9—346½); a little beyond Berwick keep to r., and it is a very good road, but rather hilly for the first 5 or 6m. by Covendrum, 339½, and Winley Stead, 340½, to which it runs near the sea coast; at about 340¾, enter Scotland.

Ayton to Cockburnspath (11½—358); it is a very good road, chiefly uphill for some miles, running past Houndwood Inn, 351, and Renton Inn, 354, and passing on the back of St. Abb's Head, then a gradual descent begins and continues for 3m., when the fall suddenly gets steeper with one or two dangerous turnings, which should not be ridden down without a reliable brake, and in any case great care must be taken, as frequent accidents to bicyclists have occurred here, and even in the old coaching days it had a similar evil reputation.

Cockburnspath to Dunbar (9½—367½); the road now runs close to the sea again, and is rather hilly but a good road through Broxburn, 366, where keep to r.

At Broxburn, on r., Broxmouth, the seat of the Duke of Roxburgh. Dunbar has been the scene of two battles; in 1296, Baliol was defeated here, and Cromwell defeated the Scotch army in the neighbourhood. There are ruins of the castle to which Mary, Queen of Scots fled, after the murder of Rizzio.

Dunbar to Linton (5½—373), is a good road through Belhaven, 368½, West Barns, 369, and Beltonford, 370; at Linton cross R. Tyne.

[Or you may avoid Dunbar by keeping to l. at Broxburn, 366, and going straight to Beltonford, 368¾.]

At Beltonford, on r., Tyningham Castle (Earl of Haddington).

Linton to Haddington (5½—378½); out of Linton there is a hill just a mile long to mount, after which the road rather deteriorates; it runs up the valley of R. Tyne.

Beyond Linton, on l., Hailes Castle. Before Haddington, on l., Amisfield (Earl of Wemyss).

Haddington to Tranent (7—385½) is a rough and very lumpy road through Gladsmuir, 382¼, to which it is chiefly uphill.

Before Tranent, 1½*m.* on *r.*, Seaton *Ho.*, and ruins of Seaton Castle.

Tranent to Musselburgh (4—389½) is a similar kind of road.

On *r.*, Preston Pans, where the young Pretender defeated the English army, in 1745. Just before Musselburgh, on *l.*, Pinkie, where the Scots were defeated, in 1547.

Musselburgh to Edinburgh (6—395½); the road is pretty good at first, but after a mile or two it becomes very bad and lumpy through Portobello, 392½, from which there is also a tramway into Edinburgh.

When going this journey it is worth bearing in mind that the north and north-east winds are more prevalent than any other on this coast, and therefore the ride *from* Berwick *to* Edinburgh is generally, on that account, not easy work.

LONDON TO EDINBURGH (by Northallerton).

This is the remainder of the Great North Road, for which the road through Leeming is substituted in the preceding route.

London to Boroughbridge (206¼)—p. 197.

Boroughbridge to Topcliffe (6½—212¾); having crossed the *R.* Ure outside Boroughbridge, keep to *r.* and through Dishforth, 210¼.

At Topcliffe, on *l.*, Newby Park.

Topcliffe to Northallerton (12½—225¼); at Topcliffe turn to *l.* and through Sand Hutton, 216¾, Newsham, 218¾, South Ottrington, 220¼, and North Ottrington, 221½.

(*Northallerton:* Black Bull; Golden Lion, *B.T.C.;* Railway; Red Lion.)
Fine Gothic *ch.* at Northallerton.

Northallerton to Enter Common (8—233¼); a pleasant road by Lovesome Hill, 229¼, through Little Smeaton, 231¼, to Great Smeaton, 232¼, after which the road becomes bad, being rutty and stony.

2 or 3*m.* W. of Smeaton was fought in 1138, the battle of the Standard, in which the Scots were completely defeated.

Enter Common to Darlington (8—241¼); keep to *l.*, and 1*m.* beyond Enter Common to *r.*; it is a good road through Dalton-on-Tees, 236¼, and Croft, 237¼, where cross the *R.* Tees; 1½*m.* before Darlington keep to *r.*, and it is macadam, very rough and lumpy, and also through the town.

[Or from *Scotch Corner*, 232¼, turn to *r.*, and it is a good road, with a descent at Middleton Lodge and another just before Stapleton, to Blackwell Bridge, 236¾ (toll to pay) over *R.* Tees; from the bridge is a short but stiff hill to mount, followed by descent to Grange road, then turn to *l.* at the cross roads, and the last 2*m.* are macadam, very rough and lumpy, into *Darlington*, 340¾.

Or from *Scotch Corner* through Middleton Tyas, 233½, to Croft, 236¾.

Or from *Catterick Bridge* through Citadella, 229¼, Scorton, 231¼, South Cowton, 233¼, North Cowton, 234¼, to Dalton-on-Tees, 236¾; good road.]

(*Dalton-on-Tees:* King William IV. Inn.—*Darlington:* Fleece.)
At Darlington, St. Cuthbert's *ch.*, built in the 12th century.

Darlington to Aycliffe ($5-246\frac{1}{4}$); by Harrow Gate, 243, and Coatham Mundeville, $245\frac{1}{4}$, is a fair granite road but hilly.

Aycliffe to Sunderland Bridge ($9-255\frac{1}{4}$); by Traveller's Rest, $247\frac{1}{4}$, through Woodham, $248\frac{3}{4}$, Rushyford, 250, Ferry Hill, $252\frac{1}{2}$, and Low Butcher Race, $254\frac{1}{2}$, is a granite road in capital order but very hilly, and requiring cautious riding; long run down out of Ferry Hill.

Sunderland Bridge to Edinburgh ($140\frac{1}{4}-395\frac{1}{2}$)—pp. 198-201.

LONDON TO KIMBOLTON (by Baldock).

London to Eaton Socon ($55\frac{1}{4}$)—p. 194.

Eaton Socon to Kimbolton ($8\frac{1}{4}-63\frac{1}{2}$); follow the Great North road to Cross Hall, $56\frac{3}{4}$, where turn to *l.*, and through Hail Weston, $57\frac{3}{4}$, Stoughton Highway *Tp.*, $60\frac{1}{2}$, and Stonley, $62\frac{1}{2}$.

LONDON TO TEMPSFORD (by Shefford).

London to Shefford ($41\frac{1}{4}$)—p. 185.

Shefford to Tempsford ($10\frac{1}{2}-51\frac{3}{4}$): turn to *r.* just before entering Shefford, and at Clifton, 43, turn to *l.* and through Stanford, 44, Upper Caldecote, 47, Brook End, 48, Beeston Cross, $48\frac{3}{4}$, where join the Great North road, and through Girtford, $49\frac{3}{4}$, to Tempsford; very fair road with a few hills, but nothing difficult. [Or turn to *r.* 3*m.* before Shefford, and through Henlow End and Henlow, $40\frac{1}{2}$, to Clifton, 42.]

LONDON TO WORKSOP AND BLYTH (by Stamford).

London to Newark ($124\frac{1}{2}$)—p. 196.

Newark to Kneesal ($8\frac{1}{4}-132\frac{3}{4}$); turn to *l.* a little out of Newark, and cross *R.* Trent just before Kelham, $126\frac{3}{4}$, and then through Camston, $130\frac{1}{4}$.

Kneesal to Ollerton ($3\frac{3}{4}-136\frac{1}{2}$); capital road but rather hilly through Ompton, $133\frac{3}{4}$, and Wellow, $135\frac{1}{4}$.

(*Ollerton:* Hop Pole; White Hart.)

Before Wellow, on *r.*, site of Jordon Castle. On *l.*, Rufford Abbey, founded in 1138 by Cistercian monks.

Ollerton to Worksop ($8\frac{3}{4}-145\frac{1}{4}$); long rise out of Ollerton, then a splendid undulating road with a surface as smooth as asphalte, across Sherwood Forest, through Budby, $139\frac{1}{2}$, and Carburton, $141\frac{1}{2}$; a stiff hill down into Worksop.

On *r.*, pass Thoresby Park, with Castle William and Thoresby *Ho.*; at Carburton, on *r.*, Clumber Park and *Ho.*

Worksop to Blyth ($6-151\frac{1}{4}$); very loose and rutty road.

LONDON TO KENDAL (by Newark).

London to Red House ($167\frac{1}{4}$)—p. 197.

Red House to Wakefield ($15-182\frac{1}{4}$); take left hand road and through North Elmsall, $171\frac{1}{4}$, Ackworth Moor Top, $174\frac{3}{4}$, Wragby, $176\frac{1}{4}$, Foulby, $177\frac{1}{4}$, Crofton, $178\frac{3}{4}$, and Agbridge, $180\frac{3}{4}$; rather hilly road.

At Wragby, on *r.*, Nostel Priory.

Wakefield to Kendal (80—262¼); through Bradford, 196¼, Keighley, 206½, Skipton, 216½, Settle, 232½, Clapham, 239¼, Ingleton, 243¼, and Kirkby Lonsdale, 250¼.—pp. 179-180.

LONDON TO RIPON (by Pontefract).

London to Red House (167¼)—p. 197.

Red House to Pontefract (9—176¼); keeping to *r.* there is a stiff hill to ascend from Red House, then rather hilly by Robin Hood's Well, 169¼, Barnsdale, 169¾, where leave the Great North road on *r.*, and go through Thorp Audlin, 172¼, and East Hardwick, 174¼.

(*Pontefract:* Green Dragon; Malt Shovel, *B.T.C.*; New Elephant; Red Lion.)

At Pontefract, on *r.*, through the town, the ruins of the castle in which Edward II. was imprisoned and barbarously murdered.

Pontefract to Oulton (8—184¼); through Houghton, 178¼, (keep to *l.*) over Methley Bridge, 180¼, and through Methley, 182¼.

Oulton to Leeds (5—189¼).

Leeds to Ripon (27½—216¾); through Harewood, 197½, Harrogate, 205, and Ripley, 209—pp. 191-2.

LONDON TO RIPON (by Knaresborough).

London to Wetherby (194¼)—p. 197.

Wetherby to Knaresborough (8—202¼); in Wetherby turn to *l.* after crossing *R.* Wharfe, and through Spofforth, 198. [Or follow the Great North Road to Kirk Deighton, 195¼, then on *l.* to Knaresborough.]

Knaresborough to Ripley (4½—206¾).

[Or beyond Spofforth keep to *l.* and through High Harrogate, 201¼, to *Ripley.*]

Ripley to Ripon (7¾—214½)—p. 192.

LONDON TO KENDAL (by Boroughbridge).

London to Boroughbridge (206¼)—p. 197.

Boroughbridge to Ripon (6—212¼); having crossed *R.* Ure outside Boroughbridge, keep to *l.* and again to *l.* at Kirkby Hill, 207¼; an undulating road through Hewicke, 210, but rather downhill for last 2*m.*; the surface is perfect.

Ripon to Masham (9½—221¾); there is a long gradual rise out of Ripon, and at first the road is good, but presently gets very bad and stony for 2*m.* before North Stainley, 216¼, through which the road falls gradually to *R.* Ure just before West Tanfield, 218¼; from here the road improves again, and there is a very long ascent to climb, on the top of which are obtained some grand and extensive views: in the last 1¼*m.* the road falls rapidly to *R.* Ure, across which Masham lies on a steep hill. [There is another road from Borough Bridge by following the Leeming lane or road as far as York Gate Inn, 213¼, as at p. 197, then turn to *l.* and through Nosterfield, 220¼, to Masham, 223¾, joining the above road 2½*m.* before it.]

(*Masham:* King's Head).

At Masham, on *l.*, Aldburgh Hall; on *r.*, Clifton Castle.

Masham to East Witton ($7—228\frac{3}{4}$); through Low Ellington, $224\frac{1}{4}$, and past Jerveaux Abbey, $226\frac{3}{4}$, the road now runs up the Ure valley, and is fairly good.

Jerveaux, called also Jervaulx, or Jervoise Abbey, was founded in 1141, and was a very rich community previous to the dissolution, since which it has been in ruins; it belongs to the Marquis of Aylesbury.

East Witton to Leyburn ($4\frac{1}{2}—233\frac{1}{4}$); the road gets rather rough over Cover Bridge, $229\frac{1}{4}$ (beyond which keep to *r.*), Ulshaw Bridge, $230\frac{1}{2}$ (*R.* Ure), and through Spennythorne, $232\frac{1}{4}$, and Harmby, $233\frac{1}{4}$.

At Cover Bridge, 1*m.* on *l.*, Middleham and ruins of castle, which was the residence of the celebrated Earl of Warwick, the king-maker. The road now enters some very pretty scenery, and follows the valley of *R.* Ure for about next 25*m.*, on the *north* bank.

Leyburn to Redmire ($4\frac{1}{2}—237\frac{3}{4}$); take the left hand road through Wensley, $234\frac{1}{4}$; bad surface.

The district here bears the name of Wensley Dale, and boasts of delightful scenery. At Redmire, on *r.*, the remain of Bolton Castle, in which Mary, Queen of Scots, was confined for 2 years.

Redmire to Askrigg ($7—244\frac{3}{4}$) through Carperby, $240\frac{1}{2}$, pretty good road in dry weather.

There are many grand and beautiful waterfalls in this neighbourhood. A little beyond Carperby, on *l.*, across the Ure is Aysgarth; 2*m.* off is Heaning Fall.

Askrigg to Hardrow ($5\frac{1}{2}—250\frac{1}{4}$); a little beyond Askrigg on *l.* across *R.* Ure, is Bainbridge. Before Hardrow on *l.* across *R.* Ure is Hawes, $250\frac{1}{2}$.

There are several pretty waterfalls or forces in the dale, as Cotter Force, Hardrow Force, &c.; near Hardrow, also, is Hardrow Scar.

Hardrow to Sedbergh ($14\frac{1}{2}—264\frac{3}{4}$); the road gradually rises, following the *R.* Ure, and for 3 or 4*m.* is quite unrideable to Thwaite Bridge, $253\frac{1}{4}$, where the Carlisle road branches off to *r.* up Ure valley, which the Sedbergh road leaves and now ascends the pass where it attains the height of 1,300ft.; having at length crossed over the ridge or watershed, the road is excellent and falls all the way down Garsdale, having Whernside Mountain on *l.*, and Bow Fell on *r.*, through Little Town, $258\frac{1}{4}$, and over Smorthwaite Bridge, $259\frac{1}{2}$, and Moorthwaite Bridge, $261\frac{1}{2}$.

(*Sedbergh:* Black Bull; Bull Inn.)

The scenery is very fine.

Sedbergh to Kendal ($10\frac{3}{4}—275\frac{1}{2}$); over *R.* Lune at Lincoln's Inn Bridge, 267, is a good road, but hilly to Kendal.

LONDON TO HAWES.

London to East Witton ($228\frac{3}{4}$)—above.

East Witton to Middleham ($1\frac{1}{2}—230\frac{1}{4}$); over Cover Bridge, $229\frac{1}{2}$, (beyond which keep *l.*), is rather rough and mostly uphill.

(*Middleham:* White Swan.)

The road now runs up the valley of the *R.* Ure for 25*m.*, through pretty and romantic scenery, keeping to the *south* bank of the river, which, however, can be crossed every few miles. At Middleham, the ruins of the castle, which was the residence of the celebrated Earl of Warwick, the "king-maker"; it is the scene of Bulwer Lytton's novel "The Last of the Barons."

Middleham to West Witton (5—235¼) is all against the collar, but otherwise a good road.
About halfway, on r. across R. Ure to Wensley, 2m., and Leyburn, 3m.; there is a toll to pay at the bridge.

West Witton to Aysgarth (3½—238¾); pretty good road through Swinethwaite, 236¼; hill to go down into Aysgarth, which is too steep to be ridden down safely.
Beyond West Witton on r. across R. Ure, to *Redmire*, 2m.; about 1½m. before Aysgarth a road turns to the left out of Wensley Dale to West Burton, 2m. passing by the way Aysgarth Force, but the surface is bad and rutty: beautiful and picturesque scenery.

Aysgarth to Bainbridge (4½—243¼); from the foot of Aysgarth Hill it is easy riding through Brush Worton, 242¼, to Bainbridge, where there is a steep pitch sharp to r. [Or ½m. beyond Aysgarth cross R. Ure to r. and go through Askrigg, 242½, a pretty good road, and 1m. further on recross R. Ure to Bainbridge, 244, which is a good road until you cross the new railway.]

Bainbridge to Hawes (4½—247¾); fair easy road.
At Hawes, on r. across R. Ure, to *Hardrow* (1¼—248½), which is 1¾m. shorter than by the preceding route.
(*Hawes*: White Hart.—*West Burton*: Black Bull.)

LONDON TO GLASGOW (by Stamford, &c.).

London to Scotch Corner (232¾)—p. 198.

Scotch Corner to Greta Bridge (10—242¾); turn to l. and follow a straight road through Smallways, 240¾.
At Smallways, on l., Barningham Hall.

Greta Bridge to Bowes (6—248¾); ½m. beyond Greta Bridge, keep to l.; very rough road.
A little beyond Greta Bridge, on r., Rokeby village, Egleston Abbey, and Barnard Castle town. Bowes was a Roman station, and has remains of a castle.

Bowes to Brough (13—261¾); the road now crosses the main Pennine range, over Stainmoor; it is nearly all a continuous uphill, some parts of the ascents being very stiff, the surface too being very rough and uneven, in many places unrideable, to Spittal House Inn, 254; then the road is up and down hill, but not quite so difficult though still rough, by Rear Cross, 254¾, and after 3 or 4m. improves gradually to Brough, approaching which is a long steep hill to descend, that should not be ridden down without a good brake. It is the best illustration of this stage, by way of comparison, that the road can only be said to be better than that from Kendal over Shap Fells to Shap.
(*Brough*: Ferry; Station.)
A little beyond Spittal Ho., on the borders of Yorkshire and Westmoreland, the road passes through the site of a Roman camp; past the moors, on l., Maiden Castle. At Brough, which was the Roman Verteræ, are ruins of a castle erected before the Conquest; the ch. is an ancient fabric, and contains a pulpit formed out of a single stone.

Brough to Appleby (8¼—270); a good but very hilly road.
(*Appleby*: King's Head; Tufton Arms.)

Appleby has been twice destroyed by the Scots, and the greater part of it was in ruins till the reign of Queen Mary. The castle was founded previous to the Conquest, but was almost all rebuilt in 1686; it contains many curious portraits and relics.

Appleby to Penrith (12¾—282¾); steep hill to mount out of Appleby, then an excellent road, but with several difficult hills, through Crackenthorp, 272, Kirkbythore, 274½, and Temple Sowerby, 276¼, (beyond which cross *R.* Eden), to the bridge over the R. Emont, 281¼, from which it is rather rough through Carlton, 281¾, into Penrith.

Just before crossing *R.* Emont, on *l.*, the ruins of Brougham Castle.

Penrith to Glasgow (113¾—396½); through Carlisle, 300¾, pp. 159—161.

LONDON TO BROUGH (by Richmond).

London to Catterick Bridge (229¼)—p. 198.

Catterick Bridge to Richmond (3¾—233); after crossing *R.* Swale, turn to *l.* at Citadella, 229¾, and it is a good gradually rising road up the valley of the Swale, through Brompton-upon-Swale, 230¼, and St. Trinians, 232.

(*Richmond:* King's Head; Queen's Head; Temperance; Unicorn.)

Richmond is beautifully situated, and surrounded by picturesque scenery; there are ruins of a castle founded soon after the Conquest, and also of St. Martin's Priory, St. Nicholas' Hospital, and of a Grey Friary.

Richmond to Reeth (9—242); continuing up Swaledale, through Marske, 237½, and Fremington, 241½, is a good and fairly level road.

Reeth to Muker (10½—252½); the road still runs up Swaledale, through Healaugh, 243½, Featham, 246, and Gunnerside, 248¾, crossing *R.* Swale at Ivey Bridge, 250½.

Muker to Kirkby Stephen (14—266½); the road runs up to the head of Swaledale, through Scar Head, 253½, Angeram, 254½, and Thorne, 255, for nearly 10*m.*, then it is all downhill through Nateby, 265¼; very hilly road, crossing over the moors most of the way.

Kirkby Stephen to Brough (4¾—271¼); by Brough Sowerby, 270.

[There is another road from *Reeth* by turning to *r.* through Argengarthdale, 245, after which the road crosses the moors, and is exceedingly hilly, and in most places very rough and bad as far as Barras, 258, thence good and mostly downhill to Brough, 262.]

About 4*m.* before Kirkby Stephen, the mountain on *r.* is called Nine Standards Hill. On *l.*, 1½*m.*, Pendragon Castle on the Askrigg road.

LONDON TO GRETA BRIDGE (by Richmond).

London to Richmond (233)—above.

Richmond to Greta Bridge (10½—243½); just before entering Richmond take the middle road at the cross roads, and through Kirkby Hill, 237½, and Smallways, 241½, it is rather hilly, but has a good surface on the whole, though inclined to be bad in places. [There is another road by taking the right fork at the cross roads and through Gilling, 235¾, a mile beyond which join the road from Scotch Corner, as at p. 205, and on to Greta Bridge, 244½.]

LONDON TO HALTWHISTLE.

London to Greta Bridge (242¾)—p. 205.

Greta Bridge to Barnard Castle (3½—246¼); ½*m.* beyond Greta Bridge keep to *r.* by Rokeby Park and Eglestone Abbey, crossing *R.* Tees just before Barnard Castle; the road is pretty good.

(*Barnard Castle:* King's Head.)

Barnard Castle is the scene of Sir Walter Scott's "Rokeby." It derives its name from a castle erected here at the end of the 11th century, but now in ruins. 2*m.* N.E. is Streatlam Castle, surrounded by beautiful scenery.

Barnard Castle to Middleton-in-Teesdale (9½—255¾); instead of going through Barnard Castle, the road keeps on the right bank of *R.* Tees all the way through Lartington, 248¾, Cotherstone, 250¼, Romald-Kirk, 252¼, and Mickleton, 254¼; it is a fair road, but bad in wet weather. Lovely scenery. [There is another road by going *through* Barnard Castle, beyond the town turning to *l.*, and through Egglestone.]

On *r.*, Lartington Hall. On *l.*, Egglestone Hall. On *r.*, Middleton *Ho.*

Middleton-in-Teesdale to Alston or Aldstone Moor (17½—273¼); up the Tees valley along the left bank, through Newbiggin, 259¼, Harwood, 265¼, across the Moors, and through Carrigillgate, 269¾, is hilly and an indifferent road; mostly uphill for about 12*m.*, and then on the fall. Wild scenery.

3*m.* beyond Newbiggin, the cataract of High Force; 4*m.* further on that of Cauldron Snout.

Alston to Haltwhistle (12½—285¾); through Whitley, 276, Thornhope, 277¾, Knaresdale, 279¾ (keep to *r.*), and by Featherstonhaugh Castle, 283¼.

At Haltwhistle, Castel Banks, Schill Hill, and Whitchester, a Roman camp.

LONDON TO TYNEMOUTH.

London to Topcliffe (212¾)—p. 201.

Topcliffe to Thirsk (5—217¾); keep to *r.* and by Thornfield Houses, 215¾.

(*Thirsk:* Fleece.)

Thirsk formerly possessed a castle, which was destroyed in the reign of Henry II., and from its ruins the *ch.* is said to have been built; the latter is a fine Gothic building with many monuments.

Thirsk to Tontine Inn (12—229¾); very lumpy road through South Kilvington, 218¾, North Kilvington, 219¾, Knayton, 221¾, Borrowby, 222¾, Leak, 223¾, by Jeator Houses, 226¼, and Mount Grace, 228¾.

At Mount Grace are the ruins of the Priory.

Tontine Inn to Yarm (8—237¾); keep to *l.*, and it is a very lumpy road through Trenholme, 231¾, Crathorne, 234¼, and Kirklevington, 235¾; through Yarm is all cobblestone paving, which will necessitate walking.

Yarm is a romantic old town. About 2*m.* S.E. is Kirk Castle.

Yarm to Stockton-on-Tees (4—241¾); after crossing the narrow bridge over *R.* Tees, there is a very steep hill to climb out of Yarm, and then it is a very lumpy road down the valley of the Tees; the streets of Stockton are macadam and very rough.

Stockton-on-Tees: Argyle; Black Lion.)

Stockton-on-Tees to Sunderland (26—267¾); very hilly road and rather rough by Norton Inn, 243¼ (where keep to *r.*), Billingham *Tp.*, 244¼, through Wolviston, 245¾, by Red Lion Inn, 249¼, through Elwick, 250¼, Sheraton, 252¾, by Castle Eden Inn, 255¼, and through Shotton, 256¼, Easington, 257½, Cold Hasledon, 260¾, Dalton-le-Dale, 261¾, Seaham, 263, Ryhope, 264¼, and Bishop Wearmouth, 267; rough cobblestone paving in Sunderland except wood pavement along High street.

(*Sunderland:* Queen's, *Hqrs.*)

At Elwick, on *r.* to Hartlepool, 5½*m*; here are some remains of a monastery of Franciscan Grey Friars, established in the 13th century; there are also considerable remains of the town walls, and on the coast several natural caverns. Castle Eden is a fine castellated mansion. At Bishop Wearmouth, on *l.*, Hilton Castle, the baronial residence of the Hiltons from the time of Athelstan to 1746.

Sunderland to Tynemouth (9¼—277); proceed along Bridge street and over the Iron Bridge, 268½, (*R.* Wear); then from the outskirts of Wearmouth, 268¾, it is a good road by Fulwell Inn, 269¾, to Fulwell *Tp.*, 270, where is Fulwell Bank to descend, rather steep, then rather shaky to to Cleadon, 271½, and pretty good undulating road through Harton, 273¼, Harton *Tp.*, 273¾, and Westoe, 274, to South Shields, 275, then cross *R.* Tyne to North Shields, 275½; there is a longish incline out of Sunderland, and run down into South Shields.

At Tynemouth are remains of the castle and priory.

LONDON TO EDINBURGH (by Coldstream).

London to Morpeth (288¾)—p. 199.

Morpeth to Glanton (21—309¾); at Loaning *Tp.*, 291, keep to *l.*, and it is a very fair road through Longhorsley *Tg.*, 295¼, over Weldon Bridge, 298¼, Low Framlington, 299, Long Framlington, 300, by Rimside House, 303½, over Rimside Moor and through Whittingham, 308.

At Weldon Bridge, on *l.*, Brinkburn Priory, formerly of the Black Canons, in the reign of Henry I.

Glanton to Wooler (10¾—320½); by Percy's Cross, 313, and Woolerhaugh Head, 318¾, is a good road.

(*Wooler:* Red Lion; Tankerville Arms.)

At Whittingham, on *l.*, Carlington Castle, Callaly Castle, and Eslington. At Wooler, 2 or 3*m.* on *r.*, Chillingham Castle, famous for the breed of wild cattle preserved here. Percy's Cross, erected in memory of Sir Ralph Percy, slain here in 1463, in a skirmish. At Wooler, on *l.*, Homildon Hill, the scene of a defeat of the Scots in 1402.

Wooler to Coldstream (14—334½); a good easy road, running down the valley of *R.* Till, through Akeld, 323¼ (keep to *r.*), Millfield, 326¼, to Pallinsburn, 329¾, then turn to *l.*, and there is a hill to mount and descend to Cornhill, 333¼, whence cross *R.* Tweed and enter Scotland.

(*Coldstream:* Newcastle Arms, *B.T.C.*)

Beyond Akeld, on *l.*, on banks of *R.* Glen, Copeland Castle. Near Millfield, on *l.*, Flodden Field, where James IV. of Scotland was defeated and slain by the English, under the Earl of Surrey, in 1513. On *r.*, across *R.* Till, Ford Castle. At Cornhill, 3*m.* on *r.*, on the banks of the Tweed *R.*, is Twizel Castle, and near it Otteaton Castle.

Coldstream to Kelso (8¾—343¼); the road is good and almost level, running up the Tweed valley; keep to *l.* at Coldstream *Tp.*, 336.

[There is another road from Cornhill by turning to *l.* and following the south bank of *R.* Tweed through Castle Wark (ruins), Carham, and Sprouston; distance about the same. Or from Akeld by turning to *l.*, following the course of *R.* Glen, by Battle Stone, 324½, through Kirk Newton, 325¾, Kilham, 328½, cross *R.* Glen, to Mindrum, 330½, and by Potts Close, 334¾, to *Kelso*, 339¼.]

(*Kelso*: Queen's Head, *B.T.C.*)

At Kelso are the remains of an abbey, founded in 1128.

Kelso to Lauder (17—360¼); through Smallholm, 349¼, and Bridge End, 356¾.

On *r.*, at Lauder, Thirlestane Castle.

Lauder to Dalkeith (18¾—379); by Carfrae Mill Inn, 364¼, Channel Kirk Inn, 366¼, Falla, 371, Costerton Inn, 372, and Path Head, 374½.

[There is another road from Coldstream to Carfrae Mill Inn by Coldstream *Tp.*, 336, Orange Lane Inn, 339¾, Plowland *Tp.*, 341¾, *Greenlaw*, 344½, Whiteburn Inn, 352, Dodd Mill, 353, Thirlestane, 354, Norton, 356¼, to Carfrae Mill Inn, 359¾.]

At Greenlaw, on *l.*, Hume Castle. At Dalkeith are Newbattle Abbey, Melville Castle, and Dalkeith Palace.

Dalkeith to Edinburgh (6¼—385¼).

[The shorter road is through Coldstream and Greenlaw to Edinburgh, 380¾.]

LONDON TO EDINBURGH (by Jedburgh).

London to Newcastle-upon-Tyne (274)—p. 199.

Newcastle-upon-Tyne to Lauder (78¼—352¼); leave Newcastle by Barrack Road, over Town Moor (west side), and it is all up and down, sharp but short hills, through Kenton *Tp.*, 277, Woolsington, 278½, to *Ponteland*, 281½, with fair surface; then by Higham Dykes, 284, and Belsay Castle, 287¼, over good surface and level road, by *Belsay*, 289 (keep to *l.*), Low *Ho.*, 289½, and *Wallington*, 292¼, to Kirk Whelpington, 295; then over Harwood Moor through Elsdon, 302¾, Otterburn, 304¾, *Ellishaw*, 308, Bagrave, 309½, Rochester, 312, Buryness, 315, Lumsden, 317¼, Carter Fell *Tp.*, 322 (enter Scotland), Doveford Bridge, 326½, *Jedburgh*, 332¼, Ancrum *Tp.*, 335¼, Newton, 341¼, and by *Fly Bridge*, 343¼, it is a give and take road, very hilly, as it crosses over the Cheviot Hills, but with good surface.

(*Jedburgh*: Red Lion.)

Beyond Wallington, 2*m.* on *r.*, Rothley Castle. At Higham Dykes on *r.*, Ogle Castle. Otterburn was the scene of the celebrated battle of Chevy Chase, in 1388; near it is Otterburn Castle. At Jedburgh are remains of the beautiful Abbey, part of it now the parish *ch.* At Fly Bridge, on *l.*, Melrose and ruins of the Abbey.

Lauder to Edinburgh (21—373¼)—above; through Dalkeith, 367.

LONDON TO JEDBURGH (by Corbridge).

London to West Auckland (246¼)—p. 198.

West Auckland to Witton-le-Wear (4½—250¾); keep first to *l.*, then to *r.*, and there is a steep climb on to Toft Hill, 248½, followed by a long descent to the bridge over *R.* Wear.

Before Wear bridge, on *r.*, Witton Castle.

Witton-le-Wear to Allan's Ford (13—263¾); keep to *l.* and by Hordon Head, 252¾, Harperley Gate or Lane Head, 253¾, Towlaw, 256¼, and Cold Rowley, 262¼.

On *l.*, Harperley Park; 3*m.* past Towlaw, on *r.*, Butsfield Abbey and Byerley Hall. At Cold Rowley, on *l.*, White Hall.

Allan's Ford to Corbridge (12—275¾); by Green Head Inn, 266, Unthank, 268¾, and Riding, 273¾, and 1½*m.* further keep to *r.* and cross *R.* Tyne. Returning, at Riding keep to *r.*

At Unthank, on *l.*, Minster Acres.

Corbridge to Colwell (7¾—283½); by Wheatsheaf Inn, 278½, where join Watling Street, and follow it to Colwell.

Beyond Corbridge, on *l.*, Sandhoe and Beaufront. On *r.*, Aydon Castle.

Colwell to Corsenside, *ch.* (9¾—293¼); by Tone Pitt Inn, 286¾, and over Woodburne Bridge, 291½.

Beyond Colwell, on *l.*, Swinburn Castle. At Tone Pitt Inn, on *r.*, Careycoats.

Corsenside to Ellishaw (4—297¼), through Troughend, 295¾.

Ellishaw to Jedburgh (24¼—321½)—p. 209.

LONDON TO SUNDERLAND (by Durham).

London to Durham (259½)—p. 198.

Durham to Houghton-le-Spring (6¾—266¼); in Durham turn to *r.* after crossing *R.* Wear once, and there is a pretty steep ascent out of the city, then good road by Blue House, 262, and through Rainton Pitt Houses or West Rainton, 263½, and East Rainton, 264½.

(*Houghton-le-Spring:* White Lion.)

Houghton-le-Spring to Sunderland (6¼—272½); steep ascent from Houghton, and then a good road, though hilly through East Harrington, 268¾, and Bishop Wearmouth, 271¾; heavy in wet weather; rough cobblestone paving through Sunderland, except the middle of the town, which is paved with wood along High street.

LONDON TO EDINBURGH (by York).

London to Bawtry (153¼)—p. 196.

Bawtry to Thorne (13½—166¾); turn a little to *r.* in Bawtry and through Austerfield, 154½, Finningley, 157¼, Blaxton, 158¼, Torne Bridge, 160¼, Hatfield Woodhouse, 163¼, and Bearwood Green, 164; for first 3 or 4*m.* undulating, then level.

(*Thorne:* Green Dragon; Greyhound; Red Lion; White Hart.)

On *r.*, at Hatfield Woodhouse, is Hatfield Chase.

Thorne to Snaith (7—173¾); level road, running near *R.* Don for 4*m.*, then over New Bridge, 171¼, and to *l.* over Turnbridge, 172¼.

(*Snaith:* Downe Arms.)

Snaith to Selby (8—181¾); cross *R.* Aire, and through Carleton, 175¾, Camblesforth, 177½, over Camblesforth Moor to Botany Bay Inn, 180¼; Selby is roughly paved.

(*Selby*: Londesborough Arms.)

At Carleton, 2 or 3m. on r., Drax Abbey. At Selby are remains of an abbey founded by William the Conqueror, whose son Henry I. was born here.

Selby to York (14¼—196¼); cross R. Ouse, and go through Barlby, 183¼ (keep to l.), Riccall, 185½, Escrick, 188¾, Deighton, 190, and Gate Fulford, 194½; it is level but not a good road, being narrow and rutty in many parts, but improves towards York. Country very flat and uninteresting.

(*York*: Black Swan; Hartrer's; North Eastern; Queen's; Scawin's; Station; White Swan Inn; York.)

York, the Roman Eboracum, is a fine city; perhaps most celebrated for its magnificent cathedral, the largest and most beautiful of its kind in the kingdom; it was founded in 626, and the present building dates from 1228. There are also remains of the city walls; the castle, including Clifford's Tower, supposed to be Roman; ruins of St. Mary's Abbey; Yorkshire Museum and Gardens; Assembly Rooms, &c.

York to Easingwold (13½—209¾); bad and heavy road through Clifton, 197¾, Rawcliff *Tp.*, 199¾, and Skelton, 200¾, to Shipton, 202¼, then capital going through Tollerton Lanes, 206, and Shire Houses, 208.

(*Easingwold*: George, B.T.C.)

Easingwold to Thirsk (10¼—220); by White Houses, 211¼, through Thormanby, 213¾, Birdforth, 214¼, and Bagby Common *Tg.*, 217.

Thirsk to Northallerton (8¾—228¾); after crossing the bridge in Thirsk keep to r., and it is a splendid road through Thornton-le-Street, 222¾; formerly it was part of the Great North Road.

Northallerton to Edinburgh (170¼—399); through Darlington, 244¾, Sunderland Bridge, 258¾, Durham, 263, Chester-le-Street, 269, Newcastle-upon-Tyne, 274½, Morpeth, 292¼, Alnwick, 311½, Belford, 326, and Berwick-upon-Tweed, 341—pp. 201-202.

LONDON TO YORK (by Tadcaster).

London to Brotherton (178½)—p. 197; keep to right entering Brotherton.

Brotherton to Tadcaster (12—190½); the road is a little easier as to hills, but still indifferent and rough to South Milford, 182¼, after which there is rather an improvement through Sherburn, 183½, Barkston, 185, and Towton, 187¼, with a nice run down when approaching Tadcaster.

(*Tadcaster*: Londesborough, B.T.C.)

At Towton, on l., Towton Field, where the Lancastrians were routed by Edward IV., in 1461.

Tadcaster to York (9—199½); keep to r. in Tadcaster, and it is a flat, uninteresting, rough, and patchy road by Street Houses, 193¾, and Dring Houses, 198¼; in wet weather very bad, improves towards York, and the last mile or two is good going.

At Dring, on r., Bishopthorpe, the palace of the Archbishop of York.

LONDON TO YORK (by Askern).

London to Doncaster (162¼)—p. 196.

Doncaster to Askorn (7—169¾); turn to *r.* just beyond Doncaster, and it is a pretty good and level road through Bentley and Owston.

Askern to Selby (13—182¼); through Haddesley, 179¾, is a very bad road, though level all the way; it is stony and rutty, being made of a soft kind of limestone, which when worn down gives a clayey surface, rough and rutty when dry.

Selby to York (14½—196¾)—p. 210.

LONDON TO GUISBOROUGH AND REDCAR.

London to Tontine Inn (229¾)—p. 207.

Tontine Inn to Stokesley (7½—237¼); keep to *r.* through Arncliffe, 230¼, and Whorlton, 232.
(*Stokesley*: Black Swan, *B.T.C.*)
At Whorlton, on *r.*, Whorlton Castle.

Stokesley to Guisborough (8—245¼); very good road through Great Ayton, 239¾, Newton, 241½, and Pinchinthorp, 242½.
(*Guisborough*: Buck; Cock.—*Great Ayton*: Temperance.)
At Newton, on *r.*, is Roseberry Topping, a remarkable hill, from which is obtained a splendid view.

Guisborough to Redcar (8—253¼); the road rapidly deteriorates to Kirk Leatham, 250¼, after which it is very bad and stony to Redcar; level.
(*Redcar*: Red Lion, *B.T.C.*)
On *r.*, Skelton Castle and Upleatham Hall.

LONDON TO KIRBY MOORSIDE.

London to York (196¼)—p. 211.

York to Stillington (11—207¼); through Wiggington, 200¾, and Sutton-on-the-Forest, 204¼, through the district formerly known as the Forest of Galtres.

Stillington to Gilling (7—214¼). On *l.* pass Crake Castle, and at Gilling on *l.* Gilling Castle.

Gilling to Helmsley—or Helmsley Blackmoor (5—219¼); level and fairly good road through Oswaldkirk, 215¼, and Sproxton, 217¾.
(*Helmsley*: Royal Oak.)
At Oswaldkirk, about 3m. on *l.*, ruins of Byland Abbey, 4m. from Helmsley, and well worth a visit, though it is only reached on foot. On *l.* of the town, Duncombe Park, Lord Feversham. 3m. N.W. are the ruins of Rivaulx Abbey, founded in 1181 by Cistercian monks.

Helmsley to Kirby Moorside (5½—224¾); turn to *r.* and through Nawton, 221¾.

LONDON TO WHITBY.

London to York (196¼)—p. 211.

York to Spittle Bridge (10¾—207); level for first 5m., then a gradual rise over Stockton Moor, and for 1½m. past Lobster House Inn, 204, and a little downhill again to Spittle Bridge; it is not a good road, being very sandy, and soft and heavy going in wet weather; railway crossing at Barton Hill Station, a little before Spittle Bridge.

At Lobster House Inn, 3*m.* on *l.*, ruins of Sheriff Hutton Castle.

Spittle Bridge to Malton (7¼—214¼); very long hill to ascend to Whitwell-on-the-Hill, 208½, then downhill for a mile, followed by a corresponding rise, and the last 3*m.* chiefly downhill into Malton; good surface, but sticky and heavy in wet weather.

(*Malton:* George; Old Globe; Rose and Crown; Royal Oak; Sun; Talbot.)

At Whitwell, 2*m.* on *l.*, Castle Howard, the magnificent seat of the Earl of Carlisle. At Malton (called also New Malton) are the remains of an ancient castle.

Malton to Pickering (8½—222¾); keep to *l.*, and it is hilly but not very rough through Old Malton, 215¼, and How Bridge, 217¾.

(*Pickering:* Black Lion; White Swan.)

Pickering contains a spacious and ancient *ch.*, and the ruins of a castle, which was besieged by the Parliamentarians. About 3*m.* N.W., at Cawthorne, are remains of 2 Roman camps, and beyond, at Cropton, of a British one. Further on are the ruins of Rosedale Abbey.

Pickering to Saltergate (8½—231¼); the road is hilly but rideable through Lockton, 227¾, with a very steep descent into Saltergate.

Saltergate to Whitby (11¾—243); the road goes over the moors for the greater part of the way and is very hilly, the hills being either too steep or too rough for riding without a brake, and in parts little better than a rough grassy track, through Silla Cross, 236¼, to Sleights, 238¾, where it leaves the moors by a tremendously steep winding hill, at the bottom of which is a level railway crossing; from here the road improves and follows the valley of *R.* Esk through Carr End, 239¼, and Ruswarp, 241.

(*Whitby:* Crown; Royal.)

At Whitby are the remains of the abbey *ch.*; also St. Mary's *ch.*, approached by 190 steps; fine piers, town-house, library, museum, baths, &c. 3*m.* distant is Mulgrave Castle (Marquis of Normanby).

LONDON TO SCARBOROUGH.

London to Malton (214¼)—above.

Malton to Rillington (4½—218¾); turn to *r.* in Malton, and there is a descent to *R.* Derwent, which cross to Norton, 214¾, and the rest is almost level, with a gentle rise to Scagglethorp *Tg.*, 217¼; the surface is not so good.

Rillington to Snainton (8—226¾); the road is still bad; about 1½*m.* beyond Rillington keep to *l.*, and there is a little downhill to Knapton Station, 221¼, where is a level railway crossing, and the rest is level over Yeddingham Bridge, 223¼ (*R.* Derwent), to Snainton.

Snainton to Scarborough (9¾—236½); out of Snainton is a slight ascent, then level, and all an excellent road, through Brompton, 228½, Wykeham, 230, Hutton Bushel, 230¾, and West Ayton, 231¼, to East Ayton, 231¾, out of which, after crossing *R.* Derwent, is a very steep hill to mount, rising 226 ft. in 1½*m.*; on the top is a good run over an excellent level road through Stepney, 233¾, and Falsgrave, 235½, and past the racecourse, with fine views of scenery; big hill to descend into Scarborough, very steep at the bottom.

(*Scarborough*: Crown; Grand; Prince of Wales; Queen; Royal; White Horse Inn.)

At Wykeham, on *r.*, Wykeham Abbey, a noble mansion, erected on the site of a priory founded 1153. Scarborough is the Brighton of the North East coast, and during the autumn is a great resort of the nobility and gentry. It combines splendid sea-bathing, with a mineral Spa: there are assembly rooms; theatre; libraries, &c.; also a ruinous old castle, built in the reign of King Stephen, and besieged twice by the Parliamentarians, who dismantled it. Beautiful and romantic scenery in the neighbourhood.

LONDON TO MARKET WEIGHTON

London to Thorne (166¾)—p. 210.

Thorne to Howden (13¼—180); level road, running near *R.* Don for 4*m.*, then over New Bridge. 171¼, and 1*m.* further keep to *r.* through Rawcliffe, 173½, and Armin, 176¾, and cross *R.* Ouse at Booth Ferry, 178¼.

At Howden are *ch.* and ancient palace of the Bishops of Durham.

Howden to Market Weighton (12—192); leaving Howden keep to *l.* through Benland, 181¾, by Howden Grange, 183½, over Welham Bridge, 185, through Holme, 187, and across Spalding Moor: quite level.

(*Market Weighton*: Half Moon, *B.T.C.*)

LONDON TO CROWLE.

London to Newark (124½)—p. 196

Newark to Newton (14¼—138¾); leaving Newark turn to *r.* along the Roman Fosse Way for a mile, and after crossing over the railway turn off to *l.* and through Winthorpe, 126½, Langford, 128, Collingham, 130, Besthorpe, 132, and Girton, 133¼.

Newton to Gainsborough (10½—149¼); through Torksey, 142¼, Marton, 144¼, Knaith, 146¼, and Lea, 147¼.

(*Gainsborough*: Black Head; White Hart.)

Gainsborough to Epworth (10¾—160); through Morton, 150¾, East Stockwith, 152½, cross *R.* Trent, through West Stockwith, 153, along the left bank of the Trent to Owston, 157, and then to *l.*

Epworth to Crowle (7—167); entering Epworth keep to *r.* and through Belton, 162.

LONDON TO BURTON-UPON-STATHER.

London to Gainsborough (149¼)—above.

Gainsborough to Scotter (8¼—157½); a little out of Gainsborough turn to *r.* and through Blyton, 152¾, and Scotton, 156¼

Scotter to Burton-upon-Stather (11½—169); through Messingham, 160, Froddingham, 164, Scunthorpe, 164½, Crosby, 165, and Normanby, 168.

LONDON TO WHITBY (by Lincoln).

London to Norman Cross (76)—p. 195.

Norman Cross to Peterborough (5¾—81¾); turn to *r.* and it is a level and good road till nearing Peterborough, when it becomes rough; just before Peterborough cross *R.* Nen; paved through the town.

(*Peterborough:* Crown; Granville Temperance.)

Peterborough is a small but well-built town; the cathedral was formerly a Benedictine abbey, founded in early Saxon times, but the present building was erected at different periods in the 12th, 13th, and 15th centuries.

Peterborough to Market Deeping (8—89¾); through Walton, 84¼, Werrington, 84¾, Glinton, 86½ (keep to *r.*), and Northborough, 88¼, is level but a rough uneven road, made with granite.

(*Market Deeping:* New Inn.)

Market Deeping to Bourn (7¾—97½); fairly level and good road through Langtoft, 92, Baston, 93¼, over Kate's Bridge, 94, and through Thurlby, 95¼.

(*Bourn:* Crown.)

About 3*m.* on *l.*, is Grimsthorpe Castle, the seat of Lord Willoughby d'Eresby, an irregular castellated building, with a beautiful chapel and a fine collection of paintings. At Bourn are traces of the site of an Augustinian priory.

Bourn to Folkingham (8¾—106¼); through Morton, 100, and Aslackby, 104¼, is a wretched road.

At Folkingham are some slight remains of a castle.

Folkingham to Sleaford (9—115¼); through Newton Goss, 108½, Osbornby, 109¼, Aswarby, 110½, and Silk Willoughby, 113¼.

(*Sleaford:* Bristol Arms; Lion.)

At Sleaford handsome *ch.* erected in the 13th century, and containing several remarkable monuments: 2 or 3*m.* on *r.* are remains of Haverholme Priory. Aswarby *Ho.*

Sleaford to Green Man Inn (9¼—124½); through Holdingham, 116¾, and Leasingham, 117¼.

Beyond Leasingham, on *r.*, Bloxham Hall. Before Green Man Inn, on *r.*, Blankney Hall.

Green Man Inn to Lincoln (8¾—133¼); the road crosses over Lincoln Heath, by Dunston Pillar, 126¾.

(*Lincoln:* Club; Great Northern; Saracen's Head; Spread Eagle; White Hart..

Dunston Pillar is a quadrangular stone shaft, about 100 feet high, erected on the heath as a guide for travellers. Beyond, on *r.*, Nocton Hall, Branston Hall, and Canwick Hall. Lincoln, the Lindum Colonia of the Romans, is one of the few cities containing part of a Roman wall, viz: the Newport Gate. The city abounds in antiquities; the chief building is the beautiful cathedral, situate on a hill whence it is visible many miles around, and containing many old monuments besides a Roman pavement, &c.; it also has a large bell, Great Tom of Lincoln; there are also ruins of the Bishop's Palace, remains of the castle erected by William the Conqueror, and the remains of John of Gaunt's Palace.

Lincoln to Spital-in-the-Street (11½—144¾); this is a continuation of the Roman Ermine street, and runs in a straight line past Midge Inn, 138¾; there is a steep ascent from Lincoln, then level with a steep descent to Spital.

About 3*m.* beyond Midge Inn, on *l.*, Summer Castle, a fine castellated mansion. Beyond it, Glentworth. Before Spital, on *r.*, Cainby Hall.

Spital-in-the-Street to Brigg, or Glanford Bridge (11¾—156½); following Ermine street for 5*m.*, and then to *r.* through Redbourne, 151¼, and Hibaldstow, 152¾, the road becomes worse and worse, being made of a whitish stone, very soft and greasy when wet; about 2*m.* beyond Hibaldstow is a level railway crossing over the M. S. & L. line, after which the road is harder; Brigg is paved; a mile before the town turn to *r.*

(*Brigg:* Angel.)

Beyond Spital, on *r.*, Norton Place. On turning to *r.*, 1*m.* before Brigg, about 4*m.* N., are the ruins of Thornham Abbey.

Brigg to Barton-on-Humber ($10\frac{3}{4}$—$167\frac{1}{4}$); leaving Brigg, keep to *l.* and again a mile further on.

(*Barton:* George.)

$3\frac{1}{2}$*m.* beyond Brigg, on *r.*, Elsham Hall. At Barton, St. Peter's *ch.* is an early Norman building, the tower having been erected about the time of the Conquest.

Barton-on-Humber to Hull (7—$174\frac{1}{4}$); through Barton to Waterside, $167\frac{3}{4}$, whence cross *R.* Humber by ferry to Hull. [There is another road by turning to *r.* in Barton and going along the lanes through Barrow, $169\frac{3}{4}$, to New Holland, $172\frac{1}{4}$, to which there is a hill to descend, and then by ferry to Hull, $175\frac{1}{4}$.]

(*Hull:* Cross Keys; George, *B.T.C.*; Paragon; Railway; Royal Station; Temperance.)

About 5*m.* E. of Barton are Thornton College and the ruins of Thornton Abbey or Priory, founded in 1139. Hull, or Kingston-upon-Hull, is the fourth seaport of England. The ancient gates of the town still remain.

Hull to Beverley (9—$183\frac{1}{4}$); through Newlands, $176\frac{1}{2}$, Dunswell, 179, and Woodmansea, $181\frac{1}{2}$, is level and fair going in fine weather.

[There is another road from *Barton* by crossing from Waterside to Hessle, $171\frac{1}{4}$, and then through Anlaby, 173, Kirk Ella, $173\frac{3}{4}$, and Skidby, $176\frac{1}{4}$, to *Beverley*, $180\frac{1}{4}$; after Anlaby it is rather hilly.]

(*Beverley:* Beverley Arms.)

Beyond Newlands, 2*m.* on *l.*, Cottingham Castle. At Beverley, the beautiful collegiate *ch.* of St. John, or Minster, containing some handsome monuments of the Percys; also St. Mary's *ch.*

Beverley to Driffield ($13\frac{1}{4}$—$196\frac{1}{2}$); going out of Beverley at the Gate keep to *r.* and again to *r.* at Molescroft, $184\frac{1}{4}$, and then through Leconfield, 186, Scorborough, $187\frac{1}{2}$, Beswick, $189\frac{3}{4}$, Watton, 191, and Hutton Cranswick, 193; good road, an improvement on the last stage, and there are no hills of any consequence except a stiff pull up a longish hill after Watton.

(*Driffield:* Bell; Buck; Keys; Red Lion.)

At Watton, on *r.*, Watton Abbey.

Driffield to Bridlington ($11\frac{1}{2}$—208); soon after leaving Driffield there is a hill to ascend followed by a steep run down, and then a succession of up hill and down, but none of any moment, through Nafferton, 199, Bracy Bridge, $201\frac{1}{4}$, Burton Agnes, $202\frac{3}{4}$, Thornholm, $203\frac{3}{4}$, Haysthorpe, $204\frac{1}{2}$, Carnaby, $205\frac{3}{4}$, and Bessingby, $206\frac{1}{2}$; good road, but rather soft and heavy after rain.

(*Bidlington Quay:* Britannia; Brunswick.)

At Bridlington are some vestiges of an Augustine priory, founded in the reign of Henry I., and to which the town owed its origin. About 1*m.* S.E., is Bridlington Quay, a great resort for sea-bathing and its mineral springs. $3\frac{1}{2}$*m.* E. of Bridlington, through Sewerby 2*m.*, is the fishing village of Flamborough, where is a ruined Danish Tower and an ancient *ch.*: 2*m.* further is the promontory of Flamborough Head.

Bridlington to Reighton ($5\frac{1}{2}$—$213\frac{1}{2}$); for the first mile or two there are some fine sea views, then the road turns inland, and is nearly all uphill, going through a bleak and somewhat desolate-looking country at the back of Flamborough Head: the road is sandy and stony, being repaired with sea pebbles, and very hilly.

Across the back of Flamborough Head is an ancient earthwork, called Danes' Dyke.

Reighton to Gristhorpe (7—220$\frac{1}{2}$); through Hunmanby, 216$\frac{1}{2}$, and Muston, 218$\frac{3}{4}$, is undulating and rather better going. [There is another road on *r.*, direct to Muston along the cliffs instead of going through Hunmanby; $\frac{1}{2}$*m.* shorter.]

1*m.* before Gristhorpe, on *r.*, is Filey, out of which, on the Scarborough road, is a hill to mount through the Fairies' Glen.

Gristhorpe to Scarborough (5—225$\frac{1}{2}$); rough and hilly road, winding over the cliffs, and just before Scarborough there are two or three sharp up and down hills, and after mounting the last stiff hill there follows a fine run down into the town past Oliver's Mount.

[There are two other routes from Driffield to Scarborough.

The first by Kendal *Ho.*, 198, Lantoft, 202$\frac{1}{2}$, Foxholes, 206$\frac{1}{2}$, Staxton, 210$\frac{3}{4}$, Seamer, 213$\frac{3}{4}$, and Falsgrave, 216$\frac{3}{4}$, to Scarborough, 217$\frac{3}{4}$, is terribly hilly, with long hill to descend into Scarborough, very steep at the bottom.

The second route is through Nafferton, 199 (shortly after keep to *l.*), Kilham, 202$\frac{1}{2}$, and North Burton, 208$\frac{1}{2}$, to Hunmanby, 212$\frac{1}{2}$, whence to Scarborough, 221$\frac{1}{2}$; rather hilly road but better than the direct one.]

Scarborough to Cloughton (4$\frac{1}{2}$—230); through Burniston, 229, the road is undulating and just passable.

At Cloughton, on *l.*, Hackness Hall.

Cloughton to Whitby (13$\frac{3}{4}$—243$\frac{3}{4}$); the road goes across the moors through Stainton Dale, 233, by Peak Alum Works, 235$\frac{1}{2}$, Mill Beck, 237$\frac{1}{4}$, and through Thorpe Town, 238$\frac{1}{2}$, Hawsker, 240$\frac{1}{2}$, and Stainsacre Lane, 241$\frac{1}{4}$; as far as Hawsker not $\frac{1}{4}$*m.* altogether can be ridden, while some of the hills are dreadfully steep; the surface is a mass of broken stones, the rains apparently washing all the earth away from them: from Hawsker to the hill leading down into Whitby the road is just passable, but the hill must be walked down.

LONDON TO LINCOLN (by Newark).

London to Newark (124$\frac{1}{2}$)—p. 196.

Newark to Lincoln (16—140$\frac{1}{2}$); in Newark turn to *r.* and the road is a continuation of the Roman Fosse Way, through Winthorpe Lane, 126$\frac{1}{2}$, by Halfway *Ho.*, 132$\frac{1}{2}$, and through Bracebridge, 138$\frac{1}{2}$; it is fairly level but a bad road, being partly a narrow lane and partly a wide grass-grown road with a mere track in the middle: the surface is very soft and heavy going; about 3*m.* before Lincoln the road is better.

LONDON TO LINCOLN (by Grantham).

London to Grantham (110$\frac{1}{4}$)—p. 195.

Grantham to Leadenham (10$\frac{1}{2}$—120$\frac{3}{4}$); in Grantham turn to *r.* and through Belton, 112$\frac{3}{4}$ (keep to *l.*), Syston, 113$\frac{3}{4}$, Barkston, 114$\frac{1}{2}$ (keep to *r*.), Honington, 115¼, Carlton Scrope, 116¾, Normanton, 117¾, Claythorpe, 119, and Fulbeck, 119¾.

Leadenham to Lincoln (12—132¾); through Welbourne, 123, Wellingore, 123½, Navenby, 124¼, Boothby Graffo, 125¼, Coleby, 126¼, Harmston, 127, Waddington, 128¼, and St. Botolph, 131¾.

LONDON TO GAINSBOROUGH (by Lincoln).

London to Lincoln (133¼)—p. 215.

Lincoln to Gainsborough (18¾—152); in Lincoln turn to *l.* and then through Saxilby, 139¼ (1¾*m.* further keep to *r.*), Fenton, 143¼, Torksey, 144¼, Marton, 146¾, Knaith, 148¾, and Lea, 150.

LONDON TO MALTON (by Hull).

London to Beverley (183¼)—p. 216.

Beverley to Bainton (10—193¼); going out of Beverley, at the Gate keep to *r.*, and at Molescroft, 184¼, to *l.*, and through Cherry Burton, 185¾, and Lund, 190¼.

Bainton to Wetwang (5½—198¾), through Tibthorpe, 194¾.

Wetwang to Malton (13—211¾); through Wharram-le-street, 204¾, North Grimston, 206¾, and Norton, 211¼.

LONDON TO BRIDLINGTON (by Leven).

London to Beverley (183¼)—p. 216.

Beverley to Leven (6¾—190); in Beverley turn to *r.*, then over Hull Bridge, 185¼, and through Tickton, 185¾, Routh, 186¾, and White Cross, 188¾, is a fairly good and almost level road.

Leven to Beeford (6½—196½); by Barff Hill, 191¼, through Brandsburton, 191¾, and by Partings Guide Post, 192½, and Warley Cross Hill, 194.

Beeford to Bridlington (10¼—206¾); by Lissit Bridge, 198, Lissit Chapel, 199, through Barmston, 200¼, by Auburn *Ho.*, 203¼, and through Hilderthorpe, 205¼. From Barmston the road runs close by the sea shore.

LONDON TO HORNSEA.

London to Leven (190)—above.

Leven to Hornsea (5¾—195¾); turn to *r.* in Leven, and it is a bad road through Catwick, 191½, Sigglesthorne, 193¼, and Seaton, 194: there are no hills.

[Or from *Hull*, 174¼ (p. 216), turn to *r.*, and through Bilton, 178¾, Sproatley, 181¼, Aldbrough, 184¼, and Mapleton, 187¾, to *Hornsea*, 191¼; the road is monotonous and level, with a rough surface. Or turn to *l.* ¾*m.* before Bilton, and go through Ganstead, 178¾, Coniston, 179¾, South Skirlaugh, 182¼, then turn to *r.* and through Rise, 183½, to Sigglesthorne, 185½.]

(*Hornsea:* Alexandra.)

LONDON TO GREAT GRIMSBY.

London to Market Deeping (89¾)—p. 215.

Market Deeping to Spalding (11½—101¼); in Market Deeping turn to *r.* and through St. James Deeping, 90¾, by Blue Bell, 94¼, New Inn, 98½, and through Little London, 100¼, the road improves to Spalding, where it is good, the granite gradually giving way to gravel : level all the way.

[Or turn off to the right ¼*m.* beyond Northborough, 88¼, and go straight to St. James Deeping, 89¾, passing Market Deeping on *l.*]

(*Spalding :* White Hart, *B.T.C.*)

At Spalding handsome *ch.* built in 1284.

Spalding to Gosberton Tp. (6—107¼); through Pinchbeck, 103½, and Surfleet, 105¼, is a very fair road, almost level.

Gosberton Tp. to Boston (10—117¼); turn to *r.* and it is a pretty fair road through Sutterton, 111, to Kirton, 113¼, whence is a splendid smooth surface to Boston: all level.

(*Boston :* Bell; Peacock; White Hart.)

At Boston, St. Botolph's *ch.* is worth seeing.

Boston to Stickney (8¾—126); in Boston take the right hand road, and it is level and pretty good by Burton Corner, 118½ (keep to *l.*), to Sibsey, 122, after which it becomes very often bad and loose.

Stickney to Spilsby (7½—133½); it is a similar kind of road through Stickford, 128, to West Keal, 131, where the first hill is met, and the road becomes good, and continues so through East Keal, 131½, to Spilsby.

(*Spilsby :* White Hart.)

At Stickford, a little on *l.*, Hagnaby Priory; beyond it Revesby Abbey.

Spilsby to Ulceby Cross (6¼—139¾); through Partney, 135¾, and Dalby *Tp.*, 137½, good surface, but very hilly.

Ulceby Cross to Louth (10¾—150½); by Calceby Beck Houses, 141½, and through Burwell, 144¾, and Dexthorpe *Tp.*, 148¾, is still hilly, the surface improving, and being very good from Burwell to Louth.

(*Louth :* King's Head; Mason's Arms.)

On *l.*, Calceby ruins. On *r.*, Burwell Park. At Dexthorpe, 2*m.* on *r.*, Legbourn Abbey.

Louth to Great Grimsby (15½—166); very good road for Lincolnshire through Fotherby, 153½, and Utterby, 154½, to Ludborough, 156¼, then fair to North Thoresby, 158¼, but gets worse through Waith, 160, Holton-le-Clay, 161¼, and Scartho, 164, up to Great Grimsby.

(*Great Grimsby :* Royal; White Hart; Yarborough.)

At Ludborough, 1*m.* on *l.*, Beesby ruins. At Great Grimsby, St. James' *ch.*, beautiful specimen of early English.

LONDON TO GREAT GRIMSBY (by Lincoln).

London to Lincoln (133½)—p. 215.

Lincoln to Langworth Bridge (6—139½); turn to *r.* in Lincoln, and the road is very bad, being usually considered to be one of the worst bits of road in the county.

At Langworth Bridge, 2*m*. S., are ruins of Barling Abbey, and 2*m*. E. are ruins of Wragby Abbey.

Langworth Bridge to Market Rasen ($9\frac{1}{2}$—$148\frac{3}{4}$); turn to *l.* and through Stainton, 140 (keep to *r.*), Snelland, 142 (keep to *r.*), Wickenby, $143\frac{1}{4}$, Lessington, $144\frac{3}{4}$, and Linwood, $146\frac{1}{2}$: it is not a good road.

(*Market Rasen:* Gordon Arms; White Hart.)

Market Rasen to Caistor ($8\frac{1}{4}$—157); through Usselby, $151\frac{1}{2}$, and Nettleton, 156.

(*Caistor:* Red Lion.)

Caistor derives its name from the Roman "Castrum," there having been an encampment here. Some Roman and Saxon antiquities have been found at Castle Hill, near to. Ancient *ch.*

Caistor to Great Grimsby ($12\frac{1}{2}$—$169\frac{1}{2}$); through Cabourn, $158\frac{1}{2}$, Swallow, 160, Irby, $163\frac{1}{2}$, and Laceby, 166.

[Or from *Market Rasen* by Walesby, $151\frac{1}{2}$, Stainton-le-Vale, $154\frac{1}{2}$, Thorganby, $157\frac{1}{2}$, East Ravendale, 160, Brigsley, $161\frac{3}{4}$, Waltham, 163, and Scartho, $164\frac{3}{4}$, to *Great Grimsby*, $166\frac{3}{4}$.]

LONDON TO LOUTH (by Sleaford).

London to Sleaford ($115\frac{1}{4}$)—p. 215.

Sleaford to Tattershall ($11\frac{3}{4}$—127); in Sleaford turn to *r.*, and go through Anwick, $119\frac{3}{4}$, Billinghay, $122\frac{3}{4}$, and over Tattershall Bridge, $125\frac{1}{2}$; very fair surface, wide and perfectly flat road.

At Anwick, on *r.*, remains of Haverholme Priory. At Billinghay, on *l.*, ruins of Catley Abbey. At Tattershall, remains of a castle erected in the 15th century, and the ruins of a *ch.*, once a magnificent structure.

Tattershall to Horncastle ($8\frac{3}{4}$—$135\frac{3}{4}$); through Coningsby, $128\frac{3}{4}$ (keep to *l.*), by Swan Inn, $129\frac{1}{2}$ (keep to *l.*), and through Haltham, $131\frac{3}{4}$; fair at first, but deteriorates nearing Horncastle, and is generally loose with deep ruts.

About 2*m*. beyond Haltham, on *r.*, Scrivelsby Court, the seat of the Dymoke family, the champions of England. At Horncastle are traces of a Roman camp.

Horncastle to Louth ($13\frac{1}{4}$—149); in Horncastle keep to *r.*, and through West Ashby, $137\frac{1}{2}$, Sambleshy, $140\frac{3}{4}$, Cawkwell, $141\frac{1}{2}$, Dovendale, $143\frac{3}{4}$, Maltby, $145\frac{1}{2}$, and Raithby, 147; the road goes over the Wolds, and is bad and very hilly: 8*m*. from Horncastle is the steep ascent of Cawkwell Hill, utterly unrideable. [A better way is to turn to *r.* $9\frac{1}{2}$*m*. from Horncastle, and go through Tathwell to Louth.]

LONDON TO SWINESHEAD.

London to Gosberton Tp. ($107\frac{1}{4}$)—p. 219.

Gosberton Tp. to Donington (4—$111\frac{1}{4}$); take the left hand road and through Quadring, 109.

At Donington, ancient *ch.*, on which are traces of a Roman inscription.

Donington to Swineshead, North End ($4\frac{1}{2}$—$115\frac{3}{4}$); through Bicker, $111\frac{3}{4}$, and Gantlet, $112\frac{3}{4}$.

(*Swineshead:* Griffin.)

LONDON TO HORNCASTLE (by Boston).

London to Boston ($117\frac{1}{4}$)—p. 219.

Boston to Revesby ($10\frac{1}{2}$—$127\frac{3}{4}$); level and pretty good road through Carrington, $124\frac{1}{4}$, and New Bolingbroke, $126\frac{1}{4}$, crossing part of the Fens. [There is another road from Stickney to New Bolingbroke, $2\frac{3}{4}$—$128\frac{1}{4}$, level and pretty good.]

At Revesby is Revesby Abbey.

Revesby to Horncastle ($6\frac{1}{2}$—$134\frac{1}{4}$); leaving Revesby bear to *l.*, through Marcham le Fen, $129\frac{1}{4}$, (turn to *r.*) Wood Enderby, $130\frac{3}{4}$, and Scrivelsby, 132; level all the way, good in parts, but generally bad and stony, and on the whole not favourable for bicycling.

At Scrivelsby, on *r.*, Scrivelsby Court, the seat of the Dymoke family, champions of England.

LONDON TO SPALDING (by Crowland).

London to Peterborough ($81\frac{3}{4}$)—p. 214.

Peterborough to Crowland ($8\frac{1}{2}$—$90\frac{1}{4}$); in Peterborough turn to *r.*, then to *l.*, and it is a good road, almost level, through Newark, $83\frac{1}{4}$, and Eye, 85, beyond which turn to *l.*, and then a straight road into Crowland. [Or follow the Lincoln road for 1m., and then turn to *r.* and through Dodsthorpe, $83\frac{3}{4}$, to Crowland, $90\frac{3}{4}$.]

At Crowland, ruins of the splendid abbey, founded in 716, part of it being still used as the parish *ch.*; also a remarkable old bridge, supposed to have been built about 860.

Crowland to Spalding ($9\frac{1}{2}$—$99\frac{3}{4}$); good level road through Cowbit, $96\frac{1}{4}$.

SECTION VIII.

From Royal Exchange; North Eastern Roads (Essex, Suffolk, Norfolk, East Huntingdonshire, and East Cambridgeshire)

LONDON TO EDINBURGH (by Ware).

(The milestones on this route are measured from Shoreditch Church.)

Royal Exchange to Tottenham High Cross (5½); asphalte pavement for ½m., along Threadneedle Street and Bishopsgate Street, and then wood paving along Norton Folgate to Shoreditch, opposite Bishopsgate Street Station, 1m., where tramway begins; then it is granite paving past Shoreditch ch., 1¼, and along Kingsland Road to Kingsland, 2½, where it gives way to ordinary macadam, rough and lumpy, through Stoke Newington, 3¾, and Stamford Hill, 4½, on the top of which, after a slight rise, the tramway ends: on the north side the descent is somewhat steeper, and then level to Tottenham High Cross, still macadam: heavy traffic, bad for bicycling.

Tottenham High Cross to Edmonton (2¾—8¼); level road through Tottenham, 6¾, and Upper Edmonton, 7¼; the macadam continues very bad, rough, and greasy; it is almost one continuous street all the way.

At Edmonton is the Bell Inn, immortalised by Cowper in his ballad of John Gilpin.

Edmonton to Waltham Cross (4¼—12½); level road, still macadam, through Ponder's End, 9¾, to Enfield Highway, 10¾, when it changes to a capital bicycling road through Enfield Wash, 11¼. At Waltham Cross on r. to *Waltham Abbey*, 1½, level, but rough macadam road.

(*Waltham Cross*: Falcon; Old Four Swans.—*Waltham Abbey*: Cock Inn; New Inn.)

At Waltham Abbey Harold was buried; from the remains of the abbey, the present fine old ch. is formed: in the neighbourhood, on the banks of the R. Lea, are several Government powder mills. Waltham Cross takes its name from the cross erected here by Edward I. in honour of Queen Eleanor.

Waltham Cross to Hoddesdon (5¾—18¼); it is level through Brook Street, 13¼, Turner's Hill, 13¾, Cheshunt or Cheshunt Street, 14¼, Cheshunt Wash, 15¼, and Wormley, 16, to the 15th ms. just beyond here, then it is undulating through Broxbourne, 17: very good road.

(*Cheshunt*: Roman Urn; Ship.—*Broxbourne*: Crown.—*Hoddesdon*: Bull Inn; Rye House.)

At Cheshunt, the Manor Ho., the residence of Cardinal Wolsey. At Hoddesdon, a little on r., the remains of Rye Ho., famous for the Rye House Plot.

Hoddesdon to Ware (4—22¼); through Amwell, 20½, is a good road; a mile before Ware is a moderate rise, with corresponding descent; in dry weather it is rather sandy and loose.

(*Ware*: Saracen's Head.)

Beyond Hoddesdon, on *l.*, Haileybury College. At Ware, St. Mary's *ch.* contains many curious monuments; in the churchyard is the tomb of Dr. Mead, who, it is alleged, died 148 years old, in 1652. At "Saracen's Head" is the "great bed of Ware." On *l.* of town the Priory.

Ware to Puckeridge (5½—27¾); in Ware keep to *r.*, and there is a long gentle rise out of the town, and easy going with sharp descent to Wade's Mill, 24, followed by a very steep hill to mount with a turn in it, then easy undulating road through High Cross, 24¾, and Collier's End, 26, and a descent into Puckeridge.

At High Cross, 2*m.* on *l.*, Sacomb Park, and near it the remains of Rowney Abbey.

Puckeridge to Buntingford (4½—32¼); keep to *l.*, and it is a good slightly undulating road.

(*Buntingford:* George.)

Beyond Puckeridge, on *l.*, Hamells and Knights Hill Parks; at Buntingford, on *l.*, Aspenden Hall.

Buntingford to Royston (6¼—38¼); good undulating road through Chipping, 34, and Buckland, 35, after which there are two stiff hills to mount followed by a considerable fall into Royston, but nothing very difficult: in Royston the High street is all downhill.

(*Royston:* Bull; Crown.)

At Royston, the *ch.* formerly belonged to a priory, and contains some old monuments. Here cross the Roman Iknield Street.

Royston to Arrington Bridge (5½—44¼); keep straight on through Royston, soon after leaving which there is a long incline, and the road is very loose, and in dry weather dusty as far as Kneesworth, 41½, and thence, though in places rather narrow, it is fairly good and level. From Royston the road runs in a straight line to Godmanchester, being the Roman Ermine Street: this route is not so good as the Great North Road.

Near North End Green, 1*m.* on *l.*, beyond Kneesworth, is an ancient entrenchment. On *r.*, Kneesworth *Ho.*

Arrington Bridge to Caxton (6¼—50½); level to Arrington, 45¾, where there is a very severe hill to mount, and then the road is very hilly, and in many places loose and stony past the Golden Lion, 48.

(*Caxton:* George.)

At Arrington, on *r.*, Wimpole Hall and Park, the residence of Lord Hardwick; a fine avenue, 3*m.* long, runs from 1½*m.* before Arrington Bridge, past the Octagon Pond to the Hall. 1*m.* beyond Golden Lion, on *r.*, Bourne *Ho.* (Earl De la Warr). At Caxton, on *l.*, some ruins called the Moats.

Caxton to Huntingdon (9½—60); the road still continues hilly, and some of the ascents are very stiff, notably one about a mile beyond Papworth St. Everard, 53½; the surface improves slightly, in many places is very fair, and after Godmanchester, 59, is splendid going to Huntingdon Bridge (*R.* Ouse), where the pavement begins through the town, and is extremely rough.

(*Huntingdon:* Crown; Fountain, *B.T.C.*; George.)

Godmanchester is supposed to have been the Roman town of Durolipons. At Huntingdon are traces of a castle built by the Saxons; before the Reformation there were 15 churches here, of which only 2 are left. Oliver Cromwell was a native of the town. 1*m.* on *l.*, Hinchinbrook *Ho.*, formerly the property of the Cromwell family.

Huntingdon to Alconbury Hill (5¼—65¼) is splendid going, though hilly; there are severe double hills at both Great Stukeley, 62¼, and Little Stukeley, 63, that going into the latter being very sharp and requiring caution.

Beyond Great Stukeley, on *r.*, Stukeley Hall.

Alconbury Hill to Edinburgh (327½—392¾); by Norman Cross, 73¼, Wansford, 81, Stamford, 86¼, Grantham, 107½, Newark, 121¾, Tuxford, 135, Bawtry, 150½, Doncaster, 159½, Wetherby, 191½, Boroughbridge, 203½, Catterick Bridge, 226½, Durham, 256¼, Newcastle-upon-Tyne, 271¼, Morpeth, 286, Alnwick, 305¼, and Berwick-upon-Tweed, 334¾—pp. 195-201.

LONDON TO HUNTINGDON (by St. Neots).

London to Tempsford (51¼)—p. 194.

Tempsford to St. Neots (4¾—56); ½*m.* beyond Tempsford keep to *r.*, and it is a fair road through Little Barford, 53¾. [Or follow the Great North Road to *Eaton Socon*, 55¼ (p. 194), and a little beyond turning to *r.* through Eaton Ford, 56, and across *R.* Ouse to St. Neots, 56¾, but the road is rather heavy, and there is a very narrow and steep bridge over the *R.* Ouse into St. Neots.]

(*St. Neots:* Angel; Cross Keys; New Inn, *B.T.C.*)

Beautiful *ch*, at St. Neots; also remains of an ancient priory. Just before the town, on *l.*, are traces of an ancient encampment.

St. Neots to Huntingdon (8¼—64¼); splendid road through Great Paxton, 59, Offord D'Arcy, 60¼, Offord Cluny, 60¾, and Godmanchester, 63¼. [Or follow the Great North Road to *Buckden*, 61¼, and ½*m.* farther keeping to *r.* through Brampton, 63¾, again turning to *r.* for *Huntingdon*, 65½, a good easy road.]

LONDON TO HUNTINGDON (by Potton).

London to Biggleswade (45¼)—p. 194.

Biggleswade to Potton (2¾—48); the Potton road strikes off to *r.* ¾*m.* before Biggleswade, and the distances are strictly 44½+3½=48.

Potton to Eltisley (8½—56½); through Gamlingay, 50½, and Waresley, 52½.

Before Potton, on *r.*, Sutton Park. On *l.*, Waresley Park. At Eltisley, on *l.*, Croxton Park and the Abbey.

Eltisley to Huntingdon (8¼—64¾); leaving Eltisley keep to *l.*, and at Kisby's Hut, 59¼, join the road from Caxton.

LONDON TO HERTFORD AND HITCHIN.

London to Hoddesdon (18¼)—p. 222.

Hoddesdon to Hertford (4—22¼); in Hoddesdon turn sharp to *l.*, and over Hertford Heath, 20½, and past Ball Park is very hilly and not such a good road. [Or to Amwell, 20½ (p. 222), and about 1¼*m.* further on turn to *l.* just before entering Ware; there is a rather stiff hill to mount, then it is fairly level, but sandy, to Hertford, 24¼.]

(*Hertford:* Dimsdale Arms, *B.T.C.*; Dunstable Arms; Salisbury Arms.)

At Hertford are remains of a castle, erected in the beginning of the 10th century.

Hertford to Watton (5¼—27½); leaving Hertford keep to *r.*, and through Waterford, 24¼, and Stapleford, 25¾; almost level.

[Or to *Ware*, 22¼ (p. 222); then by left hand road by Tunwell to *Watton*, 27¾.]

Before Watton, on *r.*, Woodhall Park.

Watton to Stevenage (6¾—34¼); out of Watton keep to *l.*, and it is almost level through Bragbury End, 30, and Broadwater, 32, where join the Great North Road.

Stevenage to Hitchin (4¼—38½); through Stevenage take the left hand road, and through Little Wymondley, 36¼.

LONDON TO HODDESDON (by Enfield).

London, General Post Office, to Newington Green (3); wood pavement for ½*m.* along Aldersgate street, then granite paving with tramway along Goswell road, past the "Angel," Islington, 1¼, along High street, and to *r.* along Essex road, where the paving soon gives way to ordinary macadam, continuing across St. Paul's road, 2¼, into Newington Green road.

Newington Green to Wood Green (2¾—5¾); leave Newington Green by the north-west corner, along Green Lanes, the tramway continuing to the Seven Sisters Road; then skirting the east side of Finsbury Park; bad macadam all the way.

At Wood Green, on *l.*, is the Alexandra Palace.

Wood Green to Enfield (5—10¾); the road is still rough for another mile, then it changes to gravel and is very good, by Palmers Green, 7¼, with a stiff rise up Bush Hill, 8¾, and a good run down on the other side; macadam and rather rough through Enfield.

1*m.* beyond Wood Green, on *l.*, Bromfield *Ho.* and Cullands Grove.

At Enfield, on *l.*, is the district formerly known as Enfield Chase, extending to the Great North road.

Enfield to Cheshunt (4½—15¼); by Forty Hill, 12, Maiden Bridge, 12½, and alongside Theobald's Park, bearing round to *r.* into the Ware road at Brook Street, 14¾, is a very fair road with no hills of any consequence.

Cheshunt to Hoddesdon (4—19¼)—p. 222.

LONDON TO SPALDING (by St. Ives).

London to Caxton (50½)—p. 223.

Caxton to St. Ives (10—60½); the road continues rather hilly through Papworth St. Everard, 53½, by Kisby's Hut, 54 (turn to *r.*), through Hilton, 57, Gallow Hill, 58½, (crossing here the Cambridge and Huntingdon road), and just before St. Ives crossing *R.* Ouse.

(*St. Ives:* Golden Lion, *B.T.C.*; Unicorn; White Horse.)

On *r.*, Papworth Hall. At St. Ives are slight remains of a priory.

St. Ives to Ramsey ($8\frac{3}{4}$—$69\frac{1}{4}$); good and almost level road to Old Hurst, $64\frac{1}{2}$, and Warboys, $66\frac{1}{2}$, beyond which is the steep descent of Shilow Hill, generally very loose, and another hill to descend at Bury, $68\frac{1}{4}$, which is rather steep at the top, but with good surface.

[Or to *Huntingdon*, 60, as at p. 223; thence turning to *r.* and through Hartford, $61\frac{1}{4}$, and Hartford *Tp.*, 65, to Hurst, $65\frac{1}{4}$. Or from Huntingdon through Ripton Regis to *Ramsey*, $69\frac{3}{4}$.]

(*Ramsey :* Crown, *B.T.C.*; George.)

At Ramsey are remains of the abbey.

Ramsey to Whittlesea ($8\frac{3}{4}$—78); by Black Swan, $73\frac{1}{4}$, and Ponds Bridge, 75.

Whittlesea to Thorney ($4\frac{1}{2}$—$82\frac{1}{2}$).

Thorney to Crowland (5—$87\frac{1}{2}$.)

Crowland to Spalding ($9\frac{1}{2}$—97)—p. 221.

LONDON TO HUNSTANTON.

London to St. Ives ($60\frac{1}{2}$)—p. 225.

St. Ives to Chatteris ($12\frac{3}{4}$—$73\frac{1}{4}$); in St. Ives turn to *r.* when over the bridge, then the road bears round to *l.*, and $\frac{3}{4}$*m.* outside the town take the left hand fork; it is a good undulating road through Somersham, $66\frac{1}{4}$.

(*Chatteris :* George; Horse and Gate.)

Somersham *ch.* is a noble edifice, containing some ancient brasses and monuments.

Chatteris to March (8—$81\frac{1}{4}$); good undulating road over Carter's Bridge, 75, and through Doddington, $77\frac{1}{4}$, and Wimblington, $78\frac{3}{4}$.

(*March :* Griffin.)

March is a long straggling town, situate on both sides of the Old Nen *R.* Before entering the town, on *l.*, is an ancient entrenchment.

March to Wisbeach ($10\frac{1}{2}$—$91\frac{3}{4}$); in March, over the bridge, turn to *l.*, and it is a good level road by Twenty Foot Bridge, $84\frac{3}{4}$, and Guyhirne Ferry, $85\frac{3}{4}$, whence it runs alongside New Nen *R.* to Wisbeach.

(*Wisbeach :* Rose and Crown; Royal; White Hart; White Lion.)

At Wisbeach, St. Mary's *ch.* is a beautiful and curious building.

Wisbeach to Lynn ($12\frac{3}{4}$—$104\frac{1}{2}$); after crossing canal or Old Nen *R.* turn to *r.*, and then through Walsoken, $92\frac{3}{4}$, Walton Highway, $94\frac{3}{4}$, Walpole Highway, $96\frac{3}{4}$, St. John's Highway, $97\frac{3}{4}$, by the Rose and Crown, $98\frac{1}{4}$ (keep to *l.*), and through Tilney-cum-Islington, $100\frac{1}{2}$, is a capital smooth level road; just before Lynn cross *R.* Ouse.

(*Lynn :* Crown, *B.T.C.*; Globe; Golden Lion; Maid's Head Inn; Norfolk-street (Fiddaman's); Railway.)

Lynn, or King's Lynn, is a considerable seaport town; St. Margaret's *ch.*, erected in 1160, is a large handsome building.

Lynn to Castle Rising ($4\frac{1}{4}$—$108\frac{3}{4}$); after leaving Lynn cross the railway, and at Gaywood, $105\frac{1}{2}$, turn to *l.*, and again at South Wootton, $106\frac{1}{2}$, whence there is a succession of hills to Castle Rising; extremely good road.

At Castle Rising are the ruins of a castle, erected about 1176, by William de Albini. Isabella, Queen of Edward II., was confined here for 38 years. The *ch.* contains an ancient ornamental font, &c.

Castle Rising to Hunstanton, *Ch.* (11¾—120½); there are some very long ascents to work up for some distance out of Castle Rising, then the road sometimes gets very loose and heavy, and full of ruts, about Sandringham, 112 (which with the Hall is passed a little on *r.*), and through Dersingham, 113; after that it is good all the way through Ingoldisthorpe, 114¼, Snettisham, 115¼, and Heacham, 117½, after which it runs along the top of the cliffs, from which there is a stiffish descent to Hunstanton. Fine scenery.

(*Hunstanton:* Golden Lion, *B.T.C.*)

At Sandringham, the gardens, grounds, and dog kennels can be seen on obtaining an order from the agent of the Prince of Wales. On *r.*, Hunstanton Hall; Hunstanton affords good sea-bathing.

LONDON TO HUNSTANTON (by Cambridge).

London to Royston (38¾)—p. 223.

Royston to Cambridge (13—51¾); in Royston turn to the right and shortly after to the left, and up a slight rise followed by a descent, and the rest is level, and all a splendid smooth road through Melbourne, 42, Harlston, 46½, Hauxton, 47½, and Trumpington, 49¼; macadam entering Cambridge, and cobble paving in the middle of the town.

This is the best road to Cambridge the only difficult hill being that at Wade's Mill.

(*Cambridge:* Bird Bolt; Castle, *B.T.C.*; Hoop; Red Lion; University Arms; Webb's Restaurant.)

Cambridge, the sister University to Oxford, contains 18 colleges and halls. It is a somewhat irregularly built town, and has not the position or the architectural beauties of Oxford; yet there are some handsome buildings, notably, King's College Chapel; besides the colleges there are the Senate House, Library, Fitzwilliam Museum, Press, Observatory, Botanic Gardens, St. Sepulchre's *ch.*, &c., &c. N. of the town, across the *R.* Cam, are the remains of the castle, and further N. is an ancient entrenchment called Arbury. The scenery is very pretty at the back of the colleges, along the *R.* Cam.

Cambridge to Stretham (11¾—63½); turn to *l.* in the middle of Cambridge, and after crossing *R.* Cam turn to *r.*; it is a good and almost level road through Milton, 55, Waterbeach, 56¾, over Stretham Bridge, 62, and across Stretham Common.

About 3*m.* beyond Waterbeach, on *r.*, Denny Abbey.

Stretham to Ely (4¼—67¾) is a good but rather hilly road, having the valley of the Old Ouse *R.* on *r.* Returning, a little out of Ely keep to *l.*

(*Ely:* Bell, *B.T.C.*; Lamb; White Hart.)

At Ely, the cathedral, erected at the end of the 11th century, and formerly belonging to the old monastery.

Ely to Littleport (5—72¾); keep to *l.* out of Ely, and except a descent to Chetisham *Tp.*, 69¾, it is fairly level, but an indifferent road past Woodhouse station, 70¾, and over Littleport Fields.

Littleport to Downham Market (12½—85¼); good level road over Littleport Bridge, 73¾, and alongside *R.* Ouse to Brandon Creek Bridge, 76¾ (cross *R.* Ouse), and by Southery Ferry, 78, to Southery, 78¾, whence it is rather hilly over Modney Bridge, 80½, through Hilgay, 81¾, Fordham, 82¾ and Denver, 84, with a hill to mount into Downham Market.

(*Downham Market:* Castle; Chequers; Crown.)

At Fordham, 3*m.* on *r.*, Dereham Abbey. At Downham Market, remains of a Benedictine Priory. At Denver, on *r.*, Riston Hall.

Downham Market to Lynn (11¼—96½); through Wimbotsham, 86½, Stow Bardolph, 87¾, South Runcton, 89½, Tottenhill, 91, Setchy, 92¾, West Winch, 94, and Hardwick, 95¼, is a good but hilly road, along a succession of avenues of trees.

On *r.*, pass Stow Hall, at Stow Bardolph; 1*m.* further, Wallington Hall and ruins of the *ch.* on *l.*: Runcton *ch.* is in ruins.

Lynn to Hunstanton (16—112½)—pp. 226-7.

LONDON TO CAMBRIDGE (by Barkway).

London to Puckeridge (27¾)—p. 223.

Puckeridge to Barkway (8—35¾); splendid road, slightly on the rise, through Braughing, 28½, and Hare Street, 31¾.

At Braughing, about 2*m.* on *r.*, Albury Hall. Beyond Hare Street, 1*m.* on *l.*, Widdiall Hall.

Barkway to Tun Bulls House (5½—41¼); very hilly road through Barley, 38¼.

At Tun Bull's *Ho.*, cross the Royston and Newmarket road.

Tun Bulls House to Hauxton (6¾—48); chiefly downhill through Foulmire, 43¼, to Newton, 46, then a short hill to rise and downhill again to Hauxton, where join the main road from Royston.

Hauxton to Cambridge (4¼—52¼)—p. 227.

LONDON TO WELLS.

London to Lynn (96½)—above.

Lynn to Hillington (7½—104); after leaving Lynn cross the railway, and at Gaywood, 97½, turn to *l.*, at South Wootton, 98½, keep to *r.*, and at Rising Lodge, 100, to *l.*

1*m.* beyond Rising Lodge, on *r.*, Roydon Hall. At Hillington, on *l.*, Hillington Hall; before, on *l.*, Cougham Hall.

Hillington to Docking (8½—112½); just beyond Hillington turn to *l.*, and through Flitcham, 105, Great Bircham, 109¾, and Bircham Newton, 110½.

[Or from Lynn to Heacham, 13—109½ (pp. 226-7), then turn to *r.* and through Sedgeford, 111½, to *Docking*, 114¾.]

On *r.*, Flitcham Abbey; in the distance Houghton Hall, formerly the residence of Sir Robert Walpole, who is interred in the *ch.*

Docking to Burnham Westgate (5½—118); in Docking turn to *r.*, and directly afterwards take the left hand road.

At Burnham Westgate, on *r.*, Burnham Thorpe, the birthplace of Nelson.

Burnham Westgate to Wells (5¾—123¾); through Burnham Overy, 118¾, by Holkham New Inn, 120¼, and Holkham Staith, 122¼, part of the way skirting Holkham Park.

(*Wells:* Crown; Globe; Railway; Ship Inn; Sun.)

On *l.*, pass a Danish encampment at Holkham Park.

LONDON TO WELLS (by South Creake).

London to Hillington (104)—p. 228.

Hillington to East Rudham, Crown (7¼—111¼); just beyond Hillington keep to right, cross Pedlar's Way, 107½, and through Harpley, 108¼, and West Rudham, 110¼. Returning, out of East Rudham keep to *r.*, and at West Rudham to *l.*

Beyond Hillington, on *r.*, Belmont. At Harpley, 1m. on *l.*, Houghton Hall; on *r.*, Rudham Grange.

East Rudham to South Creake (5¾—117); leaving East Rudham turn to *l.*, and about halfway pass Syerstone on *l.*, beyond which at Banner are some ruins.

South Creake to Wells (6½—123½); turning to *l.* in South Creake, at the "Swan," ½m. beyond, turn sharp on *r.*, and ½m. again turn to *l.*, and past Holkham Park Gate, 120½, and alongside the Park to Wells.

The road straight forward at the "Swan" leads through North Creake, 118, to *Burnham Westgate*, 121½.

At North Creake, on *r.*, Creake Abbey.

LONDON TO CAMBRIDGE (by Harlow).

(The milestones on the following routes are measured from Whitechapel Church.)

London, Royal Exchange to Stratford (4); asphalte paving along Cornhill, Leadenhall street, and Aldgate to Whitechapel *ch.*, ½, then granite paving with tramway along Whitechapel road, through Mile End, 1½, and Bow, 3, and consequently bad for bicycling; very heavy traffic as far as Mile End, beyond which the road is on a gentle rise for some distance.

Stratford to Leytonstone (2—6), is macadam and a little better road, the second mile being very fair; at the Broadway in Stratford take the left hand road: the tramway continues.

Leytonstone to Woodford Wells (3½—9½); just beyond Leytonstone keep to *l.*, and the road is now considerably better, but on a continuous rise through Snaresbrook, 7¼, to Woodford, 8½, after which it is a good gravel road through Woodford Green, 9.

(*Snaresbrook*: Eagle.—*Woodford*: Castle; George.)

[There is a better road out of London, to avoid the bad road to Stratford: either from Mile End along the Cambridge Heath road, Mare street, Hackney, to Lower Clapton, 3 (partly paved and partly macadam, with tramway); or starting from the "Angel," Islington, to Stoke Newington Green, 1¾, as at p. 225, and then from the N.E. corner along Matthias road, Barrett road, Wellington street, Shacklewell road and Downs road, and by the north side of Hackney Downs to Lower Clapton, 3¼: then turn to *r.*, along the Lea Bridge road—all macadam—to Whips Cross, 2½m., and forward to the "Castle" at Woodford Green, 2m. more; or striking off to right at Whips Cross to Snaresbrook, ¾.]

Woodford Wells to Epping (7¾—17¼); a short distance beyond Woodford Wells keep to the *r.* of the two roads, up a rise to Buckhurst Hill, followed by a long descent of that name, steep at first and generally rough, down the other side, and then level through Loughton, 12, beyond which is a moderate ascent (Church Hill) and further on a very stiff one (Golding's or Golders Hill); though more hilly and the longer road, this is in better condition; but after Golding's Hill it runs through Epping Forest for about 3m. (the first m. like a racing path), past Wake Arms, 14½, the surface beyond here being sometimes very loose. [Or beyond Woodford Wells take the left hand road, which traverses the whole length of Epping Forest, rejoining the former road at Wake Arms, 14½, and is nearly always in bad repair, being very loose and rutty, and in wet weather heavy going; no steep, though two long hills by latter route.]

(*Loughton :* Crown.—*Epping :* Bell ; Thatched House.)

1m. beyond Wake Arms, a little on *l.*, Copped Hall ; on *r.*, Ambresbury Banks, an old Roman encampment. Epping Forest is now public property, and has been secured against encroachment by the City of London Corporation.

Epping to Harlow (6½—23¾); just through Epping keep to *l.*, and there is a long descent, after which the road is undulating, but no difficult hills to mount, and the surface becomes rough and loose for a couple of miles, but improves greatly nearing Potter's Street, 21½, through which is a capital run down, and the road is then good through Bromley, 23⅜.

(*Harlow :* George ; Green Man ; Great Eastern Railway.)

At Harlow, on *l.*, Mark Hall.

Harlow to Hockerill (6¾—30½); rather long descent out of Harlow to the bridge over R. Stort, followed by one or two moderate hills through Sawbridgeworth, 26, and Spelbrook, 28; mostly good and smooth surface, but in dry weather apt to be loose. ½m. before Hockerill on *l.* to *Bishop Stortford*, (¾—30¾), rejoining the above road 1m. beyond Hockerill, but this is longer by half-a-mile ; or in Bishop Stortford from the High street turn to *r.* down a steep descent to the river, and up over the railway bridge to Hockerill.

(*Bishop Stortford :* Chequers ; George, B.T.C.)

Beyond R. Stort, on *r.*, Pishiobury Park. At Spelbrook, on *r.*, Walbury Hall. At Bishop Stortford, are ruins of the castle ; ancient *ch.* About 2m. on *r.*, on road to Dunmow, Thromhill Priory.

Hockerill to Newport (8½—39); the road is very undulating with a very good surface through Stanstead, 33¾, Ugley, 35½, and Quendon, 36½.

(*Newport :* Coach and Horses.)

At Stanstead, 1m. on *r.*, Stanstead Mountfitchet, which has an old *ch.*, and the remains of a castle, erected in the time of William I. Beyond Quendon, on *l.*, Quendon Hall. At Newport, 1m. on *r.*, Debden Hall ; fine *ch.* at Newport.

Newport to Great Chesterford (6¼—45¼); through Littlebury, 42¾, and Little Chesterford, 44¼, the road is undulating, but mostly downhill. and with a good smooth surface.

Beyond Newport, on *r.*, Shortgrove Hall ; 3m. beyond Newport, on *r.* Audley Park, the splendid seat of Lord Braybrooke, erected about 1610, on the site of an ancient abbey ; in the park is an ancient circular entrenchment, with a Druidical temple. 2 or 3m. on *r.*, is the town of Saffron Walden, with beautiful *ch.* Great Chesterford is the site of a Roman station.

Great Chesterford to Sawston (4¾—50); turning to *l.* at Stumps Cross, 46, and through Hinxton, 46¾, it is a first-rate road on the whole, with no hills, but sometimes is very loose in places.

At Stumps Cross, the Roman Icknield way crosses the road ; on *l.*, at the village of Ickleton, many Roman remains and antiquities have been found. eyond Hinxton, on *r.*, Whittlesford Hall. On *r.*, Sawston Hall.

Sawston to Cambridge (6½—56½); first-rate road with no hills through Stapleford, 51½, Great Shalford, 52¼ (keep to *r.*), and Trumpington, 54½, where join the London road through Royston.

At Stapleford, on *r.*, the Gog Magog Hills, on which is a triple circular entrenchment, supposed to be of British origin, with several tumuli.

LONDON TO CROMER.

London to Great Chesterford (45¼)—p. 230.

Great Chesterford to Bourn Bridge (4½—49¾); at Stumps Cross, 46, keep to *r.*, and it is almost a straight line, following the Roman Ickneild Way; very good road with a long rise a little after Stumps Cross, and a sharp descent to Bourn Bridge.

About 1¼m. before Bourn Bridge, on the crest of the hill looking N.E., a line of ancient ditch or entrenchment, about 3m. in length, crosses the road. At Bourn Bridge, on *r.*, Abington Hall; on *l.*, Babraham Hall.

Bourn Bridge to Newmarket (11½—61¼); by Worsted Lodge, 51, Green Man, 54¾, and Devil's Ditch, 59, a very good road with some long ascents and descents, but the last 2 or 3m., across Newmarket Heath, are very loose and bad in dry weather, the material not binding well. The country is very lonely and the scenery uninteresting,

(*Newmarket:* Rutland Arms; White Hart.)

At Worsted Lodge, cross a Roman road; on *l.*, are the Gog Magog Hills. At the 51st ms., ½m. beyond Worsted Lodge, a little on *l.*, Ely Cathedral is seen, 18m. distant; 1m. further cross Fleam Dyke or Balsham Ditch, an ancient entrenchment, several miles in extent. Just before 56th ms., on *l.*, looking backwards, you have a view of Cambridge, 9m. distant. Devil's Ditch is a line of Roman entrenchment. Newmarket derives its celebrity from being the headquarters of horse-racing.

Newmarket to Barton Mills (8½—69¾); a mile beyond Newmarket keep to *l.* and over Snailwell Heath and Kennet Heath to Red Lodge, 66¾, where is a moderate ascent; extremely bad road, being very loose and stony, except soon after heavy rain when it hardens somewhat: stiff and rough descent to Barton Mills.

At Kennet Heath, 1m. on *l.*, Chippenham Park. Beyond Red Lodge, on *r.*, Herringswell Ho.

Barton Mills to Thetford (10¾—80½); leaving Barton Mills keep to *r.*, and it is a monotonous and undulating road, over Icklingham Heath to Elvedon, 76¾, and then over Thetford Heath; extremely bad road, for miles being little better than a track across the heath, with very loose surface, in some parts covered with sand and flints, which makes the slight hills difficult. Thetford lies in a valley.

(*Thetford:* Anchor; Angel; Bell.)

On *r.*, Elvedon Hall. Thetford was the capital of East Anglia during the Heptarchy, and has been the residence of several kings of England; it possesses the remains or site of a castle, remains of a Cluniac priory, nunnery, and other religious houses; there were formerly 20 churches here.

Thetford to Larlingford (8¼—88¾); moderate hill to mount out of Thetford, and then it is an undulating road over Thetford Warren and Larling Heath; for the greater part rather stony and nearly as bad as the previous stage—a mere wheel and hoof track often filled in with flints—

for 6*m.*, when there is a level railway crossing, after which the surface improves a little; it is only decent going after rain and warm sunshine.

Larlingford to Attleborough (5¾—94½); over Fettle Bridge, 92¼, the road is somewhat of a similar character to the previous stage, but gradually improves towards Attleborough; no hills worth speaking of.

(*Attleborough:* New Inn.)

Before Fettle Bridge, on *r.*, Hargham Hall. At Attleborough, 2*m.* on r., Buckenham Abbey.

Attleborough to Wymondham (6—100½); over Morley Common is a splendid road, with no hills to speak of; about 4 or 5*m.* an hour quicker than the last 25*m.*

(*Wymondham;* King's Head, *B.T.C.*; Queen's Head; White Hart.)

Wymondham to Norwich (8½—109); there is a little uphill through and out of the former, and it is a splendid smooth road through Hethersett, 104, Thickthorn, 105, with a steep descent through Cringleford, 106½; and after crossing the bridge over the *R.* Yare, a rather steep ascent out of Eaton, 107, and another in the last mile: Norwich is paved mostly with cobblestones.

(*Norwich:* Bull Inn; Castle; Grapes, *Hqrs.*; Maid's Head; Norfolk; Rampant Horse, *B.T.C.*; Royal.)

At Norwich, the most interesting buildings are the cathedral and remains of the castle, both founded towards the end of the 11th century; there are also the Bishop's Palace, St. Peter's *ch.*, St. Julian's *ch.*, St. Andrew's Hall (formerly the nave of a *ch.* belonging to the Black Friars), Shire Hall, Erpingham's Gate, Theatres, Library, Museum, &c.

Norwich to Aylsham (11¼—120¼); through Horsham St. Faith, 112½, Newton St. Faith, 113¾, Hevingham, 117½, and Marsham, 118¼; about 2*m.* out of Norwich keep to *r.*: very good surface with no difficult hills.

(*Aylsham:* Blackboys.)

Aylsham *ch.* has some beautiful memorials.

Aylsham to Cromer (10½—130¾); by Ingworth Mill, 122, Hanworth Green, 125½, Powder Hill, 127, and Routon Windmill, 129; very good surface with no difficult hills.

[There is another road from Norwich by Catton Lodge, 111, Spixworth, 113, Maiden Bridge, 115, (¼*m.* before that keep to *r.*) Skeyton, 119½, Felmingham, 122, Antingham, 124, and Thorpe Market, 126½, to *Cromer*, 130½.

Or ¼*m.* before Maiden Bridge turn to *l.*, and through Buxton, 117¾, to *Aylsham*, 121, thence to *Cromer*, 131½—above.]

(*Cromer:* Hotel de Paris; Tucker's.)

On *l.*, Spixworth Hall. Beyond Aylsham, on *l.*, Blickling Park. On *l.*, Hanworth Hall. 2*m.* before Cromer, a little on *l.*, Felbrigg Hall. At Antingham, on *l.*, Gunton Hall (Lord Suffield). Cromer is a newly opened up watering place, and from its position has a salubrious and invigorating air; there is some pretty scenery in the neighbourhood.

LONDON TO LYNN (by Newmarket).

London to Barton Mills (69¾)—p. 231.

Barton Mills to Brandon (9—78¾); out of Barton Mills take the left of the two middle roads, and by Hobb's Cross, 72¾, over Lakenheath, and through Wangford, 75¾, and past Brandon Park.

(*Brandon:* Chequers.)

Before Brandon, on *r.*, Brandon Park; through the town, on *r.*, remains of priory.

Brandon to Stoke Ferry (10—88¾); after crossing *R.* Ouse or Brandon keep to *l.* and through Weeting All Saints, 80, is all more or less uphill across Weeting Field or Heath to Feltwell Lodge, 82¼, and then downhill and up across Methwold Warren and through Methwold, 84¾, and Whittington, 88, to which is a long descent.

[Or turn to *l.* 1*m.* before Barton Mills, and through Mildenhall, 69¾, Lakenheath, Hockwold-cum-Wilton, Feltwell St. Mary, to Methwold; about 2*m.* shorter: or turn sharp to *l.* after crossing *R.* Larke at Barton Mills.]

Past Weeting, on *r.*, Weeting Hall; on *l.*, old castle and ruins of *ch.* On *l.*, Feltwell Lodge.

Stoke Ferry to Lynn (14—102¾); ascent out of Stoke Ferry and hilly through Wereham, 90½, Stradset, 93¾, and Shouldham Thorpe, 95¼, to Fodderstone Gap, 95¾, whence nearly all downhill to Setchy, 99, West Winch, 100¼, and Hardwick, 101½.

At Wereham, 2*m.* on *l.*, Dereham Abbey; on *r.*, Stradset Hall.

LONDON TO WELLS (by Swaffham).

London to Brandon (78¾)—p. 232.

Brandon to Swaffham (14¾—93½); cross *R.* Ouse or Brandon and keep to *r.* out of the town, and 1¾*m.* further to *l.*; uphill more or less for nearly 3*m.*, then a little level over Mundford Field and downhill into Mundford, 83½, whence another long rise over Ickborough Field, and a similar descent to Hilborough, 87¾; out of here is a short stiff hill to mount, half-way up which turn sharp on *l.* (this should be descended carefully), and past Rowley Corner, and over Swaffham Heath is rather hilly.

(*Swaffham:* Crown; George.)

Swaffham *ch.* contains some curious monuments and a fine carved roof. Past Mundford, on *r.*, Lyndford *Ho.*

Swaffham to Fakenham (15¾—109¼); hilly to Newton, 97¾, then easier over Lexham Heath, through Weasenham St. Peter, 102½, by Rainham Hall, 105½, and Toft Trees, 107¼. [Or turn to *r.* 2*m.* beyond Newton and through West Lexham, 99¼, East Lexham, 100¼, Litcham, 102, Tittleshall, 104, and Pattesley Hill, 106¼, to Fakenham, 110¼.]

(*Fakenham:* Crown, *B.T.C.*; Lion.)

Before Newton, ¾*m.* on *l.*, is the village of Castle Acre, where numerous antiquities are to be seen: British earthworks, a Roman camp, ruins of a castle (erected in the reign of William I. by Earl Warren on the site of a more ancient work), and ruins of Cluniac Priory; there have also been found here a tesselated pavement, and an Anglo-Saxon cemetery, where many burial urns have been dug up. About 2*m.* W., at West Acre, remains of abbey and *ch.* Rainham Hall (Marquis of Townshend), was erected in 1636, by Inigo Jones; beyond it the ruins of Coxford Abbey.

Fakenham to New Walsingham (4¾—114), through East Barsham, 112¼, and Houghton-in-the-Dale, 113½.

At New Walsingham, the remains of a monastery of Black Canons, founded in the reign of William the Conqueror.

New Walsingham to Wells (5—119), through Wighton, 116, and by Warham Hall, 117.

LONDON TO HOLT AND CLEY.

London to Brandon (78¾)—p. 232.

Brandon to Watton (12½—91¼); cross *R.* Ouse or Brandon, and keep to *r.* out of the town, and again to *r.* 1¾*m.* further on; then by Lyndford Lodges, 82¾, West Tofts Hall, 84, through Stanford, 85½, and by Clermont or Claremont Lodge, 88½; undulating road, very loose and sandy, especially in dry weather.

(*Watton:* George.)

Watton has a remarkable old *ch.* with round tower, supposed to have been built in the time of Henry I., near the old manor *Ho.* In the vicinity is Wayland Wood, where tradition says two infants were murdered by their uncle, which gave rise to the well-known ballad. On *l.*, West Tofts Hall; at Stanford, on *l.*, Buckenham *Ho.*

Watton to East Dereham (9¾—101); in Watton turn to *l.*, and through Ovington, 92¾, Shipdham, 96, Market Street, 96¾, (at 1¼*m.* further on keep to *l.*), and Lolly Moor, 99.

(*East Dereham:* King's Arms; King's Head.)

In East Dereham *ch.* is the monument to the poet Cowper, who was buried here; also a tombstone recording the burial and subsequent removal of the remains of a Saxon princess.

East Dereham to Guist Bridge (8—109); 2*m.* beyond East Dereham keep to *l.*, and by King's Head, 105¾, and through North Elmham, 106½.

At North Elmham, on *l.*, Elmham Hall.

Guist Bridge to Holt (10¼—119¼); past Melton Park, 114¼, and through Thornage, 117.

(*Holt:* Feather; White Lion.)

Holt to Cley (4¼—123½).

LONDON TO WATTON (by Thetford).

London to Thetford (80½)—p. 231.

Thetford to Watton (12—92½); leaving Thetford, take the left of the two middle roads, and through Croxton, 82¾, over Croxton Heath, by Frogs Hall, 85¼, through Tottington, 88¾, and by Merton Hall, 90½.

LONDON TO CROMER (by East Dereham).

London to East Dereham (101)—above.

East Dereham to Reepham (10¾—111¾); leaving East Dereham keep to *r.*, and through Swanton Morley, 104½, and Bawdeswell, 107¼.

(*Reepham:* King's Arms.)

Reepham was formerly remarkable for having three churches in one churchyard.

Reepham to Aylsham (7—118¾); by Sall Hall, 113, and through Cawston, 114½, a mile beyond which cross the Norwich and Holt road.

Aylsham to Cromer (10½—129¼)—p. 232.

LONDON TO NORWICH (by Hingham).

London to Watton (91¼)—p. 234.

Watton to Hingham (6¾—98); by Carbrook Common, 93½, Upgate, 94½, and Scoulton Common *Tp.*, 96¼.

Hingham to Barford Bridge (7½—105½); through Hackford *Tp.*, 100½, and Kimberley Green, 101½, beyond which keep to *r.*, and through Carlton Forehoe, 103½.

At Kimberley Green, on *r.*, Kimberley Hall.

Barford Bridge to Norwich (7—112½); from Barford Bridge there is a steep ascent to climb, followed by a steep hill to descend, and a capital run down into Colney, 109¾; then, after crossing the *R.* Yare, there is a steep hill to climb through Earlham, 110½, to Norwich.

LONDON TO CROMER (by North Walsham).

London to Norwich (109)—p. 232.

Norwich to North Walsham (14¼—123¼); uphill to Sprowston, 111¼, then undulating and very good through Crostwick, 113¾, Horstead, 115¾, Coltishall, 116¼, and Scottow Common, 118½.

(*North Walsham:* Black Lion Inn; Black Swan Inn.)

On *l.*, Scottow Hall; further on, on *r.*, Westwick Hall, and beyond it the village of Worstead, whence the name of "worsted" is derived, as applied to woollen twists, which were first manufactured here by the Flemings, in the time of the Plantagenets; here is a beautiful *ch.*

North Walsham to Cromer (9—132¼); very good undulating road through Antingham, 125¾, and Thorpe Market, 128¾. [There is another road through Swafield, Trunch, Southrepps, and Northrepps to Cromer, 132½. Or from Trunch through Gimingham, by the cliffs, through Trimingham, Sidestrand, and Overstrand to Cromer, 133: on the rise for about 3*m.*, then all more or less downhill to Cromer, ending with a long steep descent, the last ½*m.* of which must be walked: bad road, loose and stony.]

Trimingham Point is the highest part here in Norfolk, and Norwich can be plainly seen. About 3*m.* N.E. of North Walsham is Bromholm Abbey.

LONDON TO DUNMOW.

London to Harlow (23¾)—p. 230.

Harlow to Hatfield Heath (4¼—28); turn to the right in Harlow and through Shearing Street, 26¾.

At Shearing Street, on *r.*, Downs Hall.

Hatfield Heath to Dunmow (10½—38½); through Hatfield Broad Oak, 30¼, and 3*m.* further turn to *r.*, joining the road from Bishop Stortford, and go through Little Canfield, 35½.

Beyond Hatfield Broad Oak, on *l.*, Barrington Hall. On *l.*, Little Canfield Hall; further on, Easton Hall. At Little Dunmow, 2*m.* S.E. of Dunmow, was formerly an Augustine Priory, the site being now partly occupied by the Manor *Ho.*; the tenure of Little Dunmow Manor is that of the well-known flitch of bacon.

LONDON TO DUNMOW (by Abridge).

London to Leytonstone (6)—p. 229.

Leytonstone to Chigwell (5—11); just beyond Leytonstone keep to *r*. and it is a good road, level to Woodford Bridge, 9½, then rather hilly, with a very steep hill up into Chigwell.

[To avoid the bad road through Stratford, take the alternative route at p. 229, from Mile End or the "Angel," Islington, by Lea Bridge road to Whips Cross, 5½ or 5¾, and Snaresbrook, 6¼ or 6½, whence, having crossed the main Epping road, there is a short lane on the left of the "Eagle" which goes over a level railway crossing and into the Chigwell road about 1½m. beyond Leytonstone.]

(*Chigwell*: King's Head.)

At Woodford Bridge, on *r*., Claybury Hall; beyond it, Hainault Forest extends for some miles past Chigwell.

Chigwell to Abridge (3—14) is a good road, rather hilly either way, but nothing difficult.

(*Abridge*: Stag's Head; White Hart.)

Abridge to Chipping Ongar (7½—21½); over Passingford Bridge, 16¾, and through Hare Street, 19, is a good and very undulating road, all the hills being easy to mount.

(*Chipping Ongar*: Crown; King's Head; Lion.)

At Passingford Bridge, on *r*., Albyns, and further on Suttons; 2m. further, Navestock Old Park.

Chipping Ongar to Dunmow (14—35½); beyond Chipping Ongar, after crossing the Epping and Chelmsford road, take the right-hand of the fork roads, through Fyfield, 24½, (¾m. beyond, keeping to *l*.) Leaden Roding, 29¼, (turn sharp to *l*.) and High Roding street, 32; bad road to Fyfield, then better, and nearer level, but still rather bumpy.

(*Leaden Roding*: King William IV.)

[Or there is a better route taking the left-hand road ¾m. beyond Chipping Ongar, and going through Moreton End, 24½, (turn sharp to *l*.) and Matching Green, 27½, a mile beyond which is a drop, then another one, dangerous, with corresponding descent after; surface excellent all the way to *Hatfield Heath*, 30½. Thence to *Dunmow* (10½—41), p. 235.]

LONDON TO THETFORD (by Sudbury).

London to Stratford (4)—p. 229.

Stratford to Ilford (3¼—7¼); at the Broadway in Stratford take the right hand road; the paving continues for ½m., then rough macadam: very bad for bicycling.

Ilford to Romford (5—12¼); through Chadwell Street, 9½, and by the "Whalebone," 10½, is almost a dead level, the macadam continuing all the way, very bad and rough for first 3m., then a little better; sometimes loose and dusty, and in wet weather very heavy.

(*Romford*: White Hart, *B.T.C.*)

The Whalebone belonged to a whale that is said to have been caught in the Thames the same year that Oliver Cromwell died. At Ilford, 1m. on *r*., near Barking, is an ancient Roman encampment.

Romford to Brentwood (6¼—18½); beginning with an easy rise out of Romford, the road is undulating through Hare Street, 13¼, and Brook

Street, 17, beyond which there is a long and rather steep hill to mount; the surface having now changed to gravel it is generally pretty good, but occasionally is rather loose and rough.

(*Brentwood:* George and Dragon; White Hart.)

On *r.*, Hare Hall. At Brook St., on *l.*, Weald Hall.

Brentwood to Chelmsford (11—29½); out of Brentwood good run down for 1½*m.*; through Shenfield, 19½, Mountnessing Street, 21½, Ingatestone, 23½, Margaretting Street, 25½, Stisted, 27, Widford, 28, and Moulsham, 28¾, is a good road, with a few hills, but nothing difficult.

(*Ingatestone:* George and Dragon.—*Chelmsford:* Bell; Plough; Saracen's Head, *B.T.C.*, *Hqrs.*; White Hart.)

Beyond Ingatestone, on *l.*, Hide Hall. At Stisted, on *l.*, Haylands.

Chelmsford to Little Waltham Tg. (4¼—33¾); in Chelmsford turn to *l.*, and ¾*m.* further on, when at the end of the town, turn to *r.*; it is a good road, generally very smooth, through Broomfield, 32.

Little Waltham Tg. to Braintree (7¼—41); take the right hand fork and it is rather undulating through Blackwater St. Anne's, 36¾, and Young's End, 38½, with a rather steep descent into Braintree; good road, generally very smooth.

(*Braintree:* Horn; White Hart.)

Braintree to Halstead (6—47); through Bocking Street, 41¾, and High Garret or Trotters Green, 43½ (keep to *r.*), is a smooth road, fairly level for the first 4*m.*, then all downhill, rather steep towards the end.

(*Halstead:* Bull; George, *B.T.C.*; Railway; White.)

Beyond High Garret, on *l.*, Gosfield Place, and behind it Gosfield Hall, a fine old baronial mansion.

Halstead to Sudbury (8—55): through Palmer's Street, 50, Catley Cross, 51¼, and Bulmer Tye, 52¾, is a capital road, though rather hilly; long descent into Sudbury.

[Or keep to *l.* at High Garret, and through Gosfield, 45¼, Swan Street, 47¾, to Sible Hedingham, 48¼, out of which keep to *r.*, and through Castle Hedingham, 49¼, past the Compasses, 51½, and through Bulmer Tye, 54½, to *Sudbury*, 56¾.]

(*Sudbury:* Anchor Inn; Bear; Christopher; Four Swans; Rose and Crown; White Horse.)

At Sudbury are some remains of an Augustine Priory. At Castle Hedingham is the castle.

Sudbury to Bury St. Edmund's (16½—71½); leaving Sudbury turn to *l.*, and through Redbridge, 57, Long Melford, 58½, Alpheaton, 62½, Bradfield, 66½, and Welnetham, 69, is a fairly good road; there are two or three (not more) stiffish hills.

(*Long Melford:* Black Lion.—*Bury St. Edmund's:* Angel; Bell, Everard's; Suffolk, *B.T.C.*)

Beyond Long Melford, on *l.*, Kentwell Park; on *r.*, Melford Hall. On *r.*, Bradfield Hall; further on, on *r.*, Rushbrook Hall. At Bury St. Edmund's, ruins of magnificent abbey, once the second in the kingdom.

Bury St. Edmund's to Thetford (12¼—83¾); through Fornham St. Martin, 73½, Ingham, 76, by Rymer Point, 79¾, through Barnham, 81¾, and over Barnham Cross Common.

At Fornham St. Martin, on *r.*, the Priory. At Ingham, 1*m.* on *l.*, Culford Park; further on, on *r.*, Livermere Park.

LONDON TO NORWICH (by Ixworth).

London to Bury St. Edmund's (71½)—p. 237.

Bury St. Edmund's to Ixworth (6½—78); in Bury St. Edmund's past the station, and through Barton, 74¼, it is an easy undulating road, good going, though occasionally loose in places.

At Ixworth, are ruins of the abbey; ½*m.* on *r.* of the town have been found some Roman remains.

Ixworth to Botesdale (8¼—86¼); through Stanton, 81, the road for the first 5*m.* is not so good, being sometimes loose and stony in places, and the rest is good; undulating, with a stiff ascent into Botesdale.

Botesdale to New Buckenham (11½—97¾); at the end of Botesdale turn to the left, and through Redgrave, 88, Lopham Ford Gate, 88¾ (cross *R.* Waveney), through South Lopham, 90½, North Lopham, 91¼, and Kenninghall, 93½.

At Kenninghall, on *l.*, Quidenham Park; beyond Botesdale, on *r.*, Redgrave Park. At New Buckenham, on *l.*, remains of ancient castle; 2*m.* on *l.*, Buckenham Abbey; the *ch.* contains some interesting monuments; also South Lopham *ch.*

New Buckenham to Norwich (15¼—113); very fair undulating road through Bunwell, 101¼, Tacolneston, 103¼, Bracon Ash, 106¼, Mulbarton-cum-Kenningham, 107¾, Swardeston, 108¾, Keswick, 110, and Harford Bridge *Tg.*, 110¾.

LONDON TO NORWICH (by Stowmarket).

London to Sudbury (55)—p. 237.

Sudbury to Stowmarket (15—70); leaving Sudbury keep straight on past Chilton Park, 57, through Little Waldingfield, 59, Brent Eleigh, 61½, Kettlebarston or Kettlebastone, 63¼, Hitcham, 64½, Cross Green, 65½, High Street Green or Hoisted Green, 67, and Great Finborough, 68.

(*Stowmarket:* Fox; King's Head, *B.T.C.*)

Stowmarket to Botesdale (13½—83½); by Tot Hill, 71½, Haughley Street, 73, Bacton, 77, and Furningham, 78½.

Botesdale to Norwich (26¾—110¼); through New Buckenham, 95, above.

LONDON TO NORWICH (by Ipswich).

London to Chelmsford (29½)—p. 237.

Chelmsford to Witham (8¾—38¼); in Chelmsford the road turns off to the right opposite the conduit in the middle of the street, up a slight rise, and then it is somewhat hilly but very easy riding through Springfield, 30¾, Boreham Street, 33¾, and Hatfieldbury, 35½, just beyond which is a pretty stiff hill; capital hard surface.

(*Witham:* George, *B.T.C.*; Spread Eagle, *Hqrs.*; White Hart.)

On *l.*, Springfield Place; at Boreham Street, on *r.*, Boreham *Ho.* At Hatfieldbury, on *r.*, Hatfield Priory.

Witham to Marks Tey (8¼—46½); a very good undulating road by Rivenhall End, 39¾, through Kelvedon, 41½, and Gore Pitt, 42¾.

At Kelvedon on *l.* to *Coggleshall*, (3—44½.)

At Rivenhall End, on *r.*, Braxted Park. At Kelvedon, on *l.*, Felix Hall.

Marks Tey to Colchester ($4\frac{3}{4}$—$51\frac{1}{4}$); through Stanway, $47\frac{3}{4}$, and Lexden, $49\frac{1}{2}$, is a good and almost level road: entering Colchester turn to *l.* and then sharp to *r.*, down a rather steep descent into the town, and down the High street.

(*Colchester:* Bull; George, *Hqrs.*; Shaftesbury Refreshment Rooms; Three Cups.)

On *r.*, Lexden Park. At Colchester are remains of the old walls and of the castle, a place of immense strength; ruins of St. John's Abbey, founded 1097, and of St. Botolph's Priory, &c. South of the town are the remains of an ancient encampment.

Colchester to Stratford St. Mary ($8\frac{1}{2}$—$59\frac{3}{4}$); from the High street in Colchester turn to *l.*, and follow the telegraph wires, turning to the left again after crossing the *R.* Colne; there is a steep ascent rising from the river, and then the road is rather more hilly and not so good, in some places being very loose; there is a stiff and rough descent, with a sharp curve to *l.* half-way down, to Stratford Bridge, $58\frac{3}{4}$ (*R.* Stour), after crossing which keep to *r.*

Stratford St. Mary to Ipswich, Stones End ($9\frac{3}{4}$—$69\frac{1}{2}$); stiff rise out of Stratford, and then it is a very hilly road, through Cross Green, $62\frac{3}{4}$, by Capel Station, $63\frac{3}{4}$, where there is a level railway crossing, and through Copdock, $65\frac{3}{4}$, with a long run down into Ipswich; in some places the road is very loose, mostly on the hills, and the descents require careful riding. Ipswich is paved.

(*Ipswich:* Coach and Horses, *B.T.C.*; County; Crown and Anchor; Golden Lion; White Horse.)

At Stratford, on *l.*, Hill *Ho.* Before Ipswich, on *r.*, Stoke Park, and on *l.*, The Chantry. Ipswich is a considerable seaport town, pleasantly situate on the *R.* Orwell, which, below the town, expands into an arm of the sea. Cardinal Wolsey was born here. At Stoke, 1*m.* down the right bank of the river, is capital sea-water bathing.

Ipswich to Claydon ($3\frac{1}{2}$—73); in Ipswich turn sharp to *l.*, and through Whitton Street, $71\frac{3}{4}$: good road, but in dry weather loose and stony.

Claydon to Thwaite ($11\frac{3}{4}$—$84\frac{3}{4}$); take the right hand road, over Coddenham Bridge, $75\frac{3}{4}$, through Little Stonham, 80, Brockford Green, $82\frac{1}{4}$, and Brockford Street, 84: good road.

Beyond Claydon, on *r.*, Shrubland Hall.

Thwaite to Scole ($7\frac{1}{2}$—$92\frac{1}{4}$); through Stoke, $86\frac{1}{2}$, and Yaxley, $88\frac{1}{2}$, is a good undulating road, with no difficult hills.

Beyond Thwaite, on *l.*, Major *Ho.* On *r.*, Yaxley Hall. Scole Inn was formerly noted for its singular sign of carved figure work, the size of life, and exhibiting the arms of the chief county towns and families; here also was an immense circular bed.

Scole to Long Stratton ($9\frac{1}{4}$—$101\frac{1}{2}$); through Dickleburgh, $94\frac{3}{4}$, and Titshall Green, 97, is a pretty good undulating road.

Long Stratton to Norwich (10—$111\frac{1}{2}$); through Newton Flotman, 105, and Harford Bridge *Tg.*, $109\frac{1}{4}$, is a pretty good undulating road, but chiefly on the fall.

At Newton Flotman, on *r.*, Shottesham Hall. Before Harford Bridge *Tg.*, on *r.*, at Caistor-cum-Marshall, a Roman camp.

[There is another road through Sudbury and Bury St. Edmunds to *Botesdale*, 86¼—p. 238; thence through Sturston, 91¾, to *Scole*, 93½, the road is simply perfect, smooth as a billiard table, and but slightly undulating: ½*m*. beyond Sturston join the Ipswich and Norwich Road and turn to *l*.

Or through Sudbury and Stowmarket to *Botesdale*, 83½, p. 238, whence to *Scole*, 90¾, above.

Or from Stowmarket through Thorney Green, 71½, Mendlesham, 76½, to Brockford Street, 77½, on the Ipswich and Norwich road, whence through Thwaite, 78¼, Yaxley, 82, to *Scole*, 85¾—p. 239. This is the shortest road to *Norwich*, 105.]

LONDON TO CHELMSFORD (by Epping).

London to Epping (17¼)—p. 229.

Epping to High Ongar (7½—24¾); nearly through Epping keep to *r*., and it is an easy undulating road, through Weald Gullet, 20, Tylers Green, 21, and by Bobbingworth Mill, 22: good surface, but rather stony sometimes.

¾*m*. before High Ongar on *r*. to Chipping Ongar, 24½.; or from London to Chipping Ongar, 21½—p. 236, and ½*m*. further on *r*. to *High Ongar*, 22¾.

High Ongar to Chelmsford (10—34¾); through Norton Heath, 27¼, Hoastly Hatch, 28¼, Cooks Mill Green, 29¾, Oxney Green, 31¾ (turn to *r*.), and Writtle, 32, is a good road with no difficult hills.

LONDON TO BILDESTON AND HITCHAM.

London to Stratford Bridge (58¾)—p. 239.

Stratford Bridge to Hadleigh (6¼—65); ½*m*. beyond Stratford Bridge turn to *l*., and through Higham, 60½, and Layham, 64.

Hadleigh to Bildeston (5¼—70¼); by Semer, 68¼, and Nedging, 69¼.

[Or turn to *r*. 1¾*m*. beyond Little Waldingfield, 59—p. 238, and through Chelsworth, 63, to *Bildeston*, 64.]

Bildeston to Hitcham (1½—71¾).

LONDON TO NEW BUCKENHAM (by Diss).

London to Stowmarket (70)—p. 238.

Stowmarket to Yaxley (12—82)—above.

Yaxley to Diss (4½—86½); follow the main Norwich road for 1½*m*., then turn to *l*., and through Sturston, 84½, a little beyond which cross the *R*. Waveney, and turn to *l*. at Diss Common, 85½.

(*Diss:* King's Head, *B.T.C.*)

Diss to New Buckenham (7½—94); through Shelfanger, 89, Winfarthing, 90¼, by Winfarthing Pond, 91½, and Haugh Farm, 93.

LONDON TO SCOLE (by Debenham).

London to Ipswich (69¼)—p. 239.

Ipswich to Debenham (13½—83); in Ipswich take first turn sharp to *l.*, and shortly after keep to *r.*, and through Henley, 74½, Gosbeck, 77½, and Pettaugh, 80½. [Or taking second turn to *l.*, and through Westerfield, 72, Witnesham Street, 74, Helmingham, 79½, Framsden, 80¾, and Winston, 82¼, to Debenham, 83½.]

(*Debenham:* Red Lion, *recom.* C.T.C.)

On *l.*, Helmingham Hall, a moated mansion, erected in the reign of Henry VIII.; in the *ch.* are some splendid memorials of the Tollemache family; in Debenham *ch.* are some ancient monuments.

Debenham to Eye (9½—92½); through Rishangles, 87½.

(*Eye:* White Lion, *recom.* C.T.C.)

At Eye are remains of a castle, and of a Benedictine monastery.

Eye to Scole (4½—97); through Langton Green, 93½, and Broome, 94½, ½*m.* beyond which join the main Ipswich and Norwich road.

[Or through Sudbury and Stowmarket to Brockford Street, 77½ (p. 240), whence turn to *r.*, and through Thorndon, 80, to *Eye*, 83.]

LONDON TO YARMOUTH.

London to Ipswich (69½)—p. 239.

Ipswich to Woodbridge (7¾—77¼); keep straight through Ipswich, and out of the town there is a long steep ascent to mount, easy at first, but it becomes steeper after the turn; then it is fairly level, and a very good road, but rather loose in places, through Kesgrave, 72¾, and Martlesham Street, 75½, beyond which there is a steep sandy descent and ascent.

(*Woodbridge:* Bull; Crown, *B.T.C.*; King's Arms; King's Head; Lion; Sun; White Horse.)

Beyond Kesgrave on *l.*, Kesgrave Hall. At Woodbridge, St. Mary's *ch.*, supposed to have been built in the reign of Edward III.

Woodbridge to Wickham Market (4¾—82); through Melton *Tp.*, 78¾, Ufford Street, 80, and Pettistree, 81¼, is a rather hilly road, with a steep descent into Wickham Market; good surface, but occasionally loose and sandy.

(*Wickham Market:* Vine; White Hart, *C.T.C.*)

At Pettistree, on *r.*, Loudham Hall, and beyond it the remains of Campsey Ash Abbey,; 2*m.* farther, Rendlesham *Ho.*

Wickham Market to Saxmundham (8—90); through Glemham, 85, Stratford St. Andrew, 86¾, and Farnham, 87¼, is a similar kind of road to the last stage.

(*Saxmundham:* Bell, *C.T.C.*; White Hart.)

Beyond Wickham Market, on *l.*, Glevering Hall. At Glemham, on *l.*, Marlesford Hall; on *r.*, Glemham Hall. At Saxmundham, on *r.*, Hurts Hall. About 4*m.* E. are the remains of Leiston Abbey.

Saxmundham to Blythburgh (9¾—99¾); through Kelsale, 91¼, and Yoxford, 94¼, is a good undulating road, but loose in places.

(*Blythburgh:* White Hart, *recom.* C.T.C.)

Blythburgh to Lowestoft (14¾—114½); after crossing the *R.* Blythe keep to *r.*, and through Wangford, 102¾, Wrentham, 106½, Benacre *Tp.*, 108, Kessingland, 109¾, Pakefield, 112¾, and Kirkley, 113¼, is an undulating and fairly good road till the last 2 or 3*m.*, which are heavy and sandy; after Kessingland the road runs near the sea shore, and just before Lowestoft crosses *R.* Waveney, which forms the inner harbour on *l.*, and there is an ascent over macadam road through the town.

Beyond Blythburgh first turn on *r.* to Southwold, 105½, generally a loose sandy road.

(*Lowestoft:* Globe; Royal; Suffolk, *B.T.C.*)

Beyond Blythburgh, on *l.*, Henham Hall. Beyond Wrentham, on *r.*, Benacre Hall.

Lowestoft to Yarmouth, *M.P.* (10—12½); good hard gravel road, hilly for the first 3 or 4m., and then slightly undulatory through Hopton, 119, with a mile run down to Gorleston, 122½, whence it is laid with tramway through South Town, 123½: cross *R.* Yare just before entering Yarmouth. [Or from Gorleston cross *R.* Yare by the ferry, and thus avoid the tram lines. There is also another road by turning to *r.* just out of Lowestoft, and over a common, the first mile or so being very sandy, but it becomes better near Corton, 117, where it goes almost to the edge of the cliffs; then it is but a narrow lane, with very good surface, to Hopton, 118½, where, on passing the *ch.*, a turn to *l.* must be taken leading into the main road at the "White Hart" at Hopton, 119.]

(*Yarmouth:* Angel; Bath; Crown and Anchor; Franklin's; Norfolk; Queen's; Royal; Star; Victoria.)

Yarmouth is an important seaport town, consisting chiefly of four principal streets, crossed at right angles by about 150 narrow lanes, called rows: it had formerly a moat and embattled walls, and during last century some fortifications were erected. The quay is one of the finest in the kingdom, with a broad promenade. The *ch.* was erected in 1123. Nelson's Monument. Splendid sea bathing. 2m. before Hopton, on *l.* 3m., Somerleyton Hall, containing a splendid gallery of paintings, sometimes open to the public. At Gorleston, 3m. on *l.*, ruins of Burgh Castle.

LONDON TO YARMOUTH (by Bungay).

London to Scole (85¾); through Stowmarket (p. 240).

Scole to Harleston (7—92¾); at Scole turn to *r.*, over Bilingford Common, through Thorpe Abbots, 88, Brockdish Street, 89½, and Needham, 91½, running close to *R.* Waveney. [The better way is to follow the Norwich road to Dickleburgh, 88½, which is pretty good, then turn to *r.*, and through Rushall, 90½, to *Harleston*, 93½.]

(*Harleston:* Cardinal's Hat; Magpie; Swan.)

At Brockdish, on *r.*, across *R.* Waveney, remains of Wingfield Castle. At Harleston, on *r.*, across *R.* Waveney, Mendham Priory and ruins.

Harleston to Bungay (7½—100½); dead level road through Redenhall, 94½, Wattle Wortwell, 95, by Dove Alehouse, 96, Buck Alehouse, 98, and Earsham, 99½, running close by the *R.* Waveney, and crossing it just before Bungay: good road.

(*Bungay:* King's Head.)

At Wattle Wortwell, on *l.*, Denton Ho. On *r.*, across *R.* Waveney, Flixton Hall and ruins of Abbey. At Bungay, ruins of a Benedictine Nunnery and remains of a castle. At Redenhall, on *l.*, Gandy Hall; here is a *ch.* of the 14th century. At Earsham, on *l.*, Earsham Ho.

Bungay to Beccles (5½—105¾); in Bungay turn to *r.* and then to **L** by the church; hilly but good road through Mettingham, 102, Shipmeadow, 103½, Barsham, 104½.

At Mettingham, on *r.*, ruins of castle.

Beccles to Yarmouth, *M.P.* (14¾—120½); in Beccles turn to the left and cross *R.* Waveney, then the road is fair and level through Gillingham All Saints, 107¼ (keep to *r.* twice), Toft Monks, 109½, and Haddiscoe, 111, to St. Olave's Bridge, 113¼ (cross *R.* Waveney again); after that through Fritton, 114, Bradwell, 116, to South Town, 119¾, the road is undulating, but frequently very loose and sandy, especially so in summer.

[There is another road from Bungay to Gillingham, by turning to *l.* in the former, crossing *R.* Waveney and following its left bank through Ellingham 101¾, Kirby Row, 103½, and Geldeston, 104¾, to Gillingham All Saints, 106¾.

Or from Beccles through Worlingham, North Cove, and Barnaby, a very good road, to *Lowestoft*, 112¾, whence to *Yarmouth*, 10—122¾—p. 242.]

Beyond St. Olave's Bridge, Herringfleet Hall, and the ruins of the abbey: 2*m.* on *r.*, Somerleyton Hall, containing a fine gallery of pictures, which is sometimes open to the public; very loose and sandy road to it. At Bradwell, 2*m.* on *l.*, remains of Burgh Castle.

LONDON TO FRAMLINGHAM.

London to Wickham Market (82)—p. 241,

Wickham Market to Framlingham (5¾—87¾); after crossing *R.* Deben beyond Wickham Market turn to *l.*, and through Hacheston, 84½, and Parham, 85¾, where keep to *l.*

(*Framlingham*: Crown, *B.T.C.*)

At Framlingham are the ruins of a castle, formerly a magnificent building of great strength; the *ch.* has a curious carved roof, and contains some old monuments.

LONDON TO NORWICH (by Bungay).

London to Saxmundham (90)—p. 241.

Saxmundham to Halesworth (10¾—100¾); follow the Yarmouth road for 2*m.* beyond Yoxford, 94¼, then turn to *l.* and through Bramfield, 98¾.

At Halesworth, on *r.*, Mells Chapel.

Halesworth to Bungay (9—109¾); through Stone Street, 104, St. Lawrence Ilketshall, 106¾, and St. John Ilketshall, 107¾.

Before Bungay on *r.*, ruins of Mettingham Castle.

Bungay to Norwich *M.P.* (14—123¾); through Bungay cross *R.* Waveney, then turn to *l.* at White House, 110½, and through Ditchingham, 112, Hedenham, 113, by Tumbledown Dick, 114½, Kirkstead Hall, 117, Poringland, 119¾, over Poringland Heath to Bixley, 121¼, and through Trowse *Tp.*, 122½.

On *r.*, Ditchingham Hall, Kirkstead Hall, and Bixley Park.

LONDON TO BECCLES (by Blythburgh).

London to Blythburgh (99¾)—p. 241.

Blythburgh to Beccles (10—109¾); after crossing *R.* Blythe, take the left hand road through Bulchamp, 100¾, and over a common, skirting Henham Park and through Sotherton, 103¾, to Brampton, 105; here turn to *r.* up a hill by the *ch.* and through Shaddingfield, 105¾, and Weston, 107½.

LONDON TO LODDON.

London to Bungay (100¼)—p. 242.

Bungay to Loddon (6¼—106½); keep straight on through Bungay and cross *R.* Waveney, 1½*m.* beyond which turn to *l.*, and through Broome, 102¾. [Or to *Beccles*, 105¾, (p. 242), *through* which bearing to *l.*, cross *R.* Waveney to Gillingham All Saints, 106¼, and through Stockton, 108¾, and Hales, 110, to *Loddon*, 111½.]

LONDON TO DUNWICH.

London to Woodbridge (77¼)—p. 241.

Woodbridge to Snape Bridge (10¼—87½); beyond Woodbridge turn to *r.*, and through Eyke, 81¼, Rendlesham, 82¼, and Tunstall, 85¼.

On *l.*, Rendelsham *Ho.*, and further on ruins of Campsey Ash Abbey.

Snape Bridge to Dunwich (10¼—97¾); through Snape Street, 88, Cold Fair Green, 90¾, Leiston, 92¼, and East Bridge, 94¾. [The best road to Dunwich is to follow the main Yarmouth road to Yoxford, 94¼, (as on p. 241), and then 1¼*m.* beyond on *r.*, through Darsham, 96¼, to Dunwich, 100¼.]

Beyond Leiston, on *l.*, Leiston Abbey; on *r.*, Leiston Old Abbey.

LONDON TO ORFORD.

London to Woodbridge (77¼)—p. 241.

Woodbridge to Orford (13—90¼); through Woodbridge, on the Saxmundham road turn to *r.* at Melton *Tp.*, 78¾, and then through Bromeswell, 80¼, over Sprat Bridge, 82¼, and through Butley, 84¼, Chillesford, 85¾, and Sudbourn, 88¼.

Before Sudbourn, on *r.*, Sudbourn Hall (Marquis of Hertford). At Orford, ruins of castle.

LONDON TO ALDBOROUGH.

London to Wickham Market (82)—p. 241.

Wickham Market to Aldborough (12½—94½); follow the Yarmouth road through Glemham, 85, and Stratford St. Andrew, 86¾, to Farnham, 87¼, a rather hilly road with good surface, but occasionally loose and sandy; then turn to *r.*, and through Snape, 89½, a very good road, ending with a steep descent into the town: this is the best road.

[Or turn to *r.* just beyond Wickham Market, and through Campsey Ash, Blaxhall, over Snape Bridge and through Snape Street, 1¾*m*, beyond which join above road 1*m.* out of Snape: distance about 1*m.* shorter; the road is extremely bad, being often loose and stony, made with flints.

Or to Snape Bridge, 87½ (above); thence to *Aldborough*, 93¾—above.]

(*Aldborough:* East Suffolk; White Lion.)

LONDON TO HARWICH.

London to Colchester (51¼)—p. 239.

Colchester to Manningtree (9¼—60½); from the High street in

Colchester, turn to *l.*, following the telegraph wires, and after crossing *R.* Colne keep first to *r.*, and shortly after, beyond the railway, to *l.*; then through Ardleigh, 56¼, and Wignell Street, 58¾: very bad loose hill to climb (dangerous to ride down) 3*m.* out of Colchester.

At Wignell Street, on *l.*, Lawford Hall.

Manningtree to Harwich (11½—72); through Mistley Thorn, 61¼, Bradfield, 63½, Ramsey Street, 68¼, Ramsey, 68¾, and Dovercourt, 70, running near *R.* Stour all the way.

(*Harwich:* Great Eastern; Pier; Three Cups; White Hart, *B.T.C.*)

Beyond Manningtree, on *r.*, Mistley Hall; further on, ruins of old *ch.* Beyond Bradfield, 1½*m.* on *r.*, Wicks Abbey; before Ramsey, on *r.*, Ramsey Hall.

LONDON TO HARWICH (by Great Oakley).

London to Colchester (51¼)—p. 239.

Colchester to Elmstead Market (4¼—55½); from the High street in Colchester turn to *l.*, following the telegraph wires, and after crossing *R.* Colne keep to *r.* twice for Greenstead, 52½, just out of which there is a steep and rather long hill, often covered with dust and loose stones, which must be walked up; thence (keeping to *l.* 1*m.* further on) the road is loose and dusty to Elmstead Market.

[Or turning to *r.* just entering Colchester, and along Barrack street to Hythe, a suburb of the town, and the road is good and hard to Greenstead, just before which cross *R.* Colne.]

Beyond Greenstead, on *r.*, Wivenhoe Park.

Elmstead Market to Great Oakley (9½—65); at the end of the former take left hand road through Horsley Cross, 60½, and Wicks Cross, 63; it is undulating, but very loose and bad. [Or keep to *r.* out of Elmstead Market to Frating, 57½, where turn to *l.* and go through Tendring, 62½, Weeley, 63½, Thorpe-le-Soken, 65¾ (again turn to *l.*), and Beaumont, 67¾, to Great Oakley, 70½; the road is very bad for the greater part of the way, being loose and heavy with dust, but approaching Thorpe-le-Soken it improves and after that is hilly but generally good.]

At Wicks Cross, on *l.*, Wicks Abbey; at Thorpe-le-Soken, on *r.*, Thorpe Abbey.

Great Oakley to Harwich (6—71); at Great Oakley turn to the *l.*, and through Little Oakley, 66, Ramsey, 67¾, and Dovercourt, 69; an up and downhill road, but nothing difficult, and generally in good condition.

The whole of this road to Harwich is often very bad and heavy, with thick dust and loose stones in dry weather, and in wet weather is very soft.

LONDON TO WALTON-ON-NAZE.

London to Elmstead Market (55½)—above.

Elmstead Market to Thorpe-le-Soken (10¼—65¾); at the end of the former keep to *r.* for Frating, 57½ (turn to *l.*), and through Tendring, 62½, and Weeley, 63½; the road is very bad for the greater part of the way, being loose and heavy with stones and dust, but approaching Thorpe it improves.

At Thorpe, on *r.*, Thorpe Abbey. At Frating, on *r.*, to *St. Osyth* (5*m.*—62½), where are remains of a priory.

Thorpe-le-Soken to Walton-on-the-Naze (5¼—71); at Thorpe turn to *l.*, and nearly 1*m.* beyond to *r.*, and through Kirby Soken, 69, and Walton Ashes, 71, is an excellent road. [Or at Thorpe keep straight on to Kirby Cross, 68, then turn to *l.* to Kirby Soken, 69.]

(*Walton-on-the-Naze:* Bath; Clifton, *B.T.C.*; Dorling's; Ordnance.)

LONDON TO BRADWELL AND BURNHAM.

London to Margaretting Street (25½)—p. 237.

Margaretting Street to Great Baddow (4¼—29¾); at the former turn to *r.*, and over Galleywood Common, 27½.

[Or by *Chelmsford*, 29½ (p. 237), and then to *r.* to *Great Baddow*, 31.]

Great Baddow to Maldon (8¼—38); at Great Baddow turn to *l.*, and a little after to *r.*, and through Danbury, 33¼, and Runsells, 34½.

(*Maldon:* Blue Boar; King's Head, *Hqrs.—Heybridge*; Queen's Head, *Hqrs.*)

Before Danbury, on *r.*, Danbury Place: S. of the village is an ancient Danish encampment, in which the *ch.* stands; here is a curious tomb. At Maldon, St. Mary's *ch.*, supposed to have been erected 1056. At Maldon, 1*m.* on *l.*, is Heybridge across Blackwater *R.*

Maldon to Snoreham (5—43); in Maldon turn to right.

Snoreham to Bradwell (8½—51½), through Steeple, 47.

Beyond Snoreham, on *r.* to Althorn, 45½, thence to Southminster, 48½. At Althorn on *r.* to *Burnham*, 49.

LONDON TO SOUTHEND.

London, Royal Exchange, to Barking (7½); asphalte along Cornhill, Leadenhall street, and Aldgate, to Whitechapel *ch.*, ½*m.*, then granite paving, with tramway, along High street, Whitechapel (at ¾*m.* turning to *r.*), along Commercial road, through Limehouse, 2¼, and Poplar, 3, to the East India Docks; then crossing *R.* Lea at the Iron Bridge, 3¾, it is macadam, bad and lumpy, along Barking road to Plaistow, 4¾, after which it improves, though liable to be dusty in very dry summers, to East Ham, 6½, and good to Barking: level all the way, except a slight rise from *R.* Roding into Barking; tramway extends for about 3*m.*, and the road is bad for bicycling on account of the heavy traffic. The road takes several sharp turns in Barking. [There is another road to East Ham by turning to *r.* ¼*m.* beyond Stratford, 4 (p. 229), and through West Ham, 4¾, to East Ham, 6¾.] From East Ham there is a good level road on *r.*, across the marshes, to *North Woolwich*, 3, whence Woolwich can be reached by ferry.

At Barking are remains of a nunnery, said to have been the earliest in England. About ½*m.* N. of Barking, at a farm called Uphall, on the road to Ilford, is a large Roman entrenchment.

Barking to Rainham (5½—13); level railway crossing just out of Barking, then a dip to and rise from St. Mary's or Mays Bridge, 8½, and by Ripple Side, 10, The Chequers, 10¾, Beam River *Tg.*, 11¼, and Beam Bridge, 11½; the road is flat, and generally rather loose and sandy, especially in summer, but sometimes good. [Or follow the Romford road to the "Whalebone," 10½ (p. 236), then turn on *r.*, and through Dagenham, 13¼, to Rainham, 15½.]

(*Rainham:* Angel; Phœnix; White Horse.)

Just before Mays Bridge, on *r.*, Eastbury *Ho.*, traditionally associated with the meetings of the Gunpowder Plot conspirators.

Rainham to Stifford (6—19); this is a similar description of road through Wennington, 14¼, at ½m. beyond which turn to *l.*, and there is a long stiff hill to climb, followed by a steep descent, with a turn in it, to Aveley, 16½, whence it is level over Stifford Bridge, 18¼.

Beyond Aveley, on *l.*, Belhus Park.

Stifford to Stanford-le-Hope (6—25); undulating but very good road through Baker Street, 21¼ (turn to *r.* and ½m. further to *l.*), and by the Cock Inn, 23; entering Stanford there is a level railway crossing, then a sharp rise and turn to *l.* by the King's Head. [Or at Baker Street keep straight to Orsett, 22, then turn to *r.*, rejoining the other road just before the Cock Inn. Or instead of going through Baker street turn to *r.* out of Stafford, and ½m. further to *l.*, joining the other road at 21¾; this is not so hilly.]

Stanford-le-Hope to Pitsea (5½—30½), is a very hilly road, chiefly on the rise as far as Vange, 28¾, and then undulating; very fair surface; beyond the railway bridge past Vange take the first turn to *r.*

Pitsea to Hadleigh (4¾—35¼); good undulating road past Bowers, 31¼, to the bottom of Bread and Cheese Hill, otherwise called Jarvis Hill (top of), 33¾, which is a long steep incline winding up through a wood, (and dangerous to ride *down*); from the top an excellent road runs along the top of a range of hills past Hadleigh Cross, 34¾, on Hadleigh Common.

From Jarvis Hill an extensive view is obtained over the *R.* Thames, and the opposite Kentish shore. On *r.*, the ruins of Hadleigh Castle, situate on the brow of a steep hill, overlooking *R.* Thames.

Hadleigh to Southend (5—40¼); by Leigh Elm, 37¼, is good travelling, and an easy undulating road; ½m. before Southend turn to *r.*

At Leigh Elm on *r.*, ½m. to the village of Leigh, which is worth a visit; here is Leigh Hill to descend, a steep declivity leading from the table land above the cliffs to the village and beach; it is dangerous to ride down; near the top is a right-angled turn in the steepest part, then a straight shoot down the side of the cliff, terminating in a narrow street, with a railway crossing and another turn to the beach. 1m. before Southend, ¼m. on *l.*, the village of Prittlewell, 39½.

(*Southend:* Britannia; Hope; London; Middleton; Royal, *B.T.C.*; Ship.)

Southend is much frequented as a bathing-place, &c. About 3m. E. is Shoeburyness, the locality of some of the great artillery experiments.

LONDON TO SOUTHEND (by Billericay).

London to Brentwood (18½)—p. 236.

Brentwood to Billericay (5¼—23¾); out of Brentwood there is a good run down to Shenfield, 19½, where turn to *r.*, and the road becomes bad through Hutton Street, 21, with a long and shingly ascent to Billericay.

(*Billericay:* Red Lion, *B.T.C.*)

Billericay to Wickford (5¾—29½); past South Green, 24¾, there is a long descent down Windmill Hill, steep at first, and generally rough and

stony, after which it is a good hard road through Cray's Hill, 27¼, but sometimes loose and rough; just before Wickford turn to *r.*

From Windmill Hill there is a grand view.

Wickford to Rayleigh (4¾—34¼); by Rawreth Shot, 31½, is a fairly level and good road till just before Rayleigh, when there is a very steep hill to be mounted into the town: parts of the road are sometimes bad, loose and rough.

Entering Rayleigh, on *l.*, remains of an ancient castle.

Rayleigh to Hadleigh (3—37¼); turn to *r.* at Rayleigh, and it is a fairly good and hard road through Rivers, 35, and over Thundersley Common, 36, to Hadleigh Cross, 36¾, where join the more direct London road through Pitsea.

Hadleigh to Southend (5—42¼)—p. 247.

[There is another road from Rayleigh through Prittlewell to Southend; it is a bye-road, but level and good running, except in very dry and dusty weather: at Prittlewell is a broad pathway across Prittlewell Fields to Southend: about 1½*m.* shorter.]

LONDON TO GREAT WAKERING.

London to Rayleigh (34¼)—above.

Rayleigh to Rochford (6—40¼); at Rayleigh turn to *l.*, and through Hockley, 36½.

(*Rochford:* King's Head; Old Ship.)

Rochford to Great Wakering (8—48¼); at Rochford keep to *r.*, and at Sutton, 41½, to *r.* again, to within a mile of Southend, then to the *l.*, and through South Church, 44¾, and North Shoebury, 46½.

[Or from Sutton on *l.* through the lanes to *Great Wakering*, 45¾.

Or by the direct London road through Hadleigh to the junction of the roads (½*m.* before Southend), 39¾, p. 247; here keep to *l.*, and through South Church, 40¾, and North Shoebury, 42½, to *Great Wakering*, 44¼.]

LONDON TO SOUTHEND (by Upminster).

London to Romford (12¼)—p. 236.

Romford to Upminster (3¾—16); in the middle of Romford turn to *r.*, and the road is good and level through Havering Well, 13¼ (turn to *l.*), with a hill to ride up into Hornchurch, 14½, and then down again to Upminster.

At Hornchurch, on *l.*, Langtons, and beyond it Nelmes.

Upminster to Wickford (14—30); for 10*m.* it is an almost straight lane, not passing through a single village; then, turning to *l.*, it falls into the Billericay and Wickford road, about 1*m.* before Cray's Hill, 27¾.

Wickford to Southend (12¾—42¾)—above.

LONDON TO SOUTHEND (by Purfleet).

London to Rainham (13)—p. 246.

Rainham to Purfleet (3½—16½); fairly level and very good road, but sometimes loose, to Wennington, 14¼, at the fork beyond which keep to *r.*, and with very good surface there is a decline to the railway crossing, whence is a sharp rise past the barracks and again down into Purfleet, to the river beach.

(*Purfleet:* Royal.)

Purfleet to Chadwell (6½—23); in Purfleet turn sharp to *l.*, and it is a good road slightly on the fall through Stone House, 18, and West Thurrock, 19, to 1½m. beyond, where the road to Grays Thurrock, 20¼, strikes off to *r.*; then ascend a long and rather steep hill, and from the top a slightly undulating road with a very good surface runs to Chadwell.

Beyond West Thurrock, on *l.*, Belmont Castle: from the high ground near Chadwell, capital view of Thames valley and Gravesend.

Chadwell to Stanford-le-Hope (4¼—27¼); 1¼m. beyond Chadwell keep to *l.*; it is a fairly good road, undulating with easy gradients, through Muckingford, 25, and Muckinge, 26¼.

Stanford-le-Hope to Southend (15¼—42½)—p. 247.

LONDON TO TILBURY FORT.

London to Chadwell (23)—above.

Chadwell to Tilbury Fort (3—26); ¾m. beyond Chadwell turn to right; there is a steep and loose hill to descend, and then it is a level and smooth road.

[Or to *Upminster*, 16, (p. 248); thence it is a very good road, turning to *r.* to Corbetts Tye, 17, and through South Ockendon, 20¼, to Stifford Bridge, 21½, Stifford, 22¼, where turn on *r.* to the road from Purfleet at 21½m.

Or from Upminster by turning to *l.* at Corbetts Tye and through North Ockendon, 18¾, to South Ockendon, 20½.]

(*North Ockendon:* Old White Horse; White Horse.)

From Tilbury, cross R. Thames by ferry to Gravesend; this is the best route from N. and E. London to East Kent.

CROSS ROADS.

MARGATE TO SOUTHAMPTON (by the Coast).

Margate to Ramsgate (4½), is an almost straight road; there is Chapel Hill to mount, and a fall into Ramsgate, but nothing difficult, and good surface all the way: through Ramsgate is mostly macadam. [There is another road by Broadstairs, 3½, (p. 4); thence to Ramsgate, 2—5½. Or by North Down, 1½, and Kingsgate, 2¾, to Broadstairs, 4¾.]

Margate, Ramsgate and Broadstairs, hotels, &c., pp. 3 and 4.

Ramsgate to Sandwich (6—10½); ascent out of Ramsgate and downhill out of St. Lawrence, 5¼, to Nether Court, 5¾, (¼*m.* beyond which keep to the *l.*), and Cliffs End, 6¾; from here the road is excellent and level, skirting Pegwell Bay and traversing Sandwich Marshes, past Half-way House, 8, and The Salterns, 8¾: through Sandwich is paved and bad riding. [Or instead of going through Ramsgate, turn to *r.* 2¼*m.* out of *Margate*, and through Haine, 3, and 1¼*m.* further joining the road ¾*m.* beyond Nether Court, and on to Sandwich, 9.]

Beyond Salterns, on *r.*, Richborough Castle, p. 5. Sandwich, p. 5.

Sandwich to Deal, The Castle (6½—17), is a good undulating road through St. Bartholomew, 11 (keep to the *l.*), Worth, 11½, Hacklinge, 12½, How Bridge, 13, Cottington, 13½, Sholden, 14½, and Upper Deal, 15½. [There is another and shorter route on the *l.* across the sands or marshes and close by the shore, passing Sandown Castle.]

Deal, p. 6.

Deal to Dover (8½—25½); a little way past Deal Castle turn to the *r.*, and a gentle rise begins which ends in a stiff pull through Walmer, 18¼, and Ringwould, 19¾, followed by a steep descent into a valley and a long ascent again to Dover Castle, whence there is the very steep winding descent of Castle Hill into Dover, not safe to ride down without a powerful brake: good smooth surface.

[There is another road from *Sandwich* by keeping to *r.* at St Bartholomew, 11, and through Statenborough, 12¼, Eastry, 13, whence it is rather hilly past Updown *Ho.* on *l.*, through Tilmanstone, 15¼, and Waldershare, 17, where on *r.* is Waldershare Park; 2*m.* further the top of the hills is reached and there is a ¾*m.* descent into the London road ½*m.* beyond Ewell, whence to *Dover*, 22½, see p. 6.]

Beyond Ringwould, on *l.*, Oxney Court. At Walmer, on *l.*, the Castle. Dover, p. 6.

Dover to Folkestone (7—32½); the road out of Dover leaves by the upper part of the town, and there is a long rather steep ascent past the Priory Railway Station, which continues with two or three undulations through Hougham, 28, up a long valley and over an indifferent road to the

Signal House *Tg.*, 31, on the top of Folkestone Hill; then there is a steep and dangerous descent with several sharp turns in it, and which ought not to be ridden down without a powerful brake, the surface being generally rather rough; it ends in the narrow and tortuous streets of Folkestone, through which bicyclists should keep to the right, avoiding the old or lower town.

Folkestone, hotels, &c., p. 9.

Folkestone to Hythe, *Ch.* (4½—37); there are two roads out of Folkestone to Sandgate, 34¼; the lower one next the sea is perhaps the better one, starting from the Old Town and with slight undulations skirting the base of the cliffs to Sandgate; for the other road (to the *r.*) go up the sharp hill on to the Lees in the upper part of the town, then level for a mile or so and down a long fall into Sandgate; thence the road runs alongside the sea through Shorncliff, 35¼, macadam and shaky most of the way. See also pp. 8-9.

Hythe, hotels, &c., p. 8.

Hythe to New Romney, *M.H.* (9—16); just beyond Hythe take the left hand road over the Royal Military Canal, and across Romney Marsh, running near to the sea shore the whole distance and almost dead level; it is a very fair road on the whole to Dymchurch, 42, but frequently portions are covered with loose gravel and shingle, and the remainder to New Romney is very bad for bicycling, being all made of loose stones and shingle with a cart track in the middle to ride on.

(*Dymchurch:* Ship.—*New Romney*, p. 10.)

New Romney to Rye, Strand Gate (12½—58½); follow the Appledore road for 4¼m., through Old Romney, 43, to the junction of the roads ¼m. *before* Brenzett Corner. (50½); then turn to the *l.*, and across Walling Marsh through Brookland, 51¼, and along Guldeford (or Guildford) Lane, by Kent Ditch, 54¼, to Scot's Flat, 56¼, where the R. M. Canal is recrossed: level but extremely bad for bicycling, being a continuation of the last stage, made of loose gravel and shingle, with one and sometimes two cart and horse tracks, to within 1 or 2m. of Rye, which is situate upon a hill, and has badly paved streets.

Old Romney, p. 10.—Rye, &c., p. 13.

[Instead of the bad road from Hythe to Rye, the bicyclist will do well to go inland from Hythe along the road to Ashford for 6 or 7m. (p. 8), and then bearing to the *l.* ride through the villages Aldington, &c., to Appledore, and thence through Reading Street, 2¼m. (p. 10), to Rye, 7m. (p. 14); pretty fair going on the whole, though some 4 or 5m. farther.

There is also a direct road from Appledore to Rye, 6m., alongside the Royal Military Canal, but it is a very bad road, being very grassy and full of loose pebbles, except last 2m.]

Rye to Winchelsea, Strand Gate (2—60½); very good road, dead level, except a steep winding ascent to the latter town, which is on a hill.

Winchelsea, p. 13.

Winchelsea to Hastings, Swan Inn (8¼—69¼); leaving Winchelsea a sharp turn to the *r.*, at the direction post, has to be taken, and through Icklesham, 62½, Guestling Thorn, 64½ (keep to *l.* twice), and Guestling, 66, is undulating, then there is a long, steep, winding ascent, *unrideable either way*, to Leanham, 67¼, with another short stiff rise on to Fairlight Down, then it begins to descend, and at 68m. turn sharp to *l.* into the road from Battle; about 1m. farther is a long steep hill to go down into Hastings; this stage requires careful riding in descending the hills in either direction; good road on the whole.

At Guestling Thorn on *l.*, Broomham Place. Hastings, p. 15.

Hastings to Bexhill ($5\frac{1}{2}$—$74\frac{3}{4}$); through the new town and along the Parade of Hastings and St. Leonards, $70\frac{1}{4}$, the road is level, but macadam for a couple of miles, then it turns inland and with fairly good surface is rather undulating, but chiefly on the rise; at the direction post, $\frac{1}{2}$m. before Bexhill keep to the *l.*

3m. N. of Bexhill is Crowhurst, in the churchyard of which is a large yew tree; also remains of manorial mansion. On the beach at Bexhill, a submarine forest is being left uncovered by the sea.

Bexhill to Pevensey or Pevensea, Sluice Bridge ($7\frac{1}{4}$—82); very sharp fall to Bexhill Common, $75\frac{1}{4}$, then (keeping to *l.*) long pull up, and another sharp loose descent to Little Common, 77; here keep straight on, the road being up a narrow, shingly, cart-and-hoof-track lane, uphill for nearly a mile, on to Barnhorne Hill with a couple of sharp ascents and descents to Stone Bridge, $78\frac{1}{4}$ (just before keep to *r.*); then across the marshes, over Sewers Bridge, $79\frac{1}{4}$ (where returning keep to *r.*), is level but loose and shingly road. [Or turning to *l.* at Little Common, good for a mile to the coastguard station on the beach, then very bad, simply a loose shingle bed for nearly 1m. till you cross the railway at a level, after which the surface improves across the marshes, but is still shingly; join the other road just before Pevensey.]

About 3m. N., ruins of Hurstmonceux Castle, p. 18. Pevensey, p. 18.

Pevensey to Eastbourne ($6\frac{1}{2}$—$88\frac{1}{2}$); passing by the Castle ruins and through Westham, $82\frac{1}{2}$, (where keep to *l.*, and again $1\frac{1}{2}$m. on) it is undulating and generally loose and sandy to Langley Tg., 85, and the rest level and good over Crumble Bridge, $85\frac{1}{2}$, through Bourne or Sea Houses, 87.

Eastbourne, hotels, &c., p. 18.

Eastbourne to Seaford, New Inn ($7\frac{3}{4}$—$96\frac{1}{4}$); turn to *l.* by the *ch.* in Eastbourne, and there is a long steep hill to walk up out of the town on to the top of the Downs behind Beachy Head, and after a little rough riding on the top there is a steep descent, which must be ridden down very carefully and is best walked, towards East Dean, $91\frac{1}{2}$; then a steep and loose uphill again to Friston, 92, and an easy descent, except the last part, which is rather steep and rough, through Excet, $93\frac{3}{4}$, to Excet Bridge, 94 (*R.* Cuckmere); from here is a hill to mount, then a good run down through Sutton, $95\frac{1}{4}$, to Seaford: on this stage the descents either way require very careful riding; the surface is rather rough across the Downs, but improves towards Seaford.

On *r.*, Friston Place, a mansion built in the Tudor style, but dating from the 17th century. At West Dean the *ch.* is Norman; also an old parsonage house of the 14th century. Seaford, p. 22.

Seaford to Newhaven, Bridge ($3\frac{1}{4}$—$99\frac{1}{2}$)—p. 22.

Newhaven, &c., p. 22.

Newhaven to Brighton, Aquarium (9—$108\frac{1}{2}$); keeping straight through the town there is a steep ascent out of Newhaven up to the Downs, then it is an undulating road to Rottingdean, 104½, where there is a steep descent and a corresponding rise; after that the road continues all up and down hill for 2 or 3*m*., the gradients being very steep and often rough and stony; from Kemp Town, 107, the eastern suburb of Brighton, it is a gradual slope down to the Aquarium; on the whole very good surface, though sometimes shaky. After the first mile the road runs on the top of the cliffs close by the sea shore.

From Eastbourne to Brighton this road is not so easy riding as the inland route, but following the coast there is more to see and better scenery than on the other route, for which see pp. 20-1.

Brighton, hotels, &c., p. 25.

Brighton to Old Shoreham, *Ch.* (6¾—115¾); continuing by the sea shore, along the parade or esplanade through Cliftonville, 109½, Hove, 110½, Coppard's Gap, 111¾, Southwick, 113, Kingston-by-Sea, 113½, and New Shoreham, 114½, is a very good road, nearly level; slight rise and fall in Shoreham. [There is another, the upper road, by following the London road back out of the town, and ½*m*. beyond St. Peter's *ch.* turn to the *l.* over a stiff hill, and then very undulating by Portslade, 112¾, and Buckingham House, 115, to Old Shoreham, 116. Or from the lower road turn to the *r.* beyond Coppard's Gap, and through Portslade, 112¾, to Old Shoreham, above.]

Before Coppard's Gap, on *r.*, the ruins of Aldrington *ch.* Old Shoreham *ch.* is very ancient.

Old Shoreham to Arundel, Bridge (12¼—128); take the road to *r.* across the *R.* Adur over the wooden bridge (Norfolk Bridge) at which is a toll of 2d. to pay; thence through Lancing, 117, and Sompting, 118¼, is easy going and a good road, almost level to ½*m*. before Offington House, where join the London road from Worthing (1¾*m*. on *l.*) and follow it up the hill to the next cross roads *at* Offington House, 120¼; then keep straight on, leaving the London road on the *r.*, and for the next mile it is not a good road, and there is a descent which must be taken carefully, the road bearing first to *r.* then to *l.*; the rest is undulating, and except a long stiff ascent at Patching Pond, 123½ (1¼*m*. further on turn first to *r.* then to *l.*), is all easy riding and a very good road, by Poling Cross Roads, 126, to Arundel, with a steep descent into the town.

2*m*. past Offington *Ho.*, on *l.*, Goring Lodge; before Arundel, on *r.*, Budworth Park. Arundel, &c., p. 31.

Arundel to Chichester, Market Cross (10¾—138¾); in Arundel after crossing *R.* Arun turn to *l.*; there is a good ascent out of the town, then down and up again; afterwards undulating, but nothing difficult, by Avisford Hill, 131, Ball's Hut, 132½, Crocker Hill, 134½, and through Maudlin, 136¾, and West Hampnet, 137¼: good surface, but in places loose at times. Pretty country. (On the return journey out of Chichester take the left hand road, and at Maudlin the *r.*).

1*m*. after Crocker Hill, a little on *r.*, Boxgrove, the *ch.* of which was part of a Benedictine priory, founded 1117—35. At Avisford Hill, on *r.*, Avisford *Ho*; ½*m*. on *l.*, Walberton Place. At Ball's Hut, on *r.*, Slinden *Ho.* At Maudlin, 2*m*. on *r.*, Goodwood *Ho.* and Park. Chichester, &c., p. 34.

Chichester to Havant (9—147¾); through Fishbourn, 140½, Old Fishbourn, 140¾, by Broadbridge Mill, 141¾, through Nutbourne, 144½,

and Emsworth, 145¾; almost level road, and very good going—like a racing-path.
(*Havant:* Bear; Dolphin, *C.T.C.*; Star.—*Emsworth:* Crown.)

At Broadbridge Mill, 1m. on *l.*, Bosham, with very fine Saxon *ch.*, which is a conspicuous feature in the Bayeux tapestry, as Harold sailed from here on his voyage to Normandy, and the site of his residence is still pointed out.

Havant to Cosham (4½—152); continues good going, and almost level, there being only one ascent worth mentioning, about 1m. beyond Bedhampton, 148½; it is short but rather stiff on account of its being generally loose and stony.

Beyond Bedhampton, on *r.*, Belmont Castle.

Cosham to Fareham (5—157); turn to *l.* a short distance on the Portsmouth road, then to *r.*; through Wimmering, 152½, Palsgrave, 153½, and Porchester, 154½, is the same kind of road, though sometimes rough.

Porchester Castle, &c., p. 36. On *r.* pass the three forts. Before Fareham, on *l.*, Cams Hall. Fareham, p. 41.

Fareham to Titchfield (3—160), is a good undulating road; 2m. beyond Fareham keep to *l.*

Halfway on *r.*, Blackbrook *Ho.* Near Titchfield, the ruins of Titchfield *Ho.*, where Charles I. was twice concealed.

Titchfield to Southampton (9¾—171¾); rise out of Titchfield, and pretty easy road over Titchfield Common and Sarisbury Green, 163, with a descent to Bursledon Bridge, 164, where there is a toll to pay; on the other side there is a long stiff hill to mount on to Bursledon Heath, then undulating over the Heath (keeping to *l.*), and Netley Common, to the junction with the London road from Botley, 3m. further, and over Northam Bridge, 168¾ (*R.* Itchen); Southampton is partly paved, with tramways. Returning, after Northam Bridge 1¾m., keep to *r.*, and on Titchfield Common first to *r.* then to *l.* [Or instead of going through Titchfield, you may keep to *r.* 1m. E. of it, rejoining the road on the Common 3m. further on Or beyond Bursledon Bridge turn to *l.*, and there is a long stiff hill to mount, then undulating, with one or two descents which must be taken carefully, through Netley and over Netley Common to Itchen, whence cross the river by steam ferry, which plies across every 20 minutes, to Southampton.]

At Netley, on *l.*, Netley Abbey ruins; also Netley Castle, the Victoria Hospital and Weston *Ho.* At Itchen, on *r.*, Woolston *Ho.* There are some splendid views along this road. Before Northam Bridge, on *l.*, Chewsel *Ho.*; on *r.*, Bittern Grove *Ho.* Southampton, p. 40.

CANTERBURY TO RYE.

Canterbury to Chilham (5½); in the middle of Canterbury from the London road turn to *r.*, and through the suburb of Wincheap, at the end of which, 1m. out of the town, keep to the *r.* (the left hand or old road through Shalmsford Street, 4½, being more hilly and ½m. longer), and through Thannington, 1¼, and by Howfield, 2¼, is a good undulating road.

At Chilham, on *l.*, across *R.* Stour, a circular entrenchment, supposed to be British. A little further, on *r.*, Chilham Castle.

Chilham to Ashford, Saracen's Head (8½—13¾); at the entrance of Chilham turn to *l.*, keeping close by the railway, and it is rather more hilly, but nothing very difficult through Bilton or Bilting, 8¾, Boughton Corner, 9¾, Broad Street, 10¾, Kennington, 12, and Bybrook, 13. [Or in Chilham turn to *l.* at the cross roads, by the Castle, along the old road, through Mountain Street, 6¾, and Godmersham, 7¾, to Bilton, 9, skirting Chilham Park and Godmersham Park.] Returning, ½*m.* past Bybrook keep to *r.*; surface not quite so good as the preceding stage.

At Bilton, on *l.*, Olantigh *Ho.* At Broad Street, 1*m.* on *r.*, Eastwell Park. At Boughton Corner, 1¼*m.* on *l.*, is the small old town of Wye. Ashford, p. 8.

Ashford to Ham Street (6½—20¼); turn to *l.* on the Hythe Road, and a little further turn to *r.*; passing the station and through Kingsnorth, 16¼, the road gradually rises to Bromley Green, 18, whence there are a couple of descents to Ham Street: pretty good road.

Ham Street to Brenzett Corner (4½—24¾); cross the Royal Military Canal, and over Stock Bridge, 22, through Snave, 23¾, and Brenzett, 24¼; level road. At Snave on *l.* through Ivychurch to New Romney, 8*m.*

Brenzett Corner to Rye (8¼—33)—p. 251.

[Or from *Ham Street* turn to *r.* and pretty good road through Wareborn to *Appledore*, 4½—24¾, whence to *Rye*, 6—30¾—p. 251.]

CANTERBURY TO NEWENDEN.

Canterbury to Ashford (13¾)—p. 254.

Ashford to Bethersden, *Ch.* (5¾—19½); in Ashford turn to *r.* on the Charing road, and at the end of the town turn to *l.*; good and nearly level by Buckford Mill, 15½ (keep to *r.*), to Great Chart, 16¼, through which is a short rise, then level and indifferent road, in wet weather heavy and greasy, by New Street, 17¼, beyond which keep to *r.* by Worse Bridge, 18¼. [Or *l.* by Cablehook, 17¾, and Marlin Green, 18½, to Bethersden, 19½. Returning, on entering Bethersden, also ¼*m.* farther on keep to *r.*, and not go past the *ch.*] At Marlin Green on *l.* sharp fall to Brissenden Bridge, ¼*m.*, and then uphill, with a descent into *Woodchurch*, 3½.

Bethersden to Tenterden (6½—26); out of the former is a stiff descent with rough surface, and after 1½*m.* of pretty level but still bad and heavy going, is another rather steep and longer descent, followed by a long gradual rise with better surface to High Halden, 22¼, and then level through Hocksted Green, 23, London Beach, 23¾, Bird's Isle or Boar's Isle, 24½ (except a short fall and rise at St. Michael's, 24¾), and Gallow's Green, 25¼ (keep to *r.*).

Tenterden, p. 10.

Tenterden to Rolvenden (3—29); gradual downhill for a mile out of Tenterden, ending with a steep fall to Ashbourne Mill, 27¼, then more or less uphill through Strood or Stroud Quarter, 28: bad road.

Rolvenden to Newenden (3—32); keeping to *r.* of the *ch.*, there is a long stiff descent out of Rolvenden followed by a short pull up, and downhill to Hexden Bridge, 31; again a short rise, at the top of which join the London road, and downhill into Newenden: bad surface.

CANTERBURY TO BRIGHTON.

Canterbury to Chilham (5½)—p. 254.

Chilham to Challock Lees (4½—10); keep to *r.* past Chilham

Castle, and it is generally a good hard road, rising steadily to Moldash, 9, with a steep descent to Challock Lees.

Challock Lees to Charing, *Ch.* (3¾—13¾); slight gradual rise by Paddock Street, 11, to Stockwood Head, 12¾, whence is a very steep descent into Charing; generally good road. Returning, at Stockwood Head keep to *r.* [Or past Chilham by 2nd turn on *r.*, by Shottenden Thorn, 8, Bound Gate, 10½, to Stockwood Head, 13½.]

(*Charing:* Swan, *recom. C.T.C.*)

Fine view from Stockwood Head; Canterbury Cathedral is to be seen.

Charing to Smarden (7¼—21); fairly level to Little Chart, 16, through which is a short stiff pull, and presently a sudden and very steep descent through and out of Pluckley, 17, after which it is nearly level by Ovens Green, 18¼, Maltmans Hill and Biddenden Green, 19¾: good surface.

Past Little Chart, on *l.*, Cale Hill; a little farther Surrenden.

Smarden to Biddenden (3½—24½); turn to *l.*, and the road is good to Standen, 23½, then rather rough; all level. Returning, turn to *l.* at Biddenden, and nearly 1*m.* farther (2nd fork) to *r.*

Biddenden to Milkhouse Street (4—28½); in Biddenden turn to *r.*; all but level to Three Chimnies, 26 (keep to *l.*), and after a sharp fall the rest is nearly all a long rise: not good surface.

[Or ½*m.* past Pluckley turn to *r.*, and the descent is followed by an ascent, then level for 2*m.* by Hoghill Green, descent to Hadman's Bridge, 21, and chiefly uphill to Three Chimnies, 24½.

Or at the 2nd fork road beyond Smarden keep to *r.*, joining the last road ¾*m.* past Hadman's Bridge, to Three Chimnies, 25½.]

Milkhouse Street to Cranbrook (1¾—30¼); nearly level through Willesly Green, 29¼, where keep to *l.*, with fall into the town.

Cranbrook, p. 13.

Cranbrook to Hartley (1½—31¾); long rise through and out of Cranbrook.

Hartley to Highgate (2½—34¼)—p. 14.

Highgate to Hurst Green (3½—37¾); steep descent from Highgate, then up through Hawkhurst, 35 (keep to *r.*), and from Seales Crouch, 35¼ (keep to *l.*), downhill to Rother Bridge, 36½, and uphill by Kingshill *Tg.*, 36¾, and Cooper's Corner, 37¼, where join the Flimwell road on *r.*

(*Hurst Green:* George, *C.T.C.*)

Hurst Green to Burwash Wheel (6—43¾); turn to *r.* and shortly a descent to Etchingham, 39¼, then mostly uphill to Burwash, 41¾, and level to Burwash Wheel.

Burwash Wheel to Cross-in-Hand Tp. (5¾—49½); almost level through Milkhurst Toll, 45¼, and by Heathfield Tower Hill, 47¼.

Cross-in-Hand Tp. to Ringmer (9½—59); over Waldron Down to Blackboy *Tp.*, 51¾, then downhill past Blackboy, 52¼, to Stone Bridge, 52¾, and up and down, mostly the latter, over Eason's Green, 53¾, Terrible Down, 55¼, and by Short Gate *Tp.*, 56: very heavy going. Returning, just beyond Ringmer keep to *l.*, and ¾*m.* before Cross-in-Hand, to *r.*

Ringmer to Lewes, *T.H.* (2½—61½); pretty nearly level for 1½*m.*, past Ringmer *Tg.*, 59½, then a steep descent through Cliff, 60 (where keep to *r.*), to *R.* Ouse at the entrance of Lewes, and after crossing the river a very steep hill to climb through the town. Returning, at the top of the hill above Cliff, keep to *r.*

At Ringmer, 1*m.* on *l.*, Glyndbourn. At the top of the hill, on *r.*, Malling *Ho.* Lewes, p. 22.

Lewes to Brighton, Aquarium (8¼—69¾); long stiff ascent continued out of Lewes, then undulating past Ashcombe *Tp.*, 63¼, with another long but easy ascent to Falmer, 65½, whence it is almost all downhill into Brighton to the junction with the London road at St. Peter's *ch.*; it is an easy ride between the two towns in either direction: capital surface all the way.

Beyond Falmer, on *r.*, Stanmer Park. Brighton, p. 23.

CANTERBURY TO BRIGHTON (by Lamberhurst).

Canterbury to Milkhouse Street (28½)—pp. 255-6.

Milkhouse Street to Goudhurst (4¾—33¼)—p. 13, reversed; keep straight on at the cross roads beyond Milkhouse Street.

Goudhurst to Lamberhurst (3½—36¾); out of Goudhurst is the long descent of Clay Hill, the first part best walked down, to the bridge over *R.* Teise nearly 1*m.* out of the town, then more or less uphill for 2*m.* more, when turn to *l.*, and there is a very steep ¼*m.* descent into Lamberhurst, which requires careful riding; good surface.

Lamberhurst, p. 12.

Lamberhurst to Wadhurst (4¼—41); in Lamberhurst take the right-hand road up a stiff, winding, and narrow hill, at the top of which keep to *r.* again, then after a short fall there is another steep hill to climb, and the rest pretty level through Coursely Wood Street and Turners Green, to Sparrows Green, at the entrance of the village, which is on the *l.*: narrow and rough road.

[Or from Goudhurst turn to *l.*, near top of Clay Hill, and walk down steep descent to Rise Bridge, 34¼, then uphill to Stents Corner, 35¼, where keep to *r.*, and steep descent to Beal's Bridge, 36¼, then short steep ascent, at the top of which turn to *l.*, and level for 1¾*m.* to junction of above road, ¾*m.* before Coursely Wood Street, whence to Wadhurst, 40¼.]

(*Wadhurst:* Greyhound.)

Wadhurst to Mayfield (5—46); coming back on the London road to Sparrows Green, turn to the *l.*, and 1*m.* further to *l.* again, whence it is downhill to Fidebrook, 44, then half up and half down to Coggingsmill Street, 45, and uphill into Mayfield; this is not a main highway. [The main road is very circuitous; from Sparrows Green keep straight on over a pretty level road to Mark Cross *Tp.*, 45, whence on *l.* to Mayfield, 48, as at p. 17. Fine views.]

Mayfield to Cross-in-Hand Tp. (6—52)—p. 17.

Cross-in-Hand Tp. to Brighton (20¼—72¼)—p. 256; at Cross-in-Hand turn to *r.*, or about ½*m.* before it turn to *r.* to Waldron Down, saving ½*m.*

FAVERSHAM TO ASHFORD.

Faversham to Challock Lees (6¾); through Preston, ½ (where cross the London road), and Northstreet, 2¼, the road is undulating to

Sheldwich, 3, then downhill to Sheldwich Lees, 3½, and it rises gradually through Baddlesmere Lees, 4¾, Bound Gate, 5¼, and Pearfield Green, 6.

At Sheldwich, on *l.*, Lees Court.

Challock Lees to Ashford (6—12¾); slightly uphill for 1⅛*m.*, through Challock Wood, then long descent, skirting Eastwell Park on *r.*, through Boughton Lees, 9¼, and undulating through Goatly's Lees, 10¼ (turn sharp to *l.*), and across Kennington Common, 10¾, and through Bybrook, 12. Returning, ¼*m.* past Bybrook keep to *l.*

Ashford, p. 8.

MAIDSTONE TO KEY STREET.

Maidstone to Key Street (9¾); out of the town there is a long but not steep hill to Pennenden Heath, 1¼, after mounting which a very good road, on a slight incline, runs to Deptling, 2¾, where there is a loose and rough hill, nearly a mile long, and very steep (dangerous to ride down returning); capital view; from the top is a continuous run of downhill, but not a good road, through Stockbury Valley, 6¾, and Danaway, 8¾.

Beyond Maidstone, on *r.*, Vinters Hall. At Pennenden Heath, on *r.*, Newnham Court.

MAIDSTONE TO BRIGHTON.

Maidstone to Teston (4); take the London road back through the town, and after crossing *R.* Medway keep to *l.* past the Bower, ½, and the road is uphill on to Barming Heath, 2, then down past Barming Cross, 2½, to Barming, 3, and fairly level to Teston.

At Teston, on *r.*, Barham Court.

Teston to Mereworth Cross (3—7); by Wateringbury Cross, 5, and Wateringbury, 5½.

Before Mereworth, on *l.*, Mereworth Place.

Mereworth Cross to Tunbridge (7¼—14¼); turn sharp on *l.*, and through Goose Green, 9¼, Hadlow Common, and Hadlow, 10¼, is rather hilly; awkward descent 1½*m.* before Tunbridge. Returning, after crossing the river in Tunbridge turn to *r.*

Tunbridge, p. 12.

Tunbridge to Tunbridge Wells (5¾—20) —p. 15.

Tunbridge Wells to Uckfield (14¼—34¼), crosses the Sussex Wealds, and is very bad and hilly; passing the Frant road on the *l.* and leaving the Common on the *r.*, there are a couple of hills to climb, the second a very steep one, to Eridge Green, 22¾, then a stiff descent to Hamsell Bridge, 24, after which is another long pull up to Boarshead Street, 25¼, again a little downhill to Steel Cross, 26 (where keep to *r.* and directly after to *l.*), and finally a very steep hill with loose and rough surface, riding up (or down) which is out of the question, past Boxes Gate, 26¼, and Crowborough Cross (or Mill), 27, to Crowborough Beacon *Ty.*, 28; thence a fall and rise up to Pound or Crowborough Gate, 29½, from which is a steep descent about 1*m.* long and the rest is nearly all an easy downhill and capital road by Handle (or Handell) Gate, 31, Cooper's Green, 33, and Ringles Cross, 33¾: beautiful scenery. Returning, at Ringles Cross keep to *r.*

Crowborough Beacon, on *r.*, is the highest point in Sussex, 1400ft. high. At Eridge Green, on *l.*, Eridge New Park and Castle. At Cooper's Green, on *l.*, Buxted Place. Uckfield, p. 19.

[There is another road by turning to the *r.* at the entrance of Tunbridge Wells, over Rushall Common, by Gips Cross, 21½, Lengthington Green, 21¾, with a long descent to Groombridge, 23½, out of which keep to *r.*, then to *l.* at Florence Farm, 24¼, and mostly uphill through Frayers Street, 27¼, to Ashdown Forest, where at 30*m.* join the road from Hartfield on *r.*, whence by Duddleswell Gate, 30¾, and *Maresfield*, 33½, to Uckfield, 35¼, as at p. 19.]

Uckfield to Lewes (8½—42¾)—p. 22.

Lewes to Brighton, Aquarium (8¼—51)—p. 257.

MAIDSTONE TO LAMBERHURST.

Maidstone to Teston (4)—p. 258.

Teston to Yalding (3—7); entering Teston turn to *l.*, and after crossing *R.* Medway there is a long steep hill to mount to Yalding Down, followed by downhill, the last part very steep, into Yalding.

Yalding to Horsemonden (6¼—13¼); after crossing *R.* Beult keep to *l.*, and through Denover Street, 8 (just beyond keep to *l.*), and the road is fairly level to beyond Gafford's Bridge, 11 (*R.* Teise), then chiefly uphil. to Horsemonden.

Horsemonden to Lamberhurst (3¼—16½); out of the former a short fall and rise, then turn to *r.*, and there is a steep descent, and the rest undulating, with a sharp fall into Lamberhurst.

[Or out of Yalding keep to *r.*, and over Lattingford Bridge, 7¾, to junction with road on *r.* from Wrotham, whence to Lamberhurst, through Beltering Green, Homebush Green, and Brenchley.]

MAIDSTONE TO GOUDHURST.

Maidstone to Stile Bridge (5½)—p. 10.

Stile Bridge to Marden (2¼—7¾): past Stile Bridge keep to *r.*, and through Underhill Green, 6¼; level road with one or two easy rises; entering Marden turn to *r.*

Marden to Goudhurst (4¼—12); undulating road by Marden Beach, 9, and Winchet Hill, 10¾, with long steep ascent to Goudhurst. [Or to *Horsemonden*, 13¼ (above), thence (keeping to *l.*) very hilly, 2*m.* beyond joining the London road on *r.*, and after crossing *R.* Teise the very steep ascent of Clay Hill to walk up into *Goudhurst*, 3—16¼.]

MAIDSTONE TO TUNBRIDGE WELLS (by Hale Street).

Maidstone to Teston (4)—p. 258.

Teston to Hale Street (4—8); by Wateringbury Cross, 5 (turn to *l.*), Nettlested, 6, and Nettlested Green, 7, joining the road from Wrotham on *r.* ¼*m.* before Hale Street: undulating road.

Hale Street to Pembury Green (6½—14½); crossing *R.* Medway, follow the Brenchley road for a mile, then turn to *r.*, and for 2*m.* the road is fairly level, then a stiff rise at Colts Hill, 11½, and the rest is on a gentle rise by Lower Pembury Green, 13¾.

At Hale Street, on *r.*, to Hadlow, 2½*m.*

[Or from *Teston* to *Yalding* (3—7)—p. 259; at the latter, after crossing *R.* Beult, keep to *r.*, and over Lattingford Bridge, 7¾, and 1¼*m.* further join the above road; level from Yalding; same distance.]

Pembury Green to Tunbridge Wells (3—17¼); at Wood's *Tg.*, 15¼, turn to *l.*, and the road is nearly all on the rise to Tunbridge Wells.

HASTINGS TO BRIGHTON (by Horsebridge).

Hastings to Battle, entrance of (7¼); long steep hill to climb out of Hastings to Fairlight Down, 1¼ (where keep to *l.*), the rest up and down hill, but nothing difficult, by Ore, 2¼, Beauport, 4¾, and Rose Green, 6½: rather lumpy in places. See also p. 15.

Battle, p. 14.

Battle to Ninfield (3½—10¾); turn to *l.* at the bottom of the hill entering Battle, and the road is rather up and down hill through Catsfield Green, 9¾, with a stiff pull up to Ninfield.

[Or go through Battle, then keep to *l.*, and again 1¾*m.* further, joining the other road just before Catsfield Green, 11¼.

Or from *Hastings* to *Bexhill* (5½)—p. 252; there turn to *r.*, and after descent from Bexhill is mostly uphill through Sidley Green, 6¼, to Luntsford Cross, 8, and then level through Ninfield Green, 9¾, to *Ninfield*, 10.]

Ninfield to Gardner's Street (5½—16¼); in Ninfield keep to *l.*, and from Standard Hill, 11¾, there is a descent to Boreham Bridge, 13¼, then a stiff mount to Boreham Street, 14¼, and almost level following the ridge, through Windmill Hill, 14¾.

At Boreham Street, on *l.*, by Wartling, 1½, to *Pevensey*, 4½.

Beyond Ninfield, 1½*m.* on *r.*, Ashburnham Park and *Ho.* At Windmill Hill, on *l.*, Hurstmonceux Park and Castle ruins.

Gardner's Street to Horsebridge (4—20¼); taking the left hand road, there is a good descent, then very undulating over Magham Down, 17¾, and through Amberstone Gate, 18¼.

Horsebridge to Ringmer (8½—28¾); beyond Horsebridge keep to *l.*, and after mounting a very stiff hill it is a capital undulating road over Dicker Common, Burg Hill, 23¼ (keep to *l.*), Stone Cross, 24½, and Laughton Pound, 25¼, joining the Tunbridge road on *r.* ¾*m.* before Ringmer.

Ringmer to Brighton (10¾—39½)—pp. 256-7.

LEWES TO EASTBOURNE (by Glynd).

Lewes to West Firle (4½); cross *R.* Ouse, and through Cliff, ½, where turn to *r.*, and through Southerham, 1½, and Glynd, 3½ (turn to *r.*); good undulating road. [Or at Cliff turn to *l.*, and at the top of the hill keep to *r.*, to Ringmer Gate, 2, where again to *r.*, to Glynd, 4: very hilly road.]

Before Glynd, on *l.*, Mount Caburn, on which is an old beacon. At Glynd, on *l.*, Glynd Place, and 1*m.* from Ringmer Gate, on *l.*, Glyndbourn. At West Firle, on *l.*, Firle Place.

West Firle to Polegate Green (8—12½); rather hilly to Bopeep Gate, 6½, where turn to *l.*, and fairly level over Berwick Common to Chilver Bridge, 7¼ (*R.* Cuckmere), then hilly again to Polegate Green: good surface.

Polegate Green, p. 18.

Polegate Green to Eastbourne (3½—16)—p. 18.

CUCKFIELD TO BATTLE.

Cuckfield to Hayward's Heath (2); chiefly downhill through Butlers Green, 1¼, keeping to *r.* at the entrance of the Heath just beyond.

Hayward's Heath to Chailey Common, King's Head (5—7); crossing the London road a little on *r.*, about a mile beyond is a stiff rise up to Beadles Hill, then down and up to Skeins Hill, 4½, steep fall to Pellings Bridge, 5½, and rise up to the Common.

Chailey Common to Maresfield, Cross (5½—12½); pretty level to beyond Newick Green, 9, then descent to Gold Bridge, 9½, and rather hilly over Grislands Common and Pilt Down, 10½, Batts Hill, 11, and Batts Bridge, 11½, whence a stiff hill up to Maresfield: good road.

At the beginning of Pilt Down, on *l.*, to Fletching, 1*m.*; on *r.* by Short Bridge to *Uckfield*, 2¼.

At Maresfield on *r.* Maresfield Park.

Maresfield to Cross-in-Hand Tp. (7¾—20); in Maresfield turn to *r.* by the *ch.*, down a short stiff hill to the Mill Pond, ½*m.* (beyond which keep to middle road), by Cooper's Green, 13¼, Buxted Bridge *Tg.*, 14¼, after which are two or three steep hills up and down to negotiate by Pound Green, 15¼, Five Chimneys House, 16, Curtain Hill or Hadlow Down, 17, Hadlow, 17¾, Croust Corner, 18¼ (keep to *r.*), and Gate House, 19¼ (keep to *l.*).

Beyond Cooper's Green, on *r.*, Buxted Place.

Cross-in-Hand Tp. to Wood's Corner (8—28); turn to *l.*, and again to *l.* about ½*m.* further; pretty level by Heathfield Tower Hill, 21¾, to Half Moon Inn, 22, a little beyond which turn to *r.*, and a steep descent skirts Heathfield Park on *r.*, to Cade Street, 23½, thence hilly and not a good road by the Chapel, 23¾, Punnets Town, 24½, Three Cups Corner, 25¼, and Dallington, 27½.

At the Chapel on *r.* to Warbleton, 1½*m.*; and to Rushlake Green, 1½, whence by Foul Mile, 3, Cobeech, 4½, and on *l.* to Stunts Green, 5½, to *Gardner's Street*, 6¼.

At Wood's Corner, on *l.*, to Rose Hill Park, Brightling, 1¾*m.* On *r.*, by Ponts Green, to Ashburnham, 4*m.* At Cade Street, the rebel Jack Cade was killed, 1450.

Wood's Corner to Battle (6—34); level for 1½*m.*, then descent to Darvel Hole, 30, and ascent to Netherfield Gun, 30¾, level to Netherfield Toll, 31¾, and mostly downhill through Streem, 33¼, to Battle.

Beyond Wood's Corner, on *l.*, Brightling Park. Beautiful scenery. Battle, p. 14

TUNBRIDGE WELLS TO FOREST ROW.

Tunbridge Wells to Groombridge (3½)—p. 259.

Groombridge to Hartfield (4¼—7¾); out of Groombridge keep to r., and uphill to Florence Farm, 4¼ (keep to r.), then pretty level except descent into Withyham, 6½.

At Groombridge on *l.* to Hamsell Bridge, 2*m.*, very hilly.

Before Withyham, on *l.*, Buckhurst Park.

Hartfield to Forest Row (4¼—12); beyond Hartfield keep to *r.*, and it is a rather hilly road.

GRAVESEND TO WROTHAM.

Gravesend to Meopham (5¼); turn to *r.* from the London road past the railway station, and nearly a mile further is an easy rise, with a short fall to Northumberland Bottom, 1¾, then the road rises gradually through Nursted, 3¼, and Hook Green, 4½; very good surface.

1*m.* out of Gravesend, on *r.*, New *Ho.* Before Nursted, on *l.*, Nursted Court. Meopham is pronounced Mep-ham.

Meopham to Wrotham (5¼—10½); the road continues on the rise till beyond Meopham Green, 6, then fairly level through Culversore Green, 7½, to Vigo, 8¾, half a mile beyond which a steep descent begins, on which keep to *r.*, running under the side of the hill for a mile, with short fall into Wrotham; pretty good road. [Or at Vigo turn to *l.*, down the hill to the "Kentish Drover," 9¼.]

DARTFORD TO SEVENOAKS.

Dartford to Farningham (5¼); by Hawley, 1¼, through Sutton Place, 2¼, Sutton-at-Hone, 2¾, and Sutton Street, 3¼, is a splendid road, though rather undulating, along the valley of the Darent *R.*

On *r.*, Wilnington *Ho.*, Summerhill, Oakfield Lodge, and Hawley *Ho.* Farningham, p. 7.

Farningham to Otford (5¼—10½); in Farningham turn to *l.*, cross *R.* Darent, and out of the town turn to *r.*; rather hilly road through Eynesford, 6¼, and up the Darent valley; just before Otford turn to *r.*, and descent into it. [1½*m.* before Otford on *r.* to Shoreham, ¼*m.*]

Beyond Eynesford, on *r.*, Lullingstone Park and Castle; another mile, Shoreha mCastle.

Otford to Sevenoaks (3—13½); turn to *l.* in Otford and almost level to Sevenoaks Station, 12¼, and a long stiff hill up into Sevenoaks.

Sevenoaks, p. 11.

CRAYFORD TO GREEN STREET GREEN.

Crayford to Bexley (1½)—p. 7.

Bexley to St. Paul's Cray (3¼—4¾); in Bexley turn to *l.*, cross *R.* Cray, and through North Cray, 3 (¼*m.* further cross Eltham and Farningham road), is a capital smooth road, almost level.

Beyond Bexley, on *l.*, Mount Mascal. On *r.*, North Cray Place.

St. Paul's Cray to Green Street Green (4—8¾); through the long, straggling, and narrow villages of St. Mary's Cray, 5¼, and Orpington, 6¾, is a good smooth road with slightly upward gradient: at end of St. Mary's Cray turn to *l.*, then to *r.*

(*Orpington:* White Hart.)

At Orpington, on *r.*, Broom Hill

GUILDFORD TO MAIDSTONE.

Guildford to Dorking (12); out of Guildford take the Leatherhead road on *r.*, good and level or slightly uphill to Merrow, 2, then turn to *r.* before the *ch.*, and it is a long uphill to Newland's Corner, 3½. From Newland's Corner there is a steep descent, rough in places, and best walked down, about 1*m.* long, then almost level through Shere, 5½, Gomshall, 6¼, and Abinger Hammer, 7, to Crossways Farm, 7¾, but the surface is inclined to be heavy and muddy; thence an easy ascent, followed after a little level past Wotton Hatch, 9¼, by a steep descent which requires careful riding, being rather rough and narrow at the bottom; directly after occurs a short but rough and stony rise, and the rest is nearly all more or less downhill through Westgate Street, 10½, and over Milton Heath to Dorking; good surface for last 5*m.* [Or in Guildford halfway down the hill turn to *l.* into Quarry street, taking the Cranleigh road; the pavement soon ends and there is a short descent out of the town, then fairly level through Shalford, 1, beyond which, after crossing the railway, turn to *l.* along Shalford Common and again to *l.* then to *r.*, over a level railway crossing at 3½, past Chilworth Station, 3¾, whence the road is more undulating through Albury, 5¼, and skirting Albury Park on *r.*, where it joins the upper road ¾*m.* before Shere, 7: good road but apt to be heavy and muddy when wet.]

(*Wotton Hatch:* Evelyn Arms.—*Dorking*, p. 20.)

Fine view from Newland's Corner; 1½*m.* S.W., the ruins of St. Martha's Chapel. In Albury Park, the Silent Pool. Abinger *ch.*, 1*m.* on *r.*, is early English.

Dorking to Reigate (6¼—18¼); a mile out of Dorking the road takes a sudden turn to *l.*, down a sharp but short dip which should be ridden carefully, then cross *R.* Mole and keep to *r.* over a good but rather hilly road through Betchworth, 15, and Buckland, 15¾, with a very stiff pull up to Reigate Heath, 17, whence the surface is macadam into Reigate.

2*m.* out of Dorking, on *r.*, Betchworth Park and ruins of Castle. At Betchworth, on *l.*, Tranquil Dale; in the village, on *r.*, a fine old *ch.*, Moor Place, Wonham Manor, and Broome Hall. 2*m.* beyond it, at Leigh, is Swain's Farm, an Elizabethan mansion. Reigate, p. 27.

Reigate to Red Hill (2—20¼); out of Reigate there is a hill to mount and about ¾*m.* beyond the town keep to *l.*, and it is mostly a slight decline into Red Hill: good road.

Red Hill, p. 24.

Red Hill to Godstone Green, *ms.* (4¾—25); straight across the London road, under the railway, then a very steep hill to walk up (dangerous to ride *down*), from the top of which the road is up and downhill but nothing difficult, through Nutfield, 22¼, and Bletchingley, 23½; good gravel surface.

Bletchingley formerly was a town with 7 churches and a castle, which latter was destroyed 1263, and is only represented by a mound. Godstone, p. 21.

Godstone Green to Westerham, *M.P.* (7—32); at Godstone Green turn to *l.*, and follow the London road back to Tyler's Green, 25½, then turn to *r.* by the sign-post; through Oxtead, 27¾, and Limpsfield, (end of) 29, and across the Common, good surface throughout, but there are several steep hills in each direction, and the descents require careful riding.

1m. beyond Godstone Green, on *l.*, Rooksuest H). 1m. before Oxtead, on *r.* ½m., in Tandridge churchyard, a large yew tree. Westerham, p. 19.

Westerham to River Head (4½—36½); leaving Westerham turn to *l.*, and through Brasted, 33¼, Sundridge, 34½, and Bessells Green, 35¼, is a good smooth road and easy going.

(*Brasted:* White Hart.)

A little beyond Westerham, on *r.*, Hill Park. After Brasted, on *r.*, Brasted Place; on *l.*, Comb Bank. At Bessells Green, on *l.*, Chipstead Place; on *r.* Montreal Place. River Head and Sevenoaks, p. 11.

River Head to Ightham (6—42½); turn to *l.* and directly after to *r.*, and the road is level and good for a mile beyond Sevenoaks Station, 37½, then a long ascent through and out of Seal, 39½, on to Seal Chart, 40, across which and Ightham Common the road is level for about 2m., followed by a long descent into Ightham: good smooth surface. Pretty country.

Beyond River Head, on *r.*, Bradbourn Ho. Beyond Sevenoaks Station, on *l.*, Greatness. At Seal, on *r.*, Wilderness. Ightham, p. 16.

Ightham to Wrotham Heath, Royal Oak (3⅛—45¾); through Ightham turn to *r.*; through Borough Green, 43½, a very good road but hilly.

Wrotham Heath to Maidstone, Rain's Cross (8¼—54)—p. 7.

STAINES TO BROMLEY AND FOOT'S CRAY.

Staines to Hampton (7); coming through the town Londonwards, turn to *r.* just beyond the railway, along Knowles Green, then short but stiff rise and fall over a railway bridge, after which the road is level by Ashford Ford, 1¾, except a railway bridge at Sunbury Station, 4, and a short fall approaching Hampton: very often the greater part of this road is extremely loose and sandy, especially in dry weather.

Beyond Sunbury Station, on *l.*, Kempton Park Racecourse.

Hampton to Kingston M.P. (2½—9½); level but generally sandy and heavy after leaving Hampton to Hampton Court, 8, whence to Kingston—p. 37. At Kingston Bridge macadam begins, and continues through the town.

Hampton Court, p. 37.—Kingston, p. 32.

Kingston to Ewell (5½—15); in Kingston turn to *r.* by the *ch.*, and ½m. further turn to *l.*; then there is a stiff ascent up Surbiton Hill, 10½, at the top the road improves and is level for a short distance, followed by an easy fall, and the rest is undulating and capital going through Talworth, 12, to Ewell, with a sharp descent into the town.

Ewell, &c., p. 28.

Ewell to Sutton, Cock Inn (3½—18½); nearly through Ewell take left hand fork; ½m. further the road begins to rise, and ends with a stiff pull through a cutting at Howell Hill, 16, with a fall on the other side and afterwards undulating, with good surface through Cheam, 17¼; sometimes rather rough and loose about Howell Hill.

Sutton, p. 26.

Sutton to Croydon, George Street (4¼—22¾); nearly ½m. out of Sutton there is a stiffish descent, generally with rather loose surface, after which it is an undulating and good road through Carshalton, 19½, Wallington, 20, Beddington, 21, and Waddon, 21¾; enter Croydon by Church street, turning to *r.* beyond the *ch.*, and mounting a short but very sharp pitch up Crown Hill to the London road, across which is George street: macadam through the town.

(*Carshalton:* Greyhound.—*Croydon:* p. 20.)

Before Carshalton, on *l.*, Carshalton *Ho.*; in the village, on *r.*, Carshalton Park. On *l.*, Beddington Park and Waddon Court. Croydon, p. 20.

[There is another road from *Kingston* by *Merton*, Double Gates, 14¾, reversing the route at p. 32; thence follow the Tooting road back for ¾*m.*, when turn to *r.* by a wood yard, and keeping to *l.*, it is all level except a railway bridge, and pretty good road to *Lower Mitcham*, 17. Here keep straight on across the Green, to *r.* at the pond and when over the railway bridge to *l.*, and it is level across Mitcham Common, and to the beginning of *Croydon*, 20¾, which enter over Pitlake Bridge to Church street: sometimes rather loose and sandy across the Common, otherwise good.]

Croydon to Beckenham, *Ch.* (4¾—27½); along George street, Addiscombe road (passing East Croydon Station), and Upper Addiscombe road, to Addiscombe, 23¾, where turn to *l.* (fifth turning past the station), into Havelock road, whence turn to *r.*, and past Stroud Green, 24¾, into Long Lane, and through Elmers End or Lower Elm End, 26½: after getting clear of Croydon town, the macadam changes to a pretty good gravel and flint road; in Beckenham the road twists about very much, and there is a short stiff rise up to the *ch.*, otherwise almost level.

(*Beckenham:* Rodway, *Hqrs.*)

Beckenham to Bromley. *M.H.* (1¾—29¼); turn to *r.* at Beckenham *ch.*, and keep to *l.* twice about ¼*m.* further; then there is a stiff ascent over Clay Hill, 28½, and a good descent on the other side to Shortlands Station, 28¾, whence into Bromley is a rather steep winding ascent (which requires very careful riding in descending); pretty good road: entering Bromley turn to *r.* [Or at Beckenham *ch.* keep straight on, and there is a fair road past Beckenham Place, with a good ascent and descent to Southend, 29, where turn to *r.* on to the London road from Lewisham, which follow as at p. 11 to *Bromley*, 31¼.]

Bromley, p. 11.

Bromley to Foot's Cray (5¾—35); in Bromley turn to *l.*, and it is pretty level to Widmore, 30½ (where keep to *l.*), and there is a long descent, which should be ridden down carefully to Chislehurst Station, 31¼, followed by a tremendously steep hill, ½*m.* long, to walk up to Chislehurst Common (cyclists should beware against trying to ride *down* this hill, as it is utterly impossible to do so with safety); after that is a good level road across the Common, through Chislehurst, 32½, and Perry Street, 33½, to Sidcup, 34¼, where join the London road, and a good downhill to Foot's Cray.

Foot's Cray and Sidcup, p. 7. Beyond Widmore, on *r.*, Bickley Park. At Chislehurst Common, on *l.*, Camden Place.

HOUNSLOW TO REIGATE.

Hounslow to Kingston, *M.P.* (5¾); turn sharp to *l.* entering Hounslow, and through Worton, ½, at the bridge a little further on turn to r., and past Queens Bridge, 1½, through Twickenham, 2¾, whence run close to *R.* Thames, through Teddington, 4, to Hampton Wick, 5½, through which turn to *l.*, and cross Kingston bridge into the town. Past Worton on *l.*, through Isleworth to Brentford, 3½.

(*Twickenham:* King's Head.—*Hampton Wick:* White Hart.—*Teddington:* Clarence.—*Isleworth:* Milford Arms.—*Kingston:* p. 27.)

Kingston to Ewell (5½—11¼)—p. 264.

Ewell to Burgh Heath (3½—14¾); through Ewell, at the bottom of the hill on the Epsom road turn to *l.*, and it is a good undulating road for 2*m.*, then is a steep ascent to climb to Nork Park, 13¾, and the rest is slightly downhill through Borough Street, 14½.

Burgh Heath to Reigate, *M.H.* (5¾—20½)—p. 27.

CRAWLEY TO HORSHAM.

Crawley to Horsham (7½); in Crawley turn to *r.*, and ½*m.* further to *l.*, then a moderate ascent and descent over Goff's Hill, and the rest is slightly undulating skirting the north side of St. Leonard's Forest, and through Roughey Street, 4½: perfectly good surface.

KINGSTON TO LEATHERHEAD.

Kingston to Leatherhead (8¼); from Kingston *M.P.* follow the Esher road for 1¼*m.*, all macadam, then turn to *l.* down the Brighton road, past the Surbiton race ground; a little further a stiff hill has to be mounted, and after a moderate descent the road is more or less uphill through Hook, 3¼, to Telegraph Hill, 5¼, then 1½*m.* downhill, and the rest level, with a short pull up in the town; nothing very difficult in either direction; splendid hard surface

GUILDFORD TO BRIGHTON.

Guildford to Cranleigh (8¾); in Guildford, halfway down the hill, turn to *l.* into Quarry street; the pavement soon ends, and there is a short descent out of the town, then fairly level through Shalford, 1, over Shalford Common, to Stonebridge Bar, 2; from here, after crossing the river, canal, and railway all together, the road is gently undulating, with a rather upward tendency, and running close by the railway, canal, and river, through Bramley, 3½, to Rushwood (or Rushet) Common, 5, where keep to *l.*, recross railway, river, and canal, and undulating to Cranleigh: flint road with good smooth surface. Returning, keep to *l.* about 2½*m.* out of Cranleigh. [Or on Shalford Common take left hand road, and through Wonersh, 3, and Shambley Green, 4½, and Stroud Green, 5, rejoining the other road ¾*m.* further on, to Cranleigh, 8½; more hilly and not so smooth running as the other.]

(*Cranleigh:* Onslow Arms.)

Cranleigh to Rowhook (6½—15¼); 1½*m.* beyond Cranleigh is a stiff rise and stiffer fall, otherwise mostly on a gradual incline, with good smooth surface, by Cranleigh Lane End, 12, to Ellens Green, 12¾, where turn to *l.*, and 1¼*m.* further join the road from Stone Street, and undulating to Rowhook: after Ellens Green the surface deteriorates, and for the last 1¼*m.* is rough, and in wet weather inclined to be greasy.

[Or at Rushwood Common keep to *r.*, and by Goose Green, 6¼, Leather Bottle *Tg.*, 7, Stovers Hill, 8½, *Aldfold Cross-ways*, 10, taking middle road, and Bucks Green, 13, to *Rowhook*, 15¼.]

Rowhook to Horsham (3¾—19); rather hilly road with rough surface, through Broadbridge Heath, 17¾; Horsham streets are narrow.

2*m.* beyond Cranleigh, on *r.*, Brookland *Ho.* 1½*m.* beyond Rowhook, on *l.*, Strood; before Broadbridge Heath, on *l.*, Field Place. Horsham, p. 29.

Horsham to Cowfold, *Ch.* (6¾—25¾); rather hilly but good road, by Manning's Heath, 21½, Monks Gate, 22¼, and Crab Tree, 24¼, where there is a steep descent.

Cowfold to Henfield (4¾—30½); good undulating road by Corner House *Tg.*, 28, and Mock Bridge, 28¾.

Henfield to Piecombe, Plough (5¾—36¼); a little beyond Henfield is an easy ascent to Woodmancote, 31½, and a similar descent to Terrys Cross *Tg.*, 32, then undulating to Shaves Wood cross roads, 33, (take turn to *r.*) and level to Poyning's Cross roads, where turn to *l.*, to the bottom of Dale Hill, which is a long stiff climb up through Piecombe Street, 35¾, good road.

[Or at Shaves Wood keep straight on for 1*m.* to the main London road at Muddleswood: but not so good road.]

Piecombe to Brighton, Aquarium (6—42¼)—p. 25.

GUILDFORD TO LEWES.

Guildford to Cowfold, *Ch.* (25¾)—above.

Cowfold to Albourn Green (7½—33¼); follow the Henfield road to Mock Bridge, 28¾, and ½*m.* further turn to *l.* and over Blackland Common, 30¼, and by High Cross, 32¼; rather hilly road.

Albourn Green to Ditchling (4—37¼); level through West Town, 33¾, and Hurstpierpoint, 34¼, to Stonepound Gate, 35½, beyond which is a descent and ascent to Keymer, 36½, and rest level.

Ditchling to Lewes, *T.H.* (7½—44¾); turn to *r*, and follow the Brighton road for nearly a mile to the foot of the South Downs, then turn to *l.*, and it is an undulating road through Westmeston, 39, Middleton, 39½ and Plumpton, 40, to Offham Street, 43, where join the London road from Chailey on *l.*

Lewes, p. 22.

GUILDFORD TO BILLINGHURST.

Guildford to Aldfold Cross-ways (10)—above.

Aldfold Cross-ways to Billinghurst, *Ch.* (8¼—18¼); keep to *r.* through Aldfold, 11, Loxwood Common, Loxwood, 12½, Round Street Common, 14¼, Newpound Common, 16, and over New Bridge, 16¾, entering Billinghurst at the south end.

[Or to Bucks Green, 13 (above), then turn on *r.* by Maxfields Green, 14¾, to Buckman's Corner, 15¾, whence to Billinghurst, 17¼ (pp. 30-1).

Or to Ellens Green, 12¼, (p. 266); keep straight on and through Rudgwick, 13¾, to Bucks Green, 14¾.]

WINCHESTER TO BRIGHTON.

Winchester to Petersfield (18); leave Winchester by the main Alresford road, as to which see page 39, and turn to *r.* about 3*m.* out of the town; uphill and downhill over Longwood Warren, 4½, past Hockley Farm, 6, to Hinton Ampner, 8½, then through Bramdean, 9, perfectly level road to West Meon Hut or George Inn, 11½ (where cross London to Fareham and Southampton road), after which there is a long gradual ascent, then a fine run down Bordean Hill, 15, to Langrish, 15½, through which there is a slight hill to climb, followed by a nice run down to Strood Common, 16½, (now enclosed) whence it is slightly on the rise to Petersfield; usually splendid surface, except for a few patches of stones, but heavy in wet weather.

On *r.*, Hinton *Ho.* Beyond Bramdean, on *l.*, Woodcote *Ho.*; a little further, on *r.*, Brookwood *Ho.* At Borden Hill, on *r.*, Borden *Ho.* Petersfield, p. 36.

Petersfield to Midhurst (9½—27½); keep to *l.* at the entrance to Petersfield, following the London road back to Sheet Bridge, 19½, where turn to *r.*, and through Rogate, 22½, Trotton, 24½, and across Trotton Common is rather undulating.

Midhurst, p. 34.

Midhurst to Petworth (6¼—33¾); **turn to *l.*** for Easebourn, 28½, where turn to *r.*, and through Cowdry Park for 1½*m.*, over Halfway Bridge, 30¼, and through Tillington, 32¼, is rather hilly and a moderately good road.

Petworth, p. 35. Beyond Halfway Bridge, on *l.*, Pitt's Hill.

Petworth to Fittleworth, *Ch.* (3—36¾)—p. 35.

Fittleworth to Pulborough (2¾—39½); at Fittleworth *ch.* turning to *l.*, shortly after to *r.*, the downhill continues through and out of the village, followed by a rise on to Fittleworth Common, whence there is a descent through Stopham, 133, to the *R.* Arun, after crossing which the road is pretty level to Pulborough.

(*Pulborough:* Swan.)

Pulborough to Storrington (4½—44); except a long gradual rise beyond Wickfield Bridge, 40¾, it is a fairly level and good road over Wiggonholt Common, 42, Cootham Common, 42¾, and Storrington Common.

Entrance of Storrington on *r.*, through Houghton to *Arundel*, 8½.

At Cootham Common, on *r.*, Parham Park.

Storrington to Washington Common (2¼—46¼); out of Storrington is uphill over Sullington Common, and after a short descent, last 1¼*m.* level: good road.

Washington Common to Steyning (4¼—50½); entering the Common, turn to *r.*, and ¼*m.* further to *l.*; past Wiston Park, 48, and over Broadbourn Bridge, 49¾, is a good road, with a few slight hills. Returning, keep to *l.* past Broadbourn Bridge.

Steyning to Old Shoreham, *Ch.* (4¾—55¼)—p. 28.

Old Shoreham to Brighton, Aquarium (6¾—62); reversing route on p. 253.

BRIGHTON TO BOGNOR.

Brighton, Aquarium, to **New Shoreham**, Norfolk Bridge (6½); by the sea shore, along the parade or esplanade through Hove, 2, Portslade, 3¼, and by Kingston Lighthouse, 5, is a very good road, nearly all level.

New Shoreham to Worthing, Station (6—12½); turn to *r.* at Norfolk Bridge, and directly after keep to *l.*; level to Old Shoreham *ch.*, 7, turn to *l.* and cross R. Adur, and bear to *r.* at Lancing House, and sharp to *l.* through Upper Lancing, 8¾, to Upper Cokeham, 10, where take right-hand turn, and 1m. further on turn sharp on *l.* (straight on for Arundel) to Broadwater, 11½, where turn first to *r.* and then to *l.*

Worthing, p. 30.

Worthing to Littlehampton (10—21½); in Worthing turn to *r.*, and from the end of the town there are two roads, one on *l.* through Goring, and the other through Broadwater, 12¾ (where keep to *l.*), the latter being the better and a good road, and both joining again just before Highdown Hill, 16; thence through Hangleton, 16¾, and Preston, 18; all a fairly level road, with capital surface. [Or one can go to Goring and also from beyond Preston Corner by the coast road, but it is bad for bicycling, being mostly loose shingle.

(*Littlehampton:* Norfolk; Terminus.)

Littlehampton to Bognor (7—23½); through Atherington, Middleton, and Felpham, is very bad for bicycling, being a mere beach road of loose gravel.

(*Bognor:* Norfolk.)

ALRESFORD TO BISHOP'S WALTHAM.

Alresford to Bishop's Waltham (10); in Alresford turn to *l.*, and through Cheriton, 2½, over Mill Barrow Down, 5, and Steven's Down, 7, where join the Winchester road on *r.*

1½m. past Alresford, on *r.*, Titchborne Ho. On Mill Barrow Down, on *l.*, Preshaw Ho. At Steven's Down, on *r.*, Belmore Ho. At Bishop's Waltham, on *l.*, Northbrook Ho. Bishop's Waltham, p. 42.

WINDSOR TO LEATHERHEAD.

Windsor to Egham (5); through Old Windsor Green, 2, and past the "Bells of Ouseley," 3; a pretty road, but apt to be loose and dusty, and in wet weather heavy.

Egham to Chertsey (4½—9½); in Egham turn to *r.*, and through Thorpe Lea, 6, and Thorpe, 7½; fairly level.

Chertsey, p. 38.

Chertsey to Cobham Street (7—16½); through Addlestone, 10¼, over Crockford Bridge, 11½, Ham Haw Common, through Byfleet, 13½ (turn to *l.*), and over Byfleet Bridge is a good undulating road; ½m. before Cobham Street join the Ripley to Kingston road, and there is the steepish descent of Pain's Hill.

(*Addlestone:* Duke's Head, *B.T.C.*—*Cobham Street:* White Lion.)

Cobham Street to Leatherhead (5½—22½); take the right hand road, and through Cobham, 17, to Stoke D'Abernon, 18½, is fairly level, then turn to *l.*, and the road is rather undulating to Leatherhead. [Or through Stoke D'Abernon keep to *r.*, and after a short rough descent there is a long rise to work up, thence undulating.]

Leatherhead, p. 29.

FARNHAM TO READING.

Farnham to Odiham (8); in Farnham turn to *r.* from the London road, and out of the town there is a long winding ascent past the Castle and Farnham Park, continued with one or two rests for about 2½m., then a very stiff descent through Ewshot Street, 3½, to Crondall Marsh, 4, whence keeping to *r.* there is another uphill to Itchel Mill, 5, and the rest is undulating but much easier over Rye Common, and past Dogmersfield Park, 6, on *r.*; very good surface.

Odiham, p. 52.

Odiham to Hook (3—11); through Odiham the road bears to *r.*, and is good and undulating through North Warnborough, 9 (cross canal, and ¾m. further keep to *r.*), and across Hook Common.

Hook to Reading (10¼—21¼); through Mattingley, 13, Heckfield, 15, over Heckfield Common, through Riseley, 16¼, over Sheep Bridge, 18, and by Three Mile Cross, 19¾, undulating road but nothing difficult; long gentle rise up to Heckfield Heath: good road for the most part, with perfect smooth surface.

At Heckfield, on *l.*, Highfield Park; further, on *r.*, Heckfield Place. At Heckfield Heath, a little on *l.*, the Wellington Monument at Strathfieldsaye Park.

Reading, p. 88.

BASINGSTOKE TO READING.

Basingstoke to Riseley (9½); leaving Basingstoke turn to *r.* by the station, and through Chinham, 1, Old Basing *Tp.*, 3, Sherfield, 3¾, Sherfield Green, 4½, Strathfield Turgis, 6½, and over Heckfield Heath, an excellent smooth undulating road, with no hills.

Beyond Strathfield Turgis, on *l.*, Strathfieldsaye Park.

Riseley to Reading (5—14½)—above.

ALTON TO NEWBURY.

Alton to Basingstoke (10¾); near end of Alton turn to *r.*, and through Lasham, 4, Herriard, 6¼, and Winslade, 8¼.

On *r.*, Herriard Park. Beyond Winslade, on *r.*, Hackwood Park. Basingstoke, p. 47.

Basingstoke to Kingsclere (9¾—20¼)—p. 86.

Kingsclere to Newbury (7½—27¾); over Headley Common, 23, Knights Bridge, 24, and Greenham Heath, 25.

At Greenham Heath, on *r.*, Greenham Ho.; on *l.*, Adderbury Ho., Adderbury Lodge, Newton Ho., Sandleford Priory. Newbury, p. 88.

KINGSCLERE TO WHITCHURCH.

Kingsclere to Whitchurch (8½); turn to *l.* by the *ch.*; long ascent up to White Hill, 2½, then mostly downhill: good road.

WINCHESTER TO STOCKBRIDGE.

Winchester to Stockbridge (8½); through Week, 1, past Deluge Hut, 4½, and by Woolberry Hill, 7, several steep hills especially one down into Stockbridge; not very good surface, being rough and cut up, especially in wet weather: the greater part of it is very open and exposed.

2m. before Stockbridge, on *l.*, Sombourn Park.

STOCKBRIDGE TO LYNDHURST.

Stockbridge to Romsey (10¼); through King's Sombourn, 3. Timsbury, 8, and over Timsbury Bridge, 9, is an undulating and tolerably good road.

1½m. beyond King's Sombourn, on *l.*, Compton Ho. 1½m. further, on *r.*, Mottisfont Ho. Romsey, p. 46.

Romsey to Cadnam (5¼—16)—p. 46.

Cadnam to Lyndhurst (4—20); take left hand fork and it is a good, straight, and undulating road through the New Forest. Pretty scenery.

Lyndhurst, p. 40.

LYMINGTON TO POOLE.

Lymington to Christchurch (12¾); at the end of Lymington turn to *l.*; there are two or three ups and downs, but nothing difficult by Efford Mill, 2 (cross R. Avon), to Evelton Street, 2¼, then through Downton (Royal Oak), 5, to Milton, 7½, is almost level except a short but steep winding descent beyond Downton; from Milton it is gently undulating with a sharp fall to and rise from Chewton Ford, 8½, where a stream crosses the road in a deep gully, rendering a dismount necessary; otherwise good smooth surface. Very pretty ride, but not easy to follow on account of the turns and absence of guide posts.

Beyond Efford Mill, on *l.*, Everton Ho. Before Downton, on *l.*, Newlands; beyond, on *r.*, Ashley Mount. At Chewton Bridge, on *r.*, Hinton Admiral and Hinton Ho.; 1½m. further, on *r.*, Belvidere; on *l.*, High Cliff. Christchurch p. 43.

Christchurch to Bournemouth (5¼—18); for the first 3m. through Iford, 14½ (where cross R. Stour), is almost level and a tolerably good road, though inclined to be loose and sandy; then there is a very stiff hill to mount, and the surface becomes rough and shaky approaching Bournemouth, and is rough and bumpy macadam through the town, entering which is a long descent.

Bournemouth, p. 43.

Bournemouth to Poole (7—25); steep ascent out of Bournemouth, then nearly level with a sharp fall to Parkstone Green, 23; the road is very bad, being rough and bumpy most of the way, and sometimes sandy.

Poole, p. 43.

PORTSMOUTH TO CIRENCESTER.

Portsmouth to Titchfield (7½); cross by the floating bridge ferry to *Gosport*, ⅛, then through Forton, 1½, Brockhurst Tp., 2¾ (turn to *l.*),

Rowner, 3½, and Crofton, 6, good easy road, no hills but fairish descent into Titchfield.

Tichfield, p. 254.—Gosport, p. 42.

Titchfield to Botley (6—13½), good road.

(*Botley :* Railway.)

Botley to Winchester (11—24½); good but hilly road by Fair Oak Inn, 17½, and through Twyford, 21½, to St. Cross, 23½, where join the road from Southampton, and level into Winchester.

[Or from *Gosport* follow the London road back to *Cold Harbour Tg.*, 10, as at pp. 41-2, then keep to *r.*, and ¾*m.* further to *l.*, and after mounting the hill there is a grand run down over Shidfield Common, then an undulating road, skirting the west side of Waltham Chase, with perfect surface, to *Bishop's Waltham*, 13¾; from here over Gilbert Hill, 14¼, by Belmore *Ho.*, 16¾, and Whiteflood *P.H.*, 18½, and through Morestead, 20½, to *Winchester*, 23¾, is very hilly going over the downs.

Or from *Portsmouth* follow the London road back to Cosham, 4¾,—p. 36, then (keeping to *l.*) mount the steep, rough, and loose ascent of Portsdown Hill, with long descent down the other side to Southwick, 7¾, then good and undulating to Wickham, 12¼, and *Cold Harbour Tg.*, 12¾.

Or from *Bishop's Waltham* turn to *l.* and through Upham and Twyford 21, is a first rate undulating road, with very pretty scenery.]

Winchester, &c., p. 39.—Wickham, p. 42.—Bishop's Waltham, p. 42.

Winchester to Wherwell (10—34½); nearly through Winchester turn to *l.*, then to *r.*; there is a long steep ascent out of the town (dangerous to ride down the reverse direction) and the road continues up and downhill the whole way over Worthy Down, 27½ (where keep to *l.*), and Barton Stacey Down, 31. Returning, keep to *r.* out of Wherwell.

Wherwell to Andover (3½—38); out of Wherwell turn to *r.* up a steep hill (dangerous to ride *down*) and past Harewood Forest and over Bare Down; a hilly road. Returning, in Andover turn to *r.*

Andover, p. 58.

Andover to Ludgershall (7¼—45¼)—p. 84; in Andover turn to *l.*

Ludgershall to Burbage (7—52¼); about 2*m.* beyond Ludgershall, on the Up Avon road, turn to *r.* at the bottom of a stiff hill, and through Collingbourn Ducis, 48¼, Collingbourn Sutton, 48¾, Collingbourn Kingston, 49¼, and Marr Green, 51¼, is a good road, the last 5*m.* pretty level. Returning, about 1¼*m.* out of Burbage turn to *l.* instead of going over the Downs. [Or follow the hilly Up Avon road across the Downs to East Everley, 49¾, entering which turn to *r.* and it continues very hilly till clear of the Downs, joining the other road 1¼*m.* before Burbage, 55¼.]

At East Everley, on *l.*, Everley *Ho.*

Burbage to Marlborough (6—58¼); the road continues good through Steep Green, 52¾ (keep to *l.*), and over Burbage Common to the canal, beyond which is the long and steep ascent of Leigh Hill, with a gate in the middle of it, which is generally shut, then good undulating road skirting the W. side of Savernake Forest to within 1¼*m.* of Marlborough, where is long winding descent which requires careful riding.

At Steep Green, 2*m.* on *r.*, Tottenham Park. Marlborough, p. 89.

Marlborough to Swindon (11—69¼); leaving Marlborough, keep to r., and through Ogbourn St. Andrews, 60¼. Ogbourn St. George, 61¾, and Chisledon, 64¾, is a capital road with no difficult hills. [Or by the left hand road is more hilly, over Marlborough Common and Ogbourn Downs (end of, 63¼), whence there is a steep descent, and then through Burdrop Tp., 65¾, and Wroughton, 66¾, more level. Or at Chisledon turn to l. to Burdrop Tp., 66¼.]

On r., Burdrop Park. At Chisledon, on r., Liddington Castle, an old hill fort. Swindon, p. 101.

Swindon to Cricklade (8¼—77½); undulating and good flint road by Cold Harbour Inn, 73½,—beyond which is a steep descent—Water Eaton, 76, and Corkett, 75¼. Returning, the second road to the r. must be taken, past Cold Harbour Inn.

(*Cricklade:* White Hart; White Horse, *B.T.C.*)

At Cold Harbour Inn, join the old Ermine Way; on r., beyond Broad Blunsdon, Castle Hill. At Cricklade, St. Sampson's *ch.*

Cricklade to Cirencester (6¾—84¼); in Cricklade turn to r.; through Latton, 79, and Cross Way, 80½, is a fairly level road, oolite, and inclined to be rough.

Cirencester, p. 104.

SOUTHAMPTON TO BATH.

Southampton to Romsey (7½); starting on the Totton road, ½m. out of the town turn to r.; it is a smooth road, but rather hilly. [Or follow the Winchester road for 3m., chiefly on the rise, then turn to l. and through Chilworth, 4½, to Romsey, 8; more hilly, but good road.]

Romsey, p. 46.

Romsey to White Parish (8¼—15¾); in Romsey turn to l., and after crossing *R.* Test keep to r. ½m. out of the town; from here is a long ascent, followed by several more hills to Sherfield English, 12, and undulating through Cowsfield Green, 14¾; very fair road.

Beyond Romsey, on l., Emly Park. On r., Sherfield *Ho.* Before Cowsfield Green, on l., Milshal Park; on r., Cowsfield Lodge.

White Parish to Salisbury (8—23¾); for a mile or so it is easily rideable, then there is a long steep hill to climb to the top of a deep chalk cutting on Standlinch Down, 700 ft. high, whence Salisbury Cathedral can be seen; down the other side there is a steep descent, sometimes rather rough, but otherwise safe with a good brake, to Whaddon, 19¾, and the remainder is a good road, nearly all a gentle down hill, through Alderbury, 20¾, to Salisbury. Returning, at the bottom of the hill, 1½m. before White Parish, keep to l.

[Or from *Southampton* through Totton, 3¾, p. 40; then on r., through Testwood to *Ower* or *Ous Bridge*, 8, where keep to l. over Palmer's Bridge, 9¼, by Platford Inn, 10¼, and through *Landford*, 12, and Newton, 14½, about ¾m. farther on joining the other road 1½m. past White Parish, to *Salisbury*, 21¼.

Or through *Totton* to *Cadnam*, 4½—8¼, p. 43; then on r. through Brook, 9½, and Bramshaw, 11¼, to *Landford*, 13¾.]

(*Bramshaw:* Bell.)

1½m. past White Parish, on r., Brickworth *Ho.* At Alderbury, on r., Ivychurch *Ho.*, Clarendon Lodge and Park; on l., Alderbury *Ho.* and Longford

Castle. At Landford, on r., Landford Ho.; at Newton, 1m. on l., New Ho. At Bramshaw, on r., Bramshaw Ho.; on l., Warrens. Salisbury, p. 47.

Salisbury to Fugglestone or Foulstone ($2\frac{3}{4}$—$26\frac{1}{2}$)—p. 43.

Fugglestone to Deptford Inn ($8\frac{1}{2}$—$34\frac{3}{4}$); through Chilhampton, $27\frac{3}{4}$, South Newton, $28\frac{1}{2}$, Stoford, 29, Stapleford, $30\frac{1}{2}$—just before which is a short but steep fall bearing to the left—and Steeple Langford, $32\frac{3}{4}$, is a capital bicycling road, though hilly, but there is nothing an ordinary rider need dismount for: splendid surface (chalk flint). The road runs up the valley of the R. Wiley from Salisbury, and through a pretty country.

Deptford Inn to Heytesbury ($6\frac{1}{4}$—41)—p. 82.

Heytesbury to Warminster (4—45)—p. 82.

Warminster to Beckington ($6\frac{1}{2}$—$51\frac{1}{2}$); in Warminster turn to right, 2nd turning; slight ascent out of the town, then level for about 2m., when a long, steep, and narrow descent occurs at Broomfield Tp., $48\frac{1}{2}$, followed by level past Standerwick Ho., $50\frac{1}{2}$; good road.

At Broomfield Tp., on r., Chalcot Ho.; further on, on l., Berkeley Ho.

Beckington to Stoke Viaduct ($6\frac{3}{4}$—$58\frac{1}{4}$); a stiff descent out of Beckington, then a short but stiff ascent to be mounted to Woolverton, 53, just beyond which the road to the r., called the New road, must be taken; then it is hilly but easy riding for about 4m., when the top of Stoke Hill is reached, a steep and dangerous winding descent, a mile in length, which should be ridden down with great care, the last part being steepest, and the surface sometimes loose: oolite surface, requiring great care in riding.

About 2m. beyond Woolverton, on r., Farleigh Castle ruins; further on Hinton Abbey. At Woolverton, on r., Mirfield Ho.; 1m. further, on l., Challey Ho. Fine view from Stoke Hill.

Stoke Viaduct to Bath ($4\frac{1}{4}$—$62\frac{1}{2}$)—p. 95.

[Or from Woolverton by the old road to the l., through Norton St. Philip or Philip's Norton, $54\frac{1}{2}$, Charterhouse Hinton, $56\frac{1}{2}$, Midford, $58\frac{1}{4}$, and South Stoke, $59\frac{1}{2}$, and over Odd Down, where keep to r., joining the Radstock road, with long descent into Bath, $61\frac{1}{2}$.]

Pretty scenery. At Midford, on r., Midford Castle.

SALISBURY TO CHRISTCHURCH.

Salisbury to Downton Wick ($5\frac{3}{4}$); go down Exeter street, then turn to l. after crossing R. Avon; there are three ascents and two descents, but none of them at all difficult, out of Salisbury to Bodenham, or Nunton-with-Bodenham, 3, and level through Charlton Street, $4\frac{1}{4}$: good flint road.

Before Bodenham, on l., Longford Castle. At Charlton Street, on l., Trafalgar Park and Ho., presented by Parliament to Earl Nelson. Downton lies $\frac{1}{2}$m. on l. of Downton Wick, across R. Avon. At Charlton Street, on r., Clearbury, an ancient hill fort.

Downton Wick to Fordingbridge ($4\frac{1}{2}$—$10\frac{1}{4}$), is a capital level road through South Chardford, $7\frac{1}{4}$, and Upper Burgate, 9: shortly after leaving Downton Wick the surface changes to gravel: in Fordingbridge the road bears to l. across R. Avon.

(Fordingbridge: Crown, B.T.C.; Greyhound.)

At South Chardford, on r., Breamore Ho., and beyond it Whichbury Ho., near which is Castle Ditches, a large circular entrenched hill, and the extensive earthwork called Grims Dyke or Ditch; on *l.*, across *R.* Avon, Hale *Ho.* At Upper Burgate, on *r.*, Friar's Court; across *R.* Avon, 1m. on *l.*, Castle Hill. Before Fordingbridge, on *l.*, Burgate *Ho.*; on *r.*, Packham *Ho.*

Fordingbridge to Ringwood, *Ch.* (6—16¼); out of Fordingbridge turn sharp to *r.*, and it is a capital level road through Ibbesley, 13½, and Blashford Green, 15: in Ringwood turn to *l.* Returning, in Ringwood turn to *r.* before *R.* Avon.

Before Ibbesley 1m., on *r.*, North End *Ho.*; 1m. beyond, on *l.*, Somerley *Ho.*; on *l.*, Moyles Court. On *l.*, Blashford *Ho.* Ringwood, p. 43.

Ringwood to Christchurch (9—25¼); through Lower Kingston, 18½, Avon, 20¾, Sopley, 22, and Staples Cross, is a dead level; sometimes rather sandy, otherwise a good road.

This road follows the *R.* Avon valley the whole distance. Very pretty scenery as far as Ringwood.

Beyond Lower Kingston, on *l.*, Bistern *Ho.* On *r.*, Avon Hill and Avon *Ho.*; on *l.*, Sopley *Ho.* and Winkton *Ho.* Christchurch, p. 43.

SALISBURY TO CHIPPENHAM.

Salisbury to Long Barrow Cross (7½); follow the Wilton road for a short distance past the railway, then turn to *r.* opposite the gaol, and after about a mile the road ascends to Salisbury Plain; it is hilly and good hard road past "Druid's Head" or Woodford Hut, 6, except that some of the gradients being steep at the bottom and often rough, they should be ridden down carefully.

At Long Barrow Cross, 1½m. on *r.*, is Stonehenge.

Long Barrow Cross to Red Horn Tp. (9—16½) goes straight across Salisbury Plain and is a similar kind of road; very hilly to the 13th ms., where keep to *r.* at the fork and across Black Heath, some of the ascents and descents being rough and steep; there is not a house the whole way,

About 3m. beyond Long Barrow Cross, on *r.*, is an ancient earthwork. Fine view from Red Horn Hill.

Red Horn Tp. to Devizes (5½—22); the road now suddenly leaves Salisbury Plain by Red Horn Hill, which is a long and steep descent, with a couple of sharp twists in it almost at right angles, and is dangerous to ride down; from the bottom it is pretty good but rather hilly, chiefly downhill, through Lide, 19, and Nursteed, 21: entering Devizes turn to *l.* Returning, keep to *r.* ¼m. beyond Lide.

Devizes, p. 86.

Devizes to Chippenham (10½—32½); in Devizes turn to *r.* just before the railway, and when through the town cross the canal; then keep to *r.*, and it is an easy road, with no difficult hills, through Rowde, 24 (keep to *r.*), over Chitway Heath, 26¼, by Sandy Lane, 28, and Red Hill, 29¾, (beyond which join the London road through Calne), and Derry Hill, 30¼. Returning, keep to *r.* past Derry Hill.

[There is another and much easier and better route from Salisbury along the Warminster road to Stapleford, 7—(p. 274); then keep to *r.*, and through the villages of Berwick St. James, Winterbourne Stoke, Maddington,

Shrewton, Orcheston St. George, Orcheston St. Mary, Tilshead, West Lavington, Lavington Wick, and Potterne to Devizes; about 2½m. longer.

Or at the 13th *ms.* turn to *l.* to Market Lavington, not a good road; thence by Potterne.]

At Rowde, on *r.*, Rowdeford *Ho.* At Chitway Heath, on *r.*, Bromham Battle *Ho.*; on *l.*, Nonesuch *Ho.* At Sandy Lane, on *r.*, Wands *Ho.*; on *l.*, Spy Park; on *r.*, also, the site of the Roman station Verlucio, on the line of the Roman road to Bath. A little further, on *r.*, Bowood Park. Chippenham, p. 89.

CHIPPENHAM TO WAREHAM.

Chippenham to Melksham (7¼); follow the Bath road for 1½m., then turn short on *l.*, and through Notton, 3¼, Laycock, 4¼, and Bennecar, 5¾, running near the *R.* Avon all the way. Returning, out of Melksham keep to *r.*

At Notton, on *r.*, Notton *Ho.*; on *l.*, Lackham *Ho.* Laycock Abbey on *l.* Melksham, p. 96.

Melksham to Semington (2—9¼); in Melksham cross *R.* Avon; pretty level road, oolite surface, very greasy.

Semington to Yarnbrook (3¾—13); cross the Devizes and Trowbridge road, and over Ashton Common, 10½, and through West Ashton, 12¼. [Or just beyond Semington turn to *r.*, and it is undulating through Hilperton, 11¼, with a long steepish hill through *Trowbridge*, 12¾; then after crossing the railway turn on *l.* through Studley, 12½, and North Bradley, 13¾, to Yarnbrook, 14½; level and good road, though sometimes rather rough.]

Before West Ashton, on *l.*, Rowd Ashton Park. Trowbridge, p. 85.

Yarnbrook to Westbury (2¼—15¼); turn to *l.*, and the road is level and good, though sometimes uneven.

Beyond Yarnbrook, on *l.*, Heywood *Ho.* Westbury, p. 85.

Westbury to Warminster (4—19¼); a stiff hill to descend out of Westbury, then fair undulating road; turn to *l.* just before Warminster.

Warminster, p. 82.

Warminster to Longbridge Deverill (3½—22¾); through Samborn, 19¾, and Crockerton, 21¼, is easy running.

Longbridge Deverill to Shaftesbury (11½—34¼); steady pull uphill for 1½m. from Longbridge, and then over Knoyle Downs there are several stiff hills with loose surface, to near East Knoyle, 29¼, succeeded by 4m. of good running, and a rise for 2m. to Shaftesbury. At 28m. cross Hindon and Mere road.

At East Knoyle, on *r.*, Clouds *Ho.*; on *l.*, Knoyle Park. 2m. further, on *l.*, Sedgehill *Ho.* and Hay *Ho.* Shaftesbury, p. 48.

Shaftesbury to Blandford, *M.P.* (11¼—45½); in Shaftesbury turn to *l.*, then leaving the town by the road to the *r.*—the new road—there is a long steep and winding descent, which should be ridden down very carefully and is best walked; then comes an equally long and tedious climb by Melbury Hill, from the top of which runs a capital undulating road with one or two short walks up through Fontmell Magna, 38¼, Sutton Waldron, 39, Iwerne Minster, 40, and Iwerne Courtney, 41¼, with a good descent into and through Stourpaine, 43, where enter the valley of R. Stour, and thence slightly downhill into Blandford. Returning, keep to r. 2m. out of Blandford. [Or out of Shaftesbury take the old road to *l.*, beginning with a long uphill to Melbury Abbas, 36½, and then very hilly running over the Downs, described in " Paterson " as "a summer road," and joining the Salisbury road on *l.* a short distance before Blandford: same distance. On *l.* Cranborne Chase.]

Pretty country. At Iwerne Minster, on *r.*, Iwerne Ho. and Shroton Ho. At Iwerne Courtney, on *r.*, Ranston Ho. and Steepleton Ho. ; behind, Hamilton or Hambledon Hill and Hod Hill, on which are ancient fortifications; from the former, splendid view. Blandford, p. 54.

Blandford to Spettisbury, *Ch.* (2¾—18½); at the M.P. in Blandford take the road to the *r.*, cross R. Stour, then turn to *l.*, and through Blandford St. Mary, 46¼, and Charlton Marshall, 47½, running close to R. Stour, down the valley: good road, almost level.

At Spettisbury, on *r.*, Crawford Castle.

Spettisbury to Wareham (11¾—60); at the end of Spettisbury turn to *r.*, then to *l.*, and 1½m. farther join the Bere Regis road and follow it on *r.* through Almer, 52, beyond which turn to *l.*, and through Morden, 54½, and over Gore Heath.

[Or from *Blandford* follow the Dorchester road to Winterborne Whitechurch, 50¾ (p. 54), then turn to *l.*, and through *Bere Regis*, 54½, where turn to *l.*, and over Woodbury Hill, keeping to *r.*, and Decoy Heath to *Wareham*, 61½.]

Beyond Morden, on *r.*, Morden Park. Wareham, p. 44.

RINGWOOD TO SHAFTESBURY.

Ringwood to Horton Inn (8½); cross R. Avon, and at Ashley Cross, a little beyond the railway, keep to *r.*, and over Ashley Heath, Wool Bridge, Woolbridge Common, and past Horton Park.

Horton Inn to Shaftesbury (15—23½); at 10½ m. cross Devil's Ditch, 2¼m. further cross Salisbury and Blandford road within a mile of Caishmore Inn on *r.*, and through Farnham, 15¼, and past Cranborne Chase.

CHIPPENHAM TO WAREHAM (by Frome).

Chippenham to Bradford-upon-Avon (12½); follow the Bath road for ½m. beyond Pickwick, 4, as at p. 80, then turn to *l.*
Bradford, p. 86.

Bradford-upon-Avon to Frome (9—21½); good road through Road, 17, and Beckington, 18½: rather undulating, with sharp descent into Frome.

[Or from *Chippenham* to *Trowbridge*, 12½, (p. 276); then after crossing the railway turn on *l.* and shortly after to *r.*, through Upper Studley, 13½, and Southwick, 14½, to Road, 16¼; rather more hilly, but good surface.]

Beyond Bradford, on *r.*, Farleigh Castle. Frome, p. 82. Beyond Beckington, on *r.*, Orchardleigh Ho.; 1m. on *l.*, Berkeley Ho. and Standerwick Ho.

Frome to Maiden Bradley (6—27½); there are several steep and rather long ups and downs in the first 3m., through West Woodlands, 24, then a tolerably level run of about 2m., followed by a good long ascent, a short descent, and another ascent to the village: good surface. Charming scenery.

Beyond Frome, on r., Marston Ho.; 2m. on l., West Woodlands. At Maiden Bradley, on l., Bradley Ho.

Maiden Bradley to Zeals Green (5—32½); descent through and out of the former, (at the first fork keep to r.), running under the end of Long Knoll Hill, where the surface is generally loose and dusty, but in a mile or so becomes better after crossing the Hindon and Redlinch road at the Red Lion, 30; shortly after enter the vale of Blackmere, and the church tower of Shaftesbury is visible on the hills on l.; then pass by Stour Head Ho., and Stourton village, 31, which lies off on r.

Zeals Green, p. 70.

Zeals Green to Gillingham (4—36½); following the Wincanton road (on r.) there is a descent from Zeals Green to High Cross, beyond which turn on l. and through Preston, 35; pretty level or slightly down hill.

(*Gillingham*; Phœnix, B.T.C.; South Western.)

Gillingham to East Stour (2½—39); at Gillingham turn to l., and then to r. at the station.

East Stour to Sturminster Newton (7—46); at East Stour turn to r. by the *ch.*, and through Stour Provost, 40, Moor Side, 41¼, where either to l., or to r. through Marnhull and Hinton St. Mary.

At Sturminster are remains of a castle.

Sturminster Newton to Blandford (8½—54½); through Sturminster cross R. Stour and turn to l.; hilly road through Shillingstone, 49¼, to Durweston, 51¾, then slightly downhill to Blandford: limestone road. Returning, in Blandford turn to l., and 2m. out of it again to l. over a bridge.

Before Durweston, on l., Hod Hill, an ancient entrenched hill. Blandford, p. 54.

Blandford to Wareham (14½—69)—p. 277.

[Or beyond Stourton turn to l. to *Mere*, 33¾, thence through Motcombe to *Shaftesbury* (about 7m.—40¾), whence to *Wareham*, 25¾—66¾, pp. 276-7.]

BRISTOL TO WEYMOUTH.

Bristol to Pensford or St. Thomas in Pensford (6½); leave Bristol over Redcliffe bridge and by the Bath road, turning to r. just beyond the railway; chiefly uphill through Whitchurch or Felton, 4, and downhill to Pensford.

Pensford to Farrington Gurney (5½—12); through Clutton, 9¼, and Temple Cloud, 10¼, a hilly road.

Beyond Pensford, on l., Houndstreet Park.

Farrington Gurney to Shepton Mallet (7½—19½); take the left hand fork just out of the former, and there is a steep ascent through Stone Easton, 13½, then past Old Down Inn, 15, and down again to Gurney Slade, 16, from which is another long steep climb to the top of the Mendip Hills, and long steep descent into Shepton Mallet; these gradients are dangerous to ride down.

On *l.*, Stone Easton Park; 2*m.* on *r.*, Chewton Priory. Shepton Mallet, p. 83.

Shepton Mallet to Castle Cary, Almsford Inn (6½—26); rather hilly by Cannard's Grave Inn, 20½ (keep to *l.*), to Priestleigh, 21½, then, keeping to *r.*, level to within a mile of Castle Cary. Returning, keep to *r.* a little past Almsford Inn.

Castle Cary, &c., p. 75.

Castle Cary to Sherborne (10½—36½); 1*m.* beyond Almsford Inn, keep to *r.*, through Galhampton, 28, and a little beyond turn to *l.*, and through North Cadbury, 29¾, South Cadbury, 30¾, and Corton Denham, 32¾; very hilly road, and great care must be taken in riding down some of the descents. Returning, about 2¼*m.* out of Sherborne keep to *l.* [Or there is a more favourable road through Galhampton to *Sparkford*, 30½, (p. 75); thence to Marston Magna, 34, (p. 72), where turn to *l.* to *Sherborne*, 37½ Or 1*m.* beyond Castle Cary keep straight on through Woolston and Blackford, joining the first route a little past Corton Denham, to Sherborne, about 36: not near so hilly.]

At N. Cadbury, on *r.*, Cadbury *Ho.* At Woolston, on *l.*, Yarlington Lodge. Sherborne, p. 48. Cadbury Castle, &c. p. 70.

Sherborne to Holnest (4¾—41¼); at Sherborne turn first to *r.*, through the town turn to *l.*, then steep ascent, followed by long easy descent to Leweston, 39¼, and Long Burton, 39½, and undulating to Holnest.

On *r.*, Leweston Park and Holnest Lodge.

Holnest to Dorchester (13¼—54½); undulating to Middlemarsh, 43½, then by Revels Inn, 44¾, very hilly for 3*m.* till the top of the downs is reached, after which it is undulating but chiefly downhill, with a long descent approaching Dorchester, and a stiff pull into the town. Returning, 1*m.* out of Dorchester keep to *r.* [Or beyond Holnest turn to *r.*, and it is a better road, hilly through Lyon's Gate, 43¾, to Minterne Magna, 45, then easy travelling, being mostly downhill to Cerne Abbas, 47½, after which it is good and almost level through Nether Cerne, Godmanstone, and Charminster, 53¼, just beyond which join the other road to Dorchester, 54¾. Or 1¾*m.* past Revels Inn, or *r.*, to Cerne Abbas, 47½.]

At Middlemarsh, on *l.*, Buckland and the Grange; 2 or 3*m.* distant Castle Hill and the Dungeon. On *l.*, Minterne *Ho.* At Cerne Abbas, remains of Abbey; near, on Trendle Hill, is a large entrenchment, and a figure cut in the chalk. Dorchester, p. 54.

Dorchester to Weymouth (8¼—62¾); the road is nearly level to Monkton, 57, then begins the ascent of Ridgeway Hill, which is more than a mile long, and consists of three separate stages; at the top the road commences to fall directly, the descent being steep and *dangerous* for nearly a mile, with a sharp turn in the middle at the steepest part, and another at the bottom; then through Broadway, 59½, and Radipole, 60½, the road is very undulating; flint road, good surface all the way.

Before Monkton, on *r.*, Maiden Castle; on *l.*, Herringtone Lodge. Beyond Broadway, on *r.*, Nottington *Ho.* Weymouth, p. 44.

SHEPTON MALLET TO POOLE.

Shepton Mallet to Bruton (7); rather hilly, by Cannard's Grave

Inn, 1 (keep to *l.*), Priestleigh, 2 (keep to *l.*), over Evercreech Hill, through Evercreech, 3¼ (keep to *l.*), and Milton Clevedon, 4½.

Bruton, p. 75.

Bruton to Wincanton (4¾—11¾); out of Bruton is a long uphill to Redlinch, 8½, and Stoney Stoke, 9¼, and steep descent into Wincanton.

[Or *Shepton Mallet* to *Castle Cary*, 6½, p. 279; then 1*m.* farther, keep first to *l.*, then to *r.* to *Wincanton*, 13½; not so hilly.]

On *r.*, Redlinch Park. Beyond Stoney Stoke, on *l.*, Roundhill *Ho.* Redlinch, p. 75. Castle Cary, p. 75. Wincanton, p 70.

Wincanton to Henstridge Ash (7—18¾); through Holton, 13¾ (keep to *l.* twice), Cheriton, 15½, Horsington, 16, Temple Combe, 17½, and Yeauston, 18.

Henstridge Ash, p. 48.

Henstridge Ash to Sturminster Newton (5¾—24½); through Henstridge, 19¾, and Stalbridge, 20½, and over Bagber Bridge, 22½.

(*Stalbridge:* Red Lion, *B.T.C.*)

On *r.*, Stalbridge Park. An Sturminster, remains of castle.

Sturminster Newton to Blandford (8½—33)—p. 278.

Blandford to Spettisbury, *Ch.* (2¾—35¾)—p. 277.

Spettisbury to Poole (11¼—47); by Sturminster Marshall, 36, (and 1¼*m.* farther, at the *Tpg.*, at the cross roads, keep to *l.*), and through Corfe Mullen, 38½ (turn to *r.*), and 3¼*m.* farther join the Wimborne road, and by Bushels Mill, 42¼; good undulating road.

[Or in *Blandford*, turn to *l.* before crossing *R.* Stour, through Tarrant Keynstone, 36½, Kingston Lacy, 40½, and Hill Butts, 41, to *Wimborne Minster*, 42¼, is more hilly; thence turning to *r.*, to *Poole* (6½—48¾)—p. 53.]

At Corfe Mullen, on *r.*, Hembury *Ho.* 3*m.* past Tarrant Keynstone, on the hill on *l.*, Badbury Rings, an immense ancient entrenchment of great strength. Before Kingston Lacy, on *r.*, Kingston Hall. Wimborne Minster, p. 44. Poole, p. 43.

BATH TO LYME REGIS.

Bath to Radstock (7½); there is a steep winding ascent out of Bath, about 2*m.* long (the first part very steep, and should not be ridden *down* in the other direction), to the toll gate on Odd Down, then 1½*m.* of a descent, some of which is too steep to ride down, except with a powerful brake; following this, out of Dunkerton, 4, is uphill for nearly 1½*m.*, steep and winding, most of which must be walked (and should be ridden down carefully in the opposite direction), then it is nearly level for about a mile, followed by another stiff descent of a mile into Radstock: good oolite road.

On Odd Down, 2*m.* on *l.*, Midford Castle. Before Dunkerton, on *l.*, Gumbhay. 1*m.* before Radstock, on *r.*, Camerton *Ho.* and Park; on *l.*, Woodbarrow *Ho.* Radstock, p. 86.

Radstock to Shepton Mallet (8—15½); turn to *r.* at the railway in Radstock; short but very steep ascent out of the town, then uphill for about 6*m.*, through Stratton-on-the-Fosse, 10½, and Oakhill, 13½ (except a descent into the latter), till the top of the Mendip Hills is reached, whence is a long steep descent through Downside, 14½, into Shepton Mallet. Returning, out of Downside keep to *r.*

On *l.*, Stratton *Ho.* and Downside. Shepton Mallet, p. 83.

Shepton Mallet to West Lydford (8¼—23¾); rather hilly by Cannard's Grave Inn, 16½ (keep to *r.*), through Street on the Fosse, 18¾, Wraxhill, 20¾, and Four Foot, 22¼.

At Street, on *r.*, Pylle *Ho.*; at Wraxhill, on *r.*, East Pennard Park.

West Lydford to Ilchester (6½—30¼).

Ilchester, p. 70.

Ilchester to Crewkerne (10½—40¾); straight undulating road for 5½*m.*, then turn on *l.* and through West Chinnock (Bow Gate), 33.

Crewkerne, p. 49.

Crewkerne to Marshalsea (5½—46¼)—p. 71.

Marshalsea to Lyme Regis (7¾—54); rather uphill to Lambert's Castle Hill, 48, whence undulating over Hawchurch Common, 49½ (keep to *l.*), and Uplyme Hill, with a long descent into Lyme Regis; pp. 58, 61, 71.

DORCHESTER TO GLASTONBURY.

Dorchester to Ailwell (11¼); in Dorchester turn to *r.* from the London road, and there is a sharp hill to descend out of the town, after which it is level (at 1½*m.* keeping to *l.*), crossing some marshes to Charminster, 2 (keep to *l.* again), and the road is gently undulating through Stratton, 3¼ (and turning to *r.* 1¼*m.* farther), to Grimstone Station, 4¾, whence it is rather more hilly to Ailwell.

Ailwell to Yeovil (7¾—19); through Melbury (Buck's Head), 13, and Barwick, 17½. Returning, ½*m.* out of Yeovil keep to *l.*

On *l.*, Melbury *Ho.*; on *r.*, Woolcomb Hall. Yeovil, p. 48.

Yeovil to Ilchester (4—23¼); through Yeovil, keep to *l.* at the fork roads.

Ilchester, p. 70.

Ilchester to Somerton (4¾—28); in Ilchester turn to *r.*, and out of the town keep to *l.*; about 1½*m.* farther is a steep hill to go over.

Somerton, p. 75.

Somerton to Glastonbury (7½—35½); pretty level through Littleton, 29¼, to Compton Dunden, 31, then cross Polden Hills to Street, 33½, beyond which is a rise into and through Glastonbury.

Glastonbury, p. 83.

BRISTOL TO BRIDPORT.

Bristol to Blue Bowl (9¾); leave Bristol by Victoria street for the Keynsham road, crossing *R.* Avon by Redcliffe Bridge, then turn to *r.* along Redcliffe Crescent, and to *l.* through Bedminster, 1, and 1*m.* farther past the railway again to *l.*; undulating to beyond Buishport, 2½, beyond which is a crooked ascent up to Dundry Hill, followed by corresponding descent (at 5¼*m.* keep to *r.*), and through Chew Stoke, 7.

At 5¼*m.* on *l.* to Chew Magna (1—6¼).

Blue Bowl to Wells ($7\frac{1}{2}$—$17\frac{1}{4}$); by right hand road steep ascent on to the Mendip Hills, then pretty level for 3 or 4*m.* past Castle Comfort, $12\frac{3}{4}$, and steep descent into Wells. [Or by left hand road through West Harptree, $10\frac{1}{4}$, and East Harptree, 11, entering which, turn to *r.*, and up a long steep ascent to Castle Comfort, 13.]

Wells to Glastonbury ($5\frac{1}{2}$—$22\frac{3}{4}$)—below.

Glastonbury to Somerton ($7\frac{1}{2}$—$30\frac{1}{4}$)—p. 281, reversed.

Somerton to Crewkerne (14—$44\frac{1}{4}$); entering Somerton, turn to *r.*, and through the town turn to *l.*, through Long Sutton, Long Load, Martock, and Bower Heaton, $36\frac{1}{4}$, beyond which join the road from Ilchester, p. 281.

Crewkerne to Beaminster ($7\frac{3}{4}$—52); turn 2nd on *l.*, and through Misterton, $45\frac{1}{2}$, and Mosterton, $47\frac{1}{2}$; good road with a few easy hills.
Beaminster, p. 60.

Beaminster to Bridport ($6\frac{1}{4}$—$58\frac{1}{4}$); through Bradpole, 57.
Bridport, p. 54. Beyond, on *r.*, Parnham *Ho.*

BATH TO EXETER.

Bath to Radstock ($7\frac{1}{2}$)—p. 280.

Radstock to Wells ($10\frac{3}{4}$—$18\frac{1}{4}$); turn to *r.* at the railway in Radstock; short but very steep ascent out of the town, then keeping to *r.* at $2\frac{1}{2}m.$, through Chilcompton, $10\frac{1}{2}$, and by Old Down Inn, 12 (on the Bristol and Shepton Mallet road) to Emborough, $12\frac{1}{2}$, is a gradual uphill, all of which can be ridden up; next are 2 or 3*m.* of nearly level across the top of the Mendip Hills, and the last 3*m.* are downhill, a good part of which is too steep to ride down with safety: very rutty surface, oolite, dangerously slippery when wet; heavy coal traffic.

2*m.* beyond Radstock, on *l.*, Ammerdown *Ho.* and Hardington Park; a little farther, on *l.*, Stratton *Ho.* and Mount Pleasant. At Chilcompton, on *l.*, Norton Hall. $2\frac{1}{2}m.$ beyond Emborough, on *r.*, Haydon Seat. Wells, p. 84.

Wells to Glastonbury ($5\frac{1}{2}$—$23\frac{3}{4}$); through Coxley, $19\frac{3}{4}$, and Polsham, $20\frac{3}{4}$, across East Sedge Moor and Hartlake Bridge, $21\frac{1}{4}$, is a fair road in dry weather, but being oolite, it is dangerously greasy and rutty when wet; almost level.
Glastonbury, p. 83.

Glastonbury to Piper's Inn ($4\frac{3}{4}$—$28\frac{1}{2}$)—p. 83.

Piper's Inn to Taunton ($17\frac{1}{2}$—46)—p. 81.

Taunton to South Appledore ($13\frac{1}{2}$—$59\frac{1}{2}$)—p. 73.

South Appledore to Exeter ($17\frac{3}{4}$—$77\frac{1}{4}$)—p. 76.

BRISTOL TO EXETER.

Bristol to Churchill ($13\frac{1}{4}$); leave Bristol by Victoria street for the Keynsham road, crossing *R.* Avon by Redcliffe Bridge, then turn to *r.* along Redcliffe Crescent, and to *l.* through Bedminster, 1, and 1*m.* further keep to *r.* past the railway; uphill for about first 8*m.*, then a long steep descent at Redhill, 9, which must be ridden down carefully, and the rest undulating over Perry Bridge, 10½, and through Langford, 12.

[Or *Bristol* to *Congresbury*, 12—(p. 97); then on *l.* to *Churchill*, 15¼.]

2*m.* beyond Bedminster, on *l.*, Barrow *Ho.*; a little further, 2*m.* on *r.*, Barrow Court. At Bedminster, on *r.*, Ashton Court. Before Redhill, on *l.*, Butcombe Court; beyond Redhill, on *l.*, Aldwick Court; a little farther, Menlip Lodge. On *l.*, Langford Court.

Churchill to Cross (3½—16¾); steep ascent out of Churchill, then (keeping to *r.*) undulating through Sydcot, 15, with a steep descent to Cross.

At Cross, on *l.*, to *Axbridge* (¾—17½); p. 84.

Cross to High Bridge (8¼—25); just beyond Cross turn to *l.*, and through Lower Wear, 17¾, Rook's Bridge, 20¼, East Brent, 21½, and across Burnham Level; there is not a single ascent worth mentioning.

(*High Bridge:* Railway, *B.T.C.*)

On *r.*, pass Brent Knoll hill.

High Bridge to Bridgewater (8—33); cross *R.* Brue, and through Huntspill, 26¼, to Pawlet, 28, is a similar kind of road, then undulating to Crandon Bridge (Sedgemoor Cut), 30½, before crossing which join on *l.* the Glastonbury road, and the rest is level.

On *l.*, Huntspill Court. Bridgewater, p. 81.

Bridgewater to Taunton (11—44); turn to *l.* in Bridgewater when over the bridge, and it is level for 2*m.*, then ascent through North Petherton, 36¼, and hilly through Thurloxton, 38¾, over Walford Bridge, 39¾, and through Bath Pool End, 42¼, just beyond which cross *R.* Tone; some of the hills are rather steep, and must be negotiated carefully: bad macadam road. Returning, keep to *l.* 1*m.* out of Taunton, and again to *l.* after Walford Bridge.

At North Petherton, on *r.*, Petherton Park; on *l.*, Binfords and Halswell *Ho.* On *r.*, Walford *Ho.* Taunton, p. 73.

Taunton to Exeter (31¼—75¼)—p. 282.

BATH TO WELLS (by Marksbury).

Bath to Marksbury (6¾)—p. 96.

Marksbury to Farrington Gurney (6½—13¼); by left hand road, several very stiff hills up and down through Farmborough, 7½, High Littleton, 10½, and Hallatrow, 11½. Returning, turn to *r.* ¾*m.* out of Farrington Gurney.

Farrington Gurney to Wells (7½—20¾); steep ascent out of the former, keeping to the right hand fork, and it is chiefly uphill through Chewton Mendip, 16, on to the Mendip Hills, from which, after 2 or 3*m.* of level, there is a long steep descent into Wells.

BATH TO SEATON AND BEER.

Bath to Crewkerne (40¾)—pp. 280-1.

Crewkerne to Axminster (12¼—53)—p. 71.

Axminster to Colyton (4½—57½)—p. 59.

Colyton to Seaton (2½—60); turn to *l.* and through Colyford, 58½

[Or in *Axminster* turn to *l.* before the railway and through Musbury, 56, turning to *r.* 1½m. farther on road from Lyme Regis, to Colyford, 59.]
1m. past Seaton is the village of *Beer*.

Before Musbury, on *r.*, Ash *Ho.*; at Musbury, on *l.*, Musbury Castle.

DORCHESTER TO TAUNTON.

Dorchester to Catsley Down Gate (14)—p. 60.

Catsley Down Gate to Crewkerne (8—22); keeping to *r.*, a long winding hill descends through a wood, quite safe to ride down with care; from the bottom is a good run, with two or three short hills, through South Perrott and Misterton, 20¾ (just beyond keep to *r.*): entering Crewkerne turn sharp on *l.*

Crewkerne to Chard (8—30)—p. 49.

[Or to *Broadwindsor*, 22 (p. 61); thence through Winsham and Forton to *Chard*, about the same distance.

Or at Misterton on *l.* avoiding Crewkerne.]

At Winsham, 1m. on *l.*, ruins of Ford Abbey; a little farther, on *l.*, Leigh *Ho.*

Chard to Taunton (13—43); nearly through Chard turn to *r.*; a mile ascent out of the town through Crim Chard, and the road continues hilly through Wadford, Combe St. Nicholas, by Coombe Beacon, Moor Moor, Buckland Hill, over Buckland Down, through Curland, and Staple Fitzpaine, 38½, but the ascents are nearly all rideable and the descents easy; good road on the whole, and the last 2m. are first rate.

[Or in *Chard* take first turn sharp on *r.*, chiefly downhill, through Sea, 33¼ (keep to *l.*), to Donyatt, 34, then uphill to Horton, 35, whence to *Taunton*, 46¾ (p. 74).

Or from *Crewkerne* through Hinton St. George, Dinnington, and Kingstone to *Ilminster*, 30, whence to *Taunton*, 42½ (p. 74).

Or from Crewkerne follow the Chard road for 2½m., then turn on *r.* through Kingstone to *Ilminster*, 29.]

TAUNTON TO SIDMOUTH.

Taunton to Honiton (16) crosses the Black Down Hills; chiefly uphill through Trull, 1½, Blagdon, 4 (about 3m. farther keep to *l.*), Churchingford, 8, to Beacon Hill, 10, then downhill through Upottery, 11, Rawridge, 11¾, Haynes Yard, 13, Monkton (*ch.*), 14, to Honiton.

Honiton, p. 49. 1m. out of Taunton, on *l.*, Batts; ½m. beyond Trull, on *l.*, Amberd *Ho.*, and farther on, Poundisford Lodge and Park. At Blagdon, on *r.*, Lowton *Ho.*; on *l.*, Barton Grange.

Honiton to Sidford (7½—23½); through Honiton turn to *l.*, and there is a crooked ascent of a mile or two on to Gittesham Hill, followed by a long downhill through Sidbury, 22.

At Sidbury, on *r.*, Sidbury Castle, an ancient hill fort.

Sidford to Sidmouth (1½—25) is nearly all downhill.

Sidmouth, p. 59.

TAUNTON TO EXMOUTH.

Taunton to Honiton (16)—p. 284.

Honiton to Ottery St. Mary (6—22); follow the Exeter road for 3*m*. out of Honiton, then turn to *l*. a little short of Fenny Bridges (p. 49), and through Affingham, 20; rather up and down hill.

Ottery St. Mary to Exmouth (12—34); cross *R*. Otter, then turn to *l*. through Fen Ottery, 24, Newton Poppleford, 25, and Colyton Rawleigh, 27, to East Budleigh, 29, where join the Sidmouth road, as p. 60.

(*Exmouth:* Imperial; London, *B.T.C.*; Royal Beacon; South Western.)
¾*m*. beyond Colyton Rawleigh, on *l*., Bicton Lodge.

EXMOUTH TO MINEHEAD.

Exmouth to Topsham (6¼); through Lympstone, 2¼, Exton, 4, and Ebford, 5, just beyond which turn to *l*., and over Topsham Bridge; up and down hill.

Before Lympstone, on *l*., Court Land; on *r*., Alaronde. Opposite Lympstone, across *R*. Exe, Powderham Castle; beyond Lympstone, on *l*., Nutwell Court. At Ebford, on *l*., Ebford *Ho*., Mount Ebford, and Ebford Place.

Topsham to Exeter (3¾—10)—p. 59.

[Or from Ebford keep straight on to *St. George's Clyst*, 5¾, whence to *Exeter*, 10¾—p. 59.]

Exeter, p. 49.

Exeter to Silverton (7¼—17¼); in Exeter turn to *r*., and at the suburb of St. Sidwell's, 10¼, keep to *l*.; there are one or two steep hills to climb to Stopgate, 12¼ (where turn to *l*.), then downhill over Stoke Bridges (*R*. Culm), to Stoke Canon, 14, and from Rew, 15, is again uphill.

1*m*. out of Exeter, on *l*., Stoke Hill and Duryard *Ho*. Beyond Rew, 1*m*. on *r*., Killerton Park.

Silverton to Tiverton (6¾—24); keep to *l*.; it is an undulating road slightly uphill, up the Exe valley to Bickleigh, 20½, just beyond it crossing the river, and fairly level along the right bank to Tiverton, just before which recross *R*. Exe. [Or by right hand road through Butterleigh, 21, very hilly.]

Tiverton, p. 73.

Tiverton to Bampton (6¾—30¾); in Tiverton turn to *l*., and mostly uphill to Van Post, 28¼, then down to Bampton. [Or 1*m*. out of Tiverton turn to *l*. to Botham, 25½, whence a road runs close to *R*. Exe all the way to Bampton.]

Before Van Post, 1*m*. on *r*., Huntsham Castle. Bampton, p. 78.

Bampton to Minehead (18¼—49), crosses Exmoor, and a deal of walking will be necessary; at Bampton keep to *r*., through Morebath, 33 (keep to *l*.), by Gilberts, 33¾, Bury, 35¼ (keep to *l*. and ½*m*. farther to *r*.), over Combshead Hill, Exton Hill, and Lype Hill, to Couple Cross, 43¼, then chiefly downhill to Timberscombe, 45, from which there is a steep crooked ascent of a mile on to Grabbist Hill, and downhill to Minehead.

Beyond Timberscombe on *r*. to *Dunster*, 2½; almost level.

Minehead, p. 79.—Dunster, p. 79.

EXETER TO BIDEFORD.

Exeter to Crediton (7½)—p. 68.

Crediton to Chumleigh (14—21½); in Crediton take second turn to *l.*, and a stiff hill to mount out of the town, followed by long fall to Diddy Mill, 10, then a short rise and the rest is pretty level by New Buildings, 11½, Oldburrow, 14, Morchard Bishops, 15, Red Hill, 15½, Calfs Bridge, 16¼, Eastown, 16½, Barnstaple Inn, 17¼, and through Chawleigh, 19½, with a short sharp fall to the Little Dart *R.* just before Chumleigh and similar rise into the town.

(*Chumleigh :* King's Arms, *B.T.C.*)
Beyond Crediton, on *r.*, Creedy *Ho.*

Chumleigh to Week Cross (6¼—27¾); out of Chumleigh keep to *l.*, and the road is on the decline for 1½*m.* ending with a sharp drop to the bridge over *R.* Taw, after which there is a long stiff hill up to Burrington, 24½, and the rest level.

Week Cross to Bideford (10¾—38½); turn to *l.* and by Dipford, 28, New Inn, 31, Sherwood, 31½, Cranford Moor, 32¼, Hunshaw Cross, 33¾, and Hunshaw Moor, 34¼; a few hills, but nothing difficult, except long crooked descent into Bideford.

EXETER TO BARNSTAPLE.

Exeter to Week Cross (27¾)—above.

Week Cross to Atherington (3—30¾); by right hand road, level through High Bickington, 29, and Dobbs House, 29¾ (where keep to *r.*)

Atherington to Barnstaple (6¾—37½); descent beyond Atherington into the *R.* Taw valley, then pretty level over New Bridge, 34¼, and through Bishops Tawton, 35¾.

[Or out of *Chumleigh* keep to *r.* and up on to Beacon Moor, where at 23*m.* turn to *l.* and through Chittleham Holt and Chittlehampton to Bishops Tawton: a trifle longer but much more hilly road.]

At Bishops Tawton, on *l.*, across *R.* Taw, Tawstock Court. Barnstaple, p. 74.

EXETER TO SOUTH MOLTON.

Exeter to Crediton (7½)—p. 68.

Crediton to East Worlington (11—18½); in Crediton take second turn to *l.*, mounting a stiff hill, and about 1*m.* out of the town turn to *r.*, and the road is alternately down and up through Sandford, 10, Kennersleigh, 13, by Black Boy Inn, 15, and through Thelbridge, 17.

Beyond Crediton, on *r.*, Creedy *Ho.* 1½*m.* past Sandford, on *r.*, Dowrish; at Black Boy Inn, on *l.*, Berry Castle.

East Worlington to South Molton (9—27½); uphill for 3*m.* to Meshaw Moor, then downhill to Bulls Marsh, 25, then a rise and level to South Molton.

[Or to *Chumleigh*, 21½—above; thence keeping to *r.* up on to Beacon Moor and through George Nympton, 27½, to *South Molton*, 29½; hilly road. Returning, a little out of South Molton keep to *r.*]

OKEHAMPTON TO BARNSTAPLE.

Okehampton to Hatherleigh (6¾); over Harperton Down, by Five Oaks, 1¾, and over Langabear Moor, 4, and by Bassets Gate, 6, hilly road. Returning, keep to *r.* at Bassets Gate.

Hatherleigh to Torrington (11—17½); over Hole Bridge, 8½ (*R.* Torridge), to and from which there are steep descent and ascent, and through Ash, 10, Petrockstow, 10¾, Winswell, 13¾, and Little Torrington, 16, whence a long descent to the bridge over *R.* Torridge, at the entrance of Torrington.

(*Torrington:* Globe, B.T.C.)

Torrington to Barnstaple (10¼—28); in Torrington turn to *l.* by the *ch.*, then out of the town turn to *r.* over Torrington Common, and through Hunshaw Moor, 20¼, Alverdiscott, 22¼, Newton Tracey, 23½, and Roundswell, 26¼; all up and downhill. Returning, 1m. out of Barnstaple keep to *l.* [Or at Torrington Common keep to *l.* to *Bideford*, 24¼, whence to *Barnstaple*, 8½—32½,—p. 74.]

Barnstaple, p. 74.—Bideford, p. 74.

DARTMOUTH TO PLYMOUTH.

Dartmouth to Morleigh, New Inn (8½); ascent out of Dartmouth, in places steep, nearly to Norton House, 2, then very undulating through Ditsham Cross, 3¾ (keep to *l.*), and Halwell.

Norton *Ho.* on *r.*; a little farther on *l.*, Woodbury Camp, an ancient entrenchment. Beyond Ditsham Cross, on *l.*, Weststray *Ho.*, and nearly 1m. farther, Oldstone *Ho.* Before Halwell, the road goes through an ancient camp. Just before Morleigh, on *l.*, Stanborough *Ho.*

Morleigh to Plymouth (19¼—28); through Modbury, 15½, and Brixton, 22½—(p. 64.)

NEWTON ABBOT TO TAVISTOCK.

Newton Abbot to Ashburton (7½); leave the former by the London road, and just out of the town turn to *l.*; at 3m. turn sharp to *l.*, and a little farther to *r.* to Lemonford, 4½, where join the road from Chudleigh on *r.*

Ashburton, p. 53.

Ashburton to Two Bridges (11—18½); in Ashburton turn to *r.*, and ¾m. farther to *l.*; over Holne Bridge, Hanneford Bridge, by Ash, Uppercot, Ouidsbroom, Dartmeet Bridge, and Dennebridge Pound, across part of Dartmoor, and full of steep hills.

Two Bridges to Tavistock (8—26½)—p. 65.

PLYMOUTH TO LAUNCESTON.

Plymouth to Tavistock (14); very hilly by Knacker's Knoll (or Hole) *Tg.*, 3, Bowling Green Ho., 3½, over Buckland Down to Jump, 5½, **and**

then over Rodborough Down (at 8¼m. keeping to l. at the fork roads), with a long downhill to Horra Bridge or Harrowbridge, 10¼ (cross R. Wallcomb), whence keeping to l., a couple of ascents with intervening descent through Whitchurch, 12½, to Tavistock.

2m. out of Plymouth, on r., Widey; on l., Manudon. Beyond Bowling Green Ho., on r., Derryford; a little on l., Witley Place. At the end of Buckland Down, on r., Fancy. 1m. past Jump, on r., Combe Park; a little farther, on l., Bickham, and 1m. W. of it, Mariston; 1½. N.W. of Bickham is Buckland Abbey. 1m. before Horra Bridge, on l., Pound; 1m. beyond Horra Bridge, on r., Sortridge. Tavistock, p. 65.

Tavistock to Launceston (11¾—25¾); in Tavistock turn to l., then second on r.; very hilly road over Lamerton Down, through Redford, 17½, Milton Abbots, 19½, and over Greston Bridge (R. Tamar), 22. Returning, 2¼m. out of Launceston turn to l.

At Milton Abbots, on r., Edgecumb Ho.; a little farther, 1m. on r., Kelly. At Greston Bridge, on l., Carthamartha Ho. Launceston, p. 50.

PLYMOUTH TO LAUNCESTON (by Callington.)

Plymouth to Saltash (4½)—p. 56.

Saltash to Callington (8¾—13¼); 1m. beyond Saltash keep to r., and the road is pretty level through Carkeel, 6¼, and Penter's Cross, 9 (keep to l.), to St. Mellion, 10, whence is a steep ascent to climb over Viverdon Down, and long downhill to Callington.

1m. beyond Saltash, 1m. on l., Trematon Castle. Before Carkeel, on r., Hale Ho.; at Carkeel, on r., Moditonham. At Penter's Cross, on r., Pentilly Castle. At St. Mellion, on r., Crocadon Ho. Callington, p. 65.

Callington to Launceston (10½—23¾); in Callington turn to r. by the ch., and over Hingston Down to Stoke Climsland, 16¼, and by Beal Mills, 18 (cross R. Inny), Trekenna, 19¼, Landue Mill, 20¼, and joining the Tavistock road 1¼m. farther on r.

Before Stoke Climsland, on l., Whiteford Ho. At Trekenna, on l., are some ruins. On r., Landue Ho.

BODMIN TO WADEBRIDGE.

Bodmin to Wadebridge (7¼); leaving Bodmin keep to r., and over Dunmeer Bridge, 1¾, through Washaway, 3¼, and Egloshayle, 5¾.

At Dunmeer Bridge, 2m. on r., Penhargate Castle ruins. Beyond Washaway, on r., Pencarrow. Wadebridge, p. 68.

REDRUTH TO PENRYN.

Redruth to Penryn (8); in Redruth turn to l. and again to l. ½m. farther; through Penance, Gwennap, Ponsworth, and Roscrow.

REDRUTH TO HELSTON.

Redruth to Helston (10); in Redruth turn to l. and ½m. further to r.; uphill to Forest Gate, 3, and similar descent from Tregorlands, 4; short ascent at Wendron, 7½, then level, with descent before Helston.

LAUNCESTON TO HOLSWORTHY.

Launceston to Holsworthy (13½); in Launceston go down the hill to the suburb of St. Thomas, and having crossed the river turn to *r.*; steep hill up to Dutston, 1¼, then down again to New Bridge, 1¾ (cross R. Tamar), thence through Hawkadon, 3¼, Godleigh Corner, 4½, over Beacon Moor or Chapman's Well Down, by Chapman's Well, 6¼, over Enford Moor and Belland Moor (at 8½m. keep to *l.*), through Clawton, 10¼ (cross branch of R. Tamar), and over Boarden Bridge, 11¼: hilly road, some of the gradients being steep: not a good surface.

At New Bridge, 1m. on *l.*, Werrington Ho. Holsworthy, p. 69.

LAUNCESTON TO HARTLAND.

Launceston to Blake's Cross (14½); in Launceston go down the hill to the suburb of St. Thomas, then up hill through St. Stephen's, ¾m., on to St. Stephen's Down, from which is a sharp descent to Yeolm Bridge, 1¾ (cross R. Tamar), and similar ascent to Lady Cross, 2¼, where turn sharp on *l.*; thence by Lower Langdon Bennacot, 5¼, Little Cory, 6¼, Wescott Barrow, 7¼, over Dowlsdown, by Bennets, 10, Bevil's or Bound's Hill, 11¼, Newcot, 12, and Borough, 12¼.

At St. Stephen's, on *r.*, Werrington Ho. Before Bennets, on *l.*, Whitstone Ho. At Dowlsdown, on *r.*, Wilsworthy.

Blake's Cross to Kilkhampton (3¾—18) through Grimscot, 14¾; turn to *l.* ½m. before Kilkhampton.

At Grimscot, 1m. on *l.*, Leigh Hill.

Kilkhampton to Hartland (9—27); by Crimpgate, 20¾ (keep to *r.*), over Sharston Moor, 22, Dipford Moor, by Dipford, 22¼, Little Bursdon, 23½, cross Bursdon Moor to Tosberry, 24¾ (at the bottom of the hill ¼m. farther keep to *r.*), and through Philham, 25¾.

(*Hartland :* King's Arms, *B.T.C.*)

READING TO AMERSHAM.

Reading to Henley-on-Thames (8); out of Reading, down hill to R. Thames, which cross to Caversham, 1, then turn to *r.* and through Play Hatch, 3¼, and Shiplake, 5¼, the road runs through a pretty country along the banks of the R. Thames; stillish hill out of Caversham, then nearly all downhill: excellent surface.

At Caversham, 1m. on *l.*, Caversham Park. At Play Hatch, on *r.* across Thames, Holme Park. On *r.*, Shiplake Ho. and Bell Hatch; on *l.*, Holme Wood, Crowsley Park, Blounts Court, and Harpsden Court. Before Henley, on *r.*, Boulney Court. Henley, p. 100.

Henley-on-Thames to Great Marlow (7½—15½); through Henley keep to *r.*, and through Fawley Court, 9¼, Mill End, 11¼, and Medmenham, 12¼, beyond which is a long steepish hill to climb, and then rather steep downhill which requires careful riding: splendid smooth surface. Pretty views. [Or at Henley turn to *r.*, and follow the Maidenhead road for about 1½m., then turn to *l.* through Bisham to *Great Marlow*, into which is a very steep descent : about the same distance.]

(*Great Marlow :* Crown ; George and Dragon, *B.T.C.* ; Railway.)

U

On r., Fawley Court. At Mill End, on l., Hambledon Ho. Before Medmenham, on r. across Thames, Culham Court; on r., Medmenham Abbey. 2m. farther, Harleyford Grove and Lady Place. On l., Bisham Abbey.

Great Marlow to High Wycombe (5—20½); through Great Marlow keep to l., and there is a long winding ascent to Handy Cross, 18½, shortly followed by a steep dangerous hill, or rather series of three hills, down into the town, with a turn at right angles: good surface.

1m. out of Great Marlow, on r., Westhorpe Ho. High Wycombe, p. 107.

High Wycombe to Amersham (7—27½); in Wycombe turn first to r., then to l., and a narrow street, roughly paved, leads to Wycombe Hill, a long, very steep, and rough climb, quite *unrideable up or down*; from the top is a good run of 2m. through Hazlemoor, 22½, to Deadman's Dean Bottom or Hole, into which is a steep pitch, followed by a steeper rise (either of which is barely safe to ride *down* with a powerful brake) up the opposite side, then there is a good run of about 2m. over Wycombe Heath, with a steep descent down Winchmoor Hill to the *Tpg.*, 26, and the rest an easy downhill: fair gravel surface, but in places apt to be stony, and the last 2m. loose.

[Or out of *Great Marlow* keep to r., and through Little Marlow, 17¼, is good going, then 1m. farther (keeping to l.) Woburn Hill to walk up, very steep, narrow, and winding, impossible to ride up and dangerous to ride down. Or instead of going over Woburn Hill go straight on through Cours End, 19, Woburn, 20, and Woburn Green, 20¾, out of which (keeping to r.) is a short steep ascent to Hotspur Heath, 21½, then turn to r., and a stiffish hill to mount into *Beaconsfield*, 23. Here turn to l., second turning, and it is an undulating but splendid smooth road, by Leadboroughs, 24¼, and Larkins Green, 25¾, with a steep descent into *Amersham*, 27¾.]

2m. beyond High Wycombe, 1m. on l., Hughenden, which is best reached by a road running up a narrow valley from the town. Amersham, p. 133.—Beaconsfield, p. 106.

ST. ALBANS TO STAINES.

St. Albans to Watford (7½); in St. Albans, Holywell Hill to ride down, very stiff, to R. Colne, followed by a stiff ascent, then a good road with easy hills, through St. Stephens, 1, Chiswell Green, 1¾, and by Garstons Ho., 5½.

Beyond St. Albans, on l., Sopwell, ruins of Benedictine nunnery, erected 1140; beyond it, New Barns. Past St. Stephens, on l., St. Julians. Past Garstons Ho., on l., Aldenham Abbey, Edge Grove, Munden, Wall Hall, &c. Before Garstons Ho., on r., High Elms, and 2m. off, Langley Ho. and Cecil Ho., &c. Entering Watford, on r., Nascott Ho. Watford, p. 129.

Watford to Rickmansworth (3¼—10¾) is a very good road; skirting Cashiobury Park to Cashio Bridge, 8½, then long rise, followed by very steep descent to Scots Bridge, at the entrance of Rickmansworth. [Or, past the Workhouse along some country lanes and by the side of Moor Park on l., is a good level road, nearly a mile longer.]

On r., Cashiobury Park, The Lodge, &c. On r., Scots Bridge Ho.; on l., Croxley Hall. By lower road, on r., Moor Ho.; on l., Moor Park. Rickmansworth, p. 134.

Rickmansworth to Uxbridge (8—18¾); capital road, level through Mill End, 11¾, Maple Cross, 12¼ (keep to l. of two fork roads), to West

Hyde, 13¾, after which are one or two small hills: runs close to *R.* Colne. Returning, 2*m.* out of Uxbridge, turn to *r.*

Beyond West Hyde, on *l.*, Harefield Park; 2*m.* before Uxbridge, on *l.*, Denham Place and Denham Court. Uxbridge, p. 106.

Uxbridge to Longford (6—24¾); in Uxbridge turn to *r.* past the station, and through Cowley Street, 20¼, Peachey, 21, Yewsley, 21¾, and West Drayton, 22¼, is across country, and except in winter and early spring, is in fair order: there are no hills.

Longford to Staines (3—27¾) is a good road. Returning, out of Staines turn to *l.*

About half-way on *l.*, Stanwell Place. Staines, p. 46.

BASINGSTOKE TO THAME.

Basingstoke to Aldermaston (9¼); in Basingstoke turn to *r.*, passing the ruins of the Holy Ghost Chapel, and a little farther, when clear of the town, keep to *r.*, and through Sherborne St. John, 3, Pamber End, 4¾, Tadley, 6¼, and over Silchester Common: good road. Returning, 1*m.* S. of Aldermaston keep to *l.*

Beyond Sherborne, 1*m.* on *r.*, The Vine, and a little farther, Cuffell *Ho.* and Beaurepaire *Ho.* At Silchester Common, 3*m.* on *r.*, Silchester, the remains of a Roman town; see p. 95. Before Aldermaston, on *r.*, Aldermaston Park; on *l.*, Wasing *Ho.*

Aldermaston to Jack's Booth (4—13¼); join the Bath road 1½*m.* beyond Aldermaston; all but level and good smooth surface.

Before Jack's Booth, on *l.* 1*m.*, Beenham *Ho.*; on *r.* 1½*m.*, Ufton Court, and Sulhampstead *Ho.*

Jack's Booth to Pangbourne (4½—17¾); about 1*m.* past Jack's Booth turn to *l.*, and through Englefield, 14¾, and Tidmarsh, 16½; good road.

On *l.*, Englefield *Ho.* Pangbourne, p. 99.

Pangbourne to Streatley (4—21¾)—p. 100.

Streatley to Wallingford (5—26¾); just beyond Streatley keep to *r.*, and through Moulsford, 23, is an undulating road with several sharp but short hills; flint road with splendid smooth hard surface. Runs close to *R.* Thames.

(*Moulsford*: Beetle and Wedge.)

Wallingford, p. 101.

Wallingford to Shillingford (3—29¾); 2*m.* farther cross *R.* Thames, by Shillingford Bridge, and there is a long rise into Shillingford; good road.

(*Shillingford*: Swan.)

Shillingford to Thame (12—41¾); turn to *r.* from the Dorchester road and through Warborough (*ch.*), 30½, Newington (*ch.*), 32¾, Stadhampton (*ch.*), 34¼, Little Milton, 35½, and by the Three Pigeons, 38, where cross the High Wycombe and Oxford road.

On *l.*, Newington *Ho.* On *l.*, Milton *Ho.*, and on *r.* 2*m.*, Haseley Court. Past Three Pigeons, on *l.*, Ryecote Park. S. of Thame 1*m.*, Thame Park.

NEWBURY TO ANDOVER.

Newbury to Highclere Street (5½); out of the town keep to *r.*, and over Wash Bridge, 2¼.

At Highclere Street, on *l.*, Ivy *Ho.* and Highclere *Ho.*; on *r.*, Harewood Lodge and Cell *Ho.*

Highclere Street to Andover (10½—16); stiff ascent up to Three Legged Cross, 6½, shortly followed by long descent, then through Hurstbourne Tarrant, 10¾, Kings Enham, 13¼, and Knights Enham, 14½.

Andover, p. 58.

OXFORD TO WINCHESTER.

Oxford to Abingdon (6½); cross *R.* Thames, and through South Hinksey, 2, and Bagley Wood, 3, is a good road.

Before Abingdon, on *l.*, Radley *Ho.* Abingdon, p. 105.

Abingdon to East Ilsley (11—17½); in Abingdon turn to *r.*, and when through the town to *l.*, and through Drayton, 8¾, and Steventon (Green), 10½, whence it is chiefly uphill—at 2*m.* farther crossing the Wallingford and Wantage road—through Chilton, 14½, and Kates Gore, 15¾.

At Steventon, on *l.*, Milton *Ho.*; 1*m.* farther, on *r.*, Milton Hill; at cross roads, on *r.*, Hendred *Ho.*

East Ilsley to Newbury, *ch.* (9½—27); through Beedon, 20, Chieveley, 22¼, Donnington, 26, and Speenhamland, 26¾.

At Beedon, on *l.*, Langley Hall. At Chieveley, on *l.*, Prior's Court. Newbury, p. 88.

Newbury to Whitchurch (12½—39½); just out of Newbury, after the railway, keep to *l.*, and through Newtown, 29, Whitway, 32, past Burghclere on *l.*, by Seven Barrows, and through Litchfield, 35¾, whence it is nearly all downhill to Whitchurch; rather hilly. Returning, a mile out of Whitchurch keep to *l.*

Before Newtown, on *l.*, Sandleford Priory; on *r.*, Sandleford Cottage, Newtown *Ho.*, and Hawwood Lodge. At Whitway, 1*m.* on *l.*, Sidmonton *Ho.*; on *r.*, Beacon Hill; before it, on *r.*, Highclere *Ho.* Whitchurch, p. 58.

Whitchurch to Sutton Scotney (5¼—44¾); uphill through Tufton, 40¼, and descent down Tidbury Hill, 42¼, to Upper Bullington, 43½, then slightly uphill.

Sutton Scotney to Winchester (6½—51¼), over Worthy Down. Returning, 2½*m.* out of Winchester keep to *r.*

Winchester, p. 39.

OXFORD TO SALISBURY.

Oxford to Abingdon (6½)—above.

Abingdon to Wantage (10—16½); in Abingdon turn to *r.* and through Marcham, 9¼ (about ¾*m.* farther turn to *l.*), East Hanney, 12¾, and across East Hanney Field. [Or to the cross roads 2*m.* beyond Steventon, 10½, above; then turn to *r.* and through Ardington, 14¼,—p. 101; same distance.]

On *r.*, Marcham Park. Wantage, p. 101.

Wantage to Hungerford (14—30½); beyond Wantage is a steep hill to mount, dangerous to ride down when coming the reverse direction, then mostly downhill through Great or West Shefford, 24½, and Newtown, 28¼.

[Or from the cross roads beyond Steventon, through West Hendred, 13½, East Lockinge, 14½, whence is a long steep hill to climb, and then chiefly downhill through Farnborough, 17½, to West Shefford, 23½.]

5m. past Wantage, on l., Woolley Park. On the top of the hill, beyond Wantage, on r., Letcombe Castle, an ancient entrenchment; a little farther, Letcombe Bowers. 2m. past Shefford, on r., Ploughley and Inholmes. Past Newtown, on r., Eddington *Ho.* and Chilton Lodge. Hungerford, p. 88.

Hungerford to Marton (6¼—36¾); follow the valley of the *R.* Bourn, through Shalbourn, 33¾: good road.

Marton to North Tidworth (7¾—44½); from Waxcombe, 38, the road is rather hilly, going over Waxcombe Down, Collingbourn Down, and Collingbourn Heath, to Collingbourn Ducis (Shears Inn), 41½, and about ½m. after crossing the Ludgershall road (43m.) turn to l. for North Tidworth: pretty fair road, but rather rough in places. [Or at Marton, turn to r. through East Grafton, 38½, West Grafton, 39, where turn to l., and through Collingbourn Kingston, 42¾, Collingbourn Sutton, 43½, and Collingbourn Ducis, 43¾, joining the other road 1m. before North Tidworth, 47½; capital easy road, for the latter half running down the valley of the Winterbourn.]

(*North Tidworth:* Ram; Sun.)

1m. before N. Tidworth, on r., Sidbury Hill Castle, an ancient entrenchment. Tidworth Park on l.

North Tidworth to Salisbury (15—59½); keep down the Winterbourn valley through South Tidworth, 45½, Shipton, 46¾, by Park House, 48, Cholderton, Wilbury Park, Newton Stoney, Allington, East Boscombe, Idmiston, Porton, Winterbourn Gunner, Winterbourn Dantsey, Winterbourn Earls, and Hurcot, to St. Thomas's Bridge, 57½, where join the London road, as at p. 47; capital road and undulating, with a few stiff hills. [The above is not the main road, which keeps straight on 1m. before North Tidworth, and runs direct across the downs to *Salisbury*, 58¾, but is a very hilly and bad road for half the distance, being little better than a sheep track; the latter half is also hilly, ending with a long winding descent past Old Sarum, 57½, and the hills require careful riding down as they are often loose and stony. Returning, leave Salisbury by Castle street, and outside the town past the railway keep to r.]

Salisbury, p. 47.

MARLBOROUGH TO SALISBURY.

Marlborough to Burbage (6)—p. 272; reversed.

Burbage to East Everley (5½—11½)—p. 272; reversed.

East Everley to Salisbury (16—27½); very hilly and rough road, crossing part of Salisbury Plain for 6½m., when join the Hungerford road, and thence to Salisbury it improves as to surface, but is still very hilly, ending with a long winding descent past Old Sarum, 25½, and the hills require careful riding down, as they are often loose and stony. Returning, leave Salisbury by Castle street, and outside the town, past the railway, keep to r.

[Or from *Burbage*, keep to l. 1¼m. further, and through Collingbourn Kingston, 9, Collingbourn Sutton, 9¼, and Collingbourn Ducis, 10—(above) whence forward to *North Tidworth*, 13½—above, and thence to *Salisbury*, 15—28½—above.

Or from *East Everley* turn to *l.* on the hilly Ludgershall road for $2\frac{1}{2}$*m.* to junction of above roads, then turn to *r.* to *North Tidworth*, $15\frac{1}{2}$.]

MARLBOROUGH TO SALISBURY (by Amesbury).

Marlborough to Pewsey ($6\frac{1}{4}$); more or less uphill for $3\frac{1}{2}$*m.* out of Marlborough, then steep descent through Oare, $4\frac{3}{4}$, about 1*m.* further keep to *l.*; good flint road.

(*Pewsey:* Phœnix, *B.T.C.*)

Pewsey to Up Avon (5—$11\frac{1}{4}$); through Manningford Bruce, $8\frac{1}{4}$, over Wood Bridge, $9\frac{1}{4}$, and through Rushall, $10\frac{1}{4}$; good road, level or slightly downhill.

On *l.*, Rushall Park.

Up Avon to Amesbury (9—$20\frac{1}{4}$); there are two roads, one on either bank of the *R.* Avon: the better one is that on the left or E. side of the valley running through Chisenbury, Enford, Combe, Haxton, Figeldean, Milston, and Bulford; level nearly all the way, and a capital flint road. The road by the right bank, through Chisenbury, Enford, Fyfield, Nether Avon, and Durrington, is not so easy, there being several stiff though not long hills, ending with a steep descent into Amesbury.

On *l.*, Chisenbury Priory and Chisenbury Camp. Netheravon *Ho.* Amesbury, p. 69.

Amesbury to Salisbury (8—$28\frac{1}{4}$); through Amesbury turn to *l.* instead of crossing the river, and afterwards keep to *r.*, ascending a stiff hill, with long fall on the other side to Great Durnford, $23\frac{1}{4}$, and then undulating through Salterton, $24\frac{3}{4}$, Little Durnford, $25\frac{1}{2}$, and Stratford-under-Castle, $26\frac{3}{4}$: good surface; pretty ride. [Or through Amesbury follow the Stonehenge road for $\frac{1}{4}$*m.*, then turn to *l.* through Little Amesbury, 21, Wilsford, Upper Woodford, Middle Woodford, and Lower Woodford, about 2*m.* beyond which cross *R.* Avon to Stratford-under-Castle, two or three steep hills to negotiate, and the surface is not so good as the other route, being rather rough and loose in places.] Returning, leave Salisbury by Castle street, and outside the town keep to *l.* [Or out of Amesbury keep to *l.*, and up the hill on to Salisbury Plain, a long ascent, easy at first, then steep at the top with a sharp turn in it, after which is a sharp descent and corresponding ascent, both sometimes loose and stony; then joining the Hungerford and Marlborough road, there is a good run for 2 or 3*m.* across Amesbury Down, from which is a long but gradual descent, followed at a distance of 2*m.* by a steep ascent, and finally a long winding descent, which should be ridden down very carefully; some of these slopes are often loose and stony, and require careful riding.]

At Great Durnford, on *l.*, Ogbourn Camp, an ancient hill fortress.

OXFORD TO BANBURY.

Oxford to Sturdy's Castle ($8\frac{1}{4}$); in Oxford keep to *r.* of the Woodstock road, and through Summerstown, $1\frac{1}{2}$, Kidlington (end of), $4\frac{1}{2}$, and over Langford Wharf, $5\frac{1}{2}$ (cross Oxford Canal), is for the most part pretty level riding, the few slight undulations there are being chiefly on the rise: bad road, rather narrow, and generally rutty or stony: at $7\frac{1}{2}$m. cross the London road through Islip.

Sturdy's Castle to Hopcroft's Holt (3¼—11¾) is a similar kind of road, but almost level.

1*m.* before Hopcroft's Holt, on *l.*, Maiden Bower, the site of an ancient camp. At Sturdy's Castle, cross the line of the Roman Akeman Street; on *r.*, Tackley Park. Before Hopcroft's Holt, on *r.*, Rousham Park.

Hopcroft's Holt to Deddington (4¼—16); the road continues bad, lumpy and rutty, but fairly level, to the Fox and Crown, 14, then there is a long steep descent, followed by corresponding uphill, into Deddington, and the surface begins to improve.

The road between Oxford and Deddington is mostly made of a kind of limestone, inclined to be rough when dry, and giving a clayey surface when wet, and retaining water long.

At Fox and Crown, on *r.*, North Aston Park. At Deddington, on *r.*, remains of castle or entrenchment.

Deddington to Adderbury (2¾—18¾); there are a couple of steep descents with similar intervening hills to climb, and all of which require careful riding in *descending*: the surface is somewhat better, though still not good.

On *l.*, Adderbury *Ho.*

Adderbury to Banbury (3¼—22)—p. 131.

ST. ALBANS TO WARE.

St. Albans to Hatfield (5); from the Luton road turn to *r.* in St. Albans; descent from the town, and then a gradual rise past Horseshoe Gate, and rest level: splendid smooth road.

1*m.* before Hatfield, on *l.*, Harpsfield Hall. Hatfield, p. 184.

Hatfield to Hertford (7¼—12¼); by Hatfield Mills, 6, and Coln or Cole Green, 8¾, and through Hertingfordbury, 10¾, is rather hilly; good road, but sometimes sandy.

Past Hatfield, on *r.*, Hatfield Park; on *l.*, Bush Hall. At Coln Green, on *l.*, Panshanger Park; on *r.*, Wolmers. On *r.*, Hertingfordbury Park, and Bayford Bury Park. Hertford, p. 224.

Hertford to Ware (3—15¼) is fairly level but inclined to be sandy.

Beyond Hertford, on *r.*, Balls Park. 1*m.* before Ware, on *l.*, Ware Park. Ware, p. 222.

OXFORD TO CAMBRIDGE.

Oxford to Wheatley (5½)—p. 107; reversed.

Wheatley to Thame (7½—13); descent to and long rise from Wheatley Bridge, 6½, then ¾*m.* beyond it keep to *l.* (where the right hand road goes under a railway bridge), and it is an undulating road and fair going through Aldbury, 9, and North Weston, 11. [Or beyond Wheatley Bridge keep straight on to Three Pigeons, 9¼, then turn to *l.* at the cross roads, and to *Thame*, 13¼.]

Before Wheatley, on *r.*, Shotover *Ho.*; a little farther, on *l.*, Holton Park. 2*m.* beyond Wheatley Bridge, on *l.*, Waterperry *Ho.* and Waterstock *Ho.* (*Thame*: Spread Eagle, *B.T.C.*)

Thame to Aylesbury (9¼—22¼); good and almost level road through

Haddenham, 16¼, Dinton, 18½, Stone, 19½, and Hartwell, 20¾; there is a short steep ascent to make before entering Aylesbury: paved through the town.

At Haddenham, on *r.*, Tythrope *Ho.*; 1*m.* on *l.*, remains of Notley Abbey. On *l.*, Hartwell *Ho.* Aylesbury, p. 130.

Aylesbury to Dunstable (16—38¾); sharp but short descent just before leaving Aylesbury, then level and very good road through Aston Clinton, 26¾, and over the Wendover Canal, 28, from which there is a long and rather steep ascent to climb (good and perfectly safe to ride down the contrary direction); at the top (1 *m.* short of Tring) turn to *l.* and it is a hilly road through Bulborne, 31 (cross Grand Junction Canal), and Ivinghoe (end of), 33, and over Beacon Hill, 33¾, and *R.* Ouzell, 35½; in particular a long ascent over Beacon Hill and descent into Dunstable.

From near Tring the road follows the supposed line of the old Icknield Way.

Tring, p. 130.—Dunstable, p. 138.

Dunstable to Luton (5—43¾) is a good road, gently undulating all the way.

3*m.* out of Dunstable, at Leagrave Marsh, 1½*m.* on *l.*, Wadlud's Bank, an ancient entrenchment. Luton, p. 188.

Luton to Hitchin (8½—52¼); in Luton turn sharp to *l.* past the *ch.* and station; there is a long steep hill to climb to Round Green, 44¾, and then through Lilley, 47¾, and Offley, 49¼, is good but rather hilly.

Before Lilley, on *r.*, Pulleridge Bury Park. Offley Place on *r.* Hitchin, p. 185.

Hitchin to Baldock (4¾—57); at Hitchin turn sharp to *l.*, then to *r.*, and then to *l.* again, after which through Walsworth, 53¼, and Letchworth, 55, is a very good road with no difficult hills.

At Letchworth, 1*m.* on *l.*, Wilbury Hill, a Roman camp. Baldock, p. 194.

Baldock to Royston (8½—65½), past Odsey *Ho.*, 61½, is a capital road, pretty level at first, and with one or two hills towards the end, but nothing difficult.

At Odsey *Ho.*, 2*m.* on *l.*, Harborough Banks, an ancient entrenchment. Royston, p. 223.

Royston to Cambridge (13—78½)—p. 227; in Royston take *second* turn to *l.*

OXFORD TO CAMBRIDGE (by Leighton Buzzard).

Oxford to Aylesbury (22¾)—p. 295.

Aylesbury to Leighton Buzzard (10½—33¼); pretty level through Bierton, 24¾, to Rowsham, 26½, whence is a long stiff hill to mount, then there are a couple of rises before Wing, 30¼, and long descent to Chelsea, 32¾ (turn to *r.* and cross railway and canal); good surface.

(*Leighton Buzzard:* Bell Inn; Elephant and Castle; Swan; Unicorn, *B.T.C.*)

On *r.*, Wing Park. At Leighton Buzzard, the parish *ch.*, erected in the 13th century; also handsome cross of the 14th century, recently restored.

Leighton Buzzard to Hockliffe (3¾—37); undulating, but macadam surface, rather rough.

Hockliffe to Woburn (4¼—41¼)—p. 154; keep straight through Hockliffe.

Woburn to Ampthill (7½—48¼)—p. 188; alternative route.

Ampthill to Clophill, Sluts Green (3—51¼); through Moulden, 50¼, level road.

Clophill to Shefford (5—56¾).

About 2*m.* before Shefford, on *l.*, Chicksands Priory.

Shefford to Baldock (8½—65¼); through Clifton, 58¼, and Stotfold 62¾.

[Or from *Hockliffe* to *Dunstable*, 3¾—40¾, p. 138, reversed; thence to *Baldock*, 18¼—59, p. 296].

1*m.* beyond Clifton, on *l.*, Henlow Grange. Baldock, p. 194.

Baldock to Cambridge (21½—86¾)—p. 296.

OXFORD TO CAMBRIDGE (by Bedford).

Oxford to Bicester (13); follow the Banbury road for 4*m.*, then turn to *r.* through Gosford, 4½, over Gosford Bridge, 4¾ (*R.* Cherwell), at 6¾ *m.* cross the London road through Islip, and through Wendlebury, 10; undulating road: entering Bicester turn to *r.*

A little past the London road, on *l.*, Heathfield *Ho.* 1*m.* past Wendlebury, on *r.*, Alchester, the site of a Roman town or station; also Castle Hill; on *l.*, Chesterton Lodge. Bicester, p. 132.

Bicester to Finmere (7¼—20¼); entering Bicester turn to *r.*, in middle of the town to *l.*, and leaving the town keep to *r.*, making two sides of a triangle; then through Fringford, 17, and Newton Purcell, 18¾.

1*m.* past Bicester, a little on *l.*, Caversfield *Ho.*; 1*m.* farther, on *l.*, Fringford *Ho*

Finmere to Buckingham (3½—23¾)—p. 131, reversed.

Buckingham to Stoney Stratford (8—31¾); the road runs close to *R.* Ouse all the way through Deanshanger, 29¾, to Old Stratford, 31¼ (turn to *r.*), and is almost level: good surface in dry weather. [Or 4*m.* from Buckingham turn to *r.*, cross Grand Junction Canal and *R.* Ouse, and by the right bank through Thornton, 28½, Beachampton, 29½, and Calverton, 31¼, beyond which ½*m.* turn to *l.* to *Stoney Stratford*, 32½.]

At 4*m.* on *l.*, Wicken Park. Stoney Stratford, p. 138.

Stoney Stratford to Newport Pagnell (6—37¾); in the former turn to *l.*, [if through Beachampton turn to *r.*]; very rough road but level to Wolverton, 32¾, beyond which are rise and fall over Stanton Hill to Stanton Bridge, 35¾, otherwise fairly level: for the greater part of the distance the surface is indifferent. [Or entering Wolverton keep to *r.* and past Wolverton Station, a little farther rejoining the other road again.]

(*Newport Pagnell:* Swan, *B.T.C.*)

Newport Pagnell to Bedford (13½—51¼); beyond Newport turn to *r.*, and again beyond Sherrington Bridge, 38¾, and then through Chicheley, 40½, Astwood, 43½, and Stagsden, 46¼, and over Bromham Bridge, 48¼, (*R.* Ouse), is an easy undulating road: the surface soon improves considerably, and approaching Bedford it becomes good, and there is a nice run into the town.

[Or from *Newport Pagnell*,—above, to *Olney*, 5—42¾—p. 188; out of Olney keep to *r.*, and through Cold Brayfield, 45½, to Turvey, 46½, is level running near *R.* Ouse, but liable to be flooded in wet seasons; then a rise, followed by a long descent to Bromham Bridge, 50½: very bad road.]

[Or to *Ampthill*, 48¾,—p. 297; thence to *Bedford*, 8—56¾,—p. 188.]

On *r.*, Chincheley Hall; on *l.*, 1*m.*, Astwood Bury Park; on *l.*, Bromham Hall, Bedford, p. 185.

Bedford to Great Barford (6—57½); in Bedford turn to *r.*, cross *R.* Ouse, and in the suburb of St. John's, 51¾, turn to *l.* and by Cardington Cross, 53¼, and through Willington, 55¼, is nearly level: splendid smooth surface; turn to *l.* and cross *R.* Ouse at Barford Bridge, just before Great Barford. [Or at Bedford keep straight on through Goldington Green, 52¾, to Great Barford, 57.] The roads run along the Ouse valley.

Beyond Goldington Green, on *l.*, Hawbury Hall.

Great Barford to Eaton Socon (4¾—62); stiff ascent near Roxton, 59½, otherwise capital easy road, through Wiboston, 60¾.

On *r.*, Roxton Park.

Eaton Socon to St. Neots (1½—63½)—pp. 194 and 224.

St. Neots to Eltisley (5½—69); beyond St. Neots is a long very gradual ascent, after which it is pretty level through Weald or Weld, 66½; capital surface.

About 2*m.* beyond Weald, on *r.*, Croxton Park. Eltisley, p. 224.

Eltisley to Cambridge (11¾—80¾); the road is fairly level with excellent surface, across Eltisley Field or Common and Madingley Field, beyond which is a steep hill to descend: not a village the whole way, rather a monotonous ride.

[Or at Willington, 55¼, above, turn to *r.* through Moggerhanger, 57, over Girtford Bridge, 58½, through Sandy, 59¼, Potton, 63, and Cockayne Hatley, 65¼, to *Cambridge*, 79¼.]

3½*m.* before Cambridge, at Madingley Field, on *l.*, Madingley Park Cambridge, p. 227.

OXFORD TO PETERBOROUGH.

Oxford to Middleton Stoney (11¾); follow the Banbury road for 4*m.*, then turn to *r.*, through Gosford, 4½, over Gosford Bridge, 4¾ (*R.* Cherwell), at 6¼*m.* cross the London road through Islip, and 1¾*m.* further turn to *l.*, and through Weston on the Green, 8; undulating road, with very bad surface.

A little past the London road, on *l.*, Heathfield *Ho.*; on *l.*, Weston Manor *Ho.* At Middleton Stoney, on *l.*, Middleton Park and Castle

Middleton Stoney to Baynard's Green (3¾—15½); through Ardley, 14¼, is rather more hilly.

On *l.*, Ardley Castle. 1*m.* on *l.*, is the line of an ancient entrenchment, called Avesbank, Avesditch, or Wattlebank, extending from near Kirtlington to Souldern, 6 or 7*m.*

Baynard's Green to Barley Mow Inn (3—18½) is up and down hill, the last mile crossing Cottisford Heath.

1*m.* past Baynard's Green, on *r.*, Tusmore *Ho.*

Barley Mow Inn to Brackley (2½—21); level for the first half, then a couple of falls and rises alternating into Brackley.

Before Brackley, on *r.*, Evenley Hall. Brackley, p. 136.

Brackley to Towcester (11—32); through Syresham, 25, Whittlewood Forest, and Silverstone, 28½, is a hilly road, all up and down, with one or two stiff pulls. Returning, about 2m. from Towcester turn to r.

Beyond Brackley, on r., Turweston Ho. At Syresham, on r., Biddlesden Ho. Towcester, p. 138.

Towcester to Northampton (9—41); fair road past Easton Neston Park, through Hulcote, 33½, Blisworth, 36, Middleton or Milton Alsor, 37½: there are one or two stiff hills to climb, and a long one (Hunsbury Hill) to descend into Northampton. Returning, turn to r. past the canal out of Northampton.

Northampton, p. 154.

Northampton to Wellingborough (9¼—50¼); in Northampton turn to r. at the top of the hill; it is rather hilly but always a good hard road through Abington, 42¼, Weston-Favel, 43½, Great Billing, 44¾, Ecton, 46, and Wilby, 48¾; about halfway is Barton Hill to be walked up; descent from Wilby.

On r., Abington Abbey. On r., Great Billing Ho.; on l., Billing Grange and Overstone Park. On r., Ecton Park. Wellingborough, p. 189.

Wellingborough to Finedon (3¼—54); the road now gets worse. On l., Finedon Hall.

Finedon to Thrapston (7—61); fairly good undulating road, with a steep descent before Islip, 59¾. Returning, 4m. out of Thrapston keep to l.

At the junction of the roads, on r., Woodford Lodge; on l., Twywell Lodge, and Cranford Hall. Before Islip, 1m. on l., Islip Lodge and Drayton Ho. Thrapston, p. 193.

Thrapston to Oundle (8—69): in Thrapston turn to l., and through Thorp Waterville, 63½, and Barnwell St. Andrews, 67, the road runs near the R. Nen, and crosses it before Oundle.

Before Barnwell, on l., Lilford Hall. Beyond, on r., Barnwell Castle, and ruins of a castle erected 1132. Oundle, p. 193.

Oundle to Elton (5—74); cross R. Nen and through Warmington, 72. 1m. before Warmington, on l., across R. Nen, Cotterstock Hall. At Elton, on l., Elton Hall, and 2m. distant, ruins of Fotheringhay Castle.

Elton to Peterborough (8—82); turn to r. and through Chesterton, 76½, by Kate's Cabin Inn, 77 (cross the Great North road), through Alwalton, 77¼, Overton Waterville, 79, Overton Longville or Long Orton, 79½, and Woodstone, 81, whence cross R. Nen. Returning, after crossing R. Nen turn to r.

On l., Alwalton Castle; 1m. distant, close to Great North Road the site of the Roman station, Durobrivæ. At Long Orton, on l., across R. Nen, Thorpe Hall; on r., Orton Hall. Peterborough, p. 215.

NORTHAMPTON TO STAMFORD.

Northampton to Kettering (13¾); directly out of the town a steep hill has to be mounted, and the next 10m., passing Buttock's Booth, 3¼, are almost level, over a dreary lonely road to the only village on the stage, Broughton, 11, leaving which is a sharp hill to descend.

About 5m. out of Northampton, on r., Overstone Park. Kettering, p. 185.

Kettering to Great Weldon (9—22¾); through Weekley, 15¾, Geddington, 17¼, and Stanion, 20½.

Past Weekley, on *r.*, Boughton Park and *Ho.* On *l.*, Geddington *Ho.* Before Great Weldon, on *l.*, Weldon Grange.

Great Weldon to Duddington (8½—31¼); chiefly a gradual uphill to Bulwick, 26½, and then downhill by Fineshade, 29.

Beyond Weldon, on *r.*, Weldon Park; 1m. farther, on *l.*, Deno Park. Past Bulwick, on *l.*, Bulwick Hall; on *r.*, Blatherwick Hall; on *l.*, Laxton Hall; on *r.*, Fineshade Abbey.

Duddington to Stamford (5—36½); through Colly Weston, 32¼, and Easton, 34¼. Returning, after crossing *R.* Welland turn to *r*

[Or to *Elton*, 33,—p. 299; thence straight on to *Wansford*, 36¼, and on to *Stamford*, 5¾—42½, p. 195.]

Stamford, p. 195.

BANBURY TO DEVIZES.

Banbury to South Newington (5¾): from Banbury Cross take the London road, and when leaving the town turn to *r.*; long ascent past and over Crouch Hill, then two or three rather steep hills up and down through Bloxham, 3½, and a stiff descent into South Newington: average road.

About 2m. from Banbury, on *l.*, Wykham *Ho.*

Stoke Newington to Chipping Norton (7¼—13); stiff ascent out of the former, then pretty good riding over a gently undulating road past Pomfret Castle, 9, and by Over Norton Common, 11.

At Pomfret Castle, on *r.*, Swerford Park. At Over Norton Common, 1m. on *l.*, Heythrop Park. Chipping Norton, p. 118.

Chipping Norton to Burford (11—24); nearly through the former turn to *l.*; almost level for 5m., then long downhill to Shipton-under-Whichwood, 20 (where cross *R.* Evenlode), and thence over Shipton Downs and through Fullbrook, 23¼: not a good road. Returning, out of Burford turn to *r.*

About 3m. from Chipping Norton, a little on *r.*, Sarsden *Ho.* At 3¾m., on *r.*, a circular camp and several barrows farther on. On *r.*, Shipton Court; on *l.*, Whichwood Forest. Burford, p. 108.

[Or at the fork roads, 2m. out of *South Newington*, turn to *l.*, and undulating road through Great Tew, 9½, and Church Enstone, 12, with a long fall to *Charlbury*, 16, where turn sharp to *r.*, then to *l.*, cross *R.* Evenlode, and there is a long uphill, and after that rather hilly for about 6m., on to Shipton Downs, where join the other road, and to *Burford*, 25.]

On *l.*, Great Tew Park. Before Church Enstone, 1m. on *r.*, Heythrop Park. Past Charlbury, on *l.*, Cornbury Park; 1½m. past, on the hill, on *l.*, Ranger's Lodge.

Burford to Lechlade (9—33); very steep ascent out of Burford (that requires care in riding *down*), then a gradual downhill to Broughton Poggs, 29½, crossing over the Cotswold Hills, here consisting of nothing but bare downs, and the rest level and good.

Lechlade, p. 103.

Lechlade to Highworth (5½—38½) through Inglesham, 34½.

Highworth, p. 102.

Highworth to Swindon (6½—45) through Stratton St. Margaret's 43. Returning, ¼m. out of Swindon turn to *r.*

2*m.* out of Highworth, on *r.*, Stanton *Ho.* Swindon, p. 101.

Swindon to Wroughton (2½—47½); good road, almost level: entrance of Wroughton keep to *r.*

Wroughton to Beckhampton Inn (8½—56); good smooth road through Broad Hinton, Winterbourne Basset, Barwick Basset, Winterbourne Monkton, and Avebury, 55, where keep to *r.*: undulating road.

Avebury and Beckhampton Inn, p. 89.

Beckhampton Inn to Devizes (7½—63½)—p. 95.

BANBURY TO DEVIZES (by Faringdon).

Banbury to Charlbury (16)—p. 300.

Charlbury to Witney (7½—23½); pretty level to Fawler Mill, 17¾ (cross *R.* Evenlode), whence it is uphill through Finstock, 18½, on to Finstock Heath, then after a little level, chiefly downhill again through Willy or White Oak Green, and Hailey, 21¾.

Witney, p. 108.

Witney to Bampton (5¼—28¾); nearly through Witney turn to *r.* on the Burford road, and at the three fork roads, just outside the town, take the middle one through Curbridge, 25½, and across Curbridge Common. Returning, 1¼*m.* out of Bampton turn to *r.*

[Or to *Burford*, 24 (p. 300); here turn to *l.*, and follow the Witney road for 1¾*m.*, then turn to *r.*, and through Norton Brize, 28, to *Bampton*, 30½.]

At Bampton are remains of a castle, said to have been built by King John.

Bampton to Clanfield (2¼—31); in Bampton turn to *r.*

[Or to *Burford*, 24 (p. 300); here through the town turn first to *l.* then to *r.*, and through Blackbourton, 29½, to *Clanfield*, 30½.]

Clanfield to Faringdon (4½—35½); through Radcot, 32¾, and, over Radcot Bridge, 33¼; entrance of Faringdon turn to *r.*

Faringdon to Swindon (12½—48); through Faringdon keep to *l.* and by White's Cross, 38½, through Shrivenham, 41, and over Hackron Bridge, 43. Returning, keep to *r.* twice, at ½*m.* and 1½*m.* out of Swindon.

At Shrivenham, on *l.*, Beckett Park and *Ho.*

Swindon to Devizes (18½—66½)—above.

WITNEY TO BANBURY.

Witney to Woodstock (8¾); undulating road by Ensham Demesnes 3½, through Long Handborough, 4½, over Handborough Bridge, 6 (*R.* Evenlode), and through Bladon, 6¾, a mile further joining the Oxford road, on which turn to *l.*

At 3*m.* on *r.*, Ensham Hall and Park; just before it, in Woodleys Copse, is a Roman camp. From ½*m.* before Handborough, run close to Blenheim Park, on *l.* At Bladon, on *r.*, on the hill, is a circular camp called Round Castle. At Ensham Demesnes, 1½*m.* on *l.*, is the site of a Roman villa. Woodstock, p. 118.

Woodstock to Sturdy's Castle (2—10¾); in Woodstock turn to *r.*

Sturdy's Castle to Banbury (13¾—24½)—p. 295.

MARLBOROUGH TO CIRENCESTER.

Marlborough to Wootton Bassett (12); in Marlborough turn to *r.* and across Marlborough Common, and Marlborough Downs is level or uphill for about 5*m.*, then long downhill to Broad Hinton, 7, followed by another descent at Broad Town, 8.

At 3*m.*, on *l.*, Rockley *Ho.* Wootton Bassett, p. 101.

Wootton Bassett to Cirencester (12½—24½) through Ashton Keynes, 20.

CRICKLADE TO MELKSHAM.

Cricklade to Wootton Bassett (7½); over Littleworth Bridge, 1½, through Purton Stoke, 2¼, Purton Street, 4¼, and Hooke Street, 6¼.

At Purton Street, on *l.*, Purton *Ho.* and Lydiard *Ho.* 1*m.* past Purton Street, on *r.*, Ringsbury Camp. At Hooke Street, on *l.*, Lydiard Park.

Wootton Bassett to Lyneham (4¼—11¾)—p. 101.

Lyneham to Calne (6¼—18); turn to *l.* and through Great Acre, 13¼, and Hillmarton, 14½.

Before Calne, 1*m.* on *l.*, Bassett *Ho.* Calne, p. 89.

Calne to Melksham (7¾—25¾); across Chitway Heath, 21½, and through Westbrook Green, 22¼.

Beyond Calne, on *r.*, Bowood Park. At Chitway Heath, on *r.*, Spy Park.
(*Melksham:* Kings's Arms, *B.T.C.*)

BURFORD TO CIRENCESTER.

Burford to Bibury (9¾) about 1*m.* out of Burford keep to *l.*, and through Aldsworth, 6¼.

On *l.*, Bibury *Ho.*

Bibury to Cirencester (7¼—17) through Barnsley, 13. Returning, ½*m.* out of Cirencester keep to *r.*

On *r.*, Barnsley Park. Cirencester, p. 104.

BANBURY TO DAVENTRY.

Banbury to Byfield (9¾); in Banbury go down the High street, cross canal and *R.* Cherwell, about ½*m.* farther turn to *l.*, and by Huscote, 2, through Williamscote, 4, Wardington, 5, and Chipping Warden, 6½; good road with two long steep hills.

Beyond Huscote, a little on *r.*, Chalcomb Priory. At Chipping Warden, on *l.*, Arbury, or Arberry Banks, the site of a Roman camp; on *r.*, Edgecott Hall; also Dunsmore and Wallow Bank, Roman encampments.

Byfield to Daventry (7¼—17); through Charwelton, 11¾, and Badby, 14½, is an excellent but hilly road, some of the hills stiff ones.

At Badby, on *r.*, Fawsley Park; on *l.*, Catesby Park and *Ho.*

BUCKINGHAM TO GLOUCESTER.

Buckingham to Aynho-on-the-Hill (11¼)—p. 131.

Aynho-on-the-Hill to Deddington (3—14¼); keeping to *l.*, it is 1¼*m.* downhill to *R.* Cherwell bridge, then short rise through Clifton, 13.

Entrance of Deddington, on *l.*, remains of castle or entrenchment.

Deddington to Chipping Norton (11—25¼); fairly level for a couple of miles through Hempton, 16, then a long descent with ascent again to Iron Down, 17¾, and the rest is pretty good riding over a gently undulating road, joining the Banbury road at 19½*m.*, and passing Pomfret Castle, 21¾, and Over Norton Common, 23¼.

Beyond Hempton, nearly 1*m.* on *l.*, a castle or ancient hill fort. Chipping Norton, p. 118.

Chipping Norton to Stow-on-the-Wold (8—33¼); through Salford, 27¼, to Salford Hill (or Cross Hands), 28¼, where turn to *l.*, across Chastleton Heath, and through Oddington, 31¼; steep ascent into Stow.

[Or keep straight through Chipping Norton, and through Churchill, 28¾, and Kingham, 30¼, to Stow-on-the-Wold, 34¼.]

Past Salford, on *l.*, Cornwell. On Chastleton Heath, on *r.*, an old camp, and Chastleton Hill *Ho.*; a little farther, on *r.*, Aldestrop Park, and on *l.*, Daylesford Park. On *l.*, Oddington *Ho.* Stow-on-the-Wold, p. 123.

Stow-on-the-Wold to Winchcombe (13—46¼); steep descent out of Stow, and through Lower Swell, 34¼, and Lower Guiting, 40, and Sudeley, 45¾. Winchcombe is paved.

Before Guiting, on *r.*, Guiting Park. At Sudeley, ruins of the castle.

Winchcombe to Cheltenham (6¾—53); descent out of Winchcombe, and after a little level several long inclines occur for over 2*m.*, all rideable except the last, which is steep and very rough, otherwise fairly good surface; twice at fork roads keep to *r.*; then after a run down and up, the road winds round the shoulder of Cleeve Cloud Hill, and on the other side a long descent follows leading down from the Cotswold Hills, and is dangerous to ride down without a good brake, as it is much steeper, with somewhat rough surface, and one cannot see to the bottom; after this descent, for the last 2*m.*, the road is level through Prestbury, 52¾, but rough, entering Cheltenham by Winchcombe Street.

Cheltenham, p. 109.

Cheltenham to Gloucester (9—62)—p. 109.

[Or from *Stow-on-the-Wold*, steep descent out of the town, and through Lower Swell, 34¼, where keep to *l.*, and by Naunton Inn, 39¼, to *Andoverford*, 44½, oolite road, slippery in wet weather, some steep hills, but fine run on the whole; thence to *Cheltenham*, 5¼—49¾, pp. 108-9.

Or from *Andoverford* to Kilkenny, 45¾, whence by *Birdlip*, 52½, to *Gloucester*, 59¾, p. 110.]

BANBURY TO CHIPPING CAMPDEN.

Banbury to Shipston-on-Stour (14); turn to *l.* at Banbury Cross, and through Broughton, 2¾, Lower Tadmarton, 4, Tadmarton, 4¾, Swalcliffe, 5¾, Lower Brailes, 10¼, and Over Brailes, 11, is up and down hill work nearly the whole way, and for the most part a bad road, on which pace and comfort are out of the question.

At Broughton, on *r.*, ruins of castle. Beyond Tadmarton, on *r.*, Madmarton Camp. 1½*m.* on *l.*, Tadmarton Camp and another. At Over Brailes, on *r.*, Castle Hill. Shipston-on-Stour, p. 125.

Shipston-on-Stour to Chipping Campden (7—21); through Portobello, 15½, Charingworth, 17¼, and Ebrington, 18½.

CHIPPENHAM TO CIRENCESTER.

Chippenham to Malmesbury (9½); by The Plough, 2½, Lower Stanton St. Quintin, 5¼, and through Corston, 7¼. Returning, 1½ m. out of Corston keep to *l.*

Out of Chippenham, on *l.*, Hardenhuish Park; past The Plough, on *l.*, Kingston St. Michael Priory; a little farther, 1m. on *r.*, Draycott Park. Beyond Corston, on *r.*, Cole Park. Malmesbury, p. 101.

Malmesbury to Cirencester (11—20½); in Malmesbury turn to *r.*, and a little farther to *l.*, skirting Charlton Park on *r.* and through Crudwell, 13¼, and Quelfurlong, 14½, about 2m. farther joining the Fosse Way and over Thames River Head Bridge, 17½.

Cirencester, p. 104.

BATH TO LINCOLN.

Bath to Cross Hands Inn, Old Sodbury (11); out of Bath take the London road for a little over a mile, then turn sharp to *l.*, and up a capitally engineered ascent for 3 m., not very steep and all can be ridden up, along the side of a valley, through Swainswick, 3; the rest by Toghill, 5, Dyrham Park (on *l.*), 6¾, and Toll Down Farm, 8, is an undulating road with one or two stiff hills to mount; oolite surface, very greasy when wet, and requires careful riding; pretty good for first 4 or 5 m., then deteriorates.

Leaving the London road, on *r.*, Bailbrook Ho. Before Toghill, on *l.*, Aston Lodge and Hamshill Ho. Before Cross Hands, on *l.*, skirt Dodington Park for 2m.

Cross Hands Inn to Dunkirk Tp. (3½—14½); through Petty France, 14, the road continues undulating, with the same kind of surface; pretty scenery.

On *l.*, pass two ancient encampments, and before Petty France, on *l.*, Horton Castle.

Dunkirk Tp. to Tetbury (7½—22)—p. 103, reversed; turn to *r.*, and shortly after to *l.*

Beyond Dunkirk, on *r.*, Badmanton Park. Tetbury, p. 102.

Tetbury to Cirencester (10¼—32¼); by Akeman's Inn, 27½, and over Thames River Head Bridge, 29½, is rather hilly, and there are one or two short stiff ascents: oolite surface, tolerable in dry weather when the ruts are worn down, but when wet it is very greasy and rutty, and requires careful steering.

[Said to be a better road through Chippenham, Malmesbury and Tetbury—above and p. 102].

At Akeman's Inn, join the line of the Roman Fosse Way or Akeman Street, which runs almost direct from within a few miles of Bath. At Thames Head Bridge, a short distance on *l.*, is the source of *R.* Thames; a little farther, on *l.*, remains of Trewsbury Castle. Cirencester, p. 104.

Cirencester to Northleach, House of Correction (10¼—42½); about 1 m. out of Cirencester keep to *l.*, and it is an undulating road, by Foss Cross, 38½, and Foss Bridge, 39½, to which is a stiff hill to descend, dangerous to ride down: oolite surface.

Beyond Foss Bridge, on *l.*, Stowell Park. The town of Northleach lies on the right side of the road, which only passes through one end of it, p. 108.

Northleach to Stow-on-the-Wold (8¾—51¼); by Lower Slaughter *Tp.*, 48½, is an undulating road, with a steep hill to ascend into Stow. Returning, 1*m.* out of Stow keep to *r.*

At Lower Slaughter *Tp.*, 1½*m.* on *r.*, Wick Hill *Ho.* Before Stow, on *r.*, Maugersbury *Ho.* Stow, p. 123.

Stow-on-the-Wold to Moreton-in-the-Marsh (4—55¼); long steep descent about a mile out of Stow, otherwise nearly level.

Moreton-in-the-Marsh to Halford (8¼—63½); by Stretton-on-the Foss, 58¼, and Portobello, 59¾, is hilly, the gradients being very sharp though short; the surface, however, though rather rough, is gravel. There is a tramway, which crosses the road, on two or three of the hills, and should be looked out for, and at ¾*m.* before Halford (where cross the Shipston-on-Stour to Stratford-on-Avon road) the turnings are puzzling; at Halford cross *R.* Stour.

The road now leaves the Roman Fosse Way for a time, after having followed it from Akeman's Inn.

At Moreton, on *l.*, Batsford Park.

Halford to Wellesbourne Hastings (8¾—72¼); through Upper Eatington, 65¾ (where cross Banbury to Stratford road), is rather hilly, but nothing difficult, the gradients not being so severe as the last stage.

Beyond Halford, on *l.*, Lower Eatington Hall. 3*m.* past Upper Eatington, on *r.*, Walton Hall.

Wellesbourne Hastings to Warwick (6¾—79)—p. 141.

Entering Warwick, on *r.*, Warwick Park and Castle.

Warwick to Kenilworth (5¼—84¼)—p. 142; keep straight on through Warwick when coming from Wellesbourne Hastings.

Kenilworth to Coventry (5—89¼); in Kenilworth keep to *r.*, and it is a rather hilly road, there being two good ascents and falls; splendid smooth surface, and along a fine avenue of trees nearly the whole distance. This is a noted ride both for its pretty scenery and good road.

About 2*m.* before Coventry, on *r.*, Stivichall Hall. Coventry, p. 139.

Coventry to Nuneaton (8½—97¾)—p. 156, but keep straight on at the cross streets in Coventry when coming from Kenilworth.

Nuneaton to Hinckley (5¼—103); fairly good road with no hills of any consequence: nearly 3*m.* out of Nuneaton turn to *r.* along Watling Street, and a little farther to *l.* Hinckley is paved.

[Or from *Coventry*, turning to *r.* at the cross roads, through Stoke, Sow, Anstey, Shilton, Wolvey, not very good road; about the same distance.

Or from *Coventry*, keeping straight on through Foleshill, Bell Green, Hawksbury Lane, and Bulkington to Wolvey, good and smooth.]

On *l.*, Anstey Hall; on *l.*, Hawksbury Hall. Hinckley, p. 155.

Hinckley to Leicester (13—116); very sharp ascent out of Hinckley to walk up, then pretty level to Earl Shilton, 107, beyond which is a short steep hill that it is best to walk down, and the rest is nearly level; the surface is macadam, and rather shaky for quick travelling, although generally in good order, and the latter half is sometimes reported as very good. Most of Leicester is cobble paved, with tramways.

[At Leicester the Fosse Way is again joined for a few miles; from Halford it runs straight across the county of Warwick, by Three Gates, Harwood's *Ho.*, Princethorpe, Stretton-on-Dunsmore, Frog Hall, Bretford, Brinklow, Cloudeley Bush, to Bennones or High Cross on Watling Street, at the borders of Warwick and Leicester, and thence through Narborough to Leicester; in all about 40*m.*; in most part it is but a lane in dimensions, and is hilly in places, but generally good in summer weather.]

Beyond Earl Shilton, on *l.*, Tooley Hall; on *r.*, Normanton. 3*m.* before Leicester, 1*m.* on *l.*, ruins of castle at Kirby Muxloe; a little farther, Frith Hall, and on *r.*, Braunstone Hall. Leicester, p. 166.

Leicester to Loughborough (11—127)—p. 166.

Loughborough to Trent Bridge (14—141)—p. 189; see also alternative routes to *Nottingham*, which is 1*m.* beyond Trent Bridge.

Trent Bridge to Saxondale (8—149); instead of crossing the bridge turn to *r.*; the road is undulating by Holme Lane, 143¾, and Fox and Crown, 144½, to Radcliff or Ratcliffe, 146½, then a mile and a half level, and rest downhill; surface rather rough at first, but soon gets better.

[At Saxondale again join the Old Fosse Way, which crosses the Wolds from 3 or 4*m.* beyond Leicester by Six Hills, in an almost direct line, as appears in most maps, but the greater part is disused—a mere green lane with cart ruts, and quite impracticable for bicycles.]

Beyond Trent Bridge, on *l.*, across R. Trent, Colwick Hall. At Holme Lane, on *l.*, Holme Pierrepoint; on *r.*, Cotgrave Place. On *r.*, Radcliff Lodge; on *l.*, Lamcote *Ho.*

Saxondale to Newark (11½—160½); turning to *l.*, there is a sharp descent underneath a railway bridge, then pretty level to Red Lodge, 153, and after that there are several small easy hills, with a long ascent by the side of Flintham Park, 154, to East Stoke, 156¾; thence it is level, running near the *R.* Trent for some distance, and through Farndon, 158½; good surface: entering Newark it is advisable to take the fork to the *r.*, after passing over the tramway rails to some plaster pits, as the other is a narrow and badly paved street.

The road passes through a well-wooded country, and is lined with trees on either side for miles. About 2*m.* past Saxondale, the road crosses the site of a Roman station; on *r.*, Castle Hill. On *r.*, Flintham Hall. 1½*m.* before East Stoke, on *l.*, Syerston Hall; a little farther, Stoke Hall; on *r.*, Elston Hall. Newark, p. 196.

[Or from *Trent Bridge* go forward to *Nottingham*, 142; thence very long hill (Carlton Hill) to climb, followed by descent to Carlton, 144¾, and undulating but not so good a road, through Burton Joyce, 147, Bulcote, 147¾, Gonalston, 150, Thurgarton, 151½, and Morton, to *Newark*, 160½.

Or at Thurgarton, keep straight on through Halloughton, 153¼, *Southwell*, 154¾, Upton, 157, Averham, 159¼, and Kelham, 160¼, where turn to *r.*, to Newark, 162.]

Beyond Carlton, on *l.*, Gedling *Ho.* At Thurgarton, on *l.*, the Priory. Before Southwell, on *r.*, Southwell Park, South Hill *Ho.*, Durdham Castle. At Southwell, the Minster, and ruins of the Palace. On *l.*, Norwood Hall and Park.

Newark to Lincoln (16—176½)—p. 217.

BRISTOL TO DERBY.

Bristol to Alveston (9¼); through Horfield, 2¼, Filton, 3¼, Patchway Green, 6, and Almondsbury, 7, and past the "Royal Oak," 8½; after leaving Bristol it is chiefly uphill for 2*m*., then undulating, but none of the hills difficult; good surface, rather greasy when wet.

Beyond Bristol, on *r*., Ashley Court. At Horfield, on *l*., Henley *Ho.*; on *r*., 1m., Stoke *Ho.* At Filton, on *l*., Pen Park and *Ho.* At Almondsbury, on *l*., Knowle Park. At Patchway Green, on *l*., Over Court.

Alveston to Berkeley Heath, Bell (9¾—19); by Ship Inn, 10¼ (keep to *r*.), and through Falfield, 14¾, Stone, 16, and Newport, 17¾, is rather more hilly, though generally with an excellent surface. [Or at Ship Inn on *l*. through *Thornbury*, 11½, joining the other road 2¼*m*. further on, to Falfield, 15½. Or at Stone turn to *l*. to *Berkeley*, 19, thence to *Berkeley Heath*, 20½. Or from *Thornbury* through Rockhampton to *Berkeley*, 19. Returning, out of Berkeley keep to *r*.]

At Falfield, on *r*., Torworth Court. Berkeley, p. 104.

Berkeley Heath to Hardwick (10—29); gently undulating road by Berkeley-road railway station, 20½, Cambridge Inn, 22¾, Church End *Tp*., 24½, and through Whitminster, 26, and Moreton Valence, 27; very good surface, but apt to be greasy and heavy when wet.

1½*m*. before Cambridge Inn, on *l*., Gossington Hall. Before Hardwick, on *l*., Hardwick Court. Pretty scenery.

Hardwick to Gloucester (4½—33½); through Quedgley, 30½, is level but an indifferent road.

On *l*., Field Court and Quedgley *Ho.* Gloucester, p. 105. Hempstead Court.

Gloucester to Tewkesbury (10¼—43¾); through Longford, 35, Twigworth, 36½, and Norton, 38, and by Swan Inn, 40¼, is a fairly good road, with a few easy hills; in wet weather it is apt to be greasy and rather rough: descent into Tewkesbury.

At Twigworth, on *l*., Walsworth Hall; on *r*., Hatherley Court. Tewkesbury, p. 117. Pretty country.

Tewkesbury to Worcester (16¼—60); in Tewkesbury keep to *l* twice, then cross *R*. Severn, whence a long but gradual incline up and another down again to Stratford Bridge, 48¾; after that there are two or three short easy gradients through Severn Stoke, 52¼, to Clifton, 54, and the rest fairly level through Kempsey, 55¾; splendid road on the whole, but heavy and muddy in wet weather.

The road runs near the *R*. Severn all the way. Pretty country. Past Severn Bridge, on *r*., The Mythe and Twining *Ho.* At Severn Stoke, on *r*., Croome Park. Worcester, p. 119.

[Or from *Gloucester* turn to *l*. at the *P.O.*, down a slight descent, then cross canal, and a mile out of the town, between the railway and the *R*. Severn, turn to *r*. from the Highnam road, then cross *R*. Severn 1*m*. farther on, and through Maisemore, 36 (4*m*. beyond keeping to *r*.), and Longdon, 47, to *Upton-on-Severn*, 50, is a rather hilly but good road; Bristol stone. Thence, keeping to *l*., through Hanley Castle, 51 (half a mile beyond keep to *r*.), Rhydd Green, 54¼, Powick, 58¾, and St. John's, 60¾, to *Worcester*, 61¼, is a capital road; cross *R*. Severn just before Worcester. Returning, at St. John's keep to *l*., and at Powick, and past Upton.

Or at *Upton* cross *R*. Severn to the first road, 1¾*m*. before Severn Stoke, 53.]

On *r*., Maisemore Lodge and Court. Before Longdon, on *r*., Chambers Court and Pull Court. Before Upton, 1*m*., Ham Court on *r*. At Hanley, the castle on *l.* At Rhydd Green, on *r.*, The Rhydd, Severn End, and Drake's Place on *l.*, Dripshill and White *Ho.*; 1m. farther, on *l.*, Madresfield Court. On *l.*, Powick Court. At St. John's, on *l.*, Wick *Ho.* and Boughton *Ho.*

Worcester to Droitwich (6¾—66¾); through Barbourn *Tg.*, 61, keep to *r.*, and about a mile farther there is a rather stiff ascent nearly to Fernhill, 63, otherwise fairly level or slightly undulating road; pretty good surface.

On *l.*, Barbourn *Ho.*; 1m. farther, on *r.*, Perdiswell Park. At Fernhill, on *r.*, Hinlip Hall.

Droitwich to Bromsgrove (5½—72); through Wichbold, 68¾, Upton Warren, 69¾, and Bowling Green, 70¾, is a fairly level road, except for a couple of hills: good surface but heavy in wet weather. Returning, at Bowling Green keep to *r.*

Past Droitwich, on *l.*, West Ford. At Bowling Green, on *l.*, Park Hall, Bowling Green *Ho.*, and Grafton Hall. Bromsgrove, p. 125.

Bromsgrove to Birmingham (13—85); soon after leaving Bromsgrove (1m. out of which keep to *r.*), the road goes over the Lickey Hills, which necessitate an uphill ride for 3m. to the Rose and Crown, 76; from the top it is all downhill or level through Northfield (The Ball), 79¼, by Selby Oak, 81¼, and over Bourn Bridge, 82; excellent smooth surface, except the last 2m. or so.

At Rose and Crown, 1m. on *r.*, Cofton Hall. On *r.*, Northfield *Ho.* and Pigeon *Ho.* On *r.*, Selly Hall. Past Bourn Bridge, on *r.*, Moseley Hall. Birmingham, p. 110. On *l.*, Edgbaston Hall.

Birmingham to Sutton Coldfield, *M. P.* (7¼—92¼); indifferent macadam to Aston, 86½, a suburb of Birmingham; then (keeping to *r.*) the road improves a little, but still not good, to Erdington, 88½, and after one or two little hills to Wild Green, 91, and Maney, 91½, there is an ascent to climb into Sutton Coldfield.

At Erdington, 1m. on *r.*, Pipe Hayes; on *l.*, Sutton Hall and Four Oak Hall.

Sutton Coldfield to Lichfield, Town Hall (8¾—101); through Hill, 94, Wood End *Tp.*, 96¼, and Shenstone, 97½, is an excellent road, slightly downhill or level.

Beyond Sutton, on *r*, Moor Hall. Beyond Hill, on *l.*, Little Aston Hall. On *r.*, Shenstone Park; on *l.*, Fotherley Hall. Lichfield, p. 115.

Lichfield to Burton-upon-Trent, *M. P.* (12¼—113¼); in Lichfield turn to *r.* at the cross streets, and out of the town is a short rise, and then a fall; the road now runs along the Trent valley, through Streethay, 103, Alrewas (end of), 106, by Wichnor Bridge Inn, 107¼, and through Branston, 111, and is nearly a dead level: loose and sandy in one or two places, otherwise a very good road.

On *l.*, Wichnor Lodge and Park. At Branston, on *r.*, across R. Trent, Drakelowe Hall. Burton, p. 156.

Burton-upon-Trent to Derby, All Saints' *Ch.* (11¾—125); in Burton turn to *l.*, and past the railway keep to *r.* and over Monk's Bridge, 116½, and through Little Over, 122¼: it consists mostly of long straight stretches of level road and gentle ascents and descents; for the last 2m. it is rather hilly, but nothing difficult except steep descent into Derby.

Beyond Burton, on *r.*, Wetmoor Hall. At Monk's Bridge, on *l.*, Dove Cliff *Ho.*; 2m. farther, on *r.*, Foremark; on *l.*, Egginton Hall. Derby, p. 166.

SOUTHAM TO LEICESTER.

Southam to Dunchurch (8); taking the Coventry road, ¾m. out of Southam turn to r., and it is undulating for the first 6m., by Stockton, 2, and Hardwick, 5½, then after crossing R. Leam, there is a long steep ascent to Dunchurch.

Dunchurch, p. 139.

Dunchurch to Rugby (2½—10½)—p. 182; keep straight through Dunchurch.

Rugby to Lutterworth (7—17½); cross R. Avon 1m. out of Rugby and turn to r., and again sharp to r. 1m. further on after crossing canal, and through Brownsover, 13, past Coton Ho. (on r.) 14½, half-a-mile further cross Watling Street, and through Cottesbach, 15: rather hilly, and very heavy road. Pretty country.

Lutterworth, p. 155.

Lutterworth to Leicester (13—30½); hilly through Ashby Magna, 21½, by Dog and Gun, 23¼, to Blaby, 25½, then almost level through Ayleston, 27½: good road; cobble paving through Leicester, and tramway.

Leicester, p. 106.

BATH TO LINCOLN (by Cheltenham).

Bath to Dunkirk Tp. (14½)—p. 304.

Dunkirk Tp. to Nailsworth (9¼—23¾); by Boxwell Tp., 18½, Calcott Farm, 19½, Tiltup's Inn, 22, and Barton End, 22½, the road is pretty level to the last named place, when it leaves the downs, and there is a long steep hill to walk down: oolite surface and rather bumpy. Pretty scenery. Returning, keep to l. out of Nailsworth.

On l., Boxwell Court and Lasborough Park. At Calcott Farm, on l., Kingscote Park. On l., Barton End Ho. Nailsworth, p. 104.

Nailsworth to Stroud (4¼—28); through Inchbrook, 24½, Woodchester, 26, and Rodborough, 27¼: very rough oolite road. Pretty country. Returning, at Rodborough keep to r.

On l., Woodchester Park; on r., Hill Ho. Park. At Inchbrook, on l., Parkhill Ho. At Rodborough, on l., the Fort and Stanley Park. Stroud, p. 104.

Stroud to Birdlip (8—36); through Painswick Slade, 29¾, and Ballcross, 31. Returning, keep to l. at 1m., and to r. at 2m., out of Birdlip.

[Or from *Nailsworth* on r. to *Minchin Hampton*, 2—25¾, thence through Bisley, joining the above road on l. 2m. before *Birdlip*, 36½.

Or from *Stroud*, turn to l., then to r. to Salmon's Mill, 28½, and ¼m. further on r. to *Painswick*, 31¼, where again keep to r., and also 3m. beyond, joining the principal road on r. 1m. before *Birdlip*, 37¾; long ascent out of Painswick.]

Beyond Stroud, on l., Stratford Ho.; 2m. farther, on r., Browns Hill Ho. On l., Painswick Ho. On Spenebed Hill, near Painswick, is an ancient double entrenchment, called Kimsbury Castle, King's Barrow, and Castle Godwin. Before Birdlip, on l., Witcomb Park, near which have been discovered remains of a Roman villa. 3m. past Painswick, on l., Prinknash Park. Birdlip, p. 105. Minchin Hampton, p. 104.

Birdlip to Cheltenham (5¼—41¼); pretty level for 1m. past Balloon

Inn, 37¼ (where take left hand road), then a long, winding, and dangerous descent to Leckhampton, 39¼, and the rest level.

[Or from *Painswick*, long uphill out of the town to where the Gloucester road branches off on *l.*, then by right fork some undulating road on the top of the hill, and keeping to *l.*, there is a long but not steep descent, followed after a little level by a shorter but steeper descent, after which it is level by Cross Hands, 36½, and through Shurdington, 38½, to *Cheltenham*, 41½.]

On *l.*, Leckhampton Court. Before Cheltenham, between the two roads, Charlton Park. Splendid views of Gloucester and the Severn valley. Cheltenham, p. 109.

Cheltenham to Winchcombe (6¾—48)—p. 303, reversed; Winchcombe is paved.

Winchcombe to Broadway (9¼—57¼); descent out of Winchcombe, then the road is level but rough: turn to *r.* just before Broadway.

About half-way on *l.*, Wormington Grange.

Broadway to Mickleton (6—63¼); in Broadway turn to *l.*, and through Willersey, 59 (entering which turn to *l.*, and when through it turn to *r.*), Weston-Subedge, 60¼, and Aston-Subedge, 61¼, is a good road, with one slight hill: rather difficult road to follow on account of the many turns. Returning, out of Mickleton keep to *r.*

Mickleton to Stratford-upon-Avon (9¼—72½); the road is pretty level, but with rough and rutty surface to within 2*m.* of Stratford, when there is a run down to Bridge Town, 72, whence cross *R.* Avon into Stratford. Returning, after crossing *R.* Avon take right hand road, and on crossing the railway bridge again turn to *r.* up a slight rise.

Stratford-upon-Avon, p. 125.

Stratford-upon-Avon to Warwick (8¼—80¾); after crossing *R.* Avon turn to *r.*, and the road is level for 2 or 3*m.*, then the long but gradual ascent of Black Hill, 75½, has to be mounted, shortly followed by the rather steep descent of Sherbourn Hill, which should be ridden carefully, to Morville, 78, and the rest is level through Longbridge, 79, except a sharp rise into Warwick: Black Hill rather rough, otherwise splendid smooth road. Returning, keep to *r.* at Longbridge.

1*m.* out of Stratford, on *l.* Welcombe Lodge and Clopton *Ho.* At Black Hill, 1*m.* on *l.*, Smiterfield Hall. On *r.*, Morville *Ho.* Warwick, p. 142.

Warwick to Lincoln (97½—178¼)—pp. 305-6.

BATH TO BIRMINGHAM.

Bath to Cheltenham (41¼)—p. 309.

Cheltenham to Oxenton (5¾—47); uphill for one or two miles out of Cheltenham then undulating through Bishops Cleeve, 44¼; rather rough road.

Oxenton to Sedgeborrow (7—54); keep to *r.* beyond Oxenton, and by Beckford, 50½, rather hilly and bad road.

[Or from *Winchcombe*, 48,—above; here turn to *l.* and then directly after to *r.*, and through Littleworth, 49½, to *Sedgeborrow*, 54½.]

Sedgeborrow to Evesham (3½—57½); rise out of Sedgeborrow, then mostly downhill to Bengeworth, 57¼, whence cross *R.* Avon, and there is a short steep hill to mount in the main street of Evesham; not a good road.

Evesham, &c., p. 119.

Evesham to Alcester (10—67½); long rise out of Evesham (keeping to r. at 1¼m.), then a good and gently undulating road through Norton, 60, Dunnington, 64½ and Arrow, 66¼.

Very pretty country. 1m. out of Evesham, on l., Abbey Manor *Ho.* Past Dunnington, on l., Ragley Park. Alcester, p. 125.

Alcester to Forshaw Park Tg. (11—78½); turn to l. and it is a capital smooth and almost level road through Coughton, 69½, and Spernal Ash, 70¼, to Studley, 71½, then rather uphill through Mapleborough Green, 73, Gorgot Hill, 75¼, and Braunstone Cross, 77.

On r., Coughton Court; on l., Coughton Park. On r., Studley Castle and Priory.

Forshaw Park Tg. to Birmingham (9—87½); over Truman's Heath, through Lower Inkford, 79½, Drake's Cross, 80½, over King's Norton Heath, by Holly Wood, Lane End, and Moseley, 84¼.

[Or from *Alcester* through Great Alne, 70, Little Alne, 72, Wootton Wawen, 74, to *Henley-in-Arden*, 76, whence to *Birmingham*, 15¼—91¼— p. 143.]

Birmingham, p. 140.

BATH TO MANCHESTER.

Bath to Stroud (28)—p. 309.

Stroud to Gloucester (9—37); turn to l. then to r. to Salmon's Mill, 28½, and ½m. further to l., through Pitchcombe, 30, beyond which (keeping to l.) is a steep hill to cross, dangerous to ride down either side, to Brookthrop, 32½, and then easy through Whaddon, 33½: entering Gloucester, join the Bristol road. Good views. [Or ½m. beyond Salmon's Mill on r. to Painswick, 31½, out of which is a long steep uphill (keeping to l. at the fork roads) followed by a dangerous descent down the other side, and chiefly downhill into Gloucester, 37¼.]

Beyond Stroud, on l., Stratford *Ho.* Before Pitchcombe, on r., Browns Hill *Ho.* On l. Painswick *Ho.* Gloucester, p. 105.

Gloucester to Worcester (26½—63½)—p. 307.

Worcester to Ombersley (5¾—69¼); through Barbourn *Tg.*, 64½ (take middle road), Carnmeadow Green, 65½, and over Hawford Bridge, 67, undulating road with good surface.

1½m. beyond Worcester, on r., Perdiswell Park. On r., Hawford *Ho.*; on l., Bevere. On l., Ombersley Court.

Ombersley to Kidderminster (8½—77¾); through Crossway Green, 72 (keep to r.), Hartlebury, 73½, and over Hoo Brook, 76½, is almost level: good surface. Returning, just out of Kidderminster keep to l., and 1m. beyond Hoo Brook to r.

[Or at Crossway Green on l., through *Stourport*, 74½, where turn to r., joining the above road on r. just before *Kidderminster*, 78½.

Or from *Worcester* on r. to *Droitwich*, 70¼—p. 308; here turn to l. and through Hampton Lovett and Bradford, joining the principal route 2½m. before *Kidderminster*, 79.]

On *l.*, Hartlebury Castle. Beyond Droitwich, a little on *l.*, Westwood Park. (*Kidderminster :* Lion, *B.T.C.*)

Kidderminster to Himley (9¾—87½); through Broadwater, 73¾, (keep to *l.* and 1*m.* further to *r.*), Whittington, 82, Stewponey, 83½, and Wall Heath, 87, is rather hilly, but with pretty good surface, running near *R.* Stour. Returning, at Wall Heath, turn to *r.*

At Broadwater, on *l.*, Sion Hill, Wolverley Court, and Lea Castle; 2*m.* farther, Lea Hall; on *r.*, Ismere *Ho.* At Whittington, on *l.*, Kinfare *Ho.* At Stewponey, on *l.*, across *R.* Stour, ruins of Stourton Castle; beyond, Prestwood Hall. At Wall Heath, on *r.*, Ashwood *Ho.* and Summer Hill. On *r.*, Himley Hall and Himley *Ho*

Himley to Wolverhampton (5¾—93¼)—p. 144.

Wolverhampton to Penkridge, *Ch.* (10¼—103½); by Gosbrook Mill, 94½, Ford Houses, 96½, Somerford, 99¼, and Spread Eagle, 101: undulating and good road.

On *l.*, Somerford Hall and Chillington Park. At Spread Eagle, cross Watling Street.

Penkridge to Stafford, *Ch.* (6—109½); through Dunston, 105¾, and Rowley *Tp.*, 108½, a good undulating road. Returning, out of Stafford keep to *r.*

On *l.*, Rowley *Ho.* Stafford. p. 115.

Stafford to Stone, *M.P.* (7¼—116¾); through Stafford keep to *r.*, and through Yarley, 113½, and Walton, 115¼, is excellent road with one stiff hill to go over.

Beyond Stafford, on *r.*, Tillington *Ho.*

Stone to Church Lawton (15¼—132)—pp. 151-2.

Church Lawton to Siddington, *Tp.* (10¾—142¾)—pp. 153-4.

Siddington to Manchester, St. Ann's Square (19¾—162½)—p. 165

BATH TO GLOUCESTER (by Stonehouse).

Bath to Nailsworth (23¾)—p. 309.

Nailsworth to Stonehouse (5¾—29½); very rough oolite road through Inchbrook, 24½, Woodchester, 26, and Rodborough, 27¼ (where turn to *l.*) to Cains Cross, 27¾, and thence (keeping to *l.*) good level road through Ebley, 28¼. Returning, when just out of Stonehouse turn to *l.*, and at Cains Cross to *r.*]

(*Stonehouse :* Crown and Anchor.)

On *l.*, Woodchester Park; on *r.*, Hill *Ho.* Park. At Inchbrook, on *l.*, Parkhill *Ho.* At Rodborough, on *l.*, the Fort and Stanley Park. On *l.*, Ebley *Ho.* and King's Stanley *Ho.* At Cains Cross, on *r.*, Pagan Hill *Ho.*; on *l.*, Stonehouse Court.

Stonehouse to Hardwick (4¾—34¼); through Standish, 32, good level road, though mostly macadam. Returning, at Hardwick (Cross Keys Inn) take left hand road.

On *r.*, Standish Park; 1*m.* farther, on *r.*, Haresfield Court.

Hardwick to Gloucester (4½—38¾)—p. 307.

BATH TO GLOUCESTER (by Frocester).

Bath to Dunkirk Tp. (14½)—p. 304.

Dunkirk Tp. to Kingscote, Hunters' Hall (6¾—21¼); the road is pretty level by Boxwell *Tp.*, 18½, to Calcott Farm, 19½, (where turn to *l.*): oolite surface and rather lumpy. Pretty scenery.

On *l.*, Boxwell Court and Lasborough Park. On *r.*, Kingscote Park.

Kingscote to Frocester (5¼—26½); about ¼*m.* further turn to *r.*, and through Nymphsfield, 24¼, whence the road is on the fall to Frocester: Bristol stone, fairly good surface.

[Or to *Nailsworth*, 23¾ (p. 309); then turn to *l.* by the *ch.*, and join the other road ¼*m.* beyond Nymphsfield, to *Frocester*, 27¼.]

At Nymphsfield, on *r.*, Woodchester Park.

Frocester to Hardwick (6¾—33¼): through Church End *Tp.*, 28¾ (where turn to *r.*, joining the Bristol to Gloucester road), Whitminster, 30¼, and Moreton Valence, 31½: undulating road with good surface, but apt to be greasy and heavy when wet.

On *l.*, Hardwick Court.

Hardwick to Gloucester (4½—37¾)—p. 307.

BATH TO GLOUCESTER (by Dursley).

Bath to Dunkirk Tp. (14½)—p. 304.

Dunkirk Tp. to Wotton-under-Edge (4¾—19¼); turn to *l.* and through Hawkesbury Upton, 15¾ (½*m.* beyond which keep to *r.*), Hilsley, 17¼, and Alderley, 17¾.

At Alderley, on *r.*, Wortley *Ho.* Wotton-under-Edge, p. 102.

Wotton-under-Edge to Dursley (6—25¼); in Wotton turn to *r.* and follow the Kingscote road for 3*m.*, then turn to *l.*: hilly road [Or there is a more direct road through Fordingbrook, shorter by 2*m.*]

Dursley, p. 104.

Dursley to Cambridge Inn (3¾—29); a mile out of Dursley keep to *r.*, and through Lower Cam, 26¾.

[Or from *Wotton-under-Edge*, through Smarts Green, 21½, and Stinchcombe, 23¾, to Lower Cam, 24½.]

Beyond Dursley, on *l.*, Forney Hill and Stancombe Park; on *r.*, Kingshill *Ho.* Beyond Wotton, on *l.*, Bradley *Ho.* At Smarts Green, on *l.*, Nibley *Ho.*

Cambridge Inn to Gloucester (10¾—39¾)—p. 307.

CHIPPENHAM TO GLOUCESTER.

Chippenham to Malmesbury (9½)—p. 304.

Malmesbury to Tetbury (4¾—14¼)—p. 102.

Tetbury to Minchin Hampton (6—20¼); rather rough and hilly by Upton Grove, 16, to Avening, 18½, into which a very rough and rutty hill has to be descended, unsafe to ride down; then the road becomes easier by Gatcombe Park, 19¼, where turn to *l.*

Beyond Tetbury, on r., Grove Ho.; on l., Chevenage Ho. Minchin Hampton. p. 104. Good scenery.

Minchin Hampton to Stroud (4—24½)—p. 104.
[Or at Avening turn to l. at the bottom of the hill, and the road is better with a sharp descent into *Nailsworth*, 21¼, whence to *Stroud*, 4½—25½, p. 309.]

Stroud to Gloucester (9—33½)—p. 311.

BRISTOL TO WOTTON-UNDER-EDGE.

Bristol to Iron Acton (9); nearly 2m. out of Bristol keep to l. and through Stapleton, 2½, and Hambrook, 5.
At Stapleton, on l., Heath Ho. and Stoke Giffard Park; on r., Stapleton Ho. 1m. farther, on r., Oldbury Court.

Iron Acton to Wotton-under-Edge (9½—18½); by Mudge Down, 10, Rangeworthy, 11½, Long Cross, 14.
At Rangeworthy, on r., to *Wickwar* (3¼—14¾).
At Long Cross, on l., Torworth Park.

BATH TO WICKWAR.

Bath to Cross Hands Inn, Old Sodbury (11)—p. 304.

Cross Hands Inn to Chipping Sodbury (2½—13½)—p. 97; turn to l. at Cross Hands Inn.

Chipping Sodbury to Wickwar (4—17½); turn to r.

BRISTOL TO CHIPPING SODBURY.

Bristol to Down End (4¾); through Lower Easton, 1¾, a little beyond which keep to r. and at 4m. to l.
Beyond Lower Easton, on l., Ridgeway Ho. Before Down End, on l., Oldbury Court. At Down End, on r., Hill Ho.

Down End to Nibley (4¼—9); turn to l.
Just past Down End, on l., Cleve Hill and on r., Cleve Ho.

Nibley to Chipping Sodbury (2—11); through Yate, 10.

BRISTOL TO LINCOLN.

Bristol to Sutton Coldfield, M.P. (92¼)—pp. 306-8.

Sutton Coldfield to Tamworth (7—99¼); out of the former turn to r., and it is a hilly road by Basset's Pole, 94½; cross R. Tame just before Tamworth. Returning, ½m. out of Tamworth turn to r.

Beyond Sutton, on l., Moor Hall and Ashfurlong Hall. Beyond Basset's Pole, on l., Canwell Hall. 3m. farther, 1m. on r., Drayton Park. Tamworth, p. 155.

[Or 1½m. beyond Aston, 86½ (p. 308), keep to r. and through Birches Green, 88½, Minworth, 91¾, Curdworth, 93½, ½m. past which turn to l. and 1m. farther keep to r., by Green Man, 94½; through Hunt Green, 95¾, Drayton Basset (ch.), 97¾, and Fazeley, 99, to *Tamworth*, 100¼.

Or ½m. beyond Curdworth, keep straight on through Kingsbury, 96¾, to *Tamworth*, 101¾.]

Tamworth to Measham, Union Inn (10—109¼); by Four County Gate (near Seckington), 103¼, and over Nomans Heath, 105¼.

2m. past Tamworth, on r., Amington Hall. At Four County Gate, on l., Thorpe Hall. Past Nomans Heath, on r., Appleby *Ho.* and White *Ho.* Measham, p. 156.

Measham to Ashby-de-la-Zouch (3½—112¾); keep straight through Measham.

Ashby-de-la-Zouch to Castle Donington (9½—122¼); beyond Ashby keep to *l.*, and by Breedon-on-the-Hill, 118, and through Isley Walton, 119¾.

Beyond Breedon, on r., Langley Priory. Beyond Isley Walton, on l., Donington Park and Hall.

Castle Donington to Nottingham (10—132¼); about ½m. farther cross Loughborough to Derby road, and over Harrington Bridge, 124¾, through Sawley, 125¼, Long Eaton, 126, Toton, 126½, Chilwell, 127½, Beeston, 128½, and Lenton, 130¾. Returning, ½m. before Beeston turn to *l.*

At Chilwell, on r., Chilwell Hall and Clifton Hall, across *R.* Trent. On r., Lenton Hall; on l., Wollaton Hall, Lenton Grove, and Lenton Priory.

Nottingham to Trent Bridge (1—133¼); in the *M.P.* turn to r., down Arkright street and cross the bridge to the junction of the roads.

[Or from *Ashby-de-la-Zouch*, keep to r. ¾m. farther, and through ColeOrton, 114¾, where keep to r. by Gracedieu *Tp.*, 118½, Finney Hall Wood, 120½, and Garendon Park, 121¾, to *Loughborough*, 124¾, thence to *Trent Bridge*, 138¾; p. 189.]

Trent Bridge to Lincoln (35½—168¾)—pp. 306.

KIMBOLTON TO WARWICK.

Kimbolton to Higham Ferrers (8); at the end of Kimbolton keep to *l.*, and through Tillbrook, 1½, by Three Shire Stone, 3½, and through Chelveston, 6; at Higham Ferrers, turn to *l.*, and through the town.

Higham Ferrers, p. 185.

Higham Ferrers to Wellingborough (5—13); through the former turn to r., and over Long Bridge, 12.

Between 2 and 3m. out of Higham Ferrers, on r., the site of the Roman station of Irchester. Wellingborough, p. 189.

Wellingborough to Northampton (9¼—22¼); p. 299, in the reverse direction; at Wellingborough turn to *l.*

Northampton to Weedon (7¾—30½); a little out of Northampton keep to *l.*, and by Duston, 25, Upton, 25¾, Upper Heyford, 28¾, and Floore or Flower, 29¾, a good undulating road, with easy hills; longish descent into Weedon.

Weedon to Daventry (4¼—34¾)—p. 139.

Daventry to Warwick (19¼—54)—p. 144.

CAMBRIDGE TO LEICESTER.

Cambridge to Huntingdon, *M.H.* (15½); cross *R.* Cam, and up a slight incline, after which through Girton, 3, Lolworth, 6½, Fenny Stanton, 10, and Godmanchester, 14½; it is quite a level road, with but one ascent about 2*m*. before Godmanchester, the surface is simply perfection for the greater part of the way, but sometimes in dry weather it becomes loose in places; cross *R.* Ouse entering Huntingdon, through which is ¼*m.* of paving, extremely rough. Returning, at Godmanchester turn to *l.* The road is part of the Roman Via Devana.

At Girton, 1*m.* on *l.*, Madingley Park. Huntingdon, &c. p. 223.

Huntingdon to Thrapston (16½—32); in Huntingdon turn to *l.*, through the suburb of Hinchinbrook, 16¼; hill to mount on leaving the town, then the road is almost level with simply perfect surface through Brampton, 17¼, by Creamer's Hut, 18½, and through Ellington, 20½, to Spaldwick, 22¾, after which it becomes a little lumpy and hilly, through Bythorne, 27¾, and over Mickle Hill, 29, with a steep hill to descend into Thrapston.

About 1*m.* out, on *r.*, Hinchinbrook *Ho.* On *l.*, Brampton Park. Thrapston, p. 193.

Thrapston to Kettering (9¼—41¼); cross *R.* Nen to Islip, 32¾, out of which is a steep hill to mount, then a fairly smooth undulating road through Cranford St. John, 37, Bartonfield, 39, and Barton Seagrave, 39½. Returning, a short distance out of Kettering turn to *l.*, and also at Bartonfield.

Kettering to Leicester (25¾—67)—p. 189.

WARWICK TO PETERBOROUGH.

Warwick to Princethorpe (9); at Warwick, going down the High street, turn to *r.*, through Emscote, ¾, then cross *R.* Avon, and the road is pretty level, but rather rough, skirting the north part of Leamington, 2, and through Lillington, 3, and Cubington, 4½, to Weston, 5½, and thence undulating with a little better surface. [Or from Warwick come back on the Banbury road, with a sharp descent out of the town, then cross *R.* Avon, and, turning to *l.*, it is a first-rate broad and smooth road to *Leamington*, 2¼, where turn to *l.* at the station, and straight through the town, just beyond turning to *r.*, to Lillington, 4.]

Before Weston, on *r.*, Weston Hall. Leamington, p. 114.

Princethorpe to Rugby (7½—16½); chiefly uphill for first 3*m.*, the latter part being a stiff ascent on to Dunsmore Heath (junction of the London to Coventry road, 12¼), then fairly level and fine road through Bilton, 14¾.

2*m.* past Princethorpe, on *r.*, Bourton Hall; on *r.*, Bilton Hall. Rugby, p. 182.

Rugby to Husband's Bosworth (10—26½); through Clifton, 18½, a little farther turn to *r.*, cross Watling Street, 19¾, and through Catthorpe, 20½, Swinford, 21¼, South Kilworth, 23¾, and North Kilworth, 24¾. Rather hilly. Returning, at North Kilworth turn to *l.*

At Swinford, on *r.*, Stanford Hall.

Husband's Bosworth to Market Harborough (6—32½); descent from the former, then fairly level through Theddingworth, 28, and Lubenham, 30½.

At Theddingworth, on *r.*, Holthorpe Hall. On *r.*, Thorpe Lubenham Hall. Market Harborough, p. 166.

Market Harborough to Great Weldon (14¾—47¼); hilly road through Little Bowden, 32¾, Dingley, 35, Brampton, 36½, Stoke Albany, 37¾, Wilbarston, 38¾, East Carlton, 40½, and Corby (*ch.*), 45. Returning, 3*m.* past Corby keep to *l.*

On *l.*, Dingley Hall and East Carlton Hall.

Great Weldon to Oundle (8¾—56); by right-hand road through Upper Benefield, 50¾, and Benefield, 52¾.

Beyond Great Weldon, on *l.*, Weldon Park. Oundle, p. 193.

Oundle to Peterborough (13—69)—p. 299.

BIRMINGHAM TO PETERBOROUGH.

Birmingham to Coventry (18¼)—p. 139, reversed.

Coventry to Lutterworth (15—33¼); in Coventry, after passing the cross streets at the top of the hill, keep to *l.* where the London road branches off, and ½*m.* farther take right-hand road; then through Stoke Green, 19½, Binley, 20¼ (keep first to *l.*, then to *r.*), Brinklow, 24¾ (turn to *l.*), past Stretton Station, 25¼ (keep to *r.*), through Stretton-under-Fosse, 26¾, Stretaston, 27½ (turn to *r.*), Pailton, 28½, and Cross-in-Hand *Tg.*, 31.

Beyond Binley, on *l.*, Combe Abbey and Park. At Stretton, on *r.*, Newbold Hall. Past Stretaston, on *r.*, Pailton *Ho.* At Pailton, on *l.*, Newnham Paddock. Lutterworth, p. 155.

Lutterworth to Husband's Bosworth (7—40¼); in Lutterworth turn to *r.*, and a little out of the town to *l.*, and through Walcote, 35¼, and North Kilworth, 38½, a little beyond which keep to *l.*

Beyond Lutterworth, on *l.*, Misterton Hall.

Husband's Bosworth to Peterborough (42½—82¾)—pp. 316-7.

BIRMINGHAM TO PETERBOROUGH (by Leicester).

Birmingham to Castle Bromwich (5¼); tramway and bad macadam road through the suburbs to Saltley, 2, after which it improves to Castle Bromwich.

On *r.*, Castle Bromwich Hall.

Castle Bromwich to Coleshill (4¼—9½); through Bacon's End, 8, where turn to *l.*

Before Coleshill, on *l.*, Coleshill Old Hall and Coleshill Park. Coleshill, p 145.

Coleshill to Over Whitacre (4—13½); through Shustoke, 12½, and Furnace End, 13, where turn to *r.*

Beyond Coleshill, a little on *r.*, Maxstoke Castle, chiefly erected in the reign of Edward III.; and Shustoke Hall. 1*m.* beyond Coleshill, on *l.*, Blythe Hall.

Over Whitacre to Nuneaton (8¼—21¾); turn to *l.*, and through Ansley, 16¾, Chapel End, 19¼, and Barr Green, 20¾. Returning, a little past Barr Green keep to *l.*

Beyond Ansley, on *r.*, Ansley Hall and Park.

Nuneaton to Leicester (18¼—40)—p. 305.

[Or at Furnace End, 13, keep straight on through Bently *Ty.*, 16, to *Atherstone*, 19¼; whence, turning to *r.*, to *Hinckley* (8—27¼), as at p. 155, in reverse direction; and then to *Leicester* (13—40¼)—p. 305.]

Beyond Bently *Ty.*, on *r.*, Bently Park; on *l.*, Baxterley Hall. Before Atherstone, on *l.*, Merevale Hall. Atherstone, pp. 155-6.

Leicester to Uppingham (19—59); over Saltersford Bridge, 42½, through Houghton-on-the-Hill, 46, Billesdon, 48¾, Skeffington, 50¼, Tugby, 52, East Norton, 53½, over Finchley Bridge, 54½, and through Allexton, 55½, and over Castle Hill; hilly road.

Beyond Saltersford Bridge, on *l.*, Scraptoft Hall. On *l.*, Skeffington Hall. At East Norton, on *l.*, Lodington Hall, and 2*m.* beyond it, Launde Abbey. On *r.*, Allexton Hall. Before Uppingham, on *l.*, Ayston Hall. Uppingham, p. 186.

Uppingham to Duddington (8¼—67¼); stiff descent just out of Uppingham, then pretty level through Glayston, 61, Morcot, 63, and over South Field to Tixover, 66¼, whence there is another steep descent to the *R.* Welland, before Duddington; very bad road.

On *l.*, Glayston *Ho.* and Tixover *Ho.*

Duddington to Wansford (5¾—73); turn first to *l.* and then to *r.*; very bad road.

Wansford, p. 195.

Wansford to Peterborough (7¾—80¾); turn to *l.* just before *R.* Nen, and through Ailesworth, 75½, Castor, 76½, and Longthorp, 78¾: very bad road.

Beyond Castor, on *l.*, Milton Park; on *r.*, Thorp Hall. Peterborough, p. 215.

BIRMINGHAM TO GRANTHAM.

Birmingham to Leicester (40)—p. 317.

Leicester to Melton Mowbray (15—55); tramway for first mile out of Leicester, and the road continues rather rough and uneven, but fairly level through Thurmaston, 43, to Syston, 45; after leaving Syston the surface soon improves, and through Rearsby, 47, Brooksby, 49, Frisby, 51, and Kirkby Bellars, 52½, is very good with only a few short hills, all of which are rideable; the streets of Melton are paved.

On *l.*, the valley of the *R.* Welland is parallel with the road. Just beyond Thurmaston, where the road bends to the *r.*, the road on the *l.* running almost straight on is the Old Fosse Way to Newark. On *l.*, Brooksby Hall and Rotherby Hall. Melton Mowbray, p. 186.

Melton Mowbray to Grantham (16—71); the road is hilly, being nearly all on the rise, with very rough uneven surface, requiring great caution on account of bad ruts, through Thorpe Arnold, 56¾, to beyond Waltham-on-the-Wolds, 60½, then a stiff descent and ascent to Croxton Kerrial, 64, and 2 or 3*m.* farther is a long downhill through Denton, 67½, to Harlaxton Inn, 68½, and the rest level.

Beyond Waltham, on *r.*, Croxton Park. At Croxton, 3*m.* on *l.*, Belvoir Castle, the magnificent seat of the Duke of Rutland; near, at Woolsthorpe, ruins of the old *ch.* On *l.*, Denton *Ho.*; on *r.*, Harlaxton Manor *Ho.* Grantham, p. 195.

BIRMINGHAM TO MANCHESTER.

Birmingham to Walsall, *Ch.* (8½); through Hockley Brook, 1¼, Soho, 1½ (keep to *r.*), Handsworth, 2¼, and Snails Green, 5¾. Returning keep to *r.* about 1*m.* past Snails Green. [Or leave Birmingham by Aston Park and through Perry, 3¼, joining the other road on *l.*, about 1½*m.* farther on: same distance.]

(*Walsall:* George, *B.T.C.*; Stork.)

On *l.*, Soho Park. Beyond Handsworth, on *l.*, Hamstead Hall; on *r.*, Perry Hall. At Snails Green, on *l.*, Red *Ho.* Hall; on *r.*, Barr Hall.

Walsall to Cannock (7¾—16¼); in Walsall first turn to *l.*, then keep to *r.*, and through Bloxwich, 11¼, and Great Wyrley, 14¼, to Church Bridge, 15¼, where keep to *r.*

Cannock to Stafford, *Ch.* (10—26¼); keep to *r.*, and through Huntington, 18½, and Weeping Cross, 24¼, is a hilly road along the borders of Cannock Chase, which lies on *r.* Returning, after crossing *R.* Sow, out of Stafford, keep to *l.*, and at Weeping Cross to *r.* [Or at Cannock take left hand fork to *Penkridge*, 21½, whence turning to *r.*, to *Stafford*, 27½—p. 312.]

2*m.* past Huntington, on *l.*, Teddesley Park and Hall. 1*m.* before Weeping Cross, on *l.*, Acton Hill.

Stafford to Manchester, St. Ann's Square (53—79¼)—p. 312.

KIDDERMINSTER TO DERBY.

Kidderminster to Stourbridge (6¾); by Broadwaters Inn, 1 (keep to *r.*), through Iverley, 4½, and Heath Gate, 6, is a fair road, with one or two hills to ascend.

At Broadwaters Inn, on *l.*, Sion Hill. About half-way on *l.*, Easemore Hall. Stourbridge, p. 137.

Stourbridge to Dudley (4¾—11½); following the Wolverhampton road for ¾*m.*, there is a long, stiff rise out of the town over macadam, near the top of which turn to *r.*, and through Brierley Hill, 8½. Returning, a mile out of Dudley keep to *l.*

(*Dudley:* Bush; Castle; Dudley Arms; Eagle.)

Beyond Stourbridge, on *r.*, Dennis Hill. At Dudley, the castle ruins. The road now passes through the heart of the Black Country, to beyond Walsall.

Dudley to Wednesbury (4—15½); a mile out of Dudley turn to *l.* and through Dudley Port, 12¾, Horsley, 14¼ (turn to *l.*), and Ocker Hill, 15 (keep to *r.*)

Wednesbury, p. 140.

Wednesbury to Walsall (3—18½); through Wood Green and Bescott Lane, 17, keep to *r.*

Walsall to Lichfield (10¼—28¾); through Rushall, 20, Walsall Wood, 22, Ogley Hay, 24½, Muckley Corner, 25½, and Pipe Hill, 26¾.

Beyond Walsall Wood, on *r.*, at the cross roads, Castle Old Fort, an ancient entrenchment. Lichfield, p. 115.

Lichfield to Derby, All Saints' *Ch.* (24—52¾)—p. 308.

BRISTOL TO MANCHESTER.

Bristol to Worcester (60)—pp. 306-7.

Worcester to Manchester, St. Ann's Square (99—159)—pp. 311-2.

BRISTOL TO CHESTER.

Bristol to Black Rock Inn (13½)—pp. 90-1.

Black Rock Inn to Chepstow (5—18½); beyond the railway turn to *r.*, and by St. Pierre's Park Gate, 15¾, and Poolmeyrick, 17, is an undulating road, with a long steep hill to walk down into Chepstow; rather rough for first 2*m.*, then good: rough paving in Chepstow. [Or 2½*m.* past Compton Greenfield turn to *r.* through Northwick, 10½, to *Aust Passage Inn*, 12¼, whence cross *R.* Severn by ferry to Beachley Passage House Inn, 13¼, and to *Chepstow*, 16½, turning to *l.* ½*m.* before, and crossing *R.* Wye into the town.]

Beyond Beachley *Ho.*, on *r.*, Burnsville Park and Sedbury *Ho.* Chepstow, p. 109.

Chepstow to Tintern (5½—24); at the beginning of Chepstow turn to *l.*, and there is a stiff ascent to climb, followed by another out of St. Arvans, 20½, where keep to *r.* (both dangerous to ride *down* without a good brake), to the top of Windcliff Hill, then a long descent, some parts steep, but fairly well engineered, by Tintern Abbey, 23¼; fair surface.

(*Tintern:* Royal George.)

2*m.* beyond Chepstow, on *r.*, Pierrefield *Ho.* and Park. On *r.*, the ruins of Tintern Abbey, of the Cistercian monks, founded 1131, should be visited. Splendid scenery, the road running close to *R.* Wye.

Tintern to Monmouth (10—34); continuing up the valley of the Wye through Llandogo, 26¾, over Bigswear Bridge, 27¾ (cross *R.* Wye, and 1d. toll to pay), and through Redbrook, 31½, the road is rather rough for most of the way, but with only slight gradients. Returning, after crossing *R.* Wye out of Monmouth, turn to *r.* Fine scenery. Monmouth is paved.

[Or at St. Arvans keep to *l.* over hilly road through Devauden Green, 23½, keeping to *r.* 1½*m.* further, and through Llanishen Cross, 26¼, Trellech, 28, to *Monmouth*, 33½, entering by the other end of the town. Returning, out of Monmouth turn to *l.*, and nearly 1*m.* further to *r.* Or from *Tintern* turn to *l.* to Trellech, 28.]

At Trellech are some Druidical remains. Monmouth, p. 110.

Monmouth to Wormelow Tump (11¼—45¼); through Welsh Newton, 37¾, and St. Weonard's, 41¾.

At St. Weonard's, on *l*, Treago. At Wormelow Tump, on *l.*, Bryngwyn and Moynde Park; 1*m.* before, on *r.*, Lyston *Ho.*

Wormelow Tump to Hereford (6½—51¾); through Cross-in-Hand *Tg.*, 47, and Callow, 47¾; rather rough road; macadam through Hereford. Returning, keep to *r.* past Callow.

[Or from *Monmouth* to *Ross*, 10½—44½, reversing p. 110; but if not going into Ross turn to *l.* at Wilton *Tg.*, 43¾, and a short distance further take right-hand road to *Hereford*, 56½, p. 114.]

Hereford to Leominster (12¾—64½); rather uphill road with bumpy macadam surface, through Holmer, 53½, Pipe, 54½, Moreton-on-Lugg, 55½, to Wellington, 57; a little farther is a steep ascent on to Dinmore Hill (top of, 59, followed by descent 1½*m.* long to Hope-under-Dinmore, 60½, and the remainder is hilly and rough through Wharton, 62, Elmsgreen, 63, over Broadward Bridge, 63¼, and through Bottols Green, 63¾.

On *l.*, Holmer Hall and *Ho.* At Hope on *r.*, Hampton Court. At Bottols Green, on *l.*, Rycland*s*.

Leominster to Ludlow (10—74½); through Luston, 67, Gobbits, 68¼, Portway, 70, Richard's Castle, 71½, and Overton, 73; before Ludlow cross *R.* Teme, whence there is a steep hill to mount (dangerous to descend), entering the town by a narrow archway. [Or in Leominster turn to *r.* after crossing *R.* Lugg, and there is a much better road through Stockton Cross, 66½, where turn to *l.*, Ashton, 68¾, Brimfield Cross, 71¼, Wooferton Cross, 72, and Ashford Bowdler, 73½, joining the other road at the *Tg.* a short distance before Ludlow, 75¾, where, on returning, turn to *l.*: it is fair going and pretty level, running near *R.* Teme from Brimfield, and known as the lower road.]

Before Luston, 1m. on *l.*, Eyeton Hall; at Luston, on *r.*, or before Ashton, on *l.*, Berrington Park. At Gobbits, on *l.*, Highwood *Ho.* and Birchtree. At Overton, on *l.*, Hay Park; on *r.*, Moor Park. Before Ludlow, on *l.*, Ludford Park; on *r.*, Ludford *Ho.* Ludlow, p. 120.

Ludlow to Newton Green, Guide Post (8—82½)—p. 120.

Newton Green to Church Stretton (7¾—90¼); through Halford, 83, Strefford, 84½, Felhampton, 85¾, and Little Stretton, 88¾, is rather uphill for most of the way, and rough surface for first 5m. Pretty scenery.

On *r.* is the long hill of Wenlock Edge, running N.E.; the range of hills on *l.* is the Long Mynd. 1m. before Church Stretton, on *r.*, is an old entrenched hill, called Brocards, or Brockhurst Castle; beyond the town, a little on *l.*, is another, called Bradbury Ring, and a little farther, on *r.*, is Caer Caradoc, Mount Caractacus, on the top of which is an old British camp, and embracing an extensive view.

Church Stretton to Shrewsbury (13—103¼); through All Stretton, 91½, Leebotwood, 94, Longnor, 95¼, Dorrington, 96¼, and Baiston Hill, 100¾, is a good easy road, though rather hilly in places, but chiefly downhill. Returning, after crossing *R.* Severn turn to *r.*, then to *l.* and *r.* again.

On *l.*, Longnor Hall, and a little farther, Netley Hall. Shrewsbury, p. 126.

Shrewsbury to Wem (10¼—113½); in Shrewsbury turn to *r.*, and a little further keep to *l.*, then a moderately good road through Albrighton, 106¾, with a stiff climb either way over and descent from Harmer (or Armour) Hill, 109 (where keep to *r.*), and through Broughton, 110¼.

Before Broughton, on *r.* 1m., Sansaw Hall.

Wem to Whitchurch (8¾—122¼); through Edstaston, 115¾, and Tilstock, 119¾, is a rather rough road with only one little hill. Returning, a little out of Whitchuch keep to *r.* at the railway.

[Or from Shrewsbury by the middle road through Battlefield Hadnall or Hadnall Ease, Rock Hall, Brockhurst, Dog Moor, Prees, Prees Heath, and Heath Lane, joining the other road before Whitchurch: nearly same distance.]

Whitchurch, p. 148.

Whitchurch to Chester (20—142¼)—p. 148.

BRISTOL TO CHESTER (by Worcester).

Bristol to Worcester (60)—pp. 306-7.

Worcester to Wolverhampton (29¾—89¾)—pp. 311-2.

Wolverhampton to Chester (58¾—148½)—pp. 147-8. [Or *Worcester* to *Kidderminster*, 14¼—74¼, p. 311; thence to *Shrewsbury*, 30½—104¾, p. 126; thence to *Chester*, 39—143¾—above.]

MALMESBURY TO HEREFORD.

Malmesbury to Kingscote, Hunter's Hall (10)—p. 102.

Kingscote to Frocester ($5\frac{1}{4}$—$15\frac{1}{4}$)—p. 313.

Frocester to Newnham ($8\frac{1}{4}$—$23\frac{1}{2}$); through Church End *Tp.*, $17\frac{1}{2}$, (where turn to *r.*, and $\frac{1}{2}$*m.* further to *l.*), Fretherne, $20\frac{1}{2}$, and Arlingham, $22\frac{1}{2}$, to the Three Mitres, $23\frac{1}{4}$, whence cross *R.* Severn by ferry to Newnham.

On *l.*, $1\frac{1}{2}$*m.* past the Gloucester road, Frampton Court; on *l.*, Arlingham Court.

Newnham to Mitcheldean ($5\frac{1}{2}$—29); through Little Dean, $25\frac{1}{2}$, Gun Mills, $27\frac{1}{4}$, and Abenhall or Abinghall, $28\frac{1}{4}$, is a fair road, with only one or two hills of any account. Returning, at Gun Mills keep to *r.*

At Little Dean, on *r.*, Dean Hall. Near the *ch.* is an ancient camp. At Gun Mills, on *r.* 1*m.*, Flaxley Abbey. Before Mitcheldean, on *l.*, The Wilderness.

Mitcheldean to Hereford ($18\frac{1}{2}$—$47\frac{1}{2}$); through Lea, 31, over Sandford Bridge, by Rugden Crossway, and through Mordiford, $42\frac{1}{2}$, where turn to *l.* [Or $\frac{1}{4}$*m.* beyond Lea turn to *l.*, and through Weston, $32\frac{3}{4}$, to *Ross*, 35, whence to *Hereford*, $13\frac{1}{4}$—$48\frac{1}{4}$, p. 114.]

BRISTOL TO ABERGAVENNY.

Bristol to Crick (16)—pp. 90-1.

Crick to Usk ($9\frac{1}{2}$—$25\frac{1}{2}$); turn to *l.*, and through Caerwent, $17\frac{1}{2}$ (keep to *r.*), and a mile further begins a long uphill through Llanvair Discoed, $19\frac{1}{2}$, to Went Wood, after which is a steep hill to go down, and nearly level through Llanllowel, $23\frac{1}{4}$.

On *l.*, Llanvair Castle, and on *r.*, Penhein *Ho.* On the top of the hill, at the end of Went Wood, on *r.*, Castle Troggy, or Striguil Castle. Usk, p. 113.

Usk to Abergavenny (11—$36\frac{1}{2}$); through Clytha, $30\frac{1}{2}$, Llanvihangel, $31\frac{1}{2}$, where join the Monmouth road on *r.*, and through Llangattock, $32\frac{1}{2}$, is very hilly and rough, though some parts are gravel: runs near *R.* Usk all the way.

[Or Bristol to Devanden Green, $23\frac{1}{2}$, p. 320; thence $1\frac{1}{2}$*m.* further on *l.* through Llansoy, 27, to *Raglan*, $32\frac{1}{2}$, and to Clytha, $35\frac{1}{2}$.]

Abergavenny, p. 110.

WORCESTER TO ROSS.

Worcester to Great Malvern ($8\frac{1}{4}$); cross *R.* Severn and through St. John's, 1 (turn to *l.*), Powick, $2\frac{3}{4}$ (keep to *r.*), and Newlands Green, $6\frac{1}{4}$, is a good road, but uphill nearly all the way; the last mile is a very stiff ascent; pretty country.

At St. John's on *r.*, Boughton *Ho.* and Wick *Ho.* On *r.*, Powick Court. At Newlands Green, on *l.* 1*m.*, Madresfield Court.

Great Malvern to Ledbury (8—$16\frac{1}{4}$); good smooth road with rideable undulations along the eastern slope of the Malvern Hills, through Malvern Wells, $10\frac{1}{4}$, to Little Malvern, $11\frac{1}{4}$, where keep to *r.*, and there is a half-mile walk on to the hill, and the rest, through Lower Mitchel, $14\frac{3}{4}$, is a good road, mostly downhill: this road, being all made with Malvern stone, soon dries, and is never greasy; pretty scenery.

Beyond Little Malvern, on *l.*, Herefordshire Beacon, an immense British hill fortress; a little farther, on *r.*, an old castle. At Malvern Wells, on *l.*, Belmont Lodge. At Lower Mitchel, on *r.*, Kilbury Camp. Ledbury, p. 116.

Ledbury to Ross (12—28¼).

PERSHORE TO LEDBURY.

Pershore to Upton-on-Severn (8¼); turn to *l.* and through Defford and Earl's Crome.

Upton-on-Severn to Ledbury (10½—18¾); ½m. beyond Upton keep to *r.* and through Drake Street and Little Malvern, 14½ (just beyond which turn to *l.*), and Lower Mitchel, 17¼. [Or from Upton on *r.* to Hemley Castle, 9¼, whence on *l.* to Malvern Wells, 13¾, and to Little Malvern, 15¼.]

WORCESTER TO HEREFORD.

Worcester to Ridgeway Cross (10); cross R. Severn to St. John's, 1, where turn first to *l.* then to *r.*, and through Rushwick, 2, over Bransford Bridge (R. Severn), 3, through Bransford, 4½, Leigh Sinton, 5¼ and Stiffords Bridge, 9¾.

At St. John's, on *l.*, Boughton *Ho.* and Wick *Ho.* A little farther, on *l.* Upper Wick and Langhern *Ho.* At Bransford Bridge, on *l.*, Bransford Court.

Ridgeway Cross to Newtown (7—17); by Hanleys End, 12½. over Fromes Hill, 13¼ (½m. further turn first to *r.*, then to *l.*), through Five Bridges, 14½, Eagleton or Eggleton, 16, and over Eagleton Bridge, 16½.

Newtown to Hereford (8—25); through Shucknell, 19, and over Lug Bridge, 23.

Hereford, p. 114.

NEWPORT TO ABERGAVENNY.

Newport to Mamhilad, *Ch.* (10); through Malpas, 2, and Llantarnam, 4, by New Inn, 6, and through Llanfihangel Pontymoel, 8½, good road, long hill either direction to Llantarnam. [Or to *Usk*, 11, (p. 113); thence, without crossing R. Usk, through Monkswood, 12¼, joining the other road nearly a mile before Mamhilad. 16¼.]

After crossing the canal ½ a mile before Llanfihangel Pontymoel, on *l.* to *Pontypool*, 1—9: good road.

On *l.*, Malpas *Ho.*; on *r.*, Llantarnam Abbey. On *l.*, at the division of the road, Pontypool Park.

Mamhilad to Abergavenny (7½—17½); steep hill to climb, quite unrideable, to Llanover, 13, then easy going, over Llanellen Bridge (R.Usk), 15½: good road. [Or from Monkswood on *r.* to Llanover, 16¼.]

On *r.*, Llanover *Ho.* Abergavenny, p. 110.

KIDDERMINSTER TO ABERGAVENNY.

Kidderminster to Stourport (4); almost level.

Stourport to Hundred House Inn (5—9); through Stourport cross R. Severn to Areley Kings, 4½, then the road is on the rise all the way through Dunley, 6, followed after a little downhill by a short steep ascent just before the Hundred House.

On *r.*, Areley Hall; on *l.*, Dernley Hall. At Hundred *Ho.* Inn, on *l.*, Witley Court; on *r.*, Abberley Lodge.

Hundred House Inn to Bromyard (11½—20½); keep to *l.* over Stanford Bridge, 11½ (cross *R.* Teme), through High House *Tp.*, 13¾, Upper Sapey, 14½, Tedstone Wafer, 17¼, and Sandy Cross, 18½. [Or at Stanford Bridge turn to *l.* round Stanford Park to Sapey Wood, 15, thence through Clifton, 16½, and Lower Sapey, 17¾, to just before Sandy Cross, 20¾.]

Beyond Stanford Bridge, on *l.*, Stanford Park and Court. ½*m.* before Sandy Cross, on *r.*, Saltmarsh Castle; ½*m.* beyond, on *r.* 1*m.*, Buckenhill. Bromyard, p. 121.

Bromyard to Hereford (14—34½); through Cooper's Green, 21¾ (keep to *r.*), Stoke Lacey, 24½, Burley Gate, 26½, Withington Marsh, 30¼, and over Lug Bridge, 32½. Returning, after Lug Bridge, turn 2nd to *l.*, and ¼*m.* past it.

Beyond Stoke Lacey, on *r.*, Moreton Court. Before Lug Bridge, on *l.*, New Court. Hereford, p. 114.

Hereford to Pontrilas (12—46½); through Hereford cross *R.* Wye, a short distance beyond turn to *r.*, and nearly 2*m.* farther keep to *l.*, and by Goose Pool, 38¼ (2*m.* farther turning to *l.* and then keep to *r.*), over Willcocks Bridge, 40½, and through St. Devereux, 42¼, Wormebridge, 43½, and Kenderchurch, 45¾.

2*m.* out of Hereford, on *l.*, Mountpleasant; on *r.*, Belmont. Beyond Goose Pool, on *l.*, Allensmore *Ho.* At St. Devereux, on *l.*, Didley Court and Kilpeck Castle. At Pontrilas, 3*m.* on *l.*, down the Monnow Valley, ruins of Grosmont Castle. On *r.*, running 12 or 13*m.* N.W., is the narrow valley of the *R.* Dore, called the Golden Valley. About 1*m.* from Pontrilas, is Ewias Harold Castle, and 1*m.* farther, Dore Abbey.

Pontrilas to Abergavenny (12—58½); through Rowlston, 48, Alterines, 51¼, Llanfihangel Crucornwy, 53½, and Llandilo Bertholey, 56. [Or beyond Pontrilas turn to *l.*, and by Monmouth Cap, 47½, Langue, 48, joining the other road about half-way.]

At Alterines, 2*m.* on *r.*, old castle, and 2 or 3*m.* farther, the ruins of Llanthony Abbey. Before Llandilo, 2*m.* on *r.*, the Sugar Loaf Mountain. Abergavenny, p. 110.

GLOUCESTER TO TENBURY.

Gloucester to Ledbury (16½)—p. 116.

Ledbury to Bromyard (12¾—29¼); in Ledbury keep to *l.*, and over Ledden Bridge, 18½, through Stapley, 19½, Stanley Hill, 21½, Castle Frome, 2½, Bishop's Frome, 24½, and Cooper's Green, 28¼. Returning, keep to *l.* at Cooper's Green.

Bromyard, p. 121.

Bromyard to Tenbury (10¾—40); in Bromyard turn sharp to *l.*, and leaving the town turn to *r.*, over Inkstone Bridge, 30, through Edwin Ralph, 31½, and Little Kyre *Tp.*, 35.

Beyond Inkstone Bridge, on *r.*, Buckenhill. On *r.*, Kyre Park. Before Tenbury, 1*m.* on *r.*, Kyrewood *Ho.*; 1*m.* on *l.*, Burford *Ho.* Tenbury, p. 120.

BIRMINGHAM TO BRECON.

Birmingham to Halesowen (7¾); by the Black Boy Inn, 5¼, is a good road after first 3*m*.

Before Halesowen, on *l.*, Leaseowes; beyond, Halesowen Abbey. On *r.*, about half-way, Warley Abbey. Pretty country.

Halesowen to Kidderminster (10—17¾); entering Halesowen turn to *l.*, and a little farther to *r.*, cross part of the Lickey Hills, to Hagley, 11¾, into which there is a long steep descent; the rest is easy.

On *l.*, Hagley Park and Field *Ho.*; on *r.*, Pedmore Hall. 2*m.* beyond Hagley, on *l.*, Broom *Ho.* 2*m.* before Kidderminster, on *r.*, Park Hall and Harcatt Hall. Kidderminster, p. 126.

Kidderminster to Bewdley (3—20¾) is mostly downhill. Returning, a little out of Bewdley keep to *r.*

Beyond Kidderminster, on *r.*, Summer Hill, Blakebrook *Ho.*, and The Lea; on *l.*, Spring Grove, Tickenhill *Ho.*, and Sandbourn. Bewdley lies on *R.* Severn; 1*m.* on *l.*, Ribbesford Hall.

Bewdley to Tenbury (14—34¾); keeping to *l.* 3¼*m.* out of Bewdley, the road is hilly for the first half, through Clowstop *Tg.*, 26, to Mamble, 27¾; after that it is very easy going through Newnham, 31¼, where it joins the Worcester and Droitwich road, and runs near the *R.* Teme, turning to *l.* and crossing it just before Tenbury.

On *l.*, Newnham Court. Tenbury, p. 120.

Tenbury to Leominster (9¼—44); through Leyster's Pole, 38½, Kimbolton, 41¼, and Stockton Cross, 42¼. Returning, out of Leominster, after crossing *R.* Lug, turn to *r.*

Leominster, p. 122.

Leominster to White Hill T.P.G. (8¼—52¼); in the town turn to *r.* and a mile beyond keep to *l.*, and through Monkland, 46½, and Dilwyn, 50¼.

At Whitehill *T.P.G.*, on *l.* to *Weobley* (¾—53).

Beyond Leominster, on *l.*, Ryelands. Before Dilwyn, on *r.*, Henwood Court; beyond, on *l.*, The Homme.

White Hill T.P.G. to Willersley, *Tp.* (6¼—58½); through Sarnesfield, 53¾, Kinnersley, 55¾, and Cross, 58, (where turn to *l.*)

On *l.*, Kinnersley Castle; on *r.*, Sarnesfield *Ho.* At Cross, Eardisley Park and Castle.

Willersley to Hay (7½—66): turn to *r.*, and through Winforton, 59½, Whitney, 61½, (just beyond, cross *R.* Wye), and Clifford, 63¾, to Hay.

On *l.*, Whitney Court. On *r.*, ruins of Clifford Castle; on *l.*, The Priory. At Hay, the castle.

Hay to Brecon (15¼—81¼)—p. 116.

BIRMINGHAM TO BRECON (by Kington).

Birmingham to Tenbury (34¾)—above.

Tenbury to Brimfield Cross (4—38¾); instead of turning to *l*, and crossing *R.* Teme, keep straight on, and as on p. 120.

Brimfield Cross to Mortimer's Cross (8—46¾); through

Wooferton Cross, 39½ (turn to *l.*), Comberton, 41, Portway, 41½, (turn to *l.*, and 1¼*m.* farther to *r.*), whence the road becomes hilly through Bircher, 43¾, Cock Gate, 44¼, and Lucton, 46.

At Cock Gate, on *r.*, in Croft Park, remains of Croft Castle and an ancient entrenchment. Mortimer's Cross, p. 122. At Bircher, on *l.*, Highwood *Ho.*

Mortimer's Cross to Kington (9¾—56¼); through Shobden, 48½, Staunton-on-Arrow, 50¾, Lyonshall, 54, and Penrhôs, 55. Returning, at Lyonshall, turn to *l.* [Or at Shobden turn to *r.*, through Byton Cross, 50½, where turn to *l.*, Staunton-bach, 53¼, Titley *Tp.*, 54, and Titley *ch.*, 54½, to Kington, 57¾.]

At Staunton-bach, on *l.*, Staunton Park; on *r.*, on Wapley Hill, an ancient camp. On *r.*, Shobden Court; on *l.*, Titley Court, and a little farther, on *r.*, Eywood Park. Kington, &c., p. 115.

Kington to Hay (12—68½); over Hargest Bridge, 58, by Knoll, 59, and Brilley Mountain, 62½. Returning, 4*m.* out of Hay keep to *l.*

On *l.*, Hargest Court.

Hay to Brecon (15¼—83¾)—p. 116.

BIRMINGHAM TO KNIGHTON.

Birmingham to Bewdley (20¾)—p. 325.

Bewdley to Cleobury Mortimer (8—28¾); keeping to *r.* 3¼ *m.* out of Bewdley, the road is hilly. Returning, just out of Cleobury turn to *r.*

Before Cleobury, on *l.*, Mawley Hall.

Cleobury Mortimer to Ludlow (13—41¾); after Hopton Wafers, 30¾, the road becomes very hilly, passing over part of the Clee Hills, through Hope Baggot, 36, and Caynham, 38¼. [Or 3¾*m.* past Hopton Wafers keep to *r.*, and by Henley, 38, to Ludlow, 40.]

On *r.*, Hopton Court. 2½*m.* before Ludlow, on *l.*, Henley Park. On *l.*, Caynham Court, and on *r.*, Caynham Camp. Ludlow, p. 120.

Ludlow to Walford (10—51¾); about 1¼*m.* out of Ludlow keep to *l.*, and through Bromfield, 44½, and Leintwardine, 50½; rather hilly.

At Bromfield, on *l.*, Oakley Park. 2 or 3*m.* farther, on *l.*, Downton Castle. Before Walford, on *l.*, Brandon Camp.

Walford to Knighton (7¼—59)—p. 122.

WOLVERHAMPTON TO CARMARTHEN.

Wolverhampton to Bridgenorth (13¾); leaving Wolverhampton turn to *l.* from the Shifnal road, and through Compton, 1¾, Wightwick, 3, Trescot. 4½, Shipley, 7¼, over Rudge Heath, through Bradeney, 9½, Wyken, 10½, and Roughton, 11¼, to the suburb of St. James, 13¼, whence cross *R.* Severn into the town; rather hilly road, and not particularly smooth.

At Wyken, a little on *r.*, Davenport *Ho.* Bridgenorth, p. 126.

Bridgenorth to Ludlow (19½—33¼); outside the town keep to *l.*, and by Hubbatts Mill, 15¾ (keep to *l.*), through Down, 17, Westbach, 17½, Lower Faintree, 19¼, Neenton, 20¾, North Cleobury, 22, Burwarton, 23¼, over the Clee Hills to Clee Downton, 27, by the Moor, 28¼, and through Middleton, 31, and Bock Green, 32¼. Returning, beyond Bock Green keep to *l.*

Before Lower Faintree, on *l.*, Faintree Hall; on *r.*, Neenton Hall. On *l.*, Cleobury Hall; on *r.*, Burwarton Hall. At Ludlow, on *r.*, Staunton *Ho.* Ludlow, p. 120.

Ludlow to Wigmore (8—41¼); entering Ludlow by the North end, turn to *l.*, then to *r.*, leaving the town by a narrow archway, and a dangerous steep hill to descend to *R.* Teme, beyond which turn sharp to *r.*, and through Aston, 37½, Elton, 38¼, and Leinthall Starkes, 40.

Out of Ludlow, on *l.*, Ludford *Ho.* and Ludford Park. On *l.*, Elton Hall; a little farther, on *r.*, Marlbrook Hall. At Wigmore, on *l.*, Bury *Ho.*; on *r.*, ruins of Wigmore Castle and Wigmore Hall.

Wigmore to Presteign (8¼—49½); at Wigmore turn first to *l.*, then to *r.*, hilly road through Dicken Dale, 43¼, over Deerford or Dawold Forest, through Lingen, 45¼ (bear first to *r.*, then to *l.*).

1*m.* before Presteign, on *l.*, Stapleton Castle. Presteign, p. 117.

Presteign to New Radnor (7¾—57¼); by Beggar's Bush, 51½, and Kinnerton, 54½. [Or turn to *l*,, and by Knill: about 1¼*m.* longer.]

At Beggar's Bush, 1*m.* on *r.*, Grove Hall; on *l.*, Evenjobb.

New Radnor to Bualt or Builth (14—71¼); there is a long pull up-hill through and for a mile or two beyond Llanfihangel-Nant-Melan, 60 (just beyond keep to *l.*), and then hilly, with run down for 2 or 3*m.* to Llanelwood, 70½, whence cross *R.* Wye to Builth.

Builth to Llangammarch (8¼—79½); through Llanavon, 75¾, mostly up-hill.

Llangammarch to Llandovery (14¼—93¾); through Llwydlo Fach, 84½, and Talgarth Fach, 89½.

Beyond Talgarth, on *r.*, Glan Bran Park. Llandovery, p. 111.

Llandovery to Carmarthen (26¾—120½)—p. 111.

SHREWSBURY TO HAY.

Shrewsbury to Bishop's Castle (21); through Nobold, 2, Longden, 5½, Pulverbatch, 8¼, Stitt, 11½, Bridges, 13, and Norbury, 16; no difficult hills. Returning, a little out of Bishop's Castle turn to *l.*

At 3*m.*, on *l.*, Lythwood Hall. At Stitt, on *r.*, the Stiper Stones Hill extends for 5 or 6*m.* At Norbury, 1*m.* on *r.*, Linley Hall. Bishop's Castle, p. 120.

Bishop's Castle to Clun (5½—26½); a little out of the former turn to *r.*, and through Coldbach, 22, Acton, 23½, and Colesley or Colstey, 24½.

Past Acton, on *l.*, Bury Ditches, an ancient British entrenchment. 2 or 3*m.* farther E., beyond Walcot Park, is another, called Borough Hill.

Clun to Knighton (7—33½), is rather more hilly.

Knighton, p. 117.

Knighton to Presteign (7—40½)—p. 122.

Presteign to Kington (6¼—46¾); a little out of Presteign keep to *r.*, and through Rodhurst, 39¾ (keep to *l.*), Titley *Tp.*, 41 (keep to *r.*), and Titley (*ch.*), 41½. Returning, at Titley *Tp.* keep to *l.*

On *l.*, Titley Court, and on *r.*, Eywood Park. Kington, p. 115.

Kington to Hay (12—58¾)—p. 326.

BRIDGENORTH TO TENBURY.

Bridgenorth to Cleobury Mortimer (13¼); through Oldbury, 1, Glazeley, 3¾, Deuxhill, 4½, Billingsley, 5½, and by New Inn, 9¼; rather hilly in the latter half.

Before Glazeley, on *l.*, Woodlands. At New Inn, on *r.*, Kinlet Hall.

Cleobury Mortimer to Tenbury (8—21¼); through the town turn to *l.*, and through Milsom, 16¾, and Burraston or Boraston, 19¼.

LUDLOW TO SHIFNAL.

Ludlow to Much Wenlock (20); follow the Shrewsbury road for 1½*m.*, then keep to *r.*, under the railway, and up Corve Dale; by Stanton Lacey, 3, Culmington, 5¼, Seifton, 6, and ¾*m.* farther turn short on *r.*, over Seifton Forest, through Diddlebury, or Delbury, 7½, Munslow Aston, 8¼, Munslow, 9½, Broadstone, 11, Shipton, 13½, Brocton, 15, and Burton, 17¼, it is a gentle rise nearly all the way; no hills.

Beyond Ludlow, on *l.*, Oakley Park. At Delbury, on *r.*, Molehouse Lodge. Past Munslow, on *l.*, Millichope Hall. Beyond Shipton, on *l.*, Larden Hall; and Lutwyche Hall on Wenlock Edge. Much Wenlock, p. 126.

Much Wenlock to Broseley (3½—23½); at the Marsh, 21¼, keep to *l.*

Broseley to Madeley Market (3—26½); at the beginning of Broseley turn to *l.*, cross *R.* Severn by the Iron Bridge, and through Coalbrookdale, 24½ (keep to *r.*).

The road traverses a small edition of the Black Country.

Madeley Market to Shifnal (3¾—30¼); 1½*m.* farther keep to *l.*

[Or at The Marsh, 21¼, keep to *r.*, through Barrow, 22¼., 1¼*m.* farther to *l.*, and directly after to *r.*, passing Broseley on *l.*; 2*m.* again cross *R.* Severn, a steep descent to it and steep ascent from it, and through Brockton, 26¾, joining the other road 1¼*m.* past Madeley Market to *Shifnal*, 30½].

At Barrow, on *r.*, Willey Park and Hall. Shifnal, p. 140.

BRIDGENORTH TO SHIFNAL.

Bridgenorth to Shifnal (10¾); cross *R.* Severn, turn to *l.*, and through Stockton, 4½, Norton, 5, Sutton Maddock, 6, and Brockton, 7, hilly road, with bad stony surface: ¼*m.* before Brockton on *l.*. to *Madeley Market* (2—8½).

At Stockton, on *l.*, Apley Park.

CHESTER TO BRECON.

Chester to Wrexham (11¾); cross *R.* Dee, and the road is rather rough to near Pulford, 5½, and then it improves through Rassett or Rossit, 6½, to Gresford Road, 7¾, beyond which is Marfoot Hill to mount, 1½*m.* long, rather loose, and the rest is a capital road.

(*Wrexham:* Commercial; Lion, *B.T.C.*; Wynnstay Arms.)

Before Pulford, on *l.*, Eaton Hall. At Rassett, on *l.*, Trevallyn Hall. At Gresford road, on *l.*, Horseley Hall. 1*m.* before Wrexham, on *l.*, Acton Hall.

Wrexham to Ruabon (5½—17¼); taking the right hand road, there is a steep hill out of Wrexham, and then the road is apt to be loose and heavy.

(*Ruabon:* Foxes; Wynnstay Arms, *B.T.C.*)

3*m.* beyond Wrexham, on *l.*, Erthig; on *r.*, Pentre-bychan. At Ruabon, on *l.*, Wynnstay Park.

Ruabon to Chirk (4¾—22); a mile out of Ruabon keep to *l.*, the road is pretty good over New Bridge, 19¼ (*R.* Dee), and through Whitehursts *Tp.*, 20, where join the Holyhead road.

Fine scenery. ¼*m.* beyond Ruabon, on *r.*, Plâs Madoc. At Chirk, on *l.*, Penrhos and Brynkinalt; on *r.*, Chirk Park and Castle.

Chirk to Oswestry (5¼—27¼)—p. 127; reversed

Oswestry to Llanymynech (5¾—33) through Llyngclys, 30¾.

Beyond Oswestry, on *r.*, Broom Hall; on *l.*, Belle Vue; 1½*m.* beyond, on *l.*, Sweeney Hall.

Llanymynech to Welshpool (10—43); 1¼*m.* farther cross *R.* Vyrnwy and by Four Crosses, 35½, Waerdy Bridge, 36½ (keeping to *l.* ¾*m.* farther), New Quay, 40. [Or ¾*m.* past Waerdy Bridge keep to *r.*, and through Guilsfield, where keep to *l.* to Welshpool, 44.]

Past Four Crosses, on *r.*, Rhysnant Hall. Welshpool, p. 121.

Welshpool to Newtown (14—57); 1¾*m.* farther keep to *l.*, a little beyond to *r.*, to near Berriew, 48, just before which keep to *l.*, by Garth Mill *Tg.*, 49½, and Glan Hafren, 51½.

At Garth Mill *Tg.*, on *l.*, Glan Severn; on *r.*, Vaynor Park and Garth Mill Hall. At Glan Harfren, on *r.*, Pennant; and 2*m.* farther, on *r.*, Aberbechan Hall. Newtown, p. 122.

Newtown to Llanidloes (13—70); the road follows the right bank of the *R.* Severn, through Penystrywad, 60, and Llandinam, 63¼.

(*Llanidloes:* Lion; Trewythan Arms, *B.T.C.*)

On *r.*, Penystrywad Hall; 1½*m.* farther, on *r.*, Maes Mawr Hall. 3*m.* beyond Llandinam, on *l.*, Berthddw.

Llanidloes to Rhayader (13—83); turn to *l.* (south eastward) out of Llanidloes, and it is a hilly road through St. Harmon, 79. [Or to Llangurig, 74, whence turning sharp to *l.* down the Wye valley to Rhayader, 83.]

Rhayader, p. 115.

Rhayader to Builth or Bualt (14—97); down the left bank of *R.* Wye, by Doldowlod, 87, and over Ithon Bridge, 92. Returning, from Builth keep to *l.*

Before Builth, on *l.*, Wellfield and Llanelwith Hall.

[Or just beyond *Newtown* on *l.*, chiefly uphill by Clay Hill, 58¾, to Camnant Bridge, 62, and downhill through Llanbadarn-fynydd, 65¼, Llanbister, 68¾, Llanddewi-ystrad-enny, 71¼, Llanbadarn-Vawr, 75, Llandinrod Wells, 79, to *Builth*, 86.]

At Llandinrod Wells are some mineral springs of considerable local repute.

Builth to Brecon (16¼—113¼); through Llandewr-cwm, 98, Llangynog, 100, Capel Dryffyn Honddu, or Upper Chapel, 104½, whence all downhill by Lower Chapel, 108¼, and Llandefailog, 110½. [Or at Builth turn to *l.*, keeping down the Wye valley through Capel-allt-Mawr, Erwood,

Llyswen, 109, then keep to *r.* to Bronllys, 111½, whence through Vellinvach, 114½, to Brecon, 118¾.]

CHESTER TO HAVERFORDWEST.

Chester to Ruabon (17¼)—pp. 328-9.

Ruabon to Llangollen (6—23¼); a short distance out of Ruabon there is a very steep hill where the road crosses the railway, after which it is almost all downhill to Llangollen; capital road, except at one place where it passes some ironworks, and there are two or three tram lines across the steepest part of the hill.

Llangollen to Corwen (10¼—33½)—p. 127.

Corwen to Bala (13—46½); just beyond Corwen keep to *l.* along the left bank of *R.* Dee, through Cynwyd, 36¼, Llandrillo, 38½ (keep to *r.*), to the foot of the Bala Lake or Llyn Tegid just before Bala, when turn to *r.* across *R.* Dee: undulating road. [Or beyond Corwen keep to *r.*, and cross *R.* Dee and *R.* Alwen to Druid Inn, 36½, then turn to *l.* and it is chiefly uphill by Four Crosses and up Nant-ffranan for 5*m.*, then down through Llanfor, 43½, to Bala, 44½.]

(*Bala* : White Lion Royal, *B.T.C.*)

2*m.* past Llandrillo, on *r.*, Crogen. 2*m.* farther, on *r.*, Pale and Y-Fron-heilog. 2*m.* before Bala, on *r.*, Bodweni. At the foot of Bala Lake, on *l.*, Plâs Rhiwaedog and Castle Cronw. Beyond Llanfor, on *r.*, Rhiwlas.

Bala to Dolgelly (18—64½); the road skirts the shore of Bala Lake, through Llanycil, 47½, to within a mile of Llanwchllyn, 51½; then it ascends for 3*m.*, and the rest is a gradual fall through Drwsynant, 55½, and down the Wnion Valley.

Beautiful scenery. At the head of Bala Lake, on *l.*, Glan-y-Llyn; on *r.*, a little farther, Caer Gai. At Llanwchllyn, on a hill on *r.*, ruins of Castle Carnduchan. On *l.*, Aran Mowddwy Mountain. Dolgelly, p. 121.

Dolgelly to Machynlleth (14½—79); in Dolgelly turn to *l.*, and by Cross Foxes, 67½ (keep to *r.*), Minffordd Inn, 71 (keep to *l.*), Pontabercorys, 74, and Esgair-geiliog, 75; on the rise for 5*m.*, then downhill to Minffordd Inn, and after a mile or two of uphill the rest is on the fall. For half the distance the road skirts the base of Cader Idris Mountain. Turn to *l.* and cross *R.* Dyfi just before Machynlleth.

Machynlleth, p. 122.

Machynlleth to Aberystwith (18¾—97¾); follow the Dyfi Valley down to Garreg, 85½, Eglwys-fach, 86½, then the road becomes more hilly through Trerddol, 88½, and Talybont, 90½.

Before Eglwys-fach, on *l.*, Glan-Dyfi Castle; on *r.*, Tomen-las. Aberystwith, p. 115.

Aberystwith to Llanrhystyd (9½—107¼); cross the harbour, through Piccadilly, 99¾ (keep to *r.* twice), Rhyd-y-Felin, 100¼, by Llanrhystyd Road Station, 101, and after crossing *R.* Ystwyth keep to *r*: for the last 3 or 4*m.* the road is within a mile of the sea shore.

At Rhyd-y-Felin, on *r.*, Tan-y-Castell; and ½*m.* farther, Bryn-yr-eithin.

Llanrhystyd to Aberaeron (7½—114¾); the road runs close to the sea through Llannon, 109¾, Aber Arth, 112, and Llanddewi Aberarth. 112¾.

(*Aberaeron:* Black Lion.)
At Aberaeron, on *r.*, Castle Cadwgan.

Aberaeron to Cardigan (22½—137¼); keep to *r.* and through Henfynyw, 116, Llanarth, 118¾, by New Inn, 126, through Blaenporth, 131¼, Tramam, 133¼, and Warren, 135¼.
At Llanarth, on *l.*, Noyadd. Cardigan, p. 112.

Cardigan to Eglwyswrw (6—143¼), through Llantwyd, 140¾.

Eglwyswrw to Haverfordwest (20—163¼); just beyond keep to *l.*, and through Pontynon, 144¾, Hendra Gate, 145¼, Pont Llanbiran, 146¾, Tavarn y Bwlch, 148¾; then cross the Mynydd Breseley, by New Inn, 152, to Castle Hendre or Henry's Moat, 153¼, and through Brogull, 158¼, and Prendergast, 162. Returning, keep to *r.* at Prendergast.
Haverfordwest, p. 93.

ABERYSTWITH TO CARMARTHEN.

Aberystwith to Llanrhystyd (9½)—p. 330.

Llanrhystyd to Lampeter (15½—25); turn to *l.* through Pont Hafod Peris, 11, Dyffryn Arth, 13½, Talsarn, 17¾, by King's Head, 18¾, and Foss Gwy, 22½. Returning, just out of Lampeter keep to *l.*, and at King's Head to *r.*

[Or at *Aberaeron*, 17, on *l.* up the Aeron Valley, through Llanerchaeron and Llanfihangel-ystrad to beyond King's Head; about 12*m.* longer.]
At Llanerchaeron, on *l.*, Lan Ayron. Lampeter, p. 112.

Lampeter to Carmarthen (23—48); cross *R.* Teifi, then turn to *r.* and through Pencarreg, 28½, Llan y Byther, 30¼, Pont-ceiliog, 32¼, Gwar-allt, 34¼ (keep to *l.*), New Inn, 35½, Gwyrgryg, 36½, Troed-y-rhiew, 39½, Rhyd-y-caean, 44¼, and Llangwili, 46½: very hilly road, passing over a range of mountains.
At Pencarreg, on *r.*, Llanvaughan. 2*m.* before Carmarthen, on *r.*, Cwmgwili. Carmarthen, p. 93.

ABERYSTWITH TO SWANSEA.

Aberystwith to Lampeter (25)—above.

Lampeter to Llansawyl (9—34); cross Lampeter Mountain, and it is uphill for 3 or 4*m.*, and rest downhill.
(*Llansawyl:* Black Lion.)

Llansawyl to Llandilo (10—44), through Talley, 37. Returning, a little out of Landilo keep to *l.*
2*m.* past Talley, on *r.*, Taliaris. Llandilo, p. 111.

Llandilo to Pontardulais (14—58); through Llan-dybie, 49, by Cross Inn, 51, and Llanedy, 56½. Returning, a little out of Pontardulais keep to *r.*
At Llan-dybie, on *l.*, Glyn-hir.

Pontardulais to Swansea (8½—66½). Returning, 2*m.* out of Swansea keep to *r.*

PEMBROKE TO FISHGUARD.

Pembroke to Burton (2¾); good road with one stiff hill to descend to Pembroke Dock, 2, whence cross by ferry to Burton (fare 2d., bicycle 2d.)

Burton to Haverfordwest (7¼—10); by Houghton, 3¼, Clareston, 6½, through Freystrope, 7¾, and over Mawdlin's Bridge, 9¼. Returning, after Mawdlin's Bridge keep to *l.*

[Or cross to New Milford or Neyland, a little to *l.* of Burton, and thence almost level to Hayston, out of which is a steep ascent, and down again to *Johnston*, 8, rather rough road: thence to *Haverfordwest*, 4—12 (p. 99). Returning, at Johnston turn to *l.* past the railway.]

At Houghton, on *r.*, Williamston and Benton Castle. At Freystrop, on *r.*, Boulston.

Haverfordwest to Fishguard (14¼—24¼); keeping to *l.* at Prendergast, 10½, it is a good undulating road by Mount Pleasant, 12, to Windy Hill, 12½, which will have to be walked, and then rather hilly but nothing difficult, over Trefgarn Bridge, 14¾, to Ford Chapel, 16½; after leaving Ford, the steep ascent of Wolf's Castle Hill is reached, then a slight ascent over a good hard road brings to Letterston, 19¼, and the rest is undulating over New Bridge, 20¾, and by Ffynnonstown, 23¼: good surface.

At Ford, on *l.*, an ancient camp. 2*m.* past New Bridge, on *r.*, Llanstinan Castle. Beyond Wolf's Castle, on *r.*, Scalyham. On *l.*, Trefgarn Hall. Fishguard, p. 112.

SHREWSBURY TO ABERYSTWITH.

Shrewsbury to Westbury (8¾); cross *R.* Severn and first to *l.* then to *r.*; through Cruckton, 3¾, Nox, 4¾, Yockleton or Lockerton, 6, and Stoney Stretton, 7.

Beyond Shrewsbury, on *r.*, Cadogan Place. On *l.*, Cruckton Hall. At Nox, on *l.*, Newnham.

Westbury to Montgomery (12¼—21); keep to *l.* and through Worthen, 12, Brockton, 13, Wilmington Marton, 15½ (keep to *l.*), and Chirbury, 18, is a bad road.

Beyond Westbury, on *r.*, Whitton Hall. A little farther, on *r.*, Caurse Castle, a hill fort.

[Or from *Shrewsbury* on *l.*, through Hanwood, 4, Pontesford, 6½, Pontesbury, 7½, and Minsterley, 9¼, to Brockton, 13½.]

On *r.*, Minsterley Park. At Chirbury, on *r.*, Walcot; on *l.*, Chirbury Hall and Marrington Hall. Before Montgomery, on *l.*, Lymore Park. Montgomery, p. 120.

Montgomery to Newtown (9—30)—p. 122.

Newtown to Llanidloes (13—43)—p. 329.

Llanidloes to Llangurig (4—47); chiefly uphill for 3*m.*, and then down to Llangurig.

Llangurig to Aberystwith (17½—64½)—p. 115.

SHREWSBURY TO WELSHPOOL.

Shrewsbury to Welshpool (18¾); cross *R.* Severn, keep to *r.*, and at Shelton, 1¾, to *l.*, by Pavement Gate, 4½, Cross Gate, 5¾, Cardeston, 6½, Trevenant, 12¼, and Buttington (*ch.*), 16¾.

[Or at 10½*m.* turn to *r.* and through Woolaston to Welshpool, 19¼.
Or to *Westbury*, 8¾ (above); thence on *r.* over the hills to *Welshpool*, 16¾.]

3*m.* out of Shrewsbury, on *l.*, Onslow Hall and Dinthill. On *r.*, at 2*m.*, Oxon

Hall; at 3m., Bicton Hall; at 4m., Preston Hall. Before Cardeston, on *l.*, Whistone Priory. On *l.*, Cardeston Park; a little farther, on *r.*, Rowton Castle. Welshpool, p. 121.

SHREWSBURY TO MAENTWROG.

Shrewsbury to Nesscliff (8½)—p. 126.

Nesscliff to Llanrhaiadr (18¾—27¼); at Wolf's Head, 10, keep to *l.* through Knockin, 12¼, a little farther again to *l.*, past Llyneclys station, 15¼, whence is chiefly downhill to Llan-y-blodwell, 18¼, and then up the Tanat valley, through Llangedwyn, 22¼, about 3m. beyond which keep to *r.*

Before Knockin, on *l.*, Knockin Hall; 2m. beyond, on *r.*, Moreton Hall. Before the village, on *l.*, Blodwell Hall; on *r.*, Llangedwin Hall and Plâs-nchaf. Llanrhaiadr, also called Llanrhaiadr-yn-Mochnant.

Llanrhaiadr to Bala (15—42¼); follow the valley for 2 or 3m. past Llangynnog, 32¼, when the road crosses the Berwyn Mountains, uphill for 3m., then similar long downhill towards Bala, about 4m. before which town join the Corwen road. [Or 1m. before Llanrhaiadr keep to *l.*, instead of going through it, both roads joining 2m. beyond that village.]

Bala, p. 330.

Bala to Maentwrog (20—62¼); for first half the road follows a small valley and is more or less on a moderate rise, then it crosses the mountains for about 5m., and the rest is easy downhill through Festiniog, 59¾.

SHREWSBURY TO MOLD AND FLINT.

Shrewsbury to Armour Hill (5¾)—p. 321.

Armour Hill to Ellesmere (10½—16¼); through Middle, 8, Burlton, 9½, and Cockshut, 12¼. [Or to *Wem*, 10½ (p. 321), thence turn to *l.* and by Wolverley, 13¼, and Welch Hampton, 18½, to *Ellesmere*, 21¼. Returning, 1m. out of Ellesmere turn to *l.*]

(*Ellesmere*: Bridgewater Arms, *B.T.C.*)

On *l.*, Middle Castle. Beyond Burlton, on *l.*, Pelton Hall; 1m. farther, on *r.*, Stanwardine Hall. At Wolverley, on *l.*, Loppington *Ho.* Before Ellesmere, on *r.*, Oteley Park. At Ellesmere, ruins of the castle.

Ellesmere to Wrexham (12¼—28½); through Overton, 21¼ (keep to *l.*), Eyton, 24¼, and Marchwiel, 26¼. Returning, at Marchwiel keep to *r.*

Beyond Overton, on *r.*, Bryn-y-Pees and Maegwaylod; on *l.*, Overton Brow. On *r.*, Eyton Hall, and on *l.*, Rose Hill. On *l.*, Marchwiel Hall and Erthig; on *r.*, Cefn Hall. Wrexham, p. 328.

Wrexham to Caergwrle (5¼—33¾) by the left hand road: rough and shaky, and rather hilly.

3m. past Wrexham, on *r.*, Gwersyllt Hall. At Caergwrle, the ruins of the castle.

Caergwrle to Mold (6¼—40½), through Hope, 34½.

2m. beyond Hope, on *l.*, Plâs Teg. Mold, p. 148.

Mold to Northop (3¼—43¾).

Northop to Flint (3—46¾)—p. 150.

CHESTER TO BALA (by Ruthin).

Chester to Mold (12½)—p. 148.

Mold to Ruthin (8¼—20¾); through Llanferras, 15½, and Llanbeder, 19¼ is a hilly road.

2*m.* beyond Mold, on *l.*, Colomendy Hall. On *l.* Llanbeder Hall. Ruthin, p. 149.

Ruthin to Gwyddelwern (9—29¾); turn to *l.* past the railway, and the road is more or less on the rise, running up the Clwyd valley.

Gwyddelwern to Bala (12¼—42); chiefly downhill for 3*m.*, then join the road from Corwen on *l.*, and by the Druid Inn, 34, to Bala as at p. 330.

CHESTER TO ABERYSTWITH (by Dinas Mawddwy).

Chester to Bala (46½)—p. 330. [Or to *Bala* (42)—above.]

Bala to Dinas Mawddwy (17—63½); the road skirts the shore of Bala Lake, through Llanycil, 47½, to within a mile of Llanwchllyn, 51½; there turn to *l.* by the *ch.*, and gradually ascend a narrow valley—the Cwm Cynllwyd—for about 5*m.*, and after crossing the hills the road runs down the valley of the Afon Dyfi, by Llan-y-Mowddy, 59½, and Aber-Cowarch, 62¾: wild mountain district after leaving Bala Lake.

At the head of Bala Lake, on *l.*, Glan-y-Llyn, and a little farther, on *r.*, Caer Gai. At Llanwchllyn, on a hill on *r.*, ruins of Castle Carnduchan.

(*Dinas Mawddwy:* Red Lion, *B.T.C.*)

Dinas Mawddwy to Machynlleth (11½—75)—p. 122.

Machynlleth to Aberystwith (18¾—93¾)—p. 330.

BARMOUTH TO BANGOR.

Barmouth to Harlech (10½); very bad and rough road through Llanaber, 1¼, Egryn Abbey, 3, Llandwywe, 4¾, Llanenddwyn, 5¼, Llanbedr, 7½, and Llanfair, 9½, running close to the coast most of the way.

(*Harlech:* Castle, *B.T.C.*)

Llanaber *ch.* is supposed to have been built in the 13th century. At Llanenddwyn, on *r.*, Cors-y-Gedol, and near it Carneddau Hengwm, a large Druidic remain; 2*m.* beyond, on the shores of Llyn Irddyn, are remains of an old British town, and of an old fort. Entering Llanbedr, on *r.*, the Meini Hirion cromlech. At Harlech, ruins of castle. Many British remains in the neighbourhood.

Harlech to Maentwrog (10—20½); pleasant road through Llanfihangel-y-traethau, 12½.

A mile before Maentwrog, a little on *r.*, the waterfalls Rhaiadr-du and Raven Fall.

Maentwrog to Carnarvon (21—41½)—p. 123.

Carnarvon to Menai Bridge (8—49½); very good road along the shores of Menai Straits, and through Llanfair, 44½: pretty ride.

On *l.*, Plâs Llanfair; 2*m.* farther, on *l.*, Vaynol Park and the Britannia Tubular Bridge. Menai Bridge, p. 128.

Menai Bridge to Bangor (2½—52)—p. 128: reversed.

WELLINGTON (Salop) TO WHITCHURCH.

Wellington (Salop) to Hodnet (11¾); by Sleap, 3½, Crudgington, 4, Waters Upton, 4½ (keep to *l.* and then to *r.*), Cold Hatton, 6½, and over Hodnet Heath, 10¼. Returning, out of Hodnet keep to *l.*

Beyond Wellington, on *r.*, Apley Castle. 2½*m.* beyond Cold Hatton, on *r.*, Peplow Hall. At Hodnet, 2*m.* on *l.*, Bury Walls, a Roman station.

Hodnet to Whitchurch (9¾—21½); keep to *l.*, and through Marchamley, 13, Fawles or Fauls Green, 15, Darliston, 15½, Sandford, 16½, and Heath Lane, 19. Returning, 1*m.* out of Whitchurch and again beyond Heath Lane keep to *l.*

Beyond Marchamley, on *l.*, Hawkstone Park; on *r.*, Sandford Hall. Whitchurch, p. 148.

BIRMINGHAM TO SHEFFIELD.

Birmingham to Lichfield (16)—p. 308.

Lichfield to King's Bromley (5½—21½); keep to *r.* 1¾*m.* out of Lichfield, and again 1¼*m.* farther on.

2½*m.* past Lichfield, on *r.*, Elmhurst, and a little farther, on *l.*, Haunch Hall. On *l.*, Bromley Hall.

King's Bromley to Sudbury (10½—32); keep to *l.* and over Yoxall Bridge, 22½ (*R.* Trent), through Yoxall, 23½, Needwood Forest, Christchurch in Needwood, 26½, Draycott, 30, and cross *R.* Dove just before Sudbury.

At Christchurch, on *r.*, Byrkley Lodge. 1½*m.* before Draycott, on *l.*, Holly Bush Hall. On *l.*, Sudbury Hall.

Sudbury to Ashbourne (8—40); beyond Sudbury keep to *r.*, and through Cubley, 35½, and Clifton, 39 (keep to *r.*)

[Or from *Lichfield* to *Uttoxeter*, (16¾—33¾), p. 164; thence through Rocester and Ellaston to *Ashbourne*, 10¼—44.]

Beyond Sudbury, on *r.*, Sudbury Park. Ashbourne, p. 169. Beyond Rocester, on *l.*, Burrow Hill. At Ellaston, on *r.*, Colwich Abbey.

Ashbourne to Newhaven Inn (9—49)—p. 170.

Newhaven Inn to Bakewell (5¾—54¾); keep to *r.* and through Conksbury, 53½.

Bakewell, p. 167.

Bakewell to Grindleford Bridge (6½—61¼)—p. 181.

Grindleford Bridge to Sheffield, *M.P.* (10—71¼); turn to *r.* ove, the bridge (*R.* Derwent), and there is a long ascent to Fox House Inn, 65¾ on the High Moors; cross them to Ringinglow *Tp.*, 66¾, and through Bents Green, 68, and Little Sheffield, 70, is downhill, all rideable except the last bit into Sheffield.

[Or from *Birmingham* to *Derby*, 40,—p. 308; thence to *Sheffield*, 36¼—76¼,—p. 178].

DERBY TO SHREWSBURY.

Derby to Sudbury (13¼); through Mickleover, 3, Etwall, 5¾, Hilton, 7¼, Hatton Moor, 10, Foston, 11¼, and Aston, 12¾.

On *l.*, Etwall Hall. On *l.*, Foston Hall. Sudbury, p. 165.

Sudbury to Uttoxeter (5½—18¾); beyond Sudbury keep to *l.*, and through Doveridge, 16¾.

Uttoxeter to Stafford (13½—32¼); through Blounts Green, 19¾, by Burnthurst Mill, 22¼, through Amerton, 26¼, and Weston, 27½, where cross *R.* Trent.

Beyond Blounts Green, on *l.*, Loxley Park. Beyond Burnthurst Mill, on *r.*, Chartley Park, Chartley Castle ruins, and Chartley Hall. Beyond Weston, on *l.*, Ingestrie Park and Hall. Stafford, p. 145.

Stafford to Newport (13—45¼): through Billington, 35¼, Haughton, 36¾, Gnosall, 39½, Coton, 40¾, and by Coles Mill, 43.

Newport, p. 148.

Newport to Watling Street (8½—53¾); through Lilleshall, 47¾, Donnington, 49½, Trench Lane, 50¾, and Hadley, 51¾. At Watling Street, on *r.* to *Wellington* (¾—54½).

Beyond Newport, on *l.*, Aston Hall, and the ruins of Lilleshall Abbey. A little farther, on *r.*, Longford Hall. Watling Street, &c., p. 140.

Watling Street to Shrewsbury (11½—65¼) p. 140.

[Or from *Newport*, turning to *r.* through the town, and then to *l.*, through Edgmond, 46¾, Sherry Hill, 50¾, Crudgington, 53¼, Cotwall, 55¼, High Ercall, 55¾, Ercall Mill, 56¼, Rodenhurst, 57¼, whence there is a stiff hill to cross over to Haughmond Abbey, 59¾, and level to *Shrewsbury*, 62¾.]

Before Sherry Hill, on *r.*, Stedford Castle. On *r.*, Ercall Castle. On *l.*, the ruins of Haughmond Abbey (founded 1100); and beyond it, on *R.* Severn, Uffington Castle; on *r.*, Sundorn Park and Castle.

DERBY TO WREXHAM.

Derby to Uttoxeter (18¾)—pp. 335-6.

Uttoxeter to Stone (13¾—32½); through Bramshall, 20¾, Field, 23, Coton, 26½, Milwich, 27, and Stoke, 31¾. Returning, at Stoke turn to *r.*

At Bramshall, on *l.*, Loxley Park. Before Coton, on *r.*, Birchwood Park, and on *l.*, Fradswell Hall. Beyond Milwich, on *r.*, Hilderston Hall. At Stone are the remains of a nunnery.

Stone to Woore (13½—46); entering Stone turn to *l*, and directly after to *r.*, following the Trentham road to Darlaston, 34, then keep to *l.*, and by Hatton, 38, Maer, 41½, and Irelands Cross, 45½, (where on returning keep to *l.*, and 3*m.* farther to *r.*)

On *l.*, Darlaston Hall, and 2*m.* farther, on *l.*, Swinnerton Hall.

Woore to Audlem (4½—50½); turn to *l.*, and through Buerton, 48¾.

On *r.*, Buerton Hall. (*Audlem:* Crown.)

Audlem to Whitchurch (8¾—59¼); over Cheeley Bridge, 53½, and through Burleydam, 54¼.

Beyond Burleydam, on *r.*, Combermere Abbey. Whitchurch, p. 148.

Whitchurch to Bangor (11—70¼); through Little Green, 63¼, and by Eglwys Cross, 64¼.

At Little Green, 1*m.* on *l.*, Hanmer Hall. 2*m.* beyond Whitchurch, on *r.*, Iscoed Park. 2*m.* before Bangor, on *r.*, Emral Hall.

Bangor to Wrexham ($4\frac{3}{4}$—75); cross *R.* Dee, then turn to *r.*, and through Marchwiel, $72\frac{3}{4}$, where on returning keep to *l.*
Wrexham, p. 328.

NEWPORT (Salop) TO NANTWICH.

Newport (Salop) to Hinstock ($5\frac{3}{4}$)—p. 148.

Hinstock to Market Drayton ($5\frac{1}{4}$—11); just out of Hinstock keep to *r.*
(*Market Drayton:* Corbet Arms, *B.T.C.*)

Market Drayton to Audlem ($6\frac{1}{4}$—$17\frac{1}{4}$); easy undulating road, with good surface through Adderley, $15\frac{1}{4}$. Returning, out of Audlem keep to *l.*
On *l.*, Adderley Hall. (*Audlem:* Crown.)

Audlem to Nantwich (7—$24\frac{1}{4}$); through Hankelow, $18\frac{3}{4}$, Hatherton, $20\frac{1}{4}$, Batherton, $21\frac{1}{4}$, and Stapeley, $22\frac{3}{4}$, is an easy road, with few hills, and a good surface; cobble pavement through Nantwich. Returning, 1*m.* out of Nantwich, and again at $2\frac{1}{4}$*m.*, keep to *r.*
2*m.* out of Audlem, on *r.*, Yewtree *Ho.*; and on *l.*, Hankelow Hall. Nantwich p. 146.

DERBY TO CHESTER.

Derby to Uttoxeter ($18\frac{3}{4}$)—pp. 335-6.

Uttoxeter to Stoke-upon-Trent ($17\frac{1}{4}$—36)—p. 164.

Stoke-upon-Trent to Newcastle-under-Lyme ($1\frac{1}{4}$—$37\frac{1}{4}$).
Newcastle-under-Lyme, p. 152.

Newcastle-under-Lyme to Gorsty Hill ($8\frac{1}{4}$—$45\frac{1}{2}$); turn to *r.* on the Knutsford road, to Dimsdale *Tp.*, 38, then turn to *l.*, and through Chesterton, 39, and Audley, $41\frac{1}{2}$. [Or at Newcastle, keep to *l.*, across the London road and out of the town to *r.*, then through Keel, $39\frac{1}{4}$, Little Madeley, 41 (keep to *r.*), and Betley, $44\frac{1}{4}$, to Gorsty Hill, $45\frac{3}{4}$.]
At Chesterton, on *r.*, Bradwell Hall; on *l.*, Apedale Hall. On *l.*, Keel Hall. On *l.*, Madeley Manor *Ho.*, and on *r.*, Oak Hill and Keighley Castle. On *r.*, Betley Hall, and on *l.*, Betley Court.

Gorsty Hill to Nantwich (6—$51\frac{1}{2}$), by Hough, $47\frac{3}{4}$.
[Or at Little Madeley on *l.*, through Great Madeley, $42\frac{1}{4}$, to *Woore*, $45\frac{1}{2}$, whence to *Nantwich*, 9—$54\frac{1}{2}$, p. 146.] Cobble pavement through Nantwich.
On *l.*, Hough *Ho.* 2*m.* on *r.*, Crewe Hall.

Nantwich to Chester ($19\frac{1}{4}$—$70\frac{3}{4}$)—p. 146.

MANSFIELD TO SHREWSBURY.

Mansfield to Alfreton (9); through Sutton-in-Ashfield, $3\frac{1}{4}$, where, on returning, keep to *l.*
About half-way, on *l.*, Brook Hill Hall; 2*m.* farther, on *l.*, Carnfield Hall.

Alfreton to Wirksworth, *T.H.* ($9\frac{3}{4}$—$18\frac{3}{4}$); through Alfreton, turn to *r.* from the Derby road, and by Peacock Inn, 11, through Wingfield, 12, Crich, 14 (turn to *l.*), over Hottstandel Bridge, $15\frac{1}{2}$ (cross *R.* Derwent), and through Wigwell, $17\frac{1}{2}$: the last 3*m.* hilly.
On *l.*, Wingfield Manor. At Hottstandel Bridge, on *l.*, Alderwasley Hall; on *l.*, Wigwell Grange. Wirksworth, p. 170.

Wirksworth to Ashbourne (9—27¾); after Carsington, 21, the road is hilly through Kniveton, 24¾. Returning, beyond Carsington keep to *r.*

At Carsington, on *l.*, Hapton Hall. Ashbourne, p. 169.

Ashbourne to Cheadle (13—40¾); over Hanging Bridge, 29½ (cross *R.* Dove and keep to *r.*), by Red Lion, 32½ (keep to *l.*), The Blazing Star, 36¼, and Oakmoor or Oakamore, 37½; hilly road. [Or after Hanging Bridge turn to *l.* and through Ellaston, 32½ (keep to *l.*), Dove Street, 33 (¾*m.* further keep to *r.*), Quickshill, 34¾, and Alton, 36¾, and over Alton Common to Cheadle, 40¾.]

Beyond Hanging Bridge, on *r.*, Okeover Hall. At The Blazing Star, on *r.*, Cotton Hall. Before Ellaston, on *l.*, Colwich Abbey. 1*m.* on *r.*, Alton Abbey and Alton Towers. Cheadle, p. 164.

Cheadle to Stone (10¼—51); through Fosbrook, 43¾, over Blythe Bridge or Marsh, 44¼ (keep to *l.*), by Rough Chase, 47, and Hobber Gate, 48¾. Returning, about 1*m.* past Hobber Gate keep to *r.*, and before Fosbrook to *l.*

At Fosbrook, 1*m.* on *r.*, Caverswall Castle. Stone, p. 151.

Stone to Eccleshall (5½—56½); cross canal and *R.* Trent, and through Walton, 51½, and over Norton Bridge, 54¼.

Eccleshall, p. 146.

Eccleshall to Newport (8¾—65¼); in Eccleshall turn to *l.* and through Woolton, 57¾, High Offley, 60, Littleworth, 60½, Sutton, 63, and Forton, 64.

Beyond Littleworth, on *r.*, Loynton Hall. Newport, p. 148.

Newport to Shrewsbury (20—85¼)—p. 336.

ASHBOURNE TO WREXHAM.

Ashbourne to Cheadle (13)—above.

Cheadle to Stoke-upon-Trent (10¾—23¾); through Fosbrook, 16, Blythe Bridge or Marsh, 16½ (a little farther keep to *r.*), Meere (or Mear), *Tp.*, 19, Longton, 20, Lane, 20½, Fenton or Lane Delph, 21½—p. 164.

Stoke-upon-Trent to Newcastle-under-Lyme (1¼—25).

Newcastle-under-Lyme to Woore (8¼—33¼); keep to *l.* across the London road, and out of the town keep to *r.*; then through Keel, 27, Little Madeley, 28¾ (keep to *l.*), Great Madeley, 30.

On *l.*, Keel Hall; on *r.*, Madeley Manor *Ho.*

Woore to Wrexham (29—62¼)—pp. 336-7.

SHREWSBURY TO BUXTON.

Shrewsbury to Shawbury (7); follow the Whitchurch road for 3*m.* near to Battlefield, then turn to *r*; almost level, but rather rough road.

2*m.* out of Shrewsbury, on *r.*, Sundorn Castle.

Shawbury to Hodnet (6—13); through Edgebolton, 8, and over Stanton Heath is undulating and not a good road.

On *l.*, Hodnet Hall.

Hodnet to Market Drayton (6—19); through Tern Hill, 16, and Little Drayton, 18, is almost level, but rough road.

Beyond Tern Hill, on *r.*, Buntingsdale Hall. Market Drayton, p. 337.

Market Drayton to Newcastle-under-Lyme (14¼—33¼); keeping to *r.* 2*m.* out of Market Drayton, and then by Loggerheads, 23, again 3*m.* farther keep to *l.*, and by Baldwin Gate, 27¼, through Whitmore, 29, and Millstone Green, 31, the road is undulating but mostly uphill: capital surface till nearing Newcastle. [Or 2*m.* out of Market Drayton on *l.* to Woore, 26, whence to Newcastle, 34¼, p. 338, reversed.]

2*m.* out of Market Drayton, 1*m.* on *r.*, Hales Place; on *l.*, Whitmore Hall Newcastle-under-Lyme, p. 152.

Newcastle-under-Lyme to Leek (11¼—44½); through Woolstanton, 34½, Burslem, 35¼, Norton, 37¼, and Endon, 40¼.

Burslem, p. 164. Leek, p. 169.

Leek to Buxton (12¼—56¾); through Upper Hulme, 48, Flask, 52¼, and Brand Side, 54.

Buxton, p. 167.

NANTWICH (Chesh.) TO BUXTON.

Nantwich to Church Lawton (11¾); follow the Newcastle road for 2¼*m.*, then turn to *l.* and by Crewe Park, 6¼, Butterton Lane, 7¼, Oakhanger Mere, 8¼, Alsager Heath, 9¼, and the Wilbraham Arms, 10¾.

Before Alsager Heath, on *l.*, Oakhauger Hall.

Church Lawton to Congleton (6—17¾)—p. 153.

Congleton to Smithy Green, cross roads (4¾—22½); through Bug Lawton, 20½.

Beyond Bug Lawton, on *r.*, Bug Lawton Hall; on *l.*, 1*m.*, Eaton Hall and North Rode Hall.

Smithy Green to Buxton (11¼—33¾); by Moss House, 30¾, where on returning keep to *l.*

MANCHESTER TO OSWESTRY.

Manchester to Wilmslow, *Ch.* (11¾)—p. 165, reversed.

Wilmslow to Chelford (5—16¾); by Street-Lane Ends, 13¾, and Wasford, 15.

At Wasford, on *l.*, Alderley Park.

Chelford to Holmes Chapel or Church Hulme (6—22¾); through Old Withington, 18½, and Twemlow, 21¼: Holmes Chapel is paved.

Beyond Chelford, on *r.*, Astle Hall; on *l.*, Withington Hall. At Twemlow, on *l.*, Twemlow Hall, and farther, Kermincham Hall and Lodge. Before Holmes Chapel, on *r.*, The Hermitage.

Holmes Chapel to Sandbach (4¾—27½); good smooth and level road to Brereton Green, 24¾, (whence turn to *r.*)

On *l.*, Brereton Hall. Sandbach, p. 153.

Sandbach to Nantwich (10¼—37¾); through Wheelock, 28¾, by Winterley Pool, 30, through Haslington, 31, Crewe Green, 32, Crewe Station, 33¼, Wistaston, 35½, and Willaston, 36¼. Cobble pavement through Nantwich.

Beyond Sandbach, on *r.*, Abbey *Ho.* Near Winterley Pool, on *l.*, WhiteHall. At Haslington, on *l.*, Oakhanger Hall; 1*m.* on *r.*, Clayhanger Hall. On *l.*, Crewe Hall. At Crewe Station, on *r.*, is the town of Crewe, the great manufacturing works and depôt of the L. & N. W. Ry. Co. On *r.*, Wistaston Hall. On *l.* Willaston Hall. Nantwich, p. 146.

Nantwich to Whitchurch (11—48¾); over Shrew Bridge, 38¾, through Aston Green, 42½, and Newhall Green, 43¾.

At Newhall Green, on *r.*, Wrenbury Hall, The Royals, and Combermere Abbey. Whitchurch, p. 148.

Whitchurch to Ellesmere (11½—60¼); 2*m.* out of Whitchurch keep to *l.*, and by Fenns Hall, 52¾, through Bettisfield, 54¾, and Welch Hampton, 56¼, keeping to *r.* 1*m.* before Ellesmere.

2½*m.* beyond Whitchurch, on *r.*, Iscoed Park, and on *l.*, Red Brook. On *r.* Bettisfield Hall. Ellesmere, p. 333.

Ellesmere to Oswestry (8—68¼); through St. Andrews, 62¼, over Maes Tervyn Bridge, 63½, and through Whittington, 65½.

1½*m.* beyond Ellesmere, on *r.*, Hardwick *Ho.* 1*m.* past the canal bridge, on *l.*, Halston Hall. On *l.*, ruins of Whittington castle; 1*m.* farther, on *r.*, Park Hall. Oswestry, p. 127.

SHREWSBURY TO WARRINGTON.

Shrewsbury to Whitchurch (19)—p. 321.

Whitchurch to Tarporley (13½—32½); out of Whitchurch keep to *r.*, and through Croxton Green, 26½, over Beeston Bridge, 30½, and through Four Lane Ends or Fields, 31½. [Or out of Whitchurch keep to *l.*, following the Chester road over Grindley Bridge, 21, by Bell-on-the-Hill, 22, and No Man's Heath, 24, to Hampton, 25½, where turn to *r.* at the guide post, and through Peckforton, 30¼, to Beeston Bridge, 33¼.] Through Tarporley is paved with large stones.

Before Croxton Green, on *l.*, Cholmondeley Castle. At Beeston Bridge, on *l.*, ruins of Beeston Castle.

Tarporley to Crab Tree Green (6—38½); keeping to *r.*, a steep ascent of ½*m.* out of the village is followed by a run of 3*m.* more or less downhill, to Oak Mere, 36¼, and the rest is undulating through Delamere Forest: splendid smooth surface.

Beyond Tarporley, 1*m.* on *r.*, Oulton Park.

Crab Tree Green to Warrington (12—50½); first 2*m.* downhill and often rather loose and stony, to Weaverham, 41½, and then 2*m.* farther cross *R.* Weaver and the canal, and through Bartington, 43½, Lower Whitley, 44½, Stretton, 47, and Wilderspool, 49½.

1*m.* beyond Crab Tree Green, on *l.*, Delamere *Ho.* 1½*m.* beyond Stretton, on *r.*, Appleton Hall. Warrington, p. 152.

MANCHESTER TO CHESTER.

Manchester, St. Ann's Square, **to Altrincham** (8); paved for 1½*m.* along Deansgate and Chester road, then lumpy macadam, with tramway, through Old Trafford, 2½, to Stretford, 4, after which cross *R.* Mersey and the surface improves gradually through Cross Street, 5, to good nearing Altrincham: slightly undulating road.

(*Altrincham*: Bowden; Griffin; Unicorn, B.T.C.)

At Old Trafford, on *l.*, Trafford Park and the Botanical Gardens. At Altrincham, on *r.*, Oldfield Hall.

Altrincham to Mere (5½—13½); rising ground for a mile out of Altrincham, then a good undulating macadam road over New Bridge, 10 (*R.* Bollen), by Mere End, 11, and Buckley or Bucklow Hill, 12¼.

Beyond Altrincham, on *l.*, Devisdale; on *r.*, Park Ho., Dunham Massey Park, and Barham Hall. At Mere End, on *l.*, Rostherne Mere and Denfield Hall. On *l.*, Bucklow Hall and Mere Hall.

Mere to Northwich (7—20½); good undulating macadam road through High or Over Tabley, 14½, Tabley Street, Lower or Nether Tabley, Holford Street, and Lostock Gralam, 18¾: cobble stone paving for a mile through Northwich.

At Lower Tabley, on *l.*, Tabley Park. On *l.*, Holford Hall. Northwich, p. 153.

Northwich to Tarvin (12—32½); long stiff hill to climb beyond Northwich, and after a piece of level it is followed by a hilly road with excellent surface, through Hartford, 22¼, Sandway Lane, 24, Crab Tree Green, 25½, Delamere Forest and Delamere, 28¼, when the long descent of Kelsall Brow has to be made to Kelsall, 30½, affording a fine run down, and is succeeded by a level and fair road to Tarvin.

(*Delamere*: Vale Abbey Arms.)

Fine scenery. At Hartford, on *l.*, Green Bank and Woodland Hall. Beyond Sandway Lane, on *l.*, New Park, and beyond it Vale Royal Abbey. At Delamere, on *r.*, Eddisbury Hill. At Kelsall Brow, on *l.*, Kelsborrow Castle, an ancient entrenchment; on *r.*, Ashton Hey.

Tarvin to Chester (6—38½)—p. 146.

MANCHESTER TO CHESTER (by Warrington).

Manchester, St. Ann's Square, to Patricroft (5¾); along Deansgate, then turn to *r.* along Liverpool road, Water street, and Regent road to Eccles New Road; paving and tramway for about 1½m., then macadam, rough and lumpy, through Eccles, 3¾.

At Eccles, on *l.*, across *R.* Irwell, Trafford Park; on *r.*, Hope Hall.

Patricroft to Warrington (12¾—18½); through Higher Irlam, 9, Lower Irlam or Irlam Green (Dixon's Inn), 10, Cadishead Green, 11, Hollingfare or Hollings Green, 12, Martinscroft Green *Tp.*, 15, and Woolston, 15¾, the road is undulating and fairly good, except patches of cobblestone paving through the villages; Warrington also is paved: the road runs close to left bank of *R.* Irwell and Mersey all the way.

Before Higher Irlam, on *l.*, Flixton Hall. 1m. beyond Woolston, on *r.*, Bruck Hall, and a little farther, Orford Hall. Warrington, p. 152.

Warrington to Frodsham (9½—28); cross *R.* Mersey, then keep to *r.* and through Low Walton, 20, High Walton, 20½, and Daresbury, 22½, to Preston-on-the-Hill, 24. is somewhat on the rise, presently followed by a very stiff hill to descend at Sutton, 26, and after crossing *R.* Weaver, by a steep hill up to Frodsham.

On *l.*, Daresbury Hall. At Sutton, on *r.*, Halton Castle and Norton Priory; on *l.*, Aston Park.

Frodsham to Chester (11—39); stiff ascent to Netherton, 29, then (keeping to *r.*) through Helsby, 31, Dunham-on-the-Hill, 33, Mickle Trafford, 36, Hoole, 36¾, and Flookbrook, 38¼, it is a fairly good road, except for two or three rough patches of paving. Chester is paved and very shaky.

At Mickle Trafford, on *l.*, Morley *Ho.* Past Dunham, on *r.*, Trafford Hall. On *r.*, Hoole Bank; on *l.*, Hoole Hall. Chester, p. 146.

WARE (Herts) TO COLCHESTER.

Ware to Bishop Stortford (13½); follow the Cambridge road to Collier's End, 3¾, as at p. 223, then a little farther turn to *r.*, and there is a long descent to Stondon, 6¼, and undulating through Hadham-on-Ash, 10. [Or from Ware through Widford, 5, and Much Hadham, 8, to Hadham-on-Ash, 9½, a fair undulating road. Or at Much Hadham turn to *r.* down a short descent to a stream crossing the road, and which it is best to go over by the foot bridge; then there is a long hill to ride up, and the rest is pretty level, with a steep fall through Bishop Stortford, which should be walked down; ½*m.* shorter.]

At Much Hadham, on *l.*, Moor Place. Bishop Stortford, p. 230.

Bishop Stortford to Dunmow (9—22½); out of the Stort valley the road rises sharply through Hockerill, 14, and then there are some stiff hills to climb, followed by a long run down through Takeley Street, 17½, to Bonington Green, 18½, and after another rise the rest is all downhill through Little Canfield, 20; splendid road.

(*Dunmow:* Saracen's Head, *B.T.C.*)

At Takeley Street, on *l.*, Brassingbourn Hall. At Little Canfield, on *l.*, Little Canfield Hall and Easton Park. Dunmow, p. 235.

Dunmow to Braintree (8¼—30¾); through Dunmow turn to *l.*, and through Stebbing Ford, 25½, and Rayne, 29, is a very good undulating road.

Braintree, p. 237.

Braintree to Coggleshall (5¾—36½); through Blackwater, 33¾, and Stock Street, 35¼, is a good but hilly road.

Before Blackwater, on *l.*, Stisted Hall. At Stock Street, on *l.*, Oldfield Grange.

Coggleshall to Marks Tey (4—40½); good undulating road.

Marks Tey to Colchester (4¾—45¼)—p. 239.

BRENTWOOD (Essex) TO TILBURY FORT.

Brentwood to East Horndon (4); chiefly uphill to Ingrave, 2, then downhill through Heron Gate Common, 3, on *l.* to Little Burstead, 2½*m.*

At Ingrave, on *r.*, Thorndon Hall and Park.

East Horndon to Orsett (5¾—9¾); very undulating road, but chiefly downhill, by Barnards. 5¼. Wickhouse, 6½, and Orsett Hall, 9, where turn sharp to *r.*

On *l.*, East Horndon Hall. At Wickhouse, on *l.*, Noke Hall; on *r.*, Bulphan Hall. At cross roads by Orsett Hall, on *l.*, to Horndon-on-the-Hill, 1¼*m.*

Orsett to Chadwell (3—12¾); turn to *l.* in Orsett, then to *r.*, and through Baker Street, 10½ (turn to *l.*), and over Orsett Heath.

[Or before Orsett Hall keep straight on by Rotten Row, past the Cock Inn, 9¾, by Muckinge Heath and Biggon Heath, to *Chadwell*, 11¾; good surface, with here and there a shaky bit.]

Chadwell to Tilbury Fort (3—15¼)—p. 249.

From Tilbury Fort cross *R.* Thames by ferry to Gravesend, ½*m.*

CHELMSFORD TO TILBURY FORT.

Chelmsford to Billericay (8½); take the London road back for a mile out of the town, then turn to *l.*, and past the Union house, and there is a long stiff rise on to Galleywood Common, 2½, followed by a good descent out of Stock, 5½, and a loose dangerous descent into Billericay, otherwise pretty level; good road in dry weather.

At Stock, on *r.*, Greenwood *Ho.* Billericay, p. 247.

Billericay to Langdon Hills (5½—14); keep to *r.* by the *ch.* in Billericay, and over Laindon Common (keep to *l.*), Nook Bridge, 11, and Laindon Inn, 11½, whence it is uphill more or less, ending with a steep ascent on to the Hills. Fine views.

Langdon Hills to Tilbury Fort (8½—22½); steep dangerous descent down Langdon Hill, followed by a short sharp drop, rideable, but requiring care, from Horndon-on-the-Hill, 16½, to the junction with the Southend road at 17½, then turn to *r.* and ¾*m.* farther to *l.*; then a stiff hill to mount, and after a mile of level (turning to *r.*) another to run down, and again level by Tilbury Mill, 20, to West Tilbury, 20¼, out of which is a steep hill that should be ridden down carefully; after that it is level over the marshes, with a railway crossing at 21½, and a couple of sharp dips to negotiate near Tilbury Fort.

CAMBRIDGE TO SOUTHEND.

Cambridge to Great Chesterford (11¼)—pp. 230-1, reversed.

Great Chesterford to Saffron Walden (4½—15¾); follow the London road through Little Chesterford, 12¼, to Littlebury, 13¾, entering which turn off to *l.*, and skirt Audley Park; splendid smooth road, chiefly on a slight incline. [Or at Great Chesterford turn to *l.*, and through the east end of Little Chesterford and Springwell direct to Saffron Walden; same distance.]

(*Saffron Walden:* Cross Keys; Rose and Crown, *B.T.C.*)

Saffron Walden to Thaxted (7¼—23); through Wimbish Green, 19½, is a pretty good road, but very hilly. Pretty country.

Thaxted to Dunmow (6¼—29¼); through Monk Street, 25, Great Easton, 27, and Church End, 28½, is a capital road, rather hilly, but mostly downhill. Pretty scenery.

At Great Easton, 1*m.* on *r.*, Easton Park. Dunmow, pp. 235 and 342.

Dunmow to Little Waltham Tg. (8½—37¾); through Barnston, 31½, Black Chapel, 32¾, Fourth End, 33¾, How Street, 36, and Great Waltham, 37, is a splendid undulating road, with a very steep hill to mount (dangerous to ride down) past Fourth End, and a stiff descent to Great Waltham.

Little Waltham Tg. to Chelmsford (4¼—42)—p. 237, reversed.

Beyond Barnston, on *l.*, Absoll Park. Before Great Waltham, on *l.*, Langleys. Chelmsford, p. 237.

Chelmsford to Great Baddow (1½—43½)—p. 246.

Great Baddow to Rayleigh (11¾—55¼); keep to *r.* and through Howe Green, 45¼, and Rettenden, 50¼, over Battle Bridge, 51½, through Rawreth, 52¾, and ½*m.* farther on *r.* join the Billericay road.

Rayleigh to Southend (8—63¼)—p. 248.

BRAINTREE TO ROCHFORD.

Braintree to Witham (7); through Black Notley, 1½, White Notley, 3½, and Faulkbourn, 5, is pretty level, but very loose and sandy road to Chipping, 6½, where join the Colchester road, and turn to *r.* down a stiff descent into Witham.

On *l.*, Faulkbourn Hall, and 1*m.* farther, Witham Place.

Witham to Maldon (6¼—13¼): in Witham turn to *l.*, and it is nearly level to Wickham Mills, 9½; then stiff hilly riding, the surface being loose and sandy in summer, to Langford, 11½ (just beyond over a level railway crossing); level to Heybridge, 12½, where turn to *r.*, cross *R.* Blackwater, and a steep hill to climb into Maldon (quite unrideable in either direction): good roads.

Before Langford, on *r.*, Wickham Hall; on *l.*, Langford Grove, and on *r.*, Beeleigh Abbey. Maldon, p. 246.

Maldon to North Fambridge (6½—19¾); turn first to *l.*, and by Maldon Jenkin (Royal Oak), 15¼, and Purleigh Wash, 16¼, is an excellent undulating road, except the abrupt descent of Kit Hill to walk 1*m.* before North Fambridge.

North Fambridge to Rochford (4¾—24½); cross *R.* Crouch by Fambridge Ferry (fare 6d., and bicycle 6d.), and then through South Fambridge, 21¼, and Ashingdon, 22¼.

CAMBRIDGE TO COLCHESTER.

Cambridge to Linton (11); past the station, over the Gog Magog Hills, to Babraham, 5, through Little Abington, 7, and Great Abington, 8; very hilly road.

(*Linton:* Swan.)

On the Gog Magog Hills, on *l.*, the Wandlebury, an ancient entrenchment. On *r.*, Babraham Hall. Beyond Great Abington, on *l.*, Hildersham Hall.

Linton to Haverhill (9—20); in Linton turn to *l.*, and through Horseheath, 15, and Withersfield, 18.

Beyond Linton, on *l.*, the Rivey; on *r.*, Barham Hall. 1*m.* before Horseheath, on *l.*, Horseheath Lodge; 2*m.* S. is Shudy Camps Park, and 1*m.* farther, Camps Castle, an ancient encampment.

Haverhill to Ridgewell (5½—25½); through Sturmer, 21½, and Baythorn End, 23½.

On *r.*, Sturmer Hall; on *l.*, Baythorn Park and Stoke College. Before Ridgewell, on *r.*, Whitley.

Ridgewell to Sible Hedingham (5½—31); stiff hill to descend from Ridgewell, and then nearly level through Great Yeldham, 28, to Sible Hedingham.

At Great Yeldham, on *l.*, Spains Hall. Sible Hedingham, p. **237**.

Sible Hedingham to Halstead (4—35); through Swanstreet, 31½ (keep to *l.*), and Brook Street, 33.

At Brook Street, on *l.*, Dynes Hall. Before Halstead, on *l.*, The How and Ashfield Lodge. Halstead, p. **237**.

Halstead to Colchester, Obelisk (13¾—48¾); over Blue Bridge, 36, Stone Bridge, 37½, through Earls Colne, 38½, Wakes Colne, 40½, Botsive Green, 41, Ford Street, 43, and Lexden, 46¾, where join road from London on *r.*

(*Earls Colne :* George; Lion.).

At Blue Bridge, on *r.*, Halstead Lodge; on *l.*, Colne Park and Colne Priory. On *l.*, Lexden Hall. Colchester, p. **239**.

COLCHESTER TO SUDBURY.

Colchester to Nayland (6); through Mile End, 1, Horkesley Causeway, 3½, and Great Horkesley, 4¾.

On *r.*, Horkesley Park. At Nayland, on *r.*, Tendring Hall.

Nayland to Sudbury (9¼—15¼); through Marshall's Green, 9, Assington Green, 10, and Newton Green, 12¼.

[Or at Mile End, on *l.*, through Wormingford, Bures St. Mary, and Great Cornard, to Sudbury : about the same distance.]

On *l.*, Assington Hall; on *r.*, Aveley Hall and Coddenham Hall. Sudbury, p. 237.

SUDBURY (Suffolk) TO IPSWICH.

Sudbury to Hadleigh (12¾); by Chilton Park, 2, through Great Waldingfield, 4¼ (keep to *r.*), by Edwardston Priory, 6½, through Lindsey, 9, and Kersey, 11¼.

At Kersey, on *l.*, the Priory. At Hadleigh was buried Guthrum, the Dane; fine *ch.*; p. **240**.

Hadleigh to Ipswich (8¾—21½); through Hintlesham, 16½, Sproughton, 19½, and Chauntry, 20.

On *l.*, Hintlesham Hall and Priory. Ipswich, p. **239**.

CAMBRIDGE TO YARMOUTH.

Cambridge to Newmarket (13); through Quy-cum-Stow, 4¾, and Bottisham, 7, to Devil's Ditch, 11¼, where join the London road on *r.*

On *l.*, Quy Hall and Bottisham Hall. Newmarket, p. **231**.

Newmarket to Bury St. Edmund's (14—27); keeping to *r.* 1*m.* out of Newmarket, and then through Kentford, 18, and Saxham, 23, the road is very bad and loose at first for several miles, passing through a wild, open and cheerless tract of country; then it gradually improves, and nearing Bury St. Edmund's is good.

Bury St. Edmund's, p. **237**.

Bury St. Edmund's to Botesdale (14¾—41¾)—p. **238**.

Botesdale to Scole (7½—49)—p. **240** ; alternative route.

Scole to Yarmouth, *M.P.* (34¾—83¾)—pp. **242-3**.

CAMBRIDGE TO IPSWICH.

Cambridge to Bury St. Edmund's (27)—p. 345.

Bury St. Edmund's to Stowmarket (13½—40½); in Bury turn to r., and 1m. farther to l.; very rough road through Beighton, 32½, to Woolpit, 34¾, whence it is better through Haughley New Street, 37¼, and Tot Hill, 39.

Before Beighton, on l., Rougham Hall and Rougham Place; on r., Rougham Old Hall. At Beighton, on r., Drinkstone Hall; beyond, on l., Tostock Hall. On r., Haughley Park; on l., Haughley Place and remains of the castle.

Stowmarket to Needham Market (3½—44); just beyond the former turn to l.: fairly good road but rough in places.

At Needham, on r., Airing Ho. and Barking Hall; 1m. farther, on l., Boxmere Ho.

Needham Market to Ipswich, Stones End (8½—52½); through Great Blakenham, 48, Claydon, 49, and Whitton Street, 50¼: good road, but in dry weather loose and stony. Returning, at Claydon keep to l.

At Great Blakenham, on l., Tower Hall and Shrubland Hall. Ipswich, p. 239.

WOODBRIDGE TO DEBENHAM.

Woodbridge to Otley, Ch. (6¼); through Hasketon (ch.), 1½, Burgh (ch.), 4, and Clopton (ch.), 4¾.

At Hasketon, on l., Bealings Ho. Beyond Hasketon, on l., Thorpe Hall and Grundisburgh Hall; on r., Hasketon Hall. At Clopton, on r., an ancient camp, and also at Otley, on l.

Otley to Debenham (6¼—12½); through Helmingham (ch.), 8½, Framsden (Mill), 9¾, and Winston (ch.), 11¼. Returning, at Helmingham keep to l.

On l., Helmingham Hall. On l., Winston Hall.

CAMBRIDGE TO NORWICH.

Cambridge to Newmarket (13)—p. 345.

Newmarket to Norwich (47¾—60¾)—pp. 231-2.

IPSWICH TO LYNN.

Ipswich to Stowmarket (12)—above, reversed.

Stowmarket to Ixworth (11¼—23¼); through Tot Hill, 13½, Haughley New Street, 15¼ (turn to r. and then to l.), Wetherden, 16, Elmswell, 17¾, and Norton, 20.

On r., Haughley Place and remains of the castle; a little on l., Haughley Park. On l., Elmswell Hall. On r., Norton Hall, and on l., Beaumont Hall. Ixworth, p. 238.

Ixworth to Thetford (9¾—33); through Ixworth Thorpe, 25¼, Honington, 26½, Fakenham, 27¾, by Euston Hall, 29½, and through Barnham, 31. Returning, at Barnham turn to l.

On r., Euston Park. Thetford, p. 231.

Thetford to Mundford (8—41); leaving Thetford turn to l.

Mundford to Stoke Ferry (7½—48½); through Cranwich, Little London, and Whittington, 47¾.

At Mundford, on *r.*, Lyndford *Ho.* At Cranwich, 1*m.* on *r.*, Didlington Hall.

Stoke Ferry to Lynn (14—62½)—p. 233.

[Or from Thetford take the left of the two middle roads, and through Croxton, 35¼, over Croxton Heath, by Frogs Hall, 39¾ (keep to *l.*), over Sturston Warren, through Sturston, 40½, over Tottington Warren, through Little Cressingham, 44, by the Lime Kilns, 44½, through South Pickenham, 46¾, over North Pickenham Heath, and by Corrall House, 49¼, to *Swaffham*, 51; here turn to *l.*, and there are a few short sharp hills over Swaffham Heath (at 52¾ keep to *r.*) and Narborough Field, to Narborough, 56¼, then undulating, but chiefly on a slight rise, over Pentney Common, through West Bilney, 59¼, over Winch Common, through East Winch, 61, to Middleton, 62¾, and the rest is a gentle downhill through Hardwick, 65¼, to *Lynn*, 66½: see also p. 349.]

Before Little Cressingham, on *r.*, Claremont Lodge; on *l.*, South Pickenham Hall. Swaffham, p. 233. On *r.*, Narborough Hall; on *l.*, Bilney Lodge. Lynn, p. 226.

PETERBOROUGH TO IPSWICH.

(This road crosses the Fens to Ely.)

Peterborough to Whittlesea (6¾); through Fletton, 1¼, Standground, 1½, over Horsey Bridge, 3¼, and Fieldsend Bridge, 4½, exceedingly bad road.

Whittlesea to March Bridge (11—17¾); very bad road through Eastrea, 8¼, and Cotes, 9¼. Returning, 1¼*m.* out of March keep to *l.*

March, p. 226.

March to Chatteris (8—25¾)—p. 226, in reverse: good road, with no hills to speak of.

Chatteris to Ely (12½—38¼); keep to *l.*, and through Mepal, 30½, (just before it cross Old and New Bedford Rivers), Sutton, 31¾, Wentworth, 33¾, and Witchford, 35¼. Returning, out of Ely keep to *r.*

Ely, p. 227.

Ely to Soham (5½—43¾); in Ely turn to *r.*, and through Stuntney, 39¾, and along Soham Causeway; undulating road.

Soham to Kentford (9¾—53½); through Fordham, 47¼, and by Red Lodge, 51.

Before Fordham on *l.* to *Newmarket* (5—52).

On *r.*, Fordham Abbey, and 2*m.* farther, Chippenham Park.

Kentford to Bury St. Edmund's (9—62½)—p. 345.

Bury St. Edmund's to Ipswich, Stones End (25½—88)—p. 346.

ELY TO HUNTINGDON.

Ely to Stretham (4¼)—p. 227, reversed.

Stretham to Earith (9½—13¾); turn to *r.* and mount a long hill to Wilburton, 6½, and then downhill to Haddenham, 7½, and rest undulating hrough Hill Row, along Haddenham Causeway, and by Catchwater, 9¼, and Hermitage, 13¼. [Or beyond Ely keep to *r.* and through Witchford, 3, Wentworth, 4½, Sutton, 6½ (turn to *l.*), to Hermitage, 11, where returning, keep to *l.*]

Earith to St. Ives (5½—19¼); through Bluntisham, 15, Needingworth, 17¼, and Tawdry Lane *Tg.* 18½, (keep to *l*).

St. Ives, p. 225.

St. Ives to Huntingdon (6½—25¾); in St. Ives turn to *l.*, cross *R.* Ouse, and then turn to *r.* through Hemmingford Grey, 21, Hemmingford Abbots, 22¼, and Godmanchester, 24¾. Returning, a little past Godmanchester turn to *l.*

[Or at Tawdry Lane *Tg.*, 18½, keep straight on through Houghton, 21¼, and Hartford, 22¾, to *Huntingdon*, 24. Returning, out of Hartford turn to *r.*]

Huntingdon, p. 223.

DOWNHAM MARKET TO YARMOUTH.

Downham Market to Swaffham (13¾); through Bexwell, 1¼, Crimplesham 2½ (keep to *l.*), Stradset Falgate, 3½, and Fincham, 5¼, and mostly uphill for last 4 or 5m. over Swaffham Heath.

On *l.*, Stradset Hall. Beyond Fincham, a little on *r.*, Barton Bendish Hall and Barton Abbey. At 9m., cross Devil's Dyke. Swaffham, p. 233.

Swaffham to East Dereham (12—25¾); through Necton, 17¼, Little Fransham, 19¾, Wardling, 21¾, and Scarning, 23¾, the road is chiefly on the rise with but a few short descents: splendid surface.

Before Necton, on *r.*, Necton Hall. East Dereham, p. 234.

East Dereham to Honingham (9—34¾); entering East Dereham turn to *r.*, then to *l.*, and by Tuddenham, through Esling Green, 28, and Hockering, 31, the road is mostly down hill, and the surface as a rule very good and smooth.

On *l.*, Honingham Hall.

Honingham to Norwich, *M.H.* (7—41¾); through Easton, 35¾, is a fairly good and undulating road, mostly on the fall, but no difficult hills: through Norwich is paved with cobble stones.

Beyond Easton, on *l.*, Costessey Park (Lord Stafford). Norwich, p. 232.

Norwich to Acle (11—52¾); through Thorpe, 43¾, Postwich *Tp.*, 45, Witton, 47½, Blofield, 48¼, Burlingham St. Andrew, 50¼, and Burlingham St. Peter, 52¼, is a good road and with a fair amount of up and down hill. [There is another road leaving Norwich more on the *l.*, and through Plumstead Street, South Walsham, and Upton; nearly 2m. longer.]

On *l.*, Thorpe Lodge and Mousehold Ho.; on *r.*, Crown Point. At Postwich *Tp.*, on *l.*, Gt. Plumstead Lodge. At Witton, on *l.*, Little Plumstead Hall and Plumstead Hall. On *l.*, Burlingham Hall.

Acle to Yarmouth, *M.P.*, (11½—64¼); in Acle turn first to *l.*, then second on *r.*, and over Wey Bridge, 53¾, through Burgh St. Margaret's (King's Arms), 56½, over Filby Broad, through Filby *Tp*, 57¾, Filby, 58¾, over Filby Common, through Caistor, 61¼, and White Gate *Tp.* 62½; a continuation of the same kind of road. [Or at Acle turn first to *l.*, then first to *r.*, and go across the marshes, almost in a straight line, but very flat, and through an uninteresting country, to Yarmouth, 60¾.]

Filby Broad is a large freshwater lake, where good fishing may be had. Beyond Filby, on *l.*, Ormesby Hall. At Caistor, ruins of the castle. Yarmouth, p. 242.

LYNN TO YARMOUTH.

Lynn to Swaffham (15½); through Hardwick, 1¼ (keep to *l.*), the road is on a gentle rise to Middleton, 3¾, then undulating but slightly on the fall, through East Winch, 5½, over Winch Common, through West Bilney, 7¼, over Pentney Common to Narborough, 10¼, after which over Narborough Field and Swaffham Heath there are several short sharp hills, but nothing to dismount for; the surface is fairly good, but varies considerably, but in some parts good and in others very loose and sandy. Returning, 1¼ m. out of Swaffham keep to *r.*

At West Bilney, on *r.*, Bilney Lodge, and 2 m. on *r.*, ruins of Pentney Priory. On *l.*, Narborough Hall, and 1½ m. on *r.*, Narford Hall; on *r.*, a Roman camp. Swaffham, p. 233.

Swaffham to Yarmouth, M.P. (50½—66)—p. 348.

LYNN TO YARMOUTH (by Litcham).

Lynn to Litcham (17¼); through Gaywood, 1 (keep to *r.*), over Leziate Warren or Bawsey Common, through Gayton, 6, over Gayton Field, by Gayton Windmill, 7, over Massingham Heath or Gaytonthorpe High Common, across the Pedlar's Way, 10½, and by Crow Hall Farm, 14½.

On *r.*, Gaywood Hall; 1 m. beyond Gaywood, on *r.*, Mintlyn ruins; on *l.*, Bawsey ruins. At 3 m., on *l.*, Leziate ruins; on *r.*, Leziate Hall. On *r.*, Gayton Hall. Near the Pedlar's Way, on *r.*, Gaytonthorpe High *Ho.* 1 m. before Litcham, on *r.*, Lexham Hall; on *l.*, Litcham High *Ho.*

Litcham to Bawdeswell, Bell (10¾—28); keep to *l.* of the *ch.*, and through Mileham, 19½, by Queen's Head, 20½, through Stanfield, 21, Brisley, 22, by Elmham Park, 22½, through North Elmham (King's Head), 24½, and Billingford (end of), 26½.

On *l.*, Mileham Hall. At Stanfield, on *r.*, Bilney Hall; on *l.*, Elmham Hall. On *r.*, Bawdeswell Hall.

Bawdeswell to Norwich, M.H., (13½—41½); keep to *r.*, and through Sparham, 29½, over Lenwade Bridge, 31¾ (cross *R.* Wensom), through Morton (White Horse), 33½, (again cross *R.* Wensom), Attlebridge (Bull), 33¾, and Drayton, 37½, and over Drayton Heath.

[Or from Billingford, 26½, keep to *r.* over Bylaugh Heath, 27½, to Sparham.]

Past Lenwade Bridge, on *r.*, Weston *Ho.*; on *l.*, Witchingham Hall. At Attlebridge, on *r.*, Morton Hall and Attlebridge Hall. Before Drayton, on *r.*, Taverham Hall. On *r.*, Drayton Hall and Drayton *Ho.* Norwich, p. 232.

[Or from *Litcham*, keep to *r.* through Longham, 20¼, and Great Bittering, 22, to *East Dereham*, 25½, whence to *Norwich*, 16—41½; p. 348.]

Beyond Litcham, on *r.*, Kempstone Lodge. On *r.*, Longham Hall; a little farther on, Gressenham Hall. Before East Dereham, 2 m. on *l.*, Hoe *Ho.* At 1 m. on *l.*, Quebec *Ho.*, and on *r.*, Dillington *Ho.* East Dereham, p. 234.

Norwich to Yarmouth, M.P. (22½—64); p. 348.

LYNN TO HAPPISBURGH.

Lynn to Bawdeswell, Bell (28); p. 349.

Bawdeswell to Reepham (4—32); keep to *l.* over Bawdeswell Common, and through Hackford, 31.

(*Reepham :* King's Arms.)

Reepham to Aylsham (7—39); out of Reepham keep to *l.* by Sall Hall, 33¼, where turn sharp on *r.* to Cawston, 34¾; [or straight on through Booton, 33½, to Cawston, 35;] thence over Cawston Heath (Wood Row Mill), 36, crossing the Norwich and Holt road.

Aylsham to North Walsham (6¾—45¾), by Banningham Bridge. 42¼.

North Walsham, p. 235.

North Walsham to Happisburgh (6¾—52½); by Eastgate, 46¾, Witton Mill, 47¾, and through Ridlington, 50¼.

Before Ridlington, on *l.*, Witton Park; on *r.*, Crostwich Hall and Bromholm Abbey. At Witton Mill, 1½*m.* on *r.*, Honing Hall.

LYNN TO HAPPISBURGH (by Holt).

Lynn to Hillington (7½)—p. 228.

Hillington to East Rudham, Crown (7¼—14¾)—p. 229.

[Or at Rising Lodge keep to *r.* through Grimston and Great Massingham, 12½ (where keep to *l.*), to *East Rudham*, 16¼.]

East Rudham to Fakenham (7—21¾); through Tatterset, 16¼, and Dunton, 18¾.

[Or from Great Massingham on *r.* to Weasenham St. Peter, 16½, whence to *Fakenham*, 6¾—23¼,—p. 233.]

At Tatterset, on *r.*, Brookthorpe Hall, and ruins of Coxford Abbey; farther, on *r.*, Pinkney Hall.

Fakenham to Holt (11½—33¼); over Snoring Common (Green Man), 25, through Thursford, 26½, Stock Heath, 27½, Sharrington Common (Swan), 30½, and Letheringset, 32¾, whence is a rather steep hill into Holt.

On *l.*, Thursford Hall and Wood *Ho.* Beyond Stock Heath, on *r.*, Gunthorpe Hall. Holt, p. 234.

Holt to Cromer (10¼—43½); over Sherringham Heath, 37¾, through Upper Sherringham, 38½, East Runton, 41, and West Runton, 42¼, the road is undulating, but with excellent smooth surface: pretty country. [Or at Sherringham Heath keep to *r.*, and by Beaston Heath and Felbrigg Heath to Cromer, 43¾.]

On *r.*, Fellbrigg Hall. Before Cromer, on *r.*, Cromer Hall.

Cromer to Happisburgh (14¾—58¼); by the coast through Overstrand, 45¼, Sidestrand, 46¾, Trimingham, 48½, Beacon, 49¼, Mundesley, 51, Paston, 53, Bacton, 54, Keswick, 54¾, and Walcot, 56½, the roads are bad, being hilly, loose, and stony.

At Overstrand, on *r.*, Northrepps Hall. At Bacton, on *r.*, Bromholm Abbey and Witton Park. On *r.*, Walcot Hall.

CROMER TO HUNSTANTON.

Cromer to Cley (12); through West Runton, 1¼, East Runton, 2½, Sherringham, 5, Weybourn, 7¼, and Salthouse, 10, the road runs near the sea all the way, but is hilly and for the most part loose and stony: flint road. [Or Cromer to *Holt*, 10¼—p. 350, reversed; thence turn to *r.* to *Cley*, 4¼—14½.]

Cley to Wells (9—21); the road now becomes level, skirting some marshes on the *r.*, and then steep unrideable ascent to Blakeney, 13, through Morston, 14½, over Stiffkey Bridge, 15¾, through Stiffkey, 17¼, and across Wells Marsh, 19: the surface is fair on the whole, but often loose and sandy.

On *l.*, Stiffkey Hall. Wells, p. 228.

Wells to Burnham Westgate (5¾—26¾)—p. 228, reversed.

Burnham Westgate to Hunstanton (10—36¾); ascent out of the former, turning to *r.* ¾*m.* out of the town, followed by stiff descent ¾*m.* long into Burnham Deepdale, 29¼, whence through Brancaster Staith, 30¼, Brancaster, 31½, Titchwell, 32¼, Thornham, 33¾, and Holme-next-the-Sea, 35¼, is a splendid road, almost as good as a cinder-path, and running near the sea.

On *l.*, Thornham Hall. Hunstanton, p. 227.

NORWICH TO HOLT.

Norwich to Aylsham (11¼)—p. 232.

Aylsham to Holt (11½—22¾); turn to *l.* and by Blickling *Ch.*, 12½, alongside Blickling Park, through Saxthorpe, 17, and Edgefield Green, 19½.

[Or 2*m.* out of Norwich keep to *l.* and through Horsford, 4¼, over Cawston Heath (Wood Row Mill), 10½, through Corpusty, 14½, beyond which keep to *r.*, to Saxthorpe, 15½. Returning, at Saxthorpe keep to *r.*]

PETERBOROUGH TO LYNN.

Peterborough to Thorney (7); in Peterborough turn to *r.* from the London road, and then to *l.*, and it is a good road, almost level, through Newark, 1½, and Eye, 3½, about 1*m.* farther crossing the old *R.* Nen.

Thorney to Wisbeach (14—21); across the Fens, by Boarden House Bridge, 10½, Guyhirn Ferry, 13¾, through Guyhirn, 14, and Wisbeach St. Mary, 18, good smooth road, quite level. [Or at Guyhirn Ferry cross *R.* Nen and follow the road from March along the river to Wisbeach, 19½.]

Wisbeach to Lynn (12¾—33¾)—p. 226.

OAKHAM TO LYNN.

Oakham to Stamford (11); about 2*m.* out of Oakham is Barnsdale Hill to mount; then through Whitwell, 4½, and Empingham, 6, out of which, turning to *r.*, is a steep descent; the rest undulating. [Or through Burley-on-the-Hill, 2, Cottesmore, 4½, and Greetham, 6¼, to near Ram Jam

House 8*m.*, on the G. N. Road, where turn to *r.* to Stamford, 15¼; bad road.]

At Whitwell, on *r.*, Normanton Park; 1*m.* on *l.*, Exton Park. On *r.*, Burley Park. At Greetham, on *r.*, Exton Park. Stamford p. 195.

Stamford to Market Deeping (7¾—18¾); through Uffington, 13¼, Tallington, 14½, and West Deeping, 16¾.

(*Market Deeping:* New Inn.)

On *r.*, Uffington Hall. At Tallington, 1*m.* on *l.*, Caswick Hall.

Market Deeping to Spalding (11½—30¼)—p. 219.

Spalding to Holbeach (9½—39¾); through Weston, 34, Moulton, 35¾, and Whaplode, 37¼.

(*Holbeach:* Chequers.)

Holbeach to Sutton Bridge (8¼—48); through Fleet Hard Gate, 42, and Sutton St. Mary's, 44¾, is a very good road.

Sutton Bridge to Lynn (10—58); cross *R.* Nen estuary over Sutton Bridge (3d. toll), and by Cross Keys *Ho.*, 50, through South Green, 52, Terrington St. Clement, 52½, and Clench Warton *Tp.*, 54½, and West Lynn, 57 (cross *R.* Ouse), is a level road and good hard surface all the way.

At South Green, on *l.*, Hamond Lodge. Lynn, p. 226.

DOWNHAM MARKET TO BOSTON.

Downham Market to Wisbeach (13); cross *R.* Ouse over Downham Bridge, 1, then by Salter's Lode Sluice, 2, through Nordelph, 4, Outwell, 7½, and Emneth, 11.

At Outwell, on *r.*, Beaupré Hall. At Emneth, on *r.*, Oxburgh Hall. Wisbeach, p. 226.

Wisbeach to Holbeach (13½—26½); cross *R.* Nen in Wisbeach, and when out of the town turn to *r.* past the gasworks, then by Four Gouts, 17¼, Tidd or Tydd Gout, 18¼ (cross North Level Main Drain), Tidd St. Mary's, 18¾, to Sutton St. Mary's, 21½, where join the road from Lynn, and turn on *l.* through Fleet Hard Gate, 24¼, to Holbeach.

Holbeach to Sutterton (8¾—35¼); in Holbeach turn to *r.*, and through Holbeach Clough, for a few miles the road is bad but passable, then it is good for a mile over Fossdyke Bridge, 31¾ (cross Fossdyke Wash), to Fossdyke, 32½ (turn to *l.*), and again generally very bad, being simply two smooth cart tracks worn in a bed of shingle, all the way to the junction with the main London road at Sutterton. It is much better to go round by Spalding.

Sutterton to Boston (6¼—41½)—p. 219.

STAMFORD TO BOSTON.

Stamford to Bourn (10¼); through Ryall, 2½, Carlby, 5, and Toft, 7½.

On *r.*, Ryall *Ho.* Bourn, p. 215.

Bourn to Bridgend *Tp.* (12½—22¾); through Morton, 12¾ (keep to *r.* 1½*m.* farther), Dunsby, 15¼, Dowsby, 17, Pointon, 18½, Sempringham, 19¾, Billingborough, 20¼, and Horbling, 20¾.

Bridgend to Donington (4¼—27); turn to r. at Bridgend.
Donington, p. 220.

Donington to Swineshead, North End (4½—31½)—p. 220.

Swineshead to Boston (6¾—38¼); turn to r. and through Kirton Holme.
Boston, p. 219.

BOURN (Lincoln) TO COLTERSWORTH.

Bourn to Corby (7¾); through Edenham, 2¼, and Grimsthorpe, 4.

On l., Grimsthorpe Castle (Lord Willoughby d'Eresby's seat), an irregular castellated building, with a beautiful chapel, and a fine collection of paintings. Before Corby, on r., Irnham Hall.

Corby to Coltersworth (4½—12¼).

DERBY TO LIVERPOOL.

Derby to Leek (28½)—p. 169.

Leek to Congleton (10¼—38¾); from Leek is a steep hill to descend from the Market Place (almost too steep to ride up), then the road ascends more or less all the way for 1½m. beyond Pool End, 29¼, after which there is a long steady descent most of the way for about 3m. past Rudyard Lake or Reservoir to Rushton Marsh, 33, where turn to l., and then not so hilly to Congleton.

(*Congleton*: Bull's Head; Lion and Swan.)

Congleton to Knutsford (14½—53)—p. 154.
Knutsford to Liverpool (29½—82½)—pp. 152-3.

DERBY TO BOSTON.

Derby, All Saints *Ch.*, to Nottingham (16); through Chaddesden, 2, Borrowash, 4¼, Risley, 7¼, Sandiacre, 9¼, (cross *R.* Erewash and canal), to Stapleford, 11¼, is hilly, otherwise the road is tolerably good, and after that is apt to be rather rough through Lenton, 14½; steep hill to descend into Nottingham.

[Or follow the Loughborough road back to Cavendish Bridge, 7, as at p. 166, then ½m. farther turn to l. and through Sawley and Long Eaton, to *Nottingham*, as at pp. 190 and 315.]

On l., Chaddesden Hall, and 1m. farther on, Spondon Hall. At Borrowash, on r., Elvaston Castle; 2m. farther on, on l., Hopwell Hall. On r., Risley Hall. On l., Stapleford Hall; 1m. farther, on l., Chilwell Hall; on l., Bramcote *Ho.*
Nottingham, p. 186.

Nottingham to Saxondale (9—25)—p. 306.

Saxondale to Bottesford (8¼—33¼); run down into Bingham, 26¾, out of which the road turns sharp to r., and 200 yards farther on to l., and then through Whatton, 28¼, and Elton, 30¼, it is mostly level and has a good surface; short stiff pull into Elton, which is approached beneath a fine avenue of trees.

Near Elton, on r., is seen Belvoir Castle, over-looking the lovely Vale of

AA

Belvoir. In Bottesford, is an ancient cross in good preservation; the *ch.* contains some fine monuments of the Duke of Rutland's family. At Bingham, on *l.*, Aslacton Abbey.

Bottesford to Grantham, *M.P.* (7—40¼); in Bottesford turn sharp to *l.* and again to *r.* over a bridge a few hundred yards farther on; nearly level and rather rough at first, but soon improves through Muston, 35, to Sedgebrook, 36½, then almost level to Barrowby, 38¼, when the road crosses a spur of the Belvoir range, up a long stiff hill, from the top of which is a slight descent, then another rise, shortly followed by a steep fall into Grantham, which should be taken carefully; passing under the G.N. Ry., the Great North Road is reached, and turn to *r.* for the Market Place; surface rather rough for last 2 or 3*m.*

Grantham to Bridgend, *Tp.* (15¾—56); through Spittlegate, 41, Cold Harbour *Tg.*, 43½, Nightingale, 47½, Scott Willoughby, 50½, Newton Gorse *Tg.*, 51½, and Threckingham, 52½.

Bridgend to Boston (15½—71½)—p. 353.

ASHBOURNE TO CHESTERFIELD.

Ashbourne to Wirksworth, *T.H.* (9)—p. 337.

Wirksworth to Matlock (4—13)—p. 170.

Matlock to Chesterfield (9½—22½); when over Matlock Bridge keep to *r.*, and by Kelstedge, 16¼, and Walton, 20¼: very hilly road. Returning, 1½*m.* out of Chesterfield keep to *l.*

Before Kelstedge, a little on *r.*, Overton Hall. Before Walton, on *r.*, Wingerworth Hall. Chesterfield, p. 178.

ASHBOURNE TO BELPER.

Ashbourne to Belper (11½); by Nether Starston, Bradley, Ward Gate, 5, Cross Hands Inn, 7, Turnditch, 8, and Shottle Gate, 9¼.

On *r.*, Bradley Hall.

MANSFIELD TO MATLOCK.

Mansfield to Tibshelf (6½); 1*m.* beyond Mansfield keep to *r.*, and through Skegby, 3.

On *r.*, Skegby Hall.

Tibshelf to Stretton (3—9½): through Tibshelf turn to *r.*, and through Morton, 8½.

Stretton to Matlock (6½—16); nearly 1*m.* past Stretton keep to *l.*, and through Butterley, 13, and Nether Tansley, 14½.

Matlock, p. 167.

BOSTON TO MANCHESTER.

Boston to Swineshead, North End (6¾)—p. 353, reversed.

Swineshead to Sleaford (11¼—18); through Garrick, 11, Hecklington, 13, and Kirkby Laythorpe, 16.

Sleaford, p. 215.

Sleaford to Leadenham (9—27); through Holdingham, 19¼ (turn to *l.*), and by Bayard's Leap, 24.

On *l.*, Leadenham Hall. At Bayard's Leap, cross the old Ermine Way.

Leadenham to Newark (9¾—36¾); at Leadenham turn first on *r.* and then to *l.*; through Broughton, 29¼, Beckingham, 32, and Cottington, 34½: heavy going.

On *l.*, Beckingham Hall. Newark, p. 196.

Newark to Kirklington (8½—45¼); through Kelham, 38¾ (turn to *l.*), Averham, 39¼, (turn to *r.* and 1*m.* farther keep to *r.*), and Hockerton, 42¾.

On *l.*, Kelham Hall. 2*m.* past Averham, on *r.*, Averham Park; on *l.*, Upton Lodge. On *r.*, Kirklington Hall.

Kirklington to Mansfield (9¼—54½); by Sherwood Inn, 51 (keep to *r.*), a very hilly road. Returning, at Sherwood Inn keep to *l.*

[Or from 1*m.* past Averham keep to *l.*, through Upton, 42, to *Southwell*, 44¼, p. 306; then, keeping to *r.* 1*m.* beyond, through Halam, 46, Edingley, 47, Farnsfield, 48¼, to Sherwood Inn, 52¼, where, returning, keep to *r.*]

1*m.* past Kirklington, on *l.*, Hexgrave Park. Southwell, p. 306. At Halam, on *r.*, Norwood Hall and Park. Mansfield, p. 187.

Mansfield to Chesterfield (12¼—66¾)—p. 190.

Chesterfield, p. 178.

Chesterfield to Baslow (8¾—75½); through Ash Gate, 69, and Brampton, 69¾.

Before Brampton, on *r.*, Cutthorpe Hall. Before Baslow, on *l.*, Chatsworth Park.

Baslow to Tideswell Lane End (8¼—83¾); keep to *r.* through Calver, 77¼, Stoney Middleton, 78½, and Wardlow *Tp.*, 82.

[Or 2½*m.* past Brampton, 69¼, turn to *r.* and through Corbar, 75¾, joining the above road 1*m.* farther on, to Stoney Middleton, 77½].

At Stoney Middleton, on *r.*, Stoke Hall.

Tideswell Lane End to Manchester (27¼—101)—p. 171.

BOSTON TO LIVERPOOL.

Boston to Baslow (75½)—above.

Baslow to Ashford (5—80½); cross *R.* Derwent, and then turn to *r.*, and there is a long descent to Hassop, 77¼, then to *l.*, and 1*m.* farther to *r.*

Beyond Hassop, on *r.*, Hassop Hall. On *l.*, Ashford Hall.

Ashford to Buxton (10¼—90¾)—p. 167.

[Or from *Baslow* on *l.* through Edensor, 76¾, to *Bakewell*, 79¼, thence to *Ashford*, 1¾—81,—p. 167.

Or from *Tideswell Lane End*, 83¾, above, on *l.* through Tideswell, 84¼, Hargatewall, 86¼, and Fairfield, 90¼, to *Buxton*, 91¼.]

At Edensor, on *l.*, Chatsworth Park and *Ho.*, Queen Mary's Bower, &c. Bakewell, p. 167.

Buxton to Macclesfield (11¾—102½); uphill out of Buxton by Moss House or Devonshire Arms Inn, 94¼, for about 5*m.* (quite safe to descend with a good brake) till the top of Axe Edge is reached at the Cat and Fiddle

Inn, then more or less downhill by Jackson's Smithy, 98¾, and Walker Barn (Dog Inn), 99½, in some parts very steep and rough, on which very little riding can be done; ascent into Macclesfield, through which is paved.

Pretty scenery. Macclesfield, p. 169.

Macclesfield to Chelford (6—108½); ascent out of Macclesfield, then by Broken Cross, 104, and Birtles, 106, is mostly downhill for 4*m.*; good macadam surface.

At Broken Cross, on *r.*, Upton Priory and Whirley Hall: 1*m.* farther, on *l.*, Henbury Hall. On *r.*, Birtles Hall, and beyond it, Alderley Park. 1½*m.* before Chelford, on *l.*, Capesthorn Hall. At Chelford, on *l.*, Astle Hall.

Chelford to Knutsford, *M.H.* (5¼—113¾)—p. 154.

Knutsford to Liverpool (29½—143¼)—pp. 152-3.

CHESTERFIELD TO LEEK.

Chesterfield to Baslow (8¾)—p. 355.

Baslow to Ashford (5—13¾)—p. 355.

Ashford to Longnor (7¾—21½); through Ashford keep to *l.*, cross *R.* Wye, and up long difficult ascent, then through Moneyash, 17¼, Crankston, 19½, and Crowdey Cote, 20¾.

Longnor to Leek (10—31½); through Harding's Booth, 23 (turn to *l.* 2½*m.* farther), and Upper Holme or Hulme, 28½.

WARRINGTON TO MOTTRAM.

Warrington to Altrincham (11¾); cross *R.* Mersey and it is a bad macadam road through Latchford, ¾, over a level railway crossing, a little further keep to *l.*, then better through Thelwall, 2¾, Statham, 4, Lymm, 4¾, Bollington, 8½, and Dunham, 9¾.

On *r.*, Thelwall Hall; on *l.*, Statham Lodge. On *r.*, Dunham Massey. On *r.*, Lymm Hall and Outhrington Hall. At Altrincham, on *l.*, Oldfield Hall. Altrincham, p. 341.

Altrincham to Stockport (8¾—20½); fair road through Timperley, 13¼, over Baguley Moor, and through Sharston, 15¾, to Cheadle, 17¾, and then rough to Stockport, through which is paved. Pretty country.

On *r.*, Timperley Hall. Before Sharston, on *l.*, Withenshaw Hall. Beyond Cheadle, on *l.*, Heath Bank. Stockport, p. 168.

Stockport to Mottram (7½—28); over New Bridge, 21½, through Butterhouse Green, 23½, by Hyde Chapel or Gee Cross, 25, through Greenside, 26¼, and Hattersley, 26¾.

(*Mottram*: Junction, *B.T.C.*)

At New Bridge, on *r.*, Wood Bank; 1*m.* farther, Woodbury Hall and Highfield *Ho.* On *l.*, 1*m.*, Hyde Hall. Mottram, also called Mottram-in-Longdendale.

MANCHESTER TO LIVERPOOL.

Manchester to Warrington (18½)—p. 341.

Warrington to Liverpool (17¾—36¼)—p. 153.

DERBY TO MANSFIELD.

Derby to Eastwood (11¼); in Derby turn to *r.*, and then to *l.*, and follow the Ripley road to Little Chester, 1, then turn to *r.*, and through Morley, 4¾, Smalley, 6¼, and Heanor, 9¼, just before Eastwood turning to *r.* and crossing *R.* Erewash.

At Morley, on *l.*, the Priory. At Smalley, on *l.*, Stainsley Hall. On *r.* Heanor Hall.

Eastwood to Mansfield (11—22¼); turn to *l.*, and it is a hilly road through Brinsley, 12¾ (about 1*m.* farther keep to *r.*), and Annesley, 15¾. Returning, 1½*m.* out of Mansfield keep to *r.*

On *l.*, Eastwood Hall and Brinsley Hall; on *r.*, Annesley Hall; before it, on *r.*, Felley Abbey. Mansfield, p. 187.

MANCHESTER TO SHEFFIELD.

Manchester, St. Ann's square, **to Hyde** (7¾); up Market street, along Piccadilly, down London road, through Ardwick Green, 1¾, Gorton, 3½, and Denton, 6, is a bad road, being paved nearly all the way.

Beyond Gorton, on *l.*, Audenshaw *Ho.* Before Denton, on *r.*, Hyde Hall.

Hyde to Mottram (2½—10¼); good rise for first 2*m.*, then down into and through Mottram: good macadam road, with some short patches of pavement at long intervals.

[Or from Manchester, nearly all paved through Openshaw, 3, Audenshaw, 5, to *Ashton-under-Lyne*, 7, Staleybridge, 8½ (cross *R.* Tame), and Tongfold, 10, to *Mottram*, 11¾.]

Mottram, p. 356.

Mottram to Glossop (5—15¼); dangerous descent out of Mottram, partly paved, to Hollingworth, 11 (keep to *r.*), and the rest is undulating over Woolley Bridge, 11¼ (cross *R.* Etherow), and by Glossop Hall, 14¼.

Glossop, p. 177.

Glossop to Ashopton Inn or Cock's Bridge (12—27¼); steep rises for 4*m.* over Glossop Moor, and then from Lady Clough House, 20¼, a long descent down Woodland or Ashop Dale, behind the Peak, by Snake Inn, 22, and over Alport Bridge, 24, the road being bad and rough most of the distance. Very wild scenery.

Ashopton Inn to Sheffield (11—38¼); the road soon gets rough again and there is a long steep hill up to Hollow Meadows, 32¼, on Hallam Moors, and then downhill by Rivelin Mill, 34¼, and Lidgate, 36¼.

This route is not to be recommended.

Sheffield, p. 178.

MANCHESTER TO SHEFFIELD (by Penistone).

Manchester to Mottram (10¼)—above.

Mottram to Woodhead, Crowden Bridge (5¾—16); dangerous descent out of Mottram, partly paved, to Hollingworth, 11 (keep to *l.*), then rather hilly and loose to Tintwistle, 12¼, soon after which an ascent of about 4*m.* runs up Longden Dale by Hollins, 14¼, to Woodhead; it is very rough stony and sandy, and the latter half being also steep.

Beyond Tintwistle, on *r.*, Vale *Ho.* On *r.*, Torside Reservoir.

Woodhead to Penistone (12½—28½); mostly uphill by Further Woodhead, 17¾, up to the top of the Etherow valley to Salterscroft or Salters Brook *Ho.*, 20½, and hilly but more favourable road, improving to very good approaching Thurlston, 27½.

Beyond Woodhead, on *l.*, is the Woodhead Tunnel, one of the longest in England, nearly 3*m.* long. Penistone, p. 182.

Penistone to Sheffield (12½—41)—p. 182, reversed.

[Or 3*m.* before Thurlston on *r.* through Deep Car to *Sheffield* (16—40½) —p. 182, alternative route reversed.]

SHEFFIELD TO CONGLETON.

Sheffield, *M.P.*, **to Hathersage** (9); beginning with a steep unrideable ascent out of Sheffield, then through Little Sheffield, 1¼, Bents, 3½, and Ringinglow *Tp.*, 5, is a continuous uphill to Foxhouse Inn, 6, from which there is a ½*m.* descent, followed, after a good rise to Millstone Edge, by another very steep and dangerous descent to Hathersage, impossible to be ridden down.

Hathersage to Castleton (6—15); up the valleys of the Derwent and Noe, through Hope, 13½, is almost level, and capital running.

At Castleton, on *l.*, Peak Castle. Fine scenery.

Castleton to Chapel-en-le-Frith (6—21); very steep ascent (dangerous to ride down the other direction without a brake) out of Castleton to near the Mam Tor, then (keeping to *r.*) pretty level and good road for 2*m.*, and a steady 3*m.* fall into Chapel-en-le-Frith.

Beyond Castleton, on *r.*, Odin Mine and Mam Tor, or the Shivering Mountain; on *l.*, Blue John Mine and Peak Cavern. 3 or 4*m.* on *r.*, The Peak Mountain.

Chapel-en-le-Frith to Macclesfield (13—34); through Kettleshulme and Rainow.

Macclesfield, p. 169.

Macclesfield to Congleton (8—42); rather hilly through Gawsworth; two or three stiff ascents and awkward crooked descent into Congleton.

Congleton, p. 153.

CHESTERFIELD TO GAINSBOROUGH.

Chesterfield to Barlborough (8); through Brimington, 2½, and Staveley, 4½. Returning, at Brimington keep to *l.*

Beyond Chesterfield, on *r.*, Tapton Hall and Grove. Beyond Brimington, on *r.*, Ringwood Hall. On *l.*, Barlborough Hall.

Barlborough to Worksop (7—15), through Whitwell, 11¼.

Before Worksop, on *r.*, Manor *Ho*. Worksop, p. 193.

Worksop to Retford, White Hart Inn (7¾—22¾); in Worksop turn first to *r.* and then to *l.*, and through Manton, 16¾, Ranby, 20, and Babworth, 21½.

On *l.*, Babworth Hall. Retford, p. 196.

Retford to Gainsborough (9¾—32½); turn to *l.*, and through Welham, 24 (keep to *l.*), Clareborough, 25½, Wheatley, 27¼, Saundby, 29¼, and Beckingham *Tp.*.. 30 (keep to *r.*).

LINCOLN TO WAINFLEET.

Lincoln to Langworth Bridge (6)—p. 219.

Langworth Bridge to Wragby (4¾—10¾), over Clay Bridge, 7¾, is a bad road.

(*Wragby*: Turner Arms.)

At Clay Bridge, on *r.*, Abbey ruins.

Wragby to Horncastle (10¼—21); through Langton, 12, by Midge Inn, 14¼, through Bamburgh, 17, and Eldington *Tp.*, 18½, is a wretched road: about halfway is a stiff hill to mount, after which it is mostly downhill.

On *l.*, Bamburgh Hall; on *r.*, Eldington Grove. Horncastle, p. 220.

Horncastle to Spilsby (9½—30½); take second turn to *l.* in Horncastle, and through High Toynton, 22½, Winceby, 25¼, Lusby, 26½, Mavis Enderby, 28, and Hundleby, 29½, is rather hilly and bad in places.

Spilsby, p. 219.

Spilsby to Wainfleet (9¾—40¼); through Halton Holgate, 30½, Great Steeping, 32½, Irby, 35¼, and Thorp, 38.

(*Wainfleet*: Angel.)

SHEFFIELD TO LOUTH.

Sheffield to Rotherham (6); from Ladies' Bridge is level but rough through the town to Brightside, and when clear of the suburbs is a very fair level road through Attercliffe, 1½, Carbrook, 2¼, and Tinsley, 3½; Rotherham streets are roughly paved and there is a descent down the main street, with corresponding rise up the other side.

Rotherham, p. 187.

Rotherham to Tickhill (11—17); long hill out of Rotherham, turning to *r.* through the town, then bad and bumpy macadam road to Wickersley, 10, after which it gets somewhat better, the surface being chalky, but in wet weather it is very greasy, through Bramley, 11, and Maltby, 13, after which is rather hilly.

[Or at Tinsley turn to *r.* and by Crankley Mill, 5, to Wickersley, 9].

On *l.*, Bramley Grange; on *r.*, Maltby Hall. Tickhill, p. 193.

Tickhill to Bawtry (4—21); long hill to mount at Tickhill Spittal, 18½, and descent into Bawtry: very bad road.

Bawtry, p. 196.

Bawtry to Gainsborough (13¼—34¼); through Scafforth *Tp.*, 22¼, Everton, 24¼, Drake Holes, 25¼, Gringley-on-the-Hill, 27¾, Pear Tree *Tp.*, 29¼, Beckingham, 31, and Beckingham *Tp.*, 31¾ (turn to *l.*), and cross *R.* Trent just before Gainsborough: very bad road.

At Drake Holes, on *r.* 1*m.*, ruins of Mattersey Abbey; a little farther Wiseton Park. Gainsborough, p. 214.

Gainsborough to Spital-in-the-Street (11¼—45½); through Little Corringham, 38½, and Harpswell, 43½.

Beyond Gainsborough, on *r.*, Somerby Park. At Harpswell, 1*m.* on *r.*, Glentworth. Spital, p. 215.

Spital-in-the-Street to Market Rasen (10—55½); through Glentham, 48, over Bishop's Bridge, 50, through West Rasen, 52½, and Middle Rasen, 54½.

At Market Rasen, on *r.*, 1*m.*, Lissington Park; p. 220.

Market Rason to Louth (14¾—70¼); through North Willingham, 59, Ludford, 61½, and South Elkington, 68, very bad road. Returning, 1¼m. out of Louth keep to r., and at 3½m. keep to l.

At North Willingham, on l., Willingham Hall. On r., Grange ruins. Louth, p. 219.

SHEFFIELD TO RETFORD.

Sheffield to Worksop (18); from Ladies' Bridge is level but rough through the town to Brightside; at Attercliffe, 1½, turn to r. and through Darnal, 2½, Handsworth, 4½, Aston, 8½, Conduit Hill, 9½, Todwick, 10¼, South Anston, 12, and Gateford, 16. Returning, 1m. out of Worksop keep to l.

At Handsworth, on r., Bramley Hall and Woodthorpe; on l., Orgreave Hall. Before Aston, on l., Falkner *Ho.*; on r., Aston Hall. On l., Todwick Grange. On r., Gateford Hill; on l., Walling Wells. Worksop, p. 193.

Worksop to Retford, White Hart Inn (7¾—25¾); in Worksop turn to l., and then as at p. 358.

[Or to Maltby, 13, p. 359; thence on r. by Oldcoates, the surface improves and is more sandy towards Blyth, 20½, and at Barnby Moor Inn, 23½, join the Great North Road and to *Retford*, 26½—p. 196, reversed.]

2m. beyond Maltby, on l., Sandbeck Park. On l., Blyth Hall. Retford, p. 196.

LINCOLN TO SALTFLEET.

Lincoln to Wragby (10¾)—p. 359.

Wragby to Louth (13½—24¼); turn to l. and through West Barkwith, 13, East Barkwith, 13¾, Hainton, 16, Heneage Arms, 16¾, Burgh-on-Bain, 17¾, and Welton, 20½.

On l., Hainton Hall. Louth, p. 219.

Louth to Saltfleet (10—34¼); through Grimoldby, 28, and Saltfleetby St. Peter's, 31¼.

LOUTH TO BRIGG or GLANFORD BRIDGE.

Louth to Market Rasen (14¾)—above; reversed.

Market Rasen to Caistor (8¼—23)—p. 220.

Caistor to Brigg or Glanford Bridge (9¼—32¼); through Clixby, 25½, Grassby, 26¼, Searby, 27¼, by Somerby Hall, 27¾, and through Bigby, 28½.

MANCHESTER TO GREAT GRIMSBY.

Manchester to Thurlston (27½)—pp. 357-8.

Thurlston to Barnsley (8½—36); through Hoyland Swaine, 29½, Silkstone, 32, and Dodworth, 34.

At Silkstone, on l., Banks Hall. Barnsley, p. 179.

Barnsley to Doncaster (15½—51½); through Ardsley, 38½, Darfield, 41½, Billingley Green, 43, Hickleton, 45½, Marr, 47½, and York Bar, 50, where, on returning, keep to l.

On l., Ardsley Hall. At Darfield, on l., Middlewood Hall and Edderthorpe *Ho.* At Hickleton on r., Hickleton Hall; on l., Bilham Hall. At York Bar, on r., Cusworth Park. Doncaster, p. 196.

Doncaster to Hatfield (7—58½); keep to *l.* and through Streetthorpe, 55, and Park Lane, 56½.

Beyond Doncaster, on *r.*, Green *Ho.*; on *l.*, Wheatley Hall.

Hatfield to Crowle (9¾—68¼); leaving Hatfield, keep to *r.*, and through Tudworth, 60½, over Durtness Bridge, 64¼, and Double Bridge, 66½.

Crowle to Burton-upon-Stather (8—76¼); through Eastoft, 71¼, Luddington, 73, Garthorpe, 74¾, (turn to *r.*, and ¾ *m.* farther cross *R.* Trent) and Burton Stather, 75¾.

On *l.*, Eastoft Hall.

Burton-upon Stather to Barton-on-Humber (11½—87¾); through Thealby, 77¾, and South Ferriby, 85.

Barton, p. 216.

Barton-on-Humber to Killingholme (9—96¾); through Barrow, 90¼ (turn to *r.*), and Thornton, 93¼.

On *r.*, Barrow Hall; on *l.*, Thornton Hall. Beyond, Thornton College, and ruins of the abbey or priory, founded 1139.

Killingholme to Great Grimsby (14¾—111½); through Irmingham, 98 (keep to *r.*), Habrough, 98¾ (keep to *l.*), Brocklesby, 101¼ (keep to *l.*), Keelby, 102¾ (keep to *l.*), Aylesby, 106½ (keep to *r.*), Laceby, 107¼, and by the Three Nuns, 110½. Returning, at Three Nuns keep to *r.*, out of Laceby to *r.*, beyond Aylesby to *r.*, and again at Brocklesby and Habrough. No hills, and splendid surface the whole way.

On *l.*, Brocklesby Hall; on *r.*, Spring Park. Grimsby, p. 219.

SHEFFIELD TO THORNE.

Sheffield to Rotherham (6)—p. 359.

Rotherham to Conisborough (6½—12½); when clear of the town the road is on a gradual incline for some distance, then comes a sharp descent, followed by up and down a stiff hill to Thribergh, 9, out of which is another hill to mount, and again out of Hooton Roberts, 10½, to Hilltop, whence it is level to Conisborough; good road.

Beyond Rotherham, on *l.*, Eastwood *Ho.* On *l.*, Thribergh Hall. Before Hooton Roberts, on *r.*, Ravenfield Park. At Conisborough are ruins of an old castle, which is the scene of Sir Walter Scott's "Ivanhoe." On *r.*, Crookhill Hall.

Conisborough to Doncaster (5—17½); hill to mount out of Conisborough and then through Warmsworth, 14¾, and Balby, 16: good road.

On *r.*, Warmsworth Hall, Broom *Ho.* At Balby, on *r.*, St. Catherines. Doncaster, p. 196.

Doncaster to Hatfield (7—24½)—above.

Hatfield to Thorne (4—28½); keep to *l.*

MANCHESTER TO HULL.

Manchester to Oldham (7¼); paved along Oldham street or road, and to Newton Heath, 3, then bad macadam and rising ground through Failsworth, 4¼, and Hollinwood, 5½, with steep hill to mount to Oldham:

paved through the town, tramway all the way. [Or beyond Failsworth, on *r.* through Aldershaw to Oldham, 7.]
(*Oldham :* Angel.)

Oldham to New Delph (6¼—13½); hilly road through Austerlands, 10, with a long steep downhill into New Delph: fair surface, but sandy occasionally.

New Delph to Marsden (6¼—19¾); steep ascent for 2*m.* over Diggle or Stand Edge, the top being reached (1271 ft.) just beyond Stand Edge (the first) reservoir, and then downhill into Marsden, which requires careful riding, being more or less steep, with a total fall of 640 ft. in last 2¾*m.*; very rough road, in parts loose and sandy.

[Or from Manchester by *Ashton-under-Lyne* (7)—p. 357; then outside the town keep to *l.*, and the road is uphill, and rough and bad for bicycling to Mossley, 10½, after which it is mostly downhill and good to Saddleworth, 15: from here begins the steep ascent of Diggle Edge, 1½*m.* before the top of which join the other road, to *Marsden*, 21.

Or just beyond Mossley keep to *l.* through Lidgate, joining the principal route a little past Austerlands, and on to *New Delph*, 15.]

The road here goes over Stanedge Tunnels, one railway and the other canal. About half way up the hill, ½*m.* on *l.*, a Roman camp.

Marsden to Huddersfield (6¾—26½); running down the Colne valley, the road is on a gradual fall, but with rather rough surface, through Gatehead *Tp.*, 20¼, Slaithwaite, 22¼, and Linthwaite, 22½, to Hollywell, 23¼, then after a little rise downhill again into Huddersfield: the road runs parallel with *R.* Colne, canal, and railway the whole distance: this is the new turnpike road. [The old road runs from Gatehead *Tp.* on *r.* through Bradley Brook, 22¼, and Black Moor Foot, 23¾, to Huddersfield, 26¼; more hilly.]

1*m.* out of Marsden, a little on *l.*, across the valley, is Slaithwaite Hall. Huddersfield, pp. 178 and 180.

Huddersfield to Nunbrook (4¼—31); keep down the Colne valley through Bradley, 29½, and over Cooper's Bridge, 30 (cross *R.* Calder).

At Bradley, on *r.*, Heaton Lodge. At Nunbrook, on *l.*, Kirkless Hall.

Nunbrook to Dewsbury (4—35); turn to *r.* and down the Calder valley through Christchurch, 31½.

(*Dewsbury :* Royal, *B.T.C.*)

About half way, on *l.*, Blake Hall; a little farther, on *r.*, Sands Ho.

Dewsbury to Wakefield (5—40); keep to *r.* out of the former and through Streetside, 36½; rather hilly.

[Or in *Huddersfield* turn to *r.*, cross *R.* Colne, and through Almondbury, 28½, Highgate Lane, 30, Lepton, 31, by Denby Grange, 33½, Over Shittlington, 35, over Horbury Bridge, 36½, and through Horbury, 37½, to *Wakefield*, 40.]

At Highgate Lane, on *l.*, Lascelles Hall. Beyond Lepton, on *l.*, Whitley Hall. On *l.*, Denby Grange; on *r.*, Manor Ho. Beyond Horbury, on *r.*, Lupset Hall. Wakefield, p. 179.

Wakefield to Pontefract (9¼—49¼); in Wakefield past the railway turn to *r.*, and after crossing *R.* Calder keep to *l.*, then through Agbridge, 41¼ (over canal), Crofton, 43½ (keep to *l.*), Street House *Tg.*, 45, and Purston Jacklin, 47.

At Agbridge, on *l.*, Heath Old Hall. On *r.*, Crofton Hall; and 2*m.* beyond it, Nostell Priory. At Street House *Tg.*, on *l.*, Snydale Hall. Pontefract, p. 203.

Pontefract to Snaith (12¼—61¾); at 1½*m.* cross the Great North Road and through Knottingley (end of), 52¼, Kellingley, 53¼, by Kellington Mill, 55, through Hut or Hud Green, 56¼, and Little Heck, 59.

(*Snaith:* Downe Arms.)

Snaith to Howden (9¼—71); past Cowick New Park on *r.*, over Turnbridge, 63¼, through Rawcliffe, 64½, and Armin, 67¾, and cross *R.* Ouse at Booth Ferry, 69¼.

At Howden are ancient *ch.*, and palace of the Bishops of Durham.

Howden to South Cave, *Ch.* (12—83); turn to *r.*, through Belby, 72½, Eastrington, 74¾, Gilberdike, 76½, Newport, 78, and North Cave, 81, where keep to *r.*

At North Cave, on *l.*, Hotham Hall. At South Cave, on *l.*, Cave Castle.

South Cave to Anlaby (8¼—91¼); through Riplingham *Tp.*, 86½, and Kirk Ella (*ch.*), 90¼. Returning, out of Anlaby turn to *r.*, and a little farther to *l.*

[Or from North Cave go direct on *l.* to Riplingham *Tp.*; ¼*m.* shorter.]

On *l.*, Riplingham Grange and Rowley Manor *Ho.*; 1*m.* farther, on *r.*, Raywell. On *r.*, Anlaby *Ho.*

Anlaby to Hull, *M.H.* (4¼—95½).

[Or at *South Cave* turn to *r.*, through Brough *Tp.*, 85 (keep to *l.*), Elloughton, Welton, 86, Melton, 87, North Ferriby, 88¼, and Hessle to *Hull*, 95½.

Or from North Ferriby on *l.* by Swanland, 89¾, to *Anlaby*, 92¼, and *Hull*, 96½.]

On *l.*, Welton *Ho.*; 1*m.* farther, on *l.*, Melton Hill. Before Hessle, on *r.*, Hesslewood *Ho.*; on *l.*, Tranby *Ho.*, Tranby, and Hessle Mount. Hull, p. 216.

Through Hull to Hedon, 8, thence to Patrington, 10, and on to Spurn Head, 11¼.

MANCHESTER TO HULL (by Leeds).

Manchester to Nunbrook (31)—p. 362.

Nunbrook to Leeds (11—42); through Mill Bridge, 33¼, Birstall, 35 (keep to *r.*), Bruntcliffe Thorne, 36½, Morley, 37¾, Churwell, 38¾, and Beeston, 39¾, is a harassing ride; it is very rough and there are several bad hills, the worst being that out of Birstall; for the last 3*m.* the road is almost impassable.

At Birstall, on *l.*, Oakwell Hall; on *r.*, Rydings. Leeds, p. 191.

Leeds to Selby (20¼—62¼); take the Tadcaster road to Black Bank, 43, then turn to *r.*, through Halton, 45¼, Whitchurch or Whitkirk, 46¼, West Garforth, 48½, by Peckfield *Ho.*, 52 (cross Pontefract and Wetherby road), 2½*m.* farther strike Great North Road and follow it back for a short distance (towards Ferrybridge), then turn off to *l.*, through Monk Frystone, 55¾, Hambleton, 58, and Thorpe Willoughby, 60.

Before Black Bank, on *r.*, Hall *Ho.*; a little on *l.*, The Hare Hills; beyond, on *l.*, Killingbeck Hall. At Halton, on *r.*, Temple Newsam and Park. Beyond Whitkirk, on *l.*, Austhorpe Hall. At West Garforth on *l.* Barrowly Hall. Just before G. N. Road, on *r.*, Ledstone Hall and Park. 1*m.* before Monk Frystone, on *r.*, Frysland Lodge. At Hambleton, on *r.*, Gateforth Hall. On *l.*, Thorpe Hall. Selby, p. 211.

Selby to Howdon (10—72¼); through Barlby, 63¾ (turn to *r.* and again keep to *r.* a little farther on), Hemingborough, 67¼, Barmby-on-the-Marsh, 68¾ (keep to *l.*), Asselby, 70¼, and Knedlington, 71. [Or at Hemingborough on *l.* through Newsholme, 69¾.]

Howden to Hull, *M.H.* (24½—96¾)—p. 363.

[Or from *Selby* through Barlby, 63¾, North Driffield, 67¾, Bubwith, 69¾, Harlthorpe, 71¼, Foggathorpe, 72¼, Major Bridge, 74¼, and Holme-on-Spalding Moor, 75¼, to *Market Weighton*, 80¾, the road is said to be almost impassable for a bicycle. Thence by *Beverley*, 90¼, to *Hull*, 99, see p. 216.]

LIVERPOOL TO SCARBOROUGH.

Liverpool to Prescot (8)—p. 153, reversed.

Prescot to St. Helen's (3¾—11¾); keep to *l.* and it is a bumpy macadam road; St. Helen's is paved with square setts.

(*St Helen's :* Bird-i'-th'-Hand, *Hqrs.*; Commercial, *B.T.C.*)

About half way, on *l.*, Eccleston Hall; on *r.*, the Ravenshead Glass Works. 1*m.* N. of St. Helen's is Windleshaw Abbey.

St. Helen's to Ashton-in-Makerfield (5½—17¼); the square sett paving extends a short distance out of St. Helen's, the road being slightly on the fall, then there is a short stiff rise to mount, with cobble stone paving in the middle and loose surface generally at the sides, and the rest is a fair undulating road by Black Brook, 13¾, and Ashton Cross, 15¾. Ashton is paved.

1*m.* beyond St. Helen's, on *l.*, Carr Hall. Beyond Black Brook, on *l.*, Garswood Hall. Ashton, p. 157.

Ashton-in-Makerfield to Hindley (4½—21¾). [Or turn to *l.* to *Wigan*, 22 (p. 157); thence on *r.* to *Hindley*, 24.]

Hindley to Bolton (8½—30¼); through West Houghton, 24¼ (keep to *r.*) Over Hulton, 26, and Middle Hulton, 27¼ (keep to *l.*)

[Or from West Houghton straight on through Dean, ½*m.* shorter.]

On *r.*, Hulton Park. Bolton, p. 168.

Bolton to Bury (5¾—36); through Cockley, 32¾, and Starling, 34½: steep hill to climb up through Bury from *R.* Irwell.

Bury, p. 171.

Bury to Rochdale (7¼—43¼); cross *R.* Roche and through Heywood, 39¾, and Marland, 41¼. [Or a little shorter road is over Hooley Bridge.]

At Rochebridge, on *l.*, Bridge Hall; on *r.*, Moss Hall. On *l.*, Heywood Hall, and beyond, Bamford Hall and Crimble Hall. 1*m.* beyond Marland, on *r.*, Castleton and Castlemere. Rochdale, p. 174.

Rochdale to Littleborough (3¼—46½)—p. 174.

Littleborough to Ripponden (7½—54); keeping to *r.*, the road has a long and difficult climb over Blackstone Edge for 3 or 4*m.*, then downhill by Bailings Gate, 51¼.

Before Ripponden, on *r.*, Rishworth Hall.

Ripponden to Elland (4¼—58¼); turn on *r.*, cross *R.* Ribourne, and through Greetland, 57.

Elland to Birstall (8¼—66½); through Rastrick, 60, Brighouse, 61¼ (turn to r., and through the town, keep to l.), Cleckheaton, 61¼, and Gomersall, 65½.

(*Cleckheaton*: George, *Hqrs, B.T.C.*)

Birstall to Leeds (7—73½)—p. 363.

Leeds to Tadcaster (14½—87½); by Black Bank, 74½, Halton *Tp.*, 75¾ (keep to *l.*), Seacroft, 77¾ (keep first to *l.* then to *r.*), Kiddall Lane End, 81¼, and White Hart Inn, 83½ (cross G. N. Road), is a good road but rather hilly for the first 5m.

Out of Leeds, on *r.*, Hall *Ho.*; on *l.*, The Hare Hills. Beyond Halton *Tp.*, on *l.*, Killingbeck Hall. On *l.*, Seacroft Hall. At Kiddall Lane End, on *r.*, Potterton Lodge; a little farther, on *l.*, Bramham Park. Beyond White Hart Inn, on *r.*, Hazlewood Hall. Tadcaster, p. 211.

Tadcaster to York (9—96¾)—p. 211.

York to Malton (18—114¾)—pp. 212-3.

Malton to Scarborough (22¼—137)—p. 213.

LIVERPOOL TO LEEDS (by Halifax).

Liverpool to Ripponden (54)—p. 364.

Ripponden to Halifax (5½—59½); by Triangle Inn, 55½, Sowerby Bridge, 57 (keep to *l.*), and King Cross, 58½, where, on returning, keep to *l.*

(*Halifax*: White Lion, *B.T.C.*; White Swan.)

Halifax to Bradford (8½—68½); through North Owram, 61¾, and Great Horton, 66½. Bradford is paved with granite.

On *r.*, North Owram Hall. Before Bradford, on *l.*, Little Horton Hall. Bradford, p. 179.

Bradford to Leeds (9¼—78); leaving Bradford the road is pretty level for nearly 2½m., then comes a long ascent of 1½m., which can be ridden up, through Stanningley, 72; after that it is undulating for a couple of miles, and the rest is all downhill over Kirkstall Bridge, 75, down Airedale, and through Burley, 76½, into Leeds, which is 400 ft. lower than Bradford: good macadam road outside the towns, which are granite paved.

[There is a more direct road from *Halifax* through Drighlington to *Leeds*.]

Splendid views. At Kirkstall Bridge, on *l.*, Kirkstall Abbey. Leeds, p. 191.

MANCHESTER TO SCARBOROUGH.

Manchester to Leeds (42)—p. 363.

Leeds to Scarborough (63½—105½)—above.

WAKEFIELD TO ABERFORD.

Wakefield to Oulton (5); through Stanley, 1¾, and Newmarket, 3½.

1m. out of Wakefield, on *r.*, Clark Hall; on *l.*, Garlick Hall. On *r.*, Stanley Hall; on *l.*, Hatfield Hall. At Newmarket, on *r.*, Royds Hall. On *l.*, Oulton Hall.

Oulton to Aberford (8—13); over Swillington Bridge, 6¼, through

Swillington, 7½, and over Garforth Bridge, 9. Returning, 1m. out of Aberford turn to r.
On r., Swillington Hall; on l., Leventhorpe Hall. At Garforth Bridge, on l., Barrowby Hall. Aberford, p. 197.

YORK TO HULL.

York to Grimston Bar (2¼) is macadam, and rather lumpy.

Grimston Bar to Barnby-on-the-Moor (8—10¼); keeping to r., the road improves, and has good surface in some places, over Kexby Bridge, 5½, to Wilberfoss, 7½, and then is loose and bad to Barnby.
On r., Grimston Hall.

Barnby-on-the-Moor to Market Weighton (7½—18¼); pretty level, but otherwise not good travelling, by Pocklington New Inn, 13, Hayton, 13¾, and Shipton, 16½. [Or at Barnby, on l., to Pocklington, 12¾, whence to Pocklington New Inn, 14¼.]
At Pocklington, on l., Kildwick Percy Hall. At Shipton, on l., Londesborough Park. Market Weighton, p. 214.

Market Weighton to Beverley, M.H. (10—23½); keep to l., and there is a long steep ascent before Arras, 21, then fairly level across York Wolds for about 3m., followed by a steep and loose descent into Bishop Burton, 25½, and downhill more or less to Beverley: the road is very bad and rough, and the hills very loose and steep.
Before Bishop Burton, on l., High Hall. Beverley, p. 216.

Beverley to Hull, M.H. (9—37½)—p. 216, reversed.
[Or at Market Weighton, on r., through Sancton, 20¾, and Newbald, 22½, to *South Cave*, 26¼, whence to *Hull*, 12½—33¼, p. 363.]

YORK TO BRIDLINGTON.

York to Grimston Bar (2¼) is macadam and rather lumpy.

Grimston Bar to Gate Helmsley (3½—6); keep to l., and the road is bad, being sandy and stony, through Holtby, 5.

Gate Helmsley to Garraby Street Inn (6½—12½); the road now improves, crossing the *R.* Derwent at Stamford Bridge, 7½, and is pretty level.
At Stamford Bridge, the Saxons under Harold defeated the Norwegians, previous to the invasion of England by the Normans.

Garraby Street Inn to Fridaythorpe (6—18½); from Garraby is a steep hill to walk up, the rise being about 510 feet to the mile.

Fridaythorpe to Driffield (10—28½); take the right hand road, and after the first 2 or 3m. it is chiefly downhill through Wetwang, 22½, and Garton, 25½.

Driffield to Bridlington (11½—40)—p. 216.
[From *Fridaythorpe* there is another road on l. through Fimber, 20, Siedmere, 24, then across the York Wolds to Rudstone, 36, and through Boynton, 38, to *Bridlington*, 41.]
At Sledmere, on r., Sledmere Park and Castle.

LIVERPOOL TO PRESTON.

Liverpool to Ormskirk (13½) is fairly level; paved to Walton, 3, then the cobble stones begin, and continue with alternate patches of macadam through Maghull, 8, and Aughton, 11.

(*Ormskirk*: Buck-i'-th'-Vine, *B.T.C.*; King's Arms; Wheatsheaf.)

Before Walton, on *r.*, the Priory. At Walton, on *r.*, Walton Hall. On *r.*, Maghull Hall. Before Ormskirk, on *r.*, Wimbrick Hall. Just past Ormskirk, on *r.*, Lathom *Ho.*

Ormskirk to Preston (13½—31½); through Burscough, 15½, by Burscough Bridge Inn, 16½, through Rufford, 18½, Sollom, 21½, over Tarleton Bridge, 22½, through Much Hoole, 24, Longton, 26½, and over Penwortham Bridge, 30½, is a good macadam road, hilly but nothing difficult; descent into Preston.

1m. past Ormskirk, on *r.*, Burscough Priory. At Burscough, on *r.*, Briars Hill; a little farther, on *r.*, Carr Hall. On *l.*, Rufford Hall. At Tarleton Bridge, on *r.*, Bank Hall. At Longton, on *r.*, Drumacre Hall; a little farther, on *r.*, Hutton Hall. On *l.*, Penwortham Hall. Preston, p. 158.

[From Liverpool to *Southport*, 19, is very bad, being either paved or sandy and heavy. Or from Ormskirk, on *l.*, to Southport, is a very fair road. Most of the roads about Southport are bad for bicycling.]

(*Southport*: Bold Arms, *B.T.C.*, Railway; Victoria.)

PRESTON TO WAKEFIELD.

Preston to Blackburn (11½); cross R. Ribble to Walton-le-Dale, 1¾, then take middle road and through Hoghton Lane, 4½, and Hoghton, 6½. [Or outside Preston turn to *l.*, 2½m. farther cross R. Ribble and through Samelsbury: a little shorter.] Blackburn is paved.

On *r.*, Walton Hall; beyond on *r.*, Darwen Bank and Banister's Hall. Before Hoghton Lane, on *r.*, Bradle *Ho.* On *l.*, Hoghton Tower. 2m. before, on *l.*, Witton Park and *Ho.* Blackburn, p. 173.

Blackburn to Accrington (5½—16¾); a little out of Blackburn keep to *r.* and through Church, 15¾; paved through Accrington.

About half way, on *r.*, Knuzden Hall. Accrington, p. 172.

Accrington to Burnley (6½—23¼); through Huncoat and Bentley Wood Green.

[Or beyond Blackburn keep to *l.* and by Bottom Gate, 12¾, Rushton, 14¼, Clayton-le-Moors, 16¾, Altham, 18¾, and Padiham, 20, to *Burnley*, 23½.]

Before Clayton, on *r.*, Dunken Haigh and Henfield *Ho.*; beyond, on *l.*, Clayton Hall. At Padiham, on *l.*, Huntroyd Hall. At Altham, on *r.*, Shuttleworth Hall. Burnley, p. 173.

Burnley to Todmorden (9½—32¼)—p. 174, reversed.

[Or, 1½m. out of Blackburn keep to *r.* to *Haslingden*, 19, half uphill and half down; thence nearly all downhill, and a good macadam road except for one patch of paving, to *Rawtenstall*, 21; from here up the Irwell valley by the lower road, through Waterfoot and Stacksteads to *Bacup*, 25, is fairly level, but for the greater part of the distance is three-fourths paved with square setts; out of Bacup a moderate ascent of 1½m. is followed by two steep unrideable descents into *Todmorden*, 31.]

Haslingden, p. 172. Todmorden, p. 174.

Todmorden to Halifax (12½—45¼); keep to *l.* and through Mytholm, 36¼, Hebden Bridge, 37, Mytholmroyd, 38½, Luddenden Foot, 40½, and King Cross, 43¾; running down the Calder valley all the way.

Halifax, p. 365.

Halifax to Dewsbury (10¾—56); through Hipperholm, 47¼ (keep to *r.* then to *l.*), Lightcliffe, 48¼, over Bailiff Bridge, 49, through Wommersley, 50¼, High Town, 51, Liversedge, 52, Mill Bridge, 52¾ (keep first to *l.* then to *r.*), and Heckmondwike, 54.

[Or before Luddenden Foot keep to *r.*, and through Sowerby Bridge, and Brighouse to *Nunbrook*, whence to *Dewsbury*, 4*m.* (p. 362), all close to *R.* Calder.]

Dewsbury to Wakefield (5—61)—p. 362.

PRESTON TO SCARBOROUGH.

Preston to Whalley (16½); cross *R.* Ribble to Walton-le-Dale, 1¾, then keep to *l.*, and through Samelsbury, 5½, Mellor, 8¾ (keep to *l.*), Sallisbury, 13, and Billington, 14¼; hilly road, but tolerably good surface: cobblestone paving through Whalley.

[Or to *Blackburn*, 11½, (p. 367), thence, after a long paved hill to mount out of the town, it is fairly good undulating road for over 4*m.*, and ending with a good descent to the bridge over *R.* Calder entering *Whalley*, 17¾.]

Whalley, p. 172.

Whalley to Gisburn (11—27½)—p. 172.

Gisburn to Skipton (11½—38½); through West Marton, 32½, East Marton, 33½, and Broughton, 36.

At West Marton, on *l.*, Gledstone and Ingthorpe Grange; on *r.*, Broughton Hall. Skipton, p. 179.

Skipton to Bolton Bridge (5¾—44¼)—p. 191, reversed.

Bolton Bridge to Blubberhouses (5¼—49½); very stiff uphill from Bolton Bridge for 3 or 4 miles, by Hazelwood, 45½, and across the moors: bad and hilly road.

Blubberhouses to Harrogate (10—59½); bad and hilly road over Forest Moor, by Kettlesing, 53½.

Harrogate, p. 191.

Harrogate to Knaresborough (2—61½).

Knaresborough, p. 192.

Knaresborough to Boroughbridge (7—68½)—p. 192.

Boroughbridge to Easingwold (10¼—78¾); after crossing *R.* Swale turn to *r.* and through Helperby, 72¼, over Pill Moor, and through Raskelf, 76¼.

Easingwold, p. 211.

Easingwold to Malton, *Ch.*, (19—97¾); by Bogg Hall, 81¼, through Yearsley, 84¾, Coulton, 87¼, Hovingham, 89½, Slingsby, 91½, Barton, 93¼, Appleton, 94¼, Amotherby, 94¾, Swinton, 95¼, and Broughton, 96,

Malton to Scarborough (22¼—120)—p. 213.

PRESTON TO YORK.

Preston to Skipton (38½)—p. 368.

Skipton to Otley (15—53½)—p. 191, reversed.

Otley to Harewood (8—61½); through Pool, 56½, Arthington, 58½ and Weardley, 60, running near R. Wharfe.

2m. beyond Otley, on r., Caley Hall; on l., Leathley Hall. On l., Arthington Hall. On r., Harewood Park and Ho.; also the Castle.

Harewood to Tadcaster (11—72½); good undulating road through Collingham, 66¼ (just beyond keep to r.), to Boston Spa, 68¾, then rather rough.

Beyond Collingham, on l., Beilby Grange; on r., Westwood Ho. Before Collingham, on l., Carlston Ho. and Wood Hall. Beyond Boston Spa, near the railway, on r., Oglethorpe Hall. Before Tadcaster, on r., Smaws Hall. Tadcaster, p. 211.

Tadcaster to York (9—81½)—p. 211.

[Or beyond Collingham, on l., across R. Wharfe to *Wetherby*, 67½; whence keeping to r. through Bickerton, 71, Bilton, 72½, Long Marston, 74¼, Rufforth, 76½, Acomb, 81¼, and Holdgate, 80½, to York, 82, the road is stony, loose and hilly.]

Wetherby, p. 197. 2m. beyond, on l., Swinnow Hall and Ingmanthorpe Hall; on r., Boggart Ho., and a little farther, Hall Park. On r., Bilton Hall and Manor Ho.; on l., Bilton Grange. At Long Marston, a little on r., Hutton Castle. York, p. 211.

BRADFORD (Yorks.) TO COLNE.

Bradford to Haworth, *Ch.* (8¾); through Manningham *Tg.*, 1¾ (keep to l.), Swain Royd, 4, Lingbob, 4½, and Cullingworth, 6½ (a mile farther turn to r. and afterwards to l.).

Haworth to Colne (9½—18¼); across the moors, through Stanbury, 10, Two Laws *Tg.*, 12, and over Laneshaw Bridge, 16. Returning, keep to r. a little out of Colne, and also at Laneshaw Bridge.

YORK TO BOROUGHBRIDGE.

York to Green Hammerton (10); hill to mount out of York, then through Holdgate, 1½ (keep to r.), and over Skip Bridge, 8½ (cross R. Nidd), is a level road, except one or two small hills, but very loose and rutty surface.

Before Green Hammerton, 1m. on l., Kirk Hammerton Park.

Green Hammerton to Boroughbridge (7—17); keep to r. and through Little Ouseburn, 12¼, is a bad road, up and down hill all the way; nearing Boroughbridge it improves, and there is a stiff descent into the town.

PRESTON TO YORK (by Knaresborough).

Preston to Knaresborough (61½)—p. 368.

Knaresborough to Green Hammerton (8—69½); turn to r. and a little out of Knaresborough keep to l., and through Flaxby, 64½, about ¾m.

farther join the Great North Road, and after following it back for ½m. turn on *l.* through Allerton Mauleverer, 66; a fairly level road, but bad for bicycling.

2*m.* past Knaresborough, on *r.*, Goldsborough Hall. On *l.*, Allerton Park and Hall.

Green Hammerton to York (10—79½)—p. 369, reversed.

DRIFFIELD TO MALTON.

Driffield to Sledmere (8); through Little Driffield, 1, and Garton, 3.

On *r.*, Sledmere Park.

Sledmere to Malton, otherwise New Malton (11½—19½); through Duggleslby, 13, and North Grimston, 15½, where, on returning, keep to *l.*

BRADFORD (Yorks.) TO RIPON.

Bradford to Otley (9½); through Eccleshill, 2½, over Apperley Bridge, 4¼ (*R.* Aire), through Nether Yeadon, 5¼, Upper Yeadon, 6¼ (turn to *l.*), and Guiseley, 7¾.

Beyond Eccleshill, on *l.*, Haigh Hall. Beyond Apperley Bridge, on *r.*, Upper Wood *Ho.*; on *l.*, Esholt Hall. Beyond Guiseley, 1*m.* on *l.*, Hawksworth Hall. Otley, p. 191.

Otley to Ripley (12—21½); cross *R.* Wharfe, then turn to *r.* and through Farnley, 11¼, West End, 13¼, Brackenthwaite, 16, Beckwith Shaw, 16¾, and Killinghall, 20¼, where, on returning, keep to *r.*

[Or at Upper Yeadon on *r.* to *Ripley*, 21¼, without touching Otley.]

On *r.*, Farnley Hall. Ripley, p. 192.

Ripley to Ripon (7¾—29¼)—p. 192.

LANCASTER TO SCARBOROUGH.

Lancaster to Hornby (9)—p. 176.

Hornby to Ingleton (9¼—18¼); through Melling, 10¾, Wrayton, 11½ (keep to *r.*), Cantsfield, 12¾, and Black Burton, 15¼, is a comparatively good road. Returning, a little out of Ingleton keep to *l.*

At Melling, on *r.* Wennington Hall. At Wrayton, on *l.*, Thurland Castle. On *l.*, Cantsfield *Ho.*

Ingleton to Clapham (4—22¼)—p. 173, reversed.

[Or ¼m. before Hornby, on *r.*, through Bentham, 14¾, whence over Newby Common or Moors, but the road is very bad and necessitates a deal of walking, to *Clapham*, 18¾.]

Clapham to Great Stainforth (5¾—28); turn to *l.* and through Wharfe, 24½, and Little Stainforth, 27½, in Ribblesdale.

Great Stainforth to Grassington (12—40); over Malham Moor, by Malham Water or Tarn, 32¾, Calecop, 37¼, Skirethorns, 38¾, and Threshfield, 39½, where turn to *l.*, and cross *R.* Wharfe to Grassington. [Or 1½m. past Wharfe, 24½, keep to *l.*, and over *R.* Ribble at Heath Bridge, rejoining the above road 1*m.* past Great Stainforth; 1*m.* shorter.]

On *l.*, Malham Water *Ho.*, and just before, Capon Hall.

Grassington to Pateley Bridge ($9\frac{3}{4}$—$49\frac{3}{4}$); entering Grassington turn to *r.*, and through Hebden, $41\frac{1}{4}$, over Dibbles Bridge, $42\frac{3}{4}$, and Bewerley Moor, and by Greenhow Hill, $46\frac{3}{4}$, the road is very hilly and is said to be impassable.

Before Pateley Bridge, on *r.*, Bewerley Hall. (*Pateley Bridge:* George.)

Pateley Bridge to Ripon (11—$60\frac{3}{4}$); turn to *r.* down the Nidd valley for a short distance, then turn to *l.*, and over Pateley Moor the road is frightfully hilly and rough.

About half way, on *l.*, Grantley Hall and North *Ho.* 3*m.* before Ripon, on *r.*, Studley Park. Ripon, p. 192.

Ripon to Thirsk ($12\frac{3}{4}$—$73\frac{1}{2}$); take the left hand road, and it is a stiff up and down hill ride across the Boroughbridge and Leeming road (at 65*m.*), and through Baldersby, $66\frac{1}{2}$, over Skipton Bridge, 68 (*R.* Swale), through Bushby Stoop, $69\frac{1}{2}$, and Carlton Miniot, 71.

Thirsk, p. 207.

Thirsk to Helmsley ($13\frac{1}{4}$—$86\frac{3}{4}$); beyond Thirsk take second turn on *r.*, and through Sutton-under-Whitestone-Cliff, $77\frac{1}{4}$, then a steep hill to climb over Hambleton Hill, and through Scawton (*ch.*), $82\frac{1}{4}$, and over Scawton Bridge, 84 (cross *R.* Rye); good and bad alternately.

Beyond Sutton, 1*m.* on *r.*, Osgood Hall. About 2*m.* S. of Scawton, ruins of Byland Abbey. At Scawton Bridge, on *l.*, ruins of Rivaulx Abbey. Helmsley, p. 212.

Helmsley to Kirby Moorside ($5\frac{1}{2}$—$92\frac{1}{4}$)—p. 212.

Kirby Moorside to Pickering, *Ch.* ($7\frac{3}{4}$—100); through Keldholme, $92\frac{3}{4}$, Sinnington, $95\frac{3}{4}$, Wrelton, $97\frac{1}{2}$, Aislaby, 98, and Middleton, $98\frac{1}{2}$.

On *r.*, Sinnington Manor *Ho.* Pickering, p. 213.

Pickering to Snainton, New Inn ($7\frac{1}{2}$—$107\frac{1}{2}$); through Farmanby Thornton (*ch.*), $102\frac{1}{2}$, Wilton, $103\frac{3}{4}$, Allerston, $104\frac{3}{4}$, and Ebberton, 106.

Snainton to Scarborough ($9\frac{3}{4}$—$117\frac{1}{4}$)—p. 213.

LANCASTER TO NORTHALLERTON.

Lancaster to Ingleton ($18\frac{1}{4}$)—p. 370.

Ingleton to Hawes ($16\frac{1}{2}$—$34\frac{3}{4}$); in Ingleton, turn to *l.* up the village, and the road is on the rise more or less for some 10*m.*, up the valley of the Doe or Dale Beck, with Ingleborough Hill on the right, and Whernside on the left, to Southerscales, $21\frac{3}{4}$, thence over Ingleton Fells to Geastones, $24\frac{3}{4}$, in Ribblesdale, which, follow up over Gale Moor to Newby Head Inn, $27\frac{1}{2}$, whence it is all down hill to Hawes; shockingly bad road.

(*Hawes:* White Hart.)

Hawes to Middleham ($17\frac{1}{2}$—$52\frac{1}{4}$)—p. 205, reversed.

Middleham to Bedale (10—$62\frac{1}{4}$); over Ulshaw Bridge, $53\frac{1}{2}$, through Thornton Steward, 56 (keep to *r.*), Rookwith, $58\frac{1}{4}$, and Burrill, $60\frac{1}{4}$. Returning, out of Bedale turn to *l.*

Beyond Ulshaw Bridge, on *l.*, Danby Hall and Dantzic *Ho.* On *l.*, Thornton

Grange; 1*m.* farther, on *r.*, Kilgram Grange. At Burrill, on *r.*, Thornton Hall. Bedale, p. 198.

Bedale to Northallerton (7½—69¼); at the end of Bedale turn to *l.* and through Aiscough or Aiskew, 62¼, Leeming Road *Ty.*, 63½, Morton, 65¾, and Ainderby, 66¼.

Before Morton, on *l.*, Scruton Park and Hall. Northallerton, p. 201.

LANCASTER TO STOCKTON-ON-TEES.

Lancaster to Hawes (34¾)—p. 371.

Hawes to Askrigg (6—40¾); fair easy road down Wensley Dale, through Bainbridge, 39¼, where keep to *l.*, and cross *R.* Ure.

Askrigg to Redmire (7—47¾)—p. 204, reversed.

Redmire to Richmond (11—58¾); keep to *l.*, and over Bellerby Moor by Halfpenny House, 53½, and over Barden Moor, is a hilly and rough road. [Or from Redmire to *Leyburn*, 52¼, p. 204 reversed; then turn to *l.* and through Bellerby, 53¼, to Halfpenny House, 55¼.]

At Halfpenny *Ho.*, on *l.*, Walburn Hall; 2*m.* farther, on *l.*, Hudswell Grange. Richmond, p. 206.

Richmond to Citadella (3¼—62); out of Richmond keep to *r.*, and it is a good road, on a gradual fall down the valley of the Swale, through St. Trinians, 59¾, and Brompton-upon-Swale, 61¾; see p. 206.

At Brompton, 1*m.* on *r.*, across *R.* Swale, Brough Hall.

Citadella to Enter Common, *Tp.* (9¼—71¼); through Scorton, 64, South Cowton, 66¼, North Cowton *Tg.*, 67¼, and Stragleton, 68.

At South Cowton, on *r.*, Pepper Hall.

Enter Common to Yarm (8½—79¾); first-rate road through High Worsall, 76¼, with a long and steep descent into Yarm; through the town is cobble-stone paving, which will necessitate walking.

On *l.*, Worsall Hall. Yarm, p. 207.

Yarm to Stockton-on-Tees (4—83¾)—p. 207.

KENDAL TO DALTON-IN-FURNESS.

Kendal to Staveley (10¼); by Scar Foot, 2¾, over Underbarrow Scar, through Crossthwaite, 5, Crossthwaite Green, 5¾, and over Bowland Bridge, 7, after which cross Cartmel Fells; very hilly road.

Staveley to Dalton (13¼—23½); over Newby Bridge, 11¼, through Booth, 14¼, over Penny Bridge, 16½, through *Ulverston*, 19½, and Lindal, 22—see p. 175. [Or, instead of going over Newby Bridge, turn to *l.*, by the new road through Haverthwaite, 13, to Ulverston, 19¼.]

Before Staveley, on *r.*, Town Head, on the shores of Lake Windermere. Before Haverthwaite, on *l.*, Bigland Hall. Fine scenery. See pp. 162 and 175.

About 5*m.* S. of Dalton is the new town of Barrow-in-Furness, which owes its rapid rise to the development of the iron mining.

(*Barrow-in-Furness:* Imperial, *B.T.C.*)

AMBLESIDE TO BROUGHTON-IN-FURNESS.

Ambleside to Hawkshead (4¾)); leave Ambleside on the West for the Langdale Valley, through Clappersgate, 1, out of which turn to *l* across *R.* Brathay Bridge, and shortly after is a long stiff hill to climb to Belmont, 4, and then *down to Hawkshead.*

(*Hawkshead:* Red Lion.)

At Clappersgate, on *r.*, Loughrigg Fell. On *l.*, Brathay Hall. Below Hawkshead is Esthwaite Water. Wild scenery.

Hawkshead to Coniston (3¼—8); the road does not go *through* Hawkshead, but turns to *r.* at the entrance of the town; there is a steep ascent to mount over Hawkshead Hill, 5¼, and down again to Monk Coniston, 6¼, at the head of Coniston Water, and along it to Coniston. [Or from beyond Brathay Bridge, on *r.* direct to Hawkshead Hill. Or from Clappersgate keep to *r.*, up the Langdale Valley, by the side of *R.* Brathay, and skirting the foot of Loughrigg Fell, to Skelwith Bridge, where cross *R.* Brathay; after this the road gradually ascends (a mile farther keep to *l.*), and for 2 or 3*m.* skirts the base of Oxen Fell, followed by a descent through Yewdale to Monk Coniston; about the same distance.]

(*Coniston:* Crown; Waterhead.)

On *l.*, Skelwith Force; 1*m.* farther, on *r.*, Colwith Force and Elterwater, &c. Fine scenery. Coniston Old Man, &c.

Coniston to Broughton (9¼—17¼); through Brocklebank (or Torver), 10¾, Great Riggs, 11¾, Croft End, 13¼, Owler Side, 15¼, and Hawthwaite, 16¼: hilly first half, and rest downhill.

At Broughton, on *l.*, Broughton Tower; on *r.*, the Duddon Valley.

(*Broughton-in-Furness:* King's Head, *B.T.C.*)

PENRITH TO WORKINGTON.

Penrith to Keswick (17½); turn to *r.* at the railway station, and the road is undulating to Stainton, 2½, after which a long gradual uphill begins, and continues through Penruddock, 6, to Springfield, 7½; then there is a capital ride of about 2*m.* on the top of the hills, and the rest is downhill, for the first 3*m.* more or less steep in parts, but nothing dangerous, through Moor End, 10½, uphill to Scales, 11¾, gradual descent through Threlkeld, 13¼, over New Bridge to Naddle Bridge, 14¾, where is a steep ascent, and again downhill into Keswick, the last bit very steep and best walked down; a heavy road and usually rough and stony.

At Penruddock, 2 or 3*m.* on *r.*, Greystoke Park and Castle. 1*m.* before, on *l.*, Hutton John and Hutton Park. At Threlkeld, on *r.*, Saddleback Mountain. At Stainton, on *l.*, Dalemain. Keswick, p. 162.

Keswick to Cockermouth (12—29½)—p. 176.

Cockermouth to Little Clifton (4½—34) through Brigham, 31½.

Little Clifton to Workington (3—37); through Great Clifton, 35, and Stainburn, 36.

Workington, p. 176.

CARLISLE TO WHITEHAVEN.

Carlisle to Warnell or Royal Oak (9½); through Dalston, 4½, Hawksdale, 6, Nether Welton, 7¼, and Upper Welton, 8¼, a splendid hard road, macadam made, but very smooth surface.

On *l.*, Dalston Hall. On *l.*, Hawksdale Hall, and 1*m.* farther, on *l.*, Rose Castle.

Warnell to Uldale (7¾—17¼); by Hazell Gill *Tp.*, 10½, and over Warnell, Brocklebank, and Catlands Fells, to Thorney Stone, 14½, is hilly and very bad, being chiefly country lanes.

Beyond Warnell, on *l.*, Warnell Hall; 3*m.* beyond, and 1*m.* on *r.*, Clea Hall.

Uldale to Ouse Bridge (4—21¼), by Castle Inn, 20, bad road.

Ouse Bridge (over *R.* Derwent) is at the foot of Bassenthwaite Water; on *r.*, Armathwaite.

Ouse Bridge to Cockermouth (5¾—27)—p. 176.

Cockermouth to Little Clifton (4½—31½)—p. 373.

Little Clifton to Whitehaven (9—40½); turn to *l.*, and through Crossbarrow, 32¼, Winscales, 34¼, Distington, 36½, and Moresby, 38½: see p. 176. Returning, a little out of Distington keep to *r.*

Whitehaven to Workington, p. 176.

CARLISLE TO MARYPORT.

Carlisle to Wigton (10¾); after crossing *R.* Caldew Bridge, take the road to left of Trinity *ch.*, and a short distance farther keep to *l.* to Thursley, 6½, where turn to *l.* and through Micklethwaite, 8½ (out of which, on returning keep to *r.*).

(*Wigton :* King's Arms, B.T.C.)

At Micklethwaite, on *l.*, Crofton Hall. On *r.*, Wigton Hall; on *l.*, High Moor Ho. About 1*m.* S. of Wigton is the site of the Roman station at Old Carlisle.

Wigton to Aspatria (8—18¾), through Waverton, 13, good road.

Beyond Wigton, on *l.*, Hawkrigg Hall. 2*m.* before Aspatria, on *l.*, Brayton Hall.

Aspatria to Maryport (7¾—26½), through Crosby, 23½.

2*m.* beyond Aspatria, a little on *r.*, Hayton Castle. Maryport, p. 176.

CARLISLE TO ALLONBY.

Carlisle to Wigton (10¾)—above.

Wigton to Allonby (11¾—22½); through Waverton, 13 (about 3*m.* farther keep to *r.*), and West Newton, 19.

2*m.* before West Newton, on *r.*, Langrigg Hall. 2*m.* before Allonby, on *l.* Hayton Castle.

CARLISLE TO ABBEY HOLME.

Carlisle to Kirk Bride or Leathes (11); through Newtown, 1¼, Moor Houses, 4½, Kirk Bampton, 6¼ (keep to *r.*), Fingland Rigg, 8, and Fingland, 9½.

Kirk Bride to Abbey Holme (6½—17½); through Long Newton, 13¾, and Moss Side, 15¾. Returning, out of Long Newton keep to *l.*

Holme Abbey *ch.* occupies the site of the old Cistercian Abbey, of which, however, some slight remains exist. About 3*m.* W., on the coast, are the remains of Wolsty or Wulstey Castle; near it also formerly stood the town of Skinburness, long ago destroyed by the sea.

CARLISLE TO BOWNESS.

Carlisle to Bowness (13); through Newtown, 1¼ (a little farther keep to r.), Kirk Andrews, 3½, Burgh-on-the-Sands, 5½, Longburgh, 6½, and Drumburgh Castle, 9½.

PENRITH TO HOLME ABBEY.

Penrith to Warnell or Royal Oak (14½); through Catterlin, 2¾, Thornbarrow, 3¾, Hutton, 5½, and Sebergham, 13.

On r., Hutton Hall; 1m. on l., Greystoke Park and Castle. Beyond Sebergham, on l., Warnell Hall, and on r., Holme Hill. 4½m. beyond Hutton, on l. to *Hesket Newmarket* (3¼—13¼).

Warnell to Wigton (6½—21) through Rosley. Returning, a little out of Wigton turn to l.

Beyond Rosley, 1m. on l., Clea Hall. Wigton, p. 374.

Wigton to Holme Abbey (6—27); through Wigton turn to l., and over Waver Bridge, 23 (just beyond keep to r.).

RICHMOND (Yorks.) TO DARLINGTON.

Richmond (Yorks.) to Scotch Corner (5); through Skeeby, 2, whence is a stiff hill to mount. Returning, ¼m. past Scotch Corner turn to r.

Scotch Corner to Darlington (8—13)—p. 201, alternative route.

NORTHALLERTON TO CATTERICK BRIDGE.

Northallerton to Catterick Bridge (11); through Yafforth, 1¾, Great Langton, 6, Kiplin, 7 (about 2m. farther keep to l.), and Catterick, 10, is a very fair road with good surface. [Or 2m. past Kiplin keep to r., through Bolton, 9½, and Scorton, 10, to Citadella, 11½, half-a-mile past Catterick Bridge.]

STOCKTON-ON-TEES TO WHITBY.

Stockton-on-Tees to Guisborough (12); over Stockton Bridge, 1, Acklam, 3, by Blue Bell Inn, 4, and 1m. farther turn to l., through Marton (ch.), 6, Upsall, 9, and Barnaby Grange, 10.

On l., Acklam Hall. Beyond Marton, on r., Tolesby Hall; on l., Marton Lodge, and a little farther Ormesby Lodge. Guisborough, p. 212.

Guisborough to Tranmire (10—22); by Lockwood Beck, 16¾, Harley Bash Hill, 18, Waupley New Inn, 19¾, and Scaling Dam, 20¾.

Tranmire to Whitby (10—32); through Lyth (Ch.). 27½, whence along the coast to Whitby.

At Lyth, on r., Mulgrave Castle. Whitby, p. 213.

STOCKTON-ON-TEES TO PENRITH.

Stockton-on-Tees to Darlington ($11\frac{1}{2}$); a mile out of the former the macadam improves to a very fair road, and easy going through Hartburn, $1\frac{1}{2}$, Elton, $3\frac{1}{4}$, Long Newton, $4\frac{3}{4}$, Sadberge, 7, whence is a long run down to Great Burdon, $8\frac{3}{4}$, and then an undulating and ordinary macadam road through Houghton, $9\frac{1}{2}$.

On r., Elton Hall; on l., Burnhope Ho. Darlington, p. 201.

Darlington to Pierce Bridge ($4\frac{3}{4}$—$16\frac{1}{4}$); through Low Coniscliffe, 14, and High Coniscliffe, $15\frac{1}{4}$, is a very fair undulating road, with a long hill down to Pierce Bridge, which should be descended carefully, as there is a turn at the bottom almost at right angles.

Beyond Darlington, on l., Blackwell Grange Hall.

Pierce Bridge to Winston ($6\frac{1}{2}$—$22\frac{3}{4}$); through Gainford, $20\frac{1}{2}$, is a very good road: a mile beyond Gainford is a very steep descent, followed by very stiff hill to climb into Winston.

2m. past Pierce Bridge, on l., Snow Hall. 1m. past Gainford, on r., Selaby Hall.

Winston to Barnard Castle ($6\frac{1}{4}$—29); by Arlaw Banks, 26, is all up and down, but with fair surface.

Beyond Winston, on l., Stubb Ho. Barnard Castle, p. 207.

Barnard Castle to Bowes ($4\frac{1}{4}$—$33\frac{1}{4}$); steep descent to walk down through Barnard Castle to R. Tees, which cross to Startforth, $29\frac{1}{2}$, and the rest, except one or two short dips, is all uphill, in some parts very steep.

Bowes to Penrith (34—$67\frac{1}{4}$); pp. 205-6.

YARM TO MIDDLETON-IN-TEESDALE.

Yarm to Darlington (10); cross R. Tees, then keep to l., and by Oak Tree, 5. [Or through Long Newton, $3\frac{1}{2}$, joining the road from Stockton, to Darlington, $10\frac{1}{4}$, as above.]

Darlington to Staindrop (11—21); through Cockerton, 11. Denton, 15, Summerhouse Tg., 16, Summerhouse, $16\frac{1}{2}$, and Ingleton, 19, is a rough and rather hilly road, in some places bad.

1m. before Denton, on r., Walworth Hall. At Staindrop, Raby Castle and Park.

Staindrop to Middleton-in-Teesdale ($10\frac{1}{2}$—$31\frac{1}{2}$); skirting Raby Park for 2 or 3m., then by Marwood Green and Egglestone is a rough and hilly road, bad in places. [Or from Staindrop to Barnard Castle, $5\frac{1}{2}$—$26\frac{1}{2}$; thence to Middleton-in-Teesdale, $9\frac{1}{2}$—36, p. 207.]

DARLINGTON TO ALSTON.

Darlington to West Auckland (11); through Cockerton, 1 (turn to r.), Hambleton, 4, and Houghton-le-Side, 7.

West Auckland to Witton-le-Wear ($4\frac{1}{2}$—$15\frac{1}{2}$)—p. 209.

Witton-le-Wear to Wolsingham (6½—22); keep to *l.*, and by Hordon Head, 17½, and Harperley Gate or Lane Head, 18½ (turn to *l.*), and thence close to *R.* Wear.

On *l.*, Harperley Park. At Wolsingham are remains of a monastery.

Wolsingham to Stanhope (5¾—27¾), through Frosterley, 25.

2*m.* past Wolsingham, on *r.*, Newlands Hall. At Stanhope, Castle Hill and the cavern.

Stanhope to St. John's Weardale (7½—35¼); keep up Weardale through East Gate, 30¼, and West Gate, 33½.

St. John's Weardale to Alston or Aldstone Moor (13¼—48½) by Kilhope Cross, 42¼.

(*Alston :* Blue Bell, *B.T.C.*)

DURHAM TO STOCKTON-ON-TEES.

Durham to Sedgefield (11); through Shincliffe, 2, by Fourmile Bridge, 4, Black Gate, 5¼, and the Skern River, 8¾.

On *l.*, Shincliffe Hall. At Black Gate, on *l.*, Coxhoe *Ho.* At Sedgefield, on *r.*, Hardwicke Hall; on *l.*, Mansforth Hall and Eastwell *Ho.*

Sedgefield to Stockton-on-Tees (9½—20½); through Layton, 12¾, Thorpe, 15¼, and by Norton Inn, 19.

DURHAM TO WOLSINGHAM.

Durham to Willington (6½), through Brancepath, 4¼.

On *l.*, Brancepath Castle and Park; a little farther, on *r.*, Brancepath West Park.

Willington to Wolsingham (8½—15); through Crook, 9½, and Harperley Gate or Lane Head, 11½.

Beyond Willington, on *r.*, Helmington Hall. On *l.*, Harperley Park; 2*m.* farther, on *r.*, Bradley Hall; on *l.*, across *R.* Wear, Broseley Hall. At Wolsingham, on *r.* 1*m.*, Fawnlees; on *l.*, ½*m.* before, Redgate *Ho.*

DURHAM TO HEXHAM.

Durham to Lanchester (8), through Whitton Gilbert, 3½.

Lanchester is supposed to have been a Roman station, as many remains have been found here.

Lanchester to Ebchester (7½—15½); by Maiden Law, 9½ (keep to *l.*), and Leedgate, 12¾ (keep to *r.*), and along the old Watling Street.

Ebchester to Hexham (12½—28); cross *R.* Derwent and through Whittonstall, 17½, and Riding, 22 (where, on returning, keep first to *r.* then to *l.*), and after that follow the south or right bank of *R.* Tyne to Hexham.

(*Hexham :* Old Grey Bull, *B.T.C.*)

Hexham was an important town in Saxon history, and formerly possessed a magnificent abbey, of which some ruins exist; fine old *ch.*, &c.

DURHAM TO BARNARD CASTLE.

Durham to West Auckland (14¼); by Sunderland Bridge, 4½, then by alternative route, p. 198, reversed.

West Auckland to Staindrop (5¾—20); good and easy riding through Raby, 18¾, and past Raby Park.

On *r.*, Raby Castle.

Staindrop to Barnard Castle (5½—25½); through Streatlam, 24, is a good and gently undulating road, except a longish incline about half way, and a descent into and through Barnard Castle; nothing difficult.

On *r.*, Streatlam Park and Castle. Barnard Castle, p. 207.

NEWCASTLE-UPON-TYNE TO WOLSINGHAM.

Newcastle-upon-Tyne to Lanchester (14); cross *R.* Tyne by the High Level Bridge, along which is wood pavement and good riding, to Gateshead, ½, where keep to *r.*, shortly after to *l.*, and over a moderately good road but hilly, through Norwood, 2½, Loosing Hill, 4½, Marley Hill (top of), 6, about 1*m.* farther keeping to *l.*, and through Maiden Law, 12½.

At Norwood, on *l.*, Ravensworth Castle. At Marley Hill, on *r.*, Gibside. Before Maiden Law, on *r.*, Gorecock Hall. Before Lanchester, on *r.*, Greencroft Hall and Fen Hall. Lanchester is supposed to have been a Roman station, as many remains have been found there.

Lanchester to Wolsingham (9—23); through Lanchester turn to *r.*, and through Satley, 18, and by Houselip Bridge.

Wolsingham, p. 377.

NEWCASTLE-UPON-TYNE TO SHOTLEY BRIDGE.

Newcastle-upon-Tyne to Swalwell (4½); cross *R.* Tyne over the High Level Bridge, along which is wood pavement and good riding, to Gateshead, ½, where turn to *r.*, and again a little further on; moderate road.

2*m.* past Gateshead, on *l.*, Dunston Hill.

Swalwell to Ebchester (8½—13); cross *R.* Derwent, then turn to *l.*, and good road to Rowland's Gill, and moderate surface to Ebchester, running near *R.* Derwent, and crossing it about half way.

Past Swalwell, on *r.*, Axwell Park; 3 or 4*m.* past, on *l.*, Gibside.

Ebchester to Shotley Bridge (2—15); good road.

The scenery along this route is much admired.

NEWCASTLE-UPON-TYNE TO SUNDERLAND.

Newcastle-upon-Tyne to Sunderland (12¾); from the theatre in Newcastle cross the *R.* Tyne over the High Level Bridge, along which is wood pavement and good riding, to Gateshead, 1¼; out of it turn to *l.*, and by Felling *Tp.*, 2, Felling, 2½, Heworth Bridge, 3¼, White Mare Pool, 4⅞, Boldon *Tp.*, 6, West Boldon (*ch.*), 7½, East Boldon, 8½, Fulwell *Tp.*, 10, Fulwell Inn, 10¼, Wearmouth, 11¾, and over the Iron Bridge (*R.* Wear), 12; stiff descent down Boldon Fell before West Boldon, and to Fulwell *Tp.* there is Fulwell Bank to ascend, rather steep, and a longish fall approaching Sunderland: bumpy road from end to end, the surface being much cut up with heavy traffic; cobble-stone paving in Sunderland, except in High street, which is wood paved. Returning, at Fulwell *Tp.* keep to *l.*

At Gateshead, on *r.*, Red Hough *Ho.* At Boldon *Tp.*, on *r.*, Scotch *Ho.* On *l.*, Gateshead Park. At White Mare Pool, 1½m. on *l.*, Hebburn Hall. At West Boldon, on *r.*, Hilton Castle, the baronial residence of the Hiltons from the time of Athelston to 1746. Sunderland, p. 208.

NEWCASTLE-UPON-TYNE TO CARLISLE.

Newcastle-upon-Tyne, West Gate, **to Heddon-on-the-Wall** (7); long pull uphill till West Gate *Tpg.* is reached, then steep hill down to Denton Burn, 3, and the rest is a give and take road through West Denton, 3½, and by Chapel House, 4, with moderate surface.

Heddon-on-the-Wall to Wall Houses (6—13); keep to *r.*, and through Harlow Hill, 10¾.

Wall Houses to Chollerford Bridge (8—21); through Halton, 14½, by Red House, 15¼, and Watling Street *Tg.*, 16¼, is a hilly road, and the surface in many places is bad; sharp decline to Chollerford Bridge, where cross North Tyne *R.*

From Newcastle the road runs alongside the ancient Roman or Picts' Wall, and near Chollerford are some interesting Roman remains.

Chollerford Bridge to Glenwhelt (17—38); through Walwick, 22, Carabrough, 24½, Carrow, 25½, and Loninghead, 32.

Beyond Chollerford, 1m. on *r.*, Haughton Castle, and on *l.*, Chesters. On *l.* Walwick Hall, and beyond, on *r.*, Nunwick.

Glenwhelt to Brampton (8¼—46¼); **by** Temmon Inn, 40¾, Clowsgill, 41½, and Naworth Castle (on *r.*), 43¾.

(*Brampton:* Howard Arms, *B.T.C.*)

At Brampton, the Moat or Castle Hill. About 2m. distant is a celebrated Roman inscription on a rock.

Brampton to Carlisle (9¼—55½); through Rout Holm, 48½, Crosby, 51½, and Stanwix, 54¾.

Near Rout Holm, on *l.*, Edmond Castle. Carlisle, p. 160.

NEWCASTLE-UPON-TYNE TO CARLISLE (by Hexham)

Newcastle-upon-Tyne to Heddon-on-the-Wall (7)—above.

Heddon-on-the-Wall to Corbridge (9¼—16¼); keep to *l.*, and through Horsley, 10, and by Shaw House, 13¼. [Or from *Wall Houses*, 13 (above) keep to *l.* by Aydon, 15½, to *Corbridge*, 4¼—17¼.]

Before Horsley, on *l.*, Close *Ho.* and Wylam Hall. At Shaw *Ho.*, on *r.*, Newton Hall.

Corbridge to Hexham (4¼—20½); turn to *l.*, cross *R.* Tyne, and then turn to *r.* through Dilston, 17½.

On *r.*, ruins of Dilston Castle, forfeited by the Earl of Derwentwater in 1715. Hexham, p. 377.

[There is another route to Hexham by *Swalwell*, 4½ (p. 378), thence cross *R.* Derwent, and through Bladon, 6, Ryton, 8½, Crawcrook, 9½,

Bradley, 10½, Prudhoe, 12¾ (on *r.* castle ruins), Stockfield, 15¾, Broomhaugh, 18, and Riding, 18¼, where join the road from Durham as on p. 377, to *Hexham*, 24½.]

Hexham to Haydon Bridge (6¼—26¾); gradual decline all the way; very good surface.

2*m.* beyond Hexham, on *r.*, ruins of Thirlwall Castle. At Haydon Bridge, on *l.*, Threepwood, and a little beyond it ruins of Langley Castle.

Haydon Bridge to Haltwhistle (8¾—35½); cross South Tyne *R.* to *r.*, and then beautiful road through Crowhall, 29¾, Barden Mills, 30¾, Henshaw, 31¾, and Melkridge, 33¼; only one hill to mount, and a steep ascent into Haltwhistle.

At Crowhall, on *l.*, across *R.* Tyne, Ridley Hall. At Melkridge, on *l.*, across *R.* Tyne, Unthank Hall. Haltwhistle, p. 207.

Haltwhistle to Glenwhelt (3¼—38¾) is uphill and a capital road.

About half way, on *l.*, Blenkinsop Hall, and a little farther the ruins of Blenkinsop Castle.

Glenwhelt to Carlisle (17½—56¼)—p. 379.

NEWCASTLE-UPON-TYNE TO TYNEMOUTH.

Newcastle-upon-Tyne to Tynemouth (9); the road is bumpy through Useborn, 1, Byker Hill, 2, to Wallsend, 5, then very sharp fall to Willington, and at Percy Main keep to *l.*, and the road is good through Chirton, 6½, and North Shields, 7½.

(*Tynemouth:* Grand, *B.T.C.*)

At Byker Hill, on *l.*, Heaton Hall. On *r.*, Chirton *Ho.* At Tynemouth are remains of castle and priory.

NEWCASTLE-UPON-TYNE TO BLYTH.

Newcastle-upon-Tyne to Earsdon (7½); along Jesmond road, down stiff descent of Benton Bank, and through Long Benton, 3¼; good road.

Before Earsdon, on *l.*, Backworth *Ho*

Earsdon to Blyth (6½—14); through Hartley, 10, and along the coast through Seaton Sluice or Hartley Harbour, 10½, is quite level and with good surface.

[Or Newcastle to North Shields, 7½, above; thence on *l.* through Whitley, 10, to Hartley, 12½, is a good road, and quite level. Or through Tynemouth, 9, and a pretty good road along the coast, through Cullercoats, 10¼, to Whitley, 11.]

On *l.*, Seaton Delaval Hall.

NORTH SHIELDS TO MORPETH.

North Shields to Whitridge (6½); good road through Preston, ¾, Earsdon, 3¼, and Holywell, 4¾.

Whitridge to Morpeth (10—16½); through Plessy Checks *Tp.* 10¾, and over Hartford Bridge, 11¼, and by Netherton Moor Barns, 11¾.

PENRITH TO ALNWICK.

Penrith to Alston or Aldstone Moor (18¾); through Longwathby 4½, Melmerby, 8½, and by Hartside Cross, 12¼.
At Longwathby, on *r.*, Skirwith Abbey. Alston, p. 377.

Alston to Hexham (20—38¾); good smooth surface on the whole: rather hilly to Whitfield Hall, 26¼, then on the fall for 2 or 3*m.* till the West Allen *R.* is crossed; after that the road is a little hilly again. Returning, 1¾*m.* out of Hexham turn to *l.* [Or after crossing W. Allen *R.* the better road is to keep to *l.* to Haydon Bridge, whence it is splendid road, nearly level and with very good surface, to Hexham: a little longer.]
Hexham, p. 377.

Hexham to Chollerton (6—44¾); turn to *l.*, cross *R.* Tyne, and through St. John Lee, 40¾, and Wall, 42¾, and, ½*m.* further, crossing the Picts' Wall close to Chollerford Bridge on the Newcastle and Carlisle road.
At Chollerton, on *l*, across North Tyne *R.*, Haughton Castle.

Chollerton to Kirk Harle (9½—54¼); cross Watling Street Road, 47, and through Colwell, 47½, Humbleton, 49¾, Steel Rig, 51¼, and Thrivewell, 52¾.
Beyond Chollerton, on *l.*, Swinburn Castle. Beyond Humbleton, on *r.*, Bavington Hall.

Kirk Harle to Rothbury (16—70¼); through Cambo, 57¼, Rothley Shield, 62, and Coldrife (Guide Post), 65, hilly roads, and the surface generally covered with loose stones and sand: half the distance unrideable.
(*Rothbury*: Queen's, *B.T.C.*; West End.)
Beyond Kirk Harle, on *l.*, Wallington *Ho.* Before Rothley Shield, on *r.*, Rothley Castle and Park. At Rothbury, on *l.*, Carlington Castle.

Rothbury to Alnwick (11½—81¾); the road is rideable for 2 or 3*m.* then it gets very hilly with bad surface, over Rimside Moor (Guide Post), 74¼, by Lemington Hall, 78, and over Aydon Forest.
Alnwick, p. 199.

THE CELEBRATED "IVEL" CYCLES

HOLD NEARLY ALL THE
LONG DISTANCE ROAD RECORDS OF THE WORLD.

The No. 1 ROADSTER SAFETY. Price £16.

The No. 20. ROADSTER SAFETY. Price £18.

Particulars of these and all other Patterns of BICYCLES, TRICYCLES, and TANDEMS, etc., on application to

THE IVEL CYCLE CO., LIMITED,
BIGGLESWADE, BEDS.

INDEX.

Note.—The Numbers on the Left of the Names denote Distance from London by Direct Routes. The Numbers on the Right of the Names denote the Pages.

The Sign × before a Name or Number of Page denotes that the Reference to the Pages *after it* is in the Cross Roads.

157½ ABBEY FOREGATE 120
128½ Abbots Bromley 164
171½ Abbots Chair 177
185¼ Abbots Kerswell 63
106 Abbots Moreton 135
× Abenhall 323
239¾ Aber (Carn.) 147
× Aber Arth 330
× Aber-Cowarch 334
× Aberaeron 330, 331
233¾ Aber-arad 113
192 Aberavon 92
184½ —— by Aust, 98
181½ Aberdare 99
186¾ Aberford 197, × 365
147¾ Abergavenny 110, × 322, 323, 324
145¾ —— by Rockfield 110
219 Abergele 147
212 Abergwylly 111
177¾ Aberhavesp 122
210¾ Aberystwith 115, × 330
55¾ Abingdon 105, × 292
× Abinger Hammer 263
360 Abington (Lanark) 160
× Abington (Northamp.) 299
14 Abridge 236
201¾ Accrington 172, × 307
× Acklam 373
174¾ Ackworth Moor Top 203
× Acle 318
108½ Acock's Green 143
× Acomb 369
129 Aconbury 114
68¾ Acorise or Acryse 9
165½ Acton (Ches.) 146
5 Acton (Midd.) 106
× Acton (Salop) 327
102¾ Acton Turville 97
100¾ —— by Malmesbury 103
103 —— by Great Sherston 103
69¾ Adderbury 131, × 295
× Adderley 337
170¾ Adderwater 40
214 Addingham 191
× Addiscombe 265
19¾ Addlestone 46, × 269
206½ Adlington 169
42¾ Adversane 31
180¾ Agbridge 202, × 362
124 Ailberton 109
× Ailesworth 318
× Ailwell 281
× Ainderby 372
× Aiscough or Aiskew 372
× Aislaby 371
323½ Akeld 208
58 Akeley 141
× Akeman's Inn 304
42 Albourn Green 25, × 267
130½ Albrighton 148, × 321
101½ Alcester 125, × 311
100½ —— by Banbury 135
162 Alcombe 79
159¾ —— by Rydon 81
66½ Alconbury 195
68 Alconbury Hill 195
65½ —— by Ware 223
67 Alconbury Weston 195
94½ Aldborough (Suff.) 244
93¾ —— by Snape Br. 244
70¾ Aldbourn 100
73 —— by Ramsbury 100
184½ Aldbrough, 218
× Aldbury 295
× Alderbury 273
170¾ Alderley (Ches.) 165
× Alderley (Glouc.) 313
49½ Aldermaston 95, × 291
88¾ Alderminster 125
93¾ Alderton 123
119 Aldferton 122
× Aldfold 267
× Aldfold Cross Ways 267
× Aldington 251
Aldstone Moor. *See* Alston
× Aldsworth 302
113½ Alford (Som.) 75
138¾ Alfreton 178, × 337
140 —— by Nottm. 190
316 Algirth Bridge 163
× All Stretton 321
340¼ Allanmouth 183
261¾ Allan's Ford 210
× Allerston 371
× Allerton Mauleverer 370
93¾ Allesley 139
128¾ Allestree 167, 180
× Allexton 318
× Allington 293
327½ Allonby 170, × 374
213¾ Allt Yr Odyn Arms 112
131¼ Allum (or Alam) Bdg. 126
87¼ Allum Green 42
× Almondbury 362
× Almondsbury 307
105½ Alner 57, × 277
308 Alnwick 199, × 381
305¾ —— by Ware 224
311½ —— by York 211
62¾ Alpheaton 237
174½ Alphington 55
170½ —— by Yeovil 61, 63
× Alport Bridge 357
56¾ Alresford 39, × 269
× Alrewas 308
× Alsager Heath 339
Alsop-in-le-Dale 170
273¾ Alston 207, × 377, 381
× Alterinos 324
× Altham 307
43½ Althorn 216
47 Alton 39, × 270
49½ —— by Odiham 53
× Altrincham 340, 356
122¾ Alvaston 166
× Alverdiscott 287
115¾ Alveston (Glou.) 97, × 306
92½ Alveston (War.) 136
125¾ Alvington 109
× Alwalton 299
200¾ Alwoodley Gates 191
136¾ Ambergate 167
× Amberstone Gate 260
277¾ Ambleside 162, × 372
270½ —— by Kendal 164
26 Amersham 133, × 290
25¾ —— by Pinner 134
× Amerton 336
77½ Amesbury 69, × 294
71½ Amfield 46
× Amotherby 368
83¾ Ampney Crucis 103
45 Ampthill 188, × 297
48¾ —— by Woburn 188
20½ Amwell 222
63¾ Andover 58, × 272, 292
89 Andoverford 108 × 303
261¾ Angarrack 67
251½ Angeram 206
173 Anlaby 216, × 363
310¾ Annan 163
× Annesley 357
× Ansley 317
Anslow Leys 165
× Anstey 305

93½ Ansty 48
121 Antingham 232
125¾ — by North Walsham 235
119¾ Anwick 220
× Apperley Bridge 370
113½ Appleby (Leic.) 156
281½ Appleby (Westm.) 175
270 — by Stamford 205
201¾ Appledore (Devon) 74
59 Appledore (Kent) 10, × 251, [255
× Appleton 368
31¾ Ardingley 23
57¼ Ardington 101, × 292
56¼ Ardleigh 245
× Ardley 298
× Ardsley 360
185¾ Ardwick Green 168, × 357
× Areley Kings 323
245 Argengarthdale 206
245½ Arkholme 176
× Arlaw Banks 376
× Arlingham 322
176¾ Armin 214, × 363
× Armour Hill 321, 333
230½ Arncliffe 212
51¼ Arnden 12
88½ Arnesby 181
× Arras 366
45¼ Arrington 223
44¼ Arrington Bridge 223
101¼ Arrow 135, × 311
× Arthington 369
54½ Arundel 31, × 253, 268
58¼ — by Petworth 35
× Ash (Dev.) 287
52 Ash (Hants.) 58
61½ Ash (Kent) 5
× Ash Gate 355
176 Ash Mill 73
139 Ashbourne 169, × 335, 338
54 Ashbourne Mill 14, × 255
191½ Ashburton 55, × 287
187½ — by Yeovil 56
69½ Ashbury 101
115½ Ashby-de-la-Zouch 156, × 315
114¾ — by Leicester 170
× Ashby Magna 309
76 Ashby St. Ledgers 183
100½ Ashchurch 123
126 Ashcot 81
151¾ Ashford (Derb.) 167, 171, × 355, 356
53½ Ashford (Kent) 8, × 254, 255, 258
141 Ashford (Som.) 81
× Ashford Bowdler 321
× Ashford Ford 264
136½ Ashill 74
× Ashingdon 344
47 Ashington 29
350¼ Ashkirk 183
96¾ Ashley Cross (Hants) 43
× Ashopton Inn 357
16¾ Ashtead 20
× Ashton (Ches.)
99 Ashton (Dorset) 53
× Ashton (Heref.) 321
216½ Ashton (Lanc.) 161
99½ Ashton Common 85, × 276
× Ashton Cross 364
191¼ Ashton-in-Makerfield 157, × 364
× Ashton Keynes 302
182¼ Ashton-under-Lyne 177, [× 357, 362
154 Ashtonsitch 164
151 — by Derby 169
45 Ashurst 28
169½ Askern 212
244¼ Askrigg 204, × 372
242¼ — by Aysgarth 205
104¼ Aslackby 215
× Aspatria 374
× Asselby 364
37 Assington Cross 100
× Assington Green, 345
160¼ Astbury 153
132½ Aston (Derb.) 165, × 335
× Aston (Heref.) 327
152¼ Aston (Salop) 120
× Aston (War.) 308, 314
× Aston (York.) 360
34½ Aston Clinton 130, × 296
× Aston Green 340
× Aston-Subedge 310
× Astwood 297
110½ Aswarby 215
156 Atcham 129
149 Atcham Bridge 140
99½ Atford 96
× Atherington (Suss.) 269.
187¾ Atherington (Devon) 76, × 286
185½ — by Dulverton 78
163¾ Atherleigh Mill 76
107¾ Atherstone 155, × 319
105 — by Coventry 156
× Attercliffe 360
94½ Attleborough 232
× Attlebridge 349
203½ Auburn House 218
× Audenshaw 357
× Audlem 336, 337
× Audley 337
× Aughton (Lanc.) × 367
156 Aughton (Yorks.) 187
162 — by Chesterfield 190
120 Aust Passage 98, × 320
154½ Austerfield, 210
× Austerlands 362
× Avebury 301
16½ Aveley 247
× Avening 313, 314
× Averham 306, × 355
× Avisford Hill 253
× Avon 275
96¼ Avon Bridge 143
151½ Awliscombe 74
130½ Axbridge 84, × 283
Axford 89
146½ Axminster 55, × 284
151½ — by Beaminster 61
144¼ — by Crewkerne, 71
247 Aycliffe 198
246½ — by Darlington 202
× Aydon 379
124 Aylburton 109
38½ Aylesbury 130, × 295, 296
40½ — by Amersham 133
× Aylesby 361
× Aylestone 309
120½ Aylsham 232, × 350, 351
118¼ — by Reepham 234
144¼ Aymestrey 122 [× 303
66¼ Aynho-on-the-Hill 131,
62¼ — by Bicester 132
238¾ Aysgarth 205
346½ Ayton 200
270 Ayton Bank 199

BABBACOMBE or Babbicombe 63
× Babraham 344
120¾ Babylon Hill 48
181½ Backford 151
122 Backwell West Town 97
× Bacon's End 317
× Bacton (Norf.) 350
77 Bacton (Suff.) 238
201¾ Bacup 174, × 367
× Badby 301
× Bagber Bridge 280
195½ Bagillt 150
× Bagley Wood 292
129½ Bagots Bromley 164
309½ Bagrave 209
26½ Bagshot 46
29½ — by Weybridge 46
× Bailiff Bridge 368
243½ Bainbridge 204, 205, × 372
193½ Bainton 218
× Baiston Hill 321
21½ Baker Street 247, × 342
153 Bakewell 167, × 335, 355
152½ — by Wirksworth 170
× Bala 330, 333, 334
165 Balby 193, × 301
32¾ Balcombe 24
× Baldersby 371
37½ Baldock 194, × 296, 297
× Baldwin Gate 359
4½ Balham 26
201¾ Ball Cross 64
× Ballcross 309
95 Balloon Inn 110, × 309
× Ball's Hut 253
200½ Bamber Bridge 157
209 — by Standish 158
× Bamburgh 359
159¾ Bampton (Dev.) 77, × 285
× Bampton (Oxon) 301
73 Banbury 131, × 300, 301, 303
69 — by Bicester 132
72½ — by Brackley 136
241 Banc-y-fetin 93
240½ Bangor 128, × 336
245 — by Chester 147
263¾ Banisdale Bridge 159
370½ Bankhouse Inn 184
Banner 229
× Banningham Bridge 350
Banstead 26
135½ Banwell 84
133¼ — by Bath 96
130½ Banwell Stn. 97
41½ Bapchild 3
180½ Barbrook Mill 80
× Barden Mills 380
191½ Barff Hill 218
94½ Barford 141
105½ Barford Bridge 235
87 Barford St. Martin 48
132¾ Bargate 180
62 Barham 9
7½ Barking 216
114½ Barkston (Linc.) 217
185 Barkston (York.) 211
35½ Barkway 228
142¾ Barlaston Common 165

150	Barlborough 191, × 358	140½	Bath Pool End 81, × 283		Bedhouse 160
193½	Barlby 211		Bathampton 95	96	Bedlam 117
38½	Barley 228	104	Batheaston 90	89½	Bedlam End 143
63	Barley Mow 131, × 208	×	Batherton 337	115	Bedminster 97 × 281, 282
90½	Barleythorpe 186	105½	Bathford 95	95½	Bedworth 156
×	Barmby-on-the-Marsh 364	104	—— by Melksham 96	196½	Beeford 218
×	Barming 258	103	Bathford Tg. 90	×	Beer 284
×	Barming Cross and Heath 258	106	—— by Devizes 95	209½	Beer Alston 65
222	Barmouth 121, × 334	91½	Batramsley 40	211½	Beer Ferris 65
200½	Barmston 218	×	Battisham 345		Beeston (Notts.) 190, × 315
	Barnaby 243	56	Battle 14, × 260, 261	×	Beeston (Yorks.) 363
×	Barnaby Grange 375	55	—— (by New road) 1½	×	Beeston Bridge 340
246½	Barnard Castle 207, × 376, 378		Battle Bridge 314	48½	Beeston Cross 184
		324½	Battle Stone 260	49½	—— by Shefford 202
×	Barnards 342	×	Battlefield Hadnall 321	247½	Beetham 181
148	Barnby Moor Inn 196, × 360	×	Batts Bridge and Hill 231	183½	Bector Cross 65
×	Barnby-on-the-Moor 360	52	Baughurst Street 86	59½	Begbrook 118
11½	Barnet 137	107½	Bawdeswell 234, × 349, 350	248½	Begelly 98
61½	Barnham 237, × 316	132	Bawdrip 81	44	Beggar's Bush (Oxon.) 105
171½	Barnhill 149	153½	Bawtry 196, × 359	×	Beggar's Bush (Rad.) 327
169½	Barnsdale 203	150½	—— by Ware 224	160	Beighton (Notts.) 190
×	Barnsley (Glouc.) 302	202½	Baxenden 172	×	Beighton (Suff.) 346
115½	Barnsley (Worc.) 137	64½	Baydon 100	×	Belby 363
175½	Barnsley (York.) 178, × 360	106½	Bayford-by-Mere 70	322½	Belford 200
172½	—— by Rotherham 187	111	—— by Shaftesbury 72	326	—— by York 211
192½	Barnstaple 74, × 286, 287	58½	Baynard's Green 132, × 208	99½	Belgrave 166
188½	—— by Dulverton 78	×	Baythorn End 344	308½	Belhaven 200
190½	—— by Somerton 75	×	Beachampton 207	17½	Bell Bar 184
178½	Barnstaple Cross 69	×	Beachley Passage House Inn 320	×	Bell Green 305
×	Barnstaple Inn 286	×	Beacon 350	164½	Bell-on-the-Hill 148, × 340
×	Barnston 343 [× 290	×	Beacon Hill (Bucks) 296	×	Bellerby 372
77½	Barnwell St. Andrews 193	×	Beacon Hill (Som.) 284	×	Belmont 373
102½	Barnwood 105	×	Beacon Moor 286	133½	Belper 167, × 354
×	Barr Green 317	23½	Beaconsfield 106 × 200	135½	Belper Lane End 170
258	Barras 206	×	Beadles Hill 261	259	Belsay 207
160½	Barrow (Linc.) 216, × 361	41½	Beals Bridge 12	287½	Belsay Castle 200
×	Barrow (Salop) 328	×	Beal's Bridge 257	186½	Belstone Corner 76
254½	Barrow Green 153	49	Beals Green 14	×	Beltering Green 259
×	Barrowby 354	11½	Beam Bridge 216	162	Belton (near Crowle, Linc.) 214
104½	Barsham 242		Beambridge 73		
131	Bartestree 116, × 361	136½	Beaminster 60, × 252	112½	Belton (near Grantham, Linc.) 217
×	Bartington 340	138½	Beanshurst 164		
187½	Barton (Dev.) 62	27½	Bear Green 29	370	?
219½	Barton (Lanc.) 159	90½	Bearley Cross 143	308½	} Beltonford 200
74½	Barton (Suff.) 238	36½	Bearsted 8	×	Benefield 317
×	Barton (York.) 308	164	Bearwood Green 210	54	Benges Wood 35
187½	Barton Cross 62	341	Beattock 160	95½	Bengeworth 119, × 310
×	Barton End 309	83	Beaulieu 41	181½	Benland 214
108½	Barton-in-the-Beans 157	81	—— by Basingstoke 53	×	Bennecar 278
37½	Barton-in-the-Clay 188	67½	Beaumont 245	50	Bennenden 13
69½	Barton Mills 241	59	Beauport 15, × 260	×	Bennets 289
167½	Barton-on-Humber 216, × 361	105½	Beccles 242	×	Bennones 306
		104½	—— by Blythburgh 243	46	Bensington or Benson 105
73	Barton Seagrave 185, × 316	×	Peckenham 265	×	Bentham 370
×	Bartonfield 310	×	Beckford 310	41½	Bentley Green 39
×	Barwick 281	81½	Beckhampton Inn 89, × 301	×	Bentley Wood Green 367
×	Barwick Basset 301	×	Beckingham (Linc.) 355	×	Bents 358
47½	Basildon 100	×	Beckingham (Notts.) 350	168½	Bent's Green 181, × 355
45½	Basingstoke 47, × 270, 291	103½	Beckington 85, × 274, 277	111½	Bere Regis 57, × 277
48	—— by Odiham 52	55½	Beckley by Northiam 13	114½	—— by Lytchett Minster 58
156½	Baslow 181, × 355	57½	—— by Highgate 16	111½	Berkeley 104, × 307
154½	—— by Edensor 181	×	Beckwith Shaw 370	26½	Berkhampstead 130
150½	Bassaleg 91, 99	223½	Bedale 198, × 371		Berriew 121, × 329
195½	Bassels Gate 60	221½	—— by Leeming 198	192	Berry Narbor 80
×	Bassels Gate 287	239½	Beddgelert 123	190½	—— by Rydon 81
111½	Bassets Pole 145, × 314	246	—— by Tremadoc 123	×	Berwick St. James 275
93½	Baston 215	×	Beddington 265	95½	Berwick St. Leonards 71
16½	Batchworth Heath 134	13½	Bedfont 46	337½	Berwick-upon-Tweed 200
138	Bateman Bridge 179	50½	Bedford 185, × 287	334½	—— by Ware 224
106	Bath 80, × 274, 280, 304	53	—— by Ampthill 198	341	—— by York 211
108½	—— by Devizes 95	50½	—— by Luton 189	×	Bescott Lane 319
107½	—— by Melksham 96	×	Bedhampton 254	×	Bessells Green 264
				208½	Bessingby 216

132 Besthorpe 214
189½ Beswick 216
× Betchworth 263
× Bethersden 255
236 Betheada 128
245½ Bethlem 93
× Betley 337
× Bettisfield 340
216¼ Bettws Garmon 123
220¾ Bettws-y-Coed 128
220 —— by Banbury 149
215¾ —— by Coventry 150
183¼ Beverley 216, × 366
44¼ Beverns Bridge 22
99 Beverstone 102
× Bevil's or Bound'l's Hill 289
× Bewdley 325, 326
× Bexhill 252, 260
13 Bexley 7, × 262
11¼ Bexley New Town 2
× Bexwell 348
× Bibury 302
54 Bicester 132, × 297
111¾ Bicker 220
× Bickerton 360
188 Bickington 56
161¼ Bickleigh 76, × 285
153¾ Bicknoller 78
48 Biddenden 10, × 256
× Biddenden Green 256
200¾ Bideford 74, × 286, 287
186¾ —— by Dulverton 78
189½ —— by Somerton 75
202½ Bideford Bridge 56
202 —— by Totnes 62
× Bierton 296
× Bigby 360
45½ Biggleswade 194
× Bigswear Bridge 320
157½ Bilbrook 79
70¼ Bildeston by Hadleigh 240
64 —— by Sudbury 240
31¾ Bill Hill 94
23¾ Billericay 247, × 343
× Billesdon 318
× Billingborough 352
× Billingford 349
122¾ Billinghay 220
40¾ Billinghurst 31, × 267
× Billingley Green 360
× Billingsley 328
× Billington (Lanc.) 368
× Billington (Staff.) 336
220¼ Bilsborough 158
119¾ Bilston 140
× Bilting or Bilton 255
× Bilton (War.) 316
178¾ Bilton (York.) 219, × 369
66 Binderton 34
43¾ Bines Bridge 28
29 Binfield Bridge 94
× Bingham 353
206 Bingley 179
335½ Binks 183
× Binley 317
183½ Birch 165
110¼ Bircham Newton 228
× Bircher 326
× Birches Green 314
67½ Birchington 3
14 Birchwood Corner 7
214½ Birdforth 211
97¼ Birdlip 105, × 303, 309
96¼ Birdlip by Oxford 110
51¼ Bird's Isle or Boar's Isle 10, × 255
109¾ Birdwood 110
197¾ Birkenhead 151
158½ Birley Vale 191
109¼ Birmingham 139, × 308, 311, 317, 318, 319, 325
115¾ —— by Henley-in-Arden 143
112¾ —— by Warwick 143
152½ Birmington 190
101 Birstal 166
× Birstall 363, 364
× Birtles 356
268½ Birtley 199
249¾ Bishop Auckland 198
× Bishop Burton 366
30¾ Bishop Stortford 230
267 Bishop Wearmouth 208
271¼ —— by Durham 210
× Bishop's Bridge 359
158¾ Bishop's Castle 120, × 327
× Bishops Cleeve 310
167 Bishop's Clyst 59
170 —— by Sidmouth, 60
× Bishop's Frome 324
95 Bishops Fonthill 71
20½ Bishop's Gate 94
142½ Bishop's Hull 73
145¾ Bishop's Lydeard 78
60¾ Bishop's Moat 120, 122
55¼ Bishop's Sutton 39
× Bishops Tawton 286
61¾ } Bishop's Waltham 42,
65¼ } × 289, 272
60 Bishopsbourne 9
58½ Bishopstone (Suss.) 22
71½ Bishopstone (Wilts.) 101
× Bisley 309
202½ Bittaford Bridge 56
202 —— by Totnes 62
76 Bittern 42
89¾ Bitteswell 155
111¾ Bitton 90
121¼ Bixley 213
× Blaby 309
114½ Black Boy Inn (Worc.) 144, × 325
× Black Brook 364
× Black Burton 370
× Black Chapel 343
27 Black Corner 24
305½ Black Dyke 160
× Black Moor Foot 362
× Black Notley 344
133½ Black Rock Inn 91
125¼ —— by Aust 98
73½ Black Swan 226
253¾ Black Water (Corn.) 67
× Blackbourton 301
206½ Blackburn 173, × 367, 368
305½ Blackford (Cumb.) 183
111½ Blackford (Som.) 70, × 279
189¼ Blackford Bridge 171
5 Blackheath 1
× Blackland Common 267
186 Blackley 174
233½ Blackpool 161
205 Blackrod 168
51½ Blackthorn Heath 132
× Blackwater (Essex) 312
30¼ Blackwater (Hants.) 47
89¼ Blackwater Bridge 42
30¾ Blackwater St. Anne's 237
236¾ Blackwell Bridge 201
× Bladon (Dur.) 379
× Bladon (Oxf.) 302
225½ Blaen-Bargoed 112
× Blaenporth 331
126 Blagdon 96, × 284
119 Blakeney 109, × 351
× Blake's Cross 289
103 Blandford 53, × 276, 277, 278, 280
× Blandford St. Mary 277
× Blashford Green 275
59¼ Blatchington 22
130 Blatchley Green 122
Blaxhall 244
158½ Blaxton 210
137¼ Bleadon 84
42½ Bleak Hall 194
60¼ Blean Wood 5
11½ Blendon 7
58¾ Bletchingdon 124
× Bletchingley 263
153½ Bletchley 148
56¾ Bletsoe 185
54¼ Blewberry 101
× Blickling 351
129½ Blindman's Gate 81
× Blisworth 299
125½ Blithbury 164
× Blofield 348
136¾ Bloomsbury 148
134¾ Blount's Green 164, × 3.0
Blown Sands 161
× Bloxham 300
× Bloxwich 319
× Blubberhouses 368
155½ Blue Anchor 81
91¼ Blue Bell 219
× Blue Bowl 281
× Blue Bridge 345
262 Blue House 210
191¾ Blue Pits 174
× Bluntisham 348
× Blyth (Northum.) 380
151¼ Blyth (Notts.) 212, × 360
99¾ Blythburgh 241
× Blythe Bdg. or Marsh 338
145½ Blythe Marsh 164
152¼ Blyton 214
× Boarden Bridge 289
× Boarden House Bridge 351
× Boarshead Street 258
125½ Bobbers Mill 190
38½ Bobbing 5
39¾ Bobbing Street 5
22 Bobbingworth Mill 240
× Bock Green 326
41¾ Bocking Street 237
× Bodenham 274
205 Bodfary 149
238¼ Bodinnock 66
230¾ Bodmin 50, × 298
247¼ —— by Liskeard 67
52 Bodyham Bridge 16
68 Bognor 34, × 269
65 —— by Arundel 34
65 —— by Eartham 35
28 Bol Bridge 94
191¼ Bolderstone 117
Bolehall 155
× Bollington 356

37¾ Bolney Common 25
57¼ Bolnhurst 192
198¾ Bolton (Lanc.) 168, × 364
193¾ —— by Ashbourne 171, 173
× Bolton (York.) 375
217 Bolton Bridge 191, × 369
204 Bolton Green 158
239¾ Bolton-le-Sands 159
129¼ Boninghall 140
× Bonington Green 342
168¼ Bonvilston 91
× Booth 372
178¾ Booth Ferry 214
163¼ Booth Lane Head or Boothville 153
125¾ Boothby Graffo 218
293¾ Bootle 175
× Bopeep 252
× Bopeep Gate 261
× Boraston 328
× Borden Hill 268
107¾ Bordesley 140
94½ Boreham 82
× Boreham Bridge 260
33¾ Boreham Street (Ess.) 238
× Boreham Street (Suss) 260
233¼ Borough 158, × 259
× Borough Green 264
× Borough Street 266
206¾ Boroughbridge 197, × 368, 369
220¾ —— by Sheffield 192
203¾ —— by Ware 224
196¾ Boroughstone 64
× Borrowash 353
222¾ Borrowby 207
161¼ Bosley 169
225¾ Bossiney 68
226¾ —— by Camelford 68
10¾ Bostal Heath 4
117¾ Boston 219, × 353
× Boston Spa 369
180¾ Botany Bay Inn 210
86¾ Botesdale 238
83¼ —— by Stowmarket 238
× Botham 285
348¾ Bothwell 161
71¾ Botley 42, × 272
68¾ —— by Bishop's Waltham 42
55¾ Botley Hill 108
× Botslye Green 345
× Bottesford 353
× Bottols Green 320
152¾ Bottom House 164
140¾ —— by Derby 169
182¾ Boughton (Ches.) 146
180 —— by Newport 148
69 Boughton (Northamp.) 166
× Boughton Corner 255
50¾ Boughton Hill 3
× Boughton Lees 259
49¾ Boughton Street 3
× Bound Gate 256
97¼ Bourn 215, × 352, 353
49¾ Bourn Bridge (Camb.) 231
× Bourn Bridge 308
21¾ Bourn End 130
× Bourne or Sea Houses 252
109¾ Bournemouth 43, × 271
103¾ Bourton 70
83¼ Bourton-on-the-Hill 119
183¾ Bow (Devon.) 68
180¾ Bow by Tiverton 76
3 Bow (Midd.) 229
188 Bow Bridge (near Newton Abbot) 61
194¾ —— (near Totnes) 64
× Bower 258
× Bower Heaton 282
218¼ Bowes 205, × 376
× Bowland Bridge 372
× Bowling Green 308
× Bowness (Cumb.) 375
272¼ Bowness (West.) 162
91 Bowridge 53
100¾ Box 90
98¾ Box Hill 90
23¾ Box Moor 130
106¾ Box Trees 143
× Boxes Gate 258
× Boynton 366
59¾ Bozeat 189
138¾ Bracebridge 217
× Brackenthwaite 370
62¾ Brackley 136, × 298
28 Bracknell 94
106¾ Bracon Ash 238
201¾ Bracy Bridge 216
× Bradeney 326
63½ Bradfield (Essex) 215
66½ Bradfield (Suff.) 237
× Bradford (Worc.) 311
200 Bradford (Yorks.) 179, × 365, 369, 370
196¾ —— by Newark 203
197 —— by Nottingham 187
103¾ Bradford-on-Avon 86, × 277
100¾ —— by Marlborough 95
104¾ —— by Market Lavington 86
165 Bradley (Ches.) 149
× Bradley (Derby) 354
× Bradley (Durh.) 380
× Bradley (York.) 362
× Bradley Brook 362
117¾ Bradmore 189
161¾ Bradninch 76
× Bradpole 282
51¼ Bradwell (Essex) 216
116 Bradwell (Norf.) 243
30 Bragbury End 225
132¾ Brailsford 169
41 Braintree 237, × 342, 344
289¾ Braithwaite 176
49¾ Bramber 28
× Bramdean 268
98¾ Bramfield 243
190¾ Bramham 197
× Bramley (Surr.) 206
× Bramley (Yorks.) 359
60 Bramling 5
× Brampton (Cumb.) 379
× Brampton (Derb.) 355
63¾ Brampton (Hunt.) 224, × 316
× Brampton (Northamp.) 317
163¾ Brampton (Salop) 120
105 Brampton (Suff.) 243
161½ Brampton Bryan 122
63¾ Brampton Hut 195
× Bramshall 336
× Bramshaw 273
Bramstone Cross 143, × 311
× Brancaster 351
× Brancaster Staith 351
× Brancepath 377
× Brand Side 339
205 Brandis Corner 66
78¾ Brandon 232
76¾ Brandon Creek Bridge 227
191¾ Brandsburton 218
249 Brandy Hill 193
166½ Brandy Street 79
× Bransford 323
× Branston 308
× Brasted 264
96¾ Bratton 85
Bratton Court 79
28½ Braughing 228
74¾ Braunston 139
181¾ Bray Bridge 76
67¾ Brayfield-on-the-Green 189
167¾ Brecon 111, × 329, 330
170 —— by Hereford 116
128½ Bredenbury 122
147¾ Bredwardine 116
× Breedon-on-the-Hill 315
× Brenchley 259
199½ Brent Bridge 55
61½ Brent Eleigh 238
197 Brent Harberton Ford 55
7 Brentford 46, × 266
18½ Brentwood 236, × 342
× Brenzett 255
62¾ Brenzett Corner 10, × 251, 255
124½ Brereton 145
162¾ Brereton Green 152, × 336
121¾ Bretby Park 157
× Bretford 306
189 Bretton (Flint) 146
182 Bretton (York.) 180
43 Brickhill 138
23½ Brickwall 184
237 Bridell 113
196¾ Bridestow 50
58½ Bridge 6
91½ Bridge Casterton 195
356¾ Bridge End 209
40½ Bridge Farm 24
141¼ Bridge Sollers 116
92 Bridge Town 131, × 310
94 —— by Kineton 136
157½ Bridgemore 146
181 Bridgend (Glam.) 92
173½ —— by Aust 98
× Bridgend (Linc.) 352, 354
137¾ Bridgenorth 126, × 326, 328
137¼ —— by Stourbridge 137
× Bridges 327
135½ Bridgewater 81, × 283
163 Bridgewater's Arms 99
208 Bridlington 216, × 366
206¾ —— by Leven 218
134¾ Bridport 54, × 282
× Brierley Hill 319
156½ Brigg 215
× Brigham 373
Brighouse 180, × 364
52¼ Brighton 23, × 252, 257
52¼ —— by Crawley and Cuckfield 26
51½ —— by Cuckfield 25
51¾ —— by Hand Cross 26
52½ —— by Reigate 27
48 Brightwell 101
161¾ Brigsley 220
× Brilley Mountain 328

136½ Brimfield Cross 120, × 321 325
× Brimington 358
125½ Brimpton 48
97 Brimscombe 104
70½ Brington 193
138½ Bringwyn 110
× Brinklow 306, 317
47½ Brinkshole Heath 35
86½ Brinkworth 101
× Brinsley 357
141½ Brinsop Court 115
× Brisley 349
117½ Brislington 90
× Brissenden Bridge 255
119½ Bristol by Bath 90, × 278 281, 282, 306, 314
116½ —— by Malmesbury 103
114 —— by Marshfield 97
195 Briton Ferry 92
202½ Brixham 63
196½ —— by Newton Abbot 63
210½ Brixton (Devon) 64, × 287
3 Brixton (Surrey) 20
72 Brixworth 166
166½ Broad Clyst 76
8½ Broad Green 20
125½ Broad Heath 120
× Broad Hinton 301, 302
125½ Broad Moigne (or Maine) 64
131½ Broad Oak (Salop) 137
× Broad Street 255
× Broad Town 302
47½ Broadbourn Bridge 28, × 268
35½ Broadbridge Heath 30, × 267
× Broadbridge Mill 253
156½ Broadhembury 74
75 Broadstairs 4, × 250
73½ —— by Ramsgate 4
× Broadstone 328
× Broadward Bridge 320
117 Broadwas 121
29½ Broadwater (Herts.) 194
32 —— by Hertford 225
54½ Broadwater (Suss.) 30, × 269
× Broadwater (Worc.) 312
91 Broadwater Bridge 102
× Broadwaters Inn 319
× Broadway (Dorset) 279
37 Broadway (Kent) 9
135½ Broadway (Som.) 71
90 Broadway (Worc.) 119, × 310
141 Broadwindsor 61, × 284
89½ Brockdish Street 242
89½ Brockenhurst 40
78½ —— by Basingstoke 53
83½ Brockford Green 239
84 Brockford Street 239
77½ —— by Sudbury 240
78½ Brockhurst *Tp.* 42, × 271.
× Brockhurst 321
× Brocklebank 373
× Brocklesby 361
123½ Brockley 97
10 Brockley Hill 141
Brocks Bridge 158
137½ Brockton (near Bishop's Castle) 120
× Brockton (nr. Shifnal) 328
× Brockton (near Welshpool) 332
100½ Brockworth 105
× Brocton 328
× Broken Cross 356
192 Bromborough 151
80½ Bromeswell 244
144½ Bromfield 120, × 326
54½ Bromham Bridge 189, × 297
23½ Bromley (Essex) 230
10 Bromley (Kent) 11, × 265
12 Bromley Common 11, 18
× Bromley Green 255
154 Brompton (Salop) 126
228½ Brompton (Yorks.) 213
230½ Brompton-upon-Swale 206 × 372
114½ Bromsgrove 125, × 308
113½ —— by Banbury 136
125 Bromyard 121, × 324
162½ Bronllys 116, × 330
163½ —— by Talgarth 117
× Brook (Hants.) 273
48 Brook End 202
36½ Brook Green or Street 33
97 Brook Hill 48
17 Brook Street (near Brentwood, Essex) 236-7
× Brook Street (near Halstead, Essex) 345
13½ Brook Street (Herts.) 222
14½ —— by Enfield 225
28½ Brook Street (Kent) 19
× Brookland 251
× Brooksby 318
× Brookthrop 311
102½ Broome (Norf.) 244
94½ Broome (Suff.) 241
32 Broomfield 237
101½ Broomfield *Tp.* 85, × 274
× Broomhaugh 380
23 Broomhill Hut 46
391½ Broomhouse 161
144½ Broseley 128, × 328
178½ Brotherton 197
240 Brough 177
262 —— by Richmond 206
261½ —— by Stamford 205
278½ Brough Sowerby 177
47½ Broughton (Bucks.) 154
188½ Broughton (Flint) 146
186½ —— by Malpas 148
× Broughton (Linc.) 353
× Broughton (Northam.) 299
× Broughton (Oxf.) 303
× Broughton (Salop) 321
148 Broughton (Staff.) 146
× Broughton (near Malton, Yorks.) 368
223 Broughton (near Skipton, Yorks.) 174, × 368
217 Broughton Bridge 158
252½ Broughton-in-Furness 175, × 373
× Broughton Poggs 300
7 Brown's Wells 137
× Brownsover 309
200½ Brownstone 64
17 Broxbourne 222
306 Broxburn 200
170½ Broxton 148
193½ Bruntcliff 179
× Bruntcliffe Thorne 363
242½ Brush Worton 205
108½ Bruton 75, × 279
108 —— by Warminster 83
213½ Brymind 93
257 Bryn 128
× Bubwith 364
98 Buck Alehouse 242
230½ Buckapit Bridge 56
61½ Buckden 194
194 Buckfastleigh 55
× Buckford Mill 255
55½ Buckingham 130, × 297
35 Buckland (Herts.) 223
69½ Buckland (Kent) 6
× Buckland (Surrey) 263
× Buckland Hill 284
138½ Buckland St. Mary 71
× Buckley or Bucklow Hill 341
38½ Buckmans Corner 30, × 267
× Bucks Green 267
249½ Buckshead 51
139½ Budby 202
× Buerton 336
× Bug Lawton 339
182 Bughead Cross 65
97½ Bugley 82
147½ Buildwas 129
× Builth 327, 329
× Buishport 281
× Bulborne 296
100½ Bulchamp 243
× Bulcote 306
× Bulford 294
236½ Bulk 176
× Bulkington (War.) 305
95½ Bulkington (Wilts.) 85
96½ —— by Westbury 85
38 Bullers Green 25
178½ Bullock Smithy 163
176½ —— by Derby 169
× Bulls Marsh 286
52½ Bulmer Tye 237
54½ —— by Gosfield 237
232½ Bultris 51
× Bulverhithe 252
× Bulwick 300
100½ Bungay 242
109½ —— by Halesworth 243
110½ Bunny 189, 190
32½ Buntingford 223
101½ Bunwell 238
98½ Burbage (Leic.) 155
× Burbage (Wilts.) 272, 293
85½ Burcombe 48
50½ Burcot 105
× Bures St. Mary 345
72½ Burford (Oxon.) 108, × 300, 302
133½ Burford (Salop) 120
21½ Burford Bridge 29
× Burg Hill (Sussex) 260
32½ Burgess Hill 12
15½ Burgh Heath 26, × 266
× Burgh-on-Bain 360
× Burgh St. Margaret's 348
130½ Burghill 115
110 Burleston 58
207 Burley 191, × 365
× Burley Gate 324
× Burley-on-the-Hill 351
× Burleydam 336

× Burlingham St. Andrew 348
× Burlingham St. Peter 348
× Burlton 333
Burmeston 198
80½ Burmington 124
49 Burnham (Essex) 216
× Burnham Deepdale 351
118 Burnham Westgate 228, × 351
121½ —— by South Creak 229
118¾ Burnham Overy 228
229 Burniston 217
207¾ Burnley 173, × 367
209¾ —— by Bacup 174
213½ —— by Todmorden 174
× Burnthurst Mill 336
× Burraston 328
× Burrill 371
× Burrington (Devon) 286
127½ Burrington (Som.) 96
250½ Burrow 176
25½ Burrow Green 46
132 Burrowbridge 81
× Burscough 367
× Bursledon Bridge 254
155¾ Burslem 164, × 339
× Burton (Pem.) 331
× Burton (Salop) 328
246¾ Burton (West.) 158
247½ —— by Ashbourne 171
253 —— by Manchester 169
202¾ Burton Agnes 216
118½ Burton Corner 219
× Burton Joyce 306
71½ Burton Latimer 165
103½ Burton Lazars 186
169 Burton-upon-Stather 214, × 361
123½ Burton-upon-Trent 156, × 308
121½ —— by Hinckley 157
123¼ —— by Leicester 170
250½ Burwall 175
× Burwarton 328
× Burwash Wheel 256
144½ Burwell 219
68½ Bury (Hunts.) 225
191½ Bury (Lanc.) 171, × 364
161½ Bury (Som.) 77
50½ Bury (Sussex) 31
71½ Bury St. Edmunds 237, × 345, 346
315 Buryness 209
72 Buscot 103
143¾ Bush Bank 117
178½ Bush Bridge 73
174¼ —— by Dulverton 78
8¾ Bush Hill 225
× Bushby Stoop 371
108½ Bushels Mill 44, × 280
106 —— by Cranbourn 53
110 —— by Wimborne 44
13½ Bushey 129
24¼ Buthatch Green 238
× Butlers Green 261
170½ Butley (Ches.) 169
81¾ Butley (Suff.) 244
119 Butt House 157
× Butterhouse Green 356
× Butterleigh 285
× Butterley 354
× Butterton Lane 339
× Buttington 332
× Buttock's Booth 209
165 Buxton (Derb.) 167, × 339, 355
159½ —— by Ashbourne 170
164½ —— by Wirksworth 170
117¾ Buxton (Norfolk) 232
159 Bwich 111
226½ Bwlch-clawdd 112
× Bybrook 255, 258
× Byfield 301
× Byfleet 269
× Byker Hill 380
× Bylaugh Heath 349
× Bythorne 316
154 Byton Lane 117
147 —— by Leominster 122
48 Byworth Street 35

CABBAGE HILL 94
× Cablehook 255
158½ Cabourn 220
226½ Cabus 158
113 Cadbury 70
× Cade Street 261
104¾ Cadeby 158
× Cadishead Green 341
205½ Cadleigh 56
210 Cadley 93
215½ Cadley Moor 158
84½ Cadnam 43, × 271, 273
78¾ —— by Basingstoke 53
80¾ —— by Romsey 46
207 Cadron 50
252¾ Caea Mona Inn 128
260 Caer Caeliog 128
229½ Caer Hûn Hall 150
× Caergwrle 333
144½ Caerleon 91
136½ —— by Aust 98
151 —— by Monmouth 113
160 Caerphilly 90
137½ Caerwent 91, × 332
31½ Cage Green 16
100 Cain's Cross 105, × 312
157 Caistor 220, × 360
141½ Calceby Beck Houses 219
41½ Calcot Green 88
100½ CalcottFarm 102, × 309, 313
85 Caldecot 186
207½ Calder Head 174
× Calecop 370
252 Calenick 51
12½ California 26
× Calfs Bridge 286
211½ Callington 65, × 288
131½ Callow 114, × 320
87 Calne 89, × 302
157½ Calver 181, × 355
164½ Calverleigh 73
× Calverton 297
177½ Camblesforth 210
× Cambo 381
260½ Camborne 67
51½ Cambridge 227, × 298, 316, 344, 346
52½ —— by Barkway 228
56½ —— by Harlow 231
× Cambridge Inn 307, 313
46 Camden Hill 10
223¾ Camelford 68
× Camnant Bridge 329
120 Camomile Green 114
Campsey Ash 244
130½ Camston 202
258 Canaston Bridge 98
250½ —— by Aust 98
190½ Cann Office Inn 121
× Cannard's Grave Inn 279, 281
140 Cannington 81
316 Cannobie Kirk 183
× Cannock 319
55½ Canterbury 3, × 254, 255
× Cantsfield 370
112 Canwell 145
29 Capel (Surrey) 29
190½ Capel (Mont.) 122
× Capel-allt-Mawr 329
225¾ Capel-Curig 128
226 —— by Banbury 135
× Capel Dryffyn Honddu 329
63½ Capel Stn. 239
160½ Car Top 181
× Carabrough 370
× Carbrook 369
93½ Carbrook Common 235
141½ Carburton 202
× Cardeston 332
160½ Cardiff 91
152½ —— by Aust 98
235½ Cardigan 112, × 331
244½ —— by Carmarthen 113
242½ —— —— 113
240 —— —— 113
× Cardington Cross 298
254¾ Carew 98
256¾ —— by Cold Blow 98
259¾ —— by Tenby 98
255 Carew Bridge 98
364½ Carfrae Mill Inn 209
252 Cargurrel 67
Carham 209
159 Carhampton 79
157½ —— by Rydon 81
124½ Carington 231
× Carkeel 288
× Carlby 352
294½ Carleton (Cumb.) 175
175¾ Carleton (Yorks.) 210
301½ Carlisle 159, × 373, 374, 375, 379
302½ —— by Ashbourne 171
307¾ —— by Manchester 169
300¾ —— by Stamford 206
298 Carlton (Cumb.) 159
281¾ —— by Stamford 206
107½ Carlton (Leic.) 157
× Carlton (nr. Nottingham, Notts.) 306
153½ Carlton (near Worksop, Notts.) 193
103½ Carlton Foreboe 235
× Carlton Miniot 371
131½ Carlton-on-Trent 196
116¾ Carlton Scrope 218
235 Carmarthen 92, × 331
221 —— by Aust 98
214 —— by Brecon 111
228¾ —— by Llannon 93
205¾ Carnaby 216
254¾ Carnau 51
251½ Carnarvon 123, × 334
244 —— by Banbury 135
258½ —— by Tremadoc 123
236 Carneggan 68

241¾ Carnforth 158
242¼ —— by Ashbourne 171
248 —— by Manchester 169
× Carnmeadow Green 311
185¾ Carno 122
240½ Carperby 204
239¼ Carr End 213
269¼ Carrigillgate 207
351¾ Carron Bridge 163
× Carrow 379
× Carshalton 265
93¼ Carsley Green 155
75 Carter's Bridge 226
261½ Cartmel 175
× Cashio Bridge 290
95¾ Cashmoor Inn 54, × 277
251½ Casterton 176
253¼ —— by Hornby 176
× Castle Bromwich 317
175¾ Castle Caereinion 121
111½ Castle Cary 75, × 279, 280
113 —— by Bruton 75
× Castle Comfort 282
× Castle Donington 315
255½ Castle Eden Inn 208
× Castle Frome 324
119¾ Castle Gresley 156
49½ Castle Hedingham 237
× Castle Hendre 331
301½ Castle Inn 163
108¾ Castle Rising 226
× Castleton 358
49¾ Castleton's Oak Inn 10
51½ —— by Staplehurst 11
× Castor 318
229½ Catchfrench 56
× Catchwater 347
12 Caterham Junction 20
16¾ Caterham Station 21
51½ Catley Cross 237
240¾ Caton 176
× Catsfield Green 260
133 Catsley Down Gate 60, × 284
228¾ Catterick 198, × 375
229¾ Catterick Bridge 198, × 375
226¼ —— by Ware 224
× Catterlin 375
× Catthorpe 316
111 Catton Lodge 232
191½ Catwick 218
68¾ Catworth 193
291¾ Causeway Foot 162
118¾ Cavendish Bridge 166, × 353
55¾ Caversfield 132
× Caversham 289
141½ Cawkwell 220
114½ Cawston 244, × 350
× Cawston Heath 350, 351
Cawthorne 180
50½ Caxton 223
Caynham 326
251¾ Cefn Cumyd 128
256¼ Ceirchiog 128
147¼ Cellar Head 165
206¾ Cemmes 122
× Cerne Abbas 279
211¼ Cerniogo Mawr 128
208¾ Cerrig-y-Druidion 127
× Chaddesden 353
119¼ Chaddesley Corbett 125
23 Chadwell 240, × 342, 343
6½ Chadwell Street 236
100 Chadwick End 143
42¾ Chailey 21
× Chailey Common 261
22¾ Chalfont St. Giles 133
20¾ Chalfont St. Peters 132
95¾ Chalford 104
37¾ Chalgrave 188
23¾ Chalk 2
39 Chalkwell 3
× Challock Lees 256, 257
71 Chandler's Ford Bdge. 40
360½ Channel Kirk Inn 209
× Chapel 261
197¾ Chapel Allerton 191
70 Chapel Brampton 154
× Chapel End 317
167¾ Chapel-en-le-Frith 171, × 358
164¾ —— by Ashbourne 177
72¾ Chapel House 124
164¾ Chapel Hulme 152
168 Chapel Town 178, 187
397 Chapleton 164
102¾ Chapman's Lade 85
× Chapman's Well 289
140 Chard 49, × 284
137¾ —— by Ilminster 71
47¾ Charing 8, × 256
× Charingworth 304
× Charlbury 300, 301
112¾ Charleton Horethorne 72
70¾ Charlton (near Dover, Kent) 6
7¼ Charlton (near Woolwich, Kent) 4
Charlton (near Devizes, Wilts.) 85
91½ Charlton (near Malmesbury, Wilts.) 102
93 Charlton Kings 109
× Charlton Marshall 277
× Charlton Street 274
35¾ Charlwood Gate 21
121 Charminster 60 × 279, 281
141 Charmouth 54
107¾ Charterhouse Hinton 86
106¾ —— by Devizes 86
× Charwelton 301
215¾ Chatburn 172
30 Chatham 2
73½ Chatteris 226, × 347
× Chauntry 345
× Chawleigh 286
48¾ Chawton 39, 41
179¾ Cheadle (Chesh.) 165, 356
145¾ Cheadle (Staff.) 164, × 338
× Cheam 264
140¾ Checkley 164
128 Cheddar 84
153¾ Cheddleton 164
× Cheeley Bridge 336
184 Cheetham 171, 174
171 Chelford 154, × 339, 356
29½ Chelmsford 237, × 343
31¾ —— by Epping 240
× Chelsea 296
63 Chelsworth 240
91½ Cheltenham 108, × 303, 309, 310
× Chelveston 315
116½ Chelwood 96
21¾ Cheneys 134
131¾ Chepstow 100, × 320
84⅛ Cherhill 89
× Cheriton (Hants.) 260
× Cheriton (Som.) 280
178 Cheriton Cross 49
185¾ Cherry Burton 218
200¼ Cherston 56-6
21¼ Chertsey 38, × 269
19 —— by Shepperton 38
91½ Chesford Bridge 144
26¾ Chesham 134
14¾ Cheshunt 222
15¾ —— by Enfield 225
15¾ Cheshunt Wash 222
183¾ Chester 146, × 342
181¾ —— by Malpas 148 × 378
150 Chesterfield 178, 181, × 354, 355, 358
150½ —— by Mansfield 190
265¼ Chester-le-Street 199
269 —— by York 211
151½ Chesterton 152, × 337
141¾ Chetwynd 148
× Chew Stoke 281
× Chewton Ford 271
× Chewton Mendip 283
60¾ Chichester 34, × 253
61¾ —— by Petworth 35
× Chicheley 297
93¾ Chicklade 70
38 Chiddingfold 34
137 Chidiock 54
× Chieveley 292
11 Chigwell 236
× Chilcompton 283
62¼ Childrey 101
× Chilham 254, 255
× Chilhampton 274
85¾ Chillesford 244
92¾ Chilmark 71
147 Chilson 73
88¾ Chiltern 82
× Chilton (Berks.) 292
66 Chilton Foliat 89
57 Chilton Park 238, × 345
× Chilver Bridge 261
99 Chilvers Coton 156
Chilwell 190, × 315
23 Chilwick Green 188
× Chinham 270
167¾ Chinley Head 177
× Chilworth (Hants.) 273
× Chilworth Station 263
93½ Chippenham 89, × 275, 276, 277, 304
99 —— by Swindon 102
× Chipping (Essex) 344
34 Chipping (Herts.) 223
× Chipping Campden 304
73½ Chipping Norton 118, × 300, 303
21½ Chipping Ongar 236
24¾ —— by Epping 240
108 Chipping Sodbury 97, × 314
× Chipping Warden 301
154½ Chipstable 77
× Chirbury 332
181½ Chirk 127, × 329
× Chirton 379
× Chisenbury 294
× Chisledon 273
10¾ Chislehurst 11, × 265
× Chiswell Green 290
× Chittlehamholt 283

184½ Chittlehampton 76, × 286	× Cleckheaton 365	260½ Cold Hasledon 208
× Chitway Heath 275, 302	× Cleo Downton 326	× Cold Hatton 335
24½ Chobham 46	119½ Clent 137	184½ Cold Henley 180
× Cholderton 293	× Cleobury Mortimer 326,328	262½ Cold Rowley 210
× Chollerford Bridge 379	50 Clerken Green 58	× Coldbach 327
× Chollerton 381	123½ Cley 244, × 351	× Coldrife 381
130½ Cholstry 122	49½ Cliff 22, × 256, 260	333½ Coldstream 204
172½ Chorley (Chesh.) 165	151½ Clifford 116, × 325	47½ Coldwaltham 31
204 Chorley (Lanc.) 157	× Cliffs End 250	× Cole Orton 315
204½ —— by Ashbourne 171	43 Clifton (Beds) 202, × 297	126½ Coleby 218
210 —— by Blackrod 169	42 —— by Henlow 202	121½ Coleford 113
210½ —— by Manchester 168	× Clifton (Derb.) 335	123½ —— by Mitcheldean 114
99½ Christchurch (Hants.) 43, × 271, 275	193½ Clifton (Lanc.) 168	× Coles Mill 336
	286 Clifton (Northumb.) 199	71½ Coleshill (Berks.) 102
97½ —— by Basingstoke 53	Clifton (Notts.) 190	103½ Coleshill (War.) 144, × 317
145½ Christchurch (Monm.) 91	52 Clifton (Oxon.) 105, × 303	× Colesley or Colstey 327
152½ —— by Usk 113	× Clifton (War.) 316	32 Colestock Gate 19
× Christchurch (York.) 332	281 Clifton (West.) 159	180 Colford 69
× Christchurch in Needwood 335	× Clifton (Worc.) 307	155 Colleton 74
	197½ Clifton (York.) 211	26 Collier's End 223, × 342
91½ Christian Malford 102	121½ Clifton-upon-Teme 120, × 324	× Collingbourn Ducis, C. Kingston, and C. Sutton 272, 293
182 Chudleigh 55		
178 —— by Yeovil 56	× Cliftonville 253	130 Collingham (Notts.) 214
× Chumleigh 286	214½ Clitheroe 172	× Collingham (Yorks.) 369
172½ Chunal 177	209 Cliviger 174	× Coln or Cole Green 295
× Church 367	× Clixby 360	17½ Colnbrook 87
× Church End 343	150½ Clockmill 116	214½ Colne 173 × 369
68 Church Enstone 134, × 300	42 Clophill 188, × 207	109½ Colney 245
Church Hulme. See Holmes Chapel	× Clopton 316	164 Colney Street 141
	177 Clopton Bridge 55	102½ Coltersworth 195, × 353
155½ Church Lawton 152, × 339	176 Clotton 116	116½ Coltishall 235
Church Stoke 120	× Cloudeley Bush 306	× Colt's Hill 260
× Church Stretton 321	230 Cloughton 217	224½ Colvanick 50
143½ Church Warsop 193	212 Clovelly 74	283 Colwell 210, × 331
107½ Churcham 110	148 Clown 187	129 Colwich 151
130½ Churchill 96, × 282, 293	× Clowsgill 379	221½ Colwyn 147
× Churchingford 284	× Clun 327	14½ Colyford 59, × 283, 234
201½ Churston Ferrers 63	× Clutton 276	149½ Colyton 59, × 283
× Churwell 363	× Clytha 322	× Colyton Rawleigh 285
273½ Chywoon 51	× Coalbrookdale 328	156 Combe or Cwm 117
127½ Cinder Hill 190	245½ Contham Mundeville 202	149 —— by Worcester 122
119 Cinderford 114	146½ Cobden's Ash 122	83½ Combe Bissett 53
86½ Cirencester 103, × 273, 302, 304	× Cobeech 261	10½ Combe Hill 32
	× Cobham 269	201 Combe Martin 77
89½ —— by Abingdon 106	17½ Cobham Street 33, × 269	190 —— by Lynton 80
129½ Citadella 201,206, × 372, 375	× Cock Gate 326	188½ —— by Rydon 81
× Clanfield 307	23 Cock Inn 247, × 313	× Combe St. Nicholas 284
112½ Clanville 75	× Cockayne Hatley 208	× Comberton 326
52½ Clapham (Beds.) 185	358 Cockburnspath 200	52 Compton (Berks.) 100
3½ Clapham (Surrey) 28	298½ Cockermouth 176, × 373	188½ Compton (Devon) 63
139 Clapham (York.)173, × 370	× Cockerton 376	67 Compton (Hants.) 40
130½ —— by Newark 203	50½ Cocking 34	× Compton (Staff.) 326
140 —— by Nottingham 187	195 Cockington 63	89½ Compton Chamberlain 46
× Clappersgate 372	× Cockley 364	× Compton Dunden 281
74½ Clapton 193	× Cockshut 333	126½ Compton Greenfield 91, × 329
× Clareborough 356	178½ Cockwood 62	
× Clareston 332	75½ Coddenham Bridge 239	87½ Compton Hill 48
80 Clarks Green 29	89½ Codford St. Mary 52	121½ Compton Martin 96
24 Clatterfoot End 236	26½ Codicote 155	87½ Compton Verney 136
Claughton 178	44½ Codmore Hill 31	× Conduit Hill 360
105½ Claverton 95	Codrington 103	161½ Congleton 153, × 339, 353, 358
× Clawton 289	51½ Coggers Cross 17	
× Clay Bridge 359	44½ Coggeshall 238, × 342	126 Congresbury 97 × 283
× Clay Hill (Kent) 265	× Cogginsmill Street 257	128½ Coningsby 220
× Clay Hill (Mont.) 329	51½ Colchester 239, × 345	× Conisborough 361
92½ Claybrook 155	265½ Cold Blow 93	× Coniston (Lanc.) 373
73 Claydon 239, × 348	247½ —— by Aust 98	170½ Coniston (York.) 218
119 Claythorpe 218	× Cold Brayfield 207	× Conksbury 335
108 Clayton (Lanc.) 157	220½ Cold Coniston 180	262½ Conner 67
46½ Clayton (Sussex) 23	90½ Cold Fair Green 244	85½ Connock or Coule 85
44 —— by Cuckfield 24	78 Cold Harbour Inn 102, × 273	230½ Conway 147
206½ Clayton-le-Moors 172, × 367		236 —— by Banbury 150
271½ Cleadon 208	68½ Cold Harbour Tg. 41, × 272	

221 Conwyl-Elfed 112
200¼ Cookridge 191
46¼ Cooks Bridge 22
273¼ Cook's House 162
266½ —— by Kendal 163
29¾ Cooks Mill Green 240
× Cooper's Bridge 362
× Cooper's Corner 256
× Cooper's Green (Heref.) 324
× Cooper's Green (Sussex) 258, 261
65¾ Copdock 239
× Coppard's Gap 253
180½ Copplestone 69
27¼ Copthorn Common 23
× Corbar 355
17 Corbetts Tye 249
275½ Corbridge 210, × 370, 380
× Corby (Linc.) 353.
× Corby (Northamp.) 317
121¾ Corfe Castle 45
115¾ —— by Basingstoke 53
102 Corfe Mullen 57, × 280
62 Corhampton 41
× Corkett 273
95¼ Corley 155
114½ Corlingstock 189
216¼ Cornbrow 65
333¼ Cornhill (Northumb.) 208
155¼ Cornhill (Staff.) 164
178 Corntown 92
× Corpusty 351
233½ Corsenside 210
97¼ Corsham 90
100¾ Corsley Heath 82
110¼ Corston 96, × 304
117 Corton 242
× Corton Denham 279
198½ Corwen 127
90 Coscomb Cross 123
174½ Cosgate 79
53½ Cosgrove 156
65¼ Cosham 36, × 254, 272
× Cotes (Camb.) 347
109¾ Cotes (Leic.) 189
115 Cotheridge 121
250½ Cotherstone 207
207¾ Cothy Bridge 111
× Coton (near Staff.) 336
× Coton (near Stone) 336
× Cottesbach 309
× Cottesmore 351
203¾ Cottingley 179
69 Cottington (Kent) 6, × 250
× Cottington (Linc.) 355
46¾ Cotton End 185
× Cotwall 336
103¼ Coughton 125, × 311
× Coulton 308
152 Cound 126
177¾ Countisbury 79
226½ County Stone 113
× Cours End 290
× Coursely Wood Street 257
85¾ Cove House 102
330½ Covendrum 200
91 Coventry 130, × 305, 317
99½ —— by Banbury 143
229½ Cover Bridge 204
167¾ Cowan Bridge 173
61 Cowbeach Green 12
92½ Cowbit 221
172¾ Cowbridge 91
165 —— by Aust 98
29½ Cowden Pound 19
39½ Cowfold 27, × 267
55¼ Cowley 109
170¼ Cowley Bridge 68
× Cowley Street 291
× Cowsfield Green 273
130½ Coxbench 178
× Coxley 282
212¾ Crab Tree (Dev.) 56
37¾ Crab Tree (Suss.) 27, × 267
× Crab Tree Green 340, 341
106¾ Crab's Cross 125
272 Crackenthorp 206
110 Cradley 144
223¾ Crafthole 56
219¾ —— by Yeovil 66
92¼ Cranbourn 53
22¼ Cranbourn Wood 94
47¼ Cranbrook 10, × 256
47¼ —— by Tunbridge 13, 14
132¼ Crandon Bridge 81, × 283
12¼ Cranford Bridge 87
190¾ Cranford Moor 77, × 286
× Cranford St. John 316
× Crankley Mill 359
× Crankston 356
× Cranleigh 266
× Cranwich 347
234½ Crathorne 207
× Crawcrook 380
357 Crawford 160
20 Crawley 25, × 266
29½ Crawleys Downs 23
202¼ Crawshaw Booth 173
27¾ Cray Hill 248
13 Crayford by Blackheath 2
14½ —— by Lewisham 7
73¼ Creaton 154
140 Creden Hill 114
176 Crediton 68, × 286
172¾ —— by Tiverton 76
217¼ Cremill Passage 56
150 Cressage 126
253½ Cressilly 98
× Crewe Green, Park, and Station 330
132 Crewkerne 48, × 281, 282, 284
132 —— by Amesbury 71
× Crich 337
135¾ Crick (Monm.) 91, × 322
128 —— by Aust 98
135¾ —— by Gloucester 109
79½ Crick (Northamp.) 182
116½ Crickett's Inn 156
153¼ Crickhowell 111
81¼ Cricklade 102 × 293, 302
4 Cricklewood 120
× Crim Chard 284
× Crimpgate 280
× Crimplesham 348
106¼ Cringleford 232
40¼ Cripple Crouch Hill 34, 35
53¾ Cripp's Corner 17
× Crocker Hill 253
179¼ Crockernwell 50
× Crockerton 276
× Crockford Bridge 269
23¾ Crockham Hill 19
46¼ Crockstead Green 19
139 Croes-bychan 110
101¼ Croes-ceilog 111
227¼ Croes-fford 112
237¼ } Croft 201
236¾ }
× Croft End 373
178¾ Crofton 202, × 362
130¾ Cromer 232
132¾ —— by N. Walsham 235, × 350, 351
120½ —— by Reepham 234
142¼ Cromford 167
141¼ —— by Wirksworth 170
130 Cromwell 196
× Crondall Marsh 270
243¾ Cronware 98
× Crook 377
× Crosby (near Carlisle, Cumb.) 379
× Crosby (near Maryport, Cumb.) 374
165 Crosby (Linc.) 214
× Cross (Heref.) 325.
× Cross (Som.) 283
137¼ Cross Elms 115, 117
69 Cross Ford 89
215 Cross Foxes 147, × 330
× Cross Gate 332
65½ Cross Green (near Botesdale, Suff.) 238
62¾ Cross Green (nr. Ipswich, Suff.) 239
56¾ Cross Hall 194, 195, 202
100 Cross Hands 105, × 310
134¼ Cross Hands Inn (Derby) 170, × 354
105¼ Cross Hands Inn (Glouc.) 97, × 304, 314
215½ Cross Hill 179
130¼ Cross-in-Hand *Tg.* (Heref.) 114, × 320
50¼ Cross-in-Hand *Tp.* 17, × 256, 261
207¼ Cross Inon 93
114 Cross Lane 157
× Cross Way 273
× Crossbarrow 374
361½ Crosslee *Tg.* 184
× Crossthwaite (Cumb.) 372
294½ Crossthwaite (West.) 163
× Crossway Green 311
113¾ Crostwick 235
64¼ Croughton, 131
48¾ Croust Corner 17, × 261
× Crowborough Beacon *Tg.*, Cross or Mill, and Gate 258
150¼ Crowcombe 78
× Crowdey Cote 350
× Crowhall 380
90¼ Crowland 221
87¼ —— by Ramsey 226
167 Crowle 214, × 361
45¼ Crowmarsh Gifford 100
82¾ Croxton (Norf.) 234 × 347
146 Croxton (Staff.) 146
× Croxton Green 340
× Croxton Kerrial 318
9¼ Croydon 20, × 264, 265
× Cruckton 332
× Crudgington 335, 336
× Crudwell 304
65¼ Crumble Bridge 13, × 264
× Cubington 3[illegible]

× Cubley 335	51 Dean (Hants.) 58	110½ Dishley 166
37 Cuckfield 24, × 261	× Dean (Lanc.) 364	174½ Disley 168
37½ —— by Hand Cross 26	111 Dean (Som.) 83	168½ —— by Ashbourne 170
109 Cucklington 72	160 Dean Hill 153	86½ Diss 240
115 Cuckney 193	195½ Dean Prior 55	313½ Distington 176, × 374
92½ Cuckold's Green 85	51½ Deans 22	210½ Ditchen Hills 74
51½ Culham Bridge 105	× Deansanger 207	112 Ditchingham 243
× Cullercoats 380	83 Debenham 241, × 346	44½ Ditchling 23, × 267
209 Cullingworth 189, × 360	× Deddington 295, 303	197½ Ditsham Cross 64, × 287
160 Cullompton 74	Deep Car 182, × 358	30½ Ditton 7
154½ —— by Taunton 76	263 Deeplace Bridge 93	236½ Dobwalls 57
× Culmington 323	× Defford 323	179 Deccombe 65
174½ Culverhouse 65	190 Deighton 211	112½ Docking 228
× Culversore Green 202	267½ Demmings 159	131½ Docklow 122
323½ Cumbertrees 163	33 Den Bridge 30	353 Dodd Mill 209
× Curbridge 301	209½ Denbigh 149	77½ Doddington (Camb.) 226
× Curdworth 314	208½ —— by Ruthin 149	145 Doddington (Som.) 81
105½ Curdworth Bridge 145	207 Denholme 160	118 Dodenham Lane 121
× Curland 284	× Dennebridge Pound 296	× Dodworth 360
129½ Curry Rivell 73	43½ Dennel End 188	223½ Dolaw-Saison 112
Cwm. See Comb	× Denover Street 259	244½ Dolbenmaen 123
240 Cwm-y-Glo 135	68½ Densell 9	× Doldowlod 329
192½ Cwm Ystwith 115	61½ Denton (Durh.) 376	212½ Dolgelly 121, × 330
223½ Cwmdeant 112	6½ Denton (Kent) 9	190½ Dol-y-carreg 111
× Cynwyd 330	179½ Denton (Lanc.) 177, × 357	166½ Doncaster 193, × 360, 361
	× Denton (Linc.) 318	162½ —— by G. N. Rd. 146
13½ DAGENHAM 246	66 Denton (Northamp.) 189	159½ —— by Ware 224
45 Dale Hill 25	× Denton Burn 379	111½ Donington 220, × 353
343½ Dalhousie 184	84 Denver 227	151½ Donniford 81
379 Dalkeith, 209	4½ Deptford 1	× Donnington (Berks.) 292
67½ Dallington (Northamp.) 182	60½ Deptford Inn 70, × 274	× Donnington (Salop) 336
	× Deptling 258	× Donyatt 284
× Dallington (Sussex) 261	125½ Derby 166, × 303, 335, 353, 357	119 Dorchester (Dorset.) 54, × 279, 281
× Dalston 374		
313½ Dalswinston 163	129½ —— by Ashby-de-la-Z. 170	122½ —— by Bere Regis 58
199½ Dalton Green 160	91 Derry Hill 89, × 275	49½ Dorchester (Oxon.) 105
188½ —— by Penistone 182	113 Dersingham 227	23½ Dorking 29, × 263
272½ Dalton-in-Furness 175, × 373	80½ Desborough 180	129½ Dormington 116
	324½ Detchent 200	62½ Dornford Cottage 124
261½ Dalton-le-Dale 208	× Deuxhill 338	316½ Dornock 163
236½ Dalton-on-Tees 201	199½ Devil's Bridge 115	62½ Dorringstone 9
× Danaway 258	59 Devil's Ditch (Camb.) 231, × 345	× Dorrington (near Shrewsbury) 321
33½ Danbury 246		
37 Dane Hill 21	× Devil's Ditch (Dors.) 277	154½ Dorrington (nr. Woore) 146
× Daresbury 341	90½ Devizes 66, × 275	112½ Dorsley Cross 110
× Darfield 360	88½ —— by Marlborough 95	× Double Bridge 361
142 Darlaston 151, × 336	217½ Devonport 56	98 Doughton 103
147½ Darley 167	× Dewsbury 362, 363	369 Douglas Mill 160
244½ Darlington 201, × 376	× Dicken Dale 327	112½ Doulting 83
242½ —— by Stapleton 201	91½ Dickleburgh 239	83 Dove Bridge 183
244½ —— by York 211	88½ —— by Stowmarket 242	× Dove Street 338
× Darliston 335	52½ Didcot 101	326½ Doveford Bridge 209
× Darnal 360	60 Diddington 194	143½ Dovendale 220
174½ Darrington 197	× Diddlebury or Delbury 326	71 Dover 6, × 250
94½ Darsham 244	102½ Didmarton 103	70 } Dovercourt 215
19½ Dart Bridge 55	181 Didsbury 165	69
15 Dartford 2, × 262	231 Digswell Hill 184	136½ Doveridge 165, × 336
193 Dartmouth by Newton Abbot 63, × 287	156½ Dilford 74	90 Dowdeswell 109
	× Dilston 380	15½ Down (Kent) 18
200½ —— by Torquay 63	× Dilwyn 325	× Down (Shrop.) 326
204½ —— by Totnes 64	203½ Dinas Mawddwy 121, × 334	× Down End 314
174½ Darton 180	118½ Dinder 84	85½ Downham Market 227, × 348, 352
× Darvel Hole 261	134½ Dingestow 110	
2½ Datchet 87	× Dingley 317	× Downside 281
201 Davenby 176	134½ Dinmore Hill 320	198½ Downton (Devon) 65
174½ Davenham 153	× Dinnington 284	× Downton (Hants.) 271
72 Daventry 130, × 301	× Dinton (Bucks.) 296	× Downton Wick 274
219½ Davidstow 68	80½ Dinton (Wilts.) 71	× Dowsby 352
181½ Dawlish 62	333 Dinwoodie 160	× Drake Holes 359
× Deadman's Dean Bottom 290	331½ Dinwoodie Green 100	× Drake Street 323
	× Dipford 286, 289	× Drake's Cross 311
4½ Deadman's Cross 185	210½ Dishforth 201	217 Draughton 191
73½ Deal 6, × 250		126½ Draycott (Som.) 94

144¾ Draycott (Staff.) 164, × 335
× Dra‹ton (Berks.) 292
× Drayton (Norf.) 349
75 Drayton (Oxon) 131
× Drayton Basset 314
196½ Driffield 216, × 366, 370
195 Drighlington 179, × 365
198½ Dring Houses 211
× Droitwich 309, 311
155½ Dronfield 178
89 Drove End 54
63½ Droxford 41
201¾ Druid Inn 127, × 330, 331
× Drumburgh Castle 375
× Drwsynant 330
117 Drybrook 114
× Duddington 300, 318
38¾ Duddleswell Gate 19, × 259
37¾ —— by Godstone 21
176 Duddon 146
283 Duddon Bridge 175
× Dudley 319
198 Dudley Hill 179
× Dudley Port 319
130½ Duffield 167
× Duggleaby 370
119½ Dulcot 84
163¾ Dulverton 77
162½ —— by Bridgewater 82
336¾ Dumfries 163
367½ Dunbar 200
79¾ Dunchurch 139, × 309
51½ Duncton 35
× Dunham 356
× Dunham-on-the-Hill 342
× Dunkerton 280
205 Dunkeswick 191
102 Dunkirk 101, × 304, 309, 313
104½ —— by Tetbury 103
× Dunley 324
283½ Dunmail Raise 163
× Dunmeer Bridge 288
38½ Dunmow 236, × 342, 343
41 } —— by Abridge 236
36½ }
103½ Dunnington 135, × 311
× Dunsby 352
176¼ Dunsford 65
33½ Dunstable 138, × 296
160½ Dunster 79, × 285
158½ —— by Bridgewater 81
× Dunston 312
126½ Dunston Pillar 215
179 Dunswell 216
× Dunton 350
21 Dunton Green 11, 12
201½ Dunwell Cross 64
97½ Dunwich 244
269½ Durham 198, × 377, 378
256½ —— by Ware 224
263 —— by York 211
137 Durleigh 82
169½ Durleyford 78
× Durrington 294
105½ Dursley 104, × 313
137 Durston 81
× Durtness Bridge 361
× Durweston 278
× Duston 315
× Dutston 340
207½ Duxbury 168
207 —— by Blackrod 169
× Dyffryn Arth 331
× Dymchurch 251
115¾ Dymock 116
× EAGLETON 338
6 Ealing Common 106
282½ Eamont Bridge 159
126 Eardistone 120
× Earith 347
× Earl Shilton 305
93½ Earl Stoke 85
110½ Earlham 235
× Earl's Colne 345
× Earl's Crome 323
× Earsdon 380
99½ Earsham 242
56½ Eartham 35
113¾ Earthcote Common 97
47 Easebourn 34, × 268
82¾ Easington (Glou.) 103
257½ Easington (York.) 208
209½ Easingwold 211, × 368
× Eason's Green 256
189½ East Ardsley 179
231½ East Ayton 213
× East Barkwith 360
112½ East Barsham 233
× East Boldon 378
× East Boscombe 293
× East Brent 283
94½ East Bridge 244
162½ East Budleigh 60, × 285
× East Carlton 317
65¾ East Carston 100
61 East Charlow 102
127½ East Chinnock 48, 49
26½ East Clandon 37
110½ East Cranmore 83
× East Dean 252
101 East Dereham 234, × 318, 349
75½ East Everley 65, × 272, 293, 294
× East Gate 377
× East Grafton 293
29½ East Grinstead 21
73½ East Haddon 182
6½ East Ham 246
× East Hanney 292
174½ East Hardwick 203
× East Harptree 282
268½ East Harrington 210
56 East Hendred 101
48½ East Hoathley 19
× East Horndon 342
118½ East Horrington 84
24 East Horsley 37
54 East Ilsley 100, × 292
131½ East Keal 219
× East Knoyle 276
237 East Lane End 50
57 East Lavant 34
East Leake 190
108½ East Leigh 74
100½ East Lexham 233
× East Lockinge 293
229½ East Looe 66
134 East Lyng 81
× East Marton 368
12½ East Moulsey 37
13 —— by Thames Ditton 38
× East Norton 318
264½ East Rainton 210
160 East Ravendale 220
111½ East Rudham 229, × 350
× East Runton 350, 351
8½ East Sheen 31
152½ East Stockwith 214
× East Stoke 306
× East Stour 278
53½ East Stratton 53
51½ East Tisted 41
× East Winch 347, 349
228½ East Witton 204
166½ East Wonford 49
168½ —— by Sidford 59
× East Worlington 286
66 Eastbourne 18, × 252
62¾ —— by Westerham 19
61½ —— by Godstone 21
14½ Eastburn 179
68½ Eastbury 100
59½ Eastergate 35
238½ Eastern Tap House 57
88¾ Easterton 85
× Eastgate 350
190½ Eastham 151
× Eastoft 361
× Easton (Hunt.) 300
× Easton (Norf.) 318
123 Easton (Som.) 84
95½ Easton Grey 101
× Eastown 286
× Eastrea 347
× Eastrington 363
× Eastry 250
× Eastwood 357
107 Eaton 232
136 Eaton Bridge 122
56 Eaton Ford 224
55½ Eaton Socon 194, × 295
× Ebberton 371
× Ebchester 377, 378
× Ebford 285
100½ Ebley 105
× Ebrington 304
320½ Ecclefechan 160
× Eccles 340
146 Eccles Green 115
142¾ Eccleshall 146, × 338
× Eccleshill 370
157½ Eckington 190
154½ —— by Mansfield 191
× Ecton 299
28¾ Eden Bridge 19
197½ Edenfield 171
× Edenham 353
Edensor 181, × 355
122¾ Edgarley 83
81 Edge Hill 131, 136
× Edgebolton 338
× Edgefield Green 351
153¾ Edgeton Farms 120
× Edgmond 336
8 Edgware 129
392½ Edinburgh 184
385½ —— by Coldstream 209
373½ —— by Jedburgh 209
395½ —— by Northallerton 202
395½ —— by Stamford 201
392¾ —— by Ware 224
399 —— by York 211
95½ Edington 85
× Edingley 365
8½ Edmonton 222
× Edstaston 321
× Edwin Ralph 324

Effelfach 121
× Efford Mill 271
107 Egerton 173
Egglestone 207, × 376
× Eggleton 323
18 Egham 46, × 269
× Egloshayle 288
212 Egloskerry 68
× Eglwys Cross 336
× Eglwys-fach 330
× Eglwyswrw 331
304½ Egremont 175
× Egryn Abbey 334
30¾ Elbridge 34
212¼ Elburton 64
248¾ Eldon 198
66¾ Elham 9
197½ Elland 180, × 364
× Ellaston 335, 338
304½ Ellenborough 176
× Ellens Green 266, 267
× Ellesmere 333, 340
101¾ Ellingham 243
× Ellington 316
308 Ellishaw 209
297½ —— by Corbridge 210
× Elloughton 363
× Elmers End 265
× Elmsgreen 320
65¼ Elmstead Market 245
× Elmswell 346
302¾ Elsdon 209
49 Elstow 188
11 Elstree 141
8 Eltham 7
56½ Eltisley 224, × 298
× Elton (Durh.) 376
× Elton (Heref.) 327
81½ Elton (Hunts.) 193, × 299
× Elton (Notts.) 353
354¼ Elvanfoot Inn 160
76¾ Elvedon 231
250½ Elwick 208
67¾ Ely 227, × 347
162¾ Ely Bridge 91
Emberton 188
× Emborough 282
× Emneth 352
× Empingham 351
× Emscote 316
× Emsworth 254
252 End Moor 158
× Endon 339
10½ Enfield 225
10¾ Enfield Highway 222
11½ Enfield Wash 223
× Enford 294
× Englefield 291
19½ Englefield Green 94
139½ Enmore 82
164 Ensdon House 126
69¾ Ensham 108
× Ensham Demesnes 302
60¼ Enslow Bridge 124
69 Enstone 118
68½ —— by Islip 124
233½ Enter Common 201, × 372
128¾ Enville 137
17½ Epping 229
14½ Epsom 28
160 Epworth 214
× Ercall Mill 336
× Erdington 308
× Eridge Green 258
14 Erith 4
× Erwood 329
188¾ Escrick 211
× Esgairgeiliog 330
14 Esher 32
202½ Eskynald 115
× Esling Green 348
× Etchingham 260
22 Eton 87
153¾ Etruria 164
× Etwall 335
205½ Euxton 158
× Evelton Street 271
× Evercreech 280
× Everton 359
98½ Evesham 119, × 310
68 Ewell (Kent) 6
13 Ewell (Surrey) 28, × 264, [266
179 Ewenny Bridge 92
171½ —— by Aust 93
326 Ewes Kirk 183
183 Ewloe 146
198¾ Ewood Bridge 171
× Ewshot Street 270
191¾ Exbourne 69
× Excet 252
168½ Exeter 49, × 285
166 —— by Amesbury 71
177¾ —— by Beaminster 61
172½ —— by Dorchester 55
169 —— by Hindon 71
171¾ —— by Ottery 60
167 —— by Redlinch 75
170½ —— by Sidford 59
173½ —— by Sidmouth 59, 60
170¾ —— by Taunton 76
Exilby 198
173 Exminster 62
167½ Exmouth 60, × 285
× Exton (Devon) 285
61½ Exton (Hants.) 41
85 Eye (Camb.) 221, × 351
92½ Eye (Suff.) 241
83 —— by Sudbury 241
81½ Eyke 244
× Eynesford 262
69¾ Eynsham 103
× Eyton 333

× FAILSWORTH 361
155½ Fair Cross 78
53½ Fair Oak 95
180 Fairburn 197
160½ Fairfield 177, × 355
78 Fairford 103
62½ Fairlight Down 15, × 260
204½ Fairy Cross 74
109½ Fakenham 233, × 346, 350
× Falfield 307
371 Falla 209
× Falmer 257
262¾ Falmouth 51
258½ —— by Tregony 67
235½ Falsgrave 213
216¾ —— by Lincoln 217
72½ Fareham 41, × 254
69 Faringdon 102, × 301
70½ —— by Abingdon 106
105¾ Farleigh Hungerford 86
103¼ Farleywick 95
244 Farlton 176
248¾ Farlton Lane 158
× Farmanby Thornton 371
× Farmborough 282
58 Farnborough (Berks.) 100, × 293
32 Farnborough (Hants.) 52
14 Farnborough (Kent) 11
× Farndon 306
× Farnham (Dorset.) 277
87¾ Farnham (Suff.) 241, 244
37¾ Farnham (Surr.) 34, × 270
38¾ —— by Bagshot 52, 29
17¾ Farningham 7, × 262
× Farnley 370
× Farnsfield 355
196¾ Farnworth 168
50 Farrington 41
× Farrington Gurney 278, 283
66¾ Farthingho 136
× Faulkbourn 344
109½ } Faulkland 86
108 }
47 Faversham 3, × 257
× Fawler Mill 301
× Fawles or Fauls Green 335
59¾ Fawley 100
× Fawley Court 289
114½ Fazeley 155, × 314
246 Featham 206
283½ Featherstonhaugh Castle 207
27½ Felbridge 21
× Felhampton 321
122 Felmingham 232
63½ Felpham 34, × 260
299 Felton (Northumb.) 199
× Felton (Som.) 278
Feltwell St. Mary 233
× Fen Ottery 285
184½ Fenay Bridge 182
141½ Fenny Bentley 170
155½ Fenny Bridges 49
× Fenny Stanton 316
44½ Fenny Stratford 138
143½ Fenton (Linc.) 218
× Fenton or Lane Delph 339
327½ Fenwick 200
218½ Ferensby 192
× Fernhill 308
43 Fernhurst 34
359¾ Fernielie Bridge 184
177½ Ferry Bridge 197
252½ Ferry Hill 202
× Festiniog 333
19½ Fetcham 37
92½ Fettle Bridge 232
× Ffynnonstown 332
× Fidebrook 257
× Field 336
49½ Field Green 12
× Fieldsend Bridge 347
× Figheldean 294
× Filby 348
183¾ Filleigh 74
97 Fillongley 155
150¾ Fillyford Bridge 167
56 Filmer Hill 41
× Filton 306
× Fimber 366
× Fincham 348
× Finchley Bridge 318
51½ Finden 30
69 Finedon 185, × 299

396

× Fineshade 300	12 Forty Mile 225	269½ Fulwell Inn and *Tp.* 209, × 378
× Fingland (Cumb.) 374	× Fosbrook 333	
370½ Fingland (Dumf.) 104	× Foss Gwy 331	× Furnace End 317
5½ Finmere 131, × 207	× Fossdyke 352	78½ Furningham 238
175½ Finney Green 165	62½ Foster's Booth 138	× Further Woodhead 358
× Finney Hall Wood 315	131 Foston (Derby) 165, × 335	61½ Fyfield (Berks.) 105
157½ Finningley 210	116 Foston (Linc.) 196	77 Fyfield (Wilts.) 89
× Finstock 301	153½ Fotherby 219	
× Fishbourn 253	× Foul Mile 261	26½ GADS HILL 2
41 Fishers Street 35	177½ Foulby 202	248½ Gaerwen 128
81½ Fisherton 48	43½ Foulmire 228	× Gafford's Bridge 259
87½ Fisherton-de-la-Mere 82	215½ Foulridge 173-4	66½ Gagingwell 134
252½ Fishguard 112, × 343	83½ Foulstone *see* Fugglestone	× Gainford 376
50 Fittleworth 35, × 268	× Four County Gate 315	119½ Gainsborough 214, × 358, 359
× Five Bridges (Heref.) 323	× Four Crosses (Mont.)329	
157½ Five Bridges (Som.) 76	× Four Crosses (Merio.) 330	152 —— by Lincoln 219
139 Five Lanes (Dev.) 63	× Four Foot 281	361½ Galashiels 184
148½ Five Lanes (Monm.) 91	× Four Gouts 312	231½ Galgate Bridge 158
12½ Five Oaks, 69	231½ Four Holes Cross 50	113 Galhampton 75, × 279
38½ Five Oaks Green 30	× Four Lane Ends (Chesh.) 310	27½ Galleywood Common 246, × 343
39 Five Wents 9		
194½ Fixby Hall 180	217½ Four Lane Ends (Lanc.) 158	58½ Gallow Hill 225
Fladbury Sta. 119		52½ Gallows Green 10, × 255
169 Flask (Ches.) 165	55½ Four Oaks 13	209½ Galmpton 63
117½ Flask (Staff.) 152, × 339	80 Four Shire Stone 118	191½ —— by Newton Abbot 63
120 Flax Bourton 97	43½ Four Throws 12, 14	50½ Gamlingay 224
× Flaxby 309	× Fourmile Bridge 377	141½ Gamston 196
× Fleet Hard Gate 352	× Fourth End 313	127½ Ganarew 110
41 Fleet Marston 132	90½ Fovant 48	178½ Ganstead 218
× Fletching 261	219 Fowey by Plymouth 66	112½ Gantlet 220
× Fletton 317	235½ —— by Tavistock 67	13 Ganwick Corner 194
320½ Flimby 176	× Fox House Inn 335, 358	× Gardner's Street 260, 261
14½ Flimwell 12	94½ Foxley 103	× Garforth Bridge 366
47½ —— byTunbridgeWells 16	219½ Fradden 50	224½ Gargrave 179
193½ Flint 150	247 —— by Camelford 68	× Garraby Street Inn 306
1.36½ —— by Northop 150	124½ Fragg 330	× Garreg 330
105 Flitcham 229	87½ Framlingham 243	× Garrick 354
42½ Flitwick 188	125 Frampton 60	224½ Garstang 158
185½ Flockton 180	93½ Frampton *Tp.* 104	230½ —— by Manchester 169
× Flookbrook 341	80½ Framsden 241, × 316	225½ —— by Ashbourne 171
× Floore or Flower 315	34 Frant 15	169½ Garthmyl 121, × 329
× Florence Farm 259, 263	57½ Frating 245	× Garthorpe 301
306½ Floriston 160	235½ Frayers Street 259	× Garton 370, 366
314½ Fly Bridge 209	227½ Freckleton 161	194½ Gate Fulford 211
109 Flyford Flavel 135	55 Freefolk 58	× Gate Helmsley 366
95½ Fodderstone Gap 233	211½ Fremington 206	49½ Gate House 17, × 261
× Foggathorpe 364	Freshford 95	202½ Gate Side (West.) 159
× Foleshill 305	× Fretherne 323	× Gateford 360
106½ Folkingham 215	× Freystrope 332	273 Gateshead 199, × 378
61½ Folkestone 8, × 250	42½ Friar's Oak Inn 31	349½ Gateside (Dumf.) 163
73½ —— by Bridge 9	× Fridaythorpe 366	× Gawsworth 358
× Fontmell Magna 276	30½ Frimley 52	83 Gaydon 141
12½ Foots Cray 7, × 265	× Fringford 207	52½ Gayhurst 154
181½ Ford (Dev.) 62, 63	× Frisby 318	181½ Gay's Lake 69
85 Ford (Glouc.) 121	× Friston 252	× Gayton 319
× Ford Chapel 332	114 Fritton 243	105½ Gaywood 226, × 319
× Ford Houses 312	× Frocester 313, 323	97½ —— by Cambridge 223
99 Ford Mill 96	164 Froddingham 214	× Geastones 371
× Ford Street 345	× Frodsham 341	× Geddington 299
171½ Forden 121	84½ Frog Hall 139, × 336	104½ Geldeston 243
82½ Fordham 227, × 347	88 Frog Mill Inn 108	101½ George-in-the-Tree 143
× Fordingbridge 274	85½ Frogs Hall 234, × 317	× George Nympton 283
× Fordingbrook 313	101½ Frome 82, × 277	199½ Gerah Bridge 64
345½ Forest 161	105½ —— by Westbury 85	20 Gerard's Cross 106
× Forest Gate 288	× Fromes Hill 323	28½ Gibraltar Inn 188
5½ Forest Hill 121	× Frosterley 377	212½ Gibranlwy 93
Forshaw Park 143, × 311	67½ Froxfield 83	233 Giggleswick 173
31½ Forest Row 21, × 262	44 Froyle 39	× Gilberdike 363
166½ Forfield 137	83½ Fugglestone or Foulstone 48, × 271	× Gilberts 285
7½ Forsham St. Martin 237		177½ Gileston 91
56½ Forston Green 11	119½ Fulbeck 213	245½ Gilling (Richmond) 206
77 Forton (Hants.) 42, × 271	3½ Fulham 32	214½ —— (Helmsley) 212
× Forton (Som.) 244	× Fulbrook 300	105½ Gillingham 72, × 279

107½ Gillingham All Saints 243, 244	122½ Gorleston 212	× Great Malvern 322
106½ —— by Geldeston 243	231 Gorphwysfa 135	× Great Marlow 289
47½ Gills Green 14	× Gorsty Hill 337	× Great Massingham 350
317 Gilnockie Ruins 183	× Gorton 357	31 Great Missenden 133
Gimingham 235	77½ Gosbeck 244	175½ Great Oak 6)
× Gips Cross 259	× Gosbrook Mill 312	65 Great Oakley 245
40½ Girtford 194	45½ Gosfield 237	80½ Great Oxendon 166
40½ —— by Shefford 202	× Gosford 297, 298	59 Great Paxton 224
× Girtford Bridge 294	× Gosford Bridge 297, 298	106½ Great Ponton 195
× Girton (Camb.) 316	237½ Gosforth (Cumb.) 175	× Great Riggs 373
133½ Girton (Notts) 214	277 Gosforth (Northumb.) 193	186 Great Sankey 153
221½ Gisburn 172, × 363	78 Gosport 42	64 Great or West Shefford 100
157½ Gittisham Hill 60, × 234	117½ Gost 137	97½ Great Sherston 101
382½ Gladsmuir 201	Gotham 190	232½ Great Smeaton 201
× Glan Hafren 329	42½ Goudhurst 13, × 257, 259	× Great Stainforth 370
220 Glandwr 121	Govilon 111	10½ Great Stanmore 129
× Glanford Brigg 360	110 Grafton Bridge 135	× Great Steeping 359
309½ Glanton 208	56½ Grafton Regis 156	188 Great Sutton 151
143 Glapwell 190	268½ Grampound 57	× Great Tew 300
158½ Glasbury 116	54½ Grange 189	48½ Great Wakering 249
Glascote 155	110½ Grantham 195, × 318, 354	44½ —— by Hadleigh 218
397½ Glasgow 161	107½ —— by Ware 224	× Great Waldingfield 315
410½ —— by Dumfries 164	180½ Grappenhall 152	× Great Waltham 343
403½ —— by Manchester 169	232½ Grasmere 162	× Great Weldon 300, 317
396½ —— by Stamford 206	× Grassby 300	× Great Wyrley 319
123½ Glastonbury 83, × 252	× Grassington 370	× Great Yeldham 345
× Glayston 318	33½ Graveley 194	48½ Greatham 41
× Glazeley 323	22 Gravesend 2, × 263	× Green Hammerton 369
85 Glemham 241, 244	264½ Grayrigg 175	124½ Green Man Inn 215
× Glentham 359	20½ Grays Thurrock 249	21½ Green Street (Bucks.) 131
× Glenwhelt 379, 380	38½ Gray's Wood 33	43 Green Street (Kent) 3
86½ Glinton 215	161½ Greasborough 187	15½ Green Street Green 11
× Glossop 357	131 Greasley 190	× Greenham Heath 270
175½ Glossop Hall 177, × 357	× Great Abington 344	Greenhill 160
104½ Gloucester 105, × 307, 311	× Great Acre 304	10½ Greenhill Cross 137
107½ —— by Abingdon 106	60½ Great Addington 103	18½ Greenhithe 2
103½ —— by Oxford 109	× Great Alne 311	× Greenhow Hill 371
103½ —— by Oxford and Birdlip	150½ Great Ash 118	166½ Greenoside 182
221½ Glusburn 173 [110	239½ Great Ayton 212	× Greenside 356
64½ Glympton 124	29½ Great Baddow 246, × 344	52½ Greenstead 245
× Glynd 260	× Great Barford 204	5½ Greenwich 4
× Gnosall 336	194½ Great Bebbington 151	110½ Greet Bridge 143
56½ Goatham Green 17	72 Great Bedwin 80	× Greetham 351
× Goatly's Lees 258	× Great Billing 249	× Greetland 364
× Gobbits 321	109½ Great Bircham 228	237½ Gregon 66
178½ Gobowen 127	× Great Bittering 349	127½ Greinton 81
31½ Godalming 33	× Great Blakenham 316	Grendon 155
× Godleigh Corner 289	20½ Great Bookham 67	× Gresford Road 323
69 Godmanchester 223, × 316, 348	139 Great Bridgeford 148	× Greston Bridge 258
	177 Great Budworth 153	212½ Greta Bridge 205
63½ —— by St. Neots 224	× Great Burdon 376	243½ —— by Richmond 206
× Godmanstone 279	45½ Great Chesterford 230, × 343	310½ Gretna Green 180
× Godmersham 255	× Great Clifton 373	97½ Griff 156
19½ Godstone Green 20, × 263	× Great Cornard 315	231½ Grigland 50
174½ Golbourn Bridge 148	× Great Durnford 294	× Grimoldby 360
46½ Golden Pot 52	× Great Easton 343	× Grimscott 289
89 Goldicote 131	22½ Great Effingham 37	× Grimsthorpe 353
× Goldington Green 208	64 Great Finborough 239	× Grimston 350
156 Goldthorpe 193	91½ Great Glen 166	× Grimston Bar 366
× Gomersall 365	112 Great Gonerby 196	× Grimstone Sta. 281
× Gomshall 264	166 Great Grimsby 219, × 361	159½ Grindleford Bridge 181, × 335
× Gonalston 303	166½ —— by Lincoln 220	163½ Grindley Bridge 148, × 340
125 Goodrich 110	164½	× Gringley-on-the-Hill 359
198½ Goodrington 63	96½ Great Hampton 119	220 Gristhorpe 217
× Goose Green (Kent) 259	68½ Great Harrowden 189	101½ Grooby 170
193½ Goose Green (Lanc.) 157	130½ Great Haywood 151	× Groombridge 259, 261
× Goose Green (Surr.) 267	186½ Great Heaton 171	× Guestling 251
× Goose Pool 324	× Great Horkesley 345	265½ Guildford (Corn.) 87
144½ Gore Inn 78	× Great Horton 365	27½ Guildford (Surr.) 35, × 263
42½ Gore Pitt 238	× Great Langton 376	30½ —— by Leatherhead 37
× Gorge Hill 311	× Great Madeley 337, 338	245½ Guisborough 212, × 375
× Goring 269		× Guiseley 370

109 Guist Bridge 234
273½ Gulvall 67
204½ Gulworthy 65
254½ Gumfreston 98
218¾ Gunnerside 206
× Gurney Slade 278
× Guyhirn 351
85½ Guyhirn Ferry 226, × 351
93 Guy's Cliff 142
251½ Gwalchmai 128
× Gwar-allt 331
× Gwennap 288
× Gwyddelwern 334
224 Gwydir 150
× Gwyrgryg 331

× HABROUGH 361•
84½ Hacheston 243
× Hackford 350
59¾ Hackleton 154
69½ Hacklinge 6, × 250
× Hackron Bridge 301
279 Hackthorpe 159
× Haddenham (Bucks) 296
× Haddenham (Camb.) 347
179½ Haddesley 212
178½ Haddington 200
111 Haddiscoe 243
176 Hadfield 177
× Hadham-on-Ash 342
35½ Hadleigh (Essex) 247
37¼ —— by Billericay 248
65 Hadleigh (Suff.) 240, × 345
34¾ Hadleigh Cross 247, 248
× Hadley 336
× Hadlow (Kent) 258, 260
× Hadlow (Suss.) 261
× Hadman's Bridge 256
× Hadnall Ease 321
× Hafod Peris 331
330½ Haggerston 200
121 Hagley 137, × 325
57½ Hail Weston 232
× Hailey 301
59 Hailsham 18
× Haine 250
× Hainton 360
267½ Hakin 99
× Halam 355
159½ Halberton 73, 75
246½ Hale 161
145¾ Hale Common 77
× Hale Street 259
110 Hales 244
117 Halesowen 144, × 325
100¾ Halesworth 243
27 Haley or Holly Green 91
× Halford (Salop) 321
× Halford (War.) 305
152½ Halfway 78
× Halfway Bridge 268
200½ Halifax 180, × 365, 368
198½ Halkin 146
111½ Hall End 155
112 Hall Green 143
× Hallatrow 283
× Halloughton 306
113¾ Hallow 119
218½ Hallworthy 67
58 Halnaker 35
236½ Halsar's Grave 68
47 Halstead 237, × 345
131½ Haltham 220
238½ Halton (Lanc.) 176
× Halton (Northum.) 379
× Halton (York.) 363, 365
× Halton Holdgate 359
285½ Haltwhistle 207, × 380
× Halwell 287
119½ Ham Bridge 120
46 Ham Green 132
× Ham Street 255
× Hambleton (Dur.) 363
× Hambleton (York.) 376
× Hambrook 314
380½ Hamilton (Lanark) 160
35½ Hammer Ponds 35
4 Hammersmith 46
160½ Hampton (Ches.) 148, × 340
12½ Hampton (Midd.) 38, × 264
11½ Hampton Court 37, × 261
× Hampton Lovett 311
× Hampton Wick 266
× Hamwell Bridge 258, 262
187½ Hanaford 74
33½ Hand Cross 25
× Handborough Bridge 301
184½ Handbridge 146
146½ Handford 152
176 Handforth 165
× Handle or Handell Gate 258
173½ Handley 148
122½ Handsacre 164
× Handsworth (Staff.) 318
× Handsworth (York.) 360
× Handy Cross (Bucks.) 290
147½ Handy Cross (Som.) 78
140½ Hanging Bridge 160, × 335
× Hangleton 269
162 Hangman Stone 59, 60
× Hankelow 347
62½ Hankham Street 18
149½ Hanley 164
153 —— by Longton, 164
× Hanley Castle 307
145¾ Hanmer's Cross 116
× Hanneford Bridge 287
8 Hanwell 106
× Hanwood 332
125½ Hanworth Green 232
× Happisburgh 350
300 Haraby 159
74 Haradon Hill, 69
194½ Harbertonford 64
64½ Harbledown 3
85½ Harborough Magna 182
46½ Hardham 31
× Harding's Booth 356
250½ Hardrow 204
248½ —— by Hawes 205
105½ Hardway 75
41½ Hardwick (Bucks.) 130
× Hardwick (Glouc.) 307, 312, 313
95½ Hardwick (Norfolk) 228, × 347, 349
101½ —— by Brandon 233
95½ Hardwick (War.) 143
× Hardwick (near Dunchurch, War.) 309
152¾ Hardwick Green 116
99 Hare and Hounds 103
32 Hare Hatch 88.
19 Hare Street (nr. Chipping Ongar, Essex) 238
13½ Hare Street (near Romford, Essex) 236
31½ Hare Street (Herts.) 228
203½ Harewood 191, × 369
197½ —— by Pontefract 203
126½ Harewood End Inn 114
110½ Harford Bridge *Tg.* 238
109½ —— by Ipswich 239
× Hargatewall 355
× Hargest Bridge 328
× Harlech 334
4½ Harlesden Green 133
92½ Harleston 242
69½ Harlestone 182
148 Harley 126
× Harley Bush Hill 375
13 Harlington Corner 87
23½ Harlow 230
× Harlow Hill 379
46½ Harlston 227
× Harlthorpe 384
233½ Harmby 204
× Harmer (or Armour) Hill 321
127 Harmston 218
82½ Harnham Hill 48
25 Harpenden 188
251½ Harperley Gate 210, × 377
108½ Harpley 229
× Harpswell 350
185 Harpurhey 174
× Harrington Bridge 315
210½ Harrogate 191, × 368
[illegible] —— by Pontefract 203
201½ —— by Wetherby 203
243 Harrow Gate 202
10 Harrow-on-the-Hill 133
47½ Harrowden 185
× Hartburn 376
34 Hartfield 19, × 261
× Hartford (Ches.) 341
61½ Hartford (Hunts.) 226, × 348
35½ Hartford Bridge (Hants) 47
× Hartford Bdge (Northum.) 380
× Hartlake Bridge 282
214½ Hartland 74, × 289
210½ —— by Dulverton 78
212½ —— by Somerton 75
× Hartlebury 311
46½ Hartley (Kent) 13, × 256
× Hartley (Northum.) 380
× Hartley Harbour 380
36½ Hartley Row 47
273½ Harton 208
150½ Hartrowgate 78
× Hartside Cross 381
× Hartwell 296
54 Harwell 101
58 —— by Reading 101
72 Harwich 245
71 —— by Gt. Oakley 245
263½ Harwood 207
60½ Harwood House 141
× Harwood's House 306
129½ Haselbury 49
× Hasketon 346
149 Hasland 190
40 Haslemere 33
200½ Haslingden 171, × 367
× Haslington 339

155¾ Hassop 181, × 355
62¼ }
63¼ } Hastings 15, × 251, 260
63¾ —— by Sedlescombe 17
64¼ —— by TunbridgeWells16
139½ Hatch Beauchamp 74
81½ Hatchet Gate 41
166¼ Hatchleigh 76
19¾ Hatfield (Herts) 181, × 295
× Hatfield (Yorks.) 360
30½ Hatfield Broad Oak 235
28 Hatfield Heath 235
30¾ —— by Abridge 236
× Hatfield Mills 295
163½ Hatfield Woodhouse 210
35½ Hatfieldbury 238
196¼ Hatherleigh 69, × 287
193½ —— by Tiverton 76
111¼ Hathern 166, 190
162½ Hathersage 181, × 358
× Hatherton 337
× Hattersley 356
× Hatton (Staff.) 336
95 Hatton (War.) 143
× Hatton Moor 335
93 Haugh Farm 240
Haughley Street 239, × 316
× Haughmond Abbey 336
178¾ Haughton (Chesh.) 177
× Haughton (Staff.) 336
206½ Hause Foot 159
47¾ Hauxton 227
48 —— by Barkway 228
64½ Havant 36, × 253
266 Haverfordwest 93, × 331, 332
278¼ —— by Aust 98
× Haverhill 344
13½ Havering Well 218
266½ Haverthwaite 175
190½ Hawarden 146
148 Hawchurch Common 61, × 281
250½ Hawes 204, × 371, 372
247¾ —— by Aysgarth 205
× Hawford Bridge 311
344½ Hawick 183
× Hawkadon 289
103 Hawkesbury Upton 101, × 313
48½ Hawkhurst 16, × 256
69½ Hawkinge Mill 9
× Hawksbury 305
× Hawksdale 373
× Hawkshead 372
× Hawley 262
× Haworth 369
240½ Hawsker 217
× Hawthwaite 373
× Haxton 294
154¾ Hay 116, × 325, 326
× Haydon Bridge 380, 381
12½ Hayes End 106
169½ Hayfield 177
69½ Hayling 37
× Haynes Yard 284
201½ Haysthorpe 216
× Hayston 332
× Hayton 366
38½ Hayward's Heath 23, × 261
178¾ Hazelgrove 168
176¾ —— by Derby 169
× Hazlemoor 290
× Hazlewood 368
117½ Heacham 227
43¾ Headcorn 9
197 Headingley 191
52½ Headington *Tg.* 107
107¾ Headless Cross 125
× Headley Common 270
136 Heage 180
243½ Healaugh 206
230½ Heallan 113
× Heanor 357
145 Heath 190
173½ Heath Cross 49
× Heath Gate 319
× Heath Lane 321, 335
58¾ Heathencote 138
141¾ Heathfield 77
141 Heathfield Arms 71
× Heathfield Tower Hill 256, 261
182¾ Heaton Norris 168
167¾ Heavitree 59
169 —— by Sidford 59
× Hebden 371
× Hebden Bridge 369
× Heckfield 270
× Heckington 354
× Heckmondwicke 368
× Heddon-on-the-Wall 379
113 Hedenham 243
× Hedon 363
244½ Heighington 198
194 Hele 60
162½ Hele Bridge 77, × 287
160¾ —— by Bridgewater 82
229¾ Hellifield 180
79½ Helmingham 241, × 316
219½ Helmsley 212, × 371
× Helperby 368
× Helsby 342
225¾ Helson or Helstone (near Camelford) 68
277¾ Helstone 61, × 288
154½ Hembury Fort House 74
× Hemingborough 364
× Hemley Castle 323
× Hemmingford Abbots 348
× Hemmingford Grey 348
× Hempton 303
Hen Moor 170
5½ Hendon 129
× Hendra Gate 331
265½ Hendre 112
112 Hendrew 91
× Heneage Arms 360
× Henfield (Suss.) 267
101½ Henfield (War.) 113
× Henfynyw 331
Henhurst 165
× Henley (Heref.) 326
71½ Henley (Suff.) 241
100½ Henley-in-Arden 143, × 311
35 Henley-on-Thames 103, × 289
10½ Henlow 202
44½ Henly Green 34
× Henry's Moat 331
× Henshaw 380
× Henstridge 280
110½ Henstridge Ash 48, × 280
114½ Henton 90
135¾ }
133¾ } Hereford 114, × 320, 322, 323, 324
135½ Hereford by Ledbury 116
× Hermitage 348
61¾ Herne 5
63¾ Herne Bay 5
× Heron Gate Common 342
× Herriard 270
46½ Herring Green 185
22½ Hertford 224, × 295
20½ Hertford Heath 224
× Hertingfordbury 295
226 Heskin Bridge 56-7
224¾ Hessenford 66
171½ Hessle 216, × 363
104 Hethersett 232
252¾ Heversham 158
117¾ Hevingham 232
256½ Hewes Water 57
241½ —— by Tavistock 67
210 Hewicke 203
133 Hewish 71
× Heworth Bridge 378
× Hexden Bridge 255
× Hexham 377, 379, 380, 381
Hey Houses 161
× Heybridge 344
92½ Heytesbury 82
93 —— by Deptford Inn 82
× Heywood 364
152¾ Hibalstow 215
× Hickleton 360
214½ Hick's Mill 50
40 Hicksted 25
× High Bickington 286
170 High Bostock Green 153
× High Bridge (near Bridgewater) 283
152 High Bridge (near Rydon) 81
191¾ High Bullen 77
184 High Burton 182
× High Coniscliffe 376
24½ High Cross (Herts) 223
94¼ High Cross (Leic.) 155, × 306
× High Cross (Suss.) 267
× High Ercall 336
43½ High Garret 237
× High Halden 255
292¾ High Hesket 159
158¾ High House 120
177 High Leigh 152
× High Littleton 283
123½ High Meadow 114
× High Offley 338
21¾ High Ongar 240
22¾ —— by Abridge 240
32¾ High Roding Street 236
290¾ High Side 163
19¾ High Street 12
67 High Street Green 238
× High Tabley 341
× High Town 368
× High Toynton 359
× High Walton 341
× High Worsall 372
29 High Wycombe 107, × 290
141¾ Higham (Derb.) 178, 180
60½ Higham (Suff.) 240
284 Higham Dykes 209
65 Higham Ferrers 185, × 315
× Highclere Street 291
× Highdown Hill 269
211½ Higher Bradley 173

176¾ Higher Hatton 148
× Higher Irlam 341
109½ Higher Shepton 75
255¾ Higher Sticker 57
241 —— by Tavistock 60-7
180 Higher Whitley 153
47½ Highgate (Kent) 13, × 256
48¾ —— by Goudhurst 14
4½ Highgate Archway 137
× Highgate Lane 362
109½ Highleadon Green 116
107 Highnam 116
105½ Highnam Court 109, 110, 116
231 Highway 68
170½ Highway Side 146
74½ Highworth 102, × 300
87½ Hilborough 233
[27¾ Hildenboro' 12
139¾ Hilderstone 165
205½ Hilderthorpe 218
.81½ Hilgay 227
× Hill 308
× Hill Butts 280
113¾ Hill End 116
82½ Hill Morton 182
124 Hill Ridware 164
× Hill Row 347
82 Hill Top (Hants.) 41
184¾ Hill Top (Yorks.) 180, × 361
385¾ Hillhead 184
13½ Hillingdon 106
104 Hillington 228
× Hillmarton 302
98 Hills Green 90
100¾ Hilperton 85, × 276
99¼ —— by Devizes 86
× Hilsley 313
× Hilton (Derb.) 335
57 Hilton (Hunt.) 225
127¾ Himley 144, × 312
146 Himstock 148, × 337
× Hinchinbrook 316
90½ Hinckley 155, × 305, 318
97 —— by Rugby 182
39 Hind Head Hill 35
× Hindley 364
94½ Hindon 70
96¾ —— by Salisbury 71
98 Hingham 235
Hinon 79
× Hintlesham 345
107 Hinton (Glouc.) 103
96½ Hinton (Hants.) 43
× Hinton Ampner 268
× Hinton St. George 284
× Hinton St. Mary 278
46¾ Hinxton 230
× Hipperholm 368
64½ Hitcham 238
71¾ —— by Hadleigh 240
34½ Hitchin 185, × 296
38¾ —— by Hertford 225
37½ —— by St. Albans 187
34¼ Hoad's Common 35
125¼ Hoarwithy 114
28½ Hoastly Hatch 240
× Hobber Gate 338
73½ Hobb's Cross 232
30¼ Hockerill 230, × 312
× Hockering 348
× Hockerton 355
30½ Hockley 248
× Hockley Brook 318
105½ Hockley House Inn 143
37 Hockliffe 138, × 296
× Hocksted Green 255
Hockwold-cum-Wilton 233
18½ Hoddesdon 222
19¾ —— by Enfield 225
× Hodnet (& Heath) 335, 338
160 Hog or Hug Bridge 160
× Hoghill Green 256
× Hoghton 367
67 Hoisted Green 238
× Holbeach 352
× Holdgate 369
116¾ Holdingham 215, × 355
229¾ Hole of Ellel 158
146½ Holford 81
× Holford Street 341
263½ Holker 175
122¼ Holkham Staith 228
× Hollinfare or Hollings Green 341
× Hollingworth 357
× Hollins 357
× Hollinwood 361
118¾ Hollow Cross 137
× Hollow Meadows 357
27 Holly Green 94
Holly Wood 143, × 311
× Hollywell 362
196½ Holmacot 74
186½ Holme (Lanc.) 157
248¼ Holme (Westm.) 158
187 Holme (Yorks.) 214
× Holme Abbey 374, 375
224 Holme Bridge 179
× Holme Lane 306
× Holme-next-the-Sea 351
× Holme-on-Spalding Moor 364
× Holmer 320
164¾ Holmes Chapel or Church Hulme 152, × 339
151 Holmes Marsh 115
92½ Holmesley Station 42
189 Holmfirth 177
26¾ Holmwood Station 29
× Holne Bridge 257
× Holnest 279
166 Holnicote 79
210 Holsworthy 69, × 289
206¾ —— by Tiverton 76
119¼ Holt (Norf.) 234, × 350, 351
147½ Holt (Staff.) 164
117½ Holt Heath 110
× Holtby 366
100½ Holton 70, × 230
141¼ Holton-le-Clay 210
206¾ Holwell (Dev.) 74
107 Holwell (Som.) 63
153½ Holwelslade 82
45¾ Holybourne 39
264¾ Holyhead 128
264 —— by Banbury 132
259¾ —— by Coventry 141
269 —— by Chester 147
202 Holywell (Flint) 146
198¾ —— by Flint 150
× Holywell (Northum.) 380
× Homebush Green 259
110¾ Honeywick 75
× Honingham 348
115¼ Honington (Linc.) 218
× Honington (Suff.) 346
152 Honiton 49, × 284, 285
149½ —— by Amesbury 71
156 —— by Dorchester 55
150½ —— by Redlinch 75
164¼ Honiton-Clyst 49
191½ Honley 178, 180, 182
× Hoo Brook 311
175¾ Hoo Green 152
176¼ Hoo Lane 108
132¼ Hook (Dors.) 60
39¾ Hook (Hants) 47, × 276
× Hook (Surrey) 266
× Hook Green 262
× Hooke Street 302
12 Hooking Green 134
× Hoole 342
× Hooley Bridge 364
181 Hooley Hill 177
× Hooton Roberts 361
62½ Hopcroft's Holt 134, × 295
× Hope (Derb.) 358
× Hope (Flint.) 333
× Hope Baggot 326
173¼ Hope Green 169
× Hope-under-Dinmore 320
119 Hopton (Suff.) 242
× Hopton Wafers 326
117½ Hopwas 155
× Horbling 352
× Horbury 363
252¾ Hordon Head 210, × 377
198½ Hore-down Gate 77, 80
× Horfield 306
× Horkesley Causeway 345
24 Horley 24
244¾ Hornby 176, × 370
135¾ Horncastle 220, × 350
134¼ —— by Boston 221
14¼ Hornchurch 248
59¾ Horndean 36
× Horndon-on-the-Hill 343
125 Horninglow 165
205¾ Horn's Cross (Devon) 74
17 Horn's Cross (Kent) 2
195¾ / 191¼ Hornsea 218
× Horra Bridge or Harrowbridge 288
57½ Horsebridge *Tg.* 17, × 260
54¼ —— by Westerham 19
× Horseheath 344
× Horsemonden 259
× Horsey Bridge 347
× Horsford 351
36½ Horsham 29, × 266, 267
112½ Horsham St. Faith 232
× Horsington 280
99¾ Horsley (Glouc.) 104
× Horsley (Northum.) 379
× Horsley (Staff.) 319
60½ Horsley Cross 215
115¾ Horstead (Norf.) 235
65½ Horton (Northamp.) 154
134 Horton (Som.) 71, 74, × 2[illegible]4
96¾ Horton Inn (Dorset) 63
203¾ Horwich 168
50¼ Hothfield Heath 8
111¾ Hoton 189
24¾ Hotspur Heath 107, × 290
× Hottstandel Bridge 337
279½ Hough (Westm.) 175

× Hougham 250
× Houghton (Hunts.) 318
× Houghton (Pemb.) 332
173½ Houghton (Yorks.) 203
46½ Houghton Conquest 188
51¾ Houghton Hill 31
113½ Houghton-in-the-Dale 233
× Houghton-le-Side 376
266¾ Houghton-le-Spring 210
× Houghton-on-the-Hill 318
34¾ Houghton Regis 188
9¾ Hounslow 46, × 265
× Hove 253
× Hovingham 368
68¾ How Bridge (Kent) 6, × 250
217¼ How Bridge (Yorks.) 213
44 How Green 188
× How Street 343
174 Howardtown 177
Howcleugh 160
180 Howden 214, × 363, 364
183½ Howden Grange 214
× Howe Green 344
× Howfield 254
× Hoyland Swaine 360
266½ Hubberstone 93
101¾ Hucclecote 105
195 Huddersfield 178, × 362
187¾ —— by Penistone 182
192¾ —— by Sheffield 180
109½ Hugglescote 170
127 Huish Episcopi 72
× Hulcote 299
171½ Hull 216, × 363, 364
185½ Hull Bridge 218
186¼ Hulme 157
× Humbleton 381
× Huncoat 367
199½ Hundersfield 174
196 —— by Oldham 177
× Hundleby 359
122 Hundred House Inn 119, × 323
64½ Hungerford 89, × 292
216½ Hunmanby 217
× Hunshaw Cross and Moor 286, 287
193¾ Hunslet 191
120½ Hunstanton 227, × 351
112¼ —— by Cambridge 228
× Hunt Green 314
60 Huntingdon 223, × 316, 318
64¾ —— by St. Neots 224
64¾ —— by Potton 224
111 Huntley 110
18½ Hunton Bridge 129
× Huntspill 283
152¾ Hurdlow House 170
176½ Hurlbote Green 165
166¾ Hurleston 146
32 Hurley Bottom 100
69 Hursley 45
67 —— by Basingstoke 53
45½ Hurst 226
47¼ Hurst Green 14, × 256
48¾ —— by Tunbridge Wells 16
58½ Hurstbourne Priors 58
× Hurstbourne Tarrant 292
× Hurstpierpoint 257
82¾ Husband's Bosworth 181, × 316, 317
× Huscote 302
× Hut or Hud Green 363
× Hutton (Cumb.) 375
138 Hutton (Som.) 84
230¾ Hutton Bushel 213
193 Hutton Cranswick 216
21 Hutton Street 247
× Hyde 357
× Hyde Chapel or Gee Cross 356
78½ Hythe (Hants.) 41
65½ Hythe (Kent) 8, × 251

× IBBESLEY 275
110½ Ibstock 154
× Icklesham 251
219 Ickornshaw 173
35 Idehurst 44½
61 Iden 14
44 Iden Green (near Staplehurst) 10
41½ —— near Goudhurst 13
× Idmiston 293
130½ Idridgehay Green 170
51¼ Ilford 22, × 271
25¾ Ightham 16, × 264
120½ Ilchester 70, × 281
121½ —— by Redlinch 75
7¾ Ilford 236
200¼ Ilfracombe 77
198¾ —— by Dulverton 78
197½ —— by Glastonbury 83
195¼ —— by Lynton 80
194 —— by Rydon 81
211 Ilkley 191
203 Illingworth 180
132½ Ilminster 71, × 284
133½ —— by Redlinch 75
135¼ —— by Yeovil 72
× Inchbrook 309, 312
176½ Ing Birchworth 182
23½ Ingatestone 237
76 Ingham 237
Inglebourn 64
× Ingleton (Durh.) 376
243 Ingleton (Yorks.) 173, × 370, 371
243¾ —— by Newark 203
244 —— by Nottingham 187
× Inglesham 300
114¾ Ingoldisthorpe 227
× Ingrave 342
263½ Ings 163
× Inkstone Bridge 324
33 Ippolits 185
150¼ Ipstones 164
69½ Ipswich 249, × 345, 346
163½ Irby 220, × 359
305½ Ireby 163
× Ireland's Cross 336
× Irlam Green 341
191½ Irlam-on-the-Height 168
× Irmingham 361
111¾ Iron Acton 97
145¾ Ironbridge 129
67 Irthlingborough 185, 193
99½ Isabel's Elm 123
70½ Isham 189
× Isley Walton 315
1¾ Islington 137
× Islip (Northam.) 299, 316
56 Islip (Oxf.) 123
× Ithon Bridge 329
× Iverley 319
250½ Ivey Bridge 206
× Ivinghoe 296
201¾ Ivy Bridge 55
204 —— by Totnes 62
200½ —— by Yeovil 56
256¾ Ivy Tower 98
× Ivychurch 255
41 Iwade 5
× Iwerne Courtney 276
× Iwerne Minster 276
78 Ixworth 238, × 316
× Ixworth Thorpe 316

45½ JACK'S BOOTH 88, × 291
× Jackson's Smithy 356
193 Jacobstow 69
226½ Jamaica Inn 50
226½ Jentor Houses 207
332½ Jedburgh 209
321½ —— by Corbridge 210
226¾ Jerveaux Abbey 204
185 Jews Bridge 55
51¾ John's Cross 14
262¾ Johnston 99
27½ Jolly Farmer 47, 52
Jug and Glass 170
× Jump 287
50½ Junction Inn 16

94 KATES BRIDGE 215
79½ Kate's Cabin Inn 195, × 299
× Kates Gore 292
251 Kearswick 173
129 Kedleston Inn 170
× Keel 337, 338
× Keelby 361
243¾ Keer Bridge 158
260½ Keeston Bridge 93
97¾ Keevil 85
114¾ Kegworth 166, 190
210½ Keighley 179
212½ —— by Halifax 180
206½ —— by Newark 203
207½ —— by Nottingham 187
117½ Keinton Mandeville 75
217 Kelbrook 174
120¾ Kelham 202, × 306, 355
× Kelholme 371
× Kellingley 363
× Kellington Mill 363
78 Kelmarsh 166
91¼ Kelsale 241
× Kelsall 341
343¾ Kelso 208
339½ —— by Kirk Newton 209
× Kelstedge 354
109½ Kelston 90
41¾ Kelvedon 238
× Kemp Town 253
× Kempsey 307
49 Kempston Hardwick 188
154¾ Kempton 120
235½ Kenarth 113
257¼ Kendal 158, × 372
258½ —— by Ashbourne 171
257½ —— by Beetham 163
275½ —— by Boroughbridge 204
263 —— by Clitheroe 173
268¼ —— by Halifax 180
264¾ —— by Manchester 169
259½ —— by Milnthorpe 158
262¾ —— by Newark 203
263 —— by Notts 187
266 —— by Wakefield 180

108 Kendall House 217
× Kenderchurgh 324
172½ Kenford 61
97½ Kenilworth 142, × 305
94 —— by Daventry 144
14 Kenley 204
24½ Kennersley Bridge 27
× Kennersleigh 286
93½ Kenninghall 238
× Kennington 255
1½ Kennington Gate 20, 26
3 Kensal Green 133
2½ Kensal New Town 133
1½ Kensington 46
56 Kent Street 15
57½ —— by Sedlescombe 17
× Kentford 345, 347
176 Kenton 62
171½ Kerry 123
186 Kerscot 74
× Kersey 345
93½ Kersley Green 155
72¾ Kesgrave 241
109½ Kessingland 241
14½ Keston 18
13 Keston Mark 18
293½ Keswick (Cumb.) 162, × 373
286½ —— by Kendal 176
110 Keswick (Norf.) 238, × 350
140½ Ketley Iron Works 140
74½ Kettering 185, × 299, 316
63½ Kettlebastone 238
108½ Kettleby 186
× Kettleshulme 358
× Kettlesing 368
× Kexby Bridge 366
38 Key Street 2, × 258
× Keymer 267
114½ Keynsham 90
37 Keys Green 12, 13
60 Keysoe 192
88½ Kibworth 166
× Kiddall Lane End 365
124 Kidderminster 125, × 311, 319, 323, 325
× Kidlington 294
226 Kidwelly 92
218½ —— by Aust 98
249 Kiggon Mill 51
264½ —— by Plymouth 57
402 Kilbride 164
2½ Kilburn 129
216 Kildwick 179
323½ Kilham (Northum.) 209
202½ Kilham (Yorks.) 217
× Kilhope Cross 377
89½ Kilkenny 110, × 303
× Kilkhampton 289
213½ Killinghall 192, × 370
× Killingholme 361
63½ Killingworth Castle 124
147½ Kilmington 55, 59
31½ Kiln Green 88
228 Kilrah Kilrhedyn 113
78 Kilsby 183
26 Kimberham Bridge 25
101½ Kimberley Green 235
162½ Kimberworth 187
198½ Kimbo or Point Bridge 50
× Kimbolton (Heref.) 325
64½ Kimbolton (Hunts.) 192, × 315
63½ —— by Baldock 203
28½ Kimpton 187
85½ Kineton 136
× King Cross 365, 368
33½ King Street (Berks) 94
136 King Street (Staff.) 148
118½ King Weston 75, 81
× Kingham 303
137½ King's Acre 114, 116
180 King's Bridge (Dev.) 65
113½ King's Bridge (Dors.) 44
× King's Bromley 335
× King's Enham 292
42½ King's Ferry 5
184 King's Kerswell 63
19½ King's Langley 130
× King's Sombourn 271
203½ Kingsbridge 64
101½ Kingsbury 156, × 315
55 Kingsclere 86, × 270
55½ —— by Reading 95
102½ Kingscote 102, × 313
103 Kingsdown Hill 96
× Kingsgate 250
141½ Kingsland (Hereford) 122
2½ Kingsland (Midd.) 222
147½ Kingsley Lane 164
× Kingsnorth 255
67½ Kingsthorpe 154, 166
104½ Kingston (near Poole, Dorset) 43
123½ —— (near Corfe, Dorset) 45
61 Kingston (Kent) 9
143½ Kingston (Som.) 78
10 Kingston (Surr.) 32, × 264, 265, 266
8 Kingston Bottom 32
× Kingston-by-Sea 253
62½ Kingston Inn 106
× Kingston Lacy 280
198½ Kingswear by Newton Abbot 63
206 —— by Torquay 63
× Kingstone 284
154½ Kington 115, × 326, 327
× Kinnersley 325
× Kinnerton 327
104½ Kinson or Kingston 43
112½ Kinthorn 81
× Kiplin 375
36½ Kippings Cross 12
224½ Kirby Moorside 212, × 371
103½ Kirby Row 243
69 Kirby Soken 246
68 Kirby Cross 246 [375
× Kirk Andrews (Carlisle)
313 Kirk Andrews (nr. Longtown) 183
× Kirk Bampton 374
× Kirk Bride or Leathes 374
195½ Kirk Deighton 203
173½ Kirk Ella 216, × 363
× Kirk Harle 381
130½ Kirk Langley 163
250½ Kirk Leatham 212
325½ Kirk Newton 209
295 Kirk Whelpington 209
279 / 274½ } Kirkby 175
× Kirkby Bellars 318
207½ Kirkby Hill (Boroughbridge) 197, 203
237½ Kirkby Hill (near Richmond) 206
275½ Kirkby Ireleth 175
× Kirkby Laythorpe 354
250 Kirkby Lonsdale 173
250½ —— by Newark 203
251 —— by Nottingham 187
275½ Kirkby Stephen 176
266½ —— by Richmond 206
274½ Kirkbythore 206
235½ Kirklevington 207
113½ Kirkley 241
× Kirklington 355
178 Kirkman's Green 152
314½ Kirkpatrick 160
× Kirkstall Bridge 365
117 Kirkstead Hall 243
317½ Kirtle Bridge 160
113½ Kirton 219
× Kirton Holme 353
59½ Kisby's Hut 224
54 —— by St. Ives 225
146½ Knaith 214
148½ —— by Lincoln 218
221½ Knapton Station 213
213½ Knaresborough 192, × 363, 369
202½ —— by Wetherby 203
279½ Knaresdale 207
221½ Knayton 207
29½ Knebworth 185
× Knedlington 364
132½ Kneesal 202
41½ Kneesworth 223
85 Knightlow Cross or Hill 139
184 Knighton (Dev.) 55
94½ Knighton (Leic.) 181
165½ Knighton (Rad.) 117, × 326, 327
158½ —— by Worcester 123
153½ Knighton (Staff.) 146
118½ Knighton Sutton 96
× Knights Bridge 270
× Knights Enham 292
119½ Knightsford Bridge 121
142 Knightshayne 71
149½ Knitacre 187
× Kniveton 338
19 Knockholt Pound 13
× Knockin 333
× Knoll (Heref.) 326
164 Knoll (Devon) 60
92½ Knook 82
60½ Knotting 185
× Knottingley 363
197½ Knotty Ash 153
203½ Knotty Corner 74
30½ Knowl Hill (Berks.) 88
102½ Knowle 143
61½ Knowlton 6
× Knowles Green 264
172 Knutsford 152
176½ —— by Congleton 154

166 LACEBY 220, × 361
99 / 101½ } Lackington 103
84½ Ladbroke 142
244½ Ladock 51
× Lady Cross 280
× Laindon Inn 343
42½ Lake Street 17
Lalestone 92
40 Lamberhurst 12, × 257, 259

146½ Lambert's Castle Hill 61	3'0½ Lauder 209	375½ Lesmahagow 161
116½ Lambert's Hill 83	352½ —— by Jedburgh 209	141½ Lessington 220
61½ Lambourne 100	217½ Laugharne 93	× Letchworth 296
68 —— by Newbury 100	× Laughton Pound 260	× Letheringset 350
261 Lambrigg 175	209½ Launceston 50, × 288, 289	× Letterston 332
205½ Lampeter 111, × 331	× Lavington Wick 276	147 Letton 116
201½ Lampeter Mountain 112, × 331	× Laycock 276	190 Leven 219
260½ Lamphey 98	61 Layham 210	253½ Levens Hall 158
74½ Lamport 166	× Layton 377	251½ —— by Milnthorpe 171
235½ Lancaster 158	115½ Lea (Glouc.) 322	183½ Levenshulme 163
236½ —— by Ashbourne 171	117½ Lea (Heref.) 110, × 322	300½ Low Cross 50
242 —— by Manchester 169	× Lea (Linc.) 214	49½ Lewes 22, × 256, 260, 247
× Lanchester 377, 378	150 —— by Lincoln 219	50½ —— by Uckfield 22
× Lancing 253, 269	× Leadboroughs 290	× Leweston 279
× Landford 273	29½ Leaden Roding 236	5 Lewisham 6
190 Landkey 74	120½ Leadenham 217, × 355	49½ Lexden 239, × 345
22½ Landrake 56	224½ Leak 207	233½ Leyburn 204, 205, × 372
29½ Land's End 51	94½ Leamington 142, × 316	× Leyster's Pole 325
292½ —— by Andover 58	89 —— by Southam 144	6 Leytonstone 229
307½ —— by Plymouth 57	88½ Leamington Priors 144	380½ Libberton Kirk 184
285½ —— by Redruth 67	117½ Leasingham 215	118½ Lichfield 145, × 308,319,325
291 —— by Sennen 52	18½ Leatherhead 29, × 266, 289	124½ —— by Hinckley 155
292½ —— by Tavistock 65	× Leathes 374	87½ Lide 80, × 275
× Lane 338	198 Leavengreave 174	190½ Lidford 66
190½ Lane Delph 164, × 339	15½ Leaves Green 19	× Lidgate (Lanc.) 302
119½ Lane End (Staff.) 164	63 Lechford Hut 47	× Lidgate (Yorks.) 357
Lane End (War.)143, ×291	73½ Lechlade 103, × 300	205½ Lifton 50
216½ Laneshaw Bridge 173, 365	× Leckhampton 310	× Lightcliffe 368
168½ Langaton 76	186 Leconfield 216	× Lilleshall 336
× Langdon Hills 343	119½ Ledbury 116, × 322, 323, 324	196 Lilley 296
× Langford (Essex) 314	120 —— by Stanton 118	59½ Lillingston Dayrell 141
129 Langford (Notts.) 214	120½ Ledbury Mills 116	× Lillington 316
× Langford (Som.) 283	105 Ledden Bridge (Dorset)72	171½ Lilly Bridge 49
184½ Langford Bridge (Lanc.) 157	× Ledden Bridge (Heref.)	2½ Limehouse 246
141½ Langford Bridge (Som.) 77, 78	5½ Lee 7 [334	104 Limpley Stoke 95
	206½ Lee Mill 56	19½ Limpsfield 23, × 263
× Langford Wharf 294	× Leebotwood 321	133½ Lincoln 215
97½ Langham 186	× Leedgate 377	132½ —— by Grantham 219
321½ Langholm 183	195 Leeds 191, × 363, 365	110½ —— by Newark 217
29½ Langley (Herts.) 185	188½ —— by Pontefract 203	207 Lincoln's Inn Bridge 204
38½ Langley (Kent) 9	166½ } Leek 164, × 339, 353, 350	271 Lindal 175, × 372
65½ Langley Burrell 102	195½ }	37½ Lindfield 23
65 Langley Tp. 18, × 252	154 —— by Derby 169	39 Lindridge (Kent) 12, 13
127½ Langport 72	151½ —— by Sandon 165	127½ Lindridge (Worc.) 120
126 —— by Somerton 75	95 Leek Wotton 142	× Lindsey 345
188½ Langridge 77	221½ Leeming 197	× Lingbob 369
× Langrish 268	214½ Leeming Lane 197	× Lingen 327
102 Langstone by Newton Abbot 63	156½ Lees Bottom 167	25½ Linhurst 19
	101 Leesthorpe 186	141½ Linley 128
108½ —— by Torquay 63	97½ Leicester 166, × 305,309,319	258½ Linslade 161
92 Langtoft 215	95½ —— by Welford 151	× Linthwaite 362
× Langton 359	29½ Leigh (Kent) 17	38½ Linton (Camb.) 344
93½ Langton Green 244	81½ Leigh Common 102	373 Linton (Kent) 10
125½ Langton Matravers 45	37½ Leigh Elm 247	116½ Linton (Hudd.) 200
× Langue 324	× Leigh Sinton 323	44 Linwood 220
139½ Langworth Bridge 219, × 359	150½ Leighton (Salop) 120	4½ Liphook 35
	109 Leighton (Som.) 83	234 Liskeard 56
232½ Lanivet Ford 50	× Leighton Buzzard 296	219½ —— by Tavistock 65
202½ Lantoft 217	× Leinthall Starkes 327	194 Lissit Bridge 218
30 Larkfield 7	× Leintwardine 326	102 Litcham 233, × 349
382½ Larkhall 161	92½ Leiston 244	× Litchfield 292
× Larkins Green 290	270½ Lelant 67	× Little Abington 344
83½ Larlingford 241	184½ Lemonford 55, × 287	68½ Little Addington 193
216½ Lartington 207	22½ Lemsford Mills 184	× Little Alne 311
× Lasham 270	× Lengthington Green 259	65½ Little Ann 58
386½ Laswade 184	43 Lenham 8	53½ Little Barford 224
50½ Latbbury 154	306½ Lennoxtown 160	75½ Little Barrington 108
182½ Latchford 152, × 353	× Lenton 315, 353	21½ Little Bookham 37
× Lattchford Bridge 259, 260	× Leuwade Bridge 349	75 Little Bourton 142
	137 Leominster (Heref.) 122, × 320, 325	82½ Little Bowden 186, × 317
× Latton 273	56½ Leominster (Sussex) 31	× Little Bursdon 289
	138 Lepton 180, × 362	35½ Little Canfield 235, × 342
		× Little Chart 256

DD 2

126¼ Little Chester 178, × 357
44¼ Little Chesterford 230, × 343
91¾ Little Cheverel 85
× Little Clifton 373, 374
× Little Corringham 359
× Little Cory 289
× Little Cressingham 347
267¾ Little Crossthwaite 163
127¼ Little Dewchurch 114
× Little Drayton 339
× Little Driffield 370
× Little Durnford 294
128½ Little Eaton 178
107¼ Little Elm 84
× Little Fransham 318
× Little Green 326
170½ Little Gutton 76
18¾ Little Heath Lane 184
× Little Heck 363
135¾ Little Hereford 120
43¾ Little Horsted 22
68¾ Little Houghton 189
Little Hulton 168
117 Little London (Heref.) 117
100¾ Little London (Linc.) 219
× Little London (Norf.) 347
52¼ Little London (Suss.) 17
155¾ Little Longstone 171
× Little Madeley 337, 338
× Little Malvern 322, 323
× Little Marlow 290
210¾ Little Marsden 173
× Little Milton 291
28¾ Little Missenden 133
157½ Little Norton 178
66 Little Oakley 245
× Little Ouseburn 369
× Little Over 308
58 Little Paxton 194
239½ Little Petherick 68
108¾ Little Ponton 195
168¾ Little Sheffield 181, × 375, 358
63¾ Little or East Shefford 100
231¼ Little Smeaton 201
× Little Stainforth 370
Little Stanmore 141
80 Little Stonham 239
× Little Stretton 321
63 Little Stukeley 224
× Little Torrington 287
258¾ Little Town 204
248 Little Trongrowse 67
59 Little Waldingfield 238
33¾ Little Waltham *Tg.* 237, × 343
93¾ Little Washburn 123
30¾ Little Wymondley 225
198¼ Littleborough 174, × 364
195 —— by Oldham 177
58¾ Littlebourne 5
42¾ Littlebury 230, × 343
117¾ Littledean 113
68¾ Littlehampton 31, × 209
62 —— by Petworth 35
72¾ Littleport 227
× Littleton (Som.) 281
90¾ Littleton Pannel 85
29½ Littlewick Green 88
105 Littlewood Green 125
× Littleworth (Glouc.) 310
× Littleworth (Salop) 338
× Littleworth Bridge 302
198½ Liverpool 151, × 367
201½ —— by Knutsford 153
× Liversedge 368
× Llanaber 334
× Llanarth 331
× Llanavon 327
× Llanbadarn-fynydd 329
× Llanbadarn-Vawr 320
144½ Llanbadock 113
× Llanbeder 334
× Llanbedr 334
236 Llanberis 135
× Llanbister 329
× Llanddewi Aberarth 330
× Llanddewi-ystrad-enny 330
× Llandefailog 329
229¼ Llandefeilog 92
239 Llandegai 128
243½ Llandegai 147
169 Llandegley 115
× Llandewr-cwm 320
× Llandilo Bertholey 324
199½ Llandilo 111, × 331
198½ —— by Talsarn 111
127¾ Llandinabo 114
× Llandinam 329
× Llandinrod Wells 329
× Llandogo 320
187¼ Llandovery 111, × 327
246¼ Llandowror 93
238¾ —— by Aust 98
× Llandrillo 330
Llandudno 147
221½ Llandulas 147
× Llandwywe 334
× Llan-dybie 331
223¼ Llandyfri g 112
169¾ Llandyssil 122
× Llanedy 331
× Llanellen Bridge 323
214 Llanelltid 121, 123
217 Llanelly 92
209½ —— by Aust 98
217½ Llanelnwth 113
× Llanelwedd 327
× Llanenddwyn 334
× Llanerchaeron 331
188¾ Llanerfil 121
245¾ Llanfair (Angl.) 128
× Llanfair (Carn.) 334
× Llanfair (Merion.) 334
183½ Llanfair (Mont.) 121
179¾ —— by Garthmyl 121
198½ Llanfair-Dyffryn-Clwyd 149
237¾ Llanfairfechan 147
× Llanferras 334
× Llanfihangel Crucornwy 324
165 Llanfihangel-Nant-Melan 115, × 327
× Llanfihangel Pontymoel 323
× Llanfihangel-ystrad 331
× Llanfihangel-y-treathau 334
Llanfoist 111
× Llanfor 330
193¼ Llangadock 111
× Llangammarch 327
143½ Llangattock 110, × 322
× Llangedwyn 333
228¾ Llangeler 112
223¼ Llangendrian 93
205¼ Llangervelach 93
146½ Llangibby 113
188 Llangollen 127, × 330
151¼ Llangranach 111
251 Llangristiolus 128
Llangurig 115, × 329, 332
× Llangwili 331
223¼ Llangyndeyrn 93
× Llangynnog 332
164 Llanhamlog 111
149¾ Llanhennock 113
× Llanidloes 329, 332
× Llanishen Cross 320
× Llanllowel 322
250½ Llanllyfni 123
217½ Llan-newydd 112
× Llannon (Card.) 330
216 Llannon (Carm.) 93
208½ —— by Aust 98
× Llanover 323
× Llanrhaiadr (Denb.) 333
205½ Llanrhaiadr (Mont.) 149
× Llanrhystyd 330, 331
Llanrug 135
223½ Llanrwst 150
217¼ —— by Pentre Voelas 150
161¼ Llansaintffraid (Brec.) 111
233¾ Llansantffraid-glan-Conway 150
× Llansawyl 331
× Llansoy 322
109¼ Llanspyddyd 111
× Llantarnam 323
168 Llanvaes 111
154½ Llanvair 111
× Llanvair Discoed 322
Llanvapley 110
142½ Llanvihangel 110, × 322
× Llanwchllyn 330, 334
149½ Llanwenarth 111
Llanwenog 112
Llanwinnen 112
255½ Llanwnda 123
181¾ Llanwnnog 122
× Llan-y-blodwell 333
× Llan y Byther 331
× Llan-y-Mowddy 334
× Llanycil 330, 334
× Llanymynech 329
212¼ Llougher or Llwchyr 92
× Llwydlo Fach 327
188½ Llwynjack 111
× Llyncelys 333
× Llyngelys 329
× Llyswen 330
179 Llywel 111
73¼ Lobcombe Corner 47
73¾ —— by Andover 58
326¾ Lockerbie 160
× Lockerton 332
137¾ Locking 84
13 Lock's Bottom 11
227¾ Lockton 213
193½ Lockwood 178, 180, 182
× Lockwood Beck 375
38¾ Loddington Street 10
106½ Loddon 244
111½ —— by Beccles 244
35¼ Loddon Bridge 94
233 Lofthouse (Nidderdale) 193

89¾ Lofthouse (Wakefield) 191	112½ Lotteridge 97	132½ Lugwardine 116
× Loggerheads 339	23½ Loudhams 134	203¾ Lumler Bridge 65
99 Lolly Moor 234	26½ Loudwater 107	317½ Lumsden 209
× Lolworth 316	108½ Loughborough 166, × 306, 315	190½ Lund 218
51 London Beach 10, × 255		× Luntsford Cross 260
17½ London Colney 137	12 Loughton 229	57½ Lunway's Inn 53
220½ Londonderry 197	150½ Louth 219, × 360	× Lusby 359
117 Long Ashton 97	149 —— by Sleaford 220	× Luston 321
81 Long Barrow Cross 69, × 275	24½ Lovell Hill 94	30½ Luton 188, × 276
	163 Loversall 193	88½ Lutterworth 155, × 209, 317
118½ Long Bennington 196	229½ Lovesome Hill 201	88 —— by Daventry 183
207½ Long Borrow Bridge 175	254½ Low Butcher Race 202	155½ LydburyorWalcotPark120
145 Long Bridge (Dev.) 49	× Low Conischiffe 376	66½ Lydden 6
65¾ Long Bridge (Northamp.) 189, × 315	224½ Low Ellington 204	116½ Lydford 75
	271½ Low Fell 190	122½ Lydney 109
× Long Burton 279	299 Low Framlington 208	53½ Lye (or Leigh) Green 10
77 Long Compton 124	294½ Low Hesket 159	120½ Lye, The 144
× Long Cross (Glouc.) 314	187½ Low Sticklepath 50	142½ Lyme Regis 58, × 231
101¾ Long Cross (Som.) 70	245½ Low Toft Hill 210	94½ Lymington 40, × 271
Long Eaton 190, × 315, 353	× Low Walton 341	92½ } —— by Basingstoke 53
300 Long Framlington 208	275½ Low Wood Inn 162	87½ }
103½ Long Ham 43	× Lower Brailes 303	89½ —— by Hythe 41
× Long Handborough 301	× Lower Cam 313	× Lymm 350
68½ Long Itchington 142	× Lower Chapel 329	× Lympstone 285
101½ Long Lane End 75	3 Lower Clapton 229	82½ Lyndford Lodges 234
× Long Load 282	× Lower Easton 314	85½ Lyndhurst 40, × 271
× Long Marston 369	× Lower Elm End 265	85½ —— by Basingstoke 53
68½ Long Melford 237	× Lower Faintree 326	82½ —— Road Station 70
× Long Newton (Cumb.) 374	50½ Lower Fittleworth 35	87½ Lyncham 101, × 302
× Long Newton (Durh.) 376	× Lower Guiting 303	179½ Lynmouth 79
95½ Long Newton (Wilts.) 102	16½ Lower Hallifrd 38	177½ —— by Rydon 81
227½ Long Preston 172	17¾ ——byWalton-on-Thames 38	104½ Lynn 226, × 347, 349, 354
231½ —— by Wakefield 180		102½ —— by Branden 233
101½ Long Stratton 239	60½ Lower Heyford 134	96½ —— by Cambridge 228
124½ Long Sutton 72, × 282	× Lower Inkford 311	180 Lynton 60
343½ Longbeddom 160	× Lower Irlam 341	178½ —— by Rydon 81
× Longbenton 380	× Lower Kingston 275	× Lyon's Gate 279
× Longbridge 310	× Lower Lancing 269	152½ Lyonshall 115, × 326
96 Longbridge Deverill 83, × 276	× Lower Langdon Bennacot 269	153½ —— by Weobley 115
		50 Lyss 41
× Longburgh 375	8½ Lower Mitcham 26, × 265	111½ Lytchett Minster 44
× Longden 327	× Lower Mitchel 322, 323	107 —— by Basingstoke 53
122½ Longdon (Staff.) 145	× Lower Sapey 324	113 —— by Wimbourne 44
× Longdon (Worc.) 307	77½ Lower Shuckburgh 144	× Lyth 375
121½ Longdon Green 145	× Lower Stanton St. Quintin 304	225½ Lytham 161
172½ Longdown End 65		
× Longford (Glouc.) 307	× Lower Swell 303	167 MACCLESFIELD 169, × 355, 358
15½ Longford(Midd.) 87, × 291	180 Lower Swithin 180	
93½ Longford (War.) 156	× Lower orNetherTabley311	Machen 99
114½ Longham 319	× Lower Tadmarton 303	202½ Machynlleth 122, × 330
113½ Longhope 110	141½ Lower Tean 164	213 —— by Welshpool 122
113½ Longhope Stn. 114	6 Lower Tooting 26	128½ Mackworth 169
× Longnor (Salop) 321	216½ Lower Tregunnan 68	83½ Maddington 82, × 275
× Longnor (Suff.) 356	× Lower Wear 283	× Madeley Market 328
94½ Longridge 142	× Lower Whitley 340	230½ Maentwrog 123, × 333, 334
184½ Longsight 168	× Lower Woodford 294	× Maer 336
× Longthorp 318	114½ Lowestoft 241	203½ Maes Mawr 127
× Longton (Lanc.) 367	27 Lowfield Heath 25	× Maes Teryvn Bridge 340
148½ Longton (Staff.) 164, × 338	283 Lowther Bridge 169	× Magham Down 260
310½ Longtown 183	× Loxwood 267	× Maghull 367
× Longwathby 381	× Lubenham 316	100 Maiden Bradley 83, × 277
× Longwood Warren 208	Luckbridge 64	12½ Maiden Bridge (Midd.)225
× Loninghead 379	× Lucton 326	115 Maiden Bridge (Norf.) 232
23½ Looe Mills 57	156½ Ludborough 219	152½ Maiden Down 73
57 Loose 10	× Luddenden Foot 368	26 Maiden Green 94
× Loosing Hill 378	× Luddington 361	× Maiden Law 377, 378
Lopen Head 71	× Ludford 360	127 Maiden Newton 60
88½ Lopham Ford Gate 238	70½ Ludgershall 84, × 272	26 Maidenhead 87
294½ Lorton 176	271½ Ludgwan 67	28 Maidenhead Thicket 88,100
× Lostock Gralam 341	141½ } Ludlow 120, × 321, 326, 328	56½ Maid's Moreton 141
214½ Lostwithiel 57	140½ }	34½ Maidstone 7, × 258, 264
236½ —— by Bodmin 57	98 Ludwell 48	37½ —— by Rochester 9
230 —— by Tavistock 57	× Lug Bridge 323, 324	70 Maidwell 166

225 Maingeen 93	29 Markyate Street 138	114½ Melton Park 234
105½ Maisemore 117, × 307	× Marland 364	243½ Menai Bridge 12², × 334
× Major Bridge 364	74½ Marlborough 88, × 272, 294, 302	76½ Mendlesham 240
38 Maldon 246, × 344		264½ Menehy 51
× Maldon Jenkin 344	189½ Marldon 63	× Meopham 262
× Ma'hamWater or Tarn 370	× Marley Hill 378	174½ Mere (Chesh.) 152, × 341
20½ Mallwyd 121	× Marnhull 278	160½ Mere (Wilts) 70, × 278
92 Malmesbury 101, × 304	× Marr 360	× Mere End 341
93½ —— by Cricklade 102	× Marr Green 272	97½ Meriden 139
106½ Malpas (Chesh.) 148	× Marsden 302	197½ Merivale Bridge 65
× Malpas (Monm.) 323	× Marshall's Green 345	259½ Merlin's Bridge 49
145½ Maltby 220, × 359, 360	144½ Marshalsea 61, × 281	251½ Merrington 198
214½ Malton 213, × 368, 370	137½ —— by Crewkerne 71	188½ Merripit Hill 65
211½ —— by Hull 218	118½ Marsham 232	28½ Merrow 37, × 263
× Malvern Wells 322, 323	121½ Marshes Elm 81	183½ Merrymeet 60
× Mamble 325	105 Marshfield 96	56 Mersham Hatch 8
× Mamhilad 323	257½ Marske 206	17½ Merstham 24
180½ Manchester 165, × 310, 311, 357, 361	Marston Bigot 83	62½ Merston Stream 34
	118½ Marston Magna 72, × 279	176 Merthyr Tydvil, 89
182½ —— by Ashbourne 170	× Martin Green 255	7½ Merton 28, × 265
187½ —— byChapel-en-le-Frith 171	183½ Martinhoe 80	90½ Merton Hall 234
	184½ —— by Rydon 81	160 Messingham 214
187½ —— by Derby 168	75½ Martlesham Street 241	182½ Methley 203
185½ —— by Leek 169	118½ Martley 120	84½ Methwold 233
187½ —— by Wirksworth 170	× Martock 252	102 Mettingham 242
195½ Mancravon 111	165½ Marton (Chesh.) 154	215½ Mevagissey 66
× Mancy 308	144½ Marton (Linc.) 214	× Mickle Hill 316
110½ Mangotsfield 103	146½ —— by Lincoln 214	× Mickle Trafford 342
× Manningford Bruce 294	91½ Marton (War.) 142	184 Micklefield 197
Manningham 179, × 349	× Marton (Wilts) 293	20½ Mickleham 29
× Manning's Heath 267	× Marton (Yorks.) 375	× Mickleover 335
60½ Manningtree 244	× Marwood Green 376	× Micklethwaite 374
112 Mansell Lacy 114	202½ Mary Cross 64	× Mickleton (Glouc.) 310
138 Mansfield 186, × 337, 354, 355, 357	203½ —— by Morleigh 64	254½ Mickleton (York.) 207
	3½ Maryport 176, × 374	260½ Mid-County House 93
× Manton (Notts) 358	206½ —— by Keswick 176	58 Mid Lavant 34
82½ Manton (Rutl.) 186	155½ Masborough 191	× Middle 333
× Maple Cross 200	221½ } Masham 203	198½ Middle Hulton 168, × 364
× Mapleborough Green 311	223½	× Middle Rasen 359
42½ Mapledurwell Hatch 47	104 Mason's Hill 11, 18	71 Middle Wallop 58
45½ —— by Odiham 62	27½ Matching Green 236	× Middle Woodford 294
187½ Mapleton 218	258½ Mathry 112	230½ Middleham 204, × 371
276½ Marazion or Market Jew 51	141½ Matlock 167, × 354	379½ Middleton (Edin.) 184
273½ —— by Redruth 67	143½ —— by Wirksworth 170	168½ } Middleton (Lanc.) 174
81½ March 226, × 347	142½ Matlock Bath 167	168
× Marcham 292	× Mattingley 270	× Middleton (Norf.) 317, 319
120½ Marcham le Fen 221	137 Mattock Tree, 73	× Middleton (Salop) 326
× Marchamley 335	111½ —— by Ilminster 74	× Middleton (Suss.) 267
Marchington 165	59½ Maudlin 35, × 253	× Middleton (near Bognor, Suss.) 269
× Marchwiel 333, 337	× Mavis Enderby 359	
× Marden 259	259½ Mawdlen's or Merlin's Bridge 99, × 332	257½ Middleton (Westm.) 176
× Marden Beach 259		× Middleton (Yorks.) 371
41½ Maresfield 19, × 259, 261	× Maxfields Green 267	× Middleton or Milton Alsor 299
40 —— by Godstone 21	44½ Mayfield 17, × 257	
187½ Margam Park 92	112 Mayhill 110	69½ Middleton Cheney 146
25½ Margaretting Street 237	66½ Maypole 9	255½ Middleton in-Teesdale 207, × 376
71½ Margate 3, × 250	49½ Meagrim's Hill 12	
41½ Mark Cross Tp. 17, × 257	115½ Measham 156, × 315	57½ Middleton Stoney 134, × 298
106½ Market Bosworth 157	116½ —— 157	
89½ Market Deeping 215, × 352	× Medmenham 289	233½ Middleton Tyas 201
× Market Drayton 337, 339	144½ Meere Tp. 165	107 Middlewich 143
82½ Market Harborough 166, × 316	42 Melbourne (Camb.) 227	Middopstones 182
	121½ Melbourne (Derb.) 170	× Midford 274
86 —— by Bedford 180	× Melbury 281	183½ Midgeley 180
89½ Market Lavington 85	× Melbury Abbas 277	17½ Midhurst 34, × 268
148½ Market Rasen 220, × 359	135½ Melcombe Regis 44	120½ Midway Houses 157
96½ Market Street 234	× Melkridge 360	185½ Miller Down 62
112½ Market Warsop 193	96 Melksham 96, × 276, 302	111½ Milborne Port 48
192 Market Weighton 214, × 264, 395	246½ Melling 176, × 370	110½ Milborne St. Andrews 54 × 298
	× Mellor 368	
104½ Markfield 170	× Melmerby 381	78½ Milbrook (Hants) 40
46½ Marks Tey 238, × 342	× Melton 363	69½ Mildenhall (Suff.) 233
112½ Marksbury 96, × 253	105½ Melton Mowbray 186, × 316	Mildenhall (Wilts.) 89

407

× Mile End (Essex) 345	153½ Monksilver 78	101 Mount Sorrel 163
122½ Mile End (Glouc.) 114	× Monkswood 323	× Mountain Street 255
1½ Mile End (Midd.) 229	147½ Monkton (Devon) 71, × 284	21½ Mountnessing Street 237
× Mileham 349	× Monkton (Dorset) 279	290½ Mounts 64
132 Milford (Derb.) 167	61¼ Monkton (Kent) 4	34¼ Mouse Hill 25
265½ Milford (Pemb.) 99	130½ Monmouth 110, × 325	340 Mousewald 163
132 Milford (Staff.) 115	129½ —— by Coleford 114	118½ Moxley 140
2½ Milford (Surrey) 33, 34, 35	128¼ —— by Mitcheldean 114	128½ Much Birch 114
47 Milkhouse Street 10, × 256, 257	× Monmouth Cap 324	× Much Hadham 312
	126¼ Montacute 72	× Much Hoole 267
× Milkhurst Toll 256	162½ Montford Bridge 126	146 Much Wenlock 126, × 328
256½ Mill Beck (Westm.) 158	167½ Montgomery 120, × 332	25 Muckinford 249
237½ Mill Beck (Yorks.) 217	× Moor End 373	26½ Muckinge 249
× Mill Bridge 363, 368	131½ Moor Green 190	151½ Muckleston 116
112½ Mill Cross 78	× Moor Houses 374	× Muckley Corner 219
× Mill End (Bucks.) 289	× Moor Side 278	142½ Muckley Cross 136
× Mill End (Herts.) 290	34½ Moor Street 3	× Muddiford 77
220 Millbrook (Corn.) 56	199 Moor Town 191	120½ Mudford 72
326½ Millfield 208	261½ Moorthwaite Bridge 204	380½ Muirkirk 164
340½ Millhead 163	20 Morant's Court Hall 12	252½ Muker 206
× Millstone Green 339	× Morchard Bishops 256	107½ Mulbarton-cum-Kenning-ham 234
251½ Milnthorpe (West.) 158	× Morcot 318	
249 —— by Beetham 161	× Morden (Dors.) 277	× Mundesley 356
183½ Milnthorpe (Yorks.) 179	9½ Morden (Surr.) 28	83½ Mundford 233, × 316
× Milsom 338	× Mordiford 322	× Munslow 328
× Milston 294	311½ Moresby 176, × 374	× Munslow Aston 328
55 Milton (Camb.) 227	× Morestead 272	38½ Murrell Green 47
166 Milton (Derb.) 177	25 Moreton End 236	× Musbury 284
× Milton (Hants.) 271	158½ Moreton Hall 153	359½ Musselburgh 201
× Milton Abbots 288	150¼ Moreton Hampstead 65	218½ Muston 217, × 354
× Milton Clevedon 280	81½ Moreton-in-the-Marsh 118, × 305	× Mytholm 368
55½ Milton Ernest 185		× Mytholmroyd 368
174½ Milton Green 148	× Moreton-on-Lug 320	
147½ Milverton 77	× Moreton Valence 307, 313	× NADDLE BRIDGE 373
× Milwich 336	197½ Morleigh 64, × 287	199 Nafferton 216, 217
96½ Minchin Hampton 104, × 300, 313	× Morley (Derb.) 357	107½ Nailstone 150
	× Morley (Yorks.) 363	94½ Nailsworth 104, × 309, 312, 313, 314
330½ Mindrum 209	221 Morning Star 93	
162½ Minehead 79, × 285	288½ Morpeth 199, × 389	199½ Nanmerch 118
161 —— by Rydon 81	286 —— by Ware 224	175 Nanteosel 115
223½ Minera Cross 66	292½ —— by York 211	× Nantwich 337, 339, 340
80½ Minety Station 102	203½ Morriston Bridge 92, 93	221½ Nappa 221
× Minfford Inn 330	× Morston 351	257½ Narberth 93
219½ Minskip 192	113½ Mortimer's Cross 122 × 325	× Narborough 317, 319
67½ Minster Mills 4	× Morton (Derb.) 354	265½ Nateby 206
× Minsterley 332	100 Morton (near Bourn, Linc.) 215, × 352	× Naunton Inn 303
107½ Minsterworth 109		124½ Navenby 218
× Minterne Magna 279	150½ Morton (near Gainsborough, Linc.) 214	× Naworth Castle 370
× Minworth 314		221½ Nawton 212
× Misterton 282, 284	× Morton (Norf.) 349	× Nayland 345
61½ Mistley Thorn 245	× Morton (Notts.) 306	198 Neath 93
115½ Mitcheldean 114, × 322	× Morton (Yorks.) 372	190½ —— by Aust 98
× Mitcheltroy 113	140½ Morvil 126	41½ Neatscourt 5
× Mock Bridge 267	× Morville 310	× Necton 348
22½ Mocktre 147	× Moseley 311	91½ Needham (Suff.) 212
230½ Modbury 64, × 287	× Moss House 339, 355	× Needham Market 316
80½ Modney Bridge 227	× Moss Side 374	× Needingworth 318
× Moggerhanger 298	× Mossley 362	× Neenton 326
199½ Mold 148, × 333, 334	331½ Mosspaul Inn 183	74½ Neithrop 131, 141
× Moldash 256	× Mosterton 282	354 Nellifield 184
181½ Molescroft 216, 218	× Motcombe 278	212 Nelson 173
68½ Mollen's Pond 69	8 Mottingham 11	166 Nesscliff 126, × 333
77½ Mollington 142	× Mottram 356, 357	× Nether Avon 24
× Moneynash 356	× Moulden 297	111½ Nether Broughton 186
× Monk Coniston 373	105 Moulding Bridge 112	× Nether Cerne 279
× Monk Fryston 363	× Moulsford 201	110½ Nether Compton 48
× Monk Street 313	282 Moulsham 237	70½ Nether Court 4, × 256
12 Monken Hadley 137, 184	× Moulton 352	162½ Nether Hough 187
× Monkland 325	228½ Mount Grace 207	× Nether Starston 354
× Monk's Bridge 368	151½ Mount Pleasant (Dev.) 55	144 Nether Stowey 81
× Monks Gate 267	66½ Mount Pleasant (Kent) 4	× Nether Tansley 354
61½ Monk's House 131	× Mount Pleasant (Pemb.) 333	× Nether Welton 373
107½ Monksford Street 143		102½ Nether Whitacre 150

× Nether Yeadon 370
330 Nethercleugh 160
113 Nethercote 157
× Nettlefield Gun 261
× Netherfield Toll 261
× Netherton (Chesh.) 342
191 Netherton (Dev.) 61
× Netherton Moor Barns 380
× Netley 254
68½ Nett Bridge 131
40 Nettlebed 100
× Nettlested (and Green) 259
156 Nettleton (Linc.) 220
103 Nettleton (Wilts.) 97
101½ —— by Malmesbury 103
126½ New Bolingbroke 221
× New Bridge (near Altrincham, Chesh.) 341
× New Bridge (near Stockport, Chesh.) 356
× New Bridge (near Barnstaple, Devon) 286
212½ New Bridge (near Callington, Devon) 65
205½ New Bridge (near Tavistock, Devon) 65
212 New Bridge (near Plymouth, Devon) 56
198 New Bridge (near Totnes, Devon) 61
100½ New Bridge (Dorset) 43
9?½ —— by Basingstoke 53
59½ New Bridge (Kent) 14
× New Bridge (Pemb.) 332
41½ New Bridge (Suss.) 35
× New Bridge (nr. Billinghurst, Suss.) 267
259½ New Bridge (near Sedbergh, Yorks.) 176
171½ New Bridge (near Thorne, Yorks.) 210, 214
97½ New Buckenham 238
94 —— by Diss 240
95 —— by Stowmarket 238
× New Buildings 286
382½ New Byers 184
25½ New Chapel 21
3½ New Cross 1
163½ New Dam 171
× New Delph 362
172½ New Holland 216
187½ New House 65
114½ New Inn (Derb.) 170
201½ New Inn (Devon) 50
129½ New Inn (Heref.) 122
53 New Inn (Oxf.) 124
150½ New Inn (Salop) 120
78½ New Inn (War.) 131
92½ New Inn (Wilts.) 70
62½ New Inn Green 8
× New Milford 332
182½ New Miller Dam 179
130½ New Passage 90
122½ —— by Aust Passage 93
× New Quay 329
125 New Radford 190
162 New Radnor 115, × 327
67 New Romney 10, × 251, 255
69½ —— by Rolvenden 14
68½ —— by Staplehurst 11
64½ —— by Tunbridge 13
53½ New Shoreham 28, × 253, [269
56 —— by Horsham 30
× New Street (Kent) 255
148½ New Street (Staff.) 169
114 New Walsingham 233
140½ New Ware 116
83½ Newark (Northamp.) 221, × 351 [355
124½ Newark (Notts) 196, × 306,
121½ —— by Ware, &c. 224
× Newbald 306
259½ Newbiggin 207
86½ Newbold 125
83½ Newbold-upon-Avon 182
181 Newbridge (Glam.) 92
164 Newbridge (Monm.) 99
56 Newbury 88, × 270, 291, 292
240½ Newby 173
264½ Newby Bridge 175, × 372
× Newby Head Inn 371
225½ Newcastle-in-Emlyn 112
234½ —— by Carmarthen 113
149½ Newcastle-under-Lyme 152, × 337, 338, 339
274 Newcastle-upon-Tyne 190, × 378, 379, 380
271½ —— by Ware 224
277½ —— by York 211
217½ Newchurch 112
× Newcot 289
27½ Newell Green 94
52½ Newenden 12, × 255
111½ Newent 116
274 Newgate Sands 94
× Newhall Green 340
94 Newham 83
56½ Newhaven 22, × 252
148 Newhaven Inn 170, × 335
× Newick Green 261
× Newington 291
3 Newington Green 225
36½ Newington Street 3
184½ Newland Bridge 76
176½ Newlands 216
× Newlands Corner 263
× Newlands Green 322
282½ Newlyn 52
61½ Newmarket (Camb.) 231, × 345
× Newmarket (Yorks.) 365
115½ Newnham (Glouc.) 100, × 322
120½ Newnham (Worc.) 120, × 325
209½ Newport (Corn.) 67
191½ Newport (Devon) 74
39 Newport (Essex) 230
× Newport (Glou.) 307
147½ Newport (Mon.) 91, × 323
140 —— by Aust 98
155 —— by Usk 113
245½ Newport (Pemb.) 112
140½ Newport (Salop) 147, × 336, 338
× Newport (Yorks.) 363
49½ NewportPagnell 154, × 297
218½ Newsham 201
222½ Newsholme 172
46 Newton (Camb.) 228
260 Newton (near Cartmel, Lanc.) 162
217½ Newton (near Hornby, Lanc.) 176
188½ Newton (near Wigan, Lanc.) 157
138½ Newton (Linc.) 214
97½ Newton (Norf.) 233
302½ Newton (Northumb.) 19?
341½ Newton (Roxburgh) 20?
× Newton (Wilts.) 273
241½ Newton (nr. Guisborough, York) 212
187 Newton (near Wakefield, Yorks.) 191
183½ Newton Abbot 61, × 2?7
112½ Newton Burgoland 157
105 Newton Flotman 239
108½ Newton Goss 215
149½ Newton Green (Salop) 12?, × 321
× Newton Green (Suff.) 345
× Newton Heath 361
159½ Newton Poppleford 5?, × 245
× Newton Purcell 297
173 Newton St. Cyres 68
113½ Newton St. Faith 242
110 Newton St. Loe 90, 96
× Newton Stoney 2?3
× Newton Tracey 287
× Newtown (Berks) 242
× Newtown (Cumb.) 374, 375
× Newtown (Hants) 292
× Newtown (Heref.) 323
174½ Newtown (Mont.) 122, × 329
176½ —— by Llandyssil 122
346½ Newtown (Roxb.) 183
87½ Newtown Park 41
× Neyland 332
× Nibley 314
× Nightingale 354
× Ninfield 260
166½ No Man's Heath 148, × 3?0
237½ No Man's Land 63
× Nobold 327
41½ Nock's Bridge 10
34 Nonsuch Green 15
× Nook Bridge 343
9 Norbiton 32
177½ Norbury (Ches.) 163
175½ —— by Leek 16?
× Norbury (Salop) 327
× Nordolph 352
140 Norley 128
76 Norman Cross 195
73½ —— by Ware 224
168 Normanby 214
117½ Normanton (Linc.) 218
× North Bradley 276
105 North Brewham 81
208½ North Burton 217
× North Cadbury 279
× North Cave 363
42 North Chapel 35
314½ North Charlton 200
11½ North Cheam 28
× North Cleobury 323
North Cove 243
231½ North Cowton 201
× North Cray 262
118 North Creake 229
× North Down 250
× North Driffield 364
106½ North Elmham 231, × 339
171½ North Elmsall 202
50½ North End 30

× North Fambridge 344
× North Ferriby 343
206½ North Grimston 218, × 370
182½ North Hill 74
219½ North Kilvington 207
× North Kilworth 316, 317
91½ North Lopham 238
128 North Muskham 196
18½ North Ockendon 249
221½ North Ottrington 201
× North Owram 365
× North Petherton 283
273½ North Shields 208, × 350
46½ / 44½ North Shoebury 218
North Sidborough 73
216½ North Stainley 203
187½ North Tawton 69
158½ North Thoresby 219
× North Tidworth 293, 294
123½ North Walsham 235, × 350
41½ North Warnborough 52, × 270
× North Weston 295
100½ North Witham 195
× North Willingham 369
15½ North Wood 134
North Woolwich 246
225½ Northallerton 201, × 372, 375
228½ —— by York 210
Northam 74
77½ Northam Bridge 42, × 274
65½ Northampton 154, 156, × 299, 315
71½ —— by Bedford 180
88½ Northborough 215
171½ Northbrook 60
27½ Northchurch 130
× Northfield 308
20½ Northfleet 2
54½ Northiam 13
81½ Northleach 108, × 304
195½ Northop 146, × 333
Northrepps 235
× Northstreet 257
× Northumberland Bottom 262
174 Northwich 153, × 341
× Northwick 320
353½ Norton (Berw.) 209
× Norton (Glouc.) 307
111½ Norton (Leic.) 156
147½ Norton (Notts.) 193
161½ Norton (Rad.) 117
× Norton (Salop) 328
× Norton (Staff.) 339
× Norton (Suff.) 316
× Norton (Worc.) 311
214½ Norton (Yorks.) 213
211½ —— by Hull 218
× Norton Bridge 338
× Norton Brize 301
144½ Norton Canon 114
142½ Norton Fitzwarren 77
2½ Norton Heath 240
199½ Norton House 64, × 287
243½ Norton Inn 208, × 377
107½ Norton St. Philip 86, × 274
106 —— by Devizes 86
109 Norwich 232, × 318, 319, 354
123½ Norwich by Bungay 213
112½ —— by Hingham 235
113 —— by Ixworth 238
105 —— by Mendlesham 240
110½ —— by Stowmarket 238
× Norwood 378
220½ Nosterfield 203
223½ Nottar Bridge 56
2 Notting Hill 106
124 Nottingham 186, × 306, 315, 353
123½ —— by Leicester 189
× Notton 276
× Nox 332
41½ Nuffield Heath 100, 105
× Nunbrook 362, 363, 368
99½ Nuneaton 156, × 305, 317
98½ —— by Rugby 183
52½ Nuneham Courtney 109
106½ Nunney 83
× Nunton-with-Bodenham 274
× Nursted 262
81½ Nursteed 86, × 275
× Nutbourne 253
× Nutfield 263
128½ Nuthall 190
37½ Nutley 21
183½ Nymet Tracey 68
× Nymphsfield 313
91½ OADBY 166
19 Oak End 133
× Oak Mere 340
× Oak Tree 376
95 Oakham 186, × 351
Oakhampton *See* Okehampton
× Oakhanger Mere 339
× Oakhill 280
31½ Oakingham 94
79½ Oakley Inn 185
× Oakmoor or Oakamore 338
× Oare 294
116 Oborne 48
125½ Odcomb 72
× Oddington 303
158 Oddrode 153
40½ Odiham 52, × 270
47½ Offham Street 22, × 267
× Offley 296
60½ Offord Cluny 224
60½ Offord D'Arcy 224
× Ogbourn St. Andrews 273
Ogbourn St. George 273
× Ogley Hay 319
235½ Ogwen Bank 128
230 Ogwen Lake 128
190½ Okehampton 60, × 237
191½ —— by Tiverton 76
201½ Olchfa 98
209½ Old Bell 104
61½ Old Hurst 226
257½ Old Hutton 173
215½ Old Malton 213
65 Old Romney 10, × 251
× Old Sarum 293
62½ Old Shoreham 23, × 253, 268, 269
106½ Old Sodbury 97
82½ Old Stratford 138, 155, × 297
122½ Old Swinford 137
253 Old Town 173
× Old Trafford 340
× Old Windsor Green 269
× Old Withington 339
× Oldburrow 286
× Oldbury 328
109½ Oldby 157
× Oldcoates 360
187 Oldham 177
138½ Oldmixton 84
174 Ollerton or Ollerton Gates (Chesh.) 154
136½ Ollerton (Notts.) 202
54½ Olney 189, × 297
117½ Olveston 97
× Ombersley 311
133½ Ompton 202
146½ Onibury 120
× Openshaw 357
× Orcheston St. George 276
Orcheston St. Mary 276
61½ Ore 15, × 260
90½ Orford 244
× Ormskirk 367
× Orpington 262
× Orsett and O. Hall 312
271½ Orton 175
106½ Osbaston 156
109½ Osbornby 215
127½ Osmaston 170
132½ Osmington 44
46 Ospringe 3
215½ Oswaldkirk 212
176 Oswestry 127, × 329, 340
× Otford 262
130½ Othery 81
× Otley (Suff.) 316
205 Otley (Yorks.) 191, × 369, 370
260½ Otter Bank 159
69 Otterbourn 40
304½ Otterburn 209
21½ Ottershaw 40
161½ Otterton 59, 60
160½ Ottery St. Mary 60, × 235
× Ouldsbroom 287
181½ Oulton 203, × 365
79½ Oundle 193, × 299, 317
81½ —— by Thrapston 193
× Ouse Bridge 375
× Outwell 352
202 Ovenden 180
× Ovens Green 256
104½ Over 109, 110, 116
× Over Brailes 303
202½ Over Darwen 173
199½ Over Hulton 168
66½ Over Kiddington 118
65½ —— by Islip 124
× Over Norton Common 300, 303
117½ Over Seal 156
180 Over Shepley 182
× Over Tabley 341
100 Over Whitacre 155
Overstrand 235, × 350
× Overton (Flint) 333
63 Overton (Hants.) 58
× Overton (Salop) 321
78½ Overton (Wilts.) 89
× Overton Longville or Long Orton 299
× Overton Waterville 299
92½ Ovington 234

77¾ Ower or Oux Bridge 46, × 273
× Owler Side 373
103¾ Owlerton 182
157 Owston (Linc.) 214
Owston (York.) 212
× Oxenton 310
54 Oxford 107, × 202, 294, 297, 298
58 —— by Maidenhead 109
31¾ Oxney Green 240
× Oxtead 263

62¼ PADBURY 130
× Paddock Street 236
× Padiham 367
238¾ Padstow 68
242 —— by Wadebridge 68
87 Pailton 182, × 317
195½ Paington by Newton Abbot 63
197¾ Paington by Torquay 63
× Painswick 300, 311
× Painswick Slade 300
112¾ Pakefield 241
329¾ Pallinsburn 208
220 Palmer'sBridge(Corn.) 50
× Palmer's Bridge (Wilts.) 273
7¾ Palmers Green 225
50 Palmer's Street 237
× Palsgrave 254
× Pamber End 201
45 Pangbourne 99, × 291
46¾ Pangdean 25
53½ Papworth St. Everard 223, 225
184 Paracombe 80
182¾ —— by Rydon 81
85¾ Parham 243
× Park Lane 361
297 Park Nook 175
17¾ Park Street (Herts.) 141
36½ Park Street (Suss.) 30
107 Parkstone Green 43, × 271
135¾ Partney 219
42¾ Partridge Green 27
45¾ —— by Horsham 30
16¾ Passingford Bridge 236
× Paston 350
49¾ Patcham 25
× Patchway Green 306-7
224 Pateley Bridge 192, × 371
374½ Path Head 209
× Patricroft 341
× Patrington 363
106¾ Pattesley Hill 233
× Pavement Gate 332
× Pawlet 283
× Peachey 291
114¾ Peachley 120
139¾ Peacock Inn 180, × 337
× Pearfield Green 258
29¾ Pease Marsh 33
31¾ Pease Pottage Gate 25
57½ Peasmarsh 13
× Peckforton 340
16¾ Pedham Place 7
107¾ Pedlar's Way 220, × 319
63¾ Pedlinge 8
121¾ Pedmore 137
126 Pedwell 81
195¾ Peel 168
266½ Pelaw 199
267½ Pelcomb Bridge 93
× Pellings Bridge 201
222 Pembrey 92
150½ Pembridge 117
262¾ Pembroke 98, × 331
258 —— by Carew 98
259 —— by Cold Blow 98
271¾ —— by Johnston 99
× Pembroke Dock 331
35 Pembury Green 12, × 259
193¾ Penachamawr 111
× Penance 288
× Pencarreg 331
123¾ Pencraig 110
192¾ Pendlebury 168
190 Pendleton 168
217½ Pengover 65
140¾ Penhow 91
Penistone 182, × 358
× Penkridge 312, 319
260½ Penlan 112
209¼ Penmaen 98
235½ Penmaenmawr 147
240½ Penmorfa 123
143 Penn Inn 55
121½ Penn Mill 48
206½ Pennal 122
× Pennenden Heath 258
× Penny Bridge 372
172½ Penpont 111
153¾ Penrhôs 115, × 326
212¾ Penrice 98
283½ Penrith 150, × 373, 375, 381
284¾ —— by Ashbourne 171
289¾ —— by Derby 169
282¾ —— by Stamford 206
× Penruddock 373
259¾ Penryn 51, × 288
× Pensford 278
31¾ Penshurst 17
× Penters Cross 288
137 Penters Lane 169
243½ Pentewan 66
148¾ Pentre 111
247¾ Pentre Berw 128
233 Pentre-cagyl 113
199 Pentre Halkin 146
213½ Pentre Voelas 127
212¾ —— by Banbury 150
195¾ Pentrebrunant 115
188¾ Pentrefelin 149
× Penwortham Bridge 367
171 Pen-y-bont 116
200¾ Pen-y-goes 122
229¾ Pen-y-gwryd 135
× Penystrywad 329
280¾ Penzance 51
274¾ —— by Redruth 67
313 Percy's Cross 208
249¾ Perran's Alms Houses 67
255¾ Perranwell 51
× Perry 319
× Perry Bridge 283
× Perry Street 265
163½ Perryton 69
141½ Pershall 146
102 Pershore 119, × 323
103¾ —— by Evesham 119
61¾ Pertenhall 192
81¾ Peterborough 214, × 299, 318, 351
52¾ Petersfield, 36, × 268
54¾ —— by Farnham 41
11 Petersham 32
123¾ Peterstow 114
126¾ Petherton Bridge 71
127¾ —— by Redlinch 75
129¾ —— by Yeovil 72
× Petrockstow 257
80½ Pettaugh 241
81¾ Pettistree 241
× Petty France 304
47 Petworth 34, × 268
40½ —— by Billinghurst 35
64¾ Pevensey 18, × 252, 260
× Pewsey 294
293½ Pheasant Inn 176
× Philham 280
208¾ Piccadilly 115, × 330
93¾ Picked Post 43
222½ Pickering 213, × 371
97½ Pickwick 89-90, × 277
55¾ Piddinghoe 22
114 Piddletown 54
117¾ —— by Bere Regis 58
45½ Piecombe 25, × 267
45¾ —— by Hand Cross 25
45½ Piecombe Street 25
239¾ Pierce Bridge 198, × 376
98¾ Piff's Elm 117
123½ Pig's Cross, 114
84 Pillerton Lazer 131
85½ Pillerton Priors 131
× Pilt Down 261
181¾ Pilton (Devon) 77
117¾ Pilton (Som.) 83
100¾ Pimperne 54
103½ Pinchbeck 219
242½ Pinchinthorp 212
13 Pinner 134
× Pipe Hill 319
125 Piper's Inn 80
128½ —— by Glastonbury 83
214 Piper's Pool 68
126½ Pisbury 172
× Pitchcombe 311
110¾ Pitcombe 75
36½ Pit's Head Inn 25
30½ Pitsea 247
70 Pitsford 166
66½ Pitt Pond 45
163 Pitts Moor 178
4¾ Plaistow 246
× Play Hatch 289
60½ Playden by Tunbridge 13
62½ —— by Maidstone 14
141 Pleasley 187, 190
× Pluckley 256
103½ Plumpton (Derb.) 177
× Plumpton (Suss.) 207
118¼ Plumptree 186
9½ Plumstead 4
× Plumstead Street 348
215½ Plymouth 56, × 287
216 —— by Modbury 64
215½ —— by Totnes 62
211½ —— by Yeovil 56
213 Plympton Earle 64
214 Plymstock 64
171 Pocomb Bridge 65
× Pocklington 366
× Pointon 352
62½ Polegate Green 18, × 231
Polesworth 155

263½	Polgrean 51	21½	Potter's Street 230	109	QUADRING 229
19½	Polhill Arms 11	54½	Potterspury 138	168	Quaker's Yard 99
×	Poling Cross Roads 253	48	Potton 224, × 298	135½	Quatford 126
232½	Polperro 66	33½	Potts Close 200	133½	Quatt 126
22½	Polscove 56	207½	Poulston 50	×	Quedgeley 307
×	Polsham 282	81½	Poulton (Glouc.) 103	116½	Queen Camel 72
×	Pomfret Castle 300, 303	×	Pound Green 261	45½	Queenborough 5
9½	Pouder's End 222	29½	Pound Hill 24	×	Queen's Bridge 266
299½	Ponsonby 175	33½	Pounds Bridge 17	63½	Queen's Cross 151, 156
×	Ponsworth 289	25½	Povey Cross 25	172	Queen's Head Tg. 127
×	Pont-abercorys 380	26½	—— by Reigate 27		Queenshead 180
238	Pont-Aberglasslyn 123	390½	Powburn 184	187½	Queensferry 150
227	Pont Anton 93	×	Powick 307, 322	×	Quelfurlong 304
218	Pont-ar-garfa 123	131½	Poxwell 44	36½	Quernlon 230
189½	Pont-ar-lleche 111	174½	Poynton 169	×	Quickshill 338
×	Pont-ceiliog 331	16½	Pratt's Bottom 12	106½	Quornlon 166
×	Pont Haford Peris 331	×	Prees 321	×	Quy-cum-stow 315
×	Pont Llanbiran 331	×	Prendergast 3.5, 13		
233	Pont Lychnant 147	193½	Prescot 153, × 354	×	RABY 378
206	Pont Ryffydd 140	×	Prestbury 303	170½	Rackenford 73
219½	Pont-y-berem 93	158½	Presteign 117, × 327	×	Radcliff or Ratcliffe 308
	Pont-y-bwlch 113	151½	—— by Worcester 122	×	Radcot and R. Bridge 301
247½	Pont-y-Fenny 93	196½	Preston (Dev.) 63	92	Radford (War.) 155
223½	Pont Yates 93	133½	Preston (Dorset) 44	107½	Radford (Worc.) 135
211	Pontardulais 93, × 331	46½	Preston (Kent) 3, × 257	87½	Radford Semele 144
220½	Pontdelgofylia 123	213½	Preston (Lanc.) 157, ×367, 368, 369	×	Radipole 279
176½	Pontefract 203, × 362			14	Radlet 141
281½	Ponteland 269	21½	—— by Ashbourne 171	112½	} Radstock 86, × 280
×	Pontesbury 332	219½	—— by Derby 169	113½	
×	Pontesford 332	×	Preston (Northumb.) 380	111	—— by Devizes 86
×	Pontrilas 324			109	—— by Marlborough 95
×	Ponts Green 261	90½	Preston (Rutl.) 186	347	Raecleugh 160
×	Pontynon 331	×	Preston (Som.) 278	138½	Raglan 113
×	Pontypool 323	50	Preston (near Brighton, Suss.) 25	13	} Rainham (Essex) 216
164	Pontypridd or Newbridge 99			13½	
		×	Preston (near Worthing, Suss.) 260	34	Rainham (Kent) 3
258½	Pool (Corn.) 67			105½	Rainham Hall 233
×	Pool (Yorks.) 369	146½	Preston Bower 77	190½	Rainhill 153
124½	Pool End (Heref.) 116	×	Preston-on-the-Hill 341	×	Rainow 358
155½	Pool End (Staff.) 169, ×353	123½	Preston Plucknett 48, 72	263½	Rainton Pitt Houses 210
108½	Poole 43, × 271, 280	186	Prestwich 171	147	Raithley 220
102½	—— by Basingstoke 53	103½	Prexford 77	47½	Rake 36
108	—— by Cranbourn 53	×	Priestleigh 279, 280	152	Raleigh's Cross 82
133½	Poolmeyrick 109, × 320	254½	Princes Gate 93	97½	Ram Jam House 195, ×354
52½	Popham 53	93	Princethorpe 142, × 306, 316	69	Ramsbury 89
51	Popham Lane 47			49½	Ramsdell 80
×	Porchester 254	139	Priors Lee 119	68½	Ramsey (Essex) 215
119½	Poringland 243	30½	Prittlewell 247, 249	67½	—— by Gt. Oakley 215
168	Porlock 79	261	Probus 57	69½	Ramsey (Hunts.) 226
166½	—— by Rydon 81	×	Prudhoe 380	71½	Ramsgate 4, × 250
288	Portinscale 176	27½	Puckeridge 223	230	Ramsgill 192
392½	Portobello (Edin.) 201	109	Pucklechurch 103	×	Ranby 358
21	Portobello (Kent) 7, 16	119	Pudimore Milton 72	×	Rangeworthy 314
×	Portobello (War.) 304, 305	45½	Pulborough 31, × 268	150½	Ranskill 196
×	Porton 293	×	Pulford 328	76½	Ranvild's Gate 46
65	Portsdown Hill 36	×	Pulverbatch 327	×	Raskelf 368
66½	Portsea Bridge 36	197½	Pumsant 112	×	Rassett or Rossit 323
134½	Portskewit 91	63½	Punnets Town 261	×	Rastrick 364
×	Portslade 253	16½	Purbrook 36	291½	Ravenglass 175
70½	Portsmouth 36, × 271, 272	×	Purfleet 249	54½	Ravensden 192
73	—— by Farnham 41	×	Purleigh Wash 344	112½	Ravenstone 156
206½	Portsmouth (Lanc.) 174	44	Purley 90	111½	—— by Leicester 170
126½	Portway (Dorset) 44	×	Purston Jacklin 362	270½	Ravenstonedale 176
144	Portway (near Bredwardine, Heref.) 116	×	Purton Stoke 302	173½	Rawcliffe 214, × 363
		×	Purton Street 302	×	Rawreth 344
130½	Portway (near Hereford, Heref.) 117	65½	Pusey Furze 106	31½	Rawreth Shot 249
		4	Putney 31, 32	×	Rawridge 284
×	Portway (near Ludlow, Heref.) 321, 326	5½	Putney Heath 33	200	Rawtenstall 173, × 367
		118	Putsham 84	34½	Rayleigh 218,¹ × 344
40½	Postcombe 107	128	Puxton 97	×	Rayne 342
×	Potterne 276	137½	Pye Bridge 190	9½	Raynes Park 32
14½	Potters Bar 184	85½	Pyle Inn 92	39	Reading 88, × 270, 280
51½	Potters Corner 8	110½	Pylford Bridge 28	38½	—— by Wokingham 94

EE 2

38½ Reading by Winkfield 94	96½ Ringwood 43, × 275, 277	× Roughton 326
58½ Reading Street 10, × 251	90½ —— by Basingstoke 53	× Round Green 296
254½ Rear Cross 205	135½ Ripley (Derb.) 178	× Roundswell 287
× Rearsby 318	21½ Ripley (Surr.) 33	× Rout Holm 379
163½ Red Court House 120, 122	214½ Ripley (Yorks.) 192, × 370	186½ Routh 218
17½ Red Hill (Bucks.) 106, 132	206½ —— by Knaresborough 203	× Rowde 96, × 275
20½ Red Hill (Surr.) 24, × 263	209 —— by Pontefract 203	35½ Rowhook 30, × 266, 267
87½ Red Hill (War.) 125	222½ Ripon 192, × 371	× Rowlston 324
× Red Hill (Wilts.) 275	212 —— by Boroughbridge 203	29 Rowsham 296
× Red Horn Tp. 275	214 —— by Knaresborough 203	149½ Rowsley 167
167½ Red House (Yorks.) 197	216. —— by Pontefract 203	119½ —— by Wirksworth 170
66½ Red Lodge 231, × 317	Ripperholme 180	38½ Royston 223, × 206
212 Red Well 176	10 Ripple Side 246	189 Royton 177
251½ Redberth 68	× Ripponden 364, 365	× Runbon 320, 330
25 Redbourn 138	162½ Ripway Corner 77	118½ Ruddington 189
151½ Redbourne 215	183½ Rise 218	× Rudgwick 267
79½ Redbridge (Hants) 40	× Rise Bridge 257	Rudry 89
66½ Redbridge (Suff.) 237	× Riseley 270	× Rufford 367
× Redbrook 320	87½ Rishangles 241	× Rufforth 369
253½ Redcar 212	× Risley 353	82½ Rugby 182, × 309, 316
108½ Redditch 125	× Rivelin Mill 357	81½ —— by Northampton 182
94½ Redenhall 242	99½ Rivenhall End 238	× Rugden Crossway 322
× Redford 288	22 River Head 11, × 264	128 Rugeley 145
88 Redgrave 238	40 Riverhall Bridge 16	157 Rumney Bridge 91
107½ Redlinch 75, × 220	35 Rivers 218	34½ Rumsells 218
115½ Redmarley 117	× Road 277	144 Rumwell 73
237½ Redmire 204, 205, × 372	58½ Roade Lane 156	38 Rumwood Green 9
326½ Redpath 183	158½ Roath 91	× Rusball (Staff.) 319
256½ Redruth 67, × 289	50½ Robertsbridge 14	81½ Rushall (Wilts.) 85, × 294
111½ Reepham 234, × 350	257 Robeston Wathen 93	63½ Rushden 185
242 Reeth 206	169½ Robin Hood's Well 197, 203	6 Rushey Green 11
21 Reigate 27, × 263	× Rocester 345	× Rushlake Green 261
21½ —— by Merstham 27	191½ Rochdale 174, × 364	184½ Rusholme 165
213½ Reighton 216	193 —— by Oldham 177	× Rushton 367
113½ Rempstone 189	272½ Roche 94	158½ Rushton Marsh 166, × 353
82½ Rendlesham 244	29 Rochester (Kent) 2	× Rushwick 323
152 Renishaw 191	312 Rochester (Northumb.) 200	× Rushwood or Rushet Common 266, 267
115 Retford 196, × 358, 360	10½ Rochford 245, × 314	
× Rettenden 49	162½ Rockbere 49	230 Rushyford 202
127½ Revesby 221	145½ —— by Colyford 60	241 Ruswarp 213
× Rew 285	133 Rockfield 110	408 Rutherglen 164
181 Rhayader 115, × 320	× Rockhampton 307	200½ Ruthin 149
187½ Rhodes 174	83½ Rockingham 185	326½ Ruthwell 163
198½ Rhoesmaen 111	119 Rockwell Green 73	× Ryall 352
209½ Rhossili 98	93½ Rodborough 104, × 309, 312	279 Rydal 162
204½ Rhuradar 111		151 Rydon 81
175½ Rhyd-y-Brew 111	× Rodenhurst 336	61½ Rye 13, × 251
× Rhyd-y-caean 341	× Rodhurst 327	64 —— by Cripp's Corner 17
× Rhyd-y-Felin 330	52½ Rodmill 22	62½ —— by Goudhurst 14
× Rhydd Green 307	× Rogate 268	63½ —— by Maidstone 14
215½ Rhydowen 112	52½ Rolvenden 13, × 255	65 —— by Staple Cross 16
185½ Riccall 211	252½ Romald Kirk 207	117½ Ryford 110
× Richard's Castle 321	12½ Romford 336	264½ Ryhope 208
19 Richmond (Surr.) 31	75 Romsey 45, × 271, 273	79½ Rymer Point 237
233 Richmond (York.) 206, × 372, 375	73 —— by Basingstoke 53	× Ryton (Durh.) 379
	155½ Rondcomb Gate 60	86½ Ryton (War.) 139
18 Rickmansworth 133, × 290	× Rook's Bridge 293	
148½ Ridge Cross 117	× Rookwith 371	× SADBERGE 376
15½ Ridge Hill 137	275 Roost 51	× Saddleworth 362
43½ Ridgemont 188	51½ Ropley Dean 39	× Saffron Walden 313
210½ Ridgeway 56	52½ Ropley Stoke 39	273½ Sageston 98
213½ —— by Modbury 64	× Roscrow 288	255 St. Agnes 67
× Ridgeway Cross 323	57½ Rose Green 15, × 260	20½ St. Albans 137, × 290, 295
× Ridgewell 314	× Roxley 375	19½ —— by Edgware 141
Ridgway 103	120½ Ross 110, × 322, 323	× St. Andrews 340
273½ Riding 249 × 377, 380	157½ Rossington Bridge 196	221½ St. Anthony 56
× Rillington 350	× Rothbury 381	× St. Arvans 320
211 Ridon 69	160 Rotherham 187, × 359, 361	212 St. Asaph 116
218½ Rillington 213	× Rothley Shield 381	210½ —— by Mold 149
164½ Ringinglow Tp. 151, ×335, 354	78½ Rothwell 189	214 —— by Ruthin 149
	102½ Rotten Row 143	176½ St. Athan's 91
× Ringmer 256, 260	× Rottingdean 253	253½ St. Austell 57
× Ringswould 250	× Roughey Street 266	238½ —— by Tavistock 65

× St. Bartholomew 250
249½ St. Blazey 57
131¾ St. Botolph 218
270¾ St. Breage 51
286¼ St. Buryan or Burien 52
28½ St. Catherine's Hill 33
244¼ St. Clears or St. Clare's Bridge 93
236¾ —— by Aust 98
53½ St. Clement's 107
243½ St. Columb 68
65½ St. Cross 40, × 272
169 St. David's (Devon) 68
281¾ St. David's (Pemb.) 93
274 —— by Aust P. 98
200¾ —— by Brecon 111
267½ —— by Cardigan 112
281¾ —— by Gloucester 109
272 —— by Malmesbury 103
276 —— by Marshfield 97
× St. Devereux 324
238½ St. Dogmael's 112
St. Endellion 68
268 St. Erth 67
216¾ St. George (Denbigh) 147
116½ St. George (Glouc.) 140
112 —— by Marshfield 97
168½ St. George's Clyst 59, × 283
227 St. German's 56
227½ —— by Saltash 57
221¾ St. German's Beacon 66
156¾ St. Giles 126
158½ —— by Ironbridge 129
× St. Harmon 329
× St. Helen's 364
238½ St. Issey 68
215½ St. Ive 65
270¾ St. Ives (Corn.) 67
60½ St. Ives (Hunts.) 225, × 348
136½ St. James 137, × 326
90¼ St. James Deeping 219
107¾ St. John Ilketshall 243
× St. John Lee 380
× St. John's (Worc.) 307, 322
204 St. Johns (Yorks.) 180
73 St. John's Bridge 103
40¾ St. John's Common 24
97¾ St. John's Highway 226
16½ St. John's Hole 2
× St. John's Weardale 377
254½ St. Just (nr. Falmouth) 67
288½ St. Just (nr. Penzance) 52
70¾ St. Lawrence 4, × 250
106¼ St. Lawrence Ilketshall 243
172½ St. Leonards (Dev.) 60
60¼ St. Leonards (Suss.) 15, × 252
62¼ —— by Battle 15
99¾ St. Leonard's Bridge 43
190½ St. Marks 150
228½ St. Martin's 66
194¾ St. Mary's 150
190½ St. Mary's Church 62
188½ —— by Newton Abbot 62
13 St. Mary's Cray 11, × 262
255¾ St. Mawes 67
× St. Mellion 288
155½ St. Mellons 91
243¾ St. Michael 50
56 St. Neots 195, 224, × 208
166½ St. Nicholas 91
113½ St. Olave's Bridge 243
× St. Paul's Cray 262
St. Paul's Walden 187
73¾ St. Peter's 4
× St. Sidwell's 285
210¼ St. Stephen's (Corn.) 68, × 289
× St. Stephens (Herts.) 290
227½ St. Teath 68
79 St. Thomas's Bridge 47, × 293
232 St. Trinians 206, × 372
× St. Weonard's 320
188½ Salford (Lanc.) 168
75½ Salford (Oxon.) 118, × 303
81 Salisbury 47, × 273, 274, 275, 293, 294
288 Salkeld Gate 159
× Sallisbury 368
× Salmon's Mill 309, 311
21½ Salt Hill 87
Saltaire 179
220 Saltash 56, × 288
198¾ Salter Hebble Bridge 180
231½ Saltergate 213
× Salterns 250
× Saltersford Bridge 318
× Salterton 294
× Saltfleet 360
× Saltfleetby St. Peters 360
× Salthouse 351
110¾ Samblesby 220
× Samborn 270
× Samelsbury 367, 368
155¾ Sampford Brett 78
189¾ Sampford Courtney 69
157½ Sampford Peverel 73
× Sancton 366
216¾ Sand Hutton 201
184 Sandal Magna 179
162 Sandbach 153, × 339
12½ Sanderstead 22
× Sandford (Devon.) 286
51½ Sandford (Oxon.) 109
156¾ Sandford (Salop) 148, × 335
131¾ Sandford (Som.) 96
× Sandford Bridge 322
132 Sandford Hill 96
68 Sandgate 8, × 251
50½ Sandhurst Green 12
× Sandiacre 353
36 Sandlin 9
136½ Sandon 151
23 Sandridge 187
112 Sandringham 227
× Sandway Lane 341
112¾ Sandwell Green 140
67¾ Sandwich 5, × 250
× Sandy 298
140 Sandy Brook 170
× Sandy Cross 324
181 Sandy Gate 61
× Sandy Lane 275
185 Sankey Bridge 153
364¾ Sanquhar 163
147½ Sarnesfield 115, × 325
63½ Sarre 3
× Satley 378
× Saundby 358
26 Sawbridgeworth 230
Sawley (Derb.) 190, × 315, 353
217½ Sawley (Yorks.) 172
50 Sawston 230
71½ Sawtry St. Andrews 195
× Saxham 315
130½ Saxilby 218
90 Saxmundham 211
× Saxondale 306, × 353
× Saxthorpe 351
× Scales 373
× Scaling Dam 375
× Scar Foot 372
253½ Scar Head 206
236¼ Scarborough 213
225½ } —— by Lincoln 217
217¾ }
× Scarby 360
144 Scarcliff 187
× Scarning 348
164 Scartho 219
164½ —— by Lincoln 220
× Scawton & S. Bridge 371
92½ Scole 239
93½ —— by Bury St. Edmunds 240
97 —— by Debenham 211
90¾ —— by Stowmarket 240
85¾ —— by Yaxley 240
157½ Scorborough 216
231½ Scorton 201, × 372, 375
232¼ Scotch Corner 193, × 375
234½ Scotforth 158
× Scot's Flat 251
× Scott Willoughby 354
157½ Scotter 214
156½ Scotton 214
118½ Scottow Common 235
132 Scrivelsby 221
152 Scrooby 196
164½ Scunthorpe 214
134½ Sea 71, × 284
67 Sea Houses 18, × 252
134½ Seaborough 71
45¾ Seacock's Heath 12
× Seacroft 365
59½ Seaford 22, × 252
263 Seaham 208
× Seal 264
× Seales Crouch 256
213¾ Seamer 217
× Seaton (Devon.) 283
104 Seaton (Yorks.) 218
× Seaton Sluice 380
120½ Seavington 71
× Sebergham 375
262½ Sedbergh 176
261¾ —— by Doncaster, &c., 204
× Sedgeberrow 310
× Sedgebrook 354
× Sedgefield 377
111½ Sedgeford 228
× Sedgemoor Cut 283
55½ Sedlescombe 17
94½ Seend 86
× Seifton 328
181¾ Selby 210, × 363, 364
182½ —— by Doncaster 212
× Selby Oak 308
355¾ Selkirk 183
60 Sellinge 8
136½ Selston 190
Selworthy 79
68½ Semer 240
× Semington 276
× Sempringham

299½ Sennen 52	51½ Sherrington 188	Sidestrand 235, × 350
205½ Sequer's Bridge 64	× Sherry Hill 336	156½ Sidford 59, × 284
92½ Setchy 223	× Sherwood 286	158¾ —— by Axminster 59
232½ Settle 172	203 Shield Green 199	× Sidley Green 200
232½ —— by Newark 203	× Shiere 263	158½ Sidmouth 59, × 284
233½ —— by Nottingham 187	135 Shifnal 140, × 328	193½ Sigglesthorne 218
148½ Seven Ash 78	33 Shilley Green 187	185½ —— by Ganstead 218
41½ Seven Thorns Inn 36	Shillingford (nr. Bampton Devon) 77	113½ Silk Willoughby 215
92½ Seven Wells 110		× Silkstone 360
23½ Sevenoaks 11, × 262	170 Shillingford (nr. Exeter, Devon) 55	236½ Silla Cross 213
× Sevenoaks Stn. 263, 264		40½ Silsoe 188
Severn Arms 115	47½ Shillingford (Oxf.) 105, × 201	49 Silver Hill 14, 16
× Severn Stoke 307		× Silverstone 298
57½ Seward's Bridge 39	× Shillingstone 278	× Silverton 285
× Sewers Bridge 252	× Shilton 305	53½ Singleton 34
105½ Shaddingfield 243	× Shincliffe 377	× Sinnington 371
101 Shaftesbury 48, × 276, 277, 278	28½ Shipborn 16	40 Sittingbourne 3
	96 Shipdam 234	× Six Hills 306
148½ Shakeford 149	× Shiplake 289	280 Six Mill House 199
× Shalbourn 293	× Shipley 326	111 Six Way 143
180½ Shaldon 62	103½ Shipmeadow 242	× Skeeby 375
× Shalford 266	56½ Shippon 105	× Skeffington 318
× Shalmsford Street 254	82½ Shipston-on-Stour 124, × 303	× Skegby 354
× Shambley Green 266		× Skeims Hill 261
273½ Shap 158	× Shipton (Salop) 328	200½ Skelton 211
27½ —— by Ashbourne 171	× Shipton (near Market Weighton, Yorks.) 366	119½ Skeyton 232
279½ —— by Manchester 169		176½ Skidby 216
119½ Shardlow 166	202½ Shipton (nr. York, Yorks.) 211	156½ Skilgate 77
195 Sharples 171		× Skip Bridge 369
47 Sharps Hill 132	× Shipton-under-Whichwood 300	227½ Skipton 173, × 368
× Sharston 356		226 —— by Foulridge 174
128 Shatterford 126	208 Shire Houses 211	230 —— by Leeds 191
190 Shaw (Lanc.) 177	31½ Shire Mark Hill 29	216½ —— by Newark 203
97½ Shaw (Wilts) 96	140½ Shirland 176	217½ —— by Nottingham 187
98 Shaw Hill 96	135½ Shirley Bridge 169	220½ —— by Wakefield 179
× Shawbury 339	110½ Shirley Street 143	× Skipton Bridge 371
105½ Shawclough 174	133 Shirleywick 151	× Skirethorns 370
65 Shawell 183	145 Shobden 122, × 326	162½ Skythrog 111
198½ Shawforth 174	70 Sholden 6, × 250	150 Slade's Moor Bridge 77
309 Shawton 164	8 Shooters Hill (Kent) 1	× Slaithwaite 362
26½ Shearing Street 235	143½ Shooters Hill (Staff.) 165	64½ Slape Bridge 118
67½ Shearsby 181	3 Shot-up-Hill 129	182½ Slattenslade 80
202 Sheepwash 69	× Shoreham 262	33½ Slaughter Bridge 29, 30
109 Sheepy 156	67 Shorncliff 8, × 251	115½ Slenford 215, × 354
48½ Sheerness 5	226½ Short Cross 66	× Sleap 335
51 Sheet Bridge 36, × 268	48½ Shothanger 86	× Sledmere 366, 370
162 Sheffield 178, × 335, 357, 358, 359, 360	× Shotley Bridge 378	238½ Sleights 213
	× Shottenden Thorn 250	× Slingsby 369
160½ —— by Baslow 181	× Shottle Gate 354	204½ Slough 87
169½ —— by Hassop 181	236½ Shotton 208	36 Slough Green 26
161½ —— by Mansfield 190	282 Shotton Edge 199	238½ Slyne 158
39½ Sheffield Bridge 21	95½ Shouldham Thorpe 233	196½ Smallbridge 174
38½ Sheffield Green 21	43½ Shover Green 16	9 Smallbury Green 46
41½ Shefford 185, × 297	× Shrew Bridge 340	× Smalley 357
× Sheldwich and S. Lees 258	158 Shrewsbury 126, × 321, 327, 332, 336, 338	349½ Smallholm 209
80 Shelfanger 240		210½ Smallways 205
99½ Shelford 183	153 —— by Coventry 140	241½ —— by Richmond 206
160 Shelton 126, × 332	160 —— by Ironbridge 129	299 Smalthwaite Bridge 162
19½ Shenfield 237, × 247	× Shrewton 276	46½ Smarden 10, × 256
48½ Shenley 138	62 Shripney 35	× Smarts Green 313
× Shenstone 308	× Shrivenham 301	58 Smeeth 8
2½ Shepherd's Bush 106	× Shucknell 323	13½ Smitham Bottom 24
47 Shepperton 3	× Shurdington 310	204½ Smithy Bridge 108
115½ Shepton Mallet 82, × 278, 279, 280	× Sbustoke 317	× Smithy Green (Chesh.) 339
	148½ Shute Hill 55	202½ Smithy Green (Cumb.) 176
108½ Shepton Montague 75	196½ Shutleworth 171	
252½ Sheraton 208	180½ Shutton Bridge 62	133½ Smithy Houses 178
117 Sherborne 48, 72, × 279	48½ Sible Hedingham 237, × 344	95½ Smockington 155
× Sherborne St. John 291		259½ Smorthwaite Bridge 204
193½ Sherburn 211	122 Sibsey 219	× Snails Green 318
× Sherfield 270	82 Sibson 195	220½ Snainton 213, × 371
× Sherfield English 273	11½ Sidcup 7, × 265	173½ Snaith 210, × 362
× Sherringham 241	108½ Siddington 154	89½ Snape 244

87½ Snape Bridge 244
88 Snape Street 244
7½ Snaresbrook 229
113¾ Snareston 156
61¼ Snargate 10
× Snave 255
Snead 120
142 Snolland 220
115½ Snettisham 227
43 Snoreham 246
× Snoring Common 350
× Soham 347
110¾ Soho 140, × 318
111¾ Soho Street 140
105¾ Solihull 143
× Sollom 367
279 Solva 94
138 Somercotes 190
× Somerford 312
66¼ Somersham 226
122 Somerton 75, × 281, 282
× Sompting 253
× Sopley 275
99½ Sopworth 101
103½ Sotherton 213
60¾ Souldern 132
195½ Sourton 60
× South Anston 360
154½ South Appledore 73
153 —— by Somerton 75
66½ South Berstead 34
63½ —— by Petworth 35
66¾ South Bourn 18, × 252
199 South Brent 55
195 —— by Yeovil 56
× South Cadbury 279
× South Cave 363, 366
× South Chardford 274
41¾ South Church 218
40¾ —— by Hadleigh 218
233¼ South Cowton 201, × 372
117 South Creake 229
× South Elkington 360
× South Fambridge 344
× South Ferriby 361
21¾ South Green (Essex) 217
× South Green (Norf.) 352
× South Hinksey 202
218¼ South Kilvington 207
× South Kilworth 316
90¼ South Lopham 238
182¼ South Milford 211
14¼ South Mims 137
180¾ South Molton 73, × 286
176¾ —— by Dulverton 78
179¾ —— by Somerton 75
127 South Muskham 106
× South Newington 300
× South Newton 274
20½ South Ockendon 249
220½ South Ottrington 201
× South Perrott 284
137½ South Petherton 71
× South Pickenham 347
89½ South Runcton 228
275 South Shields 208
182½ South Skirlaugh 218
217½ South Stainley 193
× South Stoke 274
18¾ South Street 19
× South Tidworth 293
110½ South Town 243
× South Walsham 318
42¾ South Warnborough 52
99½ South Witham 195
106½ South Wootton 226
98½ —— by Cambridge 228
186½ South Zeal 50
9½ Southall 106
80¾ Southam 142, × 309
82 —— by Daventry 144
76½ Southampton 40, × 254, 273
74¼ —— by Basingstoke 53
74¾ —— by Bishop's Waltham 42
78¾ —— by Botley 42
33 Southborough 15
7½ Southend (near Bromley, Kent) 11, × 265
9 Southend (near Eltham, Kent) 7, 11
40¼ Southend (Essex) 247
42½ —— by Billericay 219
42¼ —— by Purfleet 240
42¾ —— by Upminster 248
× Southerham 260
106¾ Southerleigh 68
× Southerscales 371
78¾ Southery 227
48½ Southminster 216
× Southport 367
Southrepps 235
53 Southscase 22
38½ Southwater 29
× Southwell 306, 355
× Southwick (Hants.) 272
× Southwick (Suss.) 253
× Southwick (Wilts.) 277
105½ Southwold 242
× Sow 305
× Sowerby Bridge 365
208 Spacey House 191
101½ Spalding 219, × 352
99¾ —— by Crowland 222
97 —— by St. Ives 226
× Spaldwick 316
× Sparham 349
111½ Spark Brook 143
114½ —— by Henley-in-Arden 143
115 Sparkford 70, × 279
116 —— by Redlinch 75
105¾ Sparrow Pit 171
120½ Speech House 114
57 Speen 89
56 Speenhamland 88, × 293
28 Spelbrook 230
34¼ Speldhurst 17
253½ Spennymoor 198
232½ Spennythorne 204
104½ Spernal Ash 125, × 311
107½ Spetchley Sta. 119
× Spettisbury 277, 280
133½ Spilsby 219, × 359
144¾ Spital-in-the-Street 215, × 359
207 Spittle Bridge 212
× Spittlegate 354
113 Spixworth 232
198 Spofforth 203
82½ Sprat Bridge 244
72½ Spratton 154
× Springfield (Cumb.) 373
30¾ Springfield (Essex) 238
181½ Sproatley 218
× Sproughton 345
Sprouston 209
111½ Sprowston 235
217¼ Sproxton 212
× Stacksteads 367
× Stadhampton 291
135¾ Stafford 145, × 312, 319, 336
368 Stagchall 184
× Stagsden 297
× Stainburn 373
179 Staincross 179
× Staindrop 376, 378
16½ Staines 46, × 264, 291
241¾ Stainsacre Lane 217
× Stainton (Cumb.) 373
140 Stainton (Linc.) 220
263¾ Stainton (Pemb.) 99
233 Stainton Dale 217
154½ Stainton-le-Vale 220
× Stalbridge 280
× Staleybridge 357
89½ Stamford 195, × 300, 351, 352
86¾ —— by Royston 224
179 Stamford Bridge (Chesh.) 146
× Stamford Bridge (Yorks.) 366
27¾ Stamford End (Kent) 19
4½ Stamford Hill 232
21½ Stanborough 184
99 Stanbridge Chapel 53
× Stanbury 369
× Standen (Kent) 256
63 Standen (Suss.) 45
× Standground 347
× Standish (Glouc.) 312
199 Standish (Lanc.) 158
× Stanfield 349
44 Stanford (Beds.) 202
64¾ Stanford (Berks.) 102
85½ Stanford (Norf.) 234
Stanford (Notts.) 190
144½ Stanford Bridge (Salop) 148
× Stanford Bridge (Worc.) 324
25 Stanford-le-Hope 217
27½ —— by Purfleet 249
65¾ Stanford Plain 102
× Stanhope 377
× Stanion 299
× Stanley 365
× Stanley Hill 324
262 Stanley Sands 128
Stanney Street 103
× Stanningley 365
284 Stannington 199
33½ Stanstead 230
30¾ Stanstead Borough 21
121¾ Stanton (Derb.) 156
126½ Stanton (Glouc.) 114
112¾ Stanton (near Newent, Glouc.) 117
51¼ Stanton (Oxf.) 123
81 Stanton (Suff.) 238
× Stanton Bridge 297
× Stanton Lacey 323
117¾ Stanton Wick 96
47¾ Stanway (Essex) 239
92 Stanway (Glouc.) 123
302¾ Stanwix 160, 183, × 379
163 Stapeley 146, × 337
122¾ Staponhill 156
63¾ Staple Cross 16

416

× Staple Fitzpaine 284	× Stockton (Salop) 328	× Stotfold 297
51½ Stapleford (Camb.) 231	× Stockton (War.) 309	106½ Stoulton 119
25½ Stapleford (Herts.) 225	124½ Stockton (Worc.) 120	105¼ Stour 48
× Stapleford (Notts.) 353	× Stockton Cross 321, 325	× Stour Provost 278
× Stapleford (Wilts.)274, 275	211½ Stockton-on-Tees 207, × 375, 376, 377	123½ Stourbridge 137, × 319
41½ Staplegrove 77, 78		121½ —— by Birmingham 144
43½ Staplehurst 10	2½ Stockwell 26	× Stourpaine 277
× Staples Cross 275	× Stockwood Head 256	× Stourport 311, 323
× Stapleton (Glouc.) 314	× Stoford 274	126 Stourton (Staff.) 137
102½ Stapleton (Leic.) 156	152 Stogumber 78	× Stourton (Wilts.) 278
Stapleton (York.) 201	139½ Stoke (Staff.) 151, × 336	× Stovers Hill 267
× Stapley 32½	× Stoke (War.) 305	87½ Stow Bardolph 229
177½ Star Cross 62	× Stoke Albany 317	82½ Stow-on-the-Wold 124, × 303, 305
× Starling 364	× Stoke Bridges 285	
× Startforth 376	57¾ Stoke Bruern 156	118½ Stowborough 45
29½ Starve Crow Hill 16	× Stoke Canon 285	119½ Stowey 96
× Statenborough 250	× Stoke Climsland 288	70 Stowmarket 238, × 316
× Statham 356	× Stoke D'Abernon 269	93½ Stradset 233
× Staunton-bach 326	128 Stoke Edith 116	× Stradset Falgate 343
110 Staunton Harrold 170	88½ Stoke Ferry 233, × 347	159 Straightway Head 49
× Staunton-on-Arrow 326	54½ Stoke Goldington 154	130½ Stramshall 164
154½ Staveley (Derb.) 190, × 358	× Stoke Green 317	4 Stratford (Essex) 229
263½ Staveley (Lanc.) 162, × 372	× Stoke Lacey 324	58½ Stratford Bridge(Ess.)239
261½ Staveley (Westm.)163	3½ Stoke Newington 222	× Stratford Bridge (Worc.) 307
73½ Staverton 144	104½ Stoke Rochford 195	
192½ Staverton Bridge 61	125½ Stoke Rodney 84	86½ Stratford St. Andrew 241, 244
210½ Staxton 217	149 Stoke Say 120	
× Stebbing Ford 312	110 Stoke Trister 72	59½ Stratford St. Mary 239
× Steel Cross 253	127½ Stoke-under-Hamdon 72	× Stratford-under-Castle 294
× Steel Rig 381	152½ Stoke-upon-Trent 164, × 337, 338	
133 Steen's Bridge 122		93½ Stratford-upon-Avon 125, × 310
317½ Steep Ends 163	148½ —— by Sandon 164, 152	
× Steep Green 272	104½ Stoke Viaduct 95, × 274	92½ —— by Banbury 131
47 Steeple 246	121½ Stokeford 44	94½ —— by Kineton 136
96 Steeple Ashton 85	169½ Stokeleigh Pomeroy 76	301 Strathaven 164
× Steeple Langford 274	36½ Stokenchurch 107	× Strathfield Turgis 270
213½ Steeton 179	237½ Stokesley 212	218 Stratton (Corn.) 69
× Stents Corner 257	× Stondon 342	214½ —— by Tiverton 76
233½ Stopney 213	× Stone (Bucks.) 296	122½ Stratton (Dors.) 60, ×281
31½ Stevenage 194	× Stone (Glouc.) 307	60½ Stratton (Glouc.) 105
34½ —— by Hertford 225	140½ Stone (Staff.) 151, × 312, 336, 338	× Stratton-on-the-Fosse 280
× Steventon 292		× Stratton St.Margaret's300
125½ Stewponey 137, × 312	122 Stone (Worc.) 125	5½ Streatham 20
48 Steyning 28, × 263	× Stone Bridge (Essex) 315	× Streatland 378
123 Stickford 219	90½ Stone Bridge (War.) 139	49 Streatley 100, × 291
126 Stickney 219	106 —— by Banbury 142	× Streem 261
× Stiffkey & S. Bridge 351	186 Stone Cross (Devon) 69	69½ Street (Kent) 3
19 Stifford 247	182½ —— by Tiverton 76	125½ Street (Som.) 83, × 281
22½ —— by Upminster 249	63 Stone Cross (Suss.) 18	193½ Street Houses 211
1¾ Stifford Bridge (Ess.) 247	43 Stone Crouch 12	× Street Lane Ends 339
21½ —— by Upminster 249	142 Stone Houghton 187	× Street-on-the-Fosse 281, 305
× Stiffords Bridge (Heref.) 323	18 Stone House 249	
	104 Stone Street (Suff.) 243	× Street-thorpe 361
40 Stile Bridge 10, × 259	30½ Stone Street or Ockley Green (Surr.) 30	× Streethay 308
207½ Stillington 212		× Streetside 303
75½ Stilton 195	101¼ Stonebow Bridge 110	× Strefford 321
× Stinchcombe 313	× Stonebridge Bar 266	88 Stretaston 182, × 317
27 Stisted 237	210½ Stonehouse (Devon.) 56	× Stretford 340
× Stitt 327	101¼ Stonehouse (Glouc.) 105, × 312	146½ Stretford Bridge 117
× Stock 343		63¼ Stretham 227, × 347
× Stock Bridge 255	43½ Stonepound 25	182 Stretton(Chesh.)153, ×310
× Stock Heath 350	87 Stoney Cross 43	143 Stretton (Derb.) 178, × 354
× Stock Street 342	× Stoney Middleton 355	138½ Stretton (Heref.) 114
66½ Stockbridge 47, × 271	× Stoney Stoke 280	96 Stretton (Rutl.) 195
× Stockbury Valley 253	52 Stoney Stratford 138, ×207	115½ Stretton-en-le-Field 156
× Stockfield 380	× Stoney Stretton 332	× Stretton-on-Dunsmore 306
146 Stockland 49	52 Stoning Heath 86	× Stretton-under-Fosse 317
181 Stockport 164, × 356	62½ Stonley 202	28½ Strood 2
175½ —— by Ashbourne and Buxton 170, 177	236½ Stony Bridge 93	44½ Strood Green 35
	107½ Stop Gate 76, × 285	53½ Strood or Stroud Quarter 14, × 255
179 —— by Macclesfield 169	× Stopham 268	
28½ Stock's Green 17	199½ Storridge Mill 64	99 Stroud 104, × 309, 311
106½ Stockton (Norf.) 244	× Storrington 268	

100½ Stroud by Rodborough 104
× Stroud Green 266
128½ Stroute 109
× Studley (War.) 311
102 Studley (Wilts.) 86, × 276
46 Stumps Cross 230
× Stuntney 347
× Stunts Green 261
260½ Stupelake 98
× Sturdy's Castle 294, 302
× Sturmer 344
× Sturminster Marshall 280
× Sturminster Newton 278, 280
57¾ Sturry 3
× Sturston (Norf.) 347
91¾ Sturston (Suff.) 240
84½ —— by Stowmarket 240
88¾ Sudbourn 244
133 Sudbury (Derb.) 165, × 335
55 Sudbury (Suff.) 237, × 315
8¼ Sudbury Green 133
Sude Hill 180, 182
139¼ Sugwas Pool 116
220 Summer Bridge 192
242¾ Summer Court 50
93¾ Summerham Bridge 86
91¾ —— by Marlborough 96
× Summerhouse & S. Tg. 376
55½ Summerstown 118, × 294
14¾ Sunbury 38
× Sunbury Station 264
257¾ Sunderland 208, × 378
272½ —— by Durham 210
255¾ Sunderland Bridge 198, × 378
256½ —— by Bishop Auckland 198
255½ —— by Northallerton 202
258½ —— by York 211
× Sundridge 264
24 Sunninghill 94
× Surbiton Hill 264
105½ Surfleet 219
41 Sussex Bells 34, 36
111 Sutterton 219, × 352
× Sutton (Camb.) 348
× Sutton (Chesh.) 341
41½ Sutton (Essex) 248
× Sutton (Staff.) 338
11½ Sutton (Surr.) 26, × 264
× Sutton (Suss.) 252
× Sutton-at-Hone 262
93 Sutton Benger 102
× Sutton Bridge 352
× Sutton Coldfield 308, 314
150½ Sutton Heath 148
× Sutton-in-Ashfield 337
× Sutton Maddock 328
201½ Sutton-on-the-Forest 212
133 Sutton-on-Trent 196
× Sutton Place 262
× Sutton St. Mary's 352
59 Sutton Scotney 47, × 292
× Sutton Street 262
× Sutton-under-Whitestone-Cliff 371
40½ Sutton Valence 9
× Sutton Waldron 276
93½ Swaffham 233, × 347, 348, 349
Swafield 235
× Swain Royd 369
× Swalcliffe 303
160 Swallow 220
92¾ Swallowcliff 48
× Swalwell 378, 379
47¾ Swan Street 237, × 315
127¾ Swanage 45
121¼ —— by Basingstoke 53
× Swanland 363
206½ Swansea 92, × 331
198¼ —— by Aust 98
104½ Swanton Morley 234
137¾ Swanwick 178
108¾ Swardeston 238
124½ Swarkestone 170
131½ Swell Hill 73
204¼ Swillhill End 180
× Swillington 366
77 Swindon 101, × 272, 300, 301
115½ Swineshead (Linc.) 220, × 353, 354
109½ Swineshead (Worc.) 119
234½ Swinethwaite 205
116½ Swinfen 145
× Swinford 316
59 Swinford Bridge 108
192¾ Swinton (Lanc.) 168
× Swinton (Yorks.) 368
377¾ Swirehouse 184
42 Swithland's Corner 10
× Sydcot 283
× Syresham 298
× Syston (Leic.) 318
113¾ Syston (Linc.) 217
255½ Sizergh 158

× TABLEY STREET 341
103½ Tacolneston 238
190½ Tadcaster 211, × 365, 369
158¾ Taddington 167
× Tadley 291
× Tadmarton 303
191 Taibach 92
× Takeley Street 312
230¼ Tal-y-Cafn 150
188¾ Talerthig 122
162¾ Talgarth 117
× Talgarth Fach 327
154¼ Talk-on-the-Hill 152
231 Talland 66
× Talley 331
157¼ Tallford 49
× Tollington 352
× Talsarn (Card.) 331
185¼ Talsarn (Carm.) 111
× Talworth 264
× Talybont (Card.) 370
242¾ Talybont (Carn.) 147
214½ Tamerstone Bridge 69
115¼ Tamworth 155, × 314, 315
109¾ —— by Coventry 155
240¾ Tap House (Corn.) 57
175¼ Tap House (Devon) 49
111¼ Tardebigge 125
379 Tarkill 164
× Tarleton Bridge 367
173¼ Tarporley 146, × 340
98 Tarrant Hinton 54
× Tarrant Keynstone 280
127 Tarrington 116
177¼ Tarvin 146, × 341
18 Tatling End 106, 132
× Tatterset 350
127 Tattershall 220
141 Taunton 73, × 283, 284
145 —— by Ilminster 74
142½ —— by Piper's Inn 81
139½ —— by Somerton 75
× Tavarn-y-Bwlch 331
251½ Tavernspite 93
202½ Tavistock 65, × 287
207½ —— by Okehampton 66
201½ Tavy Town 65
263½ Tears or Tier's Cross 99
269½ Tebay 175
× Teddington 266
× Tedstone Wafer 324
91½ Teffont Magna 71
182½ Teign Bridge 61
184½ Teignmouth 62
182½ —— by Haldon Hill 62
224½ Temple 50
× Temple Cloud 278
× Temple Combe 280
276½ Temple Sowerby 206
248¾ Templeton 98
51½ Tempsford 194
51¾ —— by Shefford 202
132¾ } Tenbury 120, × 324, 325, 328
130½ }
252¾ Tenby 98
62½ Tendring 245
53 Tenterden 10, × 255
56½ —— by Cranbrook 14
54¾ —— by Staplehurst 11
55¾ —— by Tunbridge 14
155½ Tern Bridge 129
148½ —— by Coventry 140
152½ Tern Hill 148, × 339
× Terrington St. Clement 352
× Teston 258, 259
× Testwood 273
97 Tetbury 102, × 304, 313
96¾ —— by Malmesbury 102
42¼ Tetsworth 107
124½ Tettenhall 140, 148
103¼ Tewkesbury 117, × 307
102½ —— by Stanway 123
× Thame 201, 295
12½ Thames Ditton 38
× Thannington Street 254
53 Thatcham 88
× Thaxted 343
× Thealby 361
43½ Theale 88
× Theddingworth 316
× Thelbridge 286
× Thelwall 356
80½ Thetford 231, × 316
83¾ —— by Sudbury 237
105 Thickthorn 232
354 Thirlestane 209
217¾ Thirsk 207, × 371
220 —— by York 211
190 Thong Bridge 178
157½ Thorganby 220
222½ Thorlby 179
213½ Thormanby 211
117 Thornage 234
× Thornbarrow 375
115 Thornbury 102, × 307
77 Thornby 154
80 Thorndon 241
255 Thorne (near Muker) 206
166¾ Thorne (near Doncaster) 210, × 361

82½ Thorney 226, × 351	160½ Tideswell Lane End 171, × 355	149½ Torworth 196
× Thorney Stone 374		× Tosberry 280
215? Thornfield Houses 207	225½ Tidiford 56	× Tot Hill 346
× Thornham 351	× Tidmarsh 291	163 Totley 181
352½ Thornhill 163	81½ Tidmington 124	191½ Totnes 61
203½ Thornholm 216	88½ Tidpit or Tipput 53	195½ —— by Ashburton 61
277½ Thornhope 207	263½ Tier's (or Tears) Cross 99	× Toton 315
290 Thornthwaite 176	26 Tilbury Fort 249, × 313	6½ Tottenham 222
× Thornton (Bucks.) 297	× Tillbrook 315	91 Tottenhill 228
× Thornton (Linc.) 361	140½ Tillington (Heref.) 115	88½ Tottington 234
244 Thornton (near Ingleton, Yorks.) 173	× Tillington (Suss.) 268	80½ Totton 40
	100½ Tilney-cum-Islington 226	50½ Towcester 138, × 298
220 Thornton (near Skipton, Yorks.) 174	× Tilshead 276	66 —— by Buckingham 141
	× Tilstock 321	250½ Towlaw 210
8 Thornton Heath 20	171½ Tilston Fernall 146	255½ Town End 161
222½ Thornton-le-Street 211	× Tilmanstone 250	187½ Towton 211
× Thornton Steward 371	× Timberscombe 285	214½ Towyn 122
× Thorp (Linc.) 359	× Timperley 356	× Tramam 331
172½ Thorp Audlin 203	× Timsbury 271	385½ Tranent 201
× Thorp Waterville 299	58 Tingewick 131	196½ Tranmere 151
× Thorpe (Durh.) 377	191 Tingley 179	× Tranmire 375
× Thorpe (Norf.) 348	305 Tinhay Bridge 50	225½ Trawsfynayd 123
× Thorpe (Surr.) 269	91½ Tinhead 85	288½ Trebear 52
88 Thorpe Abbots 242	× Tinsley 350	211½ Trobursey 50, 68
× Thorpe Arnold 318	× Tintern 320	178 Trecastle 111
65½ Thorpe-le-Soken 245	177 Tintwistle 177, × 357	150½ Tredegar House 91
× Thorpe Lee 269	30½ Tippen's Hill 94	84½ Tredington 125
126½ Thorpe Market 232	172½ Tiresford 161	236½ Tredudwell 66
128½ —— by North Walsham 235	× Titchfield 254, 271	× Trefgarn Bridge 332
	× Titchwell 351	224½ Trefriw 150
190½ Thorpe-on-the-Hill 191	144 Titensor Mill 151	137½ Tregare 110
238½ Thorpe Town 217	141½ Titherleigh 71	253 Tregear 67
76 Thorpe Waterville 193	× Titley 326, 327	259½ Tregolls 51
× Thorpe Willoughby 363	18½ Titsey (& T. Hill) 23	261 Tregony 57
73½ Thrapston 193, × 299, 316	97 Titshall Green 239	246½ —— by Tavistock 68
× Threckingham 354	104 Tittleshall 233	× Tregorlands 288
× Three Chimnies 256	162½ Tiverton 73, × 245	× Trekenna 288
× Three Cups Corner 261	163½ —— by Honiton 74	229½ Trelill 68
250 Three Gates 67	160½ —— by Somerton 75	× Trellech 320
243 Three Holes Cross 68	× Tixover 318	269 Treloweth 67
× Three Legged Cross 292	116½ Tockington 97	240 Tremadoc 123
277½ Three Mile Bridge 199	38½ Toddington (Bed.) 189	224½ Tremagennow 68
× Three Mile Cross 270	93½ Toddington (Glouc.) 123	282½ Trembeth 52
41½ Three Pigeons 107, × 291	203½ Todmorden 174, × 367	215½ Tregloss 68
× Threlkeld 373	200½ —— by Oldham 177	231½ Trenholme 207
× Threshfield 370	× Todwick 360	123 Trent Bridge 186, × 306, 315
× Thribergh 361	170 Toft (Chesh.) 152	
270½ Thrimby 159	× Toft (Linc.) 352	122½ —— by Loughborough 189, 190
× Thrivewell 381	248½ Toft Hill 210	
× Thurgarton 306	109½ Toft Monks 243	145½ Trentham 151
171½ Thurgoland 182	107½ Toft Trees 233	181½ Trentishoe 80
95½ Thurlby 215	106 Tog Hill 97, × 304	183 —— by Rydon 81
× Thurloxton 233	206 Tollerton Lanes 211	× Trerddol 330
× Thurlston 358, 360	115 Tolpiddle 58	227½ Trerule Foot 56
× Thurmaston 318	Tonbridge see Tunbridge	227 —— by Saltash 57
× Thursford 350	132 Tong 148	247½ Tresilian 51
84½ Thwaite 239	× Tongfold 357	263½ —— by Plymouth 57
7×½ —— by Stowmarket 210	229½ Tontine Inn 207	264½ —— by Tregony 57
253 Thwaite Bridge 201	6 Tooting Cross 26	168½ Tresiwon 91
× Tibshelf 354	212½ Topcliffe 201	247 Trespen 51
19½½ Tibthorpe 218	158½ Tophall 196	261 Treswithian 67
45½ Ticehurst 16	160½ Topsham 59, × 285	155½ Tretower 111
49½ Tickford End 154	191½ Tor Mohun 62, 63	264 Trevelloe 52
159 Tickhill (York.) 193, × 359	190½ —— by Newton Abbot 62	× Trevenant 332
× Tickhill Spittal 359	142½ Torksey 214	205½ Trevennen 51
165½ Tickton 218	144½ —— by Lincoln 218	291 Trevescan 52
196½ Tidaford 64	103½ Tormarton 103	215½ Trevithick Bridge 50
× Tidbury Hill 202	169½ Torne Bridge 210	251 Trewarlas 67
× Tidd or TyddGout 352	218 Torpoint 56	266½ Trewenick 51
× Tidd St. Mary's 352	192½ Torquay 62	217½ Trewint 50
129½ Tiddenham 109	191½ —— by Newton Abbot 62	252½ Trewithan 67
93 Tiddington 136	194½ Torrington 77, × 287	Trimingham 235, × 350
160½ Tideswell 171, ×× 355	194½ —— by Dulverton 78	31½ Tring 130

419

× Troed-y-rhiew 331	85½ Ugford 48	135½ Uttoxeter 164, × 335, 33
43½ Trotters Green 237	35½ Ugley 230	138½ —— by Nuneaton 165
× Trotton 268	139½ Ulceby Cross 219	15 Uxbridge 106, × 290
295½ Troughend 210	304 Uldale 163, × 371	
274½ Troutbeck Bridge 102	103½ Uley 104	× VAN POST 285
101½ Trowbridge 85, × 276, 277	230½ Ulshaw Bridge 204, × 371	28½ Vange 247
100½ —— by Devizes 86	107½ Ulverley 143	196½ Velindre (Brecon.) 111
98½ —— by Marlborough 95	268½ Ulverston 175, × 372	242½ Velindre or College(Pem.) 112
115 Troy Town 54	272½ —— by Staveley 175	
191½ Trub Smithy 174	186½ Umberleigh Bridge 76	230½ Velindre Mill 113
× Trull 284	× Underhill Green 259	165½ Vellinvach 116, × 330
123½ Trumpet (near Ledbury) 116	154½ Unston 178	199½ Venn Cross 61
	268½ Unthank 210	180½ Vicar's Cross 146
134 Trumpet (nr. Leominster) 122	80½ Up Avon 85, × 294	52½ Vine Hall 14
	94½ Upgate 235	21 Virginia Water 46
49½ Trumpington 227	191½ Upham (Devon.) 62	
54½ —— by Harlow 231	69½ Upham (Hants.) 272	43½ WADDESDON 132
Trunch 235	139½ Uphill (Kent) 9	128½ Waddington 218
250½ Truro 50	139½ Uphill (Som.) 84	× Waddon 265
258½ —— by Camelford 68	16 Upminster 248	234½ Wadebridge 68, × 288
266½ —— by Dorchester 57	× Upottery 284	24 Wade's Mill 223
251 —— by Ladock 51	Upper Allithwaite 102	× Wadford 284
60½ Tubney 105	33½ Upper Bell 9	42½ Wadhurst 15, × 257
47 Tubslake 14	× Upper Benefield 317	161½ Wadsley Bridge 182
195 Tuckenhay 64	112 Upper Broughton 186	162 Wadworth 193
× Tuddenham 318	× Upper Bullington 202	× Waerdy Bridge 329
× Tudworth 361	× Upper Burgate 274	× Wainfleet 359
× Tufton 292	47 Upper Caldecote 202	160 Waith 219
× Tugby 318	99 Upper Castlecombe 97	186 Wakefield 179, × 362, 365
114½ Tumbledown Dick 243	× Upper Chapel 329	182½ —— by Newark 202
41½ Tun Bulls House 228	71 Upper Deal 6, × 250	183 —— by Nottingham 167
30 Tunbridge 12, × 253	30½ Upper Delce 9	× Wakes Colne 315
32½ —— by Ightham 16	87½ UpperEatington 131, × 305	57½ Walberton 34
35½ Tunbridge Wells 15, × 258, 259, 260	7½ Upper Edmonton 222	× Walcot 350
	× Upper Heyford 315	86½ Walcote 155, × 317
248½ Tunstall (Lanc.) 176	18 Upper Highway 129	× Waldershare 250
85½ Tunstall (Suff.) 244	× Upper Hulme 339, 356	151½ Walesby 220
134 Tupsley 116	× Upper Lancing 269	150 Walford 122, × 326
145½ Tupton 179	7½ Upper Mitcham Green 26	138½ Walford Bridge 81, × 283
172½ Turnbridge 210, × 363	130½ Upper Penn 144	160½ Walgherton 146
× Turnditch 354	127 Upper Redbrook 114	2½ Walham Green 32
30½ Turner Hill 23	× Upper Sapey 324	× Wall 391
× Turners Green 257	× Upper Sherringham 350	139½ Wall Brook Bridge 170
13½ Turner's Hill 222	× Upper Studley 277	× Wall Heath 312
5 Turnham Green 46	83½ Upper Swell 123	× Wall Houses 379
58½ Turvey 189, × 297	180 Upper and Lower Swithen 180	46 Wallingford 100, × 291
128 Tutbury 165		202½ Wallington(Northum.)209
137½ Tuxford 196	142½ Upper Tean 164	× Wallington (Surr.) 265
135 —— by Royston 224	5½ Upper Tooting 26	× Wallsend 380
337 Tweedmouth 200	53½ Upper Waltham 35	× Walmer 250
× Twemlow 339	× Upper Welton 373	193½ Walmersley 171
108½ Twerton 90	× Upper Woodford 294	196½ Walmsley 173
12 Twickenham 31 × 206	× Upper Yeadon 370	96½ Walpole Highway 226
× Twigworth 307	× Uppercot 287	× Walsall 318, 319
191½ Two Bridges 65, × 287	89 Uppingham 186, × 318	× Walsall Wood 319
185½ Two Mile Oak 61	× Upsall 375	197½ Walshford Bridge 197
22 Two Waters 129	61½ Upstreet 3	92½ Walsoken 226
110½ Twycross 156	56 Upton (Berks.) 101	× Walsworth 296
34 Twyford (Berks.) 88	183 Upton (Chesh.) 151	163 Waltham 220
× Twyford (Hants.) 272	× Upton (Norf.) 348	14 Waltham Abbey 222
21 Tyler's Green (Ess.) 240	× Upton (Northamp.) 315	12½ Waltham Cross 222
× Tyler's Green (Surr.) 263	× Upton (Notts.) 306, 355	× Waltham-on-the-Wolds 318
277 Tynemouth 208, × 350	134½ Upton (Salop) 140	
	80½ Upton (War.) 131	× Walton (Derb.) 354
124½ UBLEY 96	× Upton Grove 313	71½ Walton (Kent) 9
43½ Uckfield 19, × 258, 261	91½ Upton Lovel 82	× Walton (Lanc.) 367
97 Uckington 117	× Upton-on-Severn 307, 323	84½ Walton (Northamp.) 215
390 Uddingstone 161	× Upton Warren 308	127½ Walton (Som.) 83
59½ Udymer 17	87½ Urchfont 85	140½ Walton(Eccleshall, Staff.) 146
× Uffington 352	× Useborn 380	
80 Ufford Street 241	144 Usk 113, × 322, 323	× Walton (Stone, Staff.) 312, 338
84½ Ufton 144	151½ Usselby 220	
179½ Ugbrook Park 61	154½ Utterby 219	71 Walton Ashes 246

94¾ Walton Highway 226
211½ Walton-le-Dale 157, × 367, 368
16½ Walton-on-Thames 37
71 Walton-on-the-Naze 246
× Walwick 379
73 Wanborough 101
5 Wandsworth 31, 32
75¾ Wangford (nr. Brandon) 233
102¾ Wangford (near Blythburgh) 241
88½ Wansford 193, × 300, 318
83¼ —— by G. N. road 195
81 —— by Royston 224
60 Wantage 101, × 292
× Warbleton 261
× Warborough 291
68½ Warboys 226
× Wardington 301
167¾ Wardle 146
× Wardling 318
158 Wardlow 171
22½ Ware 222, × 295, 349
149½ Ware Cliff House 59
× Wareborn 255
117¾ Wareham 44, × 277
111¼ —— by Basingstoke 53
34 Wargrave 100
117 Warham Hall 233
194 Warley Cross Hill 218
14½ Warlingham 22
15½ Warlingham Station 21
82½ Warmington (Northamp.) 193, × 299
78 Warmington (War.) 141
96½ Warminster 82, × 274, 276
109¼ Warmley 97
× Warmsworth 361
130½ Warmwell Cross 44
124¼ —— by Basingstoke 53
× Warnell 373, 375
60 Warnford 41
33¾ Warnham 30
× Warren 331
318½ Warrenford 200
56¼ Warrington (Bucks.) 189
183¾ Warrington (Lanc.) 152, × 340, 341, 356
188 —— by Congleton 154
185½ —— by Northwich 153
× Wartling 260
Warton (near Carnforth) 161
222½ Warton (near Lytham) 161
93 Warwick 141, × 305, 310, 316
91½ —— by Southam 144
96¾ —— by Wellesbourne Hastings 142
× Wasford 330
× Wash Bridge 291
× Washaway 288
156½ Washford 78
155 —— by Rydon 81
153½ —— by Williton 78
48½ Washington Common 29, × 268
51½ Wasing 95
158¾ Watchet 78
163 —— by Rydon 81
80½ Water Eaton 102, × 273
81½ Water Newton 195
141½ Water Pitts 82
56¾ Waterbeach 227
× Waterfoot 367
24½ Waterford 225
127¾ Watergure 71
277 Waterhead 162
× Wateringbury 258
× Wateringbury Cross 258, 259
185 Waterloo 150
× Waters Upton 335
48½ Watersfield 31
167¾ Waterside 216
14½ Watford 120, × 200
141½ Watling Street 140, × 336
130 Watnall 190
95 Wattle Wortwell 242
27½ Watton (Herts.) 225
91½ Watton (Norf.) 234
92½ —— by Thetford 234
191 Watton (Yorks.) 216
27½ Watts Cross 12, 17
× Waupley New Inn 375
41½ Wavendon 154
× Waver Bridge 375
× Waverton 374
× Waxcombe 293
× Weald or Weld 298
20 Weald Gullet 240
× Weardley 369
268¾ Wearmouth 208, × 378
102½ Weasenham St. Peter 233
× Weaverham 340
Webb Heath 125
117½ Wednesbury 140, × 319
67½ Weedon 138, × 315
114½ Weeford 145
× Week 271
× Week Cross 286
× Weekly 299
63½ Weeley 245
213¾ Weekstone Bridge 69
71½ Weeping Cross (Oxf.) 131
151½ Weeping Cross (Salop) 126
133¾ Weeping Cross (Staff.) 145, × 319
80 Weeting All Saints 233
123 Welbourne 218
× Welch Hampton 333, 340
202 Welch Whittle 158
× Weld 298
61½ Welford (Berks.) 100
80½ Welford (Northamp.) 154
× Welham 358
185 Welham Bridge 214
45½ Wellbrook 17
89½ Wellesbourne Hastings 136, × 305
10½ Welling 2
66½ Wellingborough 189, × 299 315
123½ Wellingore 218
× Wellington (Heref.) 320
Wellington (Salop) 140, × 335, 336
148 Wellington (Som.) 73
146½ —— by Somerton 75
109¾ Wellow (Som.) 86
108½ —— by Devizes 86
135½ Wellow (Notts.) 202
123¾ Wells (Norf.) 228, × 351
123½ —— by South Creake 229
119 —— by Swaffham 233
120½ Wells (Som.) 83, 84, × 282, 283
103¾ Wells Green 139
69 Welnetham 237
× Welsh Newton 320
176 Welshpool 121, × 329, 332
× Welton (Linc.) 360
× Welton (York.) 363
25½ Welwyn 184
× Wem 321, 333
× Wendlebury 297
35½ Wendover 133
× Wendron 288
14½ Wennington 247, 249
231½ Wensley 204
172¾ Went Bridge 197
× Wentworth (Camb.) 347, 348
165½ Wentworth (Yorks.) 187
146¾ Weobley 115, × 325
90½ Wereham 233
125¾ Werga 140, 148
84½ Werrington 215
× Wescott Barrow 289
137½ West Ashby 220
× West Ashton 276
246¾ West Auckland 198, × 376, 378
231½ West Ayton 213
144½ West Bagborough 82
× West Barkwith 360
360 West Barns 200
× West Bilney 317, 319
× West Bolden 378
114½ West Bromwich 140
2 West Brompton 32
208¾ West Buckish 74
West Burton 205
× West Chinnock 281
125¾ West Coker 49
54 West Dean 34
× West Deeping 352
× West Drayton 291
44 West End (Bed.) 188
× West End (Yorks.) 370
76¾ West Everley 85
171½ West Felton 127
× West Firle 260
× West Garforth 363
× West Gate 377
× West Grafton 293
42¾ West Grinstead 29
76½ West Haddon 182
4¾ West Ham 246
60½ West Hampnet 35, × 253
115¼ West Hanham 90
122½ West Harptree 96, × 282
41½ West Harrietsham 8
× West Hendred 293
190¾ West Hill 62
24½ West Horsley 37
× West Houghton 364
× West Hyde 291
55 West Ilsley 100
131 West Keal 219
79¾ West Kennet 89
× West Lavington 276
99½ West Lexham 233
307¾ West Linton 183
229½ West Looe 66
× West Lydford 281
135½ West Lyng 81
× West Lynn 352

130¾ West Markham 196
× West Marton 368
58¾ West Meon 41
207¾ West Moor 190
13¼ West Moulsey 37
× West Newton 374
120¾ West Pennard 83
203¼ West Rainton 210
× West Rasen 359
110½ West Rudham 220
× West Runton 350, 351
× West Shefford 202, 203
153 West Stockwith 214
128¾ West Stoke 72
106¾ West Stour 48
218¾ West Tanfield 203
19 West Thurrock 249
298¾ West Thurston 190
× West Tilbury 343
84 West Tofts Hall 234
× West Town 267
94 West Winch 228
100½ —— by Brandon 233
235¼ West Witton 205
× West Woodlands 278
31¼ West Wycombe 107
× Westbach 326
1¼ Westbourne Green 133
× Westbrook Green 302
60¾ Westbury (Bucks.) 136
112¾ Westbury (Glouc.) 109, 113
× Westbury (Salop) 332
124 Westbury (Som.) 84
98¾ Westbury (Wilts.) 85, × 276
99¼ Westbury Leigh 85
123¼ Westbury-on-Trym 91
64¼ Westcot Barton 134
72 Westerfield 241
21¼ Westerham, 18, × 263
× Westgate Street 263
65¼ Westham 18, × 252
26½ Westley Green 46
× Westmeston 267
274 Westoe 208
159¾ Weston (Devon) 49
118¾ Weston (Heref.) 110, × 322
× Weston (Linc.) 352
134¾ Weston (Notts.) 196
133¾ Weston (Staff.) 151, × 336
107¾ Weston (Suff.) 243
× Weston (War.) 316
145¾ Weston Coyney 165
× Westen-Favel 209
218¾ Weston Mill 56
× Weston-on-the-Green 293
× Weston-Subedge 310
141¾ Weston-super-Mare 84
139¾ —— by Bath 86
133½ —— by Bristol 97
132 Weston-under-Wood 170
41¼ Westoning 188
92¾ Westport 101
Westward Ho! 74
49 Westwell Common 8
Westwood-with-Ilford 95
194¼ Wetherby 197, × 360
184¼ —— by Royston 224
× Wetherden 316
150½ Wetley or Wetley Rocks 164
148¾ —— by Sandon 165
198¼ Wetwang 218, × 366
× Wey Bridge (Norf.) 348
× Weybourn 351
18¾ Weybridge (Surr.) 33
148 Weycroft Bridge 71
66¾ Weyhill 60, 84
135½ Weymouth 44, × 279
129½ —— by Basingstoke 53
189½ Weypre 150
× Whaddon (Glouc.) 311
× Whaddon (Wilts.) 273
171¼ Whaley Bridge 168
166 —— by Ashbourne 170
171¼ —— by Chapel-en-le-Frith 171
210¼ Whalley 172, × 368
× Whaplode 352
× Wharfe 370
201¾ Wharram-le-Street 218
× Wharton 320
105¾ Whateley 84
54¼ Whatlington 14
× Whatton 353
25¼ Wheathampstead 187
× Wheatley (Notts.) 358
48¼ Wheatley (Oxf.) 107, × 205
201½ Wheatley (York.) 180
47½ Wheatley Bridge 107, × 205
275½ Wheatsheaf Inn 210
× Wheelock 339
× Wherwell 272
9¼ Whetstone 137
289½ Whicham 175
Whimsey 103
Whip's Cross 229
169¼ Whipton 76
158 Whiston 167
290¼ Whitbeck 175
99¾ Whitbourn 82
243 Whitby 213, × 375
244¾ —— by Lincoln 217
43 Whitchurch (Bucks.) 130
× Whitchurch (Devon) 284
168¾ Whitchurch (Glam.) 99
56¾ Whitchurch (Hants.) 58, × 270, 292
126½ Whitchurch (Heref.) 110
161½ Whitchurch (Salop) 148, × 321, 335, 336, 340
× Whitchurch or Felton (Som.) 278
× Whitchurch or Whitkirk (Yorks.) 363
99 Whitcomb (Glouc.) 105
136¼ White Cross (Heref.) 114, 116, 117
128¾ White Cross (Som.) 71
188¾ White Cross (Yorks.) 218
163 White Down 74
138¾ White Gate 71
× White Hill 270
× White Hill *Tp.G.* 325
110¼ White House 243
211½ White Houses 211
131 White Lackington 71
210½ White Mill 111
× White Notley 344
× White Parish 273
91½ White Sheet Hill 48
352 Whiteburn Inn 209
127 Whitecomb 54
108¾ Whitechurch 54, × 227
173¾ Whitefield (Derb.) 177
188¾ } Whitefield (Lanc.) 171
188 }
309¼ Whitehaven 175, × 374
30½ Whiteman's Green 24
27¾ —— by Handcross 26
× White's Cross 301
50¾ Whitesmith Green 19
149¾ Whitford 59
240¾ Whitland 93
276 Whitley (near Alston) 207
× Whitley (nr. N. Shields) 380
68¾ Whitley Bridge 139
93 —— by Banbury 143
× Whitminster 307, 313
× Whitmore 339
152 Whitney 116, × 325
× Whitridge 380
56 Whitstable 5
298 Whittingham 208
248¾ Whittington (Lanc.) 176
88 Whittington (Norf.) 233, × 347
× Whittington (Salop) 340
× Whittington (Staff.) 312
108¾ Whittington (Worc.) 119
151¼ Whittington Common 178
206¼ Whittle-in-the-Woods 157
62¼ Whittlebury 141
78 Whittlesea 226, × 347
× Whitton Gilbert 377
71¾ Whitton Street 239, × 316
× Whittonstall 377
× Whitway 292
× Whitwell (Derb.) 358
× Whitwell (Rutl.) 351
208½ Whitwell-on-the-Hill 213
197¾ Whitworth 174
232 Whorlton 212
54 Wiboston 194, × 298
× Wichbold 308
107¾ Wick (Glouc.) 97
101 Wick (Worc.) 119
57¼ Wick Street 31
143¼ Wickenby 220
× Wickersley 359
× Wickfield Bridge 268
29¼ Wickford 247
30 —— by Upminster 248
× Wickham 272
82 Wickham Market 241
× Wickham Mills 344
93¼ Wickhamford Bridge 119
× Wickhouse 342
64 Wicks Cross 245
107 Wickwar 101, × 314
109½ —— by Tetbury 103
111¾ —— by Wotton-under-Edge 103
106½ Widcombe 95
28 Widford (Ess.) 237
× Widford (Herts) 342
115 Widmerpool Inn 196
× Widmore 265
196 Wigan 157, × 364
200¼ Wiggington 212
116 Wighton 233
× Wightwick 326
117¾ Wigmore 122, × 327
58¾ Wignell Street 245
92¼ Wigston 181
311 Wigton 163, × 374, 397
× Wigwell 337
× Wilbarston 317
× Wilberfoss 366
× Wilburton 347
× Wilby 299

× Wild Green 308
184¼ Wilderspool 153, × 340
55¾ Wildon 192
87½ Wiley 70
Wilford 190
156½ Willand 75, 76
× Willaston 339
× Willcocks Bridge 324
88¾ Willenhall 139
97½ —— by Banbury 143
× Willersey 310
149 Willersley 116, × 325
54¼ Willesborough 8
4 Willesden Station 133
46½ Willesly Green 10, × 256, 257
46¾ —— by Tunbridge 13
148 Willet 82
× Williamscote 301
64 Willingdon 18
× Willington (Bedf.) 298
× Willington (Durh.) 377
× Willington (Northumb. 380
156¾ Williton 78
153 —— by Rydon 81
76½ Willoughby 139
96¼ Willoughby Hedge 70
99¼ —— by Salisbury 71
113¼ Wills Bridge 90
46¾ Willshampstead 188
× Willy or White Oak Green 301
152¼ Wilmington 65
× Wilmington Marton 332
174¼ Wilmslow 165, × 339
112¾ Wilnecote 155
× Wilsford 294
84¾ Wilton (Wilts) 48
× Wilton (Yorks.) 371
345 Wilton Kirk 183
121 Wilton *Tg.* 110, 114, × 320
× Wimbish Green 343
78¾ Wimblington 226
105¼ Wimborne Minster 44, × 280
99¾ —— by Basingstoke 53
101½ —— by Cranbourn 53
86¼ Wimbotsham 228
× Wimmering 254
201¼ Win Yate or Wingates 168
107½ Wincanton 70, × 280
112 —— by Shaftesbury 72
× Winceby 359
× Winchcombe 303, 310
× Winchelsea 251
61½ Winchester 39, × 268, 271, 272, 292
62½ —— by Basingstoke 53
× Winchet Hill 259
38½ Winchfield Station 52
265¾ Windermere 163
27¾ Windlesham 46
× Windmill Hill 260
22 Windsor 87, 94, × 269
22¾ —— by Slough 87
136 Windwhistle 49
× Windy Hill 332
90½ Winfarthing 240
150 Winforton 116, × 325
× Wing 296
× Wingfield 337
175½ Wingate 79
201¼ Wingates or Win Yate 168
61¾ Wingham 5
25½ Winkfield 94
148 Winkhill Bridge 169
122¾ Winnett's Hill 113
340½ Winley Stead 200
× Winscales 374
132¼ Winscombe 84
× Winsham 284
× Winslade 270
101½ Winsley 85
48¾ Winslow 130
× Winston (Dur.) 375
82¼ Winston (Suff.) 241, × 346
× Winswell 297
124 Winterborne Abbas 54
108¾ Winterborne Thompson 58
108¼ Winterborne Whitchurch 54, × 277
107¾ Winterborne Zelstone 58
× Winterbourn Dantsey 203
× Winterbourn Earls 293
× Winterbourn Gunner 203
× Winterbourne Basset 301
× Winterbourne Monkton 301
82½ Winterbourne Stoke 70, × 275
120¾ Winterfold 125
× Winterley Pool 339
74½ Winterslow Hut 47
126½ Winthorpe 214, 217
186¾ Winwick 157
139¾ Wirksworth 170, × 337
91¼ Wisbeach 226, × 351, 352
× Wisbeach St. Mary 351
42¾ Wisborough Green 35
107½ Wishaw 145
196½ Wisket Hill 170
× Wistaston 339
× Witchford 347, 348
38¼ Witham 238, × 344
49 Withdean 25
106¼ Witherley 155
× Withersfield 344
182¾ Withington 165
× Withington Marsh 324
× Withyam 262
90¼ Withybrook 182
35 Witley (Surr.) 34
119½ Witley (Worc.) 119
74 Witnesham Street 241
65¼ Witney 108, × 301, 302
58½ Wittersham Stocks 14
× Witton 348
250¾ Witton-le-Wear 209, × 377
× Witton Mill 350
151¾ Wiveliscombe 77
40½ Wivelsfield 23
41¼ Woburn (Beds.) 154, × 296
× Woburn (Bucks.) 290
× Woburn Green 290
121¾ Wokey 84
31¾ Wokingham 94
62¾ Wollaston 189
128¼ Wolseley Bridge 145, 151
× Wolsingham 377, 378
56½ Wolvercot 118
122½ Wolverhampton 140, × 312, 326
133 —— by Alcester 143
× Wolverley 333
× Wolverton 297
92¼ Wolvey 192, × 305
245¾ Wolviston 208
129 Wombourn 144
× Wommersley 368
133½ Wonastow 110, 113
× Wonersh 266
197 Wonton 61
× Wood Bridge 294
130¾ Wood Enderby 231
5¾ Wood Green (Midd.) 225
× Wood Green (Staff.) 319
169½ Wood Hill 178
128½ Wood Park 120
77¼ Woodbridge 241, × 346
291½ Woodburne Bridge 210
166¼ Woodbury 50
× Woodchester 309, 312
× Woodchurch 255
137¼ Woodcote 148
250½ Wooden 98
50 Wooden Street 8
8½ Woodford (Ess.) 220
71 Woodford (Northamp.) 193
9½ Woodford Bridge 236
9 Woodford Green 229
× Woodford Hut 275
9½ Woodford Wells 229
60¾ Woodgate 35
248¾ Woodham 202
24¾ Woodhatch 27
180¾ Woodhead 177, × 357
192¾ Woodhouse (York.) 191
70¾ Woodhouse Station 227
× Woodhouses (Cumb.) 374
205 Woodland 56
× Woodmancote 267
181½ Woodmansea 216
× Wood's Corner 261
62 Woodstock 118
× Woodstone 299
90¾ Woodyates Inn 54
× Wooferton Cross 321, 326
123¾ Wool Bridge 44
127 Woolaston (Glouc.) 109
× Woolaston (Salop) 332
× Woolberry Hill 271
156¾ Woolcot 82
320½ Wooler 208
318¾ Woolerhaugh Head 203
49¾ Woolhampton 88
× Woolley Bridge 357
27¼ Woolmer Green 194
× Woolpit 346
278½ Woolsington 209
× Woolstanton 339
66½ Woolston (Berks.) 101
× Woolston (Lanc.) 341
× Woolston (nr. Castle Cary, Som.) 279
155¼ Woolston (near Williton, Som.) 78
× Woolton 338
52½ Woolverton (Hants) 86
× Woolverton (Som.) 274
9¾ } Woolwich 4
8½ }
149 Woonton 115
155¾ Woore 146, × 336, 337, 338, 339
83½ Wootton Bassett 101, × 302
62¾ Wootton Bridge 156
101¼ Wootton Green 142
78¼ Wootton Wawen 143, × 311

111 Worcester 119, × 307, 311, 322, 323	× Wraxhill 281	203½ Yarrow Bridge by Blackrod 169
118 —— by Alcester 135	× Wrayton 370	209 —— by Manchester 168
125 Wordesley 144	× Wrelton 371	109 Yate 97, × 314
317½ Workington 176, × 373	106½ Wrentham 241	163½ Yattington 59
150 Worksop 193, × 358, 360	52½ Wretchwick 132	97¾ Yatton Keynell 97
145½ —— by Stamford 202	× Wrexham 328, 333, 337	Yawford 78
65 Worlby Hill 47	111½ Writhlington 86	88½ Yaxley 239
131½ Worle 97	32 Writtle 240	82 —— by Stowmarket 240
Worlingham 243	24 Wrotham 7, × 262	143½ Yazor 114
183½ Worm Hill 65	26¼ Wrotham Heath 7, × 264	Yealand 161
× Wormebridge 324	× Wroughton 273, 301	208½ Yealm Bridge 64
× Wormelow Tump 320	98 Wroxall (War.) 143	209 Yealmpton 64
143½ Wormesley 115	Wroxall (Wilts.) 96	× Yeanston 280
× Wormingford 345	76 Wroxton 131	× Yearsley 368
16 Wormley 222	34½ Wych Cross *Tg.* 21	223½ Yeddingham Bridge 213
173 Worsborough 178	27¼ Wycombe Marsh 107	× Yeolm Bridge 289
170 —— by Nottingham 187	230 Wykeham 213	122½ Yeovil 48, × 291
× Worse Bridge 255	× Wyken 326	122¾ —— by Sparkford 72
51 Worsted Lodge 231	100½ Wymondham 232	251½ Yerbeston Gate 98
68½ Worth 6, × 250	102 Wyre Piddle 119	× Yewsley 291
29½ Worth Bridge 24	285 Wytheourn 162	× Yockleton or Lockerton 332
× Worthen 332		196½ York 211, × 366, 369
56 Worthing 30, × 269	× YAFFORTH 375	196¾ —— by Askern 212
60¼ Worthy 53	× Yalding 259, 260	199½ —— by Tadcaster 211
47½ Worting 58	59½ Yapton 34	× York Bar 360
170 Wortley 182	106¼ Yardley 139	29½ York Town 47
93¾ Worton 85, × 265	54¾ Yardley Gobion 156	38½ Young's End 237
× Wotton Hatch 263	64½ Yardley Hastings 189	× Yoxall and Y. Bridge 35
106½ Wotton-under-Edge 102, × 313, 314	× Yarley 312	94½ Yoxford 241, 243
× Wragby (Linc.) 359, 360	237½ Yarm 207, × 372, 376	201½ Ysceifiog 149
176½ Wragby (Yorks.) 202	124½ Yarmouth 242, × 348	Yspytty Cynfyn 115
134½ Wrantage 73	120½ } —— by Bungay 243	
100½ Wraxall 96	123¼ }	217½ ZEALLA 67
	× Yarnbrook 276	102½ Zeals Green 70, × 278
	202¼ Yarrow Bridge 157	

RAILWAY RATES FOR CYCLES.

The Rates for conveyance of cycles by train on any Railways in England (except the three Railways mentioned below) and Wales, are as follows, which include collection and delivery within usual limits.

	Up to Miles—	12	25	50	75	100	150	200	And each 50 miles beyond.
		s. d.	s. d.	s. d.	s. d.	s. d.	s. d.	s. d.	s. d.
Bicycles except Ottos and large cycle wheels.	(1) As Luggage	1 0	1 0	1 0	1 6	2 0	2 6	3 0	0 6
	(2) As Parcels at Owner's risk	1 6	1 6	1 6	2 3	3 0	3 9	4 6	0 9
	(3) As Parcels at Company's risk	2 0	2 0	2 0	3 0	4 0	5 0	6 0	1 0
Tricycles, Ottos, and Velocipedes and Sociables	(1) As Luggage	1 0	1 6	2 0	3 0	4 0	5 0	6 0	1 0
	(2) As Parcels at Owner's risk	2 0	3 0	4 0	6 0	8 0	10 0	12 0	2 0
	(3) As Parcels at Company's risk	3 0	4 6	6 0	9 0	12 0	15 0	18 0	3 0

The other portions of a bicycle, tricycle, or velocipede, when sent in pieces, are charged at ordinary parcels rate.

Sociables are charged 50 per cent more than ordinary tricycles.

Velocipedes, tricycles, and bicycles requiring a carriage truck are charged (either with owner or not):—

At Owner's risk, two-thirds of the ordinary 4-wheeled carriage rate, plus fractional parts of 6d. Where 4-wheeled carriage rates are not in operation, at 3d. per mile, fractional parts of a mile being considered a mile. } Minimum charge 5s. 0d.

At Company's risk, at the 4-wheeled carriage rate, but where 4-wheeled carriage rates are not in operation, at 4½d. per mile, fractional parts of a mile being considered a mile. } Minimum charge 7s. 6d.

The three exceptions are—the South Eastern; the London, Chatham, and Dover; and the London Brighton and South Coast Railways, whose charges are, for "bicycles and velocipedes:"—

	Not exceeding 12 miles	...	...	...	...		1s. 0d.
Above 12 and	„	25	„	...	...	...	1s. 6d.
„ 25 „	„	50	„	...	...	...	2s. 0d.
„ 50 „	„	75	„	...	...	...	3s. 0d.
„ 75 „	„	100	„	...	...	...	4s. 0d.
„ 100 „	„	150	„	...	...	...	5s. 0d.
„ 150 „	„	200	„	...	...	...	6s. 0d.
„ 200 „	„	250	„	...	...	...	7s. 0d.

These rates are for "bicycles and velocipedes," when accompanied and attended to by owner and at his own risk; if conveyed separately as parcels unaccompanied by owner, but at his risk, the rates are double the above, and the machines must be securely packed. The London, Chatham, and Dover Railway always charge for tricycles and other velocipedes and vehicles with more than two wheels at double the rates for bicycles